The Agrarian System of Mughal India 1556–1707

THIRD EDITION

Excerpts from Reviews of the First Edition

'...a fine book...a major event in South-Asian historiography.'
—P. Hardy in *English Historical Review*

'...a work developed on rigorous and diligent lines...The author reviews a century and a half of Indian agrarian history from a quite definitely socialist standpoint.'
—Luigi Pignatelli, *East and West*

'This erudite treatise...marked by wide knowledge and scrupulous accuracy... His elaborate bibliography, a model of its kind, reveals the colossal task which has been undertaken.'
—Collin C. Davies in *History*

'No serious student of the history of the sub-continent can afford to ignore the penetrating analysis of the weakness of the Mughal regime contained in the final chapter...'
—G. R. G. Hambly in *Journal of the Royal Central Asian Society*

'...a book which will be read with profit by the undergraduate as well as by the research historian of medieval India...a superb piece of work.'
—J. H. Bloomfield in *Journal of Asian Studies*

'[One] of the books on earlier epochs which have profoundly influenced the writings on modern Indian history.'
—Amiya Kumar Bagchi in *The Political Economy of Underdevelopment*

Excerpts from Reviews of the Second Edition

'Students of medieval Indian history should consider themselves unfortunate if they do not possess the volume or if they do not read it.'
—Meena Bhargava, *The Book Review*

'The reprinting of the 1963 classic is a publishing event. The book initiated a historiographical revolution in the world of medieval Indian history...What he [Irfan Habib] has done in this book is to add a tremendous amount of new evidence which enriches and deepens his original contribution.'
—Rudrangshu Mukherjee, *The Telegraph*

The Agrarian System of Mughal India 1556–1707

THIRD EDITION

IRFAN HABIB

OXFORD
UNIVERSITY PRESS

OXFORD
UNIVERSITY PRESS

Oxford University Press is a department of the University of Oxford. It furthers the University's objective of excellence in research, scholarship, and education by publishing worldwide. Oxford is a registered trademark of Oxford University Press in the UK and in certain other countries

Published in India by
Oxford University Press
YMCA Library Building, 1 Jai Singh Road, New Delhi 110 001, India

First Edition published in 1963
Second Revised Edition published in 1999
Oxford India Paperbacks 2000
Third Edition published in 2014

ISBN-13: 978-0-19-807742-8
ISBN-10: 0-19-807742-4

Typeset in Times by Muneeruddin Khan
Printed in India by Sapra Brothers, New Delhi 110 092

TO THE MEMORY

OF

MY FATHER

PROFESSOR MOHAMMAD HABIB

1895–1971

CONTENTS

ILLUSTRATIONS AND MAPS

Political and Economic Maps of the Mughal Empire at beginning and end of volume.

NOTE TO THE THIRD EDITION

The second edition of this work was published in 1999, thirty-six years after the first edition (1963). Such a long interval meant that in the second edition large portions of the text had to be rewritten to accommodate much additional matter and also to reflect the inevitable change in one's perception over time. Now that far less time has passed since the second edition, the changes made have been on a far more modest scale. Slips detected in that edition have been corrected and some references have been updated. The only major set of alterations has been due to a fresh reconstruction of the history of copper money value that became necessary after a paper published by Dr Najaf Haider. He offered conclusive proof that sources in the seventeenth century continued to mean by *paisa* or 'pice' a full *dām*, and by *ṭanka*, a double *dām*, and not half of these values respectively as had been previously thought. This has resulted in my making substantial changes not only in the text and notes of Appendix C, but also in the data and argument set out at several other places as well.

The Preface to the Second Edition, which follows this Note, explains the scope and other features of this work, which remain unaltered in the present edition. The previous edition having been cited in many publications, I have done my best to ensure that, despite changes in the text, the pages of this edition correspond to those of the second edition. The reader will thus be able readily to locate in this volume any portion of the text cited from the second edition.

Owing to the facilities provided by the Aligarh Historians Society (with Mr Muneeruddin Khan as its capable computer-operator) all the textual changes have been incorporated in the electronic text from which the camera-ready copy is to be made. Faiz Habib has drawn the Political and Economic Maps of the Mughal Empire, which had appeared in the second edition but were dropped in the paperback reprints.

Much gratitude is owed to Mr Prasun Chatterji, Commissioning Editor at the Oxford University Press, for his unruffled cheerfulness and cooperation.

Aligarh
February 2013

Irfan Habib

PREFACE

TO THE SECOND EDITION

When this book, a revised and partly rewritten version of the thesis presented at Oxford (1958), was first published (1963), I explained in the preface that the words "Agrarian System" in the title should be understood to encompass not only land revenue administration, but also agrarian economy and social structure. The chronological limits were formally set at Akbar's accession (1556) and Aurangzeb's death (1707), the two dates defining the classic period of the Mughal Empire, though one knows that, in a subject like this, there cannot be a strict adherence to such limits. By Mughal India I meant the territories which remained within Mughal control the longest, comprising what is now northern India, Pakistan and Bangladesh, and such parts of the Dakhin (the Mughal provinces of Berar, Khandesh, Ahmadnagar/Aurangabad, and Bidar), as were annexed to the Empire by 1658. This means that conditions in the southern portion of the Peninsula, comprising the Bijapur and Golkunda kingdoms, the remnants of the Vijayanagara empire ('Karnatak') and Kerala ('Malabar'), the last never annexed, were not studied, being referred to only incidentally or for comparative purposes.

The present edition maintains these limits of scope, time and territory; it also retains the original structure of treatment; and, except for Chapter IV, even the arrangement of the sections of chapters and the appendices of the first edition is preserved. I have, however, revised the entire text, rewritten it extensively and added much information from documents and texts that I have been collecting since the appearance of the first edition. As a result, despite attempts at shortening the text at many places, the length of the book has in the net expanded considerably.

In carrying out this revision I have reinforced evidence on many points, made changes where these appeared to be called for by the new evidence, and taken into account work published since 1963. In the light of the additional information, my views on the nature of the village community have changed substantially: the interpretation given in Chapter IV, Section 3, of this edition, will be found to be very different from the one in the corresponding portion (Chapter IV, Section 2) of the first edition. Elsewhere, I have deleted some polemical comments, which seemed appropriate enough in 1963, but by now have probably lost their topical interest.

The reader would find that I do not engage in debates with critics on such broad matters as the nature of the state (in respect of which since the early 1960s fashion has shifted from "Oriental Despotism" to "segmentary state" and "ritual kingship"), or the Price Revolution (on whose possible occurrence in India the first edition had touched upon), or the agrarian factors behind the decline of the Mughal empire (dealt with in Chapter IX). I have thought it best to use the space available to me mainly for presenting the further evidence that I have gathered and letting it speak for itself.

The footnotes, which account for a very large part of the book, give the required references to sources, offer explanations or discussions of terms, and sometimes also contain digressions which could not be accommodated in the main text. Readers who are not interested in these matters may ignore the footnotes and read only the main text, which, I hope, reads smoothly enough on its own.

Those whose interests lead them to the references and discussions in the footnotes may find it convenient to use the alphabetical list of Abbreviations (p.508) in order to locate the relevant entries in the Bibliography.

A complaint made in respect of the first edition was that it contained no glossary of terms. I have tried to make good the deficiency by adding short definitions and meanings to all the technical terms listed in the Index.

Since the publication of the first edition, some textual sources, cited in that edition from MSS, have been published. Wherever possible I have either replaced MS citations by references to these editions, or added references to the latter. But since tracing individual passages in these editions sometimes proved to be an excessively tedious task, I crave the reader's indulgence for being unable to provide references to printed editions in all cases, and for letting many of the previous MS citations stand as they were.

My transliteration of Persian (and Arabic) words broadly follows the system adopted by Steingass in his *Persian-English Dictionary*, with some trifling modifications. The treatment of the Arabic article *al* where it acts as a conjunctive has been made consistent in this edition, but in a simplified form, reading, e.g., *dastūru-l 'amal* (Steingass: *dastūru' l-'amal*), instead of what would be standard Arabic transliteration, *dastūr al-'amal* (cf. the hybrid *dastūr-al 'amal* of the first edition). When the article, by the rules of Arabic grammar, is assimilated in speech to the following consonant, which is thereupon doubled, this is indicated thus: 'Abdu-ṣ Ṣamad (not 'Abdu-l Ṣamad). A simplified form is adopted in case of personal names ending in *-dīn*; thus Jalāluddīn, not Jalālu-d Dīn, nor Jalālu-ddīn (though the last form may sometimes be found).

Since Steingass's system generally suits the Indian pronunciation of Persian words (especially in respect of vowel sounds), it is easier to adopt it also for Indian names and words of Indian languages, especially Hindi. This has mainly required the addition of the letters *ḍ*, *ṛ*, *ṭ* for the harder sounds of these consonants in Indian languages. In Indo-Persian writing the Indian *ṛh* is usually represented by *ḍh*; where this occurs (as when *gaḍh, gaḍhī*, is written), this has been read in this book as *ṛh*. For the few Sanskrit words, I have preferred the system used in the *Epigraphia Indica*.

Because of the possibility of confusion between the marks for *'ain* and *hamza*, on the one hand, and the single quotation marks, on the other, I have primarily used double quotation marks to enclose quotations, the single marks being mainly reserved for titles of papers, or for quotes within quotes.

Diacritical marks are applied to transliterated words and personal names throughout, not sporadically, as in the first edition. Place names do not normally carry diacritical marks, but these are furnished in the Index. The current Survey of India spellings are followed for place names except where they vary rather noticeably from the spellings in our sources: thus I read "Dehli" not "Delhi", "Ilahabad" not "Allahabad". Where these names occur in modern contexts, modern spellings are resorted to. In the event of any possible confusion, the reader may check with the Index, where both forms are given.

In quotations from English sources, the spellings are naturally those found in the texts. These differ greatly from the present-day standard, but should normally cause the reader no trouble. Where a confusion is possible, as when "coarse" is spelt "course", the modern form is furnished within square brackets.

The words "central regions" or "central provinces" wherever they occur, refer to the country around, or the Mughal provinces of, Agra and Dehli, the two major seats of the imperial court. These are to be distinguished from the British-period "Central Provinces" (largely included in the present state of Madhya Pradesh), which name when mentioned is duly capitalized. It may also be necessary to explain that "Conquered and Ceded Provinces", "North-Western Provinces" and "United Provinces", were names successively given to territories which now constitute the state of Uttar Pradesh. "Haryana" has been used for the entire plains tract between the Sutlej and the Yamuna, within the borders of pre-1947 Punjab; it may be remembered that the present state of Haryana had not come into existence when the first edition of the book was issued.

In the preface to the first edition, I especially acknowledged my debt to W.H. Moreland and P. Saran, major precursors in the field. My consciousness of the debt to them and to others like H.M. Elliot, S.H. Hodivala, Jadunath Sarkar and Ibn Hasan, has only grown with time. I have tried to give in my text and footnotes due credit for any insight or discovery to the writer in whose pages I have found it to occur first. If there is a slip or omission anywhere in such acknowledgement, it is due to inadvertence, not intention. Differences of opinion are also similarly recorded.

The acknowledgements in the preface to the first edition are reproduced after this preface. During the long period that the present edition has been in preparation I have drawn on the help and guidance of a large number of colleagues and friends, all of whom I cannot individually name. But, first of all, there is one institution to which I must render my thanks.

This institution is the Department of History (since 1968, the Centre of Advanced Study), Aligarh Muslim University. Not only has its library a very large number of rotograph, xerox, and reader-print copies, and microfilms and transcripts of MSS from various libraries in India and England (and a few from the Bibliotheque Nationale, Paris), but it has also acquired over time its own large collection of Mughal-period documents, comprising either the originals themselves or their photocopies and transcripts. Having been involved in many of these acquisitions, I can still savour those moments of excitement when an early document came to hand, or when one suddenly revealed, upon decipherment, information of a signally novel kind.

Dr Tarapada Mukherjee, of the School of Oriental and African Studies, London, sent me during the course of three or four years (1986-89), photocopies of a remarkable collection of documents relating to the Chaitanya-Vaishnavite temples of Vrindaban and the worldly transactions of their priests. Our collaborative studies (leading to the publication of three papers jointly written) were, alas, cut short by his untimely death. But thanks to his generosity, and the help of Mr Shrivatsa Goswami, I have been enabled to explore at leisure the documents of this large collection through very clear photographs. Much is owed too to Professor J.C. Wright's kindness in letting me use his unpublished transcriptions and translations of a number of Braj documents in this collection.

The late Professor S. Nurul Hasan and Professor Satish Chandra initiated studies in Rajasthani records at Aligarh; and the Department of History began to acquire transcripts from the Rajasthan State Archives. To the extent possible for me, I have tried to follow in their footsteps and complement my findings from the Persian sources with those from indigenous non-Persian material.

I was able to visit England in 1965, 1974, 1984 and 1991, and, while grateful to the British institutions that funded my travel, I am especially indebted to Miss Wenona Keane and Dr Brigid Keane for their kind hospitality on all the four occasions, which enabled me to look afresh at the rich material in British libraries.

The advantage I have drawn from daily intercourse at Aligarh with colleagues who work on different aspects of the history of the same period, and are willing all the time to inform and argue, is probably much greater than I am conscious of. A life-long friend, Professor M. Athar Ali, whom a late-detected cancer tore away from us last year, is now beyond the reach of my thanks. Shared causes have bound me over the years to Professor Iqtidar Alam Khan, whose endorsement of many conclusions of this book I so greatly value. To Professor Shireen Moosvi, pupil and then colleague, a very special debt is owed for the unstinted help she has throughout given me in the preparation of this edition.

Professor S.P. Verma, with his great knowledge of Mughal paintings, has helped me to locate relevant miniatures, from amongst which those reproduced in this edition have been selected. Professor Iqbal Husain has kindly guided me to certain Persian documents. My younger colleagues, Dr I.G. Khan, Mr Ishrat Alam, Mr S. Ali Nadeem Rezavi, Dr Farhat Hasan, Mr Jawed Akhtar and Dr S. Bashir Hasan have also helped in all manner of ways, enabling me to carry on my work with much ease of mind.

To the members of staff of the library of the Centre of Advanced Study, past and present, always courteous and cooperative, go my special thanks. I should like especially to mention Messrs Aijaz

Mohammad Khan, Jalal Abbas Abbasi, A.H. Fahmi, Abdul Haseeb, Hasan Imam Naqvi, M. Yusuf Siddiqi, Arshad Ali, H.P. Pali, R.R. Atiqi, Noor Ahmad, Bansidhar Sharma, Irfan Khan, Atamaduddin, Salman Ahmad, and Mazhar Husain.

To this list I should add the name of Mr Idris Beg, senior Office Attendant, always ready to undertake troublesome chores on one's behalf.

The initial work on the computer-processing had been carried out by Mr Sohail Ahmad, who fed in the first four chapters. The processing of the remaining text, the incorporation of numerous further changes in it made by me and the preparation of the camera-ready copy have all been the work of Mr Muneeruddin Khan, with some help in the early stages from Mr Shoaib Ahmad.

Much gratitude is owed to the Aligarh Historians Society which generously made available its excellent desktop publishing facilities for the making of the camera-ready copy.

The maps have been prepared by my son, Faiz Habib, Cartographic Assistant at the Centre of Advanced Study, in collaboration with his senior colleague, Mr Zahoor Ali Khan. Mr Ghulam Mujtaba, of the Archaeology Section of the Centre, has prepared the photographic copies from which the illustrations in this book are printed.

The page-proofs were closely scrutinized by Ms Shyama Warner, the editor assigned by the Oxford University Press, and to her many thanks are due for the corrections of linguistic and other slips. I had earlier benefited greatly from a scrutiny of the initial part of my text by Miss Salima Tyabji, then editor at the OUP. Ms Bela Malik, Commissioning Editor, OUP, has also earned my gratitude for paying so much attention to this book and for not letting me fall too far behind schedule.

My wife, Sayera, has been a source of both support and correction during all the stages this book has gone through. She had read its entire text, when it was in the form of a D.Phil. thesis, and has now read large portions of the revised version. I am particularly content that it has her approval.

IRFAN HABIB

Aligarh
30 August 1999

Excerpt from Preface to the First Edition (1963)

It is a pleasant duty for me to acknowledge the kindness of my teachers and friends from whose help and advice I have benefited. I am deeply grateful to Dr. C. Collin Davies, my Supervisor at Oxford, who allowed me the greatest latitude in respect of my views, but insisted upon precise expression and careful documentation. I can never forget the understanding and care with which he examined my work. From Professor S.A. Rashid, former Head of the Department of History, Aligarh, I received my first introduction to the subject and constant encouragement in my studies. Professor Rashid kindly went through the whole typescript of the book and suggested a number of changes in the text. He also lent me photographs and transcripts of Persian documents from the U.P. Central Record Office, Allahabad, which were in his possession. In the course of preparing the book for publication I obtained guidance and help from Professor S. Nurul Hasan, among whose pupils I have the privilege to count myself. It has been a source of pleasure and inspiration to work with my colleagues in the Department of History, Aligarh, who have allowed me to derive benefit from their work on related fields. I am particularly thankful to my friend and colleague, Dr. M. Athar Ali, who has generously helped me in seeing the book through the press. The discussions which I have had with Mr. B.R. Grover of the Delhi University, who is currently engaged in writing a detailed study of the Mughal land-revenue administration, have also been of considerable help to me. I will always cherish a grateful and happy memory of the kindness and affection my wife and I received from Miss Wenona Keane and Dr. Brigid Keane during the three years of our stay in England in which I prepared my thesis. I am, finally, grateful to my wife for correcting the entire typescript of the book and for her help in elucidating certain economic terms and ideas. None of those who have helped me are, of course, responsible for any errors that remain.

I am indebted to the authorities and staff of the Bodleian Library (Oxford), the British Museum (London), the Central Record Office (U.P.) (Allahabad), the India Office Library (London), the Indian Institute Library (Oxford), the John Rylands Library (Manchester), the Maulana Azad Library (Aligarh), the Research Library, Department of History (Aligarh), and the Royal Asiatic Society (London), for allowing me to use their collections; and to the authorities of the Edinburgh University Library for lending certain MSS to the Bodleian for my use.

CHAPTER I

AGRICULTURAL PRODUCTION

1. EXTENT OF CULTIVATION

The great cultivated expanse of the plains, valleys and hill-slopes of India has been created in the course of a stubborn struggle against Nature, which the Indian peasant has carried on for thousands of years. Forest and waste have retreated, recovered and again retreated, in endless cycles, before his hoe and plough. Every period in Indian history has had, therefore, its forest line and desert frontier, besides its political and military boundaries. For the study of Indian history in any of its aspects, this boundary line between Man's domain and Nature's is obviously of great importance. It defined the area under cultivation and, therefore, was always an index of the growth of population in the different parts of the country. It might equally be related to the existence of particular systems of production and economic organization. Hoe-cultivation, migratory agriculture, permanently settled cultivation, were all historical stages in the evolution of productive techniques, themselves in their turn so largely influenced by the extent to which virgin land was available for fresh occupation in the respective periods.

Our study of the agrarian system of Mughal India should, therefore, begin with a survey of the extent of the cultivated area in our period. General statements made on this subject by contemporaries are unfortunately not very helpful, for they are either vague or exaggerated and quite often mutually inconsistent.[1] There is sometimes information in our sources about the state of

[1] Three historians of Akbar's reign declare with one voice that the whole of the land in his Empire was fit for cultivation ('Ārif Qandahārī, 131; *Ṭabaqāt-i Akbarī*, 545; *Ā'īn*, II, 5-6). Sujān Rāi, 11, a late-17th-century writer, says more cautiously that "most of the land" of India was cultivable. But Mu'tamad Khān in his description of the empire at Akbar's death tells us that "according to the saying of the sages" only one-third of the total area was to be regarded as cultivable. He actually goes so far as to give us an estimate of the cultivable area on this basis. But he might well have spared himself, for he establishes the total area by first assuming the empire to have been a rectangle and then by taking his distances between the farthest points in the Empire for the sides of this rectangle. In working out the area from this, he makes the further error of equating 12,000 (instead of 5,000) *gaz* with the *kuroh* (*Iqbālnāma*, II, Or. 1834, f.231b.).

cultivation in particular areas, and here, perhaps, we are on surer ground. But, most important of all, records of the measured area and number of villages have survived from our period, and it is possible to use these as the basis for our survey.

The chapter entitled "Account of the Twelve Provinces" in Abū-l Fazl's *Ā'īn-i Akbarī* contains area statistics for all north Indian provinces, except Bengal, Thatta and Kashmir. These statistics are assigned to the 40th year of Akbar's reign, or 1595-6. For each of the provinces a figure is given in *bīghas* for what is called *zamīn-i paimūda* or "measured land". Then in the tables, under a column headed *ārāẓī* or "land", an entry is provided against each *sarkār* (the territorial division of a *ṣūba* or province); following this, figures are entered separately for all the *maḥals* or *parganas* composing the *sarkār*.[2] The great record of the *Ā'īn* remained unique in Mughal times; but statistics, though of a more summary kind, were compiled in the later years of Aurangzeb's reign (1659-1707). One table surviving in two or three manuscripts, gives the *raqba* or area statistics for each province, together with the number of villages, divided into those measured and unmeasured.[3] In the *Chahār Gulshan*, written by Rāi Chaturman

As for the area actually cultivated Niẓāmuddīn Aḥmad says, in explanation of the object of Akbar's administrative measures in 1574-5, that "most of the vast, inhabited area of Hindustan was lying uncultivated" (*Ṭabaqāt-i Akbarī,* II, 300). Yet Chandrabhān, writing in the last years of Shāhjahān, says that most of the cultivable area in Hindustan was in fact under the plough (*Chār Chaman,* Add. 16,863, f.32a.).

[2] The "Account of the Twelve Provinces" with its statistical tables will be found in Blochmann's edn. of the *Ā'īn,* I, 386-595. The year to which the statistics refer is mentioned on p.386. The statistics for the two Dakhin (Deccan) provinces, Khandesh and Berar, were inserted later; there are none for Ahmadnagar. In using Blochmann's edn. for these statistics, two things should be remembered. First, he has not reproduced the tables in their original form and has removed the columns with their headings altogether. Thus the figures in *bīghas* appear against each *sarkār* and *pargana* in his text without any explicit indication of what they represent. Secondly, he had only one good MS among the several on which he based his text; and besides the errors which he took on from some of his MSS, there are also a number of other typographical errors in the figures reproduced by him. I have, therefore, collated his entire text of the statistics with the corresponding portions of two of the earliest and best MSS of the *Ā'īn*, Add. 7652 and Add. 6552. Often the corrections resulting from this collation have been silently assumed in this book, unless the alterations are too large to be left unexplained. These are in general accord with the *ārāẓī* figures for *ṣūbas* and *sarkārs* as now worked out from a fresh scrutiny of the *Ā'īn's* MSS with arithmetical verification by Moosvi, 23-26.

[3] This record is preserved in two MSS, Bodl. Fraser 86, ff.57b-60b, and Edinburgh 224, ff. 1b-3b, 8a-11b. Figures from it have been abstracted and reproduced in Or.

in 1759-60, information about the area and villages is also provided separately for each *sarkār*.[4] Because its figures conform closely to those given for the provinces in the statistical table of Aurangzeb's reign, it seems certain that the *Chahār Gulshan* has reproduced statistics prepared in the last years of Aurangzeb, or very shortly afterwards. (See Table 1.1.)

The area figures in the *Ā'īn* are given in *bīgha-i Ilāhī*, while the unit in the later statistics is presumably the *bīgha-i daftarī*, which was two-thirds of a *bīgha-i Ilāhī* and came into use in the reign of Shāhjahān. The evidence brought together in Appendix A of this book suggests that the *bīgha-i Ilāhī* was 0.59 acre, or a shade less than 0.24 hectare.

The area figures of the Mughal times and of recent times can thus be converted into common units of area. But a proper comparison is impossible unless we know with some certainty what the "measured area" of the Mughal statistics represented. The Mughal administration measured the land primarily for assessing the revenue upon it. But, as we shall see in Chapter VI, the method of revenue assessment by measurement was by no means universal. Indeed, the fact that the statistics of Aurangzeb's reign, while generally showing considerable increase in area over the *Ā'īn's* figures, put down a large number of villages as unmeasured in all provinces, makes it clear that neither at the time of the *Ā'īn*, nor when these statistics were compiled, did measurement cover the entire revenue-paying area in any province. In other words, both sets of the statistics are incomplete. In the case of the later statistics, however, the stated numbers of measured and unmeasured villages offer some guidance about the total area of land that, according to the standards of the time, could have been measured.[5]

As to the kind of land covered by measurement in the Mughal

1286, ff. 310b-343a. These statistics, established after a collation of the MSS, are set out in tabular form on page 4.

[4] The *Chahār Gulshan,* ed. Chander Shekhar, New Delhi, 2011; portions translated by Jadunath Sarkar in his *India of Aurangzib,* Calcutta, 1901.

Bodl. Elliot 366 is not only the earliest among the catalogued MSS (cf. Storey, I, No. 631), but is also probably the most authoritative, being a copy of the original work and not of its later recension. Its reading has generally been preferred here to that of Sarkar's *India of Aurangzib,* which on the admission of the translator was based on a carelessly transcribed manuscript and contains many errors in the statistical portions.

[5] This is possible only in respect of provinces. The *Chahār Gulshan* does not

Table 1.1.
VILLAGE AND AREA STATISTICS OF AURANGZEB'S REIGN

Province	Total Number of Villages	Unmeasured Villages	Measured Villages	Measured Area in *bīghas* (*daftarī*)
The Empire, excluding Bijapur and Haidarabad	4,01,567	2,01,564	(2,00,003)	29,57,42,337
Bengal	1,12,788	1,11,250	1,538	3,34,775
Orissa			26,768	5,95,379
Bihar	55,376	24,036	31,340	1,27,53,156
Ilahabad	47,607	2,262	45,345	1,97,07,783
Awadh	(52,691)	18,849	33,842	1,90,27,308
Agra	30,180	2,877	27,303	4,01,00,551
Dehli	45,088	1,576	43,512	6,01,42,375
Lahor	27,761	3,192	24,569	2,43,19,376
Multan	(9,256)	4,559	4,697	44,54,203
Thatta	1,324	1,324		
Kabul	1,316	1,316		
Kashmir	5,352	5,352		
Ajmer	7,905	2,873	5,032	1,74,09,684
Gujarat	10,370	6,446	3,924	1,27,49,374
Malwa	18,678	11,742	6,936	1,29,64,538
Khandesh	6,339	3,507	2,832	88,59,325
Berar	10,878	137	10,741	2,00,18,113
Aurangabad	8,263	718	7,545	2,34,73,295
Bidar	4,526	1,007	3,519	79,06,193

Note: The figures in this table are drawn from Fraser 86, ff.57b-60b, and Edinburgh 224, ff. 1b-3b, 8a-11b. In the case of variants, Or. 1286, ff.310b-343a, and *Chahār Gulshan*, Bodl. Elliot 366, have been used to help in establishing the original figures. In the case of village statistics, readings of individual figures can be checked by comparing the total given in the MSS with the number of unmeasured and measured villages added together. Since almost all the variants are quite obviously due to errors in transcription or looseness in writing the *raqam* notation in the individual MSS, it has been thought unnecessary to set out the variants in detail. The figures for the villages may be treated as generally definitive, while in the area figures allowance should be made for possible variations in the last five digits.

period, Moreland has suggested that we should identify it with the "total cropped area" of modern statistics.[6] It included this certainly; but in this connexion we should speak more properly, perhaps, of the area sown, since the measured area also included the *nābūd*, or area affected by crop failure.[7] However, measurement does not seem to have been confined to land actually cultivated and was extended also to land regarded as cultivable.[8] Indeed, in the reign of Aurangzeb we hear of it as almost a standing complaint that the local officials sent returns only for the cultivable land and not for the land actually cultivated.[9] Some uncultivable land, such as was under habitation, tanks, nullahs, river, hill and jungle, was

provide us with area statistics for *sarkārs*, but only gives for them the total numbers of villages, without specifying how many of them were measured. The number of *maḥals* which did not return any village or area statistics is, however, often indicated for individual *sarkārs*.

The conclusions drawn by Moreland after a painstaking comparison of the *Ā'īn's* statistics with modern cropped area statistics, in respect of the western and eastern districts of the United Provinces, in the *JUPHS*, II, 1919, 1-39, and summarily stated in respect of other parts of northern India, in his *India at the Death of Akbar*, 20-22, must be substantially modified for the simple reason that they are based on the assumption that the *Ā'īn's ārāẓī* figures cover the entire area cultivated at the time. K.K. Trivedi's exercise in the same field (*Studies in History*, XIV [1998], 302-11) is fanciful in the extreme: he simply invents "gross cultivation" by flatly dividing the *Ā'īn's jama'* by 40 (p.308).

[6] *JUPHS*, II (1919), i, 3, 17. The total area cropped is obtained by adding together the land under each of the seasonal crops of the year, while the net area cropped is the total reduced by "the area cropped more than once". The latter, usually called double-cropped land, was designated *do-faṣla*, as against *yak-faṣla*, single-cropped land, in the Mughal administration. Todar Mal prescribed that both were to be measured (Memorandum of the 27th Regnal Year, *A.N.*, Add. 27,247, f.332a). For the unique perception of "double-cropped land" as one bearing a crop which "takes more than one season to mature", see Trivedi, *Studies in History*, XIV (1998), 303.

[7] For the measurement of cultivated land, see the Regulations drafted by Todar Mal in 1582: "It is known that in the *parganas* of the *k͟hāliṣa* the (recorded) area (*ārāẓī*) is less every year. Therefore, when the cultivated land has once been measured, they should, increasing it (the area measured) from year to year, establish a partial *nasaq*" (*A.N.*, III, 383; Add. 27,247, f.331b). For inclusion of *nābūd*, see the Regulations for the *Bitikchī* in the *Ā'īn*, I, 288. In the more recent of modern statistics, figures are given not for the area cropped, but for the area sown.

[8] The area of cultivable land is indicated in the measured area figures for *pargana* Merta, *ṣūba* Ajmer, dated VS1630/AD 1572-73, in Nainsī, *Vigat*, II, 77; in the draft of the *muwāzana-i dah-sāla* in the *Dastūru-l 'Amal-i 'Ālamgīrī*, f. 36b; and in the records of the village and *pargana* of Papal (Berar) of 1682-3 (1090 Fasli) described and analysed by Y.K. Deshpande, *IHRC* (1929), 84-86. See also the figures ascribed to Todar Mal's survey of Gujarat in *Mir'āt*, I, 25, where the area of the cultivable, not cultivated, land is entered.

[9] Aurangzeb's *farmān* to Rasikdās; and *parwāna* in the *Nigārnāma-i-Munshī*, ed., 77.

also measured.[10] We may assume that measurement of such land was confined to the limits of villages and settlements and was not extended to large forests or wastes, so that it must normally have accounted for a very small portion of the measured area, perhaps not exceeding a tenth of the whole.

The measured area of the Mughal records then corresponds broadly to the area covered by three categories in modern agricultural statistics: "Total area cropped (or sown)"; "current fallows"; and "cultivable wastes other than fallows". It is obvious that while the land actually cropped can be precisely determined, the word "cultivable" is open to many definitions, and it is difficult to say whether the Mughal and modern (British-Indian) statisticians used the same criteria, if, indeed, either of them used any uniform criteria at all.[11] Nevertheless, it would seem likely that the tendency of local officials, both in the Mughal and the British periods, would have been to classify only that waste as cultivable which stood on the margin of existing cultivation rather than what might be ideally cultivable, that is, cultivable if, for example, large forests were cleared or canals brought from a distance. Generally speaking, therefore, the area of cultivable waste so determined should usually bear a more or less stable proportion to the area actually cultivated, till so long, that is, as the latter does not begin to approach the limits of the total area of land. If this view is accepted, a comparison of

[10] The types of uncultivable land mentioned in the text are specified in Nainsī, *Vigat*, II, 77, for *pargana* Merta, the total uncultivable land amounting to 8.4% of the measured land. See also *Dastūru-l 'Amal-i 'Ālamgīrī*, f. 36b, where, excluding the garden land, the land designated as uncultivable amounts to just 4.1 per cent of the total measured area. In the records of the Papal *pargana* however, the uncultivable land is shown as amounting to one-fourth of the whole. But it consisted largely (430 out of 505 *netans*) of grazing land (*IHRC* [1929], 84-85). The grazing land might not really have been uncultivable, but placed in that category because it was protected from any encroachments. It was authoritatively estimated in 1928 that grazing lands then covered three-fourths of the lands classed as "culturable waste" in the official statistics, while they covered only a fourth of the waste not available for cultivation (Royal Commission on Agriculture, *Report*, 177). In the *Mir'āt*, I, 25, the uncultivable portion of the measured land, consisting of "the area under habitation, jungle, etc." is shown as amounting to nearly a third of the whole measured area. It is not clear if it included grazing land. If it did not include it, there would seem to have been little reason for measuring such vast areas of wasteland. See also Moosvi, 41-44.

[11] The Royal Commission on Agriculture, *Report*, 604-5, points out that the division between the categories "culturable waste" and "land not available for cultivation" in modern statistics is purely arbitrary, and the former sometimes includes land which is not really cultivable.

the measured area statistics of the Mughal period with the figures for the cultivable area from recent times will become useful, for then it can be taken as a rough indication of the changes that have taken place in the actual extent of cultivation in the intervening period.

There is far less danger of confusion in comparing the numbers of villages given in the statistics of the two periods. Villages are usually visibly distinct units, and one may expect that they could always be counted with precision.[12] However, the average size of the village, in population and area, might vary from locality to locality and from century to century. A comparison of the village statistics alone, therefore, cannot directly help us to form an estimate of the cultivated area in the Mughal period. But when set alongside other information, especially the area statistics, it might have some corroborative value.

For a comparative study of the Mughal and modern statistics, it is essential that the boundaries of the territorial units of the Mughal Empire be accurately determined. Detailed studies were attempted by Elliot and Beames for the location of *maḥals* listed in the *Ā'īn* under the provinces of the Gangetic basin.[13] The boundaries of these and other provinces and *sarkārs* have been drawn on the basis of the *Ā'īn's* lists in my *Atlas of the Mughal Empire*.[14] For the Dakhin provinces, an eighteenth-century work, the *Dastūru-l 'Amal-i Shāhanshāhī*,[15] has also been used here, since it gives lists of *maḥals*

[12] The statement about villages being visibly distinct units is not, perhaps, true for all parts of India. Bengal might be an exception, for instance. Modern censuses also imply a distinction between revenue and actual villages; but they themselves give figures only for the latter.

[13] For the portions of the Mughal provinces of Dehli, Agra, Ilahabad and Awadh, lying in the British 'North-western Provinces' (excluding 'Oudh'), see Elliot, *Memoirs*, II, 82-146 and 203-6 (maps facing p.203). See J. Beames 'On the Geography of India in the Reign of Akbar', Part I, *JASB*, LIII (1884), 215-32 (with map) for Awadh; and Part ii, *JASB,* LIV (1885), 162-82 (with map) for Bihar. For Bengal see Blochmann, 'Contributions to the Geography and History of Bengal (Muhammadan Period)', Part I, *JASB,* XII, (1873), 209-310; and J. Beames, 'Notes on Akbar's Subahs', *JRAS* (1896), 83-186, (with map). For Orissa, see Beames, *JRAS*, (1896), 743-65 (with map), and Manmohan Chakravarti, *JASB*, N.B., XII, 29-56. For the Punjab, I.R. Khan, 'Historical Geography of the Punjab and Sind', *Muslim University Journal*, II, No.1, 1934, pp.31-55, is helpful, though the contribution was not completed and the maps referred to in it have not been printed.

[14] *An Atlas of the Mughal Empire – Political and Economic Maps with Detailed Notes*, Delhi, 1982; reprint with additions, Delhi, 1986.

[15] Add. 22,831. This gives *maḥal*-wise statistics of villages and revenue. It also contains certain references to events of administrative history not easily found

in territory added to the Empire after the time of the *Ā'īn*. The boundaries of Mughal territorial divisions did not remain fixed. Several important changes are known to have taken place, though they were more numerous in the Dakhin, the scene of constant military operations and piecemeal annexations, than in northern India.[16] These must be taken into account especially when referring to the statistics of Aurangzeb's reign.

---

elsewhere. Similar information is also given in Lachhmī Narāin "Shafīq", *Khulāṣatu-l Hind*, transcript from Asafiya Library (Hyderabad) MS in Department of History, Aligarh.

[16] The following changes may be especially noted:

The *sarkār* of Kamrup was added to Bengal, presumably after Mīr Jumla's Assam campaign (cf. *Chahār Gulshan*, f.543a, Sarkar, 133). Shā'ista Khān's conquest of Chatgaon (Chittagong) in 1666 implied no formal change, for the territory (as a *sarkār*) was already claimed for the empire in the *Ā'īn*. Orissa, shown in the *Ā'īn* as a *sarkār* (really a sub-*ṣūba*) of Bengal, begins to appear as a separate province in the revenue records of Shāhjahān's reign, subsequent to the *Majālisu-s Salāṭīn*, ff.114a-115b.

For some time the *sarkār* of Jaunpur seems to have been transferred from the province of Ilahabad to Bihar (cf. ibid., and *Selected Documents of Shāh Jahān's Reign*, 112); but it was later restored to Ilahabad (cf. *Dastūru-l 'Amal-i 'Ālamgīrī*, f.114a).

The *sarkārs* of Tijara and Narnaul were transferred from the Agra province to Dehli before the close of Aurangzeb's reign (ibid., f.109a-b; *Chahār Gulshan*, f.35b, Sarkar, 125-6).

The *sarkār* (or sub-*ṣūba*) of Thatta was still included in the Multan province at the time of the *Majālisu-s Salāṭīn*, but, like Orissa, begins to appear as a separate province in subsequent documents. One of its former *sarkārs*, Siwistan, however, remained with Multan (cf. *Dastūru-l 'Amal-i 'Ālamgīrī*, ff.110b-111a; *Chahār Gulshan*, f. 44a-b, Sarkar, 130-131).

Kashmir's position as a *sarkār* or sub-*ṣūba* of Kabul, seems to have been from the beginning a mere matter of form; the revenue table in the *Majālisu-s Salāṭīn* is the last document of its kind in which it appears as an appendage of Kabul.

The *sarkār* of Sirohi was a part of Ajmer province at the time of the *Ā'īn*. At an uncertain date it was divided into the *sarkārs* of Bansballa, Dongarpur and Sirohi, which were all transferred to Gujarat (cf. *Mir'āt*, Supp., 225-6).

In his 8th regnal year Shāhjahān ordered the transfer from Malwa of all its territories south of the Narmada river, viz. the *sarkārs* of Baijagarh and Nandurbar and most of the *maḥals* of Handia, to Khandesh (Lāhorī, I, ii, 62-3, Ṣādiq Khān, Or. 174, ff.60a-61a, Or. 1671, ff.33b-34a; *Dastūru-l 'Amal-i Shāhanshāhī*, ff.29a, 32a, 34b). Baglana, after being annexed in 1638, was treated as a separate unit (*mulk*) for some time, but in or by 1658 was attached to Khandesh as a *sarkār* (Ṣādiq Khān, Or.174, ff.60b-61a, 87b-88a, Or.1671, ff.33b-34a, 48a; *Dastūru-l 'Amal-i Shāhanshāhī*, f.29b).

Shāhjahān separated the *sarkār* of Telangana from Berar and made it into a separate province, probably in the 8th regnal year (Lāhorī, I, ii, 62-63, 205); but towards the end of the reign, it was merged with the newly annexed territory of Bidar to form the province of Bidar (*Dastūru-l 'Amal-i Shāhanshāhī*, f.80a).

Though complete accuracy must await the time when the limits of all or almost all the *maḥals* of Mughal times can be plotted on the map, the margin of error can still be very greatly reduced by considering only large blocks of territory, placed within limits that can be defined with relatively greater exactitude. In most cases it can be so arranged that the area of the doubtful territory between two such blocks is practically insignificant in comparison with the area known to be definitely covered by either of the blocks. Thus, though it may be difficult at present to establish accurately the boundary between the Mughal provinces of Lahor and Multan, the limits of the territory covered by the Lahor province and the *sarkārs* of Multan and Dipalpur of the Multan province can be laid down with tolerable certainty. Even this case is exceptional, and most Mughal provinces, and often groups of *sarkārs* within them, can be separately treated as blocks and their boundaries put on the map without very serious danger of error.

From modern statistics one is entitled to demand greater detail as well as completeness. Fairly reliable agricultural statistics and census returns for divisions below the level of districts begin to be available from the last quarter of the nineteenth century.[17] But in the present study, for the reason that we are only considering large areas, the series of *Agricultural Statistics*, giving annual returns for districts, has been considered adequate.[18] For villages the numbers given district-wise in the census reports have been used. Both the agricultural statistics and censuses are often incomplete, especially in the earlier years, in respect of the princely states. In such cases information from later returns, or from the *Imperial Gazetteer*, has been drawn upon. It will be noticed that, as a rule, our attempt has been to use figures from the period around the beginning of the twentieth century.[19] This has been done partly because Moreland, who was the pioneer in such comparative study,

Northern Konkan, or the Talkokan-i Niẓāmul Mulkī, had been ceded to Bijapur upon the final conquest of Ahmadnagar. But it was attached to the province of Aurangabad, apparently, after Aurangzeb's 1657 campaign against Bijapur (ibid., ff.77b-78a; *'Amal-i Ṣāliḥ*, III, 262-3).

[17] The best source where these will be found, if one is not interested in statistics of any particular year, is the *District Gazetteers*.

[18] *The Agricultural Statistics of India*, issued by the Department of Revenue and Agriculture (and successors), Government of India, published at uneven intervals.

[19] The *Agricultural Statistics* mostly used are those of 1899-1900, 1909-10 and 1920-21; and the Censuses, of 1881, 1891 and 1901. Later returns have been used only where the earlier ones were either incomplete or not easily available.

worked with the figures of this period, but mainly under the conviction that this was the time when India felt the full economic effects of British rule in their most unalloyed form; and it therefore provides a good vantage point for comparison with conditions in the best days of the earlier empire.

For our regional survey, Bengal as the easternmost province of the Empire, may best serve as the starting point. The *Āʾīn* does not provide any area statistics for this province, and only an insignificant number of its villages is classed as 'measured' in the statistics of Aurangzeb's reign. Excluding Kamrup, there were 109,923 villages under Aurangzeb,[20] compared with 116,153 in the corresponding territory in 1881. It would, indeed, seem from contemporary statements that most of the province was fully occupied in Mughal times.[21] Blochmann came to the conclusion, from an examination of the *mahals* listed in the *Āʾīn*, that cultivation then extended as far down to the deltaic Sundarbans as in his own day (1873).[22] The eastern parts of the delta were, however, mercilessly ravaged and depopulated for the greater part of our period by the Magh pirates.[23] An extensive resettlement of the Bakarganj ('Backergunge') district began only after the successful Mughal expedition of 1665-6 against Arakan,[24] though the Sandwip Island had already been colonized by a rebel chieftain.[25] Further to the east the forests were probably considerably more extensive than now. In the Chatgaon ('Chittagong') territory, heavily overgrown with forest under the Maghs,[26] the extent of reclamation under the Mughals could only have been slight.[27] There were dense forests in the district of Sylhet down to the eighteenth century;[28] and it is possible that the Bhowal or Madhupur jungle covered a wider area.[29]

Unfortunately, nothing can be deduced for Orissa with any confidence. There are no *ārāẓī* statistics for it in the *Āʾīn*, and modern

[20] Both Aurangzeb's statistics and the *Chahār Gulshan* agree as to the total number of villages in the province, viz. 112,788. From this the figure for the *sarkār* of Kamrup, whose limits are uncertain, have been deducted, according as it appears in the Bodl. MS., f.53a, of the *Chahār Gulshan*.

[21] Manrique, II, 123; Bernier, 202, 441-2.

[22] *JASB*, XLII (1873), 227, 228, 231-2.

[23] *Fatḥiya ʿIbriya*, ff.122b, 123b, 164a-b, 173b; Bernier, 175; Master, II, 66.

[24] *JASB*, XLII, (1873), 228, 229, 232.

[25] *Fatḥiya ʿIbriya*, ff.142a-b, 143b, 144a, 150a. [26] Ibid., f.164a-b.

[27] *JRAS* (1896), 127. [28] *Āʾīn*, I, 391; and *JRAS* (1896), 131.

[29] The forest lay in the *sarkār* of Bazuha. Cf. *Āʾīn*, I, 390; *JRAS* (1896), 127.

statistics are also either incomplete, or, in their published form, not detailed enough for the large number of petty states in the region. However, there is good evidence for extensive forests in the province in Mughal times.[30]

For Bihar, Aurangzeb's statistics show a measured area, which on conversion from *bīgha-i daftarī* to *bīgha-ī Ilāhī*, amounts to more than three times the area shown in the *Ā'īn*. But though over a half of the total number of villages are shown to have been measured, the area under Aurangzeb still came to a fourth of the total cultivable area recorded in 1899-1900. This may be explained partly by the possibility that the Mughals confined their measurement to the narrow and densely populated belt along the Ganga, where the lands under each village would have been smaller in size than of the average village lying outside this core zone. The total number of villages assigned to the province was, however, practically equal to that counted by the 1881 Census. The *Chahār Gulshan* shows that this applied also to the case of the four *sarkārs* situated wholly to the north of the Ganga, though the figure for the easternmost *sarkār*, Mungir, which also stretched across the river into the Tarai is much smaller. It is not to be imagined, therefore, that the Tarai forest held an undisturbed sway in the region. Some *maḥals* listed in the *Ā'īn* lie close under the hills in Nepal, while large areas more to the south were then apparently under forest. Large tracts have been cleared that lay then in wilderness, but there have been previous clearings too which in late nineteenth century were overrun by the jungle.[31]

To the west of Bihar lay the two provinces of Ilahabad (Allahabad) and Awadh. The former covered large blocks of territory on both sides of the Ganga, stretching deep into Baghelkhand and also including the lower portions of the Ganga-Yamuna Doab and of the Ganga-Ghaghara Doab. Awadh extended to its north, from the river Gandhak in the east to the Ganga in the west. Only a very small part of the cultivated area of the two provinces had been measured in the time of the *Ā'īn*.[32] But measurement seems to have been considerably extended in the following century. Aurangzeb's statistics show that practically all the villages of the Ilahabad

[30] See *Atlas*, Sheet 12 & Notes, 51, cols. 1 & 2.

[31] Cf. Beames in *JASB*, LIV, 177. In the *sarkār* of Champaran the *maḥal* of Simranu stretched into Nepal and the ruins of its capital lie "among dense jungle". The territory around Bettiah, on the other hand, is said to be a more recent clearing.

[32] This can be seen from the fact that the *Ā'īn* entered nearly 4 million *bīghas*

province were covered by measurement. The measured area then was about half the cultivable area reported in 1909-10. In Awadh well over a third of the villages were unmeasured and the measured area came to about two-fifths of the 1909-10 figure.

The numbers of the villages assigned to the two provinces are considerably larger than the numbers recorded in the 1881Census – larger by one-third in Ilahabad and by one-half in Awadh. But the *sarkār* of Gorakhpur contained about the same number of villages as its territory contained in 1881; that is to say, it did not have the same numerical superiority in villages *c.*1700 over 1881 which the other parts of Awadh possessed.[33] It was, therefore, probably more backward in cultivation.[34] Indeed, in 1703 the governor of Awadh described the *sarkār* as "absolutely desolate".[35] Much of it must have been covered by the Tarai forest. From Tavernier it would appear that all was forest north of the town of Gorakhpur.[36] And we know that the forest retained its old domain up till the beginning of the nineteenth century, when, at last, a general process of reclamation began in this region.[37] Across the Ghaghara to the south, a dense forest existed along the Tons river in the eastern parts of the Azamgarh district, where there are now

---

for Ilahabad and slightly over 10 million for Awadh, while the corresponding figures in the statistics of Aurangzeb's reign converted into the same units of area, are 13.1 and 12.7 million *bīghas*. Yet over one-third of the villages of Awadh had not yet been measured in the time of Aurangzeb.

Moreland was, therfore, in obvious error when he took the *Ā'īn's* area figures to represent the entire cropped area and concluded that since its time there had been a five-fold increase in the cultivated area in the Ghaghara-Ganga Doab and a 17-fold, possibly a 40-fold, increase in the Trans-Ghaghara tract (*JUPHS*, II [1919], 18ff). Moosvi, 46-51, corrects Moreland here by a comparison of *jama'-ārāẓī* ratios, which are a good index of the extent of undermeasurement of assessed land.

33 The number of villages in the Gorakhpur *sarkār* is given in *Chahār Gulshan*. f.59a. In Sarkar, 137, the figures for this *sarkār* have been interchanged with those for Lakhnau. The *Chahār Gulshan* enters no figure for area under Gorakhpur.

34 Moosvi, 50-51, too reaches this conclusion but by an examination of *jama'-ārāẓī* ratios in the *Ā'īn*.

35 *Akhbārāt* 47/320. The *sarkār* of Gorakhpur had then been renamed Mu'aẕẕam-ābād-Gorakhpur or simply Mu'aẕẕamābād.

36 Tavernier, II, 205.

37 Muftī Ghulām Ḥaẓarat in his Persian memoir of the Gorakhpur district, written in or before 1810, says that the city of Gorakhpur was surrounded on two sides by forest and that "in certain *tappas* of the *parganas* of Unaula, Bansi, Silhat, Basti, Maghar and Gorakhpur, the country is extremely desolate, being uninhabited, owing to the scarcity of the peasants, or the jungle, or the inroads of wild elephants" (I.O.4540, f.1a). He adds, however, that the promulgation of lower revenue rates had begun to attract cultivators from the neighbouring areas (ff.9b-

no traces of any jungle.[38] There were extensive forests, again, between Jaunpur and Ilahabad,[39] and stretches of forest lay too between Ilahabad and Banaras.[40]

The Agra province comprised the central Doab and a large block of territory on the right side of the Yamuna, both north and south of the Chambal river. Almost all its villages were under measurement during the reign of Aurangzeb, though the area recorded was about the same as in the *Ā'īn* (making allowance for the transfer of Tijara and Narnaul to Dehli).[41] It amounted to about five-sixths of the cultivable area reported for the corresponding territory in 1909-10, so that the result for the whole province is practically the same as that obtained by Moreland from a comparison of the *Ā'īn* and modern 'cropped area' statistics, relating to the central Doab.[42] The number of villages assigned to the province in Aurangzeb's record was about one-third larger than the figure derived from the 1881 and later censuses.[43]

The general picture of almost full occupation of the land in the Agra province, which these statistics present, is confirmed by

---

10a). The Gorakhpur district at that time also included the districts of Basti, Gonda and Deoria.

[38] *A.N.*, III, 266-7. It would appear from this passage that the forest lay along the southern bank of the river Sarūār, i.e. the Chhoti Sarju or Eastern Tons, between Muhammadabad and Mau.

[39] The original evidence for the forest consists of the following statement by Finch, in the course of a description of various itineraries: "Thus much from Agra to Jounpore this way [i.e. via Lakhnau and Ajodhya]; from thence (returning that way to Agra) to Alabasse is 110 c. [*kos*] 30c. all which are thorow a continuall forest" (*Early Travels*, 177). It is possible to interpret this statement as meaning that the distance between Jaunpur and Ilahabad was 110 *kos*, of which 30 *kos* were covered by a forest. This is how De Laet, 65, in copying Finch, has read it. The interpretation put forward by the editor of *Early Travels*, 177*n.*, is however, that 110 *kos* represented the distance of the route from Jaunpur to Agra, via Ilahabad ('a gross under-estimate'), and 30 *kos* that part of it which lay between Jaunpur and Ilahabad.

[40] Mundy, II, 110, 119. Cf. *Atlas*, Sheet 8B, & Notes, 31 col. (b).

[41] It should be noted that Blochmann's figure in his edition of the *Ā'īn* for the *sarkār* of Agra is incorrect. Add. 7652 shows it should be 9.1 million, not 91.0 million *bīghas*. The *Ā'īn's* figure for the *sarkār* of Kalpi is some 14 lakhs lower than the total of the *pargana* figures under it. In the *Chahār Gulshan*, Sarkar, 126-7, reads "two crores" for the Agra *sarkār*, where Bodl. MS., f.39a, reads "one crore" only, and the latter is doubtless correct. Sarkar also interchanges the figures for Gwalior and Kol.

[42] *JUPHS*, II (1919), 19.

[43] The later censuses are used only where, as in the case of 'native states', sufficient details are not given in the 1881 Census.

Pelsaert, who says that in the Agra region there was a great shortage of firewood, and trees were scarce.[44] The references to a desolate zone near the Yamuna, where tigers could be hunted[45] and rebellious peasants sought refuge,[46] apply to the Chambal and Yamuna ravines which still maintain their reputation for wildness.

The province of Dehli consisted of three distinct geographical units: the country now known as Rohilkhand, the Upper Doab and the Haryana tract. By the reign of Aurangzeb practically all villages had been brought under measurement and the area recorded had grown by nearly a third over the *Ā'īn's* figure (including Tijara and Narnaul). It came, moreover, to about four-fifths of the cultivable area returned in 1909-10. At the same time the number of villages in Aurangzeb's statistics was nearly one-half larger than that recorded in the 1881 Census. The *Chahār Gulshan* shows that, compared to the conditions *c.*1910, there was no particular disparity between the Doab and Rohilkhand, such as Moreland and Moosvi, drawing on the evidence of the *Ā'īn*, have suggested.[47] There are some indications in contemporary literature which enable us to approximately trace the forest line in the north. We know that the *maḥal* of Gola in the *sarkār* of Badaun, which covered a very large tract in the present Shahjahanpur district and projected into Kheri, was almost unsurveyed at the time of the *Ā'īn*. But by 1119 Fasli or 1711, it had come to comprise ten *tappas* with 1,484 villages.[48] The explanation might be that the area was previously in the hands of local chiefs, but was now seized from them and brought under proper administration.[49] Yet it might equally indicate a real advance of cultivation at the expense of forest. In any case, the large number of settled villages assigned

[44] Pelsaert, 48. [45] *T.J.*, 279; Lāhorī, I, ii, 5. [46] *T.J.*, 375-6.

[47] While Moreland found only a "slight increase" in the Doab districts, he thought that the cropped area had increased by one-half in "Badaun, etc." and had doubled in Bareilly and nearly doubled in part of Bijnor district (*JUPHS*, II [1919], 18-19). Moosvi, 50-51, reaches similar conclusions through her calculations of *jama'-ārāẓī* ratios. The present districts of Badaun and Bareilly lay in the Badaun *sarkār*. The area given for Badaun *sarkār* in the *Chahār Gulshan* is double that given in the *Ā'īn* (after conversion into common units). This means that much of the increase postulated by Moreland could have taken place in the 17th century. For Badaun and other *sarkārs* of Dehli, only Bodl. MS. of the *Chahār Gulshan*, ff.35a-36a, should be used. The figures in Sarkar, 124-6, are very defective and must be set aside.

[48] "*Qānūngo* papers" cited by Elliot, *Memoirs*, II, 167-8.

[49] A battle between a *zamīndār* and local *jāgīrdārs* in the *ẓila'* or country of Gola and Kant (Shahjahanpur) in the reign of Shāhjahān is mentioned by Ṣādiq Khān, Or.174, f.183b, Or.1671, f.90a.

to this *maḥal* in the later record, shows that the process of reclamation had in the main been completed here by the end of our period.[50] Further to the north-west there seems to have been a ring of forest around Aonla,[51] which by early twentieth century had almost disappeared.[52] The Rampur territory was apparently well cleared,[53] but the plains of Naini Tal district lay in dense forest down to the earlier part of the eighteenth century.[54] The Dun valley, on the other hand, contained "inhabited villages and *maḥals*" and a certain amount of peasant population.[55]

Both in the Doab and Haryana the role of canal irrigation became important by the closing decades of the nineteenth century. The area thus irrigated in 1909-10 was about one-fifth of the net cropped area of the Upper Doab and about one-tenth of that of Haryana. But the British canal system provided more a safeguard against drought and a means of improving the crops, than a means of extending cultivation.[56] This might explain why the cultivated area had not materially increased in this region by *c.*1910 when large areas in Haryana were still neglected simply for lack of water, as in the earlier times.[57]

It is, in fact, further to the west, in the Indus plains, that the modern

[50] Rennell's Map of 'Oude and Allahabad', 1780, in his *Bengal Atlas*, shows that the territory around Shahjahanpur was by now well-cleared, although the territory along the upper reaches of the Gomti and its tributaries was under forest. The measured areas assigned to Aonla and surrounding *maḥals* in the *Ā'īn* do not also lend any support to the belief that a large forest was in existence in the area at that time.

[51] Yaḥyā Sirhindī, *Tārīkh-i Mubārakshāhī*, ed. M. Hidayat Husain, 187. This should have represented the situation in the 15th century, when the work was written. Cf. Elliot, *Memoirs*, II, 150, who attributes the statement to Badāūnī.

[52] It survived in name, however, for Circle III of the Aonla *pargana* was known as the "Aonla jungle" which had "large areas of dhak jungle". (Moreland, *Agricultural Conditions of the United Provinces & Districts:*Note on Bareilly, 5).

[53] Elliot, *Memoirs*, II, 138.

[54] Elliot, *Memoirs*, II, 150-51, citing the testimony of two travellers of the period, Yār Muḥammad and Tieffenthaler, about the country around and beyond Kashipur and Rudarpur. When Elliot says that in "the Mohomedan histories" all beyond Amroha, Lakhnor and Aonla is spoken of as "a desert (sic!) which the Imperial troops fear to penetrate", he has probably only the period of the Delhi Sultans in mind. This line was well breached by the time of the *Ā'īn* as a glance at Elliot's own map would show. Moreland accepted this statement as applying also to Mughal times, but suggested certain modifications (*JUPHS*, II [1919], 20).

[55] Wāriṣ, a: f.49a; b: f.142b-143b.

[56] Royal Commission on Agriculture, *Report*, 325. Cf. Moosvi, 74-79.

[57] Thevenot, 69, says of "Dehly" that "The Ground about it is excellent, where it is not neglected, but in many parts it is".

canal system brought about a fundamental change. Here, the Mughal province of Lahor covered the northern portion of the Panjab in its strict geographical sense. To the south of it stretched the province of Multan, extending down to the Indus delta in the time of the *Āʾīn,* but later on only to below Sehwan. The measured area of Lahor province does not show any noticeable alteration between the *Āʾīn* and the statistics of Aurangzeb's reign, when nine-tenths of the villages are shown to have been measured. In Multan province, the practice of measurement was apparently abandoned in the *sarkārs* of Multan and Bhakkar, but almost all the villages of Dipalpur *sarkār* had come under measurement by the later years of our period.[58]

Taking, then, the Lahor province and Dipalpur *sarkār* together, we find that the area recorded under them amounted to less than half the cultivable area of the corresponding districts and states in 1909-10. There is an interesting tradition preserved by a late seventeenth-century historian to the effect that the Panjab had been grievously laid waste and depopulated by the successive invasions of the Mongols and that a recovery began only under the Lodis, when, for example, the town of Batala was founded in the Upper Bari Doab in a clearing amidst wasteland and forest.[59] And although the province enjoyed a period of exceptional peace and security under the Mughals,[60] it is not unlikely that some of the effects of the desolation still remained. Moreover, besides the periodic havoc caused by uncontrolled rivers, when in flood, the Beas and Sutlej rivers had created in the region of Dipalpur an extensive waste, known as the Lakhi jungle.[61] The extent to which the canals are responsible for the change since those days may be seen from the fact that the proportion of land irrigated by government canals in the districts and states of the British Punjab, lying within the Mughal provinces of Lahor and Multan, was over one-third of the net area cropped in 1909-10, and, in terms of total cropping, the proportion would have been still higher. It is not to be thought, of course, that every acre irrigated by the new

[58] This is based upon a comparison of the provincial total in Aurangzeb's statistics and the provincial and *sarkār* figures in the *Chahār Gulshan*, f.44a-b, Sarkar, 130.

[59] Sujān Rāi, 66-7.

[60] This is emphasized in ibid., 88, where it is stated that in the Mughal possession of Kabul lay the key to the prosperity of the Panjab.

[61] Ibid., 63; Manucci II, 457-8 and tr.'s n. on 457.

canals was unploughed before. Indeed the canals have superseded, while the embankments have closed, most of the old inundation channels and man-made canals. But by the same means the Lakhi jungle and such other wastelands were also eliminated; and, on the balance, the extension brought about by the modern canal system by *c*.1910 was undoubtedly considerable.

Despite this increase in cultivation, the numbers of villages assigned in Aurangzeb's statistics to Lahor province and Multan and Dipalpur *sarkārs,* exceeded by over one-half the 1881 Census figure of villages for the same region.[62]

The province of Thatta was entirely unmeasured and the only data from the Mughal period that we have for it relate to the number of villages. In contrast to the position in the Panjab and other parts of Northern India, the number assigned to Thatta, together with Bhakkar and Siwistan (Sehwan) *sarkārs*, amounts to but two-thirds of the 1881 figure for Sind,[63] although the Mughal region was considerably larger. This alone may or may not mean that this region was exceptionally desolate in Mughal times. Inundation channels and canals there were, as we shall see; but still the fact that the modern Government canals irrigated nearly three-fourths of the net sown area of Sind in 1909-10, speaks for the extent of change that must have followed the spread of canal irrigation.

Like Sind, Kashmir was also unmeasured. The number of villages, as recorded in the Mughal statistics,[64] was practically the same as that of the 1901Census for the corresponding districts. Little can at the moment be said about the province of Ajmer, because while the Mughal area statistics for the province are very incomplete,[65] British agricultural statistics too cover only a part of its total area. In a recent comparison of the detailed village lists for Marwar in Nainsī's

[62] The *Chahār Gulshan* (f. 44a-b, Sarkar, 130) figures have been used for the two *sarkārs*.

[63] Including Khairpur, for which the *Imperial Gazetteer*, s.v., has served as the source.

[64] Muḥammad A'ẓam in his *Wāqi'āt-i Kashmīr khātima* (conclusion) (written, 1747) (MS in private possession), records the number of villages in each of the 37 *parganas* within the Kashmīr Valley, and gives the total number for the Valley as 3,270 only, as compared with 5,352 villages enumerated in the statistics of Aurangzeb's reign. This discrepancy needs to be investigated.

[65] This is apparent not only from the *Ā'īn* and the *Chahār Gulshan*, but also from a detailed memoir (*yāddāsht*), giving the figures for revenue and villages (in a number of cases) for each *maḥal* (Royal Asiatic Society, London: MS. Persian 173).

Vigat (early 1660s) with those of the corresponding area in the 1891 Census, it has been claimed that the number of villages remained about the same.[66]

In Gujarat the practice of assessing land revenue on the basis of measurement was superseded, partially at least, under Akbar's successors.[67] It is not surprising, therefore, that in the reign of Aurangzeb as many as 6,446 out of 10,370 villages should have been unmeasured and the recorded area amounted only to about half that of the *Ā'īn*. Besides these statistics we have a summary statement of the measured area for this province in the *Mir'āt-i Aḥmadī*,[68] allegedly based upon the survey of Todar Mal. But the total figure is very close to that in Aurangzeb's statistics and the *Chahār Gulshan*, and the specification of the unmeasured *sarkārs*, with one exception, is the same as in the latter. One can, therefore, hardly doubt that the attribution to Todar Mal's survey is imaginary and the figures are really taken from the records of Aurangzeb's reign. In the Supplement of the *Mir'āt-i Aḥmadī* we have a detailed *maḥal*-wise statement of revenue and village statistics, which is invaluable and is in broad conformity with the *sarkār* figures in the *Chahār Gulshan*. Sorath was not included in the area statistics of either the *Ā'īn* or the later records, and the number of the measured villages in Aurangzeb's statistics was half the total number of villages in the remaining territory. It would seem very likely, therefore, that at the time of the *Ā'īn*, which shows an area double that given in Aurangzeb's time, almost all the villages in the administered tracts were covered by measurement. When we compare the *Ā'īn's* area with modern returns of cultivable area from the corresponding territory,[69] the difference in favour of the latter turns out to be slight. But Moosvi, by setting the *Ā'īn's ārāẓī* against the *jama'* and map area, argues that gross cultivation *c.* 1595 was only about 58 per cent of gross cultivation in 1903-4.[70] The *Mir'āt* shows that only two-thirds of the measured area was cultivable. It

[66] B.L. Bhadani in *IESHR*, XVI (4), 416-17.

[67] *Mir'āt*, I, 217-18, 263. [68] Ibid., I, 25.

[69] These are generally drawn from the 1920-21 statistics, but the figures for Cambay and Rewa Kantha are taken from the *Imperial Gazetteer*, s.v., and relate to 1903-4. For the new Sabar Kantha district recourse has been had to the 1949-50 figures, earlier returns being unavailable. Most *maḥals* lying in Rewa Kantha district do not appear on the *Ā'īn's* list and the *Mir'āt* expressly classes them – Rajpipla, Bariya, Lunavada, etc. – as tributory territories not covered by the administrative records.

[70] Moosvi, 51-59.

is difficult to offer an explanation for inclusion of the remainder which must, from the revenue point of view, have been unnecessarily measured land unless there has been here a confusion between "cultivated" and "cultivable".[71] It is true that in 1881 the number of villages was only slightly higher than the Mughal figure.[72] Yet a Dutch observer, writing about 1629, i.e. before the great famine of 1630-32, declared that "not one-tenth of the land is cultivated", and so anyone could obtain land to till wherever he wanted.[73] The statement is an obvious exaggeration,[74] but if there is even a grain of truth in it, it would presuppose a state of affairs very different from that of the early years of the twentieth century, when practically the whole of the land was occupied. Gujarat was the province most fully described by foreign travellers, but one looks in vain for any confirmation or contradiction of this statement in their accounts.[75] The evidence that we have, then, tends, on the whole, to suggest that cultivation was much less in extent than around 1910, being quite possibly less than three-fifths of it in the time of the *Ā'īn*. It is also possible that much reclamation has taken place since Mughal times in parts of Gujarat not covered by the

[71] *Mir'āt,* I, 25. Cf. Moosvi, 56. As suggested in a previous note, the remainder might have included grazing land.

[72] The statistics of Aurangzeb's reign and the *Chahār Gulshan* put the total number of villages at 10,370. The *Mir'āt*, I, 25, gives the total as 10,465½. Its figures given under *maḥals* (ibid., Supp., 188ff), when totalled up, come to 11,563; but these include a large number of villages explicitly stated to be in ruins. The 1881 Census returned for Gujarat and Kathiawar (excluding Kachh, Rewa Kantha and the Surat states) a total of 12,545 villages. It may be mentioned that even outside the territories here excepted, the *Mir'āt* offers no village returns for certain *maḥals* in Kathiawar and in the *sarkār* of Pattan. In Commissariat, *Mandelslo*, 28, it is stated that the province of Ahmadabad "comprised within its jurisdiction 25 great towns and 3,000 villages". But here the *sarkār* has been confounded with the *ṣūba*. Geleynssen, writing a decade earlier (1629), states that there were under Ahmadabad "25 large chief-villages or small towns and below them 2,898 hamlets, etc." (*JIH*, IV, 78-9). These figures may be compared with those of the *Mir'āt* for the same *sarkār*: 25 *parganas* with villages totalling 3,497, of which 404 either were not under the control of the administration or were in ruins. The *Chahār Gulshan*, Bodl. MS., f.64a, assigns it 28 *maḥals*, with a total of 2,880 villages. It is singular that agreement in all these authorities should be so close. Similarly, Geleynssen, 75, speaks of 210 villages being "under" Baroda. *Mir'āt* has 226 villages under the *pargana* and 348 (335 in the *Chahār Gulshan*) under the *sarkār*.

[73] Geleynssen, 79.

[74] Cf. Moreland, *Agrarian System*, 129n.

[75] Mundy, 264, indeed, says that "from Agra itself... to the Gates of Ahmudavad [Ahmadabad] is a desert, barren and thievish country", but the words are, probably, not meant to stand for the entire route. He found "champion" country, mingled with woods, already before Mehsana (ibid.) and makes no reference to desolate conditions between that place and Ahmadabad.

Mughal statistics, such as the territory around Rajpipla, in whose forests wild elephants used to roam during the seventeenth century.[76]

Even though large tracts south of the Narmada had been transferred from Malwa to Khandesh by Shāhjahān, the measured area for Malwa in Aurangzeb's statistics is more than double the area recorded in the *Ā'īn.* Yet, only a third of the villages had been brought under measurement. Modern returns (1920-21) for the territory of the reduced province (omitting a few minor 'states' for which statistics are not available) show a cultivable area about three times that under Aurangzeb. But besides the fact that the latter only represented the area of a third of the villages, two-fifths of the modern figure is made up of 'Cultivable Waste', in respect of which the Mughal records are not likely to have been as complete. The number of villages, according to the 1891 and 1901 censuses, was distinctly, but not very considerably, larger than that given in the Mughal records.[77] It would seem, then, that a very large increase in cultivation cannot be postulated for this region. Malwa already enjoyed in Mughal times an established reputation for fertility and unfailing abundance.[78]

Similar deductions may, perhaps, also be drawn in respect of Khandesh. No figures are provided for the measured area of this and the other Dakhin provinces in the *Ā'īn,* but Aurangzeb's statistics show that by then 2,832 out of its total of 6,339 villages were under measurement. To judge from the 1891 and 1901 censuses the number of villages remained almost constant, while the cultivable area reported in 1920-21 amounted to about 2.5 times the measured area of Aurangzeb's reign, which was confined to less than half of the total number of villages. It would seem, therefore, that there was no material extension in cultivation in the intervening period; and this accords with the evidence of other authorities, which describe the Mughal province as well cultivated

[76] Lāhorī, I, 331; *Mir'āt*, I, 14.

[77] Aurangzeb's statistics give the number of villages for the province as 18,678, but from this 759 should be deducted as the number of those lying in the *sarkār* of Garh (cf. *Chahār Gulshan*, ff.67b-68a, Sarkar, 142), since its exact limits cannot be determined. Within the remaining territory the censuses of 1891 (used for British districts) and 1901 (for 'native states') disclosed 19,500 villages in the districts fully included in the Mughal province and 4,092 in the territories only partly covered by it.

[78] *Ā'īn*, I, 455; Mundy, 54-57, especially, 57; Tavernier, I, 47. The fame of Malwa survived till recently in the imagination of north Indian peasantry (see Crooke, *North-Western Provinces*, 171; Elliot, *Memoirs*, II, 315).

and almost fully occupied.[79]

In Berar practically all villages had been brought under measurement by Aurangzeb's reign. But though the number of villages, according to the 1891 Census, was almost unchanged, the increase in cultivable area amounted by 1920-21 to over two-thirds of, if not fully as much as, the measured area of Mughal statistics. Here, therefore, the extension of cultivation has been substantial and we may assume that it has taken place largely at the expense of the great central Indian forest, which then lay dense over the eastern regions of this province.[80]

In the Aurangabad province the total number of villages given in the Mughal records is about the same as in 1891.[81] The measured villages amounted to over nine-tenths of the total, but the measured area was only about two-thirds of the cultivable area reported in 1920-21. The neighbouring province of Bidar was very small and any comparative examination of the figures relating to it could involve a very large margin of error.

No returns of the area or number of villages are given in the Mughal statistics for the provinces of Bijapur and Haidarabad.

It might have seemed tedious to follow the Mughal statistics in such detail. But one thing emerges from this study, namely that some minor difficulties apart, the Mughal statistics are set to a fairly coherent pattern, and the amount of corroborative evidence available is not insignificant. This may entitle us to place some reliance upon the general results which our comparison with modern statistics has brought out. It seems established, first of all, that an increase in cultivation between *c.*1595 and *c.*1910 took place everywhere, though in varying degrees. The increase was the greatest, amounting to about a hundred per cent in three regions. The first region comprises Ilahabad, Awadh and Bihar

[79] "There is little left uncultivated and many of its villages look like towns" (*Ā'īn*, I, 474). See also Fitch, ed. Ryley, 95, and *Early Travels*, 16; Thevenot, 101-2; Tavernier, I, 42; Manucci, II, 429; *Dilkushā*, f.7a. The only discordant note is struck by Roe, 68, who says that the whole country from Surat to Burhanpur was "miserable and barron". Abū-l Faẓl says that most of the region was desolate in olden times, and that extensive resettlement began only under the patronage of the founder of the local dynasty, Malik Rājī, in the latter part of the 14th century (*Ā'īn*, I, 475).

[80] Cf. *Ā'īn*, I, 477-8.

[81] The figure for the number of villages in Aurangzeb's statistics, viz. 8,263, has been accepted. The *Chahār Gulshan*, f.74b, Sarkar, 151, has 5,950 only. The total of figures against individual *sarkārs* given by Sarkar, 152, is incorrect, mainly owing to a misreading of 599 as 5,599 under Parenda.

and, possibly, parts of Bengal. Here the increase has obviously been due partly to reclamation from the great sub-montane forest. The second region is that of Berar, where cultivation extended at the expense of the central Indian forest. And, finally, the Indus, basin where the extension was due almost entirely to the modern canal system. Besides these territories, the increase in cultivation seems to have varied from over one-half to one-third, or only one-fourth, much of the increase being brought about by the ploughing up of lands of inferior soils and grazing lands – a process that is still continuing.

It has been a matter of some controversy whether the average yield of the land was higher in earlier times than around 1910-11. It has been recognized that, with the traditional manuring practices continuing unaltered, two causes might have contributed to a fall in the average produce. First, the extension of cultivation over inferior lands, which it was previously uneconomical to sow; and, secondly, the continued use of clearings in the forests, where after a period of great fertility, the soil is exhausted or comes down to the level of ordinary land.[82] We have seen that if our statistical comparisons have any validity, the first factor has operated almost everywhere and the inferior land conquered by the plough after *c.* 1595 amounted by 1910-11 generally to a third, and, in some parts, half, of the area previously cultivated. We have also seen that the forests were far more extensive in the seventeenth century than in the early years of the twentieth, and this suggests that the so-called 'jhum' cultivation, in which the old clearings are abandoned once the land is exhausted, and fresh clearings are made elsewhere, was generally far more extensive than now. It is probable that this practice prevailed throughout the Tarai, as it certainly did in Gorakhpur district at the beginning of the nineteenth century.[83] As the forest has receded, this method has also lost its appeal. It is obvious, then, that in these areas, the average fertility of the land

[82] Cf. Royal Commission on Agriculture, *Report*, 75.

[83] Muftī Ghulām Ḥaẓarat, who speaks of the *chakla* of Gorakhpur with its older limits, i.e. including, besides the British district of Gorakhpur, that of Basti and a large part of Gonda, says: "The customary practice here, owing to the abundance of forest land, is that the *banjar* (previously unsown) land, which requires little to be tilled and is very productive, is sown for up to three years, whereafter it reaches the full yield and its strength declines. They then abandon it, and, instead of it, cultivate some other plot of *banjar* land. The land of the *chakla* of Gorakhpur is not as recuperative as that of the *chakla* of Azamgarh and its yield declines within three or four years (of being cultivated)" (I.O. 4540, f.10a).

actually under cultivation must have declined even more than in others.[84] We may notice, for example, Abū-l Faẓl's reference to the richness of the soil in the *sarkār* of Champaran (Bihar), where the pulse *māsh (urd)* used to require no ploughing nor any care at all in order to grow.[85] The position *c.*1910 was different only in the Indus plains and, to some extent, in the Doab, where the canals enabled high-class soils to be tilled and put to better use. But taking the area of the Mughal empire as a whole, and assuming that agricultural practices and cropping had not changed, the average hectare sown could not have been as productive around 1910 as in Mughal times. The assumption about cropping having remained unchanged cannot, however, be made without important qualifications, as we shall see in Section 3 of this chapter.

We have also referred above frequently to the village statistics of our period. A curious fact, which appears from our comparison of these with modern returns, is that in a compact group of provinces in Northern India, from Ilahabad and Awadh to Lahor and Multan, the number of villages was generally higher by half than in the final decades of the nineteenth century. On the other hand, for Bengal and Bihar and the country south of the Northern Plains, i.e. Rajasthan, Gujarat, Malwa and the Dakhin provinces, the Mughal returns are either a little below, or correspond very closely to, the numbers recorded in late nineteenth-century censuses. The reason for this relative multiplicity of villages in the Mughal north Indian provinces is not easy to discover. Quite possibly, in some areas at least, villages decreased in absolute numbers during the uncertain conditions of the eighteenth century, when many might have been laid waste, while smaller hamlets were abandoned in favour of bigger ones for better defence.[86] A more likely explanation, however, seems to be that when rings of waste and grazing land, previously marking off one village from another, were ploughed up, there could be a tendency for one village to lose its entity and merge with the other. Whatever the

[84] Cf.Moreland, *India at the Death of Akbar*, 117. His interpretation of the effects on the average yield from the elimination of forests is different from the one here advanced.

[85] *Ā'īn*, I, 417. He says also that the *banjar* lands of the sub-montane tracts are even more productive than the best category of land (*polaj*) elsewhere and the revenue officials regarded them as equivalent (ibid., 297).

[86] Crooke, *The North-Western Provinces*, 40, explains that the villages in the western part of the province look like "miniature forts" and are a relic of "the tradition of raid and rapine, when the land was harried by Sikh and Marhatta".

causes of the change, the fact to be recognized is that though the extent of cultivation in Mughal India was much less than around 1910, it maintained a larger number of villages, which, therefore, must, on average, have been much smaller in size than villages at the beginning of this century.

2. MEANS OF CULTIVATION AND IRRIGATION

Set against the great achievements of modern, scientific agriculture, it might seem difficult to imagine anything more primitive than the traditional implements of the Indian peasant. In the context of the world three hundred years ago, however, these provoked little comment. Though oxen were yoked to it, never horses, the Indian plough was no stranger to European eyes. Terry described it as the "foot-plough", a type used in England.[1] Fryer, whose observations were confined to the coastal areas, declared that the "Combies (Kumbis)... Till the Land, and dress the Corn with no remarkable difference from other Nations". He found no peculiarity in the ploughs, except that "their Coulters [are] unarmed mostly, Iron being scarce, but they have hard Wood [which] will turn their light Grounds".[2] This statement could have been true only of the coastal belt. Iron teeth would have been indispensable for the drier or harder soils inland and have obviously been in use since ancient times.[3] The remarkable dictionary, *Miftāḥu-l Fuẓalā*, compiled in Malwa in 1468-69, and illustrated in the next century, says the Hindi term *phāl* applies to the iron coulter, with which the soil is broken; and it gives a very clear illustration of a plough with such an iron coulter.[4] It is true that iron was "scarce" in our period, but its mining and manufacture were widespread

[1] *Early Travels*, 298. For the foot-plough see *OED*, s.v. *foot*-35, which gives a 1677 quotation, distinguishing between the "Foot, and Wheel-plough; Whereof the first is used in deep and clay lands, being accordingly fitted with a broad fin share". It did not thus have a wheel; nor, according to Moreland (*India at the Death of Akbar*, 160 *n*), a mould-board. Neither the inverting nor the deep-digging plough is suitable for most Indian soils (cf. Royal Commission on Indian Agriculture, *Report*, 110-112). But where a mould-board was required, e.g. in sugar-cane cultivation, the Indian peasant did employ different types of it (Elliot, *Memoirs*, II, 340-41n.).

[2] Fryer, II, 108. See also the reference in 1710 to the "wooden colter" in ploughs at Bombay (Burnell, 60-61).

[3] Thus the stricture against agriculture in the *Manusmriti*, x, 84, on account of "the wooden (implement) with iron point:, which injures the earth and its creatures" (*The Laws of Manu*, transl. Buhler, 420-21).

[4] Muḥammad bin Dāūd Shādīābādī, *Miftāḥu-l Fuẓalā*, Or. 3299, ff.16a (*phāl*),

Plough with iron-share, *Miftāḥu-l Fuẓalā* (Mālwa school: late-15th or 16th century) Or. 3299, f.145a. Courtesy: British Library.

Persian wheel (geared water-lifting device). From painting by Sānwla, 1595, in Niẓāmī's *Khamsa*, calligraphed and illustrated for Akbar's library, Or. 12,208, f.294a. Courtesy: British Museum.

and the price in terms of wheat was not more than twice the price in 1914.[5] This should not have been prohibitive for the very small amount used in the shares of Indian ploughs.[6] In one particular respect – the efficiency of traction – the hump of the Indian ox gave an advantage to the Indian plough over the European, in which the harness had often to be fixed to the horns of the beast.[7] It has, moreover, been pointed out that in certain respects, Indian agricultural methods were far from primitive when judged by the standards of the day.[8] Drill-sowing and dibbling are both described in the sources of our period.[9] Rice was transplanted.[10] Though bone manure has not been in general use, the exceptional value of fish as fertilizer seems to have been appreciated, since we are told that in Gujarat fish manure was used in sugarcane cultivation, and in Konkan, for coconut palms.[11]

The outstanding feature of Indian agriculture which impressed contemporary observers was the harvesting of two – and in some areas, three – crops in the year.[12] The larger portion of the land was

---

145a (illustration). Cf. Platts, s.v. *phāl, phālā, phālī,* "ploughshare". *Phālā* was applied to "iron share" in western U.P. (Elliot, *Memoirs*, II, 342).

5 See Moreland, *India at the Death of Akbar*, 147-51, where the conditions of the industry and the price of iron are discussed. He cites the *Ā'īn's* prices for picket-pegs, valued at 3 *dāms* a *ser* (*Ā'īn*, I, 143). Cf., however, Moosvi, 331, where a much lower price, directly given for iron in the *Ā'īn*, I, 141 (2 *dāms* a *ser*), is quoted. English iron was sold at Surat in 1613 at the rate of 3½ to 4 *maḥmūdīs* for one local *man*, or 21/3 or 22/3 *dāms* per *ser-i Akbarī* (*Lett. Recd.*, I, 235, 238, 299).

6 Francis Buchanan in his Bihar surveys (1807-16) found the plough universally provided with "a bit of iron" (*History, Antiquities, Topography and Statistics of Eastern India, etc.*, ed. Montgomery Martin, London, 1838, I, 292; II, 214-15). Earlier (1801) in the Karnataka uplands in South India, he encountered ploughs drawn by eight to sixteen oxen, with iron weighing from 7¼ and 14½ lb. (*Journey from Madras*, 342-3). A description of the forms, in which iron teeth were used in the ploughs in various localities, will be found in N.G. Mukherji, *Handbook of Indian Agriculture*, 92-3.

7 Tavernier, I, 36.

8 Cf. Elliot, *Memoirs*, II, 341-2.

9 Drill-sowing was observed on the western coast by Barbosa, I, 192, in 1516. In 1809 Elphinstone noted that "the drill-plough, which is used in India is not known [in Afghanistan]" (*Account of the Kingdom of Caubul*, I, 399). Voelcker, *Report*, 223, found the "native" seed-drill "wonderfully efficient and leaving little to be desired". In a tract on agriculture, written probably by Amānullāh Ḥusainī in the earlier part of the 17th century, dibbling is thus described: "In some places they push down a pointed peg (*mekh*) into the ground, put the (cotton) seed into the hole and cover it with earth; it grows better thus" (I.O. 4702, f.30b).

10 Burnell, 61 (Bombay island, 1710); Yāsīn's Glossary, Add. 6603, f.63b (Bengal).

11 Thevenot, 36-7; Burnell, 83.

12 *Ā'īn*, II, 5 & 6 (concerning Hindustan); I, 389 (Bengal), 513 (Dehli province);

"single-cropped" (*yak-faṣla*), being sown either for the *rabī‘* (spring) or *kharīf* (autumn) harvest, but some was "double-cropped" (*do-faṣla*) being sown with crops of both harvests in succession.[13] In the former case the land remained fallow for about half the year, and could have a repetition of the same crop.[14] In the double-cropped land, however, there was necessarily at first a two-crop cycle, since the crops of the two harvests were different. But there was knowledge of a wider rotation too. Thus in eighteenth-century Bengal there was land known as *danka-tanka* kept in continuous cultivation with a rotation cycle of rice-tobacco-cotton.[15] Early nineteenth-century English reports from south India and Awadh describe still more elaborate rotation cycles;[16] and there are general appreciations too of the Indian peasant's knowledge of the principle of crop-rotation.[17] Yet in parts of south India and in Sind there were complaints that the principle was little understood.[18] In the literature on agriculture from our period, which is in any case rather slight, the only statement of any relevance we get is that certain crops could fertilize or enrich the soil.[19]

As for the fields, the general appearance they presented seems to have been practically the same as today. Transplanted rice was put in "regular furrows".[20] There were no hedges, nothing to remind the European traveller of the growing practice of "enclosures" on his continent.[21] In Gujarat alone were thorn-bush hedges commonly raised to protect the fields; and these are noticed in our authorities

---

J. Xavier, transl. Hosten, *JASB*, N.S., XXIII, 121 (Agra region); Pelsaert, 48 (Agra region); Bowrey, 121 (Orissa coast); Sujān Rāi, 11(Hindustan).

[13] For the use of the terms *yak-faṣla* and *do-faṣla*, see Todar Mal's Memorandum, original text in *A.N.*, Add. 27,247, f.332a.

[14] Cf. Buchanan, *Journey from Madras*, II, 219. Buchanan observed (1800) that in the locality in question (in Mysore), the same field was cultivated with the same crop; he seems to overlook the fact that there would necessarily be a half-year fallow, though he argues that a full year's fallow would be better for the crop.

[15] Yāsīn's Glossary, Add. 6603, f.47b.

[16] Buchanan, *Journey from Madras*, II, 324-5; Donald Butter, *Outlines of the Topography and Statistics of the Southern Districts of Oud'h,* 63-4.

[17] Elliot, *Memoirs*, II, 342; Voelcker, *Report*, II, 233-6.

[18] Buchanan, *Journey from Madras*, I, 93, 125-6; II, 219 (South India); Hugh James's report (1847) in R.H. Thomas, *Memoirs on Sind*, II, 376.

[19] Amānullāh Ḥusainī considers the *bāqila* bean (*faba sativa*) and the Egyptian bean (*bāqila-i miṣrī* or *tarmās*) to possess fertilizing qualities (I.O. 4702, ff. 2a-b, 30a), while holding madder (*rūnās*) to improve nitrous soils (f.31a).

[20] Burnell, 61.

[21] "Their ground is not enclosed unless it be neare townes and villages" (Terry in *Early Travels*, 298).

as something of a local peculiarity.[22]

An important aspect of Indian agriculture is artificial irrigation to supplement the natural bounty of the monsoons. The principal means employed for this purpose has been the construction of wells, tanks and canals.

In the Upper Gangetic plains as also parts of the Dakhin, wells must have provided the chief source of irrigation. The different methods of drawing water out of the wells in use in India around 1900 are nearly all described by our authorities as well. East of the Jhelam, in the regions of Lahor, Dipalpur and Sirhind, there was the wooden *arhat,* or *rahat,* called by the English the 'Persian wheel', with its chain of pots and pin-drum gearing, which Bābur found such a novelty.[23] It was present in Sind; and Nainsī records Persian wheels in a number of villages of Marwar.[24] It was, however, not employed elsewhere.[25] Around Agra and further east, the *charas*, or the leather bucket lifted out of water by yoked oxen, pulling a rope thrown over a pulley, was most common.[26] Fryer, in his general account of India, describes, in addition, the *dhenklī,* based on the lever principle, which is generally in use wherever the water-level is close to the surface.[27] Most of the wells were *kachcha*, that is, made without use of masonry. These necessarily

[22] *Ā'īn* I, 485; *T.J.*, 205; Fryer, III, 158, *Mir'āt*, I, 14.

[23] *Bāburnāma*, ed., 360, 439-40; transl. S.A. Beveridge, I, 388; II, 486. In the latter passage, Beveridge omits "and Sirhind" from her translation, although it is found both in the Turki text, ed., Mano, 439, (='Haiderabad Codex', f.273b), and in 'Abdu-r Raḥīm K͟hān K͟hānān's Persian transl., Or.3714, f.376b. A description of the *rahat* appears also in Sujān Rāi, 79, as peculiar to the Punjab. The scientific name for the geared water-lifting machine is *sāqiya*. For its construction, origins and diffusion, see Thorkild Schioler, *Roman and Islamic Water-lifting Wheels*, Odense, 1973; for the history of the device in India, see I. Habib in *Aligarh Jour. of Oriental Studies*, II (1-2), 1985, 198-203. Cf. S.P. Verma, *Art and Material Culture*, 103.

[24] For Sind: Ma'ṣūm, *Tārīk͟h-i Sind*, 110, and *Maẓhar-i Shāhjahānī*, 64, for camels employed in "garden water-wheels" (*chark͟h-i bāg͟hāt*). For irrigation wheels on river-channels, see *Factories, 1646-50*, 119. Cf. M. Saleem Akhtar, *Sind under the Mughals* (transl. of *Maẓhar-i Shāhjahānī*), 285-8.

For Marwar, see the detailed village-wise statistics under *parganas* Jodhpur, Sojhat and Jaitaran in the *Vigat*, I, *passim* (as an illustration, see the village statistics for *tappa* Pali on 262-72); see also ibid., II, 116-213 (Merta).

[25] So it remained until the introduction of the metallic version of the device. As late as 1839, Butter, *Topography, etc.*, 67, found it absent in Awadh, and much later in the same century, Beames (Elliot, *Memoirs*, II, 220) noted that it was not in use "much lower down than the Upper Doab" and was "more common" there on the Yamuna side than nearer the Ganga.

[26] *Bāburnāma*, ed., 440; Bev. II, 487: "a laborious and a filthy way".

[27] Fryer, II, 94.

had to be dug, or dug afresh, every year. Pelsaert (1626) speaking with reference to the country around Agra says the wells were annually made during the rabi season; so they must have been of this type.[28] In *pargana* Merta, *ṣūba* Ajmer, out of a very large number of wells recorded in Nainsī's *Vigat* under individual villages(1664), only a few are reported as brick-lined.[29] One must remember that the higher water-table of those days made such makeshift wells more practicable than they would be today. There was, in some parts at least, a professional class of vagrant well-diggers,[30] whose work, especially when digging in sandy soil to great depth, as in the Thar Desert, is said to have been extremely hazardous.[31]

It seems clear from a reading of Abū-l Faẕl's account of the various provinces in the *Ā'īn* that he has found it superfluous to say anything about the role of irrigation if the crops depended mostly upon rainfall and only partly on wells.[32] His silence over the presence of well irrigation in particular regions should, therefore, occasion no surprise.[33] What is interesting is his statement that "most" of the province of Lahor "is cultivated with the help of well-irrigation".[34] This is repeated later (1695-96) by a historian, who himself belonged to this province.[35] One must suppose, therefore, that wells were relatively far more important at that time than around 1910 in the upper portion of the Panjab.

[28] Pelsaert, 48. [29] *Vigat*, II, 116-213.

[30] This appears from the account of an incident happening near Basawar in Agra *sarkār*, in Badāūnī, II, 243.

[31] Cf. Faiẕī Sirhindī, ff.58b-59b.

[32] As Sujān Rāi, 11, remarks of Hindustān, "although in some parts cultivation depends on wells and in some regions the land is also watered by inundations, nevertheless, most of the land is *lalmī*, which is synonymous with *bārānī* (dependent upon rain)". (The editor reads *ilāhī* for *lalmī*, but see MSS A, 11b-12a, & B, 11a-b). Cf. also *Bāburnāma*, ed. 441; Bev., II, 488. An example of how Abū-l Faẕl ignored the role of well-irrigation is offered by his remarks on the Dehli province, of which he says simply that "much of the land is irrigated by inundations (*selābī*)" (*Ā'īn*, I, 518). Sujān Rāi, 39, on the other hand, says of the same province that its cultivation is "dependent upon rain and inundation and in some places on wells".

[33] Cf., however, Moreland, *India at the Death of Akbar*, 121, for comment on the case of Awadh ("Oudh").

[34] *Ā'īn*, I, 538.

[35] Sujān Rāi, 79 (see also MSS B: f. 72a; C: 44a). He also says that the kharif harvest (the litho text reads "*kharīf* and *rabi'*"; but this is not supported by the MSS) depended mainly upon rain. Cf. also Manucci, II, 186, who noticed "an abundance of wells" around Lahor.

It is equally possible that in many tracts, especially in the central Ganga-Yamuna Doab, there was a heavy decline in the number of wells, owing to interference by modern canals with the natural drainage of the country.[36]

Archaeological remains testify to the great antiquity of irrigation tanks in peninsular India.[37] Many remains of the pre-colonial system of south Indian dams (anicuts), tanks and canals are described in Buchanan's great survey of south India in 1800-01.[38] Tavernier describes the country of Golkunda as being "full" of tanks, which are said to have been made by building dams, "sometimes half a league long," so as to enclose the water in natural depressions and use it after the rains for the fields.[39] There was the great Kamthana tank at Bidar, made by a dam built to its north, which was "verily" a "Tigris" and which freed the cultivators of the surrounding country from all dependence upon rain.[40] In the later years of Shāhjahān we find the Mughal administration proposing to advance nearly Rs 40,- to 50,000 to cultivators in Khandesh and the Painghat portion of Berar, for the purpose of erecting bunds or dams.[41] In the north, in Mewar, the very large

36 The effect of canals on wells has been of two kinds. First, the canals have appropriated to themselves, or cut off the supply of, sub-soil water of many tracts, causing a fall in the underground water-level. A number of such cases are noted by Moreland in his *Agricultural Conditions of the United Provinces and Districts*, Notes on Aligarh (p. 2), Mathura (p. 2), Agra (p. 1) and Mainpur (p.2). Secondly, in many areas, especially sandy tracts, the canals, through saturation of the sub-soil, caused "the sides of the wells to fall in, and make unsupported excavations to any depth impracticable" (*Mainpuri Dist. Gazetteer*, Allahabad, 1910, 53. Cf. Voelcker, *Report*, 69).

37 Two of the most interesting ancient examples are the Sudarshana Lake (Girnar, Saurashtra, created by a dam built under Chandragupta Maurya and furnished with conduits for irrigation under Asoka (James Burgess, *Report on the Antiquities of Kathiawar and Kachh*, 93-95, 128-38, for the epigraphic evidence, and R.N. Mehta in *Journal of the Oriental Institute*, XIII [1& 2], 20-38, for a thorough ground-survey) and the 'tremendous reservoir' at Bhojpur, Malwa, constructed by Bhoja, 11th century (Kosambi, *Introduction to the Study of Indian History*, 280-281).

38 Buchanan, *Journey from Madras*, I, 2, 3-4, 11-12, 15, 16, 70-71, 279; II, 23, 82-3, 87-90, 141, 163, 164, 190-93, 197, 218, 213-14, 235, 237-8, 245, 253, 280, 288, 291-3, 300-01, 333; III, 144, 310, 380-1, 453-4.

The *Dharwar District Gazetteer*, (1888), 257-64, gives an excellent description of similar medieval works in that district, epecially the remains of an enormous dam and irrigation lake on Kamudvati R.,with distributory canals, but left unfinished by the Vijayanagara builders owing to the collapse of one of the embankments.

39 Tavernier, I, 121-2.

40 *Ma'āṣir-i 'Ālamgīrī*, 308-9. See *Epigraphia Indo-Moslemica*, 1937-8, 1-2.

41 *Ādāb-i 'Ālamgīrī*, ed., I, 207-8; *Ruq'āt-i 'Ālamgīr*, 134.

lake of Dhebar, 16 *kurohs* in circumference, dates from our period; it is said to have supported wheat cultivation in the country around.[42]

In cases where a river rises and inundates the fields seasonally every year, both the irrigation and fertilization (if a layer of the sub-soil is left behind) are purely natural. But it is probable that the modern constructions of embankments to train the rivers for the sake of canals or railways, or for the prevention of floods, has considerably reduced the extent of land formerly enriched by this means. Abū-l Faẓl notices especially the lands thus irrigated by the Sarū (Sarju) and Ghaghara in Awadh,[43] as also the land subjected to inundations in *sarkār* Sambhal (Rohilkhand).[44] But it was the area affected by the Indus and its tributaries that offered the greatest contrast to present conditions. The seasonal inundations of the rivers, as they flowed through the parched and thirsty plains, were almost uncontrolled; and nothing reveals their range more clearly than the spectacular changes in the river courses which used to take place from time to time. In the time of the *Ā'īn,* for example, the Beas and Sutlej after uniting at, or near, their present junction bifurcated below Firozpur, the upper channel being again known as the "Beas", while the lower one, taken to be the "Sutlej", was practically identical with the present bed of the Sutlej river. The two channels, flowing for more than two hundred miles at about thirty miles from each other, united near the present confluence of the Chenab and the Sutlej.[45] Some time during the

[42] *Ā'īn*, I, 509. Sixteen *kurohs* would be about 40 miles (see Appendix A). Tod, I, 619, puts the circumference of the Dhebar Lake at no less than 30 miles. Malcolm, *Memoir of Central India*, II, 341-43, provides a detailed description of the works. The surviving dam was built in 1687-89 by Rānā Jai Singh who renamed it Jai Samund or Jaisāgar (Kavirāj Shyāmaldās, *Vīr Vinod*, I, 111-12). The *Ā'īn's* statements show that Jai Singh could only have repaired and improved the dam, giving it, for example, a marble facing; the lake and its original great dam were an earlier creation.

For other Mughal-period lakes of Mewar, see *Atlas*, Sheet 6B & Notes 19, col. c.

[43] *Ā'īn*, I, 433; also 303. It may be mentioned that the Sarju, which now meets the Ghaghara in the south-eastern corner of Kheri district, used to flow, at the time of the *Ā'īn*, past Bahraich and joined the other river at only one *kuroh* above the town of Ajodhya (ibid., 433, 435), so that it had a far longer course in the plains than now. The old channel is still traced on the maps. Jarrett's transl. (II, ed. Sarkar, 182) is seriously misleading because he has muddled up the Sai with the Sarū or Sarju.

[44] *Ā'īn*, I, 303. For Dehli province generally, see ibid., I, 513.

[45] *Ā'īn*, I, 549. This bifurcation and the courses of the two branches are established by the fact that the *Ā'īn* places towns like Dipalpur, Pakpattan, Kahror

reign of Aurangzeb the "Beas" abandoned its old bed: the bifurcation still took place, but much below the previous one and the two branches maintained a separate course only for a short distance.[46] This change must have affected cultivation in a very large area previously irrigated by the older Beas channel.

Similarly, the site of the confluence of the Chenab and Jhelam moved up by over 25 miles within the course of the seventeenth century.[47] The Panjnad did not exist and the Chenab and Beas-Sutlej met the Indus separately near Uchh.[48] The Indus shifted its course continuously, so that the huts of the villages on its banks had to be made of wood and straw.[49]

---

and Dunyapur in the Bet-Jalandhar Doab (Multan province). (Cf. I.R. Khan in *Muslim University Journal*, II, No.1, pp.34-36.) The Survey Maps show two old beds of the Beas (so called also on the maps) running quite close to each other. A detailed examinations of the *parganas* listed under the Bet-Jalandhar Doab of Multan province shows that the northern of the two 'beds' was probably the one which the Beas occupied at the time of the *Ā'īn*. (*Atlas*, Sheet 4B & Notes 11, col. b). The fact of the two main channels being known as Beas and Sutlej is not only deducible from Abū-l Faẓl's use of the word "Bet" or "Beth" for the area lying between them, but is also directly established by the account of Ṣafshikan Khān's proceedings near Multan during the pursuit of Dārā Shukoh in 1658. Marching from Multan towards Uchh, he first crossed the "Beas" and then, after traversing two stages, the Sutlej ('*Ālamgīrnāma*, 271-2).

46 As seen from the passage of '*Ālamgīrnāma*, cited in the preceding note, the old Beas bed was not yet abandoned in 1659. But writing in 1695, Sujān Rāi placed the bifurcation at a point much below Dipalpur and said that the northern channel known as Beas rejoined the Sutlej after a course no longer than "a few *farsakhs* (*kurohs*)" (Sujān Rāi, 76; *Muslim University Journal*, II, No.1,38, 40).

The Multan-Bhakkar itinerary in the *Chahār Gulshan*, Bodl. MS., f.108a, shows the route as crossing the Beas and then a branch of it, which from the position of Shujā'atpūr on its northern bank, would seem to have been flowing in the present bed of the Sutlej. This, however, does not mean that the conditions of the time of the *Ā'īn* were restored by the middle of the 18th century, but perhaps only that the *Chahār Gulshan* has copied an itinerary prepared early in the 17th century.

The abandoned channel of the Beas probably still became active during the season of inundations to merit the remark of Sujān Rāi, 63, that the river covered a few *farsakhs* in width during the season and that this created the great Lakhi Jungle in the *sarkār* of Dipalpur. See also Rennell's Map in his *Memoir of a Map of Hindustan*, London, 1792, for the numerous channels thrown out by the Beas-Sutlej river.

47 At the time of the *Ā'īn*, the confluence took place below Shorkot, which stood then in the Chanhat Doab (*Ā'īn*, I, 547, 549). Sujān Rāi, 78, however, puts it near Jhang-i-Sialan, i.e. at or near the site the confluence occupies today.

48 This appears from the *Ā'īn*, I, 549; Sujān Rāi, 76; and Rennell's map, op.cit. The Panjnad now meets the Indus near Mithankot.

49 *Ā'īn*, I, 558. Lambrick in *Journal of Sind Hist. Soc.*, III (1937), i, 15 & 16, notes that "the area annually overflowed has become far less extensive since the

The fickleness of the rivers to their beds in the soft alluvial soil has, indeed, strewn the whole of the plains with innumerable abandoned channels, many of which became active during the season of the inundations, when water from their parent rivers forced its way into them. Modern embankments, again, have closed the sources of many of these channels, but physical traces still remain to justify the supposition that the number of such natural canals in Mughal times was quite large.[50] These are usually to be distinguished from purely man-made canals by their winding courses; but so often has human effort gone into straightening or deepening them or clearing their beds of silt that in some cases, at least, the distinction will be hard to draw.[51] In the following survey an attempt has been made to present some evidence about canals whether wholly or partly man-made that were active, or were dug, during our period.

In the Dakhin the practice of leading off small canals from rivers and streams was, like that of making reservoirs, an ancient one. We are told, for example, that in Baglana "they have brought into every town and village thousands of canals, cut from the river for the benefit of cultivation";[52] and these were probably managed according to the co-operative *phad* system, which still survives in that area.[53]

But it was northern India in which some really large canals were excavated during our period. There is a tradition that the old channel of the Eastern Yamuna Canal was dug in the reign of Shāhjahān, but the canal probably dates from the earlier part of the eighteenth century.[54] On the other side of the Yamuna ran the celebrated canal of Fīrūz Shāh.[55] This was repaired during the reign

provision of an almost continuous line of river protection bunds". He thinks that "the vast bulk of cultivation in Sind from prehistoric times to the eighteenth century was *bosi*, that is, rabi crops raised on lands naturally flooded by the seasonal rise of the Indus, after its subsidence." This is exactly what Hamilton, I, 125, wrote of Sind, visited by him in 1699.

[50] Cf. Lambrick, op.cit., 16.

[51] An illustration of this is provided by the use of old river channels by Fīrūz Shāh for carrying his West Yamuna Canal to Hansi and Hisar. (See below.)

[52] Ṣādiq Khān, Or. 174, ff. 60b-61a; Or. 1671, f.34a.

[53] Royal Commission on Agriculture, *Report*, 325.

[54] See Earl of Moira's Minute (1815) in *Selections from the Revenue Records of the N.W. Provinces, 1818-20*, 349-50; Atkinson, *Descriptive, etc., Account of N.W. Provinces, etc.*, II: Meerut Division, Part I, 4-8; *Saharanpur Dist. Gaz.* (1909), 58-60. The tradition that attributes its construction to 'Alī Mardān Khān is as ill-founded as the one that supposes the same noble to have dug the *Nahr-i Bihisht*.

[55] Fīrūz Shāh's canal seems to have taken off from the Yamuna at Tajewala in

of Akbar, first by Shihābu-ddīn Khān and later by Nūru-ddīn Muḥammad Tarkhān:[56] arrangements were made to distribute water from the canal at the season of cultivation.[57] At the time of the *Ā'īn,* the canal was apparently carrying water past Hansi and only disappeared finally at Bhadra.[58] It silted up again, but Shāhjahān decided to reopen it from its mouth at Khizrabad, almost under the hills, down to Safedon and thence to dig a new channel, some thirty *kurohs*, or nearly 78 miles in length, to serve the new city of Shāhjahānābād at Delhi[59]. This was the famous "Nahr-i Bihisht" or "Nahr-i Faiẓ"[60] which must for the period be regarded as something of an achievement and though of no comparison to its modern successor, the West Yamuna Canal, it must have irrigated a considerable area.[61]

Ambala district, flowing in the bed of an old arm of the Yamuna down to Indri (*Karnal Dist. Gaz.*, 1918, A Vol., 3-4). A little beyond Safedon it ran into the old channel of Chitang river, which carried it down to Hansi, Hissar and beyond. (See Raverty in *JASB*, LXI (1892), 420; *Imperial Gazetteer*, X, 186.) This channel was not first excavated by Fīrūz Shāh as is sometimes supposed, but had been carrying Chitang river past Hansi for centuries earlier. The 13th-century Persian version of the *Chachnāma*, originally written in the 8th century, contains a definite reference to the "river of Hāsī [Hansi]" (*Chachnāma*, ed. V.M. Daudpota, 51).

[56] We are told by Wāriṣ, a:f. 401a; b:f.16b (Ṣāliḥ, III 29) that the canal had silted up by Akbar's early years; and Shihābuddīn Khān, when he was Governor of Dehli (early in Akbar's reign), repaired the canal "to extend cultivation" in his *jāgīrs*, renaming it *Shihāb Nahr*. Nūru-ddīn Muḥammad Tarkhān probably only repaired or re-excavated the bed of this canal, for according to Badāūnī, III, 198, his canal, named *Shaikhū-Nī* after Prince Salīm, was cut from the Yamuna and ran for 50 *kurohs* in the direction of Karnal and beyond (presumably past Safedon, which he himself held in *jāgīr*). The chronogram given for the construction of the canal, yields 976, while Salīm was only born in AH 977/1569). The entire problem is resolved by an interesting *farmān* of Akbar issued in 1570-71, surviving only in an English translation, published by H. Yule in *JASB, XV* (1846), 213-23, to which Abha Singh, in *Medieval India*, I, 49-61, draws attention (Yule's paper in *JASB* containing the translation is reprinted in W.E. Baker, *Memoranda on the Western Jumna Canals*, London, 1849, 95-102). This important document shows that the construction of the canal was ordered in AH 977 and designates Nūruddīn Muḥammad Tarkhān as *Mīr-i-āb* (Canal Superintendent).

[57] Akbar's *farmān* of 1570-71, op.cit. [58] *Ā'īn,* I, 514-15.

[59] Wāriṣ, a: ff. 401a-402a, 411a; b: ff. 16b-18a, 30b; Ṣāliḥ, III, 29; Sujān Rāi 29-30, 36-37. Work on the canal was started in 1638-39 and finished by 1647-48.

The *kurohs* in which the length of the canal is given, are stated to be *kuroh-i shāhī,* for which see Appendix A. 'Alī Mardān Khān had nothing to do with this canal and his name is linked with it only in later tradition, e.g. *Chahār Gulshan,* transl. Sarkar, 124, and Francklin, *The History of the Reign of Shah-Aulum,* 208.

[60] Also known simply as *Shāh-nahr*, the Royal Canal.

[61] Sujān Rāi, 36-37, says, indeed, that the canal could be said to have carried half the Yamuna and that "it conferred benefit upon the cultivation of many *parganas*

The Haryana tract, between the Yamuna and the Sutlej, is a large area not served by any perennial river. The seasonal streams which rise in or below the Siwaliks either disappear in the plains or join one of the channels leading to the Ghaggar or Hakra, the dry river of the desert. It was the practice in the region to throw dams or bunds across these streams to create an artificial inundation, or, at least, obtain some supply of water.[62] The position in the lower reaches of the rivers has naturally been precarious and this is confirmed in the case of Chitang or Chitrang by the detailed information about it, that has come down to us in a semi-official document. This is a long memorandum, prepared during the reign of Shāhjahān, proposing to clear or deepen its channel so that its water might reach Hisar, which it had failed to do for a long time, causing great distress to the country around.[63] There is, however, nothing to show that any action was taken on these proposals;[64] and no hint of such work appears in any later account.

---

and irrigated the gardens near the Capital." Francklin, op.cit., in an account of Delhi, written in 1793-4, speaks of it as "fertilising in its course a tract of more than ninety miles in length" and says that the "canal, as it ran through the suburbs of Moghul Para, nearly three miles in length, was twenty-five feet deep, and as much in breadth, cut from the quarry of solid stone..." G. Sanderson, *A Guide to the Buildings and Gardens: Delhi Fort*, 4th edn., 63-4, 65-66 *n.*, gives a good account of the alignment and engineering of Shāhjahān's canal, partly based on Major Cobin's report of 1832, reprinted in Baker, *Memoranda on Western Jumna Canals*, 79-94.

62 Thus, for example, the *band* on the 'Karnal Stream', built by Aṣālat Khān and visited by Shāhjahān in 1637-38 (Lāhorī, II, 112). Monserrate, 102, praises the groves and gardens of the plain country around Sirhind, watered from "a deep and artificial lake", filled "during the rainy season by means of irrigation channels".

63 The memorandum suggests, rather rhetorically, that the Chitang had been failing Hisar for "a hundred years". It makes no reference to any possible link with the Yamuna and traces the river to its source near Sadhaura. It contends that even if it was a seasonal river, an improved channel would enable it to reach Hisar. It also suggests that *bands* might be built on the river at two or three places in *chakla* Sirhind. This document is included among the papers collected by Bālkrishan Brahman, Add.16,859, ff.107a-109b. The papers belong to the reign of Shāhjahān and the earlier years of Aurangzeb, but this memorandum refers to "A'la Ḥaẓarat", the usual mode of address for Shāhjahān; and Abha Singh in *Medieval India-1*, 55-56, points out that the Mughal officer Bāqir Khān mentioned in the document was Governor of Dehli in 1635 only and died in 1637. It must therefore have been submitted well before the *Nahr-i Bihisht* was conceived of; that canal, in any case, had no use for the Chitang in its lower reaches.

64 It is stated that the *zamīndārs* and the peasants in *chakla* Hisar were prepared to undertake the digging of the channel through their lands or localities as soon as the water was brought up close to them. The authorities of *chakla* Sirhind, i.e. of the region of the upper reaches, were apparently not similarly enthusiastic about the project.

In the Panjab proper, a small system of canals was brought into existence in the Upper Bari Doab. The best known of these was the "Shāhnahr", also excavated in the reign of Shāhjahān. It took off from the Ravi at Rajpur (or Shahpur) close to the hills and carried water up to Lahor — a distance of about 37 *kurohs*, or 84 miles.[65] From the same point, one canal ran to Pathankot, another to Batala and a third to Patti Haibatpur. "Great benefit accrues to cultivation from these canals," says the local historian writing near the end of the seventeenth century.[66]

For the rest of the Panjab our authorities are not very enlightening. The Sidhnai reach could no longer have been a canal since it was already carrying the main stream of the Ravi.[67] We know, however, of a small canal cut from the Tavi to irrigate 'Alī Mardān Khān's garden at Sodhra near Wazirabad in the Upper Rechna Doab.[68] The presence of canals in the Multan *sarkār* is indicated by the draft of an order appointing a *mīr-i āb* (canal superintendent) for the area, which has survived in a collection of administrative documents. It requires the appointee to "dig new channels (*nāla*), clear the old channels, erect bunds on flood-torrents (*band-i sail*)" and to see to the equitable distribution of canal water among cultivators.[69] The most southerly portion of the present Sindsagar Doab, lying in "the Baluch country", was reputed for

[65] Lāhorī, II, 168-9, 233-4, 311, 315; Ṣādiq Khān, Or. 174, ff. 92a, 102a-b, Or. 1671, ff. 50b, 56a; *Zakhīrat-ul Khawānīn*, f.122b; *Ma'āṣiru-l Umarā'*, II, 806-7; Sujān Rāi, 77. Lāhorī says that the first attempt, begun under the supervision of a *protégé* of 'Alī Mardān Khān, was a failure, although the channel 48½ *kuroh-i jarībī* in length, was fully excavated. Perhaps it was given too wide a loop and the water did not reach Lahor in sufficient quantity. A second attempt at deepening the channel also proved unsuccessful. Ultimately, the whole of the first channel, except for a length of 5 *kurohs*, was abandoned, and a new one dug, which was 11½ *kurohs* shorter, and was completed by 1642-43. The distances are probably given in the earlier and shorter *kuroh* (for which see Appendix A).

[66] Sujān Rāi, 77. It is possible that the canal running to Batala occupied the first channel excavated for the *Shāhnahr*. Traces of the branch to Patti (Haibatpur) were observed in 1832 by A. Burnes, *Travels into Bokhara*, I,10.

[67] The *Ā'īn* puts Multan and Tulamba in the Bari Doab, from which one presumes that the Ravi had abandoned its old channel running past east of Multan and was flowing in the Sidhnai channel. (See also Sujān Rāi, 77.) This reach is supposed by tradition to have been originally a man-made canal, and this is supported by its remarkably straight course. Cf. *Mooltan Gazetteer*, (1883-4), 2; Raverty in *JASB*, LXI (1892), 370, note no. 365; G.R. Elsmie, *Thirty-five Years in the Punjab, 1858-93*, 354.

[68] Sujān Rāi, 74. Assuming that the Tavi then joined the Chenab at or near the present point of confluence, this canal must have been well over 30 miles in length.

[69] *Parwāna* in the *Nigārnāma-i Munshī*, ed. 151-2.

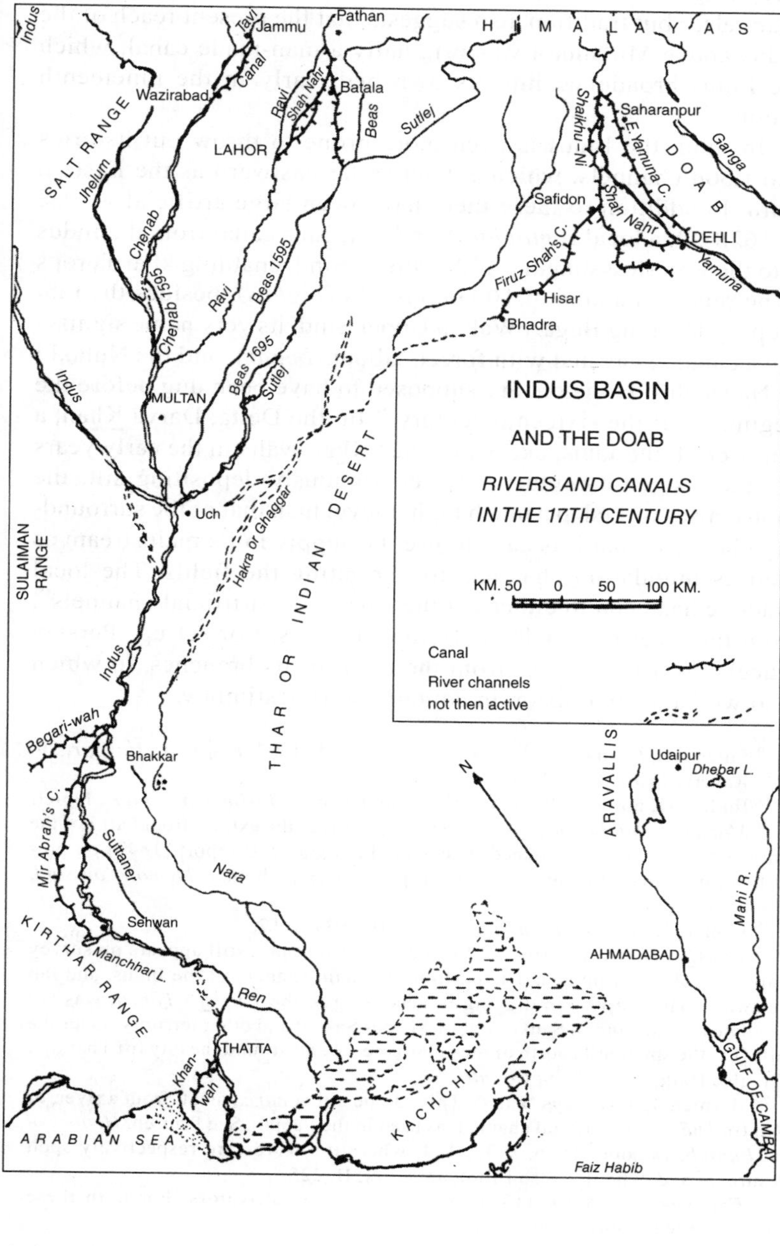
INDUS BASIN
AND THE DOAB
RIVERS AND CANALS
IN THE 17TH CENTURY
KM. 50 0 50 100 KM.
Canal
River channels
not then active
H I M A L A Y A S
SALT RANGE
SULAIMAN RANGE
KIRTHAR RANGE
THAR OR INDIAN DESERT
ARAVALLIS
DOAB
KACHCHH
ARABIAN SEA
GULF OF CAMBAY
Indus
Tavi
Jammu
Pathan
Canal
Wazirabad
Shah Nahr
Batala
Ravi
Beas
Sutlej
LAHOR
Jhelum
Chenab
Chenab 1595
Ravi
Beas 1595
Beas 1695
Sutlej
MULTAN
Uch
Hakra or Ghaggar
Saharanpur
Ganga
Shaikhu-Ni
E. Yamuna C.
Shah Nahr
Safidon
DEHLI
Yamuna
Firuz Shah's C.
Hisar
Bhadra
Begari-wah
Bhakkar
Mir Abrah's C.
Suttaner
Nara
Sehwan
Manchhar L.
Ren
THATTA
Khan-wah
Udaipur
Dhebar L.
Mahi R.
AHMADABAD
N
Faiz Habib

its fertility,[70] which Aurangzeb attributed to the inundations and well-irrigation.[71] The area is, indeed, full of abandoned river channels,[72] but tradition also suggests that the present reach of the Indus above Mithankot was originally a man-made canal, which the Indus broadened into its own bed, early in the nineteenth century.[73]

In Sind, the Indus is even more prone to throw out its arms and flood channels, which extend as far eastward as the Eastern Nara. In addition to these there have been large artificial works. In 1628-29, a local *zamīndār,* Mīr Ābra, cut a canal from the Indus into the waterless country of Northern Sind, enabling kharif crops to be raised in a area of 100,000 *jarībs* (*bīghas*), besides the rabi crops.[74] The long Begārī Wāh in Upper Sind, its very name signifying a canal excavated with forced labour (*begār*), and the Nulakhi in Naushahro Division, are supposed to have been dug before the beginning of the sixteenth century.[75] In the Delta, Daryā Khān, a minister of the Jāms, excavated the "Khān-wāh" in the early years of the sixteenth century.[76] By continuously depositing silt, the Indus raises its bed to a much higher level than that of the surrounding plains, so that it is easy to use the supply in its mainstream as well as inundation channels for irrigating the fields. The local practice has been to either cut the *kārīzs,* or "artificial channels", from the river or canals, as Bernier tells us,[77] or set up 'Persian wheels' to lift the water from the river, or its branches, to which also we have an allusion in contemporary testimony.[78]

[70] Sujān Rāi, 63, 64. [71] *Ādāb-i 'Ālamgīrī,* ed., I, 57; *Ruq'āt-i 'Ālamgīr*, 29.

[72] Raverty in *JASB*, LXI 1892, 299.

[73] Ibid., 303, note no.301; Ibadur Rahman Khan in *Muslim Univ. Jour.*, I, 569.

[74] *Maẓhar-i Shāhjahānī*, 17-18 *n*. The editor gives the extract from Part I of the work, which is yet unpublished. See also Hugh Games's report (1847) on pre-British canals in Chandaukah *pargana* (upper Sind) in Thomas, *Memoirs on Sind*, 713-17, 749-50.

[75] Lambrick in *Jour. of Sind Hist. Soc.*, III, 1937, i, 17.

[76] *Tārīkh-i Ṭāhirī*, Or. 1685, f.26a; ed., 58. This canal still appears on survey maps. It took off from near Thatta, from the main channel of the Indus, and ran westward. The purpose in digging it, according to the *Tārīkh-i Ṭāhirī*, was "to populate the *pargana* of Sankora [now Mirpur Sakro] and other territory under the hills [i.e. the small hills north of the Gharo creek] and around the city [of Thatta]". (Cf. also Haig, *Indus Delta Country,* 86, n.).

[77] Bernier, 454. He says 'kalis'. This can be either *kārīz*, a cut from a river, or *khāl* (or *khālā*), an artificial channel, as used in the Panjab. See Prinsep, *History of the Punjab*, London, 1846, I, 33, 154, where the words are respectively spelt "khureez" and "khool"; also Elliot, *Memoirs*, II, 225.

[78] *Factories, 1646-50*, 119, concerning indigo-cultivators. For both these practices, see Lambrick, op.cit., 15.

In Kashmir, Bernier described how the streams coming down from the surrounding mountains were "conducted by means of embanked earthen channels even to the top of the numerous hillocks" in the valley, thereby enabling the inhabitants to irrigate their fields of rice.[79] The Mughal emperors and nobility also laid out canals to water their gardens.[80]

Our information on the system of canal irrigation is admittedly incomplete. It is, however, obvious that while much use was made in our period of the natural inundation channels, a number of canals had also been excavated, some of them being really very large works.[81] The high-quality cropping of the Panjab and Sind, of which we hear often from contemporary authorities,[82] was probably largely to be found in tracts thus irrigated. Nevertheless, it is also clear that the natural channels could have hardly always been suitable for irrigation, which requires the level of water in the source to be generally much higher than the fields. Nor could the man-made canals of the period have offered, either in capacity or in regularity of alignment, any comparison to those built on the foundations of modern engineering. There can, therefore, be no doubt about the advance made over the Mughal canal system, even at its best, by the construction of the great network of modern canals in the Indus basin and the upper Gangetic plains, by the first two decades of the twentieth century.

3. THE CROPS AND OTHER AGRICULTURAL PRODUCE

An important feature of Indian agriculture has been the large number of crops raised by the peasants. The *Ā'īn-i Akbarī* provides revenue rates for sixteen crops of the rabi harvest cultivated in all the revenue circles of the Agra province, with three others not cultivated in some; and for twenty-five crops of the kharif harvest,

[79] Bernier, 396. The system is already referred to in Kalhaṇa's *Rājataraṅgiṇi* (12th century), transl. M.A. Stein, p.200 (verses 110-12). For a modern description, W.R. Lawrence, *Valley of Kashmir*, 323-4.

[80] Jahāngīr laid out the *Jūi Shāhī* from Lar (Sind) R. to Nūr Bāgh (*TJ*, 347), and Shāhjahān, the *Shāhnahr* (Lāhorī, I, ii, 24-5). Shāhjahān let a canal be run out of an older one to Āṣaf Khān's garden (*Bāgh-i Nishāṭ*), but on condition that water previously made available for irrigation of villages from the parent canal was not reduced (text of *farmān* given in Pir Ghulām Ḥusain Koyahāmī, *Tārīkh-i Ḥasan*, I, 292-7). Cf. *Atlas*, 103, col.(b).

[81] For an opposite view, based on rather summary considerations, see Moreland, *India at the Death of Akbar*, 107-8.

[82] *Ā'īn*, I, 538; Thevenot, 85; and Sujān Rāi, 79, for the Panjab; and *Ā'īn*, I, 556, and Manrique, II, 238, for Sind.

cultivated in all (or all but one) circles of the province with two others not cultivated in two or more circles. Allowing for two crops that were common to both harvests, as many as thirty-nine crops were thus being cultivated within the year in practically every revenue circle of the province. Lists of assessed crops are similarly extensive for the other *ẓabṭī* provinces: seventeen in rabi and twenty-six in kharif in Dehli province, and so on.[1] In southern Gujarat, near Surat, official surveyors in 1595-96 recorded as many as sixteen crops in land no larger than 80.65 *bīgha-i Ilāhī* (19.4 hectares), raised by seven cultivators.[1a] In *sarkār* Sehwan (Sind), according to a statement of 1634, the assessed crops under kharif numbered seventeen, and, under the rabi, as many as twenty-two, with six crops common to both harvests.[2] From a rather late *khasra* document (1791), giving particulars of the kharif cultivation of a strip (*pattī*) in a village in eastern Rajasthan, one learns that from amongst 42 peasants, a single peasant raised nine crops; four others, seven crops each; and another seven, six crops each. Of the remaining peasants eleven cultivated three or four crops each.[3] Clearly, the peasant of Mughal India had the knowledge and skill to deal in a large inventory of crops whose cultivation the tropical climate made possible.

In the production of foodgrains, Mughal India exhibited the same broad division into rice and wheat-and-millet zones, that we find today, with the 40-and 50-inch annual isohyets setting the dividing line. In the Assam valley,[4] in Bengal[5] and Orissa,[6] on the eastern coast[7] and in the Tamil country,[8] the narrow strip along the western coast[9] and Kashmir,[10] rice was cultivated to the virtual exclusion of wheat and millets. In Bihar,[11] Ilahabad[12] and Awadh[13] and in

[1] See the *dastūr* tables in *Ā'īn*, I, 348-85. Cf. I. Habib in *Combridge Economic History of India*, ed. T. Raychaudhuri and Irfan Habib, I, 217.

[1a] See I. Habib, 'Agriculture and Agrarian Conditions in South Gujarat, 1596', *PIHC*, 54th Session 1993, Mysore, 248-93.

[2] *Maẓhar-i Shāhjahānī*, 182-84: under kharif, *mung* should be read *mashang*; and so also *masang* under *rabī'*.

[3] S.P. Gupta, *Agrarian System of Eastern Rajasthan*, 127-29. Similar information is derived from another document of 1796 about a village in the some region, where as many as ten crops were raised, and nine out of thirty-eight peasants had sown five or more crops each in the kharif harvest (S.P. Gupta in *Medieval India – A Miscellany*, IV, 168-76).

[4] *Fatḥiya-i 'Ibriya,* f.32b. [5] *Ā'īn,* I. 389. [6] Ibid., 391.

[7] *Relations of Golconda,* 7-8; Fryer, I, 99. [8] *Dilkushā*, ff. 112b-113a.

[9] Fryer, I, 137, 139; Linschoten, I, 245-6; *Factories, 1665-67*, 45.

[10] *Ā'īn*, I, 563; *T.J.*, 300-301. The opposite was the case in Kishtwar (*T.J.*, 296).

[11] *Ā'īn*, I, 416. [12] Ibid., 423; Mundy, 91-2, 98. [13] *Ā'īn*, I, 433.

Khandesh[14] it enjoyed only a partial domain. It was grown in Gujarat, especially in the southern coastal belt;[15] and a writer of the mid-eighteenth century claimed that there had been a substantial improvement in the quality of the rice raised in the province as compared with "olden times".[16] Rice cultivation crossed its climatic limits in the dry region of the north-west in about the same way as it does now: irrigation from the Indus and its branches made it a major crop of Sind,[17] while high grade rice was sown in the Lahor province.[18]

Similarly, wheat was cultivated throughout its 'natural' region. It is interesting, however, to find that it intruded into Bengal; and although the crop obtained there was recognized to be of a low quality, it is possible that a larger quantity of it was then grown than at the present day.[19] Like wheat, barley grew most abundantly in the central plains[20] and Gujarat,[21] but could not be well cultivated in Bengal,[22] while it was not raised in Kanara[23] and Tamilnadu,[24] nor in Kashmir.[25]

The region of millets[26] coincides largely with that of wheat, but tends towards still drier zones. Thus juwār and bājrā were not cultivated in the Ilahabad province,[27] while, westwards, in the

[14] Ibid., 473; Tavernier, I, 41, 116; Thevenot, 102.

[15] *Ā'īn*, I, 493; Commissariat, *Mandelslo*, 15; Tavernier, I, 54; Thevenot, 37.

[16] *Mirā't*, I, 14.

[17] *Ā'īn*, I, 556; Manrique, II, 238; Hamilton, I, 125.

[18] Sujān Rāi, 79. Cf. also Manrique,II, 221; Thevenot, 85.

[19] Bernier, 438; Master, II, 81-2 (referring to the territory around Hugli). The Surat factors in 1616 denied "not but that Bengalla brings wheat... to Indya." (*Lett. Recd.*, IV, 327), which, however, may be due to a confusion between the port and the hinterland as the source of supply.

[20] It appears in practically all the *dastūrs* of the *ẓabṭī* provinces (Ilahabad, Awadh, Agra, Ajmer, Delhi, Lahor and Multan), except for Malwa, where it is given only in the *dastūr* circle of Raisen.

[21] Fryer, I, 297. It is noticed also in Orissa (Bowrey, 121).

[22] *Ā'īn*, I, 389. Nor in Assam (*Fatḥiya-i 'Ibriya*, f. 32b).

[23] Linschoten, I, 246.

[24] Tavernier, I, 226.

[25] *Ā'īn*, I, 389. But barley and wheat were grown in Little and Great Tibet (Lāhorī, I, ii, 287; Desideri, 75,78). Barley is often concealed in contemporary references under words like *jins-i ghalla*, or (in European sources) corn, cereals, etc.

[26] The millets listed in the *Ā'īn* (I, 293-300) are: *juwār*, *lahḍra* (i.e. *bājrā*), *sānwān* (Pers. *shāmākh*) (mod. *sawan*), *chīna* (Pers. *arzan*), *mandwa* (mod. *marua* or *ragi*), *kodron* or *kodram* (mod. *kodon*), *kangunī* (Pers. *gāl*) (mod. *kakun*), *kodirī*, or *korī* and *barṭī*. The last two cannot be identified. *Kodirī* is explicitly stated to be a low-grade crop and *barṭī* is not entered in the *dastūrs*. Perhaps, *kodirī* is a variant of *gondli* (Panicum miliare). Moreland (*India at the Death of Akbar*, 303) suggests *menjhri* or *kutki* (Panicum psilopodium) as identical with either *kodirī* or *barṭī*.

[27] *Ā'īn*, I, 423. *Juwār*, nevertheless, appears on the *dastūrs* of this province. But

Dipalpur region, juwār was the main kharif crop, with wheat sown for the rabi.[28] In Ajmer,[29] Gujarat,[30] and Khandesh,[31] millets in fact predomianted over cereals; this was not true, however, of Malwa[32] and Saurashtra.[33] In the case of pulses also it is difficult to detect any substantial change between Mughal times and *c.* 1900. What we know of the different crops from the *Ā'īn* suggests that the general pattern was very similar, if not identical.[34]

Maize, native to the New World, forms the only major addition to food crops made in India during Mughal times.[35] It was cultivated in Spain and Morocco before 1600 and afterwards spread to other parts of the Mediterranean.[36] It is, therefore, not surprising that the crop does not appear in the detailed crop lists of the *Ā'īn-i Akbarī*;[37] a suggestion that it was grown in the Vijayanagara empire has been refuted by Moreland.[38] The common Indian name for it, *makka* recalling Mecca, strongly suggests its arrival by the Red

---

lahḍra (i.e. *bājra*), together with three or four other millets, is omitted.

[28] Sujān Rāi, 63. [29] *Ā'īn*, I, 505. [30] Ibid., 485; *T.J.* 207; *Mir'āt*, I, 14.

[31] *Ā'īn*, I, 473; *Dilkushā*, f.7a. [32] *Ā'īn*, I, 455.

[33] *Mir'āt*, I, 178, though *Ā'īn*, I, 490, says *juwār* yielded three crops a year in Soraṭh.

[34] The *Ā'īn* (I, 298-300) lists the following pulses: *nakhwud* (gram) of two kinds: *Kābulī* and *Hindī*, or ordinary; *masūr* (Pers. *'adas*); *maṭar* (Pers. *mashang*, green peas); *mūng* (Pers. *māsh*); *urd* (*māsh-i siyāh*, but entered in the *dastūrs* simply as *māsh*, the *mūng* appearing under its indigenous name); *lobiyā* and *kult* (mod. *kulthi*). *Arhar* is not included in this list, but appears in the 19-years rates and the *dastūrs*. All spaces against it are left blank in the latter, except for a few circles in Awadh. In the 19-years rates also, the crop is rated only in Ilahabad, Awadh and Multan provinces and this too from only the 20th year (1575-76) and uniformly at 20 *dāms* per *bīgha*. It seems, therefore, to have been regarded as too low grade a crop to be rated in most areas. The pulse now called *khesari* is noticed as *kisārī* in its true region, Bihar; and it is said to be the food of the poor and a cause of sickness (*Ā'īn*, I, 416). *Māsh*, i.e. *urd*, could be sown without ploughing in Champaran (Bihar) (ibid., 417). *Moṭh* was seldom grown in the Ilahabad province (ibid., 423).

[35] Some earlier doubts about the New World origins of maize have been removed by archaeology. See Jacquetta Hawkes, *Prehistory*, UNESCO, 370-73; and Jose L. Lorengzo in S.J. Laet, ed., *Prehistory and the Beginnings of Civilization*, UNESCO, 627-28.

[36] Fernand Braudel, *The Mediterranean and the Mediterranean World in the Age of Philip II*, I, 424.

[37] Watt, VI, iv, 334, cites Blochmann's transl., I, 83, for an incidental reference to maize, but this is due to a misrendering of the text (I, p.97), which has *juwārī* here.

[38] *India at the Death of Akbar,* 305-6. In an important paper, P.K. Gode, *Studies in Indian Cultural History*, I, 283-94, rejects an Indian origin of maize, finding no acceptable reference to it in literature before the 17th century.

Sea route. Gode assembled convincing evidence to show that the cereal was known in Maharashtra and the Dakhin in the seventeenth century, quite possibly even before 1620.[39] It begins to appear as a kharif crop in the revenue documents of eastern Rajasthan from 1664 onwards.[40] From the scarcity of references to it in the seventeenth century, it would seem that it spread rather slowly. Its cultivation became more extensive in the nineteenth century, when it tended to displace the smaller millets on drier soils.[41]

Except for the absence of maize, our evidence for the geographical distribution of the principal food-crops shows that around 1600 it was similar to what it was towards the close of the nineteenth century. Moosvi, who has made a detailed comparison of the yield-table (*rai*') in the *Ā'īn* with the data on yields of various crops in the Dehli-Doab region during the latter half of the nineteenth century, concludes that there was little change in the yields of food crops.[42] This accords with Moreland's earlier finding, based on the *Ā'īn's* prices and assessment rates of different crops in the provinces of Awadh, Agra and Dehli, that the value of produce per acre of one food crop in terms of another did not change substantially between *c.*1600 and *c.*1910, an exception being offered by bājra which appears to have been undervalued in the earlier period.[43]

The 'cash crops' of modern classification are practically identical with what in Mughal records are termed *jins-i kāmil* or *jins-i a'lā*,[44] "high-grade crops", chiefly grown for the market. Cotton and sugarcane were the two major crops belonging to this category. Cotton cultivation is duly noticed in what later came to be known as the Bombay Cotton Tract, but especially in Khandesh.[45]

39 Gode, op. cit., 291-2.

40 S.P. Gupta, *Agrarian System of Eastern Rajasthan*, 55-59. These tables were originally presented by S. Nurul Hasan, K.N. Hasan and S.P. Gupta in *PIHC*, 28th session, 1966, Mysore, 254-7.

41 Cf. Watt, VI, iv, 334-5.

42 Moosvi, 73-86.

43 *JRAS*, 1917, 820; and 1918, 377-8; *India at the Death of Akbar*, 103 & n. Cf. Moosvi, 86-92.

44 These two terms are very frequently encountered in the revenue literature of the period from the *Ā'īn* onwards, but the sense seems everywhere to have been regarded as self-evident. Khāfī Khān classifies crops as *jins-i ghalla* (foodgrains) and *jins-i a'lā* such as "sugarcane, etc." (I, 156, 735n.). In a late 18th-century glossary of revenue terms (MS Add. 6603, f. 57a) the *jins-i kāmil* is stated to include sugar-cane, betel leaf, cotton, etc., as distinct from the *jins-i adnā*, defined as crops fetching low prices, such as the various kinds of millets.

45 For Khandesh, see *Ā'īn*, I, 473; Salbancke, *Purchas*, III, 82-3; Pelsaert 9; Thevenot, 101; and Tavernier, I, 42-3. For Berar, Thevenot, 101; for Aurangabad

It was also cultivated throughout northern India,[46] and was an important crop in Bengal,[47] where it afterwards practically disappeared.[48] The development of sea-trade and the subsequent construction of the railways were to give rise to a greater concentration of cotton-cultivation in certain regions, accompanied by a decline in others. It is possible that the average acre devoted to cotton by 1910 was better suited to the crop than in Mughal times. And from what we know of the amount of clothing available to the peasants (see Chapter III) it may also be assumed that the total yield and, perhaps, acreage as well, of cotton per head had increased considerably since *c.*1600.[49] Its relative scarcity might therefore explain the high value, in comparison to other crops, which was assigned to the yield of cotton per *bīgha* in the *Ā'īn*.[50] The change

and southern Maharashtra, Thevenot, 102; *Factories, 1655-60*, 241; *1668-9*, 270; Fryer, I, 331, 344. It also extended into Golkunda (*Relations*, 61), whose cotton was found to be better and cheaper than the cotton grown in Gujarat (*Lett. Recd,* II, 102). For Gujarat, see also Godinho de Eredia, *JASB*, Lett. IV, 1938, 549-50, *Factories, 1634-6*, 64, Commissariat, *Mandelslo*, 15, Fryer, III, 158-9; and for Kachh (Cutch), *Factories, 1636-8*, 130.

46 Manrique (II, 221) noticed cotton fields between Lahor and Multan; the Multan province was noted (Thevenot, 77) for the "plenty of Cotton" it yielded; and "vast quantities" of cotton were "collected" in the territory of Thatta (Manrique, II, 238-9). Salbancke (*Purchas*, III, 84) noticed "store of cotton-wools" in villages on the Bayana-Merta route (Rajasthan). Roe, 322, found cotton fields on the way from Ajmer to Mandu near Toda; and Mundy, 56-57, in Malwa. It was apparently an important crop in the Agra region (*Factories, 1655-60,* 118), and there is a reference to its cultivation in the territory of Sirsa, in Haryana (Bālkrishan, f.63a). The inclusion of cotton in the *dastūrs* for almost all circles in Ajmer, Ilahabad and Awadh shows that it was being cultivated in these provinces as well. We know from *Factories, 1618-21*, 192-3, and Mundy, 134, that its cultivation extended up to Patna, and there are references to cotton grown in Orissa (Fitch: Ryley, 114, *Early Travels, 26; Ā'īn*, I, 391).

47 Linschoten, I, 95; Fitch: Ryley, 25, 28, *Early Travels*, 112, 118; Bernier, 402, 439; Master, II, 81-2; Bowrey, 132-4.

48 An official report of 1886-87, quoted by Watt, IV, 134, says: "Cotton was formerly grown in the Dacca and Mymensingh districts, in a large tract of land ... very well suited to the plant. The cotton raised here ... was the finest known in the world and formed the material out of which the Dacca ... muslin was manufactured. Since the decline of that celebrated fabric, the cultivation of cotton has almost entirely ceased in the tract."

49 Cf. Moreland, *India at the Death of Akbar*, 105, for the same conclusion.

50 This is worked out in ibid, 105, and *JRAS*, 1918, 381. Moosvi, 76,82, compares the *rai'* (standard crop-yield) in the *Ā'īn* with the yields of cotton estimated in 1892 for Delhi and various districts of western U.P., and finds the *rai'* to be distinctly higher in both irrigated and unirrigated lands. The average yield, however, turned out to be almost the same when she compared the *rai'* with estimates for the same region in the 1870s. But when she compared the *dastūrs* for cotton with

in the comparative value of sugarcane was far less substantial.[51] Its cultivation was certainly quite widespread in Mughal times, even more so, perhaps, than that of cotton.[52] The Bengal sugar was then pre-eminent both in volume of output and quality.[53] The cultivation of sugarcane subsequently declined in Bengal, although it still remained by 1910 one of the important crops of the province.

The small amount of information that we have concerning the different oilseed crops, does not indicate any notable difference in their geographical distribution. They were prominent in Bengal[54] and appear with some minor exceptions in the *dastūrs* or revenue-rates of all the provinces from Ilahabad to Multan.[55] Rapeseed

the value of output as estimated in the 1870s for the same localities, there immediately appeared a great decline. Taking the value of output of wheat as the standard, cotton output was valued in Agra at 129.99% of wheat in Akbar's time, but at only 66.67% in 1870-71 (ibid., 88).

[51] *India at the Death of Akbar*, 103. Moosvi, 76, 82, found the sugarcane output per acre to be lower in Akbar's time than the estimated output for sugarcane in Delhi and western UP in 1870s and 1892. But in three out of five localities the value of output (with that of wheat as standard) still remained about the same; it had fallen in the other two localities (Moosvi, 88).

[52] For Bihar, *Ā'īn*, I, 416; Mundy, 134. It is listed (distinguished as of two grades, ordinary and thick *(paunda)*, practically without exception in the *dastūrs* of all the *ẓabṭī* provinces in the *Ā'īn*. Bayana and Kalpi (Agra province) and Maham (in the *sarkār* of Hisar Firuza, Dehli province) are specially noted for the sugar produced there (*Ā'īn*, I, 442, 527). Steel and Crowther (*Purchas*, IV, 268) say of "all the Country betwixt Agra and Lahore" that "it yeelds great store of poudered Sugar..." See also *Factories, 1646-50*, 255, & *1655-60*, 118, for Agra; Bernier, 282, and Thevenot, 68, for Dehli; *Bāburnāma*, ed., 360, Bev., I, 388; *Factories, 1637-41*, 134-5, Thevenot, 85 and Sujān Rāi, 79, for Lahor province; Pelsaert, 31, and Thevenot, 77, for Multan; and *Ā'īn*, I, 455, for Malwa. For Sind, see Linschoten, I, 56. For Gujarat, Linschoten, I, 60, Tavernier, I, 54, Thevenot, 36, and Fryer, I, 266; there was, however, no surplus for export (*Lett. Recd.*, V, 115; VI, 280). For Khandesh, Mundy, 48. For Baglana, Ṣādiq Khān, Or. 174, ff. 60b-61a; Or. 1671, f.34a. For Berar, Manucci, II, 429. For Aurangabad province, Thevenot, 102. For Konkan, Careri, 168-9, 179. The sugar of the Dakhin and of Lahor was much esteemed for quality (Sujān Rāi, 79; Thevenot, 85).

[53] Linschoten, I, 97; *Haft Iqlīm*, 94, 97; *Factories, 1630-33*, 323, *1646-50*, 255: Bernier, 437, 442. Assam produced white, red and black sugar, sweet, but hard (*Fatḥiya-i 'Ibriya*, f.32b).

[54] Bernier, 442, says "mustard sesame for oil" was grown in this province. The *arindi* silk in Bengal was dependent upon the castor-plant. See also Master, II, 81-2; Bowrey, 132-33.

[55] The *Ā'īn* lists five oilseed crops: safflower, linseed, mustard, sesame or rapeseed and *toryā*. Of these the first, third and fourth seem to have been universally cultivated; the second is omitted from the *dastūrs* of the Agra province; and the last is given only in those of Awadh, Agra, Lahor and Ajmer (central, eastern and south-eastern parts only). Monserrate, 214, says that flax was grown in "the neighbourhood of the Indus". But see Thevenot, 51, who denies its presence, an error

and, perhaps, the castor-plant were noticed also in Gujarat.[56] Flax was grown mainly for the linseed, i.e. for its oil, although its fibre-producing quality was known.[57] It was acknowledged, however, that it grew better and in greater quantity in Europe and the Ottoman Empire.[58] Groundnuts were not grown in Mughal times.[59] Compared with foodgrains, the prices of the oilseeds, especially linseed, were much lower than in *c*.1910 owing to the importance gained by them in the nineteenth century as items of export.[60] It would be surprising if their production per head of population was not substantially higher around 1910 than in Mughal times. And yet, rather surprisingly, there is evidence that the value of output of these crops was distinctly less towards the close of the nineteenth century than around 1600.[61]

Among the fibre-yielding crops, *san,* or sunn-hemp, probably far outstripped jute in our period. The *dastūrs* in the *Āʼīn* assume its cultivation in almost every portion of the *ẓabṭī* provinces. Jute was obviously produced in Bengal for the local market alone.[62] The enormous extension of its cultivation in Bengal, in fact, took place largely in the course of the nineteenth century, at the expense of rice and sugar, a circumstance which was undoubtedly connected with the chronic food shortage which later affected the province.

---

probably due to the fact that its fibre was not used in India. For the decline in the cultivation of safflower, which also yielded a dye, see below.

56 Fryer, I, 297.

57 "*Kattan* (Flax): They sow it in the *kharīf* season, either for oil or for rope or for linen." (Tract on Agriculture, I.O.4702, f.30b). Linen was, however, never produced in any noticeable quantity in Mughal India.

58 "In the countries of Rūm and Farang" (ibid).

59 Watt, *Dict. of Commercial Products,* 74-75, finds the earliest reference to groundnut cultivation in Buchanan's survey of south India (1800).

60 Moreland, *India at the Death of Akbar,* 103-4; *and JRAS*, 1918, 378-9. See also Moosvi, 327,332.

61 That is, in terms of wheat. This is what I deduced (this book, first edition, 432) by comparing the *Āʼīn's dastūrs* for the Meerut circle with the values of output given in *Meerut Dist. Gaz.,*1922, 44-45. Moosvi, 87-88, corroborates this deduction by citing evidence from Aligarh district for 1872-73 (where, however, she recognises that the figure for the yield of mustard is dubious). It is difficult to explain such a change in the value of output of oilseed crops.

62 Master, II, 81-2, where among the products of the territory around Hugli are listed "course hempe, gunneys, and many other commodityes". Moreland, *India at the Death of Akbar*, 119, following Jarrett takes a product of *sarkār* Ghoraghat, viz. *ṭāṭband* (*Āʼīn*, I, 390), to mean sack-cloth, i.e. jute. This was accepted by me in the first edition of this book, 41 & n. As, however, the *ʻAlamgīrnāma*, 724, makes clear, *ṭāṭband* was a kind of silk ('eri'). (See *Atlas*, 70, col.c.)

The dye-yielding crops are now of little account; but this was certainly far from the case in the seventeenth century; and indigo, especially, looms large in the commercial literature of the time. The best indigo grew in the Bayana tract near Agra,[63] while that of a lower quality was cultivated in the Doab, around Khurja and Kol (Aligarh).[64] The second place was generally assigned to the indigo of Sarkhej near Ahmadabad.[65] But that of Sehwan in Sind was thought to be better than it in many respects.[66] The indigo of Telangana in the Dakhin occupied a mid-way position between these fine varieties and the coarser sorts of indigo which were grown practically everywhere, from Bengal to Khandesh.[67] So profitable were the crops of the Bayana and Sarkhej tracts that the stalks were kept in the fields to give three cuttings in two years, a practice frequently described by contemporary authorities,[68] though largely abandoned in later days.[69] Indigo is, perhaps, the only crop

[63] *Ā'īn*, I, 442; Finch, *Early Travels*, 151-2; Pelsaert,13-14; Mundy 222, 234; Tavernier, I, 72.

[64] Pelsaert, 15; Mundy, 96; *Factories*, *1630-33*, 325.

[65] *Ā'īn*, I, 486; Finch, *Early Travels*, 174; Jourdain, 171-3; Broeke, transl. Moreland, *JIH*, X, 246.

[66] *Factories*, *1637-41*, 274; *1646-50*, 29. Cf. also Withington, *Early Travels*, 218; Roe, 76; *Factories*, *1634-36*, 129, *1637-41*, 136-7, *1642-45*, 203, *1646-50*, 12-13, 33, 119.

[67] For the Telangana indigo, see *Lett. Recd.*, II, 102; Foster, *Supp. Cal.*, 93; *Relations*, *35-36*, 61; *Factories*, *1665-7*, 164.

Indigo was grown in Bengal (Tavernier, II, 8) as well as Bihar (Mundy 151, 153). The crop is listed in the *dastūrs* of all the *ẓabṭī* provinces in the *Ā'īn*. It was grown near Gwaliar (*Factories*, *1646-50*, 122), in Mewat (Pelsaert, 15) and near Dehli (Thevenot, 68). Mundy, 235, 240, noticed "base Indico" being cultivated at Lalsot and near Sambhar in the Ajmer province; and Salbancke (*Purchas*, III, 84, 88) found "store of course [coarse] Indico" in some villages between Bayana and Merta. Apart from Sarkhej, other parts of Gujarat, e.g. the territory around Khambayat, Baroda and Baroch, also produced indigo (Jourdain, 173-4; Commissariat, *Mandelslo*, 15; Tavernier, I, 54). For indigo grown in Khandesh, see Thevenot, 101, and Tavernier, II, 42. Indigo was also an important crop in southern Coromandel (T. Raychaudhuri, *Jan Company in Coromandel*, 9).

[68] Finch, *Early Travels*, 152-3; *Lett. Recd.*, IV, 240-41; Pelsaert, 10-13; Mundy, 221-3. All these descriptions apply only to the Bayana tract, but from such passages as *Factories*, *1655-60*, 76, it appears that the practice was also followed in the country around Sarkhej. Tavernier, II, 8-9, is probably as mistaken in taking it to be the universal practice in India as in asserting that "it is cut three times a year". The tract on agriculture, already cited, says clearly that the general method of cultivating it much resembled that of cotton; only it was cut earlier (I.O. 4702, f. 31a). Linschoten's description of the method of cultivation in Gujarat (II, 91) is also in accord with this. Neither refers to more than one cutting from the same stalks.

[69] Not entirely, however: the practice of taking off two cuttings survived in the

for which contemporary estimates of production are available, though the output must naturally have varied greatly each year according as the seasons were favourable or otherwise. From the various estimates in our sources, it would seem that the annual production of the dye in the three principal indigo tracts of the empire, viz. Bayana-Doab-Mewat, Sarkhej and Sehwan, amounted in favourable years to some 1.8 million lb. avdp. (816.4 metric tons).[70] This excludes the yield of such regions as parts of Gujarat (besides Sarkhej), Khandesh, and Bihar, for which no estimates are recorded. But even allowing for this, the total indigo production of the empire could hardly have exceeded a third, or even a fourth, of the output in the 1880s when foreign demand

---

North-Western Provinces or U.P. (Watt, IV, 407), while in Khandesh "a two-year and sometimes a three-year crop" was grown to "a very small extent" (ibid., 412). The principal cause of this change seems to be that in the old indigo tracts the extra remuneration from the second cutting, which was much better than the first, did not justify the land's being left exclusively under indigo for two years which this method required. Moreover, the Bayana indigo was cultivated with the help of well irrigation and much of its special quality was held to derive from the well water (Pelsaert, 13-14). Under canal irrigation the quality deteriorated considerably (Watt, IV, 406).

[70] Contemporary estimates are given either in bales, churls or fardles, or in *mans*. Both sets of units were subject to regional variations and the *mans* were also altered from time to time. In this note the original figures are all converted into their equivalents in lb. avdp. on the basis of information brought together in Appendix B.

Pelsaert, 13-15, put the yield of the Bayana tract at 884,800 lb. in favourable times and half of it in bad years. In addition, the Doab and Mewat contributed, in his judgement, some 221,200 lb. each annually. In 1633 the output of the "whole of Hindustan", i.e. presumably the central regions of the empire, was estimated at nearly 830,000 lb., and of this the Bayana tract was thought to contribute one-third (*Factories, 1630-33*, 325).

The quantity produced at Sarkhej seems to have reached or exceeded 332,000 lb. in good years like 1615, and to have fallen, excepting the period of famine, to about 221,400 lb. in indifferent years such as 1644 (*Lett. Recd.*, III, 51; *Factories, 1624-29,* 232; *1630-33*, 125, 178; *1634-36*, 73, 292; *1642-45*, 163-4).

The production in the Sehwan tract appears to have fallen steadily. This decline is not only mentioned explicitly in *Factories*, *1642-5*, 136, but is also reflected in estimates of the output; 132,600 lb. in 1635; 73,760 lb. in 1639; and only 29,480 lb. in 1644 (*Factories*, *1634-36*, 129; *1637-41*, 136-7; *1642-45*, 203).

The estimate of 1.8 million lb. given in the text is made up of Pelsaert's estimates for Bayana, Doab and Mewat, and the estimated output of Sarkhej in 1615 and of Sehwan in 1635. The favourable years were, however, not always the same everywhere and the total yield was probably lower in most years. There is a statement in *Factories*, *1637-41*, 92, from Surat, that according to "general report" the "proceed of the lease" of indigo in the empire in 1638 was going to be 40,000 "maens", i.e. if the Gujarat *man* is meant, about 1,476,000 lb.

was at its height.[71] It is, however, not to be compared with the position only one or two decades later, when indigo cropping was in rapid decay and due soon to disappear completely, owing to the manufacture of a synthetic substitute in Europe. Its elimination has had an adverse effect on other crops as well, especially wheat and cereals, for it had great fertilizing properties and did not necessarily conflict with the rabi cropping.[72]

The fate of indigo had been anticipated by that of *āl* (morinda citrifolia), yielding a red dye and cultivated in the lower Doab and Bundelkhand,[73] and around Sironj in Malwa.[74] This was also completely eliminated owing to manufactured dyes.[75] The cultivation of safflower, which yields a purple dye, also declined considerably by early twentieth century.[76]

Britain's Opium Wars with China helped establish opium as the premier item of India's export by the 1850s; thereafter it declined gradually in relative importance. Though its great day had yet to come, it was grown almost everywhere in the Mughal empire, but especially in Malwa and Bihar.[77] True hemp (*siddhī*

[71] This is based on the assumption that the total produce in 1880s was about 12 million lb. avdp. (5,442 metric tons) in the area covered by the Mughal empire. This is deduced from the figure of 10.8 million lb. exported from the ports of Bengal, Bombay and Sind and the total domestic consumption for the *whole* of India, estimated at 2 million lb. (Watt, IV, 421-2). The Mughal-Indian production was far less impressive, particularly since the indigo was obtained by the evaporation method and was therefore less concentrated than indigo obtained from boilers, its cost in modern times being about half that of the latter (Moosvi, 84-5).

[72] Cf. Moreland, *Agricultural Conditions of the United Provinces & Districts*, Note on Bulandshahr, 5-6, for the adverse effect of its disappearance on wheat. For its value as a preparatory crop for wheat, see also Voelcker, *Report*, 361. Indigo refuse or "seet" possessed great value as manure (ibid. 106). Cf. also Watt, IV, 407.

[73] No rates are given against this crop anywhere in the *Ā'īn* except for the *dastūr*-circles of Kalpi, Phapund and Erach in Agra province and Kutya and Kalinjar in Ilahabad. (So in the MSS. Blochmann wrongly assigns the rates to Korra and Jajma'u instead of Kutya and Kalinjar.)

[74] George Roques's MS report (1678-80) on textile crafts in India (in French), commentary & transl. (extracts) in Paul R. Schwartz, *Printing on Cotton at Ahmadabad, India, in 1678*, 12-13. Cf. Malcolm, *Memoir of Central India*, II. 77, where it is stated that "aul" was exported from Malwa in considerable quantities.

[75] Moreland, *India at the Death of Akbar*, 102-3. The dye-yielding seeds of the plant used to be exported in Mughal times (*Bahār-i 'Ajam*, s.v., *āl*).

[76] The dye is known as *kusum* and is extracted from the flower. For the decline in its cultivation, see *Meerut Dist. Gaz.*, 47, and *Bulandshahr Dist. Gaz.*, 37.

[77] For Malwa see *Ā'īn*, I, 455; Finch, *Early Travels*, 142; Jourdain, 149; *T.J.*, 179. Cf. *Imperial Gazetteer*, IX, 36. For Bihar, Fitch: Ryley 110, *Early Travels*,24; Marshall, 414. Opium is also noticed in Bengal (Bernier, 440; Master, II, 81-2)

or the *bhang* plant) was also widely cultivated,[78] although Aurangzeb ordered it to be completely eradicated,[79] possibly with the same lack of success as has attended later efforts.

The introduction and rapid extension of the cultivation of tobacco was a notable feature of the agricultural history of the seventeenth century. Tobacco is not mentioned anywhere in the *Ā'īn*; but within a decade of its compilation pious pilgrims returning from Mecca had brought news of the novelty to the court; and in 1603 an imperial envoy coming back from Bijapur, where the use of tobacco had already become common, was able to present to Akbar a hookah (*chilim*) well and properly made in every respect.[80] The addiction spread fast: Jahāngīr's prohibition was, perhaps, merely formal and, in the event, totally ineffective.[81] By Shāhjahān's reign tobacco had found a place in the perfumery of aristocratic households.[82] In the following reign, "Mahomedans" are said to have taken to consuming "a great deal of this article";[83] and another writer bemoans the fact that the infection had seized the rich and poor alike, without distinction.[84] He also alleges that in the beginning only a small quantity of tobacco used to come from Farang (Europe), so that it was not very common. But ultimately the peasants took to cultivating it with such enthusiasm that it began to predominate over other crops, a change which, according to him, took place during Jahāngīr's reign.[85] That this is substantially true is shown by the fact that by 1613 a "great quantity" of tobacco was being grown in villages near Surat;[86] and

---

and finds a place in almost all the *dastūrs* of the *ẓabṭī* provinces in the *Ā'īn*. For Multan, see Pelsaert, 31; Thevenot, 77. For Sehwan, *Factories, 1634-36*, 129. For Marwar, Mundy, 247. For Mewar, Manucci, II, 432. For Gujarat, Linschoten, I, 60; For Berar, Manucci, II, 429.

78 Monserrate, 214; Linschoten, I, 60 (refers to Gujarat only).

79 Aurangzeb's order of May 1659, addressed to the *dīwān* of Gujarat, forbidding its cultivation, is preserved in the *Mir'āt*, I, 247. Late in his reign we find the *faujdār* of Kuch Bihar acknowledging the receipt of a similar order for its eradication (*Matīn-i Inshā'*, f.12a-b). Cf. also Fraser 86, f. 92b.

80 Asad Beg, Memoirs, Or. 1996, f. 21a-b. He says the use of tobacco had the approval of "the wise men of Europe (*Farang*)".

81 *T.J.*, 183. Sujān Rāi, 455-56, writing some eighty years later, says the lips of some of the tobacco addicts of Lahor were cut off for defying this order.

82 *Bayāẓ-i Khwushbū'ī*, I.O. 828, f. 11b. 83 Manucci, II, 175.

84 Sujān Rāi, 454. 85 Ibid.

86 *Lett. Recd.*, I, 299-300. Cf. Fryer, I, 266, for its cultivation in the same region. It had spread to Golkunda "a few years" before Methwold's time, 1618-22 (*Relations*, 35-36).

Terry affirms that it was sown "in abundance" in his time (1616-19).[87] It was recorded among the taxed crops of *sarkār* Sehwan (Sind) in 1634, when it was observed that it had appeared there within the previous six years.[88] Its cultivation soon became universal and two revenue manuals belonging to the seventeenth century record its presence in regions so far inland as Sambhal and Bihar.[89]

Coffee as a beverage had become familiar to aristocratic and polite society.[90] It used to be imported from the Arabian peninsula and Abyssinia through Mocha and was not as yet properly acclimatized in India.[91] Still, an apparently unsatisfactory variety was being grown in southern Maharashtra.[92] Tea was just coming to be known, but was not cultivated anywhere,[93] not even in Assam, where it must have existed in a wild state.[94]

Among spices, pepper was commercially the most important article. Long pepper grew chiefly in Bengal, but the best, the round or black pepper, an item of world trade, was produced outside the limits of the Mughal Empire, in the southern ranges of the Western Ghats.[95] Capsicum or chilli, now so widely grown and an indispensable ingredient of practically every Indian meal, was unknown

[87] *Early Travels*, 299. He says (what the *Lett. Recd.*, op.cit., implies) that as yet the peasants knew "not how to cure and make it strong as those in Western India [West Indies]". Cf. also Methwold, *Relations*, 35-6.

[88] *Maẓhar-i Shāhjahānī*, 184. Tobacco began to be grown, it says, during the administration of Dīndār Khān (1628-34).

[89] *Dastūru-l 'Amal-i Navīsindagī*, f. 182a-b; *Dastūru-l 'Amal-i 'Ālamgīrī*, f.36b.

[90] Ovington, 180. The discovery of coffee or *qahwa* is referred to in the *Haft Iqlīm*, 14, but the beverage is mentioned neither in the *Ā'īn*, nor in the *Bayāẓ-i Khwushbū'ī* of Shāhjahān's reign. It is likely, therefore, that it became popular only in the latter part of the 17th century. In the later years of Aurangzeb it appears as a suitable article of gift at the court (*Akhbārāt* 44/269 and 49/25). There is a careful description of the seed and beverage in the mid-18th century work, *Mir'ātu-l Iṣṭilāh*, f. 218a.

[91] Tavernier, II, 20; Ovington, 180; *Mir'ātu-l Iṣṭilāh*, f.218a.

[92] *Factories, 1655-60*, 241. In Ma'mūrī, f. 202a (Khāfī Khān, II, 501), coffee plants are mentioned among the tress surrounding the fort of Khelna, captured by Aurangzeb in 1702.

[93] Qāẓī bin Kāshifuddīn Muḥammad Yazdī, *Risāla-i Chūb-i Chīnī*, Add. 19,169, ff.155b-156a. In this tract, written in or before 1629 in Iran, tea is called *chā*, and the question is raised whether it comes from China. See also *Factories, 1655-60*, 276; Ovington, 181.

[94] Nothing like tea is described or referred to in the *Fatḥiya-i 'Ibriya*, which contains a detailed account of the country.

[95] For long pepper grown in Bengal, see *Ā'īn*, I, 390; *Haft Iqlīm*, 94,97; Fitch: Ryley, 189, *Early Travels*, 46; Bernier, 440; Bowrey 134. It grew also in Kuch

to Mughal India. It was acclimatized in India only about the middle of the eighteenth century.[96]

One can discern little difference from the present day in the cultivation of betel leaf or *pān*, which was grown practically all over India.[97] Perhaps, the improved means of transport have helped to substantially extend its cultivation; but we have no definite proof.

Another crop grown entirely for the market was saffron. Its cultivation was confined, as now, to Kashmir, where it had greatly declined by the end of the nineteenth century.[98]

Vegetables were widely cultivated in Mughal India. Urban demand put a premium on their cultivation in plots near the towns, and it was characteristic of the Indian social structure that a particular caste, that of "Mālīs", should have specialized in this.[99]

(Kuch Bihar) (*Haft Iqlīm*, 100) and in the forests of Champaran (Bihar) (*Ā'īn*, I, 417). Tavernier, II, 12, is alone in saying that "without going beyond the territories of the Great Mogul there is enough [of long pepper] to be obtained in the Kingdom of Gujarat". But he has, perhaps, the re-exports, rather than the produce, of Gujarat in mind. For the round pepper produced in Bijapur, Kanara and Kerala, see Linschoten, I, 66, 67, 71-74; Fitch: Ryley 186, 188, *Early Travels*, 45, 46; *Factories, 1622-23*, 51; *1624-29*, 2-3; *1634-36*, 212; *1637-41*, 93; *1668-69*, 112, 224-5; Tavernier, II, 11; Fryer, I, 139, II, 42; Ma'mūrī, f. 202a.

[96] The two commonest varieties, *capsicum frutescens* and *capsicum annum* are both natives of South America (Watt, II, 134-5, 137-8, etc.). Āzād Bilgrāmī, writing in 1762-3, says that chilli or *mirch-i surkh* was unknown in Hindustan (i.e. northern India) ten or twenty years earlier and was taken there by the Marathas, who were greatly addicted to it; "some people of Hindustan" had now also learnt to use it in their meals (*Khizāna-i 'Āmira*, 48).

[97] For *pān* cultivation, see *Ā'īn*, I, 80-82, and Tract on Agriculture, I.O.4702, f. 27a-b. The *pān* leaves of the following regions are especially noticed in the *Ā'īn*: Bengal (from which came the *Bangla* leaf) (I, 80), Orissa (I, 391), Bihar (*Maghī*) (I, 416), Banaras (*Kapūrkānt*) (I, 80), Agra province (I, 441), especially Antri (near Gwaliar) (I, 449), Malwa (I, 455), especially Bajalpur in Sarangpur *sarkār* (I, 462), and Khandesh (I, 473). References in other literature abound.

[98] See *A.N.* III, 648; *Ā'īn*, I, 98, 565; *T.J.*, 45, for saffron grown in the Valley; *T.J.*, 296, and Pelsaert, 35-36, for saffron grown in Kishtwar. Within the Valley, saffron cultivation has remained largely confined to the vicinity of Pampur, where, according to the *Ā'īn*, I, 565, it was raised on 10,000 to 12,000 *bīghas*, or 2,400 to 2,880 hectares. But by the survey of 1887-93, the measured "saffron land" in the Valley was found to be 4,527 acres (= 1,832 hectares) of which only 132 acres (= 53 hectares) were actually sown with saffron (Lawrence, *Valley of Kashmir*, 342-3, 451).

[99] See a report in *Waqā'i' Ajmer* 235: "One Baja by name, belonging to the caste of *Mālī*, i.e. of gardeners who engage themselves in the cultivation of pot-herbs and vegetables, had remained outside the City [of Ajmer] for the night in order to guard a field of egg-plants (or brinjal) and was kidnapped by thieves," etc. Cf. Ānandrām Mukhliṣ, *Safarnāma-i Mukhliṣ*, 37, for fields of egg-plants around the town of Hasanpur (Rohilkhand). For the caste of *mālīs*, see *Tashrīḥu-l Aqwām*, ff. 231b-233a.

Among the vegetables the introduction of the sweet and the ordinary potato probably represents the most notable change since Mughal times.[100] Varieties of yams were, however, known,[101] and formed an article of popular diet in parts of the Dakhin and so possibly also in northern India.[102] Tomato and okra are well-known newcomers. With these exceptions, the vegetables commonly grown were practically the same as now;[103] and they impressed European travellers with their variety and abundance.[104]

The cultivation of roses seems to have received strong impetus in the seventeenth century from the demand for rose-water and the newly invented rose-essence (*'iṭr-i jahāngīrī*).[104a]

In fruit-growing it was natural that the most diverse features should have been observed. Many fruits grew wild in the jungles and were only gathered for sustenance by the poor.[105] Others, notably the melon (*kharbūza*), were cultivated as seasonal crops by the peasants.[106] Trees bearing the better class of fruits such as quality mangoes were usually planted in groves, in carefully

[100] The problem of the origin of the potato and its introduction in India is best discussed in Watt, III, 115-122.

[101] Two species of yams are mentioned in the *Ā'īn* among the fruits, viz. *tarrī* and *pindālū* (I, 79-80). In the tables of prices the former is listed among "fruits proper, while the latter, with another yam, *kachālū*, appears in the list of "fruits eaten after being cooked" (I, 70, 72). Linschoten, II, 42, says: "There grow in India many Iniamos and Batatas"; and a similar statement is made by Careri, 206. As Watt, op.cit., points out the "Iniamo" and "Batata" of Linschoten are only different species of yam and his "Batata" does not mean sweet potato. In the English literature of the time, 'potato' either meant a sweet potato or an ordinary potato (*OED*, s.v. potato), but English travellers seem often to have confounded the yam with the sweet potato. Thus Methwold *Relations*, 8, and Terry, *Early Travels* 297.

[102] Fryer, II, 76, noted that in Kanara "Potatoes [yams?] are their usual Banquet". In the 1655 edition of his work Terry added that "potatoes excellently well-dressed" were served at a banquet given by Āṣaf Khān in 1617 (London, 1777, p.197; *Early Travels,* 297, n.).

[103] The most comprehensive list of the vegetables then in the market will be found in the *Ā'īn*, I, 63-4, 72-3, classified into vegetables proper and fruits eaten after being cooked.

[104] Terry, *Early Travels*, 297; Pelsaert, 48; Mundy, 310; Manucci, I, 66; Fryer, I, 297-8; Careri, 206.

[104a] See I. Habib in *Mughal Gardens*, 130-31.

[105] Jungles of mangoes, khirni and tamarind were encountered when entering Gujarat via Dohad (*T.J.*, 205) and "faire woods of Kheernee, Peelooes etts.", as well as "mangooes", when entering the province from the direction of Sirohi (Mundy, 260-2, 265). "Wild date trees" grew between Baroch and Surat (Finch, *Early Travels*, 175).

[106] The *Ā'īn* lists both the *Wilāyatī* (Central Asian) and Indian melons in the *dastūrs*, but doubtless the latter were more widely grown. In the Dakhin "helpless

measured rows.[107] The groves might belong to the peasants,[108] but it is probable that quite often they were owned by richer people, who seasonally rented them out to cultivators or professional fruit-sellers, as is the custom even today.[109] Members of the aristocracy and officials possessed orchards to have fruits not only for their own consumption but also to sell for profit.[110] Many, if they were Muslims, built their graves amidst groves of fruit trees, the income from which went to support their descendants or the guardians of their graves.[111]

Our sources are far from reticent on the subject of fruits, especially in regard to their taste. But much of what they have to say – on, for example, the regions where the best mangoes grow[112] or the extraordinary usefulness of the coconut palm,[113] and so on – may with equal truth be said today. It is best to turn our attention chiefly to the changes that appear to have taken place in the products and practices of horticulture during and since our period. These changes stemmed, first of all, from the new species of fruits introduced from the New World through the agency of the Portuguese. The most notable was the pine-apple (*ananas sativa*),

---

and destitute people grow the muskmelons (*kharbūza-i garmā*) in the sand upon the banks of rivers" (Ma'mūrī, f. 184b; Khāfī Khān, II, 405).

[107] The Tract on Agriculture, I.O. 4702, f. 28b, recommends that mango trees be planted in an orchard (*būstān*) at a distance of 23 *gaz* (yards) from each other.

See also Mundy, 97: "Round about Kera [Kara, Ilahabad province]...wee sawe and past through many groves of Mango trees Sett in Rancke by measures."

[108] This would appear from *T.J.*, 251-2, where it is stated that anyone who converted his cultivated land into an orchard, was entitled to get all his revenue remitted. Allahabad 1198 (of AD 1674-75) refers to an orchard laid out by two *muqaddams* (headmen) of a village.

[109] This was the case in Goa, where the Portuguese "let out (their coconut tress) unto the Canariins", some of these rentiers having as many as "300 or 400 trees or more" (Linschoten, I, 187). In the Mughal empire even the great imperial garden at Sirhind was yearly rented out "for fifty thousand rupias" (Finch in *Early Travels*, 158).

[110] An imperial *farmān*, issued in the 8th regnal year of Aurangzeb, recites: "15. Officials and government servants grow in their gardens and those of the crown (*sarkār-i wālā*) every kind of vegetables and fruits and give them to the greengrocers at double the rates and extort the price by force" (*Mir'āt*, I, 261).

[111] Pelsaert, 5; *Mir'āt*, I, 263-4; *Nigārnāma-i Munshī*, f. 200a, ed., 152; and *Durru-l 'Ulūm*, ff. 55b-56a.

[112] Specified in the *Ā'īn*, I, 75-76, as Bengal, Gujarat, Malwa, Khandesh and Dakhin. One may, however, note the omission of Awadh, where the grafted mango has now become commercially so important.

[113] "In the whole world there is not a tree more profitable than this tree is" (Caesar Frederick: *Purchas*, X, 91). Cf. *Ā'īn*, I, 79; Manucci, III, 185-6.

which spread throughout the length and breadth of India with striking rapidity. Grown in the beginning in the Portuguese possessions on the western coast,[114] it had by the end of the sixteenth century become common enough in Bengal[115] and Gujarat and Baglana,[116] to be noticed among the important products of these regions. It figures prominently among the Indian fruits described by Abū-l Faẓl,[117] and during Jahāngīr's reign many thousands of pine-apples were gathered every year in the imperial gardens of Agra.[118] Papaya and cashew-nut were introduced from the same source, but took more time to spread.[119] Guava, another alien, was probably introduced after our period.[120] The Portuguese were also probably the first to create varieties of the mango by grafting.[121] Grafted mangoes are reported from Bengal only in the eighteenth century;[122] and the practice might have been brought there by the Portuguese.

Secondly, the court and the aristocracy made great endeavours to grow almost every variety of fruits in their gardens.[123] The attempt

[114] Linschoten, II, 19; *T.J.*, 173; della Valle, I, 134-5. It is remarkable that the Brazilian name of the fruit, *ananas*, should also have been taken over in both Persian and the various Indian languages.

[115] *Haft Iqlīm*, 94. Cf. also *'Ālamgīrnāma*, 691-2; Bernier, 438; Manucci, III, 183. In the 1660s pineapple of a very good quality was found growing in Assam (*Fatḥiya-i 'Ibriya*, f. 32b).

[116] *Ā'īn*, I, 488, 492. [117] Ibid., I, 69, 76. [118] *T.J.*, 173.

[119] Della Valle (I, 134-5) tasted these two fruits in Daman in 1623. He goes too far, however, in attributing an American origin also to the mango and 'Giambo' (either *eugenia jambolana* or *eugenia jambos*). Linschoten, II, 27, had already found the cashew-nut growing in the Portuguese possessions and noted that it had been transplanted from Brazil. Thevenot, 102, noticed it growing along the route from Surat to Aurangabad.

[120] It may be mentioned that *amrūd* in the literature of the time, e.g. *Ā'īn*, I, 68, or the Tract on Agriculture above cited, I.O. 4702, f.16b-17a, signified a pear, not guava. The name was transferred to the latter fruit much later.

[121] "Afonso", the famous grafted mango of the western coast, is ascribed to one Niculao Afonco of Goa by Manucci, II, 169; III, 380. For the absence of grafted mangoes before the Portuguese experiments, see P.K. Gode, *Studies in Indian Cultural History*, I, 452-54.

[122] A passage interpolated in the I.O.MS of *Nuskha dar Fan-i Falāḥat* (I.O.4702, f. 28a-b), but omitted in the Aligarh MS (Lytton: Fārsiya 'Ulūm 51, f.13b), mentions the grafting methods used at Murshidabad in raising mangoes. The reference to Murshidabad makes it certain that the interpolation was made in the 18th century. The tract in its original text states that grafting is possible, but not essential, in the case of the mango.

[123] Praising the mangoes of Muqarrab K͟hān's garden at Kirana (between Dehli and Sirhind), Mu'tamad K͟hān says that Muqarrab K͟hān "had obtained seeds of mangoes from the Dakhin, Gujarat and other distant parts of which he had heard any praise, and planted them here". He adds that this garden, covering an area of 140 *bīghas* or 33.6 hectares, contained "a large number of trees native to warm

to grow Central Asian fruits had begun with Bābur;[124] and it was claimed during the reign of his grandson (Akbar) that melons and vines as good as those of Turan and Iran were being grown in the plains around Agra.[125] But the success was confined only to the imperial gardens and the orchards of the nobility, where their cultivation was often superintended by Central Asian gardeners[126] and the seeds were constantly imported from abroad,[127] not to mention the special irrigation facilities that were provided.[128] Nevertheless an important practice was popularized from these efforts at horticultural emulation. Sweet cherry was not grown in Kashmir before Akbar's reign, but now Muḥammad Qulī Afshār introduced it from Kabul by means of grafting. By the same method, apricot trees which were formerly few, now became plentiful.[129] Apparently for reasons of prestige, the practice was restricted for some time to imperial gardens only, but Shāhjahān lifted this ban for both "the select and the masses". Remarkable results are said to have followed from its wider application. The quality of the oranges, the *sangtara, kola* and *nārangī*, was very greatly improved.[130] How far grafting was a new practice in India or only a case of new experiments on the lines of an old principle, it is hard to say.[131] Bernier's remarks suggest that by the sixties of the century, it was either not being followed at all or followed only very slovenly in Kashmir, the very site of the first experiment.[132]

---

and cold climates" (*Iqbālnāma*, Nawal Kishor ed., III, 557).

[124] *Bāburnāma*, ed., 607; Bev., II, 686.

[125] *Ā'īn*, I, 441; II, 6. Cf. also *Ma'āṣir-i Raḥīmī*, II, 604, for planting of melons, alleged to have been previously unknown in Khandesh, in 'Abdur Raḥīm Khān Khānān's garden at Balakvada.

[126] This appears from *Bāburnāma*, op.cit.; *Ā'īn*, II, 6; and Ṣādiq Khān, Or. 174, f. 102a, Or. 1671, f. 56a.

[127] Pelsaert, 48; Bernier, 249-50. Cf. *Ma'āṣir Raḥīmī*, II, 604.

[128] The water-works of Mughal gardens are justly famous. Even Roe recognized that "the King and nobility have as excellent and artificial waterworks of their own as can be desired" (*Lett. Recd.*, VI, xxvi). See also C.M. Villiers Stuart, *Gardens of the Great Mughals*, 14-15 and passim. On the staff, wells, and oxen in Mughal gardens see I. Habib in *Mughal Gardens*, 132-34.

[129] *T.J.*, 299. Cf. I. Habib in *Mughal Gardens*, 129 & n.

[130] Ṣādiq Khān. Or.174, f. 102a; Or. 1671, f. 56a.

[131] The practice was common in Persia and Central Asia. In the Tract on Agriculture, I.O. 4702, the method is discussed in detail and the grafting of fig on mulberry, apple on pear, peach on plum, apricot on almond, and vine on apple, is recommended. All this is taken, however, from the much earlier work, *Risāla-i Falāḥat* (Add. 1771, ff. 157-269, etc.), which was written in Persia.

[132] Bernier, 397. Hugel found in 1835 that grafting was "unpractised ... probably unknown" in Kashmir (*Kashmir and the Punjab*, 96-97).

Indian sericulture notoriously suffered a great decline in the nineteenth century. Ovington has left behind a detailed account of Indian sericulture: from the local terms used in it, it obviously relates to Bengal. The silkworm was multivoltine with six crops in the year.[133] Bengal also produced the largest quantity of silk.[134] Sericulture was also practised in Kashmir[135] and rather dubiously in Sind.[136] Anything like an estimate of the volume of production comes only from Tavernier, who says that Qasimbazar in Bengal alone could furnish about 22,000 bales, which at his equation of a bale with 100 *livres* might mean 2.4 million lb. avdp.[137] Since Tavernier goes on to give a figure for Dutch export of Bengal silk which is practically double the maximum Dutch exports in any year during the 1660s, one may hesitate to accept his estimate.[138] Yet a later (1752) French estimate put the total exports of Bengal silk annually at 12,000 to 15,000 "mounds", or 0.9 to 1.1 million lb. avdp.,[139] and if this represented as much as half of Bengal's production, it should confirm Tavernier's figures. In 1963 the total Indian production of mulberry silk was only 2.7 million lb. avdp.[140] It is

[133] J. Ovington, *A Voyage to Suratt in the Year 1989, etc*., London, 1696, 599-606. This portion ("observations concerning the nature of the silk-worms") is omitted in Rawlinson's edn., London, 1929, which I have otherwise used. Was the Bengal silkworm originally imported from south China? It is interesting to read: "In South China, a 'tropical' variety of silkworm could produce several generations each year; its silk was softer and shinier, but coarser than the central Chinese variety" (Dieter Kuhn, *Science and Civilization in China*, ed. Joseph Needham, V (9), 305).

[134] *Ā'īn*, I, 390; *Haft Iqlīm*, 94, 97; Bernier, 202, 439, 441; Master, II, 81-2; Bowrey, 133. The quality of Bengal silk was not as good as that of Persia or Syria, but it was much cheaper; and it was thought that if "well selected and wrought with care", it might improve in quality as well (Bernier, 439-40). Silk was also produced in "Kūch" or Kuch Bihar (*Haft Iqlīm*,100).

[135] *Ā'īn*, I, 562-3; *T.J.*, 300.

[136] Manrique, II, 239; Hamilton, I, 125. Not fine, says Hamilton. No modern authority.

[137] Tavernier, II, 2. A bale of Bengal silk weighed, according to Dutch records, 143 lb. avdp., while 100 French *livres* of the time would have come to less than 109 lb. avdp. See Appendix B.

[138] Cf. Om Prakash, *The Dutch East India Company and the Economy of Bengal*, 54 & *n*. The Dutch exports, says Tavernier, amounted to 6,000-7,000 bales (or 6,54,000 to 7,63,000 lb.avdp), while, according to Om Prakash, the maximum annual procurements of the Dutch during the 1660s remained under 300,000 Dutch lb, or about 3,27,000 lb. avdp.

[139] Bal Krishna, *Commercial Relations between India and England*, 198.

[140] Commonwealth Economic Committee, *Industrial Fibres-a Review,* 127-8. Cf. Maxwell-Lefroy's estimate of 3 million lb. avdp. (1917), cited by Moreland, *India at the Death of Akbar*, 174, 195.

probable, then, that there was an absolute fall in the volume of silk produced in Bengal, besides a much greater fall per head of population.

Besides the true or mulberry silk, there were other semi-domesticated or semi-wild varieties which must have accounted for a large portion of Indian silk production.[141] Tasar ("herba") was collected in Bengal, Orissa and possibly parts of the Dakhin;[142] eri in Assam, Bengal and Orissa;[143] and 'muga' and 'champa' in Assam.[144]

Lac-culture was also a prominent occupation in Mughal times, but there is no evidence of any particular difference in its position then as compared to that in early twentieth century.[145]

Where the seventeenth-century peasant enjoyed a distinctly superior position to his descendant was in respect of cattle and draught animals. From what we know about the extent of cultivation during that period, it is obvious that the land available for grazing, both waste and forest, was far greater in extent than around 1910.[146] Even in so densely cultivated a province as Bengal,

[141] In 1963 the production of such silks was estimated at 1.3 million lb. as against the true-silk production of 2.7 million lb. (Commonwealth Economic Committee, op.cit.).

[142] For identification of the "herba" in European sources with tasar silk, see *Atlas*, 69, col.c. For its production in Bengal: Laval, I, 328-9; *Factories, 1655-60,* 295; Orissa: Caesar Frederick in *Purchas*, X, 113; Fitch, *Early Travels*, 26; Master, II, 845. For the Dakhin, the references in Abbé Carre, II, 326, and Bowrey, 111, are probably to tasar (cf. *Atlas*, 62, col.c).

[143] For 'eri' silk the word in Persian sources is *ṭāṭband* (*Atlas*, 70 col.c). Assam: '*Ālamgīrnāma*, 724; *sarkār* Ghoraghat and Bengal: *Ā'īn*, I, 390; Master, II, 299-300; Orissa: *Ā'īn*, I, 107.

[144] Tavernier, II, 281; '*Ālamgīrnāma*, 724. Cf. *Atlas*, 53, col.c.

[145] The lac produced in Bengal was the best, the cheapest and the most abundant (*Factories, 1630-33*, 323, *1634-6*, 146; Tavernier, II, 18; Bernier, 440; Bowrey, 132). It was also abundant, Tavernier (II, 221) adds, in Assam; it was produced in Orissa (Bowrey, 121-2) and Bihar, but that of the latter region was neither very good nor very cheap (Mundy, 151, 153). It was also collected in Gujarat (*Lett. Recd.*, I, 30; Commissariat, *Mandelslo*, 16) and in Bijapur and Malabar (Linschoten, II, 90; *Factories, 1624-29*, 258). This geographical distribution accords largely with the one existing in modern times, though in the British Central Provinces too it was to be had "abundantly" (cf. Watt, IV, 570). Lac yielded a red dye and served as sealing wax and varnish (*Lett. Recd.*, I, 30; Commissariat, *Mandelslo*, 16-17; Travenier, II, 18, 221). As a dye it has now ceased to be of any value owing to chemical competitors.

[146] Cf. Moreland, *India at the Death of Akbar*, 106-7; and Royal Commission on Agriculture, *Report*, 201-2. The extension of cultivation into the Tarai forests also greatly curtailed the excellent grazing land available there to the professional breeders (Moreland, *Agricultural Conditions*, 28-31).

a traveller found "pasturages" with "enormous herds" a noticeable feature of the rural scene.[147] We need not read much into the statement made by contemporary European observers about the great numbers of cattle found in the various parts of India,[148] since cattle were particularly scarce in most parts of Europe, where satisfactory methods of keeping them fed and alive through the winter were yet to be discovered. When, however, Abū-l Faẓl says that the number of tax-free cattle allowed per plough was four bullocks, two cows and one buffalo,[149] it is difficult to resist the impression that an ordinary peasant had, compared with later days, a more numerous stock to work with.[150]

The larger number of working cattle per head of population is perhaps even better demonstrated by the obvious plenitude of clarified butter or *ghī*. In the Agra region, we are told, butter, with rice, formed "the food of the common people" and there was no one in Agra who did not eat it.[151] Similarly, butter was produced in such plenty in Bengal that besides being part of the diet of the masses, it was also exported.[152] In terms of wheat and millets it was considerably cheaper than at the beginning of the twentieth century.

[147] Manrique, II, 123.

[148] Linschoten, I, 300-301; *Relations*, 63, 86; Roe 67; Terry in *Early Travels*, 296; Pelsaert, 49; Manrique, II, 123, 329.

[149] *Ā'īn*, I, 287. The average number of cattle per yoke in the United Provinces in 1924-5 was 2 bullocks, 1.1 cows and one buffalo; and in the Punjab, 2 bullocks, 1.3 cows and 1.4 buffaloes (figures worked out from the tables given in the *Report* of the Royal Agricultural Commission, 181-2). For the United Provinces, see also Moreland, *Agricultural Conditions*, 26-27.

[150] S.P. Gupta, *Agrarian System of Eastern Rajasthan*, 255-68, introduces us to a memorandum of 1666, giving figures of cultivated area (*jot*), peasants (*asāmī*) and yoke-bullocks (*hal-bail*) in *pargana* Chatsu: In the eleven villages (including the township of Chatsu) covered, there were 2,448 peasants and 6,200 bullocks, i.e. 2.53 bullocks per head. Another similar document of the same year, giving particulars of 13 villages of Mauzabad, counts 1,184 peasants and 4,000 bullocks, or 3.38 bulloks per head (ibid., 63, 67).

There is an interesting memorandum on the number of new peasants, with their bullocks, settled in certain *parganas* in the Aurangabad province assigned as *jāgīr* to Aurangzeb during his viceroyalty of the Dakhin (*Selected Documents*, 245). The total figures for the peasants and bullocks are 251 and 310 respectively. It was estimated that in Bombay, including Sind, there were, in 1924-5, 10 bullocks to every 8.1 cultivators (male workers) (Royal Commission on Agriculture, *Report*, 182), thus giving the same ratio of cattle to men. But one would expect the migratory peasants of the Mughal document to have belonged generally to the poorer strata.

[151] J. Xavier, transl. Hosten, *JASB, N.S.*, XXIII, 1927, 121.

[152] Bernier, 438,440.

In the *Ā'īn* it is rated 8.75 times dearer than wheat,[153] and the same ratio is found in the prices reported officially from Agra in 1669.[154] In 1875-76 the prices of four varieties of *ghī* (two of cow's *ghī*, and two of buffalo's) at Agra ranged from 11.6 to 13.1 times that of wheat.[155] Moreland calculated the average price of *ghī* at Agra, Delhi and Lahore in 1910-12 as 13.9 times that of wheat.[156] In the Dakhin the "selling" prices of *ghī* ranged from about 6.5 to 8 times those of wheat, according to official price-lists from Aurangabad (May 1661), Dharur (August 1661) and Ramgir (February 1662), with abnormally high prices (13.4 and 14.9 times of wheat) reported from Udgir (August-September 1662).[157] In 1952 the ratio was about 1:9 in the region, comparing, however, the harvest price of wheat with the city market price of *ghī*.[158]

It may be supposed that with more fodder and grass available, the average quality of the cattle should also have been much better, but the traditional aversion to slaughtering useless cattle[159] makes it unlikely that the breeds were much superior.[160] The milk yield

[153] *Ā'īn*, I, 60, 65.

[154] *Ma'āṣir 'Ālamgīrī*, 98. For *raug̱han* in the printed text, Add. 19,495, f.54b, reads *raug̱han-i zard*, this being the more specific word for *ghī*. A report of prices, dated August 5, 1678, from Ajmer, puts the price of *ghī* at as low as 5.5 times that of wheat, but this was probably because grains were then fetching exceptionally high prices owing to a failure of the rains (*Waqā'i'-i Ajmer*, 14).

[155] *Prices and Wages in India*, 12th issue, 251 (prices paid by the Army). Cf. Moosvi, 329,332.

[156] *JRAS*, 1918, 820.

[157] For the price-lists, see *Waqā'i' Dakhin*, 37-44, 75-77, 108-14, 147-50.

[158] The ratio has been worked out from a comparison of the price of *ghī* in the Hyderabad market in February 1952 and the harvest price of wheat for the whole state as well as for the Bidar district. Source: *Agricultural Prices in India, 1951 and 1952* and its supplement, *Farm (Harvest) Prices of Principal Crops, 1947-48 to 1951-52.*

[159] This sentiment was strongest in regions like Bengal (Fitch: Ryley, 119, *Early Travels*, 28), Gujarat (Roe, 67) and the Dakhin (*Relations*, 17; *Factories, 1655-60*, 261; Tavernier, II, 169) particularly, of course, in respect of cow-slaughter. Cow-slaughter was also administratively discouraged by Akbar and Jahāngīr, which seems to have had some effect in northern India (Pelsaert, 49; *Taẕkira Pīr Ḥassū Teli*, Aligarh MS, f. 36b). Here, however, the existence of Muslim communities created a large market for meat (cf. Tavernier, I, 38). Sind, in fact, exported hides (Linschoten, I, 56; Manucci, II, 427).

[160] The point has, however, been made that the best Indian breeds were the result of the efforts of the special castes of professional breeders, who were nomadic and took cattle to graze over long distances. The extension of cultivation has either seriously curtailed or completely eliminated their occupation (Royal Agricultural Commission, *Report*, 198-9). Hisar, the home of the famous 'Hissar' breed of oxen, has an old history as an exporter of cattle: cf. Bālkrishan Brahman,

of the cows and buffaloes in the imperial stables,[161] at the maximum, does not exceed that given by the best breeds in recent times, and a Dutch observer noted that the cattle gave "nothing like so much milk" as those of his own country,[162] where the general slaughter before every winter enforced a remorseless selection.

The wool of the Indian sheep also was not of a quality that could impress European travellers: it was coarse and fit only for blankets.[163] The goat's hair from which the famous shawls of Kashmir were woven, was imported from Ladakh and Tibet.[164]

If, as we have suggested above, the cattle population per capita was larger than around 1910, one would expect the peasant of our period to have a more abundant supply of cattle manure. Moreover, since waste-land and jungles were far mor extensive and firewood, therefore, more easily available, cow-dung would probably have done its proper duty as a fertilizer and not been consumed as fuel.[165] Still, in the more densely cultivated regions like the Agra province, where firewood was scarce, "the poor" commonly used to burn cow-dung for domestic purposes.[166]

It is not possible for us to consider in any detail the subsequent developments in Indian agriculture. But in so far as tracing them may help us to mark the particular features of agricultural production in our period, it may be useful to recall where the changes between *c.*1700 and *c.*1900 were most pronounced. In the inventory of food crops, the only additions were maize and potato; and, among oilseeds, groundnuts. The important difference was in the proportionate increase in the acreage devoted to the cash crops at the expense of foodgrains. The increase in their acreage went hand in hand with a considerable concentration of

ff.59b-60a, concerning the despatch of two batches of 349 and 652 *gāo* (cows, bulls and/or bullocks) to an unnamed potentate at the price of about Rs7½ per head, from the *chakla* of Hisar.

161 "A cow gives daily 1 *ser* to 15 *ser* [1.4 to 20.7 lb. avdp.] of milk and a buffalo from 2 to 30 *ser* [2.8 to 41.5 lb.]" – *Ā'īn*, I, 151. The buffalo of the breed of Mahur (Berar) gave one *man* (55.32 lb.) or more of milk (every day) (ibid., 477).

162 *Relations*, 86. The statement relates only to Golkunda.

163 Terry, *Early Travels*, 297; *Lett. Recd.*, VI, 200.

164 *T.J.*, 301. Cf. Mohibbul Hasan, *Kashmir under the Sultans*, Calcutta. 1959, 245-6.

165 Cf., however, Moreland, *India at the Death of Akbar*, 107, where it is argued that the droppings of cattle on the grazing land might not have been collected at all, and so much of the fertilizer lost, owing to the extensiveness of the waste lands.

166 Pelsaert, 48; Ovington, 183.

particular crops in certain tracts. The twin processes arose in the nineteenth century with the destruction of important Indian hand-industries, chiefly textiles, and the conversion of the Indian agrarian economy into a source of raw materials for Britain.[167] The same impulse led to the ultimate disappearance of indigo and a decline in sericulture.[168] But on the whole it may be said that the new distribution of crops enabled land to be devoted to crops for which it was better suited, in contrast to Mughal times, when a tendency towards self-sufficiency in the main crops was to be observed in almost every region. Besides, the predominant emphasis on food crops in those times must have led to useless surpluses in favourable years. We had concluded at the end of Section 1 that, were other things to remain the same, the fertility of the average acre under the plough should have declined since the Mughal period. It is possible now to argue that the better distribution of crops must in a very large part have mitigated the effects of this decline; and this is why in the case of most crops a higher average yield in the Mughal times cannot be indisputably established. But average yield per acre is not the same thing as average yield per head. In conditons where the total extent of cultivation was far smaller than it was in *c*.1900, the available land per head was likely to have been larger, and so too the grazing lands. We are, therefore, entitled to imagine the average peasant as tilling larger fields and possessing more numerous cattle and so getting a larger size of product (in value) than his successor in 1900.[169] What he was able to keep out of it for himself is, however, another matter.

4. AGRICULTURAL MANUFACTURES

The combination of purely agricultural work with manufacturing processes was a notable feature of peasant life in Mughal India. The destruction of the rural cottage industries forms one of the most violent chapters in the economic history of British rule in India.[1] From the evidence for the nineteenth century, when the

[167] Cf. Karl Marx, *Capital*, I, 453-4.

[168] We have not included the introduction of tobacco and pine-apple in the changes since Mughal times, because they were introduced early in the 17th century, and it is not clear how far their per-capita production increased between then and 1900. The tea and coffee plantations of today lie largely outside the limits of the Mughal empire. Opium was still important in 1900.

[169] Cf. I. Habib in *Cambridge Economic History of India*, I, 220-21.

[1] See Romesh Dutt, *The Economic History of India under Early British Rule*, 6th ed., London, n.d., 256 ff., and *The Economic History of India in the Victorian*

elements of the older system still survived, it is possible to obtain a general picture of these industries which could be held true for Mughal times. But the following outline is mainly based on contemporary evidence.

It is to be supposed that in the case of foodgrains, the peasant's part in the productive process generally ended with the threshing of the corn.[2] The milling of flour (by hand) and rice-husking took place usually in the household of the consumer and were confined, in that of the peasant, to whatever was meant for the consumption of his own family.[3] It was chiefly in respect of the cash crops that not only the existing techinques, but also the conditions of transport, made it necessary for certain manufacturing processes to be carried out before the produce left the hands of the peasant or, at least, the precincts of the village. Thus cotton was picked and ginned by the peasants,[4] and then cleaned or carded with a bow by a special class of itinerant labourers, called *dhunyās*.[5] Thereafter it was spun

---

Age, London, 1950, 99-123; also D.R. Gadgil, *The Industrial Evolution of India*, London, 1944, 33-47. For a defence of the thesis of 'de-industrialization' in the 19th century against recent criticisms, see I. Habib, *Essays*, 320-22, 340-51.

[2] Of which the methods were practically the same as were universal at the time of Independence. A description of these is given by Fryer, II, 108, who especially notes threshing with the aid of yoked oxen in the "Open Fields". Why he should describe this as the practice of "Moor-men" (Muslims) and threshing with a "Stick" as that of "Gentues" (Hindus) is obscure.

[3] "The *Indian* Wives dress their Husbands Victuals, fetch Water, and grind their Corn with an Hand-Mill, when they sing, chat and are merry". (Fryer, II, 118. Cf. also Linschoten, I, 246, 261.) Only in this (twentieth) century has the establishment of power mills modified this universal picture of the Indian woman's daily work in the home. In the *Dastūru-l 'Amal-i 'Ālamgīrī*, f.57a-b, there is an account of the milling of 4 *mans*, 4 *sers* of wheat. The flour obtained amounted to 4 *mans* and the wages of the grinder came to 3 annas per *man*, representing according to the price of wheat given in the same manual, 3¾ *sers* of the grain. Ordinary wheat flour (*khushka*) is priced a quarter above wheat in the *Ā'īn*, I, 63. See also the prices in the *Waqā'i' Dakhin*, 37, 42-43, 75, 77. In 1630 we find the English planning to buy 7000 maunds of "paddye (which when beaten there will be reduced to somewhat above 4,500 *maunds* ryce)" (*Factories, 1630-33*, 62).

[4] The seed was separated from the cotton by the Indian gin (*charkhī*) with two worm-rollers. See a late 18th-century account of cotton cultivation in Add. 19,503, f.52b.

[5] This is the Hindi name, the process being known as *dhunnā*. The Arabic-Persian term for the carder is *naddāf*. His bow is illustrated in *Miftāḥu-l Fuẓalā*, Or. 3299 (text dated 1468-69, but illustrated in the 16th century), ff.126b, 259b.

That the carder was itinerant and moved from "village to village" with his family, appears from Thevenot, 10; *Mir'āt*, I, 260; and *Ẓawābiṭ-i 'Ālamgīrī*, Ethé 415, f.181b; Or. 1641, f. 136a; Add. 6598, f. 189a. The caste is also described in James Skinner's *Tashrīḥu-l Aqwām*, written in 1825 (ff.302b-303a). In cases where

into yarn within the peasant households,[6] and so became ready for sale to be passed on to the weaver. With the transfer of its ultimate destination to the textile factories in Lancashire or Bombay, the processes of ginning, cleaning and spinning were all largely lost to the countryside, the picked crop being ususally sent straight off to the ginning mills. Sugar and *guṛ* manufacture constituted another important village industry: The juice was obtained from the cane by use of worm-geared wooden rollers worked by oxen in the southern regions,[7] and by the stone mortar-and-pestle mill, also turned by oxen, in the Gangetic zone.[8] These mills were replaced by iron-rollers only by the close of the nineteenth century.[9] The juice used to be put in iron cauldrons serving as boilers; and *guṛ* and various varieties of sugar were produced by different degrees of refining.[10] Except for the making

---

cotton wool, not yarn, was put on the market, cotton was not carded, because it would then have swelled and become too bulky for transport (*Factories, 1665-67*, 174. Cf. also ibid, *1630-33*, 19-20).

[6] "It (yarn) is made or spun in the out villadges by the porest sort of people; from whence it is gleaned up by persons that trade in it" (*Factories, 1661-65*, 112).

[7] "Sugar canes Press'd between two great wooden Roulers turn'd about by Oxen, whence they come out thoroughly suqeez'd" (Careri, 169: area around Bassein).

[8] "A stone sugar-press" with a Sanskrit inscription dated Samvat 1609/AD 1553 was found at Azamgarh (U.P.) (A. Fuhrer, *Monumental Antiquities and Inscriptions in the North-Western Provinces and Oudh*, 319); a dated "stone mill" of Samvat 1636/1579 from Pratapgarh district (Ibid., 187) is also probably the stone mortar of a sugar mill. "Great stone sugar mills" of olden days were found in the Satpura valleys of Khandesh where sugar was no longer widely cultivated (Watt, VI, ii, 304, quoting *Bombay Gazetteer*, XII, 226). I have discussed 19th-century evidence for both the rollers and mortar-and-pestle mills in *Indian Historical Review*, V (1-2), 155-58.

[9] Watt, VI, ii, 303; Voelcker, 276-7; Crooke, *North-Western Provinces*, 332.

[10] The process of refining the sugar by boiling it in iron couldrons is referred to in Careri 169; *Mir'āt*, I, 287; and *Durru-l 'Ulūm*, f.61b. *Gur* (Persian, *qand-i siyāh*) must have been the most common of all varieties of sugar. Abū-l Faẓl (*Ā'īn*, I, 77) mentions it, but does not give its price.

From the Dutch Company's factors' accounts at Agra, analysed by Moreland, it appears that the average price of *guṛ* (based on monthly rates) was 4.1 times the price of wheat flour ("meal") in 1637 and 2.4 times in 1638 (*JUPHS*, III, 151-2; cf. Brij Narain, *Indian Economic Life, Past & Present*, 17). The prices reported from Aurangabad in 1661 and Ramgir in 1662 show it to have been worth about twice the price of wheat (*Waqā'i' Dakhin*, 37, 43, 75, 76; *Daftar-i Dīwānī o Māl o Mulkī*, 173). This implies that it was relatively more expensive than in recent times, when its price has seldom exceeded anywhere one and a quarter of wheat.

Careri, 169, saw white sugar being manufactured in the villages and Abū-l Faẓl lists four varieties besides *guṛ*: red and white (powdered) sugar, white candy (or crystals) and the best refined *nabāt* (*Ā'īn*, I, 65, 77). Moreland finds their prices

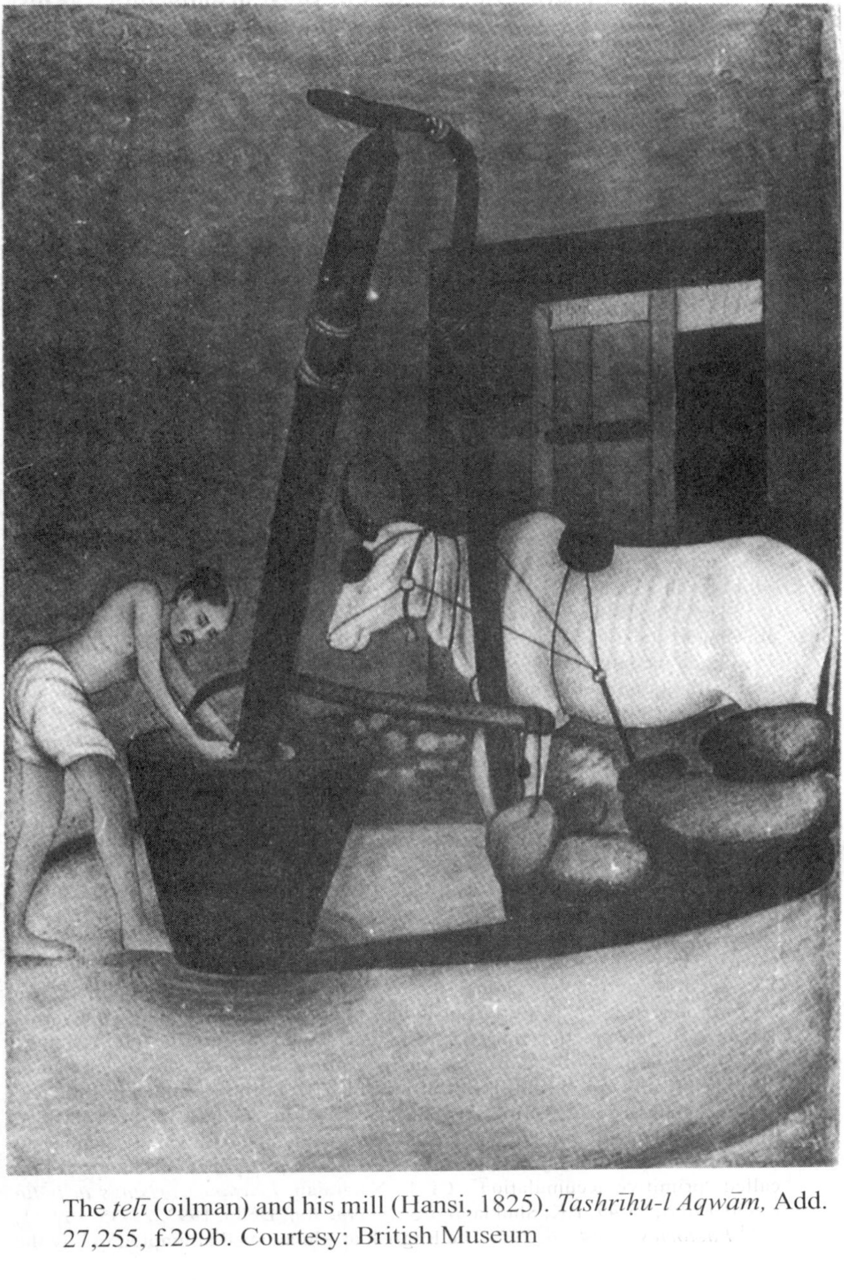

The *telī* (oilman) and his mill (Hansi, 1825). *Tashrīḥu-l Aqwām,* Add. 27,255, f.299b. Courtesy: British Museum

of *guṛ*, the entire string of processes of sugar manufacture was lost to the village by the coming of the refineries which began directly to buy the cane. The extraction of oil from the oilseeds also used to take place within the village at the hands of members of the semi-itinerant caste of *telīs*, oilmen, working with the help of ox-driven presses.[11] With the extensive export of oilseeds by 1900, much of the oil-pressers' work too was lost. Finally, there was the manufacture of dyes. In the Agra region, at least, the indigo dye was manufactured in the villages. The method, described in detail by contemporaries, involved the building of two levels of masonry vats with well cemented walls.[12] It appears, however, that in Gujarat the peasants frequently sold the leaf to a class of middle-men who arranged for the extraction of the dye and finally put it on the market.[13] The industry has now long been extinct along with the crop. Not to be ignored also are the rural industries based on

---

as given in the *Ā'īn* to be also much higher in relation to wheat than in *c.*1910 (*JRAS*, 1918, 379; *India at the Death of Akbar*, 157-8). Moosvi, 327, 332, shows the sugar prices were already on a much lower level in respect of wheat during the 1860s in the Agra region. The lower level could not be attributed to metallic crushers which came into use later.

[11] The Arabic-Persian word for *telī* is *'aṣṣār*, who, like the cotton-carder, is presumed to be itinerant in occupation in a *farmān* of Aurangzeb (*Mir'āt*, I, 260). The similar economic position of the *dhunyā* and the *telī* is probably responsible for the tradition that the former sprang from the latter (*Tashrīḥu-l Aqwām*, op.cit.; the *telī* is portrayed and described on ff.299b-301a).

[12] Finch, *Early Travels*, 153-4; *Lett. Recd.* IV, 241; Pelsaert 10-11, 15; Mundy, 221-3; Tavernier, II, 8-9. Professor Iqtidar Alam Khan has explored the surviving indigo vats at Bayana and at localities in the Doab. They conform fairly well to the descriptions in our sources. The process of manufacture consisted, to put it briefly, in putting the stalks into one large vat and, when it had absorbed the dye, running off the water into a lower vat where the dye was first fully dissolved by stirring the water continuously and then allowed to settle at the bottom. It was then collected and spread on cloth to dry. Salbancke, *Purchas*, III, 84 (closely copied by Coverte, 66-67) says the stalks were laid out to rot, then the indigo taken out by being trodden upon by oxen; this was ground and "boiled in furnaces". This is entirely erroneous, though the reference to boilers seems to anticipate a step introduced later by European indigo planters. Except for this innovation (Moosvi, 84), the practice of the Anglo-Indian planters, as described, for example, in N.G. Mukherji's *Handbook of Indian Agriculture*, 301, showed no basic change from the process followed by the peasants of the 17th century. Voelcker's *Report*, 261-5, contains a detailed criticism of the manufacturing methods of these planters. The indigo planters' place in Indian history rests not on their inventive genius but on their record of robbery, torture and murder, those pretty methods of what Marx called "primitive accumulation". Cf. L. Natarajan, *Peasant Uprisings in India (1850-1900)*, 33-47; P.K. Shukla, *Indigo and the Raj*, Delhi, 1993, 25-35, 109-31.

[13] *Factories, 1634-36*, 292. The English at Ahmadabad attempted to buy the

distillation, whether of liquor or rose-water, rose essence or other perfumes.[14]

Facts such as these should help us to appreciate the degree to which the wholesale separation of industry from agriculture intensified, even if it did not wholly create, the problem of seasonal unemployment in the villages. And if we look still more closely, we will notice that the manufactures we have mentioned covered some of the most important needs of the peasant's family. When a village spun its own yarn and obtained its own sugar and oil,[15] and when the rural weaver, carpenter, blacksmith and potter sufficed for practically everything that a peasant's household required, – the clothing, the plough and the few farming tools and earthen pots,[16] – there would have been little, indeed, left that the peasants would need to get from outside the village limits.

---

leaf themselves and manufacture the dye with the aid of hired labour, but the experiment proved uneconomical (ibid., *1646-50*, 77-78, 189, 202-3; Roques, transl. Indrani Ray, *IHR*, IX, 119).

[14] See for detailed discussion and references Gode, *Studies in Indian Cultural History*, I, 15-37; I. Habib in *Aligarh Jour. of Oriental Studies*, II (1-2), 205-10; idem in *Mughal Gardens*, 130-31.

[15] It might be best to remember here that the cultivation of cotton and sugarcane was, in geographical terms, far more widespread than now.

[16] "In each aldea (village) they have all the occupations and their menials, to wash clothes, to remove refuse, a blacksmith, etc." (Monserrate, *Informacion*, tr. Hosten, *JASB*, N.S., XVIII, 352). This, written in 1579, refers to the Salsette Island (Goa) and the Konkan. See also Chapter III, Section 1, for the few material possessions of the peasant of Mughal India.

CHAPTER II

TRADE IN AGRICULTURAL PRODUCE

1. LONG-DISTANCE TRADE

A consideration of the extent and organization of the market for agricultural produce is naturally essential to any serious study of an agrarian economy. The available evidence on the internal trade of Mughal India is by no means small. It tends, however, to emphasize the trade in high-value goods, with which we are not directly concerned. Besides, with attention rightly paid to regional studies, an all-India perspective is often lacking in recent work. At the moment, avoiding details which will take us too far outside our sphere, a description is offered of the main features of the trade carried on in agricultural produce.

The closely knit national market of today is clearly the creation of the railways. The most obvious limitations to long-distance trade in our period were set by the means of transport.[1] Bullock-carts, camels and pack-oxen carried goods on roads that were little more than tracks, though distinguished in the case of the major highways, at any rate, by a system of *sarāis*, or walled lodging- and store-houses, mainly for passing the nights.[2] The traffic passed

[1] A very effective proof of this lies in how the foodgrain prices, which earlier had a very large range over the different parts of the country, began to cluster together as the railway network extended during the latter half of the 19th century. Zahoor Ali Khan offers an ingenious cartographic exposition of this process in *Indian Historical Review*, IV(2), 336-53.

[2] A systematic construction of *sarāis* on the routes is attributed to Sher Shāh ('Abbās Khān, ff.108b-109a; *Ṭabaqāt-i Akbarī*, II, 106; Badāūnī, I, 363, 384; Aḥmad Yādgār, 227-8). The *sarāis* are described frequently by European travellers, e.g. Steel & Crowther, *Purchas*, IV, 268; Manrique, II, 99-101; Bernier, 233; Tavernier, I, 45; Bowrey, 117; Manucci, I, 68, 69, 116 – Bernier is alone in his sneers. There is no contemporary complaint about the charges paid for lodging in the *sarāis*, and from Withington, *Purchas*, IV, 174, and Marshall, 117-18, these would appear to have been nearly nominal. For two recent surveys of surviving remains of Mughal-period *sarāis*, see Iqtidar Alam Khan, *IHR*, XIV (1-2), 111-37, and M.S. Ahluwalia and Subhas Parihar, *Panjab Past and Present*, XVI(1) (1982), 108-25. Some of the routes were marked by avenues of trees, wells at short distances and minarets set up at intervals of *kurohs*. (See, besides 'Abbās Khān and other Persian texts cited above in this note: *A.N.*, III, 111; Finch in *Early Travels*, 160, 185-6; Steel & Crowther, op.cit.; Coryat in *Early Travels*, 244; *T.J.*, 277; Roe, 493; Mundy, 82-84, 86, 92; Bernier, 284; Thevenot, 57, 85; Tavernier, I, 78.)

over some of the small rivers by masonry bridges.[3] The roads were used by *qāfilas* or caravans of merchants carrying articles of higher values. The transport on land of goods of bulk, like foodgrains, sugar, butter and salt, was organized mainly by the famous caste of *banjāras* who practically held a monopoly of this trade.[4] Their method consisted of driving enormous herds of pack-laden bullocks, feeding on pasturages along the routes.[5] The *banjāras* were themselves nomads and lived with their families in camps or *ṭānḍas*. A large *ṭānḍa* might contain as many as 600 or 700 souls and up to 12,000 or 15,000 or even 20,000 bullocks,[6] which would have carried about 1,600 to 2,700 tons.[7] On occasions such as when a large army had to be supplied, the *banjāras* might collect 1,00,000 bullocks or more.[8] On the whole, the volume of

[3] Local officials were asked to build bridges over *nālas* or streams and channels, wherever these presented difficulties to the traffic passing on the routes (*Nigārnāma-i Munshī*, ed., 98-99). The great imperial highway running across the plains was carried over the Degh, the Black Bein, the West Yamuna Canal, the Sengar, Rind, and Kudra by stone or brick bridges (Monserrate, 98; Steel and Crowther, *Purchas*, IV, 267-8; Mundy, 89, 91, 129; Tavernier, I, 120; Sujān Rāi, 72; Cunningham, *Archaeological Survey Reports*, XI, 120-23). Similarly, the route leading from Agra to the Dakhin, crossed the Utangan and Kuwari on such bridges (Mundy, 64-5; Tavernier, I, 3), and, later on, the Sind (Manucci, II, 322; Cunningham, *Archaeological Survey Reports*, II, 325-7). See *Atlas*, 'B' sheets & notes, passim, for these and other Mughal bridges; also Jean Deloche, *Ancient Bridges of India*. The larger rivers were almost all unbridged (Bernier, 380), except for the great Jaunpur bridge over the Gomti; boat-bridges were thrown across the Yamuna at Agra and Dehli (*A.N.*, III, 151; Bernier, 241). Most of the smaller streams were probably crossed at fords. As a result, during the rains, while some routes, like the Agra-Patna route, became difficult or unsuitable for wheeled traffic (*Factories, 1618-21*, 258, 283; Mundy, 143-4), flooded rivers closed the Agra-Burhanpur route altogether for the whole season (Tavernier, I, 31).

[4] Cf. *T.J.*, 345; *Factories, 1624-29*, 270; Mundy, 55, 95; Tavernier, I, 33-34. The classification of the *banjāras* by Tavernier into four distinct castes, each respectively carrying corn, rice, pulse and salt is entirely fanciful. They took to any region such goods as it was in need of and returned with those of which it had a surplus (Mundy, 96, 98-9; cf. also *Aḥkām-i 'Ālamgīrī*, f.83a). They traded largely on their own account, but were ready on occasions to carry goods for others (Mundy, 95-6).

[5] Mundy, 96. Among the exactions declared illegal by Aurangzeb are listed the fees levied on the *banjāras* for grazing their animals (*Mir'āt*, I, 287; Fraser 86, f. 93a; Khāfī Khān, I, 87).

[6] Roe, 67; Mundy, 95-6; Tavernier, I, 32-3.

[7] A bullock seems to have normally carried about 4.2 *man-i Shāhjahānī*, or 310 lb. avdp. (*Factories, 1655-60*, 63). Mundy, 95, puts the load at 4 *man-i-Jahāngīrī*, i.e. 265.5 lb. only, and Marshall, 425, at 4 *man-i Shāhjahānī* (or 295 lb.). Tavernier, I, 32, on the other hand, thought it to be as much as 300 or 350 *livres*, i.e. 327 to 390.5 lb.

[8] *T.J.*, 345; *Aḥkām-i 'Ālamgīrī*, f.83a.

goods transported annually by them must have been very considerable, large enough, probably, to be expressed in terms of hundreds of thousands of tons. The costs of transport under this system were obviously much lower than those of other methods of land transit,[9] but the pace was also much the slowest;[10] and the necessity of finding grazing lands along the routes must have severely limited the *banjāras'* operations during the summer and in the drier tracts.[11]

It was the rivers which in fact offered the cheapest means of transport.[12] In Bengal,[13] Sind[14] and Kashmir[15] goods were mostly conveyed on boats. From Agra, barges of great burthen – of 300 to 500 "tonns" – sailed to Patna and Bengal down the Yamuna and the Ganga, performing the downward journey during the rains and taking the rest of the year to come up again.[16] Similarly, Lahor and Multan were river-ports from which rather smaller craft went

[9] This may be deduced, for instance, from *Factories 1618-21*, 102, and *1655-60*, 63. The low costs were not primarily due to the use of bullocks. Pack oxen hired in the ordinary way were more expensive in terms of weight carried than carts (Marshall, 117-118), which in turn were distinctly more expensive than camels (*Lett. Recd.*, IV, 237-8). The real savings affected by the *banjāras* arose from the fact that in their *ṭānḍa* fifty to hundred bullocks might be looked after by just one family, while by allowing time to their animals to graze along the route they did not normally have to spend anything on fodder.

[10] "Not above 6 or 7 miles a daye att most" (Mundy, 96). Otherwise pack-oxen provided the quickest transport (Tavernier, I, 33). A laden cart normally took 35 days to reach Agra from Patna in the dry season (*Factories 1618-21*, 191, 199), and both carts and camels 50 days to perform the journey between Agra and Surat (*Lett. Recd.*, IV, 237-8).

[11] The whole subject of *banjāras* has been discussed by me, with use of further evidence, in James Tracy (ed.), *Rise of Merchant Empires*, 371-79.

[12] This may be illustrated by the transport charges quoted in 1639: "Freight or cartage of goods" from Agra to Multan was Rs 2½ per "maen"; but from Multan to Thatta, a slightly longer distance, the freight by boat amounted to only Rs ¾ "per maen" (*Factories, 1637-41*, 135-6).

[13] *Ā'īn*, I, 389.

[14] Ibid., 555. It is stated that there were some 40,000 boats "small and big" plying in the *sarkār* of Thatta, or Sind below Bhakkar. See also *Tārīkh-i Ṭāhirī*, Or. 185, f.58a-b; ed., 130.

[15] Ibid., 563; *T.J.*, 298. Abū-l Fazl says there were 30,000 (*rect.* 3,000?) boats in Kashmir (*A.N.*, III, 550), while Jahāngir, op.cit., gives the number as 5,700 for "the city (Srinagar) and the *parganas*."

[16] Jourdain, 162; Mundy, 87-88. Moreland puts the "tun" of the English records of the time at 4/10 to 6/10 of the net registered ton of modern shipping (*India at the Death of Akbar*, 310-12). Bowrey, 225, speaks of "great flat bottomed Vessels of an Exceeding Strength ... called Patellas", plying between Patna and Hugli, each of which brought down 4,000 to 6,000 "Bengala maunds", or about 130 to nearly 200 tons in weight. Cf. also Hamilton, II, 20-21.

down to Thatta.[17] To judge from the fact that 10,000 "tonns" of salt alone were annually transported on boats from Agra to Bengal,[18] the rivers must have borne a very great volume of traffic. The capacity of the coasting fleet too, considering the circumstances of the time, was impressive,[19] and it was extensively used for the transport of goods of bulk, including foodgrains.[20] It was very vulnerable, however, to piracy from European shipping which now dominated the Indian seas.[21]

The broad effects imposed upon trade by contemporary conditions of transport may best be appreciated by a study of transport costs set by the side of the prices then prevailing. For example, the cost of a *man*-load carried on camel's back from Agra to Surat in the early years of the seventeenth century amounted to no less than four times the *Ā'īn's* price of wheat of that weight, but only half of that of white sugar.[22] Unfortunately, the costs incurred by the *banjāras* are nowhere stated,[23] but we can still form some idea

[17] Steel and Crowther, *Purchas*, IV, 268; *Factories, 1634-36*, 244; *1637-41*, 135-7. The burthen of these boats is put variously at 40 to 50 "tunnes", "100 tonns and upwards" and 500 to 2000 "maens" (i.e. up to 65 tons in weight). (Salbancke, *Purchas*, III, 85; *Factories, op.cit.*). According to Hamilton, I, 123, the largest of these "flat-bottomed" vessels ("Kisties") could "lade about 200 Tuns".

[18] Jourdain, 162.

[19] The English factors at Surat in 1648, speak of "the greate quantity of shipping these country merchants are already possessed of" and "consequently" of their own fear that if they offered the Company's ships for sale, "though serviceable and good ships, how exceedingly they would be undervallued" (*Factories, 1646-50*, 190). Cf. Moreland, *India at the Death of Akbar*, 227ff., and *Akbar to Aurangzeb*, 81ff.

[20] In October 1705 the *Dīwān* of Gujarat received an order to despatch 200,000 *mans* of foodgrains by sea for Aurangzeb's army operating on the western coast (*Akhbārāt* A 182). If the quantity is expressed in terms of *man-i Shāhjahānī*, it would have been about 6,690 metric tons, but, if the *man* of Gujarat is meant, only 3,345 tons. A similar order for despatching 100,000 *mans* by sea had been issued a year or two earlier (*Mir'āt*, I, 354).

[21] The licensing system instituted by the Portuguese, and later by the Dutch and the English, not only imposed a great financial burden on Indian shipping, but was also used to exclude Indian ships from certain lines of trade. Thus the Dutch forcibly prevented them from carrying cotton or opium to Malabar or bringing pepper from there (see below). In 1677 they blocked all sea-borne exports of rice from the Gingelly or Kalinga coast (T. Raychaudhuri, *Jan Company in Coromandel*, 67-8).

[22] The rates quoted per *man-i Jahāngīrī* in three consecutive years are as follows: Rs 1.56 (Rs 1.3 *Jahāngīrī*) in 1617; Rs 1.40 in 1618; and Rs1.40 and 1.67 in 1619 (*Lett. Recd.*, VI, 238; *Factories 1618-21*, 47, 51, 73-4). See *Ā'īn*, I, 60, 65, for prices of wheat and white sugar.

[23] As has been said above, the transport by the *banjāras* was undoubtedly the cheapest on land. In 1656 saltpetre was despatched from Agra to Surat, apparently, through the agency of the *banjāras* and the saving resulting therefrom is particularly

of the charges of river-transport. The cost by boat from Multan to Thatta in 1639, for the same quantity, was nearly twice the *Ā'īn's* price of wheat but only about one-sixth of that of white sugar.[24] Clearly, the divergence in prices between distant markets had to be very great before movement in foodgrains and similar goods of bulk could take place, while in articles of higher value the relative divergence needed to be much smaller. Moreover, price differences should have tended to be far less along rivers than over land.

But there were also other factors, besides the means of transport, which greatly influenced carrying trade. Of these, transit dues may be assigned cardinal importance. A series of imperial orders issued by Akbar and his successors declare all such imposts – indiscriminately termed *bāj*, *tamghā* and *zakāt* – abolished, either entirely or with some exceptions.[25] It is possible that such prohibitions did result in the elimination of a number of tolls and taxes, many of them probably inherited from the annexed kingdoms.[26] Nevertheless, despite the comprehensive phraseology of the orders, they do not seem to have had more than partial effect. Duties of all types continued to be collected: either this was done illegally, for the benefit of the *jāgīrdārs* or other officials; or what had been

emphasized. The amount paid was Rs 2.7 per *man-i Shāhjahānī*. This included transit dues, so that an exact comparison is not possible. But it was certainly not inexpensive (*Factories, 1655-60*, 63).

24 *Factories, 1637-41*, 135, 136. The cost of transit amounted to one-ninth and one-thirteenth, respectively, of the current prices of white sugar at Lahor and Multan, quoted in the same document. The current price of wheat is not given, but the cost of transit came to about two-thirds of the price given for wheat at Lahor at the end of the century (*Khulāṣatu-s Siyāq*, f.90b; Or. 2026, f.57a).

25 Akbar issued a *farmān* to this effect in the early years of his reign ('Ārif Qandahārī, 32-3). The text of the *farmān* issued in 1582-3 is preserved in the *Inshā'-i Abū-l Faẓl*, 67-8, and *Mir'āt*, I, 171-3. (See also *A.N.*, III, 295-6; *Ṭabaqāt-i Akbarī*, III, 347; *Ā'īn*, I, 284.) Jahāngīr refers to a similar order of his own on his accession in *T.J.*, 4 (cf. Asad Beg, f.30a). Shāhjahān's *farmān* is given in Ṣaliḥ Kambū's *Bahār-i Sukhun*, Add. 5557, ff.23b-24a; Or. 178, ff.51a-53a. (Cf. also *Chār Chaman-i Barhaman*, A: f.25a; B: f.16a-b.) Aurangzeb's *farmān*, issued in the year of his accession, is reproduced in *Durru-l 'Ulūm*, ff. 37b-38b, and is mentioned in *Mir'ātu-l 'Ālam*, Aligarh MS, ff.138b-139a; *'Ālamgīrnāma*, 435-9; *Mir'āt*, I, 249, 251-2; *Ma'āṣir-i 'Ālamgīrī*, 530-31; Khāfī Khān, II, 87-90. For another order enumerating the forbidden dues, see *Mir'āt*, I, 286-7.

26 For some success in enforcing these orders, see Monserrate, 79-80, and *Jahāngīr and the Jesuits*, 36. It is probable that the Mughal Empire represented in this respect a great improvement on conditions under the provincial kingdoms. Thevenot, 131, by implication, favourably compared the Mughal toll system with that of Golkunda. It similarly comes out in a better light in comparison with the

abolished by one hand was authorized by the other.[27] One ought apparently to distinguish between two categories of such taxes. In the big marts, frontier towns and ports, all goods sent out or in transit had to pay a duty of 2.5 per cent *ad valorem*,[28] though in some places it was more, in others less.[29] Aurangzeb raised the rate to 5 per cent for Hindus, but kept it at the old percentage for Muslims, except for a period of fifteen years (1667-82) when they were exempted altogether.[30] Foodgrains, like other commodities,

---

regimes of the tributary chiefs. Thus transit dues between Agra and Patna, with no chieftaincies intervening, are said to have amounted to Rs 14 and, at most, to Rs 20 per cart in 1621 (*Factories, 1618-21*, 269-70). Twelve years later the duties on the Agra-Ahmadabad route, passing through territories of important Rajput chiefs, but traversing no greater distance, could only be compounded for Rs 45 per cart (Mundy, 278). In an English document of 1616, the "customes and extortions" on this route are described as "intollerable" and the alternative route Surat-Burhanpur-Agra, which passed almost entirely through imperial lands, is preferred as "safer, speedier and cheaper" (Foster, *Suppl. Cal.*, 89). For other complaints of imposts levied in the chiefs' territories, see Tavernier, I, 31; *Factories, 1646-50*, 192-3; and *Waqā'i' Ajmer*, 12-13, 196.

27 According to *A.N.*, III, 670, it was reported in 1595-6 that despite the *tamghā* having been abolished, money was still being collected on the routes under the pretence of this tax, and officers had to be deputed to suppress this practice. They could not have been very successful because upon his accession, Jahāngīr noted that such dues were being exacted in "every province and every *sarkār*" (*T.J.*, 4). Despite Jahāngīr's own prohibition, more sweeping than that of his father, we find Nūr Jahān's own agents collecting transit dues right opposite Agra (Pelsaert, 4). Khāfī Khān remarks that Aurangzeb's order forbidding the collection of these duties remained a dead letter, because, first, no one found guilty of levying illegal cesses was seriously punished; and, secondly, the expected yield from the banned imposts was often included in the *jama'* of the assigned *jāgīrs*, so that the *jāgīrdārs* had no option but to collect them to make up their sanctioned income (Khāfī Khān, II, 88-9).

28 This rate is given for the ports in *Ā'īn*, I, 204. A similar duty was levied at Multan for goods conveyed to Qandahar or Thatta in the reign of Shāhjahān (*Factories 1637-41*, 81); it was also imposed on goods purchased in upper Sind (*1655-60*, 81). Aurangzeb in his *farmān* abolishing transit dues, specifically excludes from its terms, "the established *zakāt*, which on frontiers and in particular towns is fixed and instituted in accordance with imperial orders" (*Durru-l 'Ulūm*, ff. 37b-38b). The goods paid duty upon an estimate of their value according to the official report of the retail prices prevailing in the local market (Pelsaert, 43; *Factories 1637-41*, 136; *Mir'āt*, I, 318-19, 339-40; *Khulāṣatu-s Siyāq*, ff.90a-92b, Or.2026, ff.57a-59a).

29 3.5 per cent "inwards and outwards" at Surat and 1.25 or 1.5 per cent at Baroch (Foster, *Supp. Cal.*, 47, 86; Pelsaert, 42, 43; Commissariat, *Mandelslo*, 9). Only 0.25 per cent was paid at Thatta for clearance from the *ghāṭ* or channel, it being supposed, presumably, that the main duty had been paid on up-country goods at Multan (*Factories 1637-41*, 136).

30 See *Mir'āt*, I, 258-9, 265-6, 298-9; *Factories 1665-67*, 266; *Durru-l 'Ulūm*, ff. 59b-60a.

were subject to this duty,[31] though they might be exempted in times of scarcity.[32] The second and, perhaps, more burdensome category comprised the various tolls and cesses – generally called *rāhdārī* – which were exacted by the various authorities controlling the routes. These were apparently mostly proportionate to the value of goods carried,[33] though in some cases like river crossings a uniform rate might be levied.[34] Imperial edicts emphasize the desirability of freeing foodgrains and articles of mass consumption from the burden of such imposts.[35] While the levies on these goods might not have been heavy in normal circumstances, these, paradoxically enough, tended to become very severe in conditions of scarcity or famine. Then, not only did their amount rise dramatically, but it is possible also that under the pretence of collecting them, the officials held up the trade till they had extorted a large share out of the merchants' profits expected from the high prices.[36] Moreover, it is almost certain that with the relaxation of central authority towards the close of our period, the incidence of these cesses rose enormously.[37]

[31] Cf. *Khulāṣatu-s Siyāq*, op.cit.; Fraser 86, f. 74a-b.

[32] Khāfī Khān, II, 88, Or. 6574, f.33b; *Mir'āt*, I, 309, 315.

[33] Thus the English factors at Surat, writing to their colleague in Burhanpur, 1616, declare that as regards "the customes etc. aryseing on cartes on the way, wee conceave that severall comodities pay different customes" (Foster, *Supp. Cal.*, 66).

[34] *Ā'īn*, I, 204; Tavernier, I, 96.

[35] See the texts of the *farmāns* of Akbar, Shāhjahān and Aurangzeb, abolishing transit duties, cited in footnote 25 above.

[36] The famine in Dhaka in Bengal in 1662-3, was attributed to "the heavy burden of the *zakāt*, the oppression of the *rāhdārs* (officers in charge of the routes) and the exactions of the *chaukīdārs* (men posted at *chaukīs* or toll and guard stations)", and the consequent inability of the merchants to bring grain to the city. Ultimately Dāūd Khān, the acting governor of Bengal, was constrained to exempt foodgrains from all such duties on his own authority, and his action was later upheld at the court (*Fatḥiya-i 'Ibriya*, ff.79b-80a, 110b-111a). Although the text of the general *farmān* of Aurangzeb (as given in the *Durru-l 'Ulūm*) is silent on the point, all chroniclers commenting upon it agree that it was meant to give relief, especially in view of the scarcity conditions prevailing over large parts of the empire. In Sind, traffic used to be held up in normal times, professedly for the collection of dues, but really to extort bribes (*Factories 1637-41*, 137; *1655-60*, 81). Such a profitable system could not have been confined to Sind alone. In Aurangzeb's later years, when high prices prevailed in his camp in the Dakhin, the *mutaṣaddī* of Surat extorted Rs 2 per bullock and his agent, Re 1, from the *banjāras*, before allowing them to take grain to the imperial army (*Aḥkām-i 'Ālamgīrī*, f.148b).

[37] Khāfī Khān, II, 87-90, portrays the situation in detail and says that the imposts and cesses levied in Aurangzeb's reign surpassed those of the past, and the *zamīndārs* also became bold enough to collect tolls everywhere. A commodity taken inland from the ports might have to pay as much duty as the price it had been

As for the general state of law and order which determined the levels of "protection costs", it is worth noticing that the organization of the caravans and *sarāis*, of the *ṭānḍas* of *banjāras*, who went armed,[38] and, possibly, of flotillas in the rivers[39] was mainly designed to met the threat of robbery on the routes.[40] The protection of the routes was moreover regarded as one of the foremost duties of the administration and it was a well-established law of the Mughal Empire that the officer in whose jurisdiction an incident of robbery or theft occurred was bound to either recover the goods lost or himself pay compensation to the victims.[41] The officers met this obligation by pursuing a policy of ferocious reprisals and sacking the suspected villages, methods by no means unprofitable to themselves.[42] This, however, was true only of the plains and the territories closely controlled by the imperial government. In or near the hills, ravines and desolate country, such a policy could not be successfully carried out; and here robbers and rebels often became indistinct, levying what might be regarded as either ransom or tribute upon merchants passing through their territories.[43] In general, however, one gains the impression, from

---

bought for. Aurangzeb himself writes of the exactions of the *amīn* and *faujdār* of Seoni (Khandesh): "This is not *rāhdārī*, but *rahzānī* (highway robbery)" (*Ruq'āt-i 'Ālamgīrī*, Kanpur, 14). Cf. also Manucci, IV, 16.

[38] Mundy, 262. For their readiness to fight, see Tavernier, I, 33.

[39] Moreland, *India at the Death of Akbar*, 167-8.

[40] This may be the reason why *ṭhagi* or organized strangling became such a menace to trade and travel in the late 18th century, when the old organization of transport had been very greatly disrupted. Of the European travellers of our period, only Thevenot, 58, and Fryer, I, 244-5, refer to this crime. Cf. also *Waqā'i' Ajmer*, 405, for reference to "highway robbers known in Hindi as *ṭhags*."

[41] "Owing to the justice and management of this great Government, such peace is maintained on the routes and halting places that merchants and traders and travellers journey forth to (distant?) parts in tranquillity of heart and joy. If at any place anything is lost, the officers who have jurisdiction (*'amal-dārān*, MS. var. *'ummāl*, revenue officials) there are obliged to pay compensation as well as a fine for their negligence" (*Chār Chaman-i Barhaman*, A:f.25a-b; B: 16b). The *Ā'īn*, I, 284, imposes such an obligation on the *kotwāl* (police head of the town) only, but since the revenue collector (*'amalguzār*) was expected to perform all the duties of the *kotwāl*, where that official was not separately appointed (ibid., 288), this must apply to him as well. Manucci, II, 451, says that "should any merchant or traveller be robbed in daylight" on the roads, the *faujdār* (commandant of the area) was "obliged to pay compensation". See also *Akhbārāt* A, 193. A similar responsibility seems to have devolved upon the *jāgīrdārs* as well (*Factories, 1646-1650*, 300-302). Cf. *Durru-l 'Ulūm*, f.64b-65a.

[42] For the wide employment of these methods, see Chapter IX, Section 2.

[43] "He (Jahāngīr) can be regarded as King of the plains or open roads only, for

the experience of European commerce in India, and especially from contemporary rates of insurance for goods in inland transit, that whatever dangers a lonely traveller might have to face, caravan trade was normally fairly safe over the larger portion of the Mughal empire.[44]

A positive element in the situation was the exceptionally well-developed system of finance and credit.[45] The use of *hunḍīs* or bills of exchange was widespread, and the rates, considering the times, were certainly moderate.[46] There was, besides, an organized system of insurance, which could cover the risks of loss in transit,[47] but also the incidence of taxes.[48]

It is not easy to assess with precision the effects on trade of each of the factors described above. It would seem, however, that none of these modified to any great extent the relative possibilities of trade set by the means of transport, which, to repeat, were more favourable to the transit of goods of higher value than of goods of bulk and to transit along rivers than over land. Perhaps, the transport of foodgrains was sometimes encouraged by the administration, but we have also seen that it might as often be retarded.

---

in many places you can travel only with a strong body of men, or on payment of heavy tolls to rebels" (Pelsaert, 58-59). For threats to traffic on the routes, see specific reports of encounters with Rajputs of Baghelkhand and the Kolis in Gujarat, in Mundy, 110-11, 117-20, 259, 263-4, 269-70. For Gujarat see also Geleynssen, 73, 74, 79, 81; and for the Indus delta, Hamilton, I, 116-18.

44 The impressions of individual travellers vary. It is possible to set against the unfavourable account of Finch the experiences of such travellers as Manrique and Tavernier. Moreover, some routes might be safer than others. Thus the Agra-Patna route was "not very daingerous for robbers" (*Factories, 1618-21*, 269); and Mundy would not have met any had he proceeded via Jaunpur (Mundy, 110). For a favourable view of the maintenance of law and order under the Mughals, see Saran, 399-403.

The insurance rate on cochineal sent from Surat to Agra in 1655 was only 2½% (*Factories, 1655-60*, 15). In 1646 treasure was insured at 1% to cover its conveyance from Daman to Surat (*Factories, 1646-50*, 88). Malcolm quotes insurance rates prevalent about 1795 between various places in central India and between these and cities in other parts of the country; they appear quite moderate (*Memoir of Central India*, II, 366-69). Cf. I. Habib, *Essays*, 223-24.

45 Sujān Rāi, 25, describes it enthusiastically, regarding it as one of the wonders of India.

46 See I. Habib in *PIHC*, 33rd session, 1972, Muzaffarpur, 290-303.

47 Sujān Rāi, 25, who says this was known as *bīma*. Cf. I. Habib, in T. Raychaudhuri, ed., *Contributions to Indian Economic History*, I, 15-17.

48 Cf. Mundy, 278, 291: the men who undertook this were called "adowyaes", apparently professional "Carters". According to the *ẓimn* of Aurangzeb's *farmān* of 1665, reproduced in *Mir'āt*, I, 261, the *adhwayas* were persons who let out carts on hire for long distances.

And though transport across land was itself costlier, it was still more vulnerable to the exactions of chiefs and rebels, as on the Rajasthan route.[49]

Reports of prices of agricultural produce have not survived in sufficient abundance for us to tabulate prices at various places on the same dates so as to determine what degrees of price difference could be tolerated between regions under the existing conditions of transport and trade. Two illustrations can, however, be offered: (1) An unemployed Mughal official, who kept a diary, tells of scarcity felt "all over the country" in the summer of 1718. He was at Illahabad, where he records prices prevalent during 10-16 July; he then came to Agra, where too he records prices prevalent in August-September. A rupee had fetched 14 *sers* of wheat at Illahabad, but only 7 *sers* at Agra; *ghī* (clarified butter) sold at 2½ *sers* at Illahabad, and at 2 *sers* at Agra. Clearly, *ghī* as the more expensive product moved more easily than wheat; and so the smaller price difference in its case. When the official went the same month (Shawwāl/September 1718) from Agra to Dehli, about 125 miles away, he found the prices substantially higher there than at Agra. Ordinary rice at Agra sold at 7 *sers* and the fine (*bāsmatī*) at 5 *sers*; at Dehli even the ordinary rice sold at 4 *sers*. Wheat flour at Agra was 7 *sers* to the rupee; at Dehli gram flour sold at 5 *sers*. At Agra the rate for *ghī* was 2 *sers* to the rupee; at Dehli, 1¼ *sers*.[50] (2) S. Nurul Hasan and S.P. Gupta traced in the *arsaṭṭhas* the harvest prices prevailing in 1730 in two *parganas* of eastern Rajasthan, their headquarters only about 40 miles apart. While the range of rabi prices in the two *parganas* coincides fairly well, one notices quite substantial differences in the kharif prices, possibly owing to transport difficulties in the rainy season.[51]

We have, then, to begin with the premise that long-distance trade became possible only when the price differences in these markets became so large as to accommodate the high costs of transport. In the following pages, a description is attempted of long-distance trade in major items of agricultural produce, as came to be ordinarily established, very much in the manner of Schumpeter's "circular flow", sustained by stable price differences between the various regions.

[49] See note 26 above.

[50] *Mir'ātu-l Ḥaqā'iq*, Bodl. 257 (Fraser 124), ff.135a, 138b, 139a.

[51] *PIHC* (29th Session, Patiala, 1967), 348. The two *parganas* are Chatsu and Malarna.

There is no doubt that Bengal stood out in our period for low prices[52] and had a large surplus in provisions available for export. There was a regular coastal trade in rice, sugar and butter, carried to Coromandel[53] and, around Cape Comorin, to Kerala.[54] Sugar was shipped to Gujarat[55] and even to Persia,[56] while opium was chiefly exported to Kerala.[57] Sometimes wheat was also sent from its ports to southern India[58] and the Portuguese possessions.[59] Opium, long pepper, ginger and tobacco were exported on Indian "trading Shipping",[60] and gunny bags sent by sea to Persia.[61] Orissa annually exported by sea over 40,000 tons of grain (rice), together with butter and lac to the Coromandel ports.[62] The imports into Bengal from the Coromandel coast included cotton yarn and tobacco.[63]

In the course of the seventeenth century, an important sea-borne trade developed in Bengal silk, notably through the agency of the

[52] Linschoten, I, 94-5; *Ā'īn*, I, 389; Bowrey, 193-4; *Kālimāt-i Ṭaiyabāt*, f.50a. An English factor declares in 1650; "At Hugli may be procured beeswax, pepper, civet, rice, butter, oil and wheat; all at about half the price of other places" (*Factories, 1646-50*, 338).

[53] *Relations*, 40, 60; *Factories, 1634-36*, 41; Bernier, 437; *Early Annals*, I, 399. Other exports included gingeli (sweet oil) seeds, long pepper, gum-lac, wax, and silk (cf. also Caesar Frederick, *Purchas*, X, 114). The export of rice to Coromandel, a rich rice-growing area itself, is remarkable. Methwold (*Relations*, 40) thought it looked like "coales carried to New-castle, yet here they sell them to contented profit".

[54] Fitch, Ryley, 185, & *Early Travels*, 44; *Relations*, 60. And also to the Portuguese possessions on the western coast, for which see Fitch, Ryley, 110, & *Early Travels*, 24, 28; *Lett. Recd.*, IV, 327 (here the editor seems to be mistaken in suggesting that "Indya" means Hindustan; to the English of the period it usually meant Portuguese India).

[55] Pelsaert 19; *Factories*, N.S., III, 256; Glamann, *Dutch-Asiatic Trade*, 160, & n.

[56] Bernier 437; *Factories, 1668-69*, 179; Om Prakash, 173-76. In 1680-81, the Dutch factors from Hugli exported to Persia a "record amount" of 1.46 million ponds, or about 1.6 million lb. avdp., of sugar (Om Prakash, 176).

[57] *Factories, 1661-64*, 355. The Dutch forcibly imposed their monopoly over this trade (Om Prakash, 169-70).

[58] The Mughal army operating in 'Karnatak' (coastal Tamilnadu) obtained its wheat from Bengal (*Dilkushā*, ff.113b-114a). For the export of wheat from Bengal (as well as from Surat) to the English settlement of Madras, see Hamilton, I, 367-68.

[59] *Lett. Recd.*, IV, 327.

[60] Hamilton, II, 21.

[61] Ibid., II, 17 ("Gunnies... for embaling goods").

[62] Bowrey, 121-2. Cf. also Caesar Frederick, *Purchas*, X, 112-13; *Relations*, 54; Hamilton, I, 368.

[63] *Relations*, 60.

Dutch, who exported it to Japan and Holland. They are said to have taken 6,000 or 7,000 bales yearly (possibly an exaggeration) from the Qasimbazar market; they would have taken even more if the merchants from other parts of the Mughal Empire and Central Asia had allowed them to do so.[64] Silk was also a "staple" export to Coromandel.[65] In the latter part of the century, cotton yarn and sugar also began to be exported to Europe.[66]

Up the Ganga, Bengal exported rice and silk to Patna,[67] receiving wheat, sugar and opium in return.[68]

There was brisk trade on and along the Ganga and Yamuna up to Agra. Agra not only imported raw silk and sugar from Bengal and Patna, but also obtained such provisions as rice, wheat and butter from the eastern provinces, without which, it was said, it could not have fed itself.[69] In return, salt was carried down by river to Bengal, where it was very scarce, together with cotton and opium.[70]

From Agra again, sugar and wheat and Bengal silk were carried to Gujarat.[71] As a mart, however, Agra owed much of its prominence to the indigo trade. What was reputed to be the best indigo

[64] Tavernier, II, 2. He says their rivals took as much as the Dutch, the balance remaining for local consumption in Bengal. Tavernier's figures for the Dutch purchases of silk seem exaggerated: the peak year of the Dutch Company's export of Bengal silk was 1662, when the quantity was equal to 278,000 lb. avdp. (Om Prakash, 126). Bengal raw silk exports to Holland picked up later, supplies ordered in the 1690s generally exceeding 230,000 lb. avdp. a year (ibid., 198-9, 210-11).

[65] *Early Annals*, I, 399.

[66] *Factories, 1655-60*, 179, 297; *Factories*, N.S., II, 331; Hedges, I, 75.

[67] *Factories, 1618-21*, 193-4; Mundy, 153; Bernier, 153, 437. Patna seems to have been an important mart for Bengal silk probably owing to its convenient position in relation to Agra (cf. Pelsaert, 7).

[68] Fitch, Ryley, 110 & *Early Travels* 24; Bowrey, 225.

[69] Pelsaert, 4-5, 9; Mundy, 95-6, 98-9. The imperial court obtained its supply of *sukhdās* rice from Bahraich (*Ā'īn*, I, 53). The *dastūrs* of rice in the *ṣūbas* of Illahabad and Awadh are substantially lower than those in Agra; the difference in the *dastūrs* of wheat are, however, marginal (Moosvi, 121-24). If the *dastūrs* varied according to local prices, we might suppose that Agra could have obtained rice, but not much wheat, from the east.

[70] Jourdain, 162; Pelsaert, 9. For the dearness of salt in Bengal, see *Ā'īn*, I, 390. It was scarcer still in Assam (*Fatḥiya-i 'Ibriya*, f.32b).

Agra must have obtained the salt it sent eastwards from two major sources: the Salt range beyond Lahor (*Ā'īn*, I, 539; Marshall, 414-15; Sujān Rāi, 75) and the Sambhar Lake (Sujān Rāi, 55). Salt was also extracted from nitrous soils by a caste known as Nūnias (*Tashrīḥu-l Aqwām*, ff.354b-356a); but it is unlikely that this was taken to any point beyond the local market.

[71] *Factories, 1618-21*, 102; *1624-29*, 235-6; Pelsaert, 19; Tavernier, II, 2. As Pelsaert and Tavernier tell us, there was a large silk-weaving industry at Ahmadabad which was wholly dependent upon Bengal silk.

in the world grew in its neighbourhood, at and near Bayana, and, besides being sent to all parts of India, it had an international market. Formerly, it used to be taken to Lahor for sale to merchants from the Middle East,[72] but with the opening of the direct sea-borne commerce with Europe, Agra became its chief, if not sole, emporium.[73] The European trade became very important in the first half of the seventeenth century, after which it experienced a sharp decline.[74]

Apparently, wheat could be taken to the Lahor market from as far as Muradabad, and high-quality rice from Sirhind.[75] From Lahor and Multan, sugar and ginger were sent down on boats to Thatta, whence these returned laden with pepper and dates.[76] Butter for export was brought down by river to Thatta from Bhakkar.[77] Indigo was carried in the same way from Sehwan for shipment to Basra[78] and, occasionally, via Surat to Europe.[79] For some reason, however, the Basra trade decayed,[80] and the English did not succeed in replacing it.[81]

Kashmir exported saffron to Agra[82] and other parts of India, entering into competition at Patna with the saffron brought from Nepal.[83] In return, it imported salt, pepper, opium, cotton and yarn.[84]

72 Pelsaert, 30.

73 The best or Bayana indigo was largely bought by the Dutch and the English as well as the Armenian, "Mughal" and Persian merchants, who also took much of the indigo grown in the Doab near Khurja and Kol. The variety grown in Mewat was meant mainly for local consumption and for markets in India (Pelsaert, 15, 18; *Factories, 1642-45*, 136).

74 This was largely due to the rise in the price of Agra indigo and the competition from the slave-worked plantations established in the West Indies (*Factories, 1646-50*, 32, 76-7; *1655-60*, 322, 336; *Factories*, N.S., III, 245. Cf. Moreland, *Akbar to Aurangzeb*, 112-113). There was some recovery in the trade later on, because in 1684-5 the English company ordered 500 bales from Agra though only 212 could be procured (*Factories*, N.S., III, 285).

75 See the account of dues levied at Shahdara-Lahor in *Khulāṣatu-s Siyāq*, ff.90a-92b, Or. 2026, ff.57a-59a.

76 Pelsaert, 31-2; *Factories, 1637-41*, 136.

77 *Factories, 1637-41*, 136. The butter produced in Sind is praised by Linschoten, I, 56, and *Ā'īn*, I, 556. Hamilton, I, 126, speaks of "great Quantities of Butter" exported from Sind; and Manucci, II, 427, says it was exported to Musqat.

78 *Factories, 1637-41*, 136-7.

79 For trade in it by the Portuguese, see Roe, 75; for trade by the English, *Factories, 1637-41*, 274; *1642-5*, 203, etc.

80 *Factories, 1642-5*, 136.

81 Ibid., 203; *1646-50*, 12-13, 29, 33.

82 Pelsaert, 35.

83 Marshall, 413. Cf. also Fitch, Ryley, 116, & *Early Travels*, 27, for "saffron like the saffron of Persia" produced in Bhutan.

84 *T.J.*, 300, 315; Pelsaert, 36.

The most important feature of trade in western India was the position of Gujarat as a great importer of foodstuffs. It obtained wheat and other foodgrains from Malwa and Ajmer and rice from the Dakhin.[85] Indeed, it provided a market for the produce of so distant a region as Gondwana,[86] while rice was also brought by sea from Malabar.[87] On the other hand, its major exports consisted of high-grade crops. Of these, cotton was by far the most important. The crop raised between Surat and Burhanpur (Khandesh) supported an extensive trade to Agra.[88] Cotton and cotton yarn were sent by sea to the Persian Gulf and the Red Sea ports[89] and down the coast to Kerala.[90] It was also occasionally exported to Europe.[91] The indigo produced in Gujarat, especially the Sarkhej variety, was exported to both Europe and the Middle East.[92] A large quantity of opium was shipped to Kerala[93] and tobacco to Thatta,[94] Persia[95] and the Red Sea ports.[96] Among re-exports, sugar was frequently sent to Europe,[97] silk to the Middle East,[98] and saffron to Malabar.[99]

Along the western coast, pepper was probably the most important article of commerce. From certain areas in Mahārashtra

[85] *Ā'īn*, I, 485. And also from Agra, as we have seen.

[86] Speaking of Garh, in the province of Malwa, Abū-l Faẓl says: "By its cultivation, the Dakhin and Gujarat obtain relief" (*Ā'īn*, I, 456).

[87] van Twist, 76. And this despite the fact that Kerala itself does not seem to have had a superfluity of rice (cf. Fitch, Ryley, 185; *Early Travels,* 44). Other goods imported from Kerala were coconuts, coir, palm-sugar, betel-nuts, etc., besides pepper (Pelsaert, 19; van Twist, 76; Fryer, I, 136).

[88] Pelsaert, 9.

[89] Fryer, I, 282.

[90] van Twist, 76; *Factories, 1665-67*, 101.

[91] Cf. *Akbar to Aurangzeb*, 137-8, concerning exports of yarn. On cotton wool, see *Factories, 1624-29*, 212; *1655-67*, 174. We are not, of course, speaking here of piece-goods, which accounted for a very large part of the trade to Europe.

[92] *Ā'īn*, I, 486; *Factories, 1630-33*, 19-20; Fryer, I, 282. Most of the Sarkhej indigo was exported. Even when its output was low, estimated at 6,000 (Gujarat) *mans* only, the proportion locally required was no more than one-sixth (*Factories, 1642-45*, 163-4).

[93] Linschoten, II, 113; van Twist, 76; *Factories, 1661-64*, 355; *1665-67*, 99-101. It is possible that much of the opium that Gujarat exported came from Malwa. The Dutch purchased it at Burhanpur for conducting their pepper trade (Tavernier, I, 19).

[94] *Factories, 1646-50*, 60.

[95] Ibid., *1637-41*, 126.

[96] Ibid., *1618-21*, 63.

[97] Although sugar was produced in Gujarat, it was not sufficient for local consumption, let alone for export. The English often contracted for its supplies with *banjāras* from Agra (*Lett. Recd.*, V, 115; VI, 280; *Factories, 1618-21*, 102; *1624-29*, 235-6, 270. Cf. also *Akbar to Aurangzeb*, 138-9).

[98] Fryer, I, 282.

[99] van Twist, 76.

and Upper Kanara there was brisk overland trade to Agra,[100] but the traditional trade of Malabar had been with Gujarat, pepper sent by sea in exchange for opium and cotton. This commerce was completely disrupted by the Dutch in the 1660s; they forcibly monopolized the trade in all the three commodities, raising opium in Malabar and pepper at Surat to almost impossible prices.[101] The international trade in pepper, produced in Kanara and Kerala, lies outside the limits of this study.

It will be noticed that we have seldom been able to speak in terms of the actual volume of goods transported. On the basis of some rather general statements by Tavernier, the quantity carried by the *banjāras*, the seventeenth-century specialists in long-distance transport, has been estimated at 821 million metric-ton miles a year, which may be compared with the Indian railways' carriage of 2,500 metric-ton miles in 1882.[102] Though thus admittedly of a much smaller size than what it came to be after only the initial stages of railway construction, the volume transported in the earlier century was by no means insignificant; and production for distant markets was, therefore, an aspect of Mughal Indian agriculture that has always to be borne in mind. Over large regions – as indicated particularly by the exports from Bengal and the imports into Gujarat – even food crops were affected by the demands of long-distance trade. This was naturally truer still of the cash crops; and in certain tracts specializing in the cultivation of high-grade products, such as Bayana and Sarkhej in indigo, and Pampur (Kashmir) in saffron, the peasant's dependence on trade must undoubtedly have been very great.

2. LOCAL TRADE; THE PEASANT AND THE MARKET

It is obvious that although the volume of agricultural produce carried from one region to another was in the aggregate substantial, it could never have accounted, under the existing conditions of transport, for more than a small share in the total value of agricultural production, and a still smaller one in terms of volume. For the mass of the peasantry, the local market must have been of incomparably greater significance; and local trade largely consisted of the trade between town and surrounding country.

[100] *Factories, 1646-50*, 255; *1661-64*, 344.

[101] *Factories, 1661-64*, 261; *1665-67*, 99-101, 151, 174.

[102] I. Habib in Tracy (ed.), *Rise of Merchant Empires*, 376-77. Cf. Tavernier, I, 33-34.

Among the sources of the period we often encounter statements that suggest the presence of a large urban population: thus the multitudes of artisans, "peons" and servants found in the towns provide a topic of comment to foreign observers.[1] In Akbar's empire, we are told by a contemporary historian, there were 120 big cities and 3,200 townships (*qaṣbas*), each having under it from a hundred to a thousand villages.[2] The largest Indian city in the seventeenth century was undoubtedly Agra, with a population estimated at 500,000 and 660,000 in the days when it contained the court.[3] It still remained larger than Dehli, when the court shifted to the latter,[4] though Dehli was now (1660s) held to be as populous as Paris, which then had a population approaching 500,000.[5] Lahor in its days of glory had been described as second to none in Asia or Europe, and may, therefore, be reasonably thought to have a population not smaller than a third of a million, at the least.[6] Dhaka and Patna had, in 1630-31, estimated populations of 200,000 each;[7] and Thatta was assigned

1 "Another good thing [in Hindustan] is that it has unnumbered and endless work-men (*ḥarfa-gar*) of every sort" (*Bāburnāma*, ed. 469, Bev., II, 520; "in Hindustan" is implied in the text, but not actually mentioned, as in Beveridge's transl.). Among European authorities, see della Valle, I, 42, and Pelsaert, 61.

2 *Ṭabaqāt-i Akbarī*, III, 545-6.

3 The former estimate is given in a letter of 1609 from Agra by J. Xavier (transl. Hosten, *JASB*, N.S., XXIII, 1927, 121); and the latter by Manrique, II, 152, who says that it excludes strangers. In 1583-6, Agra and Fatehpur Sikri were each judged to be larger than London (Fitch, Ryley, 97-8; *Early Travels*, 17-18; cf. also Salbancke, *Purchas*, III, 84, for Fatehpur Sikri). This was before Agra finally wrested supremacy from Lahor. In Aurangzeb's early years when the court was at Dehli, Thevenot, 49, contended on hearsay that though "a great Town", Agra was not such "as to be able to send out Two hundred thousand men into the Field". But this gives little positive indication of its population, beyond suggesting a ceiling of about 800,000 to allow for women, old men and children.

4 Bernier 284; Tavernier, I, p.86.

5 Bernier 281-2, for the comparison with Paris. The population of Paris has been estimated at 500,000 in *c.*1700 (Cipolla, *Before Industrial Revolution*, 303).

6 Thus Monserrate, 159-60, who visited Lahor in 1581. In 1615 Coryat (*Early Travels*, 243) declared that it was "one of the largest cities of the whole universe" and "exceedeth Constantinople" (which he had seen) "in greatnesse". He adds that it was then larger than Agra. See also *Ā'īn*, I, 538. It declined subsequently (Pelsaert, 30; Tavernier, I, 74, 77). Among European cities, Paris with 300,000, and London and Naples with 250,000 each, appear to have had the largest populations in *c.*1600 (Cipolla, op.cit., 302-4).

7 Manrique, I, 44-45; II, 140. On the basis of a detailed report from the *kotwāl* of Patna, the number of Muslims buried at the Governor's expense in the famine of 1671, Marshall estimates that in all 90,720 inhabitants of the town perished in it. Earlier, but apparently less reliable, reports from the *kotwāl's chabūtra* put the

50,000 houses, and so about 200,000 people or more in 1635.[8] Ahmadabad in the early years of the seventeenth century was stated to be as big as London with its suburbs, which in 1600 contained about 250,000 inhabitants.[9] The population of Surat was put at about 100,000 in 1663, and 200,000 in 1700.[10] For the other large cities like Rajmahal, Multan and Burhanpur no such estimates have been provided. But outside the empire, Masulipatnam (Machilipatnam) had a population estimated at 200,000 in 1672.[11] Such data suggest that the fixing of the ratio of urban to the total population of the country at 15:100 is not unreasonable; and from what we know of the depopulation of the towns in the nineteenth century, it is unlikely that this ratio was exceeded until the twentieth century.[12]

The towns had not only to be fed, but had also to be supplied with raw materials for their crafts. In respect of food alone, they required a much larger portion of rural produce (in value) than would have been consumed by an equivalent rural population. For one thing, the court and the aristocracy, their dependants, merchants, and other richer elements in the towns, required a much higher proportion of the more expensive products – more wheat than coarser grains; more fine than ordinary rice; more sugar than *guṛ*; more cattle for meat; more sesame, spices, etc., and similarly more expensive drugs: opium, better-quality tobacco. For another, transport costs would favour movement of food supplies of higher than lower values. In addition, the towns had large numbers of

---

number of the dead at 135,400 and later on at 103,000 (Marshall, 152, 153). These numbers go to confirm Manrique's estimate.

[8] Bocarro, *Jour. Sind Historical Soc.*, IV, 201.

[9] *Lett. Recd.*, II, 28; Withington, *Early Travels*, 206. For the population of London, Cipolla, op.cit., 304. For Ahmadabad, see also Hamilton, I, 142 ("in Magnitude and Wealth ... little inferior to the best Towns in Europe").

[10] Godinho, 47; Hamilton, I, 147. Cf. Ashin Das Gupta, *Indian Merchants and the Decline of Surat*, 29-30.

[11] Fryer, I, 90.

[12] Arguing on the basis of the physical composition of the extracted surplus, I have suggested that, though considerable, the urban population in Mughal India did not probably exceed one-sixth of the total, being perhaps around 15% (I. Habib, *Essays*, 211-12, and in *Cambridge Economic History of India*, I, 168-69; cf. Moosvi, 299-305). This seems reasonable in view of the fact that, notwithstanding a probable decline in the absolute size of the urban population during the 19th century and a considerable increase in the total population in the same period, the urban population, was about 10% of the total (Burma excluded) in 1901. For de-urbanization during the 19th century, see I. Habib, *Essays*, 347-51.

artisans who needed raw materials to enable them to work at their crafts, such as cotton, indigo, other dye crops, and silks. If, then, there was an urban population in Mughal India, forming 15 per cent of the total, it might well have required for itself as much as 30 per cent of the rural produce (in value), if not more.[13]

When such a large portion of the peasant's produce was ultimately put on the market to be supplied to the towns, his own relations with the market are naturally well worth investigating. Sometimes he parted with this portion in lieu of land revenue and in such cases it was the potentates – the *jāgīrdārs* or their agents – who must have arranged for its sale;[14] and they, whenever they could make use of their authority, were probably able to obtain a much higher price than the peasant ever could.[15] But in most provinces the peasant was obliged to pay the revenue in cash[16] and there he must have had to sell the produce himself. This he must have often done by carting his produce to the local market or the towns.[17] Or, in the case of a high-grade crop like indigo, he would be approached in the village by merchants interested in the trade.[18]

But it is possible that a very large number of peasants were not able to reach the open market at all, being compelled to sell on contracted terms to their creditors. Whether the creditors were merchants or the village money-lenders, the result was always to

[13] Cf. I. Habib, *Essays*, 200-13, esp. 202-3.

[14] On such arrangements, evidence from eastern Rajasthan is especially significant. See S.P. Gupta, *Agrarian System of Eastern Rajasthan (c.1650-c.1750)*, 92-102: in most cases, the collected grain (or the claim to revenue in kind?) appears to have been sold within the village to the village *banya* or *mahājan* (money-lender) or to peasants (*raiyat*), the arrangement being designated *bichotī*.

[15] A particular phrase, "to sell *ba-ṭarḥ*", was used for the practice of sale of stocks at enforced high prices by the potentates either to "peasants and servants" or to "the men of headquarters (*ṣadr*) and shop-keepers" (*Mir'ātu-l Iṣṭilāḥ*, f.55a). In a proclamation issued in 1686 the *faujdār* of Sorath (Saurashtra) pledged himself not to follow his predecessors in selling "the foodgrains (*g͟hallāt*) of his *jāgīr* by force (*ba-ṭarḥ*), i.e. by *udaira* (?), to the merchants" (*Epigraphia Indica, Arabic & Persian Supplement*, 1955 & 1956, 100-101).

[16] See Chapter VI, Section 5.

[17] "The peasants of the *pargana* of Patlad, etc., come to Ahmadabad to sell cartloads of foodgrains" (*Ak͟hbārāt* A, 77). In 1630 we find a headman (*paṭel*) negotiating with the English at Surat for the sale of 1,000 (Gujarat) *mans*, half belonging to him and half to others of a (or his?) village near Baroch; the proposed place of delivery is not stated (*Factories, 1630-33*, 91). See also S.P. Gupta, op.cit., 103.

[18] *Lett. Recd.*, VI, 220, 234-5, 248-9; Pelsaert, 15-16, all references being to the Bayana tract.

depress the price received by the peasant.[19] Yet peasants not bound in this manner were also probably not able to obtain anything like a fair return. Their urgent need for cash to pay the revenue and keep themselves alive, forced them to sell as soon as the harvest came into their hands, while the merchants could usually afford to wait.[20] On the way to and in the market, again, the peasants might be obliged to pay various dues and perquisites.[21] In the process of sale, they were probably commonly defrauded in the weighing of their produce[22] and

[19] *Lett. Recd.*, II, 106; Pelsaert, 16. In 1628 the English were able to obtain indigo from villages near Bayana "by money advanced beforehand" at Rs 24½ per *man* when the prevailing market rate was Rs 36½ – a substantial difference even if the country indigo was "green", i.e. more wet and more liable to lose in weight from drying than the indigo supplied by the local merchants (*Factories, 1625-29*, 208). In the cotton-producing villages near Surat, merchants in league with the brokers of the English used to give "out old worme eaten decayed corn in the severall neighbouring villadges; which they take out in yearne and in parcells bring it to [Surat]" (ibid., *1661-65*, 112).

[20] This point is made by Roe in explaining the advantages the local merchants enjoyed over the English in buying indigo from the cultivators (*Lett. Recd.*, VI, 220).

[21] For example, in *Akhbārāt* A, 77, already cited, the complaint is made that the peasants bringing grain from Patlad had to pay Rs 2 per cart as *rah-dārī* to the *nākadārs* and *chaukīdārs* stationed by the *faujdār* of the environs (*gird*) of Ahmadabad. *Mir'āt*, I, 259-64, contains Aurangzeb's *farmān* of 1665 which lists and forbids a number of such exactions reported from Gujarat, especially at and around Ahmadabad, e.g. for feeding bullocks, whether drawing carts or carrying loads, when brought from outside the city, a fee of one *ṭanka*; on carts bringing grass and straw, one copper coin; on those bringing firewood, five *sers* of the same; and on each ox-load, four almonds exacted at various places *en route* to the town. Again, "poor people and peasants bring all sorts of cattle to sell in the city and its suburbs; something is exacted from them twice; first, in the name of 'entry' and then at the time of sale; and if no sale is effected and they wish to take it (the cattle) back, something has to be paid on account of 'Departure'." In Pattan, on each cartload of bananas and sugarcane they levied Rs 4 to 5. And so on. Cf. S.P. Gupta, op.cit., 103, 106-7, for similar dues and taxes in eastern Rajasthan.

[22] Pelsaert, 16-17, describes how in the indigo trade the peasants were by this means made to part with 47 *sers* or more instead of 40. He says, however, that with the rise in the demand for their produce, the peasants were becoming more vigilant against this abuse. In Indian markets it was customary to have a third party for weighing the goods when changing hands. The weighman was known as *bayā* or *kayāl* (cf. Elliot, *Memoirs*, I, 236). This person received perquisites from both sides, but as often as not was to be found in league with the merchant, whether purchaser or seller. (Cf. Royal Agricultural Commission, *Report*, 388-9.) A *parwāna* of 1646 shows the importance attaching to his position. The *bayā'ī* of the *mandavī* or grain-market at Gokul was till then in the hands of the agents of Gosāin Bithal Rāi. One Nāthā offered to pay as much as Rs 175 annually to the authorities if this function was transferred to him. This was refused on representations that Nāthā was seeking this privilege as a means of monopolizing the market

in the cash paid out to them.[23]

Finally, there was the scourge of monopoly and engrossing, *iḥtikār*, alike denounced by moralists[24] and prohibited officially.[25] When it was a case only of a few persons cornering the stocks it was not the peasant, but the townsman, who suffered from it.[26] But often in order to establish a monopoly, local authorities prevented the peasant from selling his produce to anyone except the favoured buyer or group of buyers, so that he too was victimized. Such local monopolization seems to have been a common phenomenon, though it is possible that, being usually disapproved of at the court, it could not ordinarily have been carried beyond certain limits.[27] In 1633 an imperial indigo monopoly was established, covering the whole empire and due to run for three years.

---

and driving away other merchants (Jhaveri, Doc. IX). *Kayālī* appears among the forbidden cesses in the *Ā'īn*, I, 301. Probably, by this is meant not the perquisites of the weighman, but the amount he was obliged to pay to the authorities for the exercise of his privilege.

23 Tavernier, I, 24-25.

24 Badāūnī, *Nijātu-r Rashīd*, 349-51. See also *Ā'īn*, I, 291, where it is declared to be the meanest of all occupations.

25 *Inshā'-i Abū-l Faẓl*, 65 (*Mir'āt*, I, 169-70); *Ā'īn*, I, 284.

26 Such official or purely commercial monopolies were the more readily established in conditions of scarcity. Thus in 1657 when an abundant harvest was unexpectedly obtained in the Agra region, it was stated that "many sheroffs and others, who, allured with the sweetness of former yeares gaines, have ingrossed great quantity of sugar, corne and cotton are like to bee (see?) scarce one third part of the mony they disbarced..." (*Factories, 1655-60*, 118).

27 A *farmān* issued in 1665 by Aurangzeb and addressed to the *dīwān* of Gujarat lists the following among the forbidden practices: "13. Officers and *seṭhs* (merchants) and *desāīs* (headmen) of most *parganas* of the said province do not allow others to buy the newly harvested grain. They first buy it themselves and whatever be rotten or spoilt they pass on to the tradesmen (*byūpārīs*) by force and compel them to pay them the price at the full rates for (good) grain ... 23. In Ahmadabad and its suburbs and the *parganas* of the said province some people have monopolized the sale and purchase of rice. No one can sell or buy without their sanction. Owing to this, rice bears a high price in Gujarat" (*Mir'āt*, I, 260-262). In 1647 we find the English factors at Ahmadabad apprehensive of the Governor, Shā'ista Khān's ambitions of becoming "the sole merchant of this place" and declare that if he succeeded in engrossing the indigo "wee may then expect shortly to fetch our butter and rice from him" (*Factories, 1646-50*, 130). This shows that till then these commodities had not been monopolized, and it is possible that the tendency became more marked under the scarcity conditions prevailing during the early years of Aurangzeb. Shā'ista Khān carried his commercial ambitions later on to Bengal. His panegyrist declares that before his arrival there "the officers of this province monopolized (the trade in) most articles of food and clothing and all merchandise and goods and sold them at whatever rates they wished .... This glorious commander, the founder of the foundation of justice and generosity,

But it was abandoned in the second year, not the least, perhaps, because "many of the cultivators (being in general a resolute harebrained folk)" rooted up their plants in protest.[28]

The peasant's indebtedness, the various cesses, the malpractices in the market and the imposition of monopolies must all have worked to enlarge the margin between the price obtaining in the secondary market and that paid to the peasant. The prices paid to the peasants themselves varied: *arsattha* documents from eastern Rajasthan show that village harvest prices could differ from the mean of such prices in the whole *pargana* by as much as 5 per cent or more.[29] Nevertheless the village and the local town market prices must generally have maintained a certain proportion. If the margin of difference became too large, merchants and buyers from the secondary market would try to buy from the peasants direct;[30] and it was noticed in such cases that the latter were shrewd enough to raise their prices immediately.[31] In fact we find cultivation responding closely, almost desperately, to market demand: the peasants of Gujarat replaced cotton with food crops under the incentive of high food prices following the great famine of 1630-2.[32] Similarly, in Sind and Bayana in the 1640s a slump in indigo

did not follow this ignoble practice and ordered that whosoever so wishes may buy and sell" (*Fathiya-i 'Ibriya*, f.127b). How far this order was seriously meant may be judged from the account of another contemporary witness: "The Nobobs [Shā'ista Khān's] Officers oppress the people, monopolize most Commodityes, even as grass for Beasts, canes, firewood, thatch, etc., nor doe they want wayes to oppress those people of all sorts who trade, whether natives or Strangers ..." (Master, II, 80).

[28] *Factories, 1630-33*, 324-5. The peasants referred to are those of the Agra province. The Dutch and English also banded together to oppose the monopoly, but climbed down very soon (ibid., *1630-33*, 327-8; *1634-36*, 1, 12). The monopoly also extended to Gujarat; the re-introduction of 'free trade' there is referred to in ibid., *1634-36*, 70, 142. The actual text of the *farmān* abolishing the imperial monopoly of "the purchase of indigo" is contained in Blochet, Suppl. Pers. 482, f.98a (date missing).

[29] See table 3 in S.P. Gupta, *Agrarian System of Eastern Rajasthan*, 85. The prices are for the years 1664 and 1730 in *parganas* Chatsu and Malarna.

[30] This is clear from our information for the indigo trade at Agra, where foreign merchants had the option of buying either from the local merchants or the peasants. See especially Pelsaert, 15-16. When grain became very scarce in Dehli in the early years of Aurangzeb's reign, "the people of the city flocked to the villages where grain was sold" (*'Ālamgīrnāma*, 611).

[31] As in the indigo tract near Agra. Cf. *Lett. Recd.*, VI, 235, 249; Pelsaert, 16.

[32] "Which ['great price' yielded by 'graine'] hath undoubtedly disposed of the country people to those courses which hath been most profitable for them and so discontinued the planting of cotton which could not have vented in proporcion of

prices caused a corresponding decline in indigo cultivation.[33] The most remarkable example of the peasant's readiness to cultivate anything which could sell better is offered by the rapid expansion of tobacco cultivation, where it appeared to a contemporary that the peasants, in fact, anticipated the market.[34]

Until now we have considered only the flow of goods from the villages to the towns. What of any reverse flow? There were some commodities for which towns served as distributive centres: salt, brought from distant places of extraction, must necessarily have passed through town markets, before reaching the hands of pedlars, who sold it in the villages; so too *guṛ*, in demand in villages which could not grow their own sugarcane.[35] When cloves – an article of import from overseas – became cheap in Agra, the low price induced everyone to buy, and in the villages "women and children wore necklaces made of cloves".[36] An important question is whether there was a rural demand for products of urban crafts as well. We may assume that the more prosperous *zamīndārs* must have sought superior quality cloth, jewellery and weapons fashioned in the towns.[37] But whether the peasants also contributed

former tymes, because the artificers and mechaniques of all sorts were so miserably dead or fledd ..." (*Factories, 1634-36*, 64).

[33] The fall in the demand for Sehwan indigo in the Middle East "hath soe admirably declined its vallue where it is made that the planters are almost beggered thereby, and therefore doe annually more or lesse reduce the wonted quantities made by them" (*Factories, 1642-45*, 136). For Bayana, see ibid., 202.

[34] Sujān Rāi, 454. See also Moreland, *Akbar to Aurangzeb*, 190-192, on the general tendency of the peasants "to follow the markets".

[35] The village pedlars are thus described in the *Tashrīḥu-l Aqwām* (1825), ff.167b-168a: "Carrying *ghī* or oil in a small jar in the hand, and salt and *guṛ* with balance, etc., in two pieces of coarse cloth, which they call *palla*, one put on the head, the other on the back, they go from house to house selling their wares in the villages." These hawkers are said to have belonged to "the poor" among the class of traders known as Bedehaks, Sārth-bāhaks or Banjīwālas. For information about *pherī-wāls*, pedlars, taking *guṛ* and salt from urban markets in Rajasthan, gleaned from records of early 19th century, see B.L. Gupta, *Trade and Commerce in Rajasthan during the 18th Century*, 78-79.

One would have liked to have earlier evidence. The nearest I have is Abū-l Faẓl's contemptuous remark about Hemū that he belonged to the "lowliest" Banya (*baqqāl*) caste of Dhūsars, and "with a thousand of indignities (*be-namakī*) had sold brackish salt (*namak-i shor*) in the streets" (*A.N.*, I, 337).

[36] Pelsaert, 24-25 (referring to large supplies of cloves in the later years of Akbar's reign).

[37] Cf. Moosvi, 301 & n. The demand may explain such statements as that of Salbancke (1609) about Sukkar, which is said to have consisted of "Weavers and Diers, which serve the Country round about" (*Purchas*, III, 85).

to such demand to any recognizable extent may well be doubted.[38] On the whole, the trade was heavily in one direction – from villages to town.

3. MOVEMENTS OF AGRICULTURAL PRICES

Before setting forth on our exploration of the evidence on agricultural prices, some words of caution are necessary. Agricultural prices varied sharply with the seasons and quality of harvests. Moreover, there were enormous differences in the prices prevailing in different regions. These facts greatly depreciate the value of much of the small amount of evidence that we possess. Nevertheless, where the prices quoted belonged to years of normal harvests, it should be permissible to draw comparisons. Similarly, from our study of the pattern of long-distance trade, we may claim to have obtained a little insight into the relative levels of prices in some of the provinces for a few important commodities; and with the help of this knowledge inter-regional comparisons can also be of use in establishing price trends.

The most detailed list of prices coming down from our period is to be found in the *Ā'īn*. From the words used by Abū-l Faẓl it seems clear that these are prices regarded as normal at the imperial court.[1] When the *Ā'īn* was written, Lahor had been the seat of the court for some years, but it may be a mistake to regard the prices as those ordinarily current in that city, for we are told that the arrival there of the court had greatly raised the prices of agricultural produce in the Panjab, so as to justify an increase in the revenue demand in the *ṣūba* by 20 per cent; this was withdrawn only when the court left that city.[2] The *Ā'īn's* prices are, therefore, likely to

[38] See the perceptive remarks by Tapan Raychaudhuri in *Cambridge Economic History of India*, I, 327. Moosvi, 307 n., seems to have missed this passage while commenting on Raychaudhuri's views.

[1] Abū-l Faẓl prefaces his price lists with the following explanation: "*Ā'īn* of the Prices of Provisions: Although during marches and the rains, etc., they vary greatly, yet some mean prices are tabulated below so that enquirers may find the means to be enlightened therein" (*Ā'īn*, I, 60). Moreland (*JRAS*, 1917, 815ff.) thought the prices given are those which the *mīr bakāwal* (superintendent of the imperial kitchen) deemed reasonable and adopted for buying provisions. This is unlikely because the *mīr bakāwal* seems to have made his purchases from distant areas, apparently where the best was available (*Ā'īn*, I, 53). The prices paid by him in such transactions would not have been affected by the journeys of the court, while this would naturally have been the case with the market of the camp from where the soldiers and others accompanying the court made their purchases.

[2] *A.N.*, III, 747.

be higher than those prevailing at Lahor in ordinary times by as much as a fifth. For comparison with later prices at Lahor, we have only one document, professedly abstracted from the register of market-dues at Shahdara-Lahor, dated January 1702.[3] We have unfortunately no knowledge of what the harvest had been like that year in the Panjab. The foodgrain prices that can be compared are as follows (all stated in rupees per *man-i-Shāhjahānī*, the necessary conversions having been made):

	Ā'īn-1 (Lahor:Court)	*Ā'īn*-2 (Lahor:Without Court)	January 1702 Lahor
Wheat	0.40	0.33	1.14
Sukhdās Rice	3.33	2.77	2.00
Mūng	0.60	0.50	1.00
Moṭh	0.40	0.33	1.00

With the exception of the *sukhdās* rice, a fine variety with a limited market,[4] the prices at Lahor appear to have increased substantially over the century – assuming that 1702-3 was a normal year, and allowing for the fact that January, preceding the rabi harvest, is undoubtedly a time when wheat, a rabi crop, should have fetched a higher price than the monthly average price for the year.

Since it happens that we have better price data for Agra during the seventeenth century, it is important to consider what relation the prices thought to be normal for Lahor when it contained the court (1586-98), bore to those prevalent at Agra. If the cash revenue-rates for the major crops are an index of the price levels between the two cities before 1586 – the rates were framed before that year – then the prices at Lahor were significantly lower than those at Agra; but the maximum differences in the rates of major crops did not exceed 20 per cent.[5] This continued to be the

[3] *Khulāṣatu-s Siyāq*, f.90a-b; Or.2026, ff.57a-59a.

[4] The *sukhdās* variety, praised by Sujān Rāi, 11, cannot now be identified.

[5] With the Agra *dastūrs* as 100, the Lahor *dastūrs* for major crops are: wheat: 81.99; gram, 80.05; barley, 93.50; mustard, 93.33; jowar, 89.98; lahdra, 99.87; rice, 81.50; sugarcane, 98.48; cotton, 92.59; indigo, 100.26 (Moosvi, 121, 124). The table in ibid., 100, shows that the Lahor *dastūrs* are conversions of the pre-1586 rates

case in the decade preceding the completion of the railway network (1861-70): with the Agra prices as 100, wheat at Lahor was 90.1, barley 86.9, and Jowar 90.2.[6] If the official assumption that the coming of the court raised Lahor prices by 20 per cent was at all justified by the prices which actually prevailed at Lahor after 1586, then we must assume that the *Ā'īn's* prices were probably a little higher than those that were current at Agra before 1586; they could not in any case have been lower.

If the *Ā'īn's* prices, then, represent the ceiling for the prices ordinarily prevalent at Agra before 1586, we may, on that basis, compare them with the prices we have for that city for the years 1637, 1638, 1670 and 1718. The prices for 1637-38 come from the books of the Dutch factory at Agra, stated month by month. For most of 1638 scarcity prevailed, the price rise being duly reflected in the monthly prices. The monthly accounts are complete for the years 1637 and 1638; quotations have also survived for January 1639 which are ignored below.[7] The 1670 prices are those of February-April, at the time of collection of the rabi harvest; these were apparently thought to be exceptionally low and to betoken plenty.[8] The prices reported from Agra in August-September 1718 were those of a period of considerable scarcity.[9] The various available prices are tabulated in Table 2.1.

(before the introduction of the *gaz-i Ilāhī* in that year), made according to the official schedule, which Moosvi, 91, 119-20, has convincingly reconstructed. The rates themselves are therefore unaffected by the 20%-enhancement in revenue, which was presumably made simply through raising the total assessments made on the basis of these rates.

6 Calculated from the 1861-70 prices indexed in Moosvi, 115-116.

7 The Dutch evidence for the Agra prices, 1637-38, was presented by Moreland in *JUPHS*, III (I), 146-161, esp. 149-50, 152-54. A fuller table of data abstracted from the same source is given in H.W. van Santen, 97. There are a few differences between Moreland and van Santen; I have generally followed the latter. What Moreland renders as "meal" is "gestemeel" (barley flour) in van Santen. I am grateful to my colleague, Mr Ishrat Alam for guiding me to van Santen and for explaining his text and tables.

8 "The household officers (*bayūtāt*) reported the grain prices of the capital, Akbarābād (Agra), to the Emperor, by whom joyous the Appearance and the Heart, happy the Faith and the World! ... [Prices quoted]. People sang their paeans of thanks on the harps of prayer...." (*Ma'āṣir-i 'Ālamgīrī*, 98). The printed text which has *raughan* only should be corrected by reference to MS. Add. 19,495, f.54b, which has *raughan-i zard*, i.e. ghee or *ghī*.

9 *Mir'ātu-l Ḥaqā'iq*, f.138b. For the prevalent scarcity, see ff.135a, 139a.

Table 2.1

Food Prices: Agra, 1638-1718, all in Rs per *man-i-Shāhjahānī*

	A'in	Annual average of monthly rates 1637	1638	Feb.-April 1670	August-September 1718
Wheat	0.40	-	-	1.14	-
Wheat flour	0.50	-	-	-	5.71
Barley flour	0.37	1.08	1.72	-	-
Gram	0.27	1.05	1.70	0.95	5.16
Moth	0.40	0.97	1.54	-	-
Mūng	0.60	-	-	-	6.15
Sukhdās rice	3.33	-	-	2.86	8.00
Ghī	3.50	8.39	9.52	10.00	20.00
Guṛ I	-	4.32	4.07	-	6.15
Guṛ II	-	3.41	2.55	-	5.41

A further comparison can be made of the rabi prices (March) of 1637, 1638 and 1670:

	Ā'īn	1637	1638	1670
Gram	0.27	1.00	1.82	0.95
Ghī	3.50	8.46	8.73	10.00

In studying the prices tabulated above, we have to bear in mind the fact that 1638 and 1718 were years of scarcity, while 1670 had a plentiful harvest. The ascent in prices is therefore unmistakable. By 1637, which seems to have been a normal year, prices were two to three times higher than the ceiling for pre-1586 Agra prices represented by the *Ā'īn*. In 1670, a year of plenty, the prices were about the same as in 1637; and prices of wheat, gram and *ghī* now were about three times those of the *Ā'īn* (the *sukhdās* variety of rice again forming the sole exception, as in the case of Lahor). Clearly, a great rise had occurred between 1586 and 1637; and the level attained seems to have continued till 1670.

The price of sugar is not infrequently quoted in the English commercial records of the period, and it may be worthwhile to trace its progress in some detail. Apart from a very highly refined product, called *nabāt*, and the red sugar, the *A'īn* gives the rates for two other varieties, white sugar candy (*qand-i safed*) and white (powdered) sugar (*shakkar-i safed*), viz. 7.33 and 4.27, respectively, in terms of rupees per *man-i-Shāhjahānī*.[10] In 1615 the latter variety seems to have fetched but Rs 2.75 to 3 in the region "betwixt Agra and Lahore".[11] Yet in 1639 the price of "candy" at Lahor was no less than Rs 11, and the best (powdered) "sugar" was quoted at Rs 7, coarser varieties being obtained for Rs 5.75 and 6.[12] In 1646 a "super-fine" variety of the latter fetched Rs 6;[13] and in 1651 the price was said "not to exceed" Rs 6.[14] Thus within the earlier part of the seventeenth century, sugar had risen by about 40 per cent or more, in the central regions of the Empire.

Finally, a word about the price of indigo, for which our information is much greater. What was reputedly the best variety in India was cultivated at and around Bayana in the vicinity of Agra. The details of its price history, gleaned largely from English commercial literature, may be relegated to a footnote.[15] So clear is this evidence that it should not be necessary to enter more than

[10] *Ā'īn*, I, 65.

[11] Steel and Crowther, *Purchas*, IV, 268. I take it that the "great Maund of fortie", in terms of which the price is quoted, is the *man-i Jahāngīrī* and not *man-i Akbarī*. In case the latter unit was still in use in the sugar trade, the rates, when stated in terms of *man-i Shāhjahānī*, would amount to Rs 3.33 to 3.66 per *man*.

[12] *Factories, 1637-41*, 135.

[13] Ibid., *1646-50*, 135.

[14] Ibid., *1646-50*, 62. Higher prices (Rs 9 and 8) had prevailed in Agra in 1638, but that was a scarcity year (van Santen, 95).

[15] Before setting out the information in tabulated form it may be noted that the *man-i Akbarī* remained in use for indigo at Agra throughout our period, and the prices are usually expressed in it. Where some other unit is used, the rate is converted into Rs per *man-i Akbarī* for convenience of comparison. If the indigo is of the growth of some other place than the Bayana tract proper, the place of origin comes first under description; if the price given is the price of Bayana indigo on delivery at Agra, Surat or Swally, this is indicated by putting the name of the place at the end.

Year	Rs per *man*	Description	Source
1595-6	10 to 16	Usual	*Ā'īn*, MSS (Add. 7652, 6552, 5645, &c.). Blochmann, I, 442 reads Rs 10 to 12 per *man*.
1609	16 to 24	Usual	*Lett. Recd.*, I, 28.
,,	25	Paid	Ibid.
1614	31	Paid, Surat(?)	Ibid., II, 194.
1614-5	34 & 36	Quoted	Ibid., III, 69-70
1615	36	Quoted, Agra	Steel & Crowther, *Purchas*, IV, 267.
1615	27 & 28	,,	*Lett. Recd.*, IV, 327.
1616	35	,,	Ibid., IV, 239, 327.

a few comments. Admittedly, the price curve is full of troughs and crests, but this is hardly surprising for a crop which was very

1616	29 to 33	Paid	Ibid., IV, 239.
,,	36 & 38	Price always at Agra	Ibid.
,,	36 & 37	Paid, Surat	Ibid., V, 110.
,,	30½ & 30	Paid, Agra	Foster, *Suppl. Cal.*, 109.
1617	28 to 36; average 33¼	Paid	*Lett. Recd.*, VI, 234-5, 245, 249.
1618	35	Assumed	*Factories,1622-23*, 284-5.
1624-5	28 to 32	Quoted	*F.1624-29*, 63.
1626	30	Usual	Pelsaert, 15.
1627	33¾ to 35	Paid	*F. 1624-29*, 189.
,,	35 to 36½ & 30	,,	Ibid., 208.
1627-8	32½ to 35	,,	Ibid., 228.
1628-9	36 & 37	,,	Ibid., 335.
1630	38	,,	*F. 1630-33*, 131.
1633	61	Paid. Monopolist's Price	*F. 1634-36*, 1, 2.
1633-4	62 plus 2	,,	Ibid., 12.
1635-6	45 to 56	Paid	Ibid., 206.
1639	45	Estimate, Swally	*F. 1637-41*, 192.
1640	40 & above	Paid	Ibid., 278.
1643	33 & below	,,	*F. 1642-45*, 136.
1644	26 to 31½	,,	Ibid., 202.
1644-5	37 to 40	,,	Ibid., 254.
1645	33	Koria. Quoted	Ibid., 304.
1645-6	40	Paid	*F.1646-50*, 33.
1646	42	Expected	Ibid., 62.
1646-7	43 & above	Quoted	Ibid., 114.
1647-8	40¾ to 43¾	Paid	Ibid., 202.
1648	42	Half dry. Quoted	Ibid., 219.
,,	43 5/8	Hindaun. Quoted	Ibid.
,,	36 & 37	Doab. Paid	Ibid.
1648-9	40 to 46	Quoted	Ibid., 276.
1649	35 & 36	,,	Ibid.
1650	47 & above	Hindaun. Quoted	*F. 1651-54*, 9.
,,	46	,, ,,	Ibid., 51.
1651	45¾	Khurja. Quoted	Ibid., 302.
1653	48	Quoted	Ibid., 221.
1655	33 & 38	Khurja. Paid	*F. 1655-60*, 18.
1655-6	33	Hindaun. Quoted	Ibid., 63.
1658	38	Paid	Ibid., 153.
1662	46 & 47	Quoted	*Journal Van Dircq van Andrichem's, etc.*, 204.
1663-4	100½	Quoted, Surat	*F. 1661-64*, 320.
1665	97 4/5	Paid, Surat	*F. 1665-67*, 5.
1667	52	Quoted, Surat	*F. 1668-69*, 3.
1668	51	Paid	Ibid., 6-7
1669-70	55	Expected, Surat	Ibid., 194.

vulnerable to natural disasters[16] and was raised predominantly for distant markets. Nevertheless, through all these fluctuations a steady rise is unmistakable; this continued even when the European demand began to fall off in the 1660s.[17] The year 1669-70 was one of plentiful harvests, as we have seen, and Bayana indigo was then stated to be "indifferent cheap",[18] but the anticipated price was about three times the one regarded as the maximum by Abū-l Faẓl, and twice the normal highest limit for the price set in 1609.

The Amber territories belonged largely to *ṣūba* Ajmer, but their proximity to Agra makes it natural for us to consider the comparatively rich price data from that area in the context of price movements in Agra and its immediate vicinity. Unluckily, the Amber material on prices begins after 1650, so that it tells us nothing about the trends in the first half of the seventeenth century. S. Nurul Hasan, K.N. Hasan and S.P. Gupta presented detailed data

---

If the 1669-70 price is as per delivery at Surat, the Agra price could not have been less than Rs 47 per *man*. Judging from the fact that in 1651 the transport charges of a camel load from Agra to Ahmadabad amounted to Rs 15, annas 3, or about Rs 1.7 per *man-i Akbarī* (*Factories, 1651-54*, 52), it may be assumed that the cost of transit between Agra and Surat could not have exceeded Rs 2.5 per *man*. Moreover goods carried on behalf of the English were exempt from all transit dues on this route (ibid., *1665-67*, 266), but they had to pay a brokerage of ten per cent to their own agents (ibid., *1668-69*, 7).

Tavernier, II, 7, says that "one generally pays" Rs 36 to 40 per *man* for the Bayana indigo. His experience of India ranged from 1640 to 1667, but he visited Agra only twice, in 1640-43 and in 1665-67. We can see that his statement could not have applied to the latter years and he is probably recollecting the prices current at the time of his earlier visit.

It is unfortunately not possible to trace the Bayana indigo prices after 1669-70 from the published English records.

van Santen, 15-16, offers a table of Bayana indigo prices from Dutch sources. It supplements our table by supplying prices for some years for which there is no quotation in English records. On the whole, it corroborates the English evidence pretty well. van Santen's table, however, lacks any quotations for the years 1664 to 1678, and thus omits any indication of the great ascent in indigo prices in the mid-1660s. It furnishes, on the other hand, quotations for two subsequent years, 1679 (Rs 34½) and 1686 (about Rs 40½). These prices, though lower than the price expected in 1669-70, are still twice and two and a half times the maximum set in the *Ā'īn-i Akbarī*.

[16] Cf. Pelsaert, 13.

[17] See table of quantities of Bayana indigo annually purchased by the Dutch East India Company in van Santen, 140.

[18] *Factories, 1668-69*, 194: Bayana indigo here appears under the designation "Lahore indigo", a survival from the earlier times when Lahor was the main mart for it for overland merchants.

on prices of major foodgrains drawn from *arasaṭṭhas* for the period *c.*1650-1750; and then S.P. Gupta and S. Moosvi compiled price indices of all crops, weighted according to tax values, for the period 1665-50.[19] The weighted price indices show a fair long-term stability (with the expected large annual fluctuations) from 1665 to 1706. A steep rise occurs thereafter, so that the long-term price level established during 1706-50 seems to have been twice as high as the one prevailing before 1706. The same trend is apparent in the prices of Amber indigo: while five quotations from the years 1667-90 yield an average price of Rs 26.29 per *man*, twelve quotations from the years 1712-37 yield an average of Rs 45.17.[20]

For Gujarat we are lucky to have price data from both halves of the seventeenth century. van Twist tells us that before the 1630-32 famine, wheat ordinarily sold there at a rate equal to Re 0.79 per *man-i-Shāhjahānī*.[21] This is corroborated by a stray quotation for Surat in 1618 (Re 0.77).[22] If we disregard the high prices reported during the 1630-32 famine and its aftermath, we still find prices at a substantially raised level in the 1640s. van Santen has collected nine quotations for wheat from the Dutch records for various months during the four years 1641-4: these range from Re 0.87 to Rs 2.50, but the average is Rs 1.33 per *man-i Shāhjahānī*.[23] A similar rise is indicated in the case of rice from van Santen's quotations. It was sold at Surat in 1609 at Rs 1.15-1.20 and in 1611 at Rs 1.14 per *man-i Shāhjahānī*. There are ten quotations for rice at Surat during the years 1641-4, the rates ranging from Rs 1.32 to Rs 3.00, the average Rs 1.61-1.85.[24] For the second half of the century, the published quotations from the English and Dutch records are too few to enable us to say anything with confidence, but van Santen's tables suggest, at any rate, that there was no decline in wheat and rice prices from the levels reached in the 1640s.[25] In 1726 (28 February), when cheapness was gratefully

[19] *PIHC* (Patiala Session, 1967), 345-68; *IESHR*, XII (2) (1975), 183-93.

[20] *PIHC* (Patiala Session, 1967), 353; S.P. Gupta, *Agrarian System of Eastern Rajasthan*, 86. No prices are quoted for the years between 1690 and 1712.

[21] van Twist, 68.

[22] van Santen, 93. In 1611, it is true, the English purchased wheat at Surat for Rs 1.36 per *man-i Shāhjahānī* (*Lett. Recd.*, I, 141); but, as Moreland (*Akbar to Aurangzeb*, 171) points out, the transaction was made at a disadvantage and at a season when wheat must have been selling at peak prices. In February 1619 "corn" put aboard a Bantam-bound vessel was invoiced at an equivalent of Re 0.91 per *man-i Shāhjahānī* (*Factories, 1618-21*, 83).

[23] van Santen, 93. [24] Ibid., 92. [25] Ibid., 92-93.

recorded at Ahmadabad, wheat cost Rs 1.77 per *man-i Shāhjahānī* and rice Rs 1.66.[26]

The trend in foodgrains is paralleled in van Santen's table for *ghī*. The prices quoted from the years 1615-16 to 1623 (four quotations) for Surat are in the range Rs 6.99-7.99 per *man-i Shāhjahānī*, averaging Rs 7.64-7.89. There are nine quotations for the years 1641-4: the range, Rs 6.81 to 10.16, and the average Rs 8.70.[27] In 1700 the price quoted was Rs 16.54;[28] but in 1726, at Ahmadabad, the price ranged within the year from Rs 11.86 to Rs 16, the lower price prevailing when provisions were reported to be cheap.[29]

The upward movement is discernible in Gujarat sugar prices as well. In 1613 "powder sugar" sold at Rs 4.44 per *man-i Shāhjahānī* at Ahmadabad;[30] and Terry, whose experience was confined to Gujarat and Malwa (1616-19), calculates on the basis of its being usually priced at Rs 4.93.[31] In 1622, however, sugar was declared to be "very dear" at Ahmadabad, and the price quoted was the equivalent of Rs 9.11;[32] subsequently, in 1628 the rates quoted kept to between Rs 8 and 9.[33] The price at Surat in 1618 was Rs 9.24;[34] next year, it was Rs 7.11 or 8.[35] In 1635, after the famine, it stood at Rs 11.77.[36] van Santen's nine quotations for the years 1641-4 yield an average of Rs 8.51 to 9.31 from a range of Rs 4.42 to 10.51.[37] The 1726 price at Ahmadabad was Rs 10.00.[38] The quotations for *guṛ* are scantier, but they indicate a consistent upward movement: Rs 3.07 in 1623; Rs.3.31(average of eight quotations), 1641-4; Rs 5.50 in 1645 – all from Surat.[39] In 1726 at Ahmadabad it fetched Rs 5.71.[40]

[26] *Mir'ātu-l Ḥaqā'iq*, f.384a. On 6 May the same year at the same city, wheat fetched Rs 2.96 and on 23 August Rs 3.64 per *man-i Shāhjahānī*; rice cost on these dates Rs 1.41and Rs 2 (ibid., ff.405a, 437b). I have assumed that the original quotations are in the Gujarat *man*.

[27] van Santen, 94. [28] Ibid. [29] *Mir'ātu-l Ḥaqā'iq*, ff.384a, 405a, 437b.

[30] *Lett. Recd.*, I, 305-6.

[31] Terry, *Early Travels*, 296-7: "after it is well refined, [sugar] may be bought for two pence the pound or under". He usually reckons 1 Re as equal to 2s. 6d. (ibid., 284, 302).

[32] *Factories, 1622-23*, 109. [33] Ibid., *1624-29*, 221; *1630-33*, 61.

[34] van Santen, 95.

[35] *Factories, 1618-21*, 102. Unless the reference is to candied sugar, the price given in *Lett. Recd.*, VI, 280, for Surat is impossibly high. It works out at Rs 14.00 to 15.00 for a period before 1617. Sugar candy fetched Rs 12.44 in 1616 at Surat (ibid., IV, 299).

[36] *Factories, 1634-36*, 177. [37] van Santen, 95.

[38] *Mir'ātu-l Ḥaqā'iq*, f.437b. [39] van Santen, 95.

[40] *Mir'ātu-l Ḥaqā'iq*, f.437b.

Moreland offers a detailed study of the price history of Sarkhej indigo, the best variety of that dye grown in Gujarat.[41] His interpretation of the evidence is, however, coloured by the belief that the "standard" price prevailing before 1613 was Rs 18 for the Gujarat *man*, equal to half a *man-i Shāhjahānī*. Once he accepts this as the earlier standard, he can observe no rise in the normal price during the period down to the 1660s.[42] But reflection suggests that the "standard" price of Rs 18 could hardly have prevailed in Akbar's later years. This is because the Bayana indigo was much superior in quality to the Sarkhej, and, therefore, much more expensive;[43] yet the *Ā'īn's* normal price for Bayana indigo, converted into the same Gujarat *man*, was only Rs 6 - 9.60; and in 1609 the "usual" price quoted for it was, for the Gujarat *man*, Rs 9.60 to 14.40.[44] Surely, then, it is out of the question for Sarkhej indigo to have borne a price above Rs 8 in 1595 or Rs 12 in 1609. Indeed, in 1609 its actual price was reported to be just Rs 10 to 12.[45] Moreover, Moreland's "standard" price occurs in English factors' statements made in 1613 and 1614,[46] so that, at best, it could have been true only of the years after 1609. Moreland's table of Sarkhej indigo prices largely corroborates Tavernier's statement of its normal price, Rs 15 to 20 for the Gujarat *man*, during the period of his stay in India, 1640-67.[47] Given this level, the ascent in its price after 1595 was surely substantial. Unluckily, there are no price data at hand for Sarkhej indigo after 1667.

There has been some dispute about price trends in seventeenth-century Bengal. Moreland, who believed that prices did not rise in India generally, argued that Bengal was an exception, for here prices rose in the 1650s to remove previously existing price differences between Bengal and other regions.[48] Susil Chaudhuri has taken issue with this and shown that even after the 1650s Bengal maintained a much lower price-level than other parts of the country.[49] In his last years Aurangzeb could still refer to the reputed "cheapness" prevalent in Bengal and Bihar.[50] But cheapness

[41] *Akbar to Aurangzeb*, 160-64.

[42] Ibid., 164.

[43] See, e.g., Tavernier, II, 7. The Bayana indigo, he says, cost in his time, from Rs 36 to 40 per *man-i Akbarī*, while the Sarkhej variety fetched Rs 22½ to 30 (rate adjusted to the same weight).

[44] See table in footnote 15 of this section.

[45] *Lett. Recd.*, I, 28.

[46] Ibid., I, 305-6; II, 152.

[47] Tavernier, II, 7.

[48] *Akbar to Aurangzeb*, 178-81.

[49] *Trade and Commercial Organisation in Bengal, 1650-1750*, 241-48.

[50] *Kalimāt-i Ṭaiyabāt*, f.50a.

is a relative matter: if prices rose in other parts of the country, they might also rise in Bengal though not so greatly as to equalize. It is, therefore, difficult to dismiss out of hand the English factors' report from Hugli in 1658 that provisions were "now three times as deare as formerly", so as to necessitate enhancements in the allowed expenses.[51] Quotations in English records for sugar prices at Hugli in 1650, 1661 and 1683 show them ranging from Rs 3 to 5 per *man-i Shāhjahānī* during seasons other than the rainy season, when prices normally rose.[52] This indicates that prices for sugar in Bengal were now about the same as had prevailed in the central regions and Gujarat in the early years of the century. If Bengal prices had always been lower than those farther inland, an increase in its price level must have taken place by the middle of the century. For the second half of the century, we have Om Prakash's table for prices of rice, wheat, *ghī* and sugar, derived from Dutch invoices of Bengal exports for the period 1657-58 to 1713-14. There are great gaps in respect of both years and commodities. As they stand, they show no recognizable trend and may suggest stability over the period.[53] The evidence from Bengal thus parallels that from eastern Rajasthan, which too, as we have seen, exhibits a similar stability for the years 1665-1706.

Evidence for foodgrain and other prices comes from other areas as well; but much of it consists of stray reports or statements and does not enable us to trace price movements over time.[54]

[51] *Factories, 1655-60*, 407. Om Prakash's disbelief in this statement rests squarely on the assumption that "the Madras prices did not rise between 1650 and 1661" (*Dutch East India Company and the Economy of Bengal, 1630-1720*, 251 n.); he makes no allusion to Susil Chaudhuri's earlier criticism of Moreland on identical grounds.

[52] *Factories, 1646-50*, 337; C.R. Wilson, ed., *Early Annals of the English in Bengal*, I, 380; Hedges, I, 75. The rates are based on a conversion of "bale" into *man-i Shāhjahānī*, for which see Appendix B.

[53] Om Prakash, 251-3.

[54] Bhīmsen recalled in his old age that in 1658, some fifty years before he wrote his memoirs, "foodgrains such as wheat and gram were selling at 2½ *mans* per Rupee and *juwār* and *bājrī* at 3½ *mans*". He adds that in the second regnal year of Aurangzeb (1659-60) in the Dakhin generally wheat and gram sold at 2 *mans* per rupee (*Dilkushā*, ff.15b, 20b). But either his memory was playing him false or the low prices did not prevail for long. We are fortunate in possessing an official report of prices at the Aurangabad market in May 1661. This shows that wheat was then selling at ¾ *man* per Re and gram at just under one *man*. *Juwārī* was priced at a little above one *man* per rupee and *bājrī* at a little less than one *man*. The report, however, agrees with Bhīmsen in rating *guṛ* at 20 *sers* per Re and *ghī* at 4 *sers*, although it gives these prices for the lowest grades only (*Waqā'i' Dakhin*, 37-44.

Our study of such evidence as is usable for the purpose suggests that there were two substantial ascents in long-term price levels: one during the early decades of the seventeenth century, with the wave affecting Bengal possibly slightly later; and the other after the middle of the century.[55] The factors behind these ascents need to be examined. Since these could lie at least partly in the supply of the money-metal, room has been found in Appendix C for a detailed scrutiny of the gold and copper prices of the silver rupee, the standard coin of the Mughal Empire in the seventeenth century. It will be seen that the evidence for a general fall in the value of the rupee relative to gold is quite definite, and it is possible to work out this decline in some detail. We find, for example, that if the price level expressed in silver was 100 at the time of the *Ā'īn*, it should have risen to over 150 in the 1620s; another ascent in the 1650s and 1660s put it somewhere around 178. Thereafter it fell a little and stood at about 146 by the end of the century. It may be observed that, not only do the data of agricultural prices (as in Eastern Rajasthan and Bengal) confirm this later recovery in silver, the agreement between the earlier trends in silver prices and agricultural prices (as established from evidence from the central regions and Gujarat) is also quite close.

Owing to massive demonetization of copper in the Mughal Empire, copper prices fell heavily during *c.* 1600-20 (see Appendix C). But after 1620 silver steadily fell in value relative to copper as well; and so copper too now became an index of rising price-level.

In our study of agrarian trade we found that while the village did not materially depend on the produce of the towns, the towns absorbed a large portion of the produce of the village. This was

---

Cf. also the prices-report from the *sarkār* of Ramgir, 1662, *Daftar-i Dīwāni*, 171-5; *Waqā'i' Dakhin*, 75-77).

Grain prices are also quoted for various dates during 1678-80 in *Waqā'i' Ajmer*, 14, 148, 343, 599, 703. But in the absence of earlier data relating to the same area, the information is of hardly any use for our present purpose.

See Arasaratnam, *Merchants, Companies and Commerce,* 335-38, for the "steady increase in the price of rice" in Coromandel from the beginning of the 17th century to mid-18th century.

[55] A view contrary to these conclusions has been put forward by S. Subrahmanyam, ed., *Money and the Market in India, 1100-1700*, 203-9. The reader may compare the two discussions and judge for himself.

largely made possible because of the heavy land-revenue demand. Land revenue pumped back into the towns the money that had gone out to draw food and raw materials from the countryside, or, when the tax was received in kind, simply caused these necessary supplies to be carted to the towns. When an increase in agricultural prices took place, the balance could not be restored merely by an increase in the prices of urban manufactures, since they had a very limited market in the villages. It could be restored only by an increase in land-revenue collections in money or by a shift to crop-sharing. Since the land revenue accounted for by far the larger portion of the peasant's surplus, it follows that each tax increase in terms of money would correspondingly neutralize any advantage that the peasant might obtain through a rise in the price of his produce.[56]

[56] Conversely, the peasant would be in trouble if the prices fell even temporarily. The Surat factors in November 1644 reported advices from Agra "of the small quantity of [indigo] seed sowed this year (occationed by the mean price that indico hath in Agra been sold for the two passed years, at which rates people under so great taxations cannot subsist)" (*Factories, 1642-45*, 202).

CHAPTER III

MATERIAL CONDITIONS OF THE LIFE OF THE PEASANTRY

1. GENERAL DESCRIPTION

"The common people", declares a Dutch observer during the reign of Jahāngīr, live in "poverty so great and miserable that the life of the people can be depicted or accurately described only as the home of stark want and the dwelling place of bitter woe."[1] To attempt a description of the normal articles of consumption of the peasant in our period is really tantamount to outlining the lowest possible level of subsistence – a dictum with which most contemporary writers would probably have readily agreed.[2]

It is a pity that on the very important subject of the quantity of food consumed by the peasants our sources are not very helpful. We are, however, slightly better served with regard to the kinds of food which entered into popular diet. It is naturally to be expected that in Bengal, Orissa, Sind and Kashmir, rice, being the major crop, should have formed the staple diet of the masses;[3] a similar position was enjoyed by rice, *juwārī* and *bājrā* in Gujarat.[4] But, generally speaking, it was the coarsest varieties out of his produce which the peasant was able to retain for his own family. We know that in Kashmir the rice eaten by the ordinary people was very coarse;[5]

[1] Pelsaert, 60.

[2] To what, asks Bhīmsen, did southern India owe its innumerable temples, some of them without a peer in the world? To the fact, says he, that the soil is immensely productive while the expenses of the inhabitants on bare subsistence are so little. This was the reason why the *rājas* seizing the surplus, could devote enormous resources to the construction of the great temples of the country (*Dilkushā*, ff.112b-113b). This passage would have better illustrated Marx's argument that a larger surplus could arise owing to lower costs of subsistence, than the statement for Egypt that he quotes from Diodorus (*Capital*, I, 521-2). Shivājī is reputed to have said concerning "the Common People": "Money is inconvenient for them: give them Victuals and an Arse-Clout, it is enough" (Fryer, II, 66).

[3] For Bengal, *Ā'īn*, I, 389; Fitch, Ryley, 119, and *Early Travels*, 28; Bernier, 438. For Orissa, *Ā'īn*, I, 391; for Sind, ibid., 556; and for Kashmir, ibid., 564.

[4] *Ā'īn*, I, 485. "Some Doll and Rice being mingled together and boyled, make Kitcheree, the common Food of the Country" (Hamilton, I, 161). Fryer, II, 119, says in general of India, but probably thereby meaning only Gujarat and the western coast, that "Boil'd Rice, Nichany [the ragi millet], Millet and (in great scarcity) Grass-Roots are the food of the ordinary People".

[5] *T.J.*, 300.

and in Bihar the "indigent" were compelled to eat the "pea-like grain", *kisārī*, which used to cause sickness.[6] In *sarkār* Sehwan (Sind), the peasants (*ra'īyat*) lived on the seeds of a wild grass (locally called *dair*) growing around Lake Manchhar, for quite a long period each year.[7] Despite the fact that wheat flourished best in the Agra-Dehli region, it did not form part of the "food of the common people", which here consisted of rice, millets and pulses.[8] Similarly, though Malwa, as we have seen, had wheat enough for export, Terry, whose experience was mainly gained there, says that "the ordinary sort of people" did not eat wheat, but used the flour of "a coarser grain" (probably *juwār*).[9]

Foodgrains were generally supplemented by a few vegetables or pot-herbs.[10] Fish entered into the mass diet in such provinces as Bengal, Orissa, Sind and Kashmir.[11] On account of both indigence and religious scruples (against beef and pork), meat was but rarely consumed by the peasant.[12]

6 *Ā'īn*, I, 416.

7 *Maẕhar-i-Shāhjahānī*, 70-1. The author says that if the peasants did not have this resource to fall back upon, they would not have survived under certain (oppressive) *jāgīrdārs*.

8 J. Xavier, tr. Hosten, *JASB*, NS, XXIII (1927), 121; Bernier, 283. Pelsaert, 60-61, speaking specifically of the workmen of Agra, says: "For their monotonous daily food they have nothing but a little *khichrī* ('kitchery' in the text), made of green pulse [*moṭh*] mixed with rice... eaten with butter in the evening; in the day time they munch a little parched pulse or other grain, which they say suffices for their lean stomachs." (See, however, Brij Narain, *Indian Economic Life, Past and Present*, 14-15, for a criticism of this passage.) It is curious that none of our sources should mention barley, which must also have been commonly eaten. Its price in the *Ā'īn*, I, 60, is the same as that of ordinary gram.

9 "Both toothsome, wholesome and hearty" and "made up in round broad and thick cakes [*chapātīs*]" (Terry, *Voyage to East India*, reprint [London, 1777], 87, 199). This statement does not occur in the first version of Terry's journal, reprinted in *Early Travels*.

10 Beans and other vegetables were usually on sale in the smallest villages, according to Tavernier, I, 38, 238. In Bengal "three or four sorts of vegetables" were included among "the chief [articles of] food of the common people". (Bernier, 438). In Orissa the brinjal was commonly eaten (*Ā'īn*, I, 391). "Vegetables of different kinds" were eaten in Kashmir (ibid., 564; *T.J.*, 300).

11 *Ā'īn*, I, 389, 391, 556, 564. Manrique, I, 65, however, says of Bengal: "fish is little eaten, especially by those who live inland."

12 "In the large village there is generally a Musalman governor and there you find sheep, fowl and pigeons for sale," but not "in the places where there are only Banians [Hindus]" (Tavernier, I, 38). Roe, journeying from Surat to Burhanpur, complains that despite the country being "plentifull, especially of cattle", the Banians "that will kyll nothing inhabiting all over, yet by the same reason they would sell us none" (Roe, 67). In Agra the workmen "know little of the taste of

It has been suggested earlier that the output of *ghī* per capita was higher in Mughal times than now. This is shown among other things by the fact that it was a constant part of the staple diet in the Agra region[13] and western India,[14] and was consumed by the better-off in Bengal.[15] The people of Assam were, however, utterly unfamiliar with it and regarded it with abhorrence.[16] In Kashmir too, the common people cooked their food in water; and walnut-oil and *ghī* were regarded as delicacies.[17]

Tavernier declares that "even in the smallest villages ... sugar and other sweetmeats, dry and liquid, can be procured in abundance".[18] And one may assume from this that *guṛ* at any rate was commonly consumed in the villages. As for salt, its price in terms of wheat quoted in the *Ā'īn* was lower than those at Agra and Lahor in the 1860s; but the railways brought about a substantial reduction in salt prices, so that in 1894 at the two places salt was worth in wheat a little over half of what it was worth in 1595-96.[19] By *c.*1900, then, salt consumption per capita should have been substantially higher than in Mughal times. In the seventeenth century, costs of transport made salt exceptionally scarce and dear in Bengal;[20] and in parts of Bengal and in Assam, people were

---

meat" (Pelsaert, 60). In Bengal "they will eate no flesh, nor kill no beast" (Fitch, Ryley 119, *Early Travels*, 28). Manrique was held at a distance by the villagers in Orissa as belonging to a people "who eat fowls as well as cows' and pigs' flesh"; the slaughter of peacocks by members of his party aroused the greatest indignation (Manrique, II, 105-13). The people of Assam, however, had no such inhibitions and ate almost everything (*'Ālamgīrnāma*, 726; *Fatḥiya 'Ibriya*, f.36a). The people of Badrinath territory in the Himalayan kingdom of Srinagar ate mutton, "which makes them stronger than Hindus" (Antonio de Andrade, 1624, quoted in C. Wessels, *Early Jesuit Travellers*, 52). For meat as a principal article of diet in Ladakh, see Desideri, 78.

13 Xavier, 124; Pelsaert, 61. 14 Terry, *Early Travels*, 296; 1777 reprint, 198-9.

15 Manrique, I, 64-5. Cf. Bernier, 438. Fitch, Ryley, 119, *Early Travels*, 28, speaks of "milke" not butter. In 1810-11, in Bhagalpur district (Bihar), bordering on Bengal, *ghī* was reported to be "a luxury the daily use of which falls to a very small proportion of the community" (Buchanan, *Bhagalpur Report*, 186).

16 *'Ālamgīrnāma*, 726; *Fatḥiya 'Ibriya*, f.36a, ed., 68. 17 *T.J.*, 300-1.

18 Tavernier, I, 238. Cf. also Terry, *Early Travels*, 325: he says the vegetarian "Gentiles" live upon "herbs and milke and butter and cheese and sweet meates, of which they make divers kindes". In view of these statements, it is surprising that Moreland should believe "the large consumption of sweetmeats" to be "a comparatively modern feature of Indian life" (*India at the Death of Akbar*, 272).

19 Moosvi, 329-30. The best contemporary description of the methods used in the Sambhar Lake and the Salt Range is in Sujān Rāi, 55, 75. The disappearance now of the caste and industry of the *nūnias*, who obtained salt from nitrous soils, is obviously due to the decline in its price.

20 *Ā'īn*, I, 39.

driven to use as substitute a bitter salty substance extracted from the ashes of banana stalks.[21] The use of capsicums or chillies, today a necessary ingredient in every meal, however humble, was not then known.[22] Spices such as cumin seed, coriander seed and ginger were probably occasionally within the peasant's reach,[23] but cloves, cardamoms and pepper were obviously far too expensive for him, at least, in the central regions.[24] When cloves were cheapest, before the Dutch imposed their monopoly on sea-borne trade with Indonesia, they were looked upon by the villager, not, apparently, as an article of food, but as ornaments fit to adorn the necks of his wife and children.[25]

During certain seasons, the peasants were presumably able to enjoy fruits of the more common kind as well as those growing wild.[26]

There is practically no information as to the prevalence of *pān* eating in the countryside, and one may doubt if the habit could have been indulged in by the mass of the people. The intoxicant, *tāṛī* or toddy (sap-wine), was frequently noticed – and consumed – by European travellers, but it is obvious that its consumption

21 *Haft Iqlīm*, 95; *Fatḥiya 'Ibriya*, f.32b, ed., 62. 22 See Chapter I, Sec.3.

23 As may be judged from the prices given in the *Ā'īn*, I, 55-6. Cumin seed (*zīra*), coriander seed (*siyāhdāna*, or *kalaunji*) and aniseed (*ajwā'in*) appear in the *dastūrs* as well. For ginger, see also Terry, *Early Travels*, 324, and 1777 reprint, 198.

24 Prices given in the *Ā'īn*. Tavernier, II, 10, says cardamom "is only used in Asia at the tables of nobles". Terry, declares in his second version (1777 reprint, 198) that "the meaner sort of the people there eat rice with green ginger and a little pepper".

25 Pelsaert, 24-5. He is speaking of the early years of the 17th century, when, according to him, cloves fetched Rs 60-80 per "maund" at Agra. Allowing for the difference between the *Akbarī* and *Jahāngīrī* weights, this accords with the rate given in the *Ā'īn*, viz. Rs 60 for *man-i Akbarī*. As Moreland has shown, the *Ā'īn's* price works out, in terms of wheat, to at least 15 times the modern price for cloves (*JRAS*, [1918], 379).

26 Thus, in the Mewar hills cultivation was rare, but mangoes plentiful: not so sweet and tasty as elsewhere, they formed (in the season, obviously) the staple diet of the "humble masses", who got sick thereby (Badāūnī, II, 234-5). Fruits were more commonly eaten in Bengal (Fitch, Ryley, 119, *Early Travels*, 28); and in Assam, oranges were so common as to sell at the rate of 10 for one copper coin (*Fatḥiya 'Ibriya*, f.26a-b, ed., 48). Coconut was, of course, on a different plane altogether, but the areas (e.g. Malabar: cf. Tavernier, I, 197) where it formed part of the staple diet, largely lay outside the limits of the Mughal empire. In 1897 it was said of the poorer strata in the villages of Uttar Pradesh that "the many jungle fruits and roots in addition to the village mango crop ... innutritious as they are" helped to keep them alive in the critical period before the standing crop was harvested (Crooke, *North-Western Provinces*, 274).

was less widespread inland than in Gujarat and the Dakhin.[27] The extent of the use of opium is difficult to judge. Abū-l Faẓl speaks of the practice of the doping of small children by "the high and low" as if it was a peculiar custom confined to Malwa,[28] whereas in more recent days it was found to be much more widespread. Tobacco smoking had already become a mass habit by the end of the seventeenth century. Speaking ostensibly of India in general, but really of Gujarat and the western coast, Fryer refers to "the ordinary People" smoking "a Pipe of Tobacco",[29] while we know that by this time the "poore sort" had taken to smoking the cheroot in Coromandel.[30] From Sujān Rāi's rhetoric one may assume that people in northern India were also rapidly learning to smoke.[31]

The facts we have adduced above do not easily lend themselves to the purpose of an exact comparison. But, speaking generally, if we take only the middle and poorer strata of the Indian peasantry, at around 1900, the change in diet would seem to have been inconsiderable. The peasant of Mughal times was more fortunate with *ghī*; his modern descendant had more salt and three entirely new articles of food, maize, potatoes and chillies. But this was nearly all.

In regard to clothing, our authorities are generally brief and precise. Of Hindūstān, the country "from Bhera to Bihar", Bābur observes: "Peasants and the poor (*ra'īyat o reza*) go about completely bare-footed. They tie on a thing called *langūta*, a decency-clout which hangs two spans below the navel. From the tie of this pendant, another clout, beneath it, is passed between the thighs and made fast behind. Women also tie on a cloth (*lung*), one-half of which goes round the waist, the other is thrown over the head".[32]

[27] For Gujarat see Finch in *Early Travels*, 175; Mundy 32-3; Ovington, 142-3. For the Dakhin (western coast), see Abbé Carre, I, 227; he carefully distinguishes between toddy, a wine, and "arrack", which was "a spirit made out of toddy which they distil". Bābur noticed villagers collecting date-toddy liquor in the Chambal valley between Bayana and Dholpur, and he describes the method of extracting this as well as the *tāṛī* proper (*Bāburnāma*, ed., 458-9; Bev., II, 508-9). Mundy, when passing near Banaras, but to the south of the Ganga, came across "aboundance of Tarree trees" which he had not seen for the previous twenty days of his journey from Agra. He was told, however, that the trees were grown for their leaves, used for mats, and not for the liquor (Mundy, 124-5).

[28] *Ā'īn*, I, 455.

[29] Fryer, II, 119. See also Abbé Carre's observation, on the western coast (1673), of the porters "always smoking" tobacco (Abbé Carre, I, 227).

[30] Bowrey, 97.

[31] Sujān Rāi, 454.

[32] *Bāburnāma*, ed., 467-68. Mrs Beveridge's translation, II, 519, and Thackston's 351, need to be considerably modified in the light especially of 'Abdu-r Raḥīm

In other words, just the shortest dhoti sufficed for men and a sari for women; and nothing or little else was worn. In Jahāngīr's reign an English factor at Agra declared that "the plebeian sort is so poor that the greatest part of them go naked in their whole body [save] their privities, which they cover with a linen [cotton] coverture".[33] Fitch says the same thing while speaking of Banaras, and adds that in winter, in lieu of wool "the men wear quilted gowns of cotton like to our mattraces and quilted caps".[34]

The clothing of the ordinary people was even more brief in Bengal. "Large numbers of men and women", says Abū-l Faẓl, "go naked and do not wear anything except for the loin-cloth (*lung*)."[35] Furthermore, in Orissa "women do not cover anything except for the privy parts and a large number make their coverings from leaves of trees".[36]

On the other side, in Sind, "the people of the countrye (I meane those which inhabitt out of the cities) are of moste part verye rude, and goe naked from the waste upwards, with turbants on their hedds".[37] In Kashmir cotton was not worn at all; both men and women put on just a single woollen garment, called *pattū*, which came down to the ankles. They kept it unwashed on their bodies for three or four years till it was completely tattered.[38]

In Gujarat the women's attire was described as comprising "a *Lungy* being tied loose over their shoulders Belt wise and tucked between their Legs in nature of short Breeches", and a short bodice, these two "being all their Garb, going constantly without Shooes

Khān-i Khānān's standard Persian translation (Or. 3714, ff.411b-2b).

33 *Lett. Recd.*, VI, 187.

34 Fitch, Ryley, 107; *Early Travels*, 22. Salbancke, writing from Agra, says: "indeed woollen cloth is so rare a matter to be seen worn by the people of this country, by reason of the dearness of it and the cheapness of their own cotton" (*Lett. Recd.*, VI, 200). This was substantially true even about 1900, and the lowest price of a woollen blanket as given in the *Ā'īn*, I, 111, was only slightly higher in terms of wheat than that obtaining at the beginning of the 20th century (*JRAS*, 1918, 381; Crooke, *North-Western Provinces*, 273).

35 *Ā'īn*, I, 389. Cf. Fitch, Ryley, 118-9, *Early Travels*, 28; Manrique, I, 61-2.

36 *Ā'īn*, I, 391. Cf. Bowrey, 208: "The Ourias... are very poore, weare no better habit than a Lungee, or a white cloth made fast about their waste."

In Assam, we are told, "it is not the custom to wear the turban, gown, drawers or shoes or to sleep on cots; they tie a piece of *kirpāsī* [calico] on the head and *lungī* on the waist and put a scarf round their shoulders. In winter some of the wealthy people wear a *nīm-jāma* [waist-coat] of the fashion of *Ya'qūb-khānī*" (*Fatḥiya 'Ibriya*, f.47a, ed., 70; *'Ālamgīrnāma*, 727; Tavernier, II, 223).

37 Withington in *Early Travels*, 218.

38 *Ā'īn*, I, 564; *T.J.*, 301; Pelsaert, 35.

and Stockins".[39] Though we have no direct evidence bearing upon the point, conditions were probably similar in the Mughal Dakhin, a large cotton-growing area. On the other hand, the scantiness of clothing became very marked as one went into Golkunda and southern India.[40]

There can, therefore, be little doubt that the change by 1900 in respect of clothing had been substantial, pitiful as conditions still were. Bābur's description, for example, might yet have held true of parts of eastern Uttar Pradesh, but not for the Doab or Panjab. Similarly, despite the great poverty of the Bengal villages, the sari worn by women, at any rate, ruled out a statement from being made any longer in the strain of Abū-l Faẓl.

The available information concerning the dwelling places of the peasants may be rapidly surveyed. In Bengal the ordinary hut is said to be, as "in the most part of India", "very little and covered with straw";[41] it was made by roping bomboos together[42] upon "walls" or rather plinths of mud excavated at the site.[43] In Orissa the walls were made of reeds.[44] In Bihar "most houses" had roofs of earthenware tiles.[45] The huts of the peasants of the Doab are

[39] Fryer, II, 116-7. Though he purports here to be giving a description of "East-India", his knowledge is patently restricted to Gujarat and the western coast. For clothing worn in the territory of Daman, see Careri, 162 (with editor's correction, 340).

[40] Bhīmsen was a native of Burhanpur and spent a large part of his life at Aurangabad. The contrast between the ordinary clothing seen in Mughal Dakhin and that in southern India is reflected in the disdain with which he describes the latter. Speaking of the "Karnatak of Bijapur and Gulkunda" (Tamilnadu), he says: "Men tie up a dirty scarf on their head and a small piece of cloth for hiding (the privy parts), and one sheet of calico (*kirpās*) [thrown over their shoulders] suffices for years... and women wear a cloth three or four cubits long round the waist, like a *lung*, leaving the head and breasts bare..." (*Dilkushā*, f.113a). In this description Bhīmsen is supported by other contemporary authorities, e.g. Fitch, Ryley, 94, *Early Travels*, 16; *Relations*, 76-7; Bowrey, 97, for Golkunda and Coromandel; Linschoten, I, 260-1, for Kanara; Fitch, Ryley, 186, *Early Travels*, 47; Tavernier, I, 97; and Fryer, I, 137-8, for Kerala; and Manucci, III, 39-41 for southern India, generally. In the Salsette Island "They go Naked, both Men and Women covering their Privities with a Clout, and their Breasts with another... leaving the Arms, Thighs and Legs bare" (Careri, 179). We may presume this applied generally to the Konkan.

[41] Fitch, Ryley, 119, *Early Travels*, 28. See also Manrique, I, 64.

[42] *Ā'īn*, I, 389.

[43] Master, II, 92-3. Cf. *Imperial Gazetteer*, VII, 241. In Assam "rich and poor make their habitations and houses out of wood, bamboo and straw" (*'Ālamgīrnāma*, 727).

[44] *Ā'īn*, I, 391. [45] Ibid., 416.

described as "badd mud walled ill thatched covered howses".[46] The villages on the banks of the Indus consisted of "houses of wood and straw", which could always be shifted.[47] In Ajmer province "the common people live in tent-shaped bamboo huts".[48] Round about Sironj (Malwa) the peasants lived "in small round huts", "miserable hovels".[49] The houses in Gujarat were roofed with tiles (*khaprail*) and often built of brick and lime.[50] In Khandesh and Bidar, however, the huts were again mud-walled and thatched.[51] All this sounds familiar, and it is obvious that there was practically no change in the housing conditions of the peasant, for better or worse, during the subsequent period of colonial rule. The peasants' huts were made with materials that were most easily procurable and without the use of much building skill, so that the kind of material used, together with the climate and soil, bore almost the entire responsibility for such regional variations as existed.

There was little within the hovel to attract the attention of contemporary observers. "Furniture there is little or none, except for some earthenware pots to hold water and for cooking and two beds [i.e. cots] one for the man, the other for the wife."[52] This is said of workmen in Agra, and there is no reason to expect that the peasants' possessions were on any better scale. From Terry's testimony we may add to this brief list of domestic articles "the small iron hearths" used by "the common people" for baking their cakes of bread.[53] We are also told that in southern India "their plate is a leaf ... or a small plate of copper, of which the whole family eats".[54] Linschoten says the peasants in Kanara "commonly

46 Mundy, 73. He is speaking specifically of the country around Kol; he calls the peasants "Gauares" (*ganwārs*) and "Labourers" (for his use of the latter word see also ibid., 90). The Agra workmen too lived in houses "built of mud with thatched roofs" (Pelsaert, 61).

47 *Ā'īn*, I, 550; Sujān Rāi, 64.

48 *Ā'īn*, I, 505. In a "Towne", i.e. village, of Marwar, Mundy, 249, noticed "every howse standinge by itselfe, in form like our round Corne Stacks in the feild though not so bigg nor soe high".

49 Monserrate, 21.

50 *Ā'īn*, I, 485. As Mundy left the Abu hills behind on his way to Ahmadabad, he noted, "the howses begin to be covered with Tiles" (Mundy, 258).

51 Fitch, Ryley, 94-5, *Early Travels*, 16; Roe, 68.

52 Pelsaert, 61.

53 *Early Travels*, 296. He means the round iron plate, the *tawā*, on which the *chapātī* is baked. See also Abbé Carre, I, 227, for millet cakes baked by the poor on "iron plates".

54 Manucci, III, 43.

drinke out of a Copper Canne with a spout ... which is all the metell they have within their houses."[55] Presumably, from the fact that the great copper mines lay in northern India the peasants within the Mughal empire were a little better served with this metal. But the *Āʾīn's* price for copper has been computed to be five times higher, in terms of wheat, than its price in 1914.[56] This explains why Pelsaert refers only to earthen vessels even for cooking. The earthen vessels were in fact "almost universal" among the peasants of the central regions till the earlier part of the nineteenth century; and it is only since then that they "have entirely been replaced by (utensils of) brass or other metal".[57] Apart from cots there was probably little other wooden or bamboo furniture, except perhaps, the low stool, called *chaukī*, the use of which was a traditional part of village etiquette.[58] Tin boxes and a few little trinkets were indeed all that would be needed to complete the picture of the peasant's domestic possessions around 1900.[59] And at both times, filth and poverty made the peasant's family constantly vulnerable to smallpox and other dreaded diseases.[60]

As for jewellery, the custom of converting savings into women's ornaments was apparently universal, and foreign travellers note almost everywhere the extraordinary amount of ornaments which women might wear.[61] Their descriptions of these are very general as a rule, but from them and from a specific statement by Fryer,[62] it would appear that for the poorer people ornaments consisted of copper, glass or conch shells[63] or even, as we have seen, at one time, of cloves.

[55] Linschoten, I, 261-2, also 226.

[56] In the Lucknow market (Moreland in *JRAS* [1918] 381-2). Cf. Moosvi, 331.

[57] Moens, *Settlement Report for the Bareilly District*, 55, cited by Crooke, *North-Western Provinces*, 276. Cf. also Moreland, *India at the Death of Akbar*, 273-4.

[58] Mushtāqī, f.21a: "It is the custom of a class of villagers (*dihqān*) that when a guest comes to their house, the wife of the host gives him water to wash his hands and feet and puts the *chaukī* before him."

[59] Cf. Crooke, 268; Moreland, *India at the Death of Akbar*, 277-8.

[60] Of fifty-nine villagers, whose personal descriptions recorded before *qāzīs*, 1653-1717, survive in the Vrindaban Docs., as many as eighteen bore the scars of small pox.

[61] Cf. Fitch, Ryley, 107, 109, 118-9, *Early Travels*, 22-3, 28; Fryer, II, 117; Ovington, 188-9, etc.

[62] "The Rich (women) have their Arms and Feet Fettered with Gold and Silver, the meaner with Brass and Glass and Tuthinag, besides Rings at their Noses, Ears, Toes and Fingers" (Fryer, II, 117). Cf. Careri, 162 (editor's corrections, 340).

[63] As in Orissa (Bowrey, 208-9). Here men wore ornaments in the same way as women (*Āʾīn*, I, 391).

To judge from the frequent accounts of rites, festivals and pilgrimages preserved for us in contemporary accounts, it is obvious that these played a noticeable part in the peasant's life.[64] Such occasions, the marriages of his children, the funeral rites for the dead, and the visits to riverside festivals, must have consumed a part of his meagre resources or increased his debt.[65] Indeed, a contemporary Dutch observer especially castigates the people of Gujarat, who in years of good harvests "spent and squandered" their "surplus" "on their devilish festivals" – for which, he says, God, in His usual way, chastised them with the great famine of 1630-32.[66]

2. FAMINES

We have so far seen the peasant only in the poverty and squalor that were his lot in a normal period. But the monsoons upon which his harvest depended were not always constant in showering their bounty. All might be lost if the rains failed at the crucial time or poured down in such excess as to drown the crops. The railway network in time offered the means whereby foodgrains could be rapidly transported from the surplus to the scarcity areas. This benefit conferred by the railways added in due course another item to the well-publicized list of achievements of British administration, viz. the conversion of "food famines" into "work famines". With this claim we have, of course, no concern here; but in so far as attempts have been made to present the famines under British rule in a softer light than those under the Mughals, a few necessary comments are relegated to a footnote.[1]

[64] Pelsaert, 24-5.

[65] The authorities saw in these pilgrimages yet another means of extortion. Akbar abolished the pilgrim levy, called *kar* (*A.N.*, II, 190; *Ā'īn*, I, 301), but it was later silently re-imposed. The *Nigārnāma-i Munshī*, f.97a-b, Bodl. f.73a, ed., 76 (defective), contains a *parwāna* to Muḥammad Momin, *amīn*, reminding him of the impending "season of the gathering of Hindus in multitudes on the banks of the river Gang, which in the Hindwī language is called Ganga, and which they cross after every few years"; and that "at such a time considerable revenue is obtained from the *maḥal* of *sā'ir* [taxes other than land revenue]". The *parwāna* underlines the necessity of obtaining exact information as to the routes and places of worship so that none might evade payment. And yet the "revenue from bathing in the Ganga" is included in the list of the forbidden cesses under Aurangzeb (*Ẓawābiṭ-i 'Ālamgīrī*, Ethé 415, f.181b, Or. 1641, f.136b; Add. 6598, f.189b).

[66] van Twist, transl. Moreland, *JIH*, XVI, 66.

[1] The "horrible picture" of the Gujarat famine of 1630-2 provided Vincent A. Smith, the *doyen* of Anglo-Indian historians, with an opportunity to underline "the immensity of the difference in the conditions of life as existing under the rule of

An idea of the frequency and violence of these calamities in our period may be gained from the following chronicle of famines and scarcities, compiled from contemporary sources. We must, however, remember that this can have no pretensions to completeness and the list will probably extend as more evidence becomes available.[2]

Our period began at the tail-end of a terrible famine which, for two successive years, 1554-5 and 1555-6, had ravaged "all the eastern parts of Hind", particularly the territories around Agra, Bayana and Dehli. People died in groups of tens and twenties and more, and the dead received "neither graves nor coffins": "the common people lived on the seeds of Egyptian thorn, wild dry grass and cowhides". Badāūnī claims to be an eyewitness to acts of cannibalism. Most of the affected country "was rendered desolate, cultivators and peasants disappeared, and rebels plundered the towns of the Muslims".[3] Agra itself was desolated with only some houses remaining.[4] Abū-l Faẓl says that the scarcity was over by the time of Akbar's accession in February 1556,[5] probably owing to a successful rabi crop.

---

the Mogul dynasty when at the height of its glory and those prevailing under the modern British government" (*Oxford History of India*, 394). This "modern" government opened its regime in India with a famine which swept off one-third of the population of Bengal into the other world. Smith is all indignation that only "one-eleventh of the assessment of land revenue" was remitted by Shāhjahān in 1630-2. Contrast this (imagined) heartless miserliness with the benevolence shown by the English in 1769-70: "In a year when thirty-five per cent of the cultivators perished, not five per cent of the land tax was remitted, and ten per cent was added to it for the ensuing year (1770-1)" (Hunter, *Annals of Rural Bengal*, 39). Moreland, who is generally cautious in making such statements, could still say in 1923 that under British rule "the very idea of a food-famine has been banished from all but the few tracts still inaccessible" (*Akbar to Aurangzeb*, 210). Less than thirty years earlier 5.15 million people were carried away by the famine of 1896-7, and twenty years later (1943) some 1.5 million, if not more, were to die of starvation in Bengal (cf. L. Visaria and P. Visaria in *Cambridge Economic History of India*, II, 530-31). See also Brij Narain, *Indian Economic Life*, 85-107, for a critique of Moreland. On Michelle McAlpin's arguments in her *Subject to Famine* against the nationalist criticisms of British taxation and trade policies as factors behind famine mortality, see my comments in *Essays*, 290-91 & nn.

2 Coromandel, which was specifically prone to famines is not included in this survey, being outside the limits of our study.

3 Badāūnī, I, 428-9; *A.N.*, II, 35. The latter also refers to cannibalism. See also Abū-l Faẓl's autobiography in *Ā'īn*, II, 264, for an account of this famine.

4 *Ā'īn*, II, 264.

5 *A.N.*, II, 35. But see *Ā'īn*, II, 264, where Abū-l Faẓl himself says the famine raged during the first year of Akbar's reign.

Severe scarcity seems to have affected Gujarat some time during the 1560s; it became common, during its visitation, for parents to sell their children for trifles.[6] There is an allusion to a very acute famine around Sirhind in or about 1572-3.[7] In 1574-5 there was again a serious famine in Gujarat, this time accompanied by pestilence; and large numbers of people, both "lowly and respectable", migrated from the province.[8] There was also a general apprehension of drought this year in northern India, but the danger was averted by timely showers.[9] Some parts of it, however, seem to have experienced scarcity in 1578-9.[10] In 1587 and 1588, locusts destroyed crops in the Bhakkar territory (Sind): "most people migrated and the Samja and Baluch, plundering both sides of the river, did not let a single place of habitation escape them."[11] In 1589-90 drought caused a famine in the same locality.[12]

There was a general insufficiency of rain in 1596: "High prices plunged a world into suffering", and Akbar ordered free kitchens to be opened in every city.[13] While repeating these statements, another historian describes the same drought and famine as of extreme severity, the scarcity continuing for three or four years in "Hindūstān". There was considerable mortality and people were driven by hunger to eat carrion.[14] In 1597 there was an acute scarcity from drought in Kashmir, where destitute people "having no means of nourishing their children, exposed them for sale in the public places of the city".[15]

[6] Caesar Frederick, *Purchas*, X, 90. This Italian traveller visited Khambayat, where he witnessed this scarcity, between 1563 and 1567.

[7] A family in this area took to cannibalism and, when finally apprehended, explained that they had acquired the habit in this famine (Faiẓī Sirhindī, f.121a-122a).

[8] 'Ārif Qandahārī, 198-99; *Ṭabaqāt-i Akbarī*, II, 301; Badāūnī, II, 186; Faiẓī Sirhindī, f.122a-b. The last two obviously derive their information from the *Ṭabaqāt-i Akbarī*; but while the *Ṭabaqāt-i Akbarī* is silent about the scale of mortality, Badāūnī adds that countless people died.

[9] *A.N.*, III, 106-7. [10] *A.N.*, III, 224. [11] Ma'ṣūm, *Tārīkh-i Sind*, 249.

[12] Ibid., 250. [13] *A.N.*, III, 714.

[14] Nūru-l Ḥaqq Dihlawī, *Zubdatu-t Tawārīkh*, Or. 1650, f.256b. In Elliot & Dowson, VI, 193, "Men ate carrion" is rendered as "Men ate their own kind". There is a reference to this famine also in Banārasī Dās, *Ardha Kathānak*, ed. & transl. Lath, 16, 231-2. The author, then at Jaunpur, says the famine began in Samvat 1653 (AD 1596-7): owing to high prices "the world became miserable (*be-hāl*)". By Māgh S. 1654 (Jan.-Feb. 1598) the scarcity had passed – a statement that conflicts with the very long duration assigned to the famine by Nūru-l Ḥaqq.

[15] *Akbar and the Jesuits*, 77-8. Cf. *A.N.*, III, 727; Sabzwārī, *Rauẓatu-ṭ Ṭāhirīn*, Or.168, ff.560b-561a.

Writing in 1615-16, Jahāngīr refers to the spread of bubonic plague from the Panjab to Sirhind, the Doab and Dehli in this and the preceding year. He cites a learned opinion that this was due to the excessive drought which had been experienced for two years (1613-4 and 1614-5?), but no particulars about the scarcity are supplied.[16]

The great famine of 1630-2 was probably the most destructive of all the recorded calamities in Mughal India and certainly one which left the deepest impression on contemporaries. It affected Gujarat and most of the Dakhin.[17] There was first a complete failure of the rains in these areas in 1630; the next year, the crops were promising in Gujarat, but were first attacked by mice and locusts and then destroyed by excessive rain,[18] while in the Dakhin the drought seems to have continued.[19] Pestilence followed close in the wake of the famine to carry away those who had escaped starvation. The most harrowing scenes were witnessed. Parents sold their children. There was a wholesale migration in the direction of the less affected lands, but few could even complete the first

[16] *T.J.*, 161-2.

[17] This famine is described by Qazwīnī (Add. 20,734, pp.442-4; Or. 173, ff.220b-221a) and Ṣādiq Khān (Or. 174, ff.29a-32a; Or. 1671, ff.17a-18b), both of whom claim to have been eye-witnesses, being apparently present at the court, which had its seat then at Burhanpur. Lāhorī, I, 362-3, merely summarizes Qazwīnī, so that the acceptance of his account as the only contemporary description in Persian and then the criticism of its contents as pure rhetoric are both undeserved (Saran, 427 ff.). Khāfī Khān, I, 444-9, copies Ṣādiq Khān verbatim, omitting or altering only the personal references. The principal European sources are Mundy, passim; *Factories, 1630-33*, passim; and van Twist, 65-9. Their statements apply mostly to Gujarat.

[18] Here the European authorities have been followed: *Factories, 1630-33*, 134-5, 158, 165, 181, 193; Mundy, 38; van Twist, 66, 68.

[19] Qazwīnī says that though there was a deficiency of rain in 1630 in "most of the *maḥals* of Bālāghāṭ, especially the region around Daulatabad", the drought was much more widespread in 1631. Ṣādiq Khān, on the other hand, says probably inverting the true order, that there were excessive rains in 1630, which spoilt the crops and that this was followed by a complete drought in 1631. In the third year, he adds, mice and locusts caused great damage to the crops. As noted above, both these writers had personal experience only of the conditions in the Dakhin, and it is possible that the famine continued there in 1631 owing to a cause directly opposite to that in Gujarat. Nature behaved differently again in Coromandel. Here the famine began, as elsewhere, in 1630 (*Factories 1630-33*, 73, 268); the drought continued into 1631, but "abundance of raigne" fell at last in August 1632 (ibid., 203-4, 228). However, there was too much of it in 1633: "such aboundance of rain as rotted... a great part of the corne in the fields ere 'twas halfe ripe" (*Factories 1634-36*, 40).

stages of the journey before death overtook them; the dead blocked the roads. In the first year the poor largely perished, but in the second the turn of some of the rich also came.[20] Cattle-hide and hog-flesh were eaten; the crushed bones of the dead were mixed and sold with flour, and ultimately cases of cannibalism became common.[21] The transportation of grain by the *banjāras* to Gujarat from Malwa and beyond was hampered in 1630 by the task of feeding Shāhjahān's army encamped at Burhanpur.[22] But though the army was dispersed and the *banjāras* were reaching Surat with large supplies in the following year,[23] the prices still remained prohibitive.[24] Unprecedented gains accrued to the imperial treasury in Malwa, by the sale of grain for supply to the Dakhin.[25] As was the usual practice of the administration, *langars* or free kitchens were opened in the major cities,[26] more as a gesture of charity, however, than with any ambition of providing substantial relief. The land revenue remission, of necessity, was considerable.[27]

Of all the affected provinces, Gujarat suffered the most heavily.[28] Three million of its inhabitants are said to have died during the ten months preceding October 1631; while a million reputedly perished in the country of Ahmadnagar.[29] The cities of Gujarat were, by death or flight, reduced to almost one-tenth of

[20] This is emphasized by both Ṣādiq Khān and van Twist.

[21] Saran, 429-31, suggests that the references to cannibalism in Lāhorī and van Twist are products of literary flourish and hearsay. Both speak of cases where parents ate their own children. Mundy, 276, returning to Gujarat on the very morrow of the famine, makes a similar statement. Ṣādiq Khān refers to a report made to the court of a woman, who had brought a complaint before the *qāẓī* of Ahmadabad, against a neighbour, who after killing her son with her consent, had denied her a share in his flesh. That reports of such acts as well as murders for cannibalistic purposes, were widely credited, shows that the practice of feeding on corpses at least was resorted to during the famine.

[22] Mundy, 56; *Factories, 1630-33*, 165.

[23] *Factories, 1630-33*, 196; *1634-36*, 224-5.

[24] In January 1632 "graine" at Surat was selling at 6¼ and 6 ½ *maḥmūdīs* per *man*, said to be a lower rate than formerly owing to the supplies brought by the *banjāras* as well as by sea (*Factories, 1630-31*, 196). In September 1631 the rate had been no less than 16 *maḥmūdīs* per *man* (ibid., 165). The normal price of wheat before the famine had been only 1 *maḥmūdī* for 1 1/8 *mans* (van Twist, 68).

[25] *Zakhīratu-l Khawānīn*, f.120b.

[26] Qazwīnī, Add. 20734, 444; Or.173, f.221a; Lāhorī, I, 363; Ṣādiq Khān, Or. 174, f.31b, Or.1671, f.18b; Khāfī Khān, I, 448-9.

[27] See Chapter VI, Section 8.

[28] Lāhorī, I, 363.

[29] As reported by the Portuguese Viceroy to his sovereign (*Factories, 1630-33*, xxi).

their former state.[30] The villages could hardly have fared much better. Ṣādiq Khān declares that "the *parganas* of Sultanpur, Nandur, Mandu, Ahmadabad and indeed the [entire] province of Khandesh and some *parganas* of Bālāghāṭ were rendered utterly desolate", and peasants had to be brought in from other areas to settle there. Late in 1634, after three good seasons, it was reported from Gujarat that although the towns were recovering in population "the villages fill but slowly".[31] In 1638-9 the "marks" of the famine could yet "be seen everywhere";[32] and cultivation had obviously not recovered fully till even the end of the second decade of Shāhjahān's reign (1647).[33]

In 1636-7, the Panjab was reported to be suffering from famine and scarcity.[34] High grain prices prevailed at Agra in the summer of 1638, but there is no evidence of famine conditions.[35] In 1640 excessive rain and the resultant inundations detroyed the kharif crop in Kashmir;[36] and in 1642 famine conditions prevailed there again from the same cause, forcing about 30,000 people to flee in distress to Lahor.[37] The latter year also witnessed a prolonged drought in Orissa which disrupted its customary exports of grain to Coromandel.[38]

During the 1640s the rains failed repeatedly in parts of Northern India. In 1644, Agra province was thus affected, though famine conditions are not reported.[39] In February 1646 it was represented

[30] Cf. Mundy, 276, instancing the case of the weavers; also *Factories, 1630-33*, 180: in December 1631 only "10 or 11 famillyes" were left out of 260 formerly inhabiting the village of Swally.

[31] *Factories, 1634-36*, 65. See also ibid., 146 (a report sent in January 1636).

[32] Commissariat, *Mandelslo*, 7. But see an optimistic report of January 1640 in *Factories, 1637-41*, 235: "This country is restored to its pristine plenty."

[33] Lāhorī, II, 711-2, writing under the 20th year of Shāhjahān (1646-7) declares that Gujarat and the Dakhin provinces were so adversely affected by the famine that their *jama'* (or assessed revenue) was still at a lower pitch than formerly.

[34] Lāhorī, II, 29.

[35] See Moreland's analysis of the Agra Dutch factories' accounts in *JUPHS*, III,(1), 149-50, 153, and table on 152.

[36] Ibid., 204-5; Ṣādiq Khān, Or. 174, f.96a, Or. 167, f.52b.

[37] Lāhorī, II, 382-3; Ṣādiq Khān, Or. 174, f.99b, Or.167, f.54a-b; Khāfī Khān, I, 587.

[38] Moreland, *Akbar to Aurangzeb*, 208; Raychaudhuri, *Jan Company in Coromandel*, 45.

[39] *Factories, 1642-45*, 202. An *'arẓdāsht* of Khān Jahān Bārha (Add. 16,859, ff.1b-2b), sent to the court in the month of Jumāda I, refers to the collection of revenue from the rabi harvest in his *jāgīr* in Gwalior and adds that during the current year "the calamity of drought was so heavy that the yield (*ḥāṣil*) was very

at the court that the indigent were being forced to sell their children owing to the high prices of foodgrains in the Panjab; but the distress was apparently limited.[40] In 1646 drought was experienced at Agra and Ahmadabad.[41] In 1647 the rains failed utterly in Marwar, which "hath occasioned a famine, insoemuch that those parts are, either [by] mortality or peoples flight, become wholly depopulate and impassable".[42] In 1648 there was again a "partial failure of the rains" in the Agra region.[43] Bengal, on the other hand, was visited with an excess of rain in 1644-5 and 1648, spoiling its sugarcane crops.[44]

In 1650 there was a failure of rain in all parts of India.[45] The "dearth of corne" was reported from Awadh;[46] and the scarcity affected the country between Agra and Ahmadabad.[47] In 1651 in the Panjab the crops were harmed first by drought and then by excessive rain, so that grain prices became very high and the peasants were unable to pay the full revenue.[48] In Multan province the rabi crop of 1650 had been spoilt by locusts and the kharif, as elsewhere, by drought, while the rabi of 1651 also suffered from inundations.[49]

In 1655 the kharif crop in parts of the Bālāghāṭ region of Mughal Dakhin was damaged by late and heavy showers.[50]

A prolonged period of scarcity in Northern India began in 1658. Caused initially perhaps by the ravages of the War of Succession,

---

much lower than in the previous years". Though the year is not given, from its contents the report can be assigned to the 18th regnal year of Shāhjahān, and accordingly, since the month is given, to June-July 1645. The harvests affected by drought must therefore have been the kharif of 1644 and rabi of 1645.

40 Lāhorī, II, 489. The limited extent of the scarcity is shown by the fact that Shāhjahān ordered all children sold by their parents to be repurchased at the original price at the cost of the exchequer and to be restored to their families, a measure hardly to be thought of had large numbers been involved. Probably the prices rose only temporarily, pending the gathering of the rabi harvest.

41 *Factories, 1646-50*, 62, 99.

42 Ibid., 192-3; also 157.

43 Ibid., 219.

44 Raychaudhuri, 179.

45 *Factories, 1646-50*, 322; *1651-54*, 29.

46 Ibid., *1651-54*, 9-10.

47 Ibid., 26.

48 Wāriṣ, A: f.445a, B: f.76a-b; Ṣādiq Khān, Or. 174, ff.168a-169a, Or. 1671, f.84b; Ṣāliḥ, III, 125. A letter in Bālkrishan Brahman's collection, Add. 16,859, (ff. 39a-b, 37a, folios misplaced) about drought in Hisar is perhaps to be assigned to this year.

49 *Ādāb-i 'Ālamgīrī*, 202a-b, ed., II, 801, 804, *Ruq'āt-i 'Ālamgīr*, 227-8. The letters are addressed to Jahān Ārā and are datable only by inference.

50 *Ādāb-i 'Ālamgīrī*, ff.54b, 55b, ed., II, 213, 217; *Ruq'āt-i 'Ālamgīr*, 140-1, 166-7.

it was sustained for the first four or five years of Aurangzeb's reign by the vagaries of the monsoons. The scarcity was felt particularly in the regions around Agra, Dehli and Lahor, and in or before the 4th regnal year (1661-2) *langars* had to be established on a large scale by the administration in these cities.[51] The worst sufferer, however, was Sind, where famine and plague raged in 1659-60 and "swept away most part of the people".[52] Gujarat suffered from drought in 1659, 1660 and again in 1663,[53] raising foodgrain prices so greatly that in 1664 it was thought that another failure of the rains would "utterly dispeople all these parts",[54] a fear which happily did not materialize.[55] Even Malwa – the land of perpetual plenty – was affected, for owing to the War, the kharif crop of 1658 was largely destroyed.[56] Eastwards, in Bengal, a local famine developed in 1662-3 in Dhaka, the distress from which was intensified owing to interference with the transport of foodgrains by officials' exactions and obstructions on the routes.[57] But, generally speaking, except for Sind, there is no suggestion that large-scale mortality or the usual scenes of horror marking a serious famine were observed anywhere.

In 1670, the kharif crop failed completely in Bihar from want of rain and during the succeeding year an acute famine ravaged the territory extending from the west of Banaras to Rajmahal. We have an eyewitness account of how multitudes perished on the routes and in the city of Patna, and how parents sold their children. In Patna alone, 90,000 were estimated to have died and of "the townes near Patana, some [were] quite depopulated, having not any persons in them".[58] About the same time a severe drought affected Raybagh territory in Bijapur, resulting in migration and sale of children.[59]

[51] *'Ālamgīrnāma*, 609-11; Khāfī Khān, II, 87, 124 (cf. var. Or.6574, f.33a); Bernier, 433, 437. Bihishtī Shīrāzī in his *Āshob-i Hindūstān,* quoted by Durgā Prasād, *Gulistān-i Hind*, II (Supplement), 105, speaks of famine and pestilence ravaging the whole of India, after the imprisonment (in 1658) of Prince Murād Bakhsh, whose servant Bihishtī was.

[52] *Factories, 1655-60*, 210 & n., 307. Cf. 'Alī Sher Qāni' Tattawī, *Tuḥfatu-l Kirām*, III, 196.

[53] *Factories, 1655-60*, 306-7, 320; *1661-64*, 25, 200, 257, 329. Cf. *Mir'āt*, I, 251.

[54] *Factories, 1661-64*, 320-1.

[55] Ibid., 323.

[56] *'Arzdāsht* of Ja'far Khān in *Jāmi'u-l Inshā'*, f.10b, and *Faiyāẓu-l Qawānīn*, Or. 9617, Vol. I, f.130b.

[57] *Fatḥiya 'Ibriya*, ff.79b-80a, 110b-111a.

[58] Marshall, 125-7, 138, 149-53. Cf. also Bowrey, 226-7.

[59] Abbé Carre, I, 233, 264.

Late in 1678, grain prices were reported to have risen very greatly at Lahor,[60] but no account of the distress is available. There was drought also in Ajmer province, resulting in migrations towards Malwa; but showers later in the season averted disaster.[61] In 1682 "famine and scarcity" prevailed in Gujarat and there was a popular riot against the governor at Ahmadabad over the high grain prices.[62] Drought was also experienced in the Dakhin, where plague began to rage in the towns from this year.[63] The crops failed again in the peninsula in 1684, and prices are stated to have risen greatly.[64]

Gujarat too continued to be subject to scarcity conditions. In 1685, the prices of foodgrains rose so much that all duties on them had to be remitted, and there was a riot in Ahmadabad against the *qāẓī*, who was thought to be in league with the engrossers.[65] The high prices continued into the following year owing to drought.[66] The drought extended to the whole of the Dakhin in 1686, so that "what happened to the poor and indigent cannot be recorded".[67] Sind was also probably affected at the same time since a very severe scarcity accompanied by epidemic occurred there during a Governor's term that lasted from 1684 to 1688.[68] In 1691 both famine and pestilence visited Gujarat[69] and scarcity was experienced there again in 1694-5.[70] The region around Dehli also felt the scarcity of 1694-5, but the worst affected was the Bāgar tract on the north-eastern edge of the Thar Desert. Its inhabitants migrated to other parts, eating carrion, selling their children, and dying in thousands.[71] There was also a famine in Orissa during 1695.[72] In 1696-7 drought affected parts of Gujarat and Marwar, and not a trace of grass or water could be found between Pattan and Jodhpur.[73] It also extended to Sind where 80,000 persons in Thatta alone reportedly died of plague following the drought.[74]

60 *Ma'āṣir-i 'Ālamgīrī*, 169. 61 *Waqā'i' Ajmer*, 16, 20, 21, 25.

62 *Mir'āt*, I, 300-1; *Factories*, N.S., III, 277.

63 Ma'mūrī, ff.155b-156a; Khāfī Khān, Add. 6574, f.105a-b.

64 Khāfī Khān, II, 317. 65 *Mir'āt*, I, 309. 66 Ibid., 315.

67 Khāfī Khān, II, 236-7. 68 Qāni', *Tuḥfatu-l Kirām*, III, 97.

69 *Mir'āt*, I, 325. 70 Ibid., 329-30.

71 Yaḥyā Khān, *Tazkiratu-l Mulūk*, Ethé 409, f.108a-b. He says that they first came to Dehli and then moved on towards Ujjain. Are the present settlements of Bāgarīs in eastern Malwa the result of this migration? See Elliot, *Memoirs*, I, 9,10.

72 Wilson, *Early Annals of Bengal*, I, 401. 73 *Mir'āt*, I, 335-6.

74 Hamilton, I, 122. Hamilton says the drought had begun three years before he came to Thatta, which was in 1699.

A great famine began in the Dakhin in 1702. In February it was reported to the court from Sangamner (Aurangabad province) that owing to drought "most of the villages" had been rendered desolate.[75] In the course of the year "in the whole of the Dakhin no rain fell that was in keeping with the interests of cultivation";[76] in fact, the rains were so prodigious as to devastate the kharif harvest.[77] Great scarcity prevailed everywhere south of the Narmada, and people were compelled to migrate from their ancestral homes.[78] The next year (1703) brought no relief, for owing to the excessive winter rains the rabi crop was also damaged, wheat suffering particularly from blight.[79] Then drought came. A historian speaks of it as the year, for Maharashtra, of "famine and scarcity owing to drought, the mortality of the poor and the wail of the weak".[80] Drought, with its close companion, plague, continued into 1704.[81] In the two years, 1702-3 and 1703-4, in the Dakhin "there expired over two millions of souls; fathers, compelled by hunger, offering to sell their children for a quarter or a half of a rupee, and yet forced to go without food, finding no one to buy them".[82]

It will be observed that the evidence in our possession shows considerable variations in the frequency of famines in various regions. In part, this may be due to the fact that we are better informed about some provinces (say, Gujarat) than others. But this will not, for example, explain why Bengal, for which our information during the latter half of the seventeenth century is considerable, has practically no serious famine on record: indeed, the 1662-3 scarcity at Dhaka was described as an unprecedented phenomenon for that province.[83] Similarly, Malwa seems to have largely lived up to its reputation for being perennially free from scarcity.[84] The Upper Gangetic region was not so fortunate, but the one great famine involving large-scale mortality took place just before the beginning of our period. Only one famine of similar dimensions is recorded for Bihar. On the other hand, the provinces in the Indus basin, Gujarat and Mughal Dakhin seem to have been much more vulnerable to natural calamities and suffered repeatedly.

75 *Akhbārāt*, 46/12. 76 *Dilkushā*, f.146a.

77 Manucci, III, 423; Ma'mūrī, f.202b; Khāfī Khān, II, 510.

78 *Dilkushā*, f.146a. 79 Ma'mūrī, f.202b; Khāfī Khān, II, 510-11.

80 *Ma'āṣir-i 'Ālamgīrī*, 477.

81 See *Akhbārāt* A, 245 (22 July 1704) for reference to "scarcity of grain and lack of rain" throughout the Dakhin.

82 Manucci, IV, 97. 83 *Fatḥiya 'Ibriya*, f.80a. 84 Mundy, 57.

It is, perhaps, needless to emphasize the extent of distress a famine imposed upon the mass of the people. Years of large-scale mortality might have been few, but when they did come, the amount of depopulation could have been frightful. Not only did people die of starvation, they also fell victim to all kinds of pestilence, particularly the dreaded plague, which followed in the wake of even the lesser scarcities.[85] It is not possible to estimate exactly the degree to which these calamities counteracted the natural growth of population. It is possible to exaggerate their effects in this respect. The famine of 1630-2 might have denuded large portions of Gujarat of living beings, but for the next three generations, at any rate, nothing like it occurred. Similarly, the central provinces had a full hundred and fifty years, within our period, to recover from the depopulation suffered in the 1554-6 famine. There were, however, other miseries besides death which the famines heaped upon the poor. Their consumption fell dangerously below the necessary level of subsistence, and we have occasionally a glimpse of what they were forced to eat in times of dearth. Fryer considered it an accepted fact that "(in great Scarcity) Grass Roots" became "the common Food of the ordinary people".[86] The wasted fields drove peasants from their homes to seek sustenance in distant regions, and each scarcity was marked by a phenomenal glut in the slave market.[87] The famines, from time to time, introduced into the stolid isolation of agricultural production, a terrible element of fluidity and devastation. If there had been nothing else, this alone would have sufficed to explain the migratory characteristics of the peasantry, which were such a marked feature of the agrarian life of the time.

[85] Jahāngīr's reference to the association of plague with drought has already been mentioned. The belief, based upon experience, was commonly held. Thus in 1664 the English factors at Surat wrote: "The passed yeare(s) dearth these people affirme to be the cause of the intemperature of the aire so what alwayes faollowes a scarcity of raine and corne. All the townes and villages hereabouts are full of sickness, scarce a house free" (*Factories, 1661-64*, 329).

[86] Fryer, II, 119.

[87] Apart from the instances noted above, the sale of children by parents is recognized as a usual consequence of famine and distress in Akbar's orders cited by Badāūnī, II, 391. Cf. also Fitch, Ryley, 57, *Early Travels*, 12; Manucci, II, 451; Raychaudhuri, *Jan Company in Coromandel*, 166-7.

CHAPTER IV

THE PEASANT AND THE LAND; THE VILLAGE COMMUNITY

1. AGRARIAN PROPERTY: THE PEASANT AND THE LAND

European travellers visiting India in the sixteenth and seventeenth centuries held unanimously to the view that the king was the owner of the soil in India.[1] The doctrine was passed on to British officials, who maintained that the East India Company had inherited a universal right of ownership over the land from its predecessors.[2] Yet, as Wilson observed in his criticism of James Mill's influential assertion of this doctrine, there was no sanction for such a claim in ancient Indian law; nor, as Kovalevsky added, in Muslim law.[3] No such pretensions were put forward on behalf of the Mughal rulers in any official documents. When Abū-l Faẓl sets himself the task of justifying the imposition of taxes on "the peasant and the merchant", he does not argue that the tax on land flows from the sovereign's right of ownership; he appeals, on the contrary, to a social contract, by which the sovereign obtains his "remu-neration" through taxation in return for providing protection and justice to his subjects.[4]

It is only in the eighteenth century that we have an assertion of the king's right to ownership. A famous lexicon (1739-40) takes the term k͟harāj to signify the land tax, "which accrues to the king because of his ownership (*milkiyat*) of the land".[5] In an interesting

[1] Xavier, 121-22; 105; *Relations*, 10-11; Bernier, 5, 204, 226, 232, 238; *Factories, 1668-69*, 184; Fryer, I, 137; Careri, 240-41; Manucci, II, 46.

[2] E.g. James Grant, 'Analysis of the Finances of Bengal' (1786), *Fifth Report*, 251; James Mill, *History of British India*, I, 137-40, 251; Baden-Powell, *Indian Village Community*, 223.

[3] Cf. Rosa Luxemburg, *Accumulation of Capital*, 372 & 373-3 n.

[4] *A'īn*, I, 290-91.

[5] Tek Chand 'Bahār', *Bahār-i 'Ajam*, s.v. *k͟harāj*. A similar statement appears in one of the Persian replies to questions asked on agrarian rights by English officials, *c*.1789 (Add.19,503, f.46a). Another respondent, 'Abdu-sh Shakūr held (25 May 1789) that previously the *rājas* and *zamīndārs* were owners of the land; but now the emperor held the right of ownership, because he could depose them (Add. 19,502, f.339a; Add. 19,504, f.68a). Cf. another response, Add. 19,504, ff.64a-62a (folios numbered conversely). By this time, the ideas of English officials must have begun to colour the views of their Indian subordinates. One respondent

theoretical tract a Muslim jurist of about the same time (*c*.1745) avers that in olden times the Hindu peasants did indeed believe their *rājas* to be "the owners (*mālik*) of the entire land", but according to law (*shar'an*), the cultivated, tax-paying land could not be held to be the property of the ruler (*sulṭān*).[6] He admitted rather significantly that in his own time the peasants regarded the *zamīndārs* (the reputed descendants of the *rājas*) as proprietors; and this was reinforced by the peasants' allowing the *zamīndārs* the right to expel them from the land.[7] Yet, he says, this was a false claim on the part of the *zamīndārs*, since what the sultan realized (*maḥṣūl*) from the *zamīndārs* and peasants was not really land tax (*kharāj*), for it exceeded all legally allowable limits; it was, in fact, rent (*ujrat*). In India neither the peasants nor the *zamīndārs* could be deemed to be tax-paying proprietors, since the sultan was not called upon to make any provision for them out of the *maḥṣūl*, should they abandon, or be removed from, the land, as would have been necessary had they truly been proprietors.[8] One would think that the Qāẓī was now reaching the very conclusion that he had at the start contested, namely that as rent-receiver the king should be deemed to be the proprietor; he just manages to avoid this by arguing that land was to be seen rather in the light of "spoils" (*fai'*) and as belonging to the Muslim public treasury (*baitu-l māl*), though this too was under the control and administration of the sultan.[9]

In essence, Qāẓi A'la's arguments coincide with the conclusions of the European travellers: the king was either the proprietor or possessor of the entire land, since what was received by him or on his behalf was so large a share of the produce of the land as to approximate legitimately to rent rather than to anything recognizable as tax. This view could also have been influenced by the *jāgīr* system. The *jāgīrdārs* were the most natural counterparts of the great lords in Western Europe, who by the sixteenth century

---

did say, however, that the land belonged to the person who brought it under cultivation, whether he be the peasant (*ra'īyat*) or the king's assignee (*ḥākim*) (Add. 19,504, f.66a).

6 Qāẓī Muḥammad A'lā, *Risāla Aḥkām al-Ārāẓī*, MS Aligarh, f.43a-b. Unluckily, the tract is not dated, but according to 'Abdu-l Ḥaī, *Nuzhatu-l Khawāṭir*, VI, 278, he was the author of *Kashshāf-i Iṣṭilāḥātu-l Funūn*, written in 1745. (I owe guidence to this reference to the late Maulana Sibtul Hasan, head of the MSS section of M.A. Library, Aligarh).

7 *Risāla Aḥkām al-Ārāẓī*, f.44a.

8 Ibid., ff. 47a-48a.

9 Ibid., ff.47b-49a.

were already well on their way to establishing their position as full landowners of their manors and fiefs. If the Mughal emperor could so routinely transfer the *jāgīrdārs* from their *jāgīrs* or terri-torial charges, then, he, and not the assignees, had to be seen as the true owner.[10]

Since the concept of the king's ownership of the land was based only on the size of the land tax, and not on any claims put forward by the king himself (or his officials), this could not even theoretically preclude the existence in the towns of a system of private property in land, as was expressly noted by Bernier.[11] Our records not only show townsmen as *māliks* selling plots to each other, but also selling lands to the king, or even disputing their possession with him.[12] A private proprietor seems to have had the full right to levy rent and to evict the occupant.[13]

Less easy to explain in the framework of the theory of royal ownership of land are the even more numerous sales of agricul-tural land in villages by *zamīndārs* and others, whom the documents themselves often style *māliks* or proprietors. As we shall see in Chapter V these sale-deeds clearly show that extensive private property existed in rights over shares in such produce of the land as was left after the payment of land revenue, which latter comprised a very large part of the surplus. The rather low values

[10] Cf. Saran, 330-31, 333. Such a line of argument seems to lie especially behind Bernier's perception of the Mughal emperor's position as owner of the soil.

[11] See his reference to "some houses and gardens which he ['the Great Mogol'] sometimes permits his subjects to buy, sell and otherwise dispose of, among themselves" (Bernier, 204). Roe, 105, was, therefore, obviously exaggerating when he said that, apart from the king, "no man hath a foote".

[12] For disputes between the state and private owners or occupants, see *Waqā'i' Dakhin*, 50-51; *Waqā'i' Ajmer*, 386, 432, 440; NAI 2671/14. Documents recording acts of sale of urban lands and houses are too numerous for one to attempt even a representative selection, but the following may be offered as specimens; *Ma'āṣiru-l Ajdād*, 517-18 (Maham, *sarkār* Hisar, 1590), 521-7 (same locality, 1631); Blochet, Suppl. 482, ff.210b-211b, 222a-223a (sale-deeds of "a one-storeyed house with land", place and date not stated, but pre-1648); document of 1669 in *Tārīkh-i Amroha*, 311-12; and I.O.4438: 64 (double-storeyed house, Batala, 1707-8?). Numerous trans-actions relating to urban property are recorded in Vrindāban Documents. In *Ādāb-i 'Ālamgīrī*, ed., II, 880 (doc. of *c.*1655), it is stated of houses near the fort of Agra: "Those houses (*ḥavelīs*) are either *nuzūlī* (state owned) or have owners; ... in the latter case, they must be of one of two kinds: either the owners themselves live in those houses, or have given them out on rent."

[13] For house-rents by private owners, see Foster, *Suppl. Cal.*, Surat, 1616, Doc. no.295; NAI 2671/13 (Mathura, 1675) & 2671/14 ("4 houses and 2 shops", Mathura, 1694). See also *Ādāb-i 'Ālamgīrī*, op.cit. For eviction of an occupant by a lawful owner, see *Waqā'i' Ajmer*, 386-7, and NAI 2671/13.

in relation to annual land revenue (Chapter V, Section 1) tell us that what was held by the *zamīndārs*, could not have been the right to full surplus or rent, but only to a secondary share out of it. In such circumstances whether the *zamīndārs*, even if styled *māliks* in the documents, and accepted as such by peasants, could be proprietors of land in the strict sense of the word must remain questionable.

There is, most important of all, the question of the rights and status of the peasants themselves. It has been argued, but without adducing much evidence, that the peasants were the ultimate proprietors of land in pre-colonial India.[14] To some extent one could supply the deficiency in evidence. Aurangzeb's *farmān* to Muḥammad Hāshim[15] uses the terms *mālik* and *arbāb-i zamīn* (landowners) for the actual cultivators of the land. The testimony of the *farmān* is, however, suspect since it was expressly drafted to set out the laws of the *Sharī'at*, which bore little relevance to the agrarian conditions in India.[16] But it is by no means alone among official documents in assuming peasants to possess ownership rights.[17] A document (1611) from the middle Doab, tracing the right of *zamīndārs* of a village, alleges that this had been purchased from certain *māliks*, who, in turn, had purchased the village "from the ancient *māliks*, who were Kāchhīs and Chamārs", and who, to judge by their castes, could only have been cultivators and labourers.[18] Eighteenth-century evidence from eastern Rajasthan tells us of superior peasants, expecting concessional revenue rates, buying up lands of ordinary cultivators (*pāltīs*), and either leasing them out on share-cropping or cultivating them with the aid of hired labour.[19] The specific cases are reinforced by the general statement of the historian K͟hāfī K͟hān, who speaks of "the proprietary (*milkī*) and hereditary lands" of the peasants, though in the context of these being seized and sold away by oppressive revenue officials.[20] On the other hand,

[14] Saran, 328-35.

[15] See text in *JASB*, NS, II (1906), 238-49, and *Mir'āt*, I, 268-72.

[16] Cf. Moreland, *Agrarian System*, 133, 139-40.

[17] See, e.g., *Nigārnāma-i Munshī*, ed., 143-4; *Durru-l 'Ulūm*, ff.46b-47a.

[18] Shamsabad Doc.4. The Kāchhīs were traditionally low-caste cultivators of market or garden crops, and the Chamārs the lowliest cultivators and labourers. Even if in this particular case, the original purchase was fictitious, the claim would not have been put forward had such a transaction been regarded by contemporaries as impossible (cf. I. Habib in *IESHR*, IV (3), 215-16, 230-32).

[19] Dilbagh Singh in *IHR*, II (2), 304-6.

[20] K͟hāfī K͟hān, I, 157-8; Add. 6573, ff.96b-70a.

Qāẓī Muḥammad A'lā, as we have seen, tells us that peasants, far from claiming to be *māliks*, admitted the *zamīndārs* to be the proprietors of their lands.[21] For the Dakhin, Munro was to make a similar statement in 1807 about the peasants' abstention from claiming ownership over their land.[22]

The crux of the matter really is whether the substance, not merely the designation, of the peasant's relationship to the land he cultivated, was such as to deserve the application of the term 'proprietary'.

Certain statements in our sources suggest recognition of the peasant's right to permanent and hereditary occupancy. The *farmān* addressed to Muḥammad Hāshim provides that if the cultivator-*mālik* was found incapable of cultivating the land or abandoned it altogether, it was to be given to another for cultivation, so that there was no loss of revenue. But if at any time the original *mālik* recovered his ability to cultivate the land, or returned to it, the land was to be restored to him.[23] That this was not an abstract principle is shown by its adoption in an imperial *sanad* in the specific case of a village, where cultivation had been abandoned. A person is said to have offered to repair its wells and restore cultivation. The *sanad* declares that the offer was to be declined wherever the *mālik* was present and capable of undertaking cultivation. Only failing this was the offer to be accepted, but provided the consent of the *mālik* was first obtained.[24] Akbar's regulations exhorted the revenue officials to ensure that the revenue grantees did not convert "peasants' holdings" (*ra'īyat-kāshta*) into

[21] *Risāla Aḥkām al-Ārāẓī*, f.44a.

[22] "In the Ceded Districts and throughout the Deccan, the ryot has little or no property in land – he has no possessory right; he does not even claim it. He is so far from asserting either a proprietary or a possessory right that he is always ready to relinquish his land, and take some other which he supposes is lighter assessed" (*Fifth Report*, 947).

[23] This is the burden of Art. 3. It concerns land under *kharāj-i muwaẓẓaf*, or a fixed rate of revenue. But Art. 17 declares that if the *mālik* of the land, paying *kharāj-i muqāsima*, or revenue varying with the produce, was able to cultivate it no longer (*Mir'āt*, I, 272), or, by another reading, died heirless (*JASB*, NS, II, 1906, 243; *Durru-l 'Ulūm*, f.142a), the land would be dealt with in the same way as that under *kharāj-i muwaẓẓaf*. In 1800 Buchanan observed this being precisely followed in practice: "The cultivator is nevertheless considered as having a claim to certain lands; and even if he have been absent for a number of years, he may return and reclaim the lands formerly occupied by his family" (*Journey from Madras*, I, 388). A similar practice was noticed by Malcolm in 1821 in respect of the low-caste Kurmi peasants in the Bagar tract of Malwa (*Memoir of Central India*, II, 76 n.).

[24] *Nigārnāma-i Munshī*, ed., 143-4.

their own "personally cultivated holdings" (*khwud-kāshta*),[25] the significance of this being brought out exceptionally well by a survey (1596) of a revenue grant in Navsari, near Surat, in which the two categories of holdings are sharply distinguished.[26] Jahāngīr's accession decrees prohibited the revenue officials themselves from forcibly converting the land of the peasants (*zamīn-i ri'āyā*) into their own holdings (*khwud-kāshta*).[27]

More: When the *Ā'īn* says of the king's obligation to protect peasants "who hold cultivated lands for generations", the assumption of hereditary claims to land among peasants seems to be tacitly admitted.[28] The *farmān* to Muḥammad Hāshim, Art.11, might not be raising an irrelevant issue when it discusses how the land revenue was to be realized from heirs on the death of a cultivating *mālik*. Moreover, the same *farmān* suggests that land could be sold by the cultivators so that one has to assume that the peasant's occupancy claim could sometimes even be worth someone's buying.[29]

That the peasant's right had in fact the potential for conversion into a saleable right is proved by some sixteenth- and seventeenth-century records of sales of land occupancies by peasants in and around Vrindāban, the temple-town which grew up in the area of the village of Dosaich and its hamlets, near Mathura. The township created an increasing demand for land for houses and gardens; and we find in 1594, the rate of Rs 2.75 per *bīgha* quoted for determining the price of cultivated land (*zamīn-i zirā'atī*) sold by two Gaurava peasants; next year another peasant sold such land

25 *A'īn*, I, 287.

26 See my analysis of this doc. in *PIHC*, 54th Session, 1993, Mysore, 252-4.

27 *T.J.*, 4. The first version of Jahāngīr's Memoirs makes the sense of the order still more explicit. "The *karorīs* [imperial revenue officials] and *jāgīrdārs* are not to seize the land of the peasants (*zamīn-i ri'āyā*) and not to make it their own land (*zamīn-i khwud*) and get it cultivated" (Aligarh transcript of Riza Library MS [Persian, History: 175], p.11). The spurious Memoirs contained in R.A.S., Morley 117, Pers. Cat. 122, f.11a), follow the first version closely here.

28 *A'īn*, I, 290.

29 See Art. 13, which deals with the problems of realizing the revenue from the seller or buyer in case of sale during the year. The commentator on the *farmān*, whom Sarkar introduces to us, doubts the whole assumption of peasant proprietorship manifest in its terminology and provisions. He argues that if the peasant's right to land was saleable, none of the peasants would have fled without first selling the land, and then the problem of land abandonment by peasants (cf. Art.3) would not have arisen (*JASB*, NS, II [1906], 244). One can counter this by saying that although the peasant's right might be deemed saleable and be occasionally

at Rs 2.35 per *bīgha*.[30] Yet the very same year much higher rates prevailed elsewhere in the same township: Rs 14.40 for cultivated and Rs 4 for waste (*banjar*).[31] Subsequently, prices rose further. In 1611, what is described as "cultivators' land" was sold at Rs 12.35 per *bīgha*;[32] in 1653 cultivated land, with *muqaddamī* claims, sold at Rs 17;[33] in 1654 cultivated land, at Rs 13.33,[34] and in 1702, at Rs 20.36.[35]

Such an advantageous situation, not only in respect of the price of land, but also owing to proximity of market, as well as other favourable circumstances, such as tax-concessions or especially productive soil, could also create the possibility of the field-holder being different from the actual cultivator, working the land on lease. Such conditions obviously existed in 1596 near Navsari, southern Gujarat, where the names of the cultivating lessees appear under the main holders in the entries under *ra'īyat-kāshta* (peasant-cultivated) in the survey of land under a grant.[36]

It is likely that the peasant's right to land, with the potential of becoming a saleable right, in the manner we have just outlined, could exist only in areas which were *ra'iyatī*, that is, where the peasants were unencumbered with any claims of *zamīndārs* over them. The *zamīndārs*, as we shall see, were often credited with the right to determine peasant occupancies, the peasants acknowledging them as proprietors (Chapter V, Section 1). But Qāẓī Muḥammad A'lā also gave to the king the power to take away land from peasants. If the peasants flee, he says, the king assigns their lands to others, allowing the former cultivators no share in

sold in practice as well, yet, owing to the abundance of land and the heaviness of the revenue burden, he would not often succeed in finding buyers.

30 IVS 208 and 180 A & B.

31 IVS 209 A & B and 210. In the former document I take 22½ *tankas* to mean 22½ *dāms*.

32 NAI 2691/1: *zamīn-i ẕail muzāri'ān*.

33 Govind-dev, 39.

34 Govind-dev (unnumbered)

35 Govind-dev (unnumbered). Prices of other plots of land, not described as cultivated or waste, or not involving persons easily identifiable as peasants, are not considered here. These could be much higher: in one transaction of 1594, the price works out at Rs 102 per *bīgha* (Govind-dev, unnumbered, & Wright 6). In a sale per deed of 1653-4, the *bīgha* used is defined as *bīgha-i Ilāhī*, but otherwise the *bīgha* is left undesignated in the documents.

36 See I. Habib in *PIHC*, 54th session, 1993, Mysore, 252-4. A. Siddiqi cites reports from the 1820s of two villages in Doab, in one of which all "the proprietors" worked their land "assisted by their families", there being no other cultivators; but in the other there were 26 "members of the [peasant] brotherhood", and six "mere tenants" (*Agrarian Change in a North Indian State*, 32).

the produce of the land abandoned by them. Even if the peasants remain but are unable to till the land, the king gives it to other peasants, on whom the revenue is then levied.[37] It is, however, possible to argue that this right only accrued to the king and his officials when the peasant failed to pay the revenue, or did not raise the produce out of which the revenue could have been paid.[38] No right of eviction at will is claimed on the king's behalf, even by Qāẓī Muḥammad A'lā, who otherwise seems keen to discern marks of the king's possessory control over all land.

If the peasant could not, under contemporary conceptions of justice or equity, be removed from his land, he did not equally have the free or absolute right to remove himself from it. There was, observed a European traveller in respect of the Gujarat peasants, "little difference between them and serfs such as are found in Poland, for here [too] the peasants must all sow ...."[39] Aurangzeb's *farmān* to Muḥammad Hāshim, Art. 2, insists upon this obligation of the peasants when it says that, "if after investigation, it appears that despite their capacity to undertake cultivation and [the availability of] irrigation, they have withdrawn their hands from cultivation", the revenue officials should "coerce and threaten them and visit them with imprisonment and corporal punishment". The draft of a specimen bond from village officials, given in a manual of revenue administration (1730-31), offers a confirmation of the principles set forth in Aurangzeb's *farmān*. The *zamīndārs* and village officials here bind themselves "not to allow any cultivator to leave his place"; if some cultivators did nevertheless abscond, they undertook to distribute the land of the absconders among those who remained.[40]

Documents dealing with specific cases show how the peasant's obligation to remain in his original place to cultivate the soil was

[37] *Risāla Aḥkām al-Arāzī*, ff.47b-48a. (Qāẓī Muḥammad A'lā makes no reference to peasants' selling away their rights to land.) Careri, 241, speaks of "the poor Peasants who have sometimes the Land they have cultivated taken from them, and that which is untill'd given in lieu of it" by the government of the "Great Mogul".

[38] This is the burden of Buchanan's observations (1800) on cultivators' rights in Mysore, after its seizure from Tipu Sultan (*Journey from Madras*, I, 124, 271). A similar practice prevailed in Sonda territory (North Kanara), where the land was considered "the property of the government" (ibid., III, 242).

[39] Geleynssen, *JIH*, IV, 78. One may remember that Poland was the classical land of Second Serfdom.

[40] Bekas, f.67b. The bond (*muchalka*) was given by *zamīndārs*, *muqaddams* (village headmen) and *paṭwārīs* (village accountants). All documents in Bekas are drawn from records of *sarkār* Sambhal, *ṣūba* Dehli.

insisted upon. In 1646 the emperor ordered the *jāgīrdārs* of Broach, Baroda, etc., to return the peasants who within the previous five years had migrated from *sarkār* Surat and *pargana* Olpad in the *jāgīr* of Princess Jahān Ārā.[41] Earlier in 1632 when seventy peasants had fled from *pargana* Maqbulabad into Jahān Ārā's *jāgīrs* in southern Gujarat, she had ordered that they be handed over to the men of the *jāgīrdār* of *pargana* Maqbulabad.[42] Two interesting cases of individual peasants come from the same collection of documents. In a document of 1617-18, we read how Khānjī, a cultivator (*muzāri'*) of a village in *pargana* Batlari, quarrelling with headmen of his village, had fled to the neighbouring *pargana* of Uklesar (Ankleshwar) in *sarkār* Broach, and was detained for two months by its *shiqqdār* (revenue collector) and then handed over to the headman of yet another village, presumably to engage in cultivation. Orders were issued that he should be immediately returned to his original village.[43] In another document (1635-38) we find a cultivator, Isḥāq, reporting that he had left his original village Khanchauli in *pargana* Chaurasi, *sarkār* Surat, a few years earlier to go to Daman, and had returned thence to Bulsar to engage in cultivation on short leases (*ganvat*); when the *desāī* of Bulsar tried to fix a permanent rate (*ẓabṭī*) on him, he went to village Rajwara, *pargana* Chikli; and from here the *desāī* of *pargana* Chaurasi finally took him to his original place. But the *desāī* of Bulsar now laid claim to his person, and was pressing the headman of Rajwara to produce him. Orders were now issued that the *desāī* of Bulsar could not claim him just on account of the two years of short-lease cultivation; he rightfully belonged to his original village in *pargana* Chaurasi.[44]

It was probably because of the importance of the tie to one's original village that a very widespread distinction came to be made between the original place where one was under an obligation to cultivate under compulsion and any other place where one went voluntarily as an outsider. Such an outsider would be called *pāikāsht* or *pāhī*.[45] An imperial order of 1634 to the governor of

[41] Blochet, Suppl. Pers. 482, f.94b.

[42] Ibid., ff. 98b-99b. See also ibid., ff.40b-42a, 50a-b, 154a and 163b-164a, 169b, where officials ask others for return of peasants who had left their original places.

[43] Ibid., 152a-b.

[44] Ibid., f.1660b. For *ganvat*, see A. Rogers, *Land Revenue of Bombay*, I, 172.

[45] According to what is probably a mid-18th century text, "*pāikāsht* peasants

Gujarat recites that some peasants from *pargana* Khambayat had gone into *pargana* Patlad to cultivate the land by way of *pāi-kāshta*. When some of them died, the agents of the governor and other *jāgīrdārs* of *pargana* Patlad tried to compel other peasants of *pargana* Khambayat to cultivate the land they had tilled, or to force the surviving *pāikārs* (*pāikāsht* peasants) to cultivate more land. Both the actions were held improper and so prohibited.[46] Clearly, the *pāikāsht* peasants were thought to be exempt from the obligation to stay on and cultivate the land to which the native peasants were subject.

But as migrants they could always be forced to return to their original places. Thus in 1641 the Jām of Navanagar was compelled, after a successful expedition against him, "to expel peasants belonging to the territory around Ahmadabad, who had migrated into his country so that they might return to their homes and [native] places".[47] Late in Aurangzeb's reign, the *faujdār* of Kalyan is found justifying his military action against the Portuguese on the ground that the peasants whom he had brought back to their original lands from the territories of the *zamīndārs* had been enticed afresh by the "Farangīs" to settle in their dominions.[48] This right could also be converted into a licence to one *jāgīrdār* to raid the territory of another for obtaining "cattle and men", so much so that Jahāngīr was obliged to forbid this practice in his accession edicts.[49]

[are] those who have their homes in villages different from the one where they carry on cultivation", contrasted with *khwud-kāsht* peasants, who had homes in the same *pargana* (? village) (*Risāla-i Zirā'at*, ff.76-8a). See also Yāsīn's glossary, Add. 6603, ff.52a, 81a. The term *pāhī* for such peasants appears extensively in Nainsī's *Vigat* (*c*.1664), e.g., II, 125, 126, 165, 179, 195, 211, in the chapter on *pargana* Merta. Satish Chandra, indeed, prefers the reading *pāhī-kāsht* to the usual *pāi-kāsht* (*IHR*, I (1), 51-64). Cf. Fallon, s.v. *pāhī*, where the definition "non-resident cultivator" is given, and *pāhī āsāmī*, *pāhī-kāsht* and *pāi-kāsht* are listed as alternative forms. *Pāhī* is derived from Old Hindi *pākhī*, from Sanskrit *paksh*, side. Derivation from Persian *pāi*, "foot, low", would suggest a class of subordinate cultivators.

[46] Blochet, Suppl. Pers. 482, f.43a.

[47] Lāhori, II, 232; *Mir'āt*, I, 214.

[48] *Kārnāma*, ff.238a-239a, 243a-244b. The Portuguese themselves went a step further and introduced a rigorous serfdom in their dominions. Describing conditions in Salsette "Island" (Goa), Careri (1695) says; "The Peasants are worse than Vassals to the Lords of the Villages; for they are bound to till the land, or to farm as much as may put them in a condition to pay the Landlord; thus like slaves, if they fly from one village to another, their landlords bring them back by force" (Careri, 179: original English translation amended according to editor's corrections).

[49] Thus, at least, according to the first version of his Memoirs (Aligarh transcript,

The willingness of the state to recognize the peasant's right of occupancy, and its anxiety to prevent him from leaving the land, were both natural in an age when land was relatively abundant, and peasants scarce. We have seen in Chapter I that in Mughal times the area under cultivation was in many regions probably only a half and in others two-thirds to three-quarters of the area under cultivation at the beginning of the twentieth century. There were always stretches of virgin land beckoning to the peasant, while with his low level of subsistence and primitive huts he had few immovable possessions to tie him to his old place of habitation.

"In Hindustān", observed Bābur, "hamlets and villages – even towns – are depopulated and set up in a moment. If a people of a large town, who have lived there for years, flee from it, they do it in such a way that not a sign or trace of them remains in a day or a day and a half. On the other hand, if they fix their eyes on a place in which to settle, they need not dig water-courses or construct dams because their crops are all rain-grown. The population is unlimited. A group collects together, they make a tank or dig a well; they need not build houses or set up walls – *khas* grass abounds, trees (are) innumerable, and straightway there is a village, or town."[50]

The propensity to abandon the land whenever he could was so marked a feature of the peasant's normal conduct that Kabīr (*c.*1500) could liken the five senses to the *krisanwā* (=*kisāns*, peasants) who have fled the village, leaving the soul, as the headman (*mahatau*), to render the accounts.[51] Such migrations could be over long distances. We even read of a Rathor peasant from Marwar coming to settle in Bihar.[52] In 1665 an official reported that as a result of famine the peasants (*raiyatīs*) of four *parganas* in eastern Rajasthan had migrated to distant parts such as Malwa and Burhanpur and Pūrab (Ilahabad and further east) and Pilibhit, and that he was trying to bring them back.[53] But, ordinarily, the migrations must have been limited to adjoining areas, as in

---

op.cit., 11; see also the spurious Memoirs, R.A.S., Morley 177, Pers. Cat. 122, f.11a). No reference to it occurs in the corresponding passage in *T.J.*, 4.

[50] *Bāburnāma*, ed., 440-1; Bev., II, 487-88. I have considerably modified the translation by referring also to 'Abdu-r Raḥīm's Persian version, Or. 3714, f.377b.

[51] *Gurū Granth Sāhib*, Nagari text, II, 1104; *Kabīr Granthāvalī*, 299; Macauliffe, VI, 250-51.

[52] Ḥasan 'Alī Khān, *Tārīkh-i Daulat-i Sher Shāhī*, in *Medieval India Quarterly*, I (1) (July 1950), Persian text, 3.

[53] Doc. quoted in S.P. Gupta, *Agrarian System of Eastern Rajasthan*, 121-2.

cases we have just seen described in documents from southern Gujarat. Surveying Mysore in 1800, Buchanan was to consider such migrations an important check on "arbitrary oppression" under "native governments".[54]

The position of the peasant in Mughal India in relation to land thus offers a sharp contrast to that of his descendant living under modern landlordism created under British rule. The great weapon in the hands of the modern landlord has been the threat of evicting his tenantry. The abandonment of his land by any of his tenants came to hold no terrors for him. But even in 1819 this was not the case: writing of what is now Uttar Pradesh, Holt-Mackenzie noted that "land being more abundant than labour, in general, the zamindar has greater reason to dread the desertion of his Ryots than they to fear expulsion from their lands".[55] The situation changed as a result of two parallel processes. First, the *zamīndār* turned into the main rent-expropriator as the share of the colonial state in the agricultural surplus directly claimed in tax declined during the latter half of the nineteenth century.[56] Second, the pressure on land increased as sources of livelihood outside agriculture stagnated or disappeared under the impact of Britain's conquest of the Indian market. The two processes handed over larger numbers of peasants, bound hand and foot as tenants-at-will, to the landlord; and land at last became scarce and human beings superfluous.

It is time now to turn for a last glance on the vexed question of 'property' in land in Mughal India. In so far as the peasant recognized the *zamīndār's* right of choice in giving land to him to till (Chapter V, Section 1), he was not, in such lands at least, the proprietor. In these and other (*ra'īyati*) areas, his right of occupancy was counterbalanced by the constraints legally set on his mobility. To that degree, he was a semi-serf, not a free agent. And his right, such as it was, was seldom saleable. It is, therefore, not possible to discern the emergence of any substantive peasant property in Mughal India. Rather one could say that there was no exclusive right of property vesting in anyone;[57] instead the system

[54] *Journey from Madras*, I, 298. [55] *Revenue Selections*, 96 (cf. also 252).

[56] This did not mean an absolute decline in the tax burden, however, since indirect taxes increased (I. Habib, *Essays*, 280-1).

[57] One cannot, therefore, quarrel with Maine when he said (*Village Communities in the East and the West*, 3rd ed., 157-8 & ff.) that "property" in India is not to be understood in the sense of "the same assemblage of rights which constitutes the

contained a network of transferable rights and obligations, with different claimants (the king or his assignee; the *zamīndār*; and, finally, the peasant) to differently defined shares in the produce from the same land.

2. PEASANTS AND LABOURERS

The peasant, together with his family, universally appears in our documents as a separate, individual producer, tilling his own fields. What was said by a revenue manual of the early nineteenth century of the Dehli and Agra region would have been as true in the seventeenth: "The cultivating peasants (*āsāmīs*), who plough up the fields, mark the limits of each field, for identification and demarcation, with borders of [raised] earth, brick and thorn, so that thousands of such fields may be counted in a village."[1] The general statement can be illustrated by lists of peasant-fields such as the one contained in a survey of a revenue grant near Navsari, south Gujarat, from 1596, with each peasant holding divided up among fields, each with different crops, averaging 2 *bīghas, 9 biswas Ilāhī* or less than 0.6 hectare;[2] or in a document of c.1757 from the township of Maham, in *sarkār* Hisar of *ṣūba* Dehli;[3] or, again, in *khasras* of villages of about the same time from eastern Rajasthan now preserved at the Rajasthan State Archives at Bikaner.[4] The evidence for cultivation of separate holdings by individuals in eastern Rajasthan is reinforced by official censuses of plough-oxen (*hal-bail*), one of which for *pargana* Chatsu, of as early a date as 1666, lists about seventy peasants (*āsāmī*) per village in a sample of ten villages, each person on average owning 2.8 bullocks.[5] In Gujarat we read of peasants "setting their fields apart" by raising fences of thorn-bush.[6] When Buchanan carried out his

---

modern English ownership of land in fee simple;" though it is another matter whether this was due, as he asserted, to the fact that "the feudalism of India" was never "completed."

[1] Chhatar Māl, *Dīwān Pasand*, Or. 2011, f.8a.

[2] Cf. I. Habib in *PIHC*, 54th Session, 1993, Mysore, 248-50 (text of doc. between pp. 256-7).

[3] Printed in *Ma'āṣiru-l Ajdād*, 560-62.

[4] See S.P. Gupta, *Agrarian System of Eastern Rajasthan*, 294-309, for the text of such a *khasra* of village Morara, *pargana* Naraina, of 1745.

[5] The document is described by S.P. Gupta, 255-6, and partly printed, ibid., 257-268. The sample we have taken is that of the ten villages listed in the table in S.P. Gupta, 256, and excludes the figure of the *pargana*, as a whole, as well as of the township of Chatsu. For other similar cattle censuses, see ibid., 131-133.

[6] *TJ*, 205.

wonderfully detailed surveys of southern and eastern India in the first decade of the nineteenth century he similarly found individual farming to be the dominant mode, together with landlord 'estate'-farming here and there, but with no trace of communal cultivation anywhere.[7] Such conditions explain why the assumption of individual peasant cultivation so universally underlies the revenue regulations of the Mughal administration, such as those that insist on separate assessment of the holdings of each peasant as against the imposition of an aggregate figure for the whole village.[8]

Individual peasant farming can never be egalitarian. The relative abundance of land might be thought to have been a factor inhibiting the increase of wealth in the hands of a few by their monopoly of the land. But, as Marx pointed out in the second draft of his letter to Vera Zasulich, "the possession of chattels, an element which is playing an increasingly important part in agriculture itself, progressively differentiates the fortune of the members of the commune [village community]," once they have taken to "parcel farming of the land".[9] Not only the possession of cattle, but also of seed, wells, water-wheels, sugar-mills, indigo-vats, and so on, would determine how much land and what and how many crops a peasant could cultivate, with his own or with hired labour. With the extension of market relations, and so of usury, differentiation would intensify further. The retrogressive nature of the land tax (Chapter VI, Section 1) was also likely to assist the process of differentiation even if there was not the further factor of the richer transferring their tax burden on to the shoulders of their poorer brethren.

The differentiation has undoubtedly left its mark on official classification of the rural population. We first of all have the all-

[7] The only possible survival of communal farming that could possibly be detected in Buchanan's surveys (1800) is his description (*Journey from Madras*, III, 319-20) of the "singular" manner of letting out lands at Pollachi in Coimbatore district (Tamilnadu): "the fields are divided into three qualities according to the goodness of this soil; and they are then divided among the cultivators by an assembly of these people." But the "farmers" complained that they were allotted more lands than they could till; and it would seem therefore that the method was actually forced upon the village by a heavy revenue demand.

[8] *A'īn*, I, 285-6, 288; Aurangzeb's *farmān* to Rasikdās, Art. 3, etc. See also Chapter VI, Section 4.

[9] Marx and Engels, *Collected Works*, XXIV, 363. Cf. also Utsa Patnaik's critique (*The Long Transition*, 1-62) of Chayanov's theory of the egalitarian nature of the "peasant economy".

embracing term *ri 'āyā* or *ra 'īyat*, standing for subjects, tax-payers and peasants (according to context). The bulk of this mass seems to consist of *reza ri 'āyā*, or small peasants, contrasted with the big men, *muqaddams* (headmen), etc.[10] There is a further term *muzāri '* (cultivator) which occurs frequently in the documents, alongside *ri 'āyā* and *ra 'īyat*, and represents more specifically the cultivating peasant.[11]

These distinctions were based essentially on the resources of the peasants of the various categories. The verses of Gurū Arjan (d.1606) tell us of the *khasam* (master) of the field, who sets a watchman (*rākhā*) over his field; and of the *kirsān* (peasant) who orders about the reapers (*lāvās*) who cut his crop.[12] The presence of the rich peasant, using hired labour, is unmistakable here. Some two hundred years later, the *Dīwān Pasand* drew this picture of the *muqaddams* as peasants:

> Most *muqaddams*, who undertake cultivation on their own (*khwud kāsht*), engage labourers as servants and set them to the tasks of agriculture; and taking from them the work of ploughing, sowing, reaping the harvest, and drawing water from the well, while paying them fixed wages, whether in cash or in grain, they become masters of the produce of cultivation and thus appear as both *muqaddams* and *āsāmīs* [peasants].[13]

There is much evidence for this stratum of peasants in seventeenth- and eighteenth-century documents from eastern Rajasthan. They bore the designation of holders of *khud-kāsht*(=*khwud-kāshta*), or *gharu-hālā* ("of home-plough"), and employed hired labourers (*majūrs*) to till their lands or sometimes gave their lands out on a share-cropping basis.[14]

With such rich peasants at one extreme, a *farmān* of Aurangzeb introduces us to those at the other: small peasants (*reza ri 'āyā*) who "engage in cultivation but are wholly in debt for their subsistence and seed and cattle". They were numerous enough for the

[10] Cf. Aurangzeb's *farmān* to Rasikdās, Art. 9.

[11] Thus in a late-18th-century response to a questionnaire, it is stated that a cultivator who has his house on his own land is called *ra 'īyat* or *muzāri '*, but one who has his house on the land of another is only a *muzāri '* (Add. 19503, f.64a).

[12] *Gurū Granth Sāhib*, Nagari text, 143, 179.

[13] *Dīwān Pasand*, Or. 2011, f.8a.

[14] I follow the analysis of the evidence by S.P. Gupta, *Agrarian System of Eastern Rajasthan*, 118, and Dilbagh Singh in *IHR*, II (2), 303-6. Gupta's evidence relates more to the 17th century, and Dilbagh Singh's to the 18th. The term *riāyatī* (Pers. *ri 'āyatī*), or concessional rate-holders, for the superior peasants, which Dilbagh Singh gives, does not occur in Gupta's study. I do not recall seeing this term used for any category of peasants in Mughal documents either.

emperor to take special cognizance of them, and, classifying them as "indigent", to declare them exempt from the *jizya* (poll-tax).[15] Indebtedness certainly increased indigence: a mid-eighteenth century work from Bengal states that "most" peasants contracted debt to pay the land revenue and other imposts, and that the high rates (12½ per cent per month), compounded after short periods, led to their utter ruin.[16] From Maharashtra comes the evidence, taken just at the end of Maratha rule (1820), of widespread peasant indebtedness and of ruinously high rates charged on the smaller loans.[17] Because of their diminishing means, the pauperized peasants could be compelled to plough lands of other peasants, from whom presumably they had obtained some assistance (e.g. loan of plough) in return, later, for payments out of the produce. Such sub-peasants were called *kaljana* in Bengal.[18] They had their counterparts in eastern Rajasthan, among the *pāltīs*, who tilled the lands of *zamīndārs* and superior peasants as mere share-croppers, being subject to eviction at will by the landholders.[19]

The differentiation among the peasantry is well brought out by the *jizya* (poll-tax) returns from two villages near Lahor (1697-8), which are reproduced in two administrative manuals. Here out of a total of 280 non-Muslim males, 73 were tax-exempt, being minors, affected by illness, physically handicapped, mentally deficient, or absent. Out of the remaining 207 males, 13 are shown in Class I, that is each with possessions worth over Rs 2500; 35 in Class II, each with possessions worth over Rs 50; and 137 in Class III, each with possessions worth less than Rs 50. Twenty males were "absolutely indigent", and, on that account, exempt from tax.[20] Here one may see in Class I the small group consisting of

[15] *Nigārnāma-i Munshī*, ed., 139 (collated with Or.1735, f.180a-b, and Bodl. ff.143b-144a). The reading *kāh* (straw) in the printed text is to be corrected to *gāu* (cattle), as in the MSS. See also *Ma'ārif*, XL (1937) (No. 4), 237 (but otherwise defective, reading *zamīndār* for *z̲immī-i nādār* and *farẓ* for *qarẓ*).

[16] *Risāla-i Zirā'at*, ff.10b-11a.

[17] Thomas Coats, 'Account of the Present State of the Township of Lony', 1820, *Transactions of the Literary Society of Bombay*, III, 212-3. Out of 87 families of cultivators in this village, all except 15 or 16 were in debt, the sums borrowed ranging from Rs 40 to 200. The usual interest rate on cash loans was 24% per annum but on smaller sums it was 2 'pice' per rupee per month or 40% per annum.

[18] *Risāla-i Zirā'at*, f.8a.

[19] Cf. Dilbagh Singh, *IHR*, II (2), 305.

[20] *K̲h̲ulāṣatu-s Siyāq*, Aligarh MS, f.41a-b; Or.2026, f.56a-b. The totals given in the *K̲h̲ulāṣatu-s Siyāq* MS are erroneous, since they do not match its own detailed figures; Or.2026 is correct throughout.

zamīndārs, usurers and grain merchants; in Class II, the rich peasants; in Class III, the bulk of the peasantry, the *reza ri'āyā*; and among the "absolutely indigent", the poorest peasants (identified as indigent in Aurangzeb's *farmān*) and landless labourers.

A number of Rajasthani documents give us illustrations of peasant stratification in quantitative terms. Official censuses of plough-oxen (*hal-bail*) are particularly significant since these show the varying access to one of the basic resources for cultivation. In 1641, in a village of *pargana* Mauzabad, *sarkār* Ajmer, out of 114 *āsāmīs* (cultivators), 55 had one or two bullocks each, to a total of 128, while 25 had more than three each, to a total of 134 bullocks.[21] The plough statistics are still more revealing. In 1665 in a village in Chal Kalana, *sarkār* Narnaul, in *ṣūba* Dehli, 34 out of 52 *āsāmīs* had either a half or one plough each, making a total of 30½ ploughs, while 15 had two ploughs each, a total of 30.[22] The richer peasants' larger command over ploughs was still better marked in another village of *sarkār* Tijara in the same province. Here in 1666 out of 38 *āsāmīs*, 26 had one plough each, but two had three each, and another two had five each.[23]

The differentiation is similarly visible when we consider statistics of produce. In rabi 1711 in a village in *pargana* Tonk (*ṣūba* Ajmer), three peasants out of thirty-nine produced over 100 *mans* each, comprising over 23 per cent of the total barley crop of the village. On the other hand, as many as nineteen obtained less

---

The values of the possessions of the three classes of assessees are given in *dirhams* in Aurangzeb's *farmān* imposing the *jizya* (*Mir'āt*, I, 296). I have converted the figures into rupees taking 12 *dirhams* as equal to Rs 3, as. 2, the sanctioned rate for Class III. Īsardās, f.74a-b, gives the scales of values in rupees, but makes a slip in regard to Classes II and III. He has over Rs 2,500 as the worth of the possessions of Class I assessess, over Rs 250 for Class II and just Rs 52 for Class III.

[21] S.P. Gupta, *Agrarian System of Eastern Rajasthan*, 131-2 (tables marred by printing slips). Satish Chandra has a similar analysis of a census of plough-oxen of a village in *pargana* Chatsu, *sarkār* Ajmer (1666), in *IHR*, III (1), 93. There, out of 159 *āsāmīs*, 109 had only one or two bullocks each (total, 184), while the remaining 50 had 3 to 7 bullocks each (total, 198). Figures for 26 villages in the *pargana* are tabulated in ibid., 97.

[22] *IHR*, III (1), 87-8, 94-5. Satish Chandra also analyses figures for the aggregate of 94 villages of the *pargana* in this census. Nearly 80% of the peasants had half or one plough each; but 16½% had two or three.

[23] *IHR*, III (1), 96. In another village from the same census, whose figures are analysed, the maximum number of ploughs owned by any one *āsāmī* was five, such *āsāmīs* being but four out of forty-three (ibid., 97).

than 10 *mans* each.[24] The analysis of a *khasra* of kharif 1791 of a village in *pargana* Jaipur, shows that out of 42 cultivators, one raised as many as nine crops in the kharif harvest; four, seven crops each; and seven, six crops each, cotton being cultivated by all. Eleven raised three or four crops each, thus comprising the middle stratum. At the bottom, as many as nineteen raised one or two crops only, but cotton was cultivated by none.[25] Obviously, the size of lands actually cultivated by peasants of the different strata must have varied accordingly. Naturally, the peasants who raised the larger number of crops usually cultivated larger areas of land. This is brought home to us by the Navsari revenue-grant survey of 1596 (south Gujarat). Here three large cultivators with an average holding of 22.25 *bīghas Ilāhī* raised ten crops, while the remaining four cultivators, with an average holding of only 3.48 *bīghas* each, raised only six crops, none of them growing sugarcane, safflower or cotton – the major cash crops sown in the fields of the larger cultivators.[26]

There is other evidence too of large agricultural holdings. A master dyer of Akbar held in a village near Agra 37 [pre-*Ilāhī*] *bīghas* or about 8 hectares as his "self-cultivated holding (*zirā'at-i khāṣa*)", on which, according to a *farmān* of 1562 he was hitherto paying tax.[27] Later in Akbar's reign, peasants of some villages in *pargana* Sopa, *sarkār* Surat, Gujarat, are found reporting that a *desāī* had a *khwud-kāsht* cultivation "worth nearly 3,000 *maḥmūdīs*" (or about Rs 1,250) in *jama'* or annual revenue.[28] He must surely have used large numbers of ploughs and much hired labour, to raise crops on which so much tax could be due. Southern India, outside the area of our study, had similar conditions: Buchanan in his enquiries in Karnataka and Malabar in 1800-01, found a high degree of differentiation among "farmers" practically everywhere,

[24] S.P. Gupta, *Agrarian System of Eastern Rajasthan*, 128-9.

[25] Ibid., 127-9. See also another *khasra jamabandī* of January 1796, giving data of kharif 1795 for a village in *pargana* Chatsu. Sixteen out of 36 cultivators raised only one crop, none sowing cotton. Three *paṭels*, on the other hand, cultivated six to eight crops each, including cotton in every case (S.P. Gupta, *Medieval India – A Miscellany*, IV, 168-76: read "three" for "two" *paṭels* in Gupta's analysis on p.170).

[26] See my analysis of the document in *PIHC*, 54th Session, 1993, Mysore, 248-52: read 3 *bīghas* 9½ *biswas* for 3 *bīghas* 14½ *biswas* on p. 250, l.5.

[27] For a facsimile of this *farmān*, see I. Habib, ed., *Akbar and his India*, 285 (read '*Farmān* II' for '*Farmān* I' beneath the facsimile); and for its transl., ibid., 282-4.

[28] *Parwāncha* of Ṣādiq Khān in Blochet, Suppl. Pers. 482, ff.170b-171b.

his informants usually employing as their yardstick the numbers of ploughs that the peasants owned.[29]

The existence of cultivation by *zamīndārs* and rich peasants implied, as we have seen, the use of hired labour. Gurū Arjan had spoken of the watchmen (*rākhā*) and reapers (*lāvās*) employed by the *khasam* or *kirsān*, the peasant; the *Dīwān Pasand* tells us how the hired labourers performed all the tasks of agriculture for the *muqaddams* or headmen; and *majūrs* (labourers) appear in records of eastern Rajasthan as necessary aids to cultivation by superior landholders. A large reserve of such labour was undoubtedly supplied by the so-called "menial" castes. Their members not only undertook work considered abhorrent by the caste peasants, such as tannery, scavenging, etc., but were also, in a large measure, agricultural workers. Buchanan noted in his report on the Patna-Gaya district (Bihar) in 1811-12 that the "Chamars, or Muchi, who are tanners and workers of leather... when not employed in their profession, cultivate the land, chiefly as day labourers".[30] In Haryana in 1825, Skinner observed of the same caste that "they worked for wages in the fields of cultivators and *zamīndārs*".[31] The Dhānuks, constituting a still lower caste, were supposedly so called because they husked rice (*dhān*) and also "laboured at cutting and carrying the crops of the cultivators".[32] They were known as Thorīs in the Ajmer province, and Balāhars elsewhere.[33] The latter name is specially significant because it takes us back to the fourteenth century, when Ẓiyā' Baranī used it to denote the lowliest of the cultivators.[34] That the number of people belonging to these castes was quite large can be argued on the basis of modern censuses.[35] For the Mughal empire we can reasonably assume a

[29] *Journey from Madras*, I, 389-90; II, 216-17, 320, 495; III, 35, 139-40, 181, 281, 320-21, 428, and 349.

[30] *Patna-Gaya Report*, I, 350 (*Eastern India*, I, 180). He adds: "but some have farms".

[31] *Tashrīḥu-l Aqwām*, f.182a.

[32] Ibid., ff.101b-102a. Wilson derives the name of this caste from Sanskrit *dhanushka*, a bowman (Ibbetson, *Punjab Castes*, 295).

[33] The identification of Dhānuks with Thorīs is made in the *Tashrīḥu-l Aqwām*, f.188a, and of Thorīs with Balāhars in a report of 1679 in *Waqā'i' Ajmer*, 131. Same authorities for their traditional occupation; also Add. 6603, ff.51b-52a, and Elliot, *Memoirs*, II, 249.

[34] In contrast to khoṭs: Baranī, *Tārīkh-i Fīrūz-shāhī*, Bib. Ind., 287.

[35] See table in S.J. Patel, *Agrarian Labourers in Modern India and Pakistan* (Bombay, 1952), 65. Patel took his figures from the *Report* of the Simon Commission, I, 40-41, which presumably drew upon the 1921 Census.

similar size, and cite a piece of contemporary evidence for support: an official census of households in a group of four villages in a *pargana* of *sarkār* Agra in 1641, shows the Chamārs alone as constituting 23 out of 249 households, or 9.2 per cent of the total.[36]

In addition, there must have been villagers belonging to the peasant castes too, who, becoming pauperized, could not even be share-croppers and turned into wage-labourers. It was surely they who formed the pool of *ghair-jam'ī* peasants, that is peasants not cultivating land and so not yet paying any tax, from amongst whom the authorities were expected to draw cultivators for newly settled villages.[37] Buchanan noted in 1811-12 that in the Patna and Bihar districts "poor people of the cultivating tribe (Chasas) or artificers" saw no disgrace in letting themselves out as day-labourers, although "people of high caste" did not do so.[38] Similar conditions prevailed in the territories of southern India that he had surveyed in 1800-01.[39]

We rarely encounter in our sources any rural slaves who could have augmented the class of agricultural labourers. The *jizya* returns of 1697-8 from villages in the vicinity of Lahor that we have cited above do not record any slaves under the tax-exempt categories where they should have been recorded had they been present.[40] Nor do slaves appear in the abundant documentation relating to eastern Rajasthan as a recognizable element of agrarian society, to judge from modern studies based on this documen-tation.[41] The only reference to a slave who could possibly have been working in the fields that I have been able to find from Gujarat is contained in an official's order of 1637 issued on the complaint of a cultivator (*muzāri'*), against two other cultivators, who had allegedly seized a slave of his.[42] The very limited use of slaves in agriculture in eastern India is confirmed by Buchanan's detailed

36 Satish Chandra and Dilbagh Singh, *PIHC*, 33rd Session, 1972, Muzaffarpur, 198-9. The villages belonged to *pargana* Wazirpur, now in Rajasthan.

37 *Nigārnāma-i Munshī*, ed., 81, 114.

38 *Patna-Gaya Report*, II, 559.

39 At Kolar (Karnataka), the farm servants and labourers were drawn from the ranks of "all castes except Brahmans and Mussulmans" (*Journey from Madras*, I, 298). Around Cannanore (Kerala) the hired men were "Nairs, Moplays and Tiars" (ibid., II, 562).

40 *Khulāṣatu-s Siyāq*, Aligarh MS, f.41a-b; Or. 2026, f.56a-b.

41 That is the studies of Satish Chandra, S.P. Gupta and Dilbagh Singh already cited.

42 Blochet, Suppl. Pers. 482, f.165a. The slave-owning peasant belonged to a village in *pargana* Maroli, *sarkār* Surat.

surveys, even if only because the number of slaves, including those employed as domestics, was so small. Still, in Bhagalpur district (1810-11) most men slaves were found to be employed in agriculture,[43] while in Purnea (1809-10), Hindus "of rank" had their "small free estates" and rented farms cultivated by slaves.[44] In his journey through southern India, 1800-01, Buchanan found agrestic slavery to be strongest in Kerala, of less importance in coastal Kanara, and barely traceable in the remainder of Karnataka and Tamilnadu.[45] It may be inferred from both the negative and positive evidence that while in the Mughal empire, rural slavery was not wholly absent, it was numerically only a very minor source of agricultural labour even in the areas where it was found.

The existence of a rural proletariat in Mughal India, which Moreland had assumed,[46] and for which we have now presented some evidence, touches an important aspect of our pre-colonial history. Modern landlordism and the commercialization of agriculture under the colonial regime vastly expanded the ranks of the landless in the nineteenth century and later;[47] but this process was essentially one of enlargement, not of creation, of the class. Its previous existence was undoubtedly inherent in two pre-existing facts.

In the first place, if we assume that land was then abundant, then, on an average, the peasant's holdings must have been larger than in later days when the population pressure on land increased. In a larger holding, the peasant would need extra hands, especially at harvesting, but these would be the very times when other peasants too would be occupied. The additional hands could come only from the lower or menial castes, whose members were prevented by the caste system from turning into peasants, and who were therefore obliged perforce to work at depressed wages (customary or not). The existence of 'untouchables' was thus a pillar of Indian peasant agriculture from very early times, ever since, that is, the food-gatherers and the forest folk were humbled and subjugated by settled

43 *Bhagalpur Report*, 193. 44 *Purnea Report*, 162.

45 See *Journey from Madras*, I, 19; II, 361-2, 370-72, 495, 562; III, 140, 226-7, 280-1.

46 "It appears to me to be certain that in the sixteenth century, as at the present day, the rural population included a large number of landless labourers" (*India at the Death of Akbar*, 112).

47 S.J. Patel, *Agricultural Labourers of India and Pakistan*, esp. 9-20. Cf. I. Habib, *Essays*, 331, 361.

agricultural communities.[48] It would not, indeed, be surprising if the actual status of many of them in Mughal India too was semi-servile, implying some kind of bondage, including the obligation to render forced labour (*begār*) to *zamīndārs* and upper caste peasants.[49]

Secondly, the process of differentiation, as it enlarged the resources of one stratum and reduced those of the other, forced a number of peasants to abandon cultivation and hire themselves out to their richer neighbours. It is possible that so long as one had an opportunity to settle in fresh lands, with borrowed seed and cattle,[50] the numbers of such labourers, recruited from pauperized peasants, might remain limited: the great change would come when, under the colonial regime, by the latter half of the nineteenth century, the impoverished peasant, once thrown out of his land, lost the capacity of ever setting up as peasant again.

3. THE VILLAGE COMMUNITY

The village in Mughal India stood in a dual position in its relationship with the world outside. A large amount of its produce had to be marketed outside, in order to meet tax claims; and thus a part at least of its economy was dominated by the requirements and vicissitudes of commodity production. At the same time, since the village had few claims upon anyone outside its limits, its own inhabitants' needs had to be met very largely from within itself, and it had, therefore, to function as a self-sufficient unit.[1] The twin circumstances dictated that a system of individual peasant production (a seeming variant of Marx's "petty mode") with resultant

[48] Cf. I. Habib, *Essays*, 124-25. For the status of the Chanḍālas and the origin of untouchability, see V. Jha, *IHR*, XIII (1-2), 1-36.

[49] *Begār* was a practical symbol of the menial and lower castes' subjugation. The *Waqā'i' Ajmer*, 131, contains a report of the flight of a party of Rājpūts with a wounded comrade: in each village they requisitioned the services of the Thorīs (menial caste) of the local *zamīndārs*, who carried the cot of the wounded man to the boundary of the next village, where the Thorīs of that village took over. The Chamars were known as Begārīs because they had to work as porters without payment (*Tashrīḥu-l Aqwām*, ff.181b, 182a). On the other hand, we read of a Gūjar, who refused to render *begār* to some Rājpūts, apparently because he felt he was not liable to it; he was beaten to death in punishment (*Waqā'i' Ajmer*, 187). For *begār*, see also Add. 6603, ff.516-520; *Tashrīḥu-l Aqwām*, f.188a. For the semi-servile status of the menial castes in more recent times, see Crooke, *North-Western Provinces*, 208; cf. Moreland, *Agrarian System*, 160.

[50] See Aurangzeb's *farmān*, already cited, in *Nigārnāma-i Munshī*, ed., 139, where the indigent peasants are said to be in debt "for subsistence, seed and cattle".

[1] This is a restatement of conclusions already set out in Chapter I, Section 4, and Chapter II, Section 2.

differentiation (see preceding section) should coexist with the organization of the village as a "community", a network of caste divisions and customary service or barter relationships.[2]

The bulk of the population of the ordinary village must have consisted of peasants, who were usually identified by their caste, or *qaum*. When, says Qāẓī Muḥammad A'lā, "the inhabitants of a village" are unable to cultivate the land, the king could expel and settle another *qaum* in their stead.[3] An actual description of peasants by their caste occurs in a document of 1611 where we are told that "the ancient *māliks* (proprietors)" of a village in Central Doab had been Kāchhīs and Chamārs, the former a caste of reputedly skilled cultivators, the latter of tanners and labourers.[4]

This could be a middling case because even today in the Doab one can identify villages with single dominant peasant castes (Jāṭs, Gūjars, Thākurs, etc.) or with fair mixtures of castes, the territorial caste-limits always overlapping. Nainsī, in his village-wise survey of Marwar in the *Vigat* (*c.*1664), records the inhabitants of each village by their peasant castes. "Menial" castes do not at all appear among the recorded village inhabitants, and the artisan castes only on those rare occasions apparently when they constituted a significant portion of the peasantry as well.[5] When a village is reported to be in ruins, the *Vigat* often carefully records the caste or castes, which "carry on cultivation" (*khet kharai*) in its lands. The *Vigat* survey could well help us to map the peasant castes of Marwar. It shows that villages of Marwar were divisible into two zones. In the northern zone, most villages had a single peasant caste each; in the south, such villages as contained two or more peasant castes each formed the more numerous portion.[6] The existence of

[2] Cf. Marx, *Capital*, I, tr. Moore and Aveling, 350-52. Caste was the source of the "unalterable division of labour" of which Marx speaks here. For Marx's "petty mode of production", see ibid., 787.

[3] *Risāla Aḥkām al-Ārāẓī*, f.48a.

[4] Shamsabad Docs. 4. Cf. I. Habib in *IESHR*, IV (3), 215-16.

[5] The most frequently specified artisan caste among village inhabitants in the *Vigat* is that of *kumbhārs* or potters (recorded with other castes in 23 out of 184 villages in *pargana* Sojhat and 17 out of 121 in Jaitaran). Other professional castes that appear are *mālīs* (gardeners), and more rarely still *kalāls* (wine-distillers), *telīs* (oil-pressers), *sūtdhārs/sūtārs* (carpenters) and *luhārs* (ironsmiths).

[6] In the northern zone, single-caste villages account for 259 out of 319 villages for which the requisite data are given in *pargana* Merta; 513 out of 735 in *pargana* Jodhpur; and 40 out of 48 in Phalodi (for *pargana* Merta, see the village-wise survey in *Vigat*, II, 116-277; for Jodhpur, Nainsī's own tabulation from his village-wise survey, ibid., I, 190-95; and for Phalodi, his summary of the data,

single-caste villages in northern Marwar is also attested by statements like the one that appears in a Mughal report of 1679 about a village in *pargana* Merta, whose people are said to have been Jāṭs. They complained that some Rājpūts came at night, and demanded the surrender of an indigent Rājpūt, who had settled in the village "owing to distressed circumstances". They then killed him to pass off his head as that of the murderer of two official messengers.[7] Clearly, a Rājpūt who went to settle in a village where there were no members of his own caste, could lose all sympathy of his peers.[8]

The predominance of a single peasant caste in particular villages, together with multiplicity of such castes in others, forms a pattern which may perhaps be said to be universal in India.[9]

From the caste of the peasant inhabitants, the *Vigat* leads us to another distinction: whether the peasants were settlers (*basī*) brought in by potentates, or the original, native folk (*lok/log*, *basīwāṁn/basewān lok*, *desī lok*).[10] The former appear in a relatively small number of villages, often with the formula: "There are no *lok*. The *basī* inhabited by such-and-such (caste)."[11] The *basī* were a group of peasants, belonging to a variety of castes, who were bound to a potentate as patron, through debt or other assistance previously received, or, expected to be received, and so, if Tod is right, tied down to the settlement established by their patron.[12] What, then, of the folk, or *lok*? They were, first, pre-

ibid., II, 10-12). In the southern and south-eastern *parganas* single-caste villages numbered but 30 out of 184 villages (excluding those in ruins, but including grant villages) in Sojhat; 12 out of 121 in Jaitaran; and 40 out of 115 in Siwana (ibid., I, 425-89, 509-53; II, 232-77).

[7] *Waqā'i' Ajmer*, 122.

[8] There were, however, as many as 21 villages in *pargana* Merta, in *Vigat's* survey, where both Jāṭs and Rājpūts appear as inhabitants side by side.

[9] For this pattern in as distant an area from the Doab and Marwar as the Tirunelveli (Tinnevelly) district in Tamilnadu, see David Ludden, *Peasant History in South India*, 66-7.

[10] The distinction is borne upon us by the following entry under one village: "The *basīwāṁn lok*, Jāṭs; the people (*log*) of the *basī* of Rā[o] Gopāldās Sundardās [live] in the eastern part" (*Vigat*, II, 199).

[11] For a group of villages, where this formula repeatedly occurs, see *Vigat*, I, 526-32.

[12] Tod, *Annals and Antiquities*, I, 143-46. See also II, 593-4, where Tod points out that "*Bussie*, or properly *vasi*, means a 'settler', an 'inhabitant' from *vās*, 'a habitation', and *vasna*, 'to inhabit', but it does not distinguish between free settlers and compulsory labourers; but wheresoever the phrase is used in Rajwarra, it may be assumed to apply to the latter. Still, strange to say, the condition includes none

eminently peasants, for in a village their settlement was distinguished from that of the mercantile caste of Bohauras (Bohras).[13] And, unlike the *basī*, they were not tied to any potentate, but derived their claims to land from the very fact of being natives of a particular village.

When we speak of the *basī* and, especially, the *lok*, as peasants, we should, perhaps, make clear a further distinction. Communities so designated included castes whose members either did not undertake the actual labour on the land, or undertook it only partially. Higher castes, such as Rājpūts, Brahmans, Chārans and Banyas, would not touch the plough, following Manu's famous injunction.[14] And yet Rājpūts accounted for 167 out of 513 single-caste villages in *pargana* Jodhpur. One cannot but assume that they either cultivated the land through extensive use of wage-labour (especially perhaps menial-caste labour), or exercised some kind of authority over the actual cultivators, whose castes, since they were in a subordinate position, Nainsī does not care to report. In other areas, peasant castes proper, whose members never had the luxury of entertaining scruples about pollution from the plough, appear in a numerically dominant position. In *pargana* Merta, Jāṭs are recorded in 242 out of 319 single-caste villages (as against only six where Rājpūts alone are recorded); and they are prominent enough in Jodhpur (215 out of 513), Jaitaran and Sojhat, though tending to be replaced by Patels in Siwana.[15] All this is in accord with the picture of rural differentiation we ourselves have drawn, except that here some of the differentiation came from the caste system itself.[16]

---

of the accessories of slavery; there is no task-duty of any kind, nor is the individual accountable to anyone; he pays the usual taxes, and the only tie upon him appears to be that of compulsory residence in his *vās* ..." Cf B.L. Bhadani in *PIHC*, 50th Session, 1989-90, Gorakhpur, 236-55.

13 *Vigat*, I, 246.

14 *Manusmriti*, X, 84; tr. G. Buhler, 420-21. Cf. Ibbetson's description (*Panjab Castes*, 134-5) of the Rājpūt peasant of Haryana: "he cultivates badly, for his women are more or less strictly secluded and never work in the fields, while he considers it degrading to actually follow the plough, and will always employ hired ploughmen if he can possibly afford it."

15 Other peasant castes recorded in the *Vigat* include Sīwīs, Mers, and, less often, Gūjars.

16 Maine, *Village Communities in the East and West*, 176-7, was, therefore, not wrong in insisting on the intensely hierarchical nature of the Indian village community. There is very little to cavil at, when Baden-Powell, *The Indian Village Community*, 399-400, 403, 418-23, asserts that the "false" notion of communal

It is in the light of such varied differentiation that we may look at the internal structure of the village. On this matter evidence of signal importance has come to us from documents relating to the temple establishments at Vrindāban, going back to the sixteenth century. A series of documents, in Persian and Braj, record purchases of land in the village of Aritha (now Radhakund), some distance from Mathura and Vrindāban. Here we find the same seven named persons, all sons of different fathers, selling different plots of land at various dates (many of the dates being fictitious, however, the real transactions taking place in 1579 and 1588). In the Braj documents they style themselves "the village-resident *panch*", and "*panch mukadamman*", or, as we may say, the village oligarchs.[17] In the Persian documents they appear simply as "village residents", but in the last comprehensive document they are referred to as *muqaddams* or headmen. They do not here sell land cultivated or owned by them as individuals, but alienate plots of "village land" (*zamīn-i mauẓa*') in five transactions and "land of the *kund* (pond)" in one. In one document all the six plots are stated to be "waste land". The sales put a total of 238 *bīghas* of land in the hands of Raghunāth and Jīv Gosāin, who became its private owners with no rights remaining to the sellers to dispose of the land in any way. This was admitted by the *muqaddams* of the village (five named persons "and others") in 1641 while referring to the land sales of their "ancestors" (*buzurgān*).[18] Clearly, they were the successors of the earlier *panch*. In a land sale in village Vrindāban the sellers, numbering four, are styled *panch* in the Braj version (1558) and *muqaddams* in Persian (1569).[19] The small number accords with the position of the *panch* as village oligarchs. Even when the number was larger, as in Nagu, hamlet of village Dosaich, where we have as many as thirteen sellers

---

property arose out of the operation of "the more developed idea of the joint-family", whose members' control over the village often derived from conquest and subjugation of the earlier inhabitants, resulting, in other words, in an hierarchy imposed by force.

[17] For *panch* and *panchāyat* in 19th-century Hindustani usage, see Fallon, s.v. *panch*, n.m., and *panchāyat*.

[18] The Braj documents are Wright 1A, 1, 2 (from Rādhādāmodar Temple); and the Persian, Madan Mohan 6, 7, 8, 10, 11,14, 17, 18, and Rādhādāmodar 9, 11. The collection to which the original of the document of AH 996/1588, issued by Raghunāth, giving details of the six plots, belongs, is not indicated in the photograph, but a copy exists in Madan Mohan 1.

[19] Wright 3 (two copies in Rādhādāmodar: Ser. 5, Acc. 3 and Ser. 21, Acc. 37) and Rādhādāmodar (Ser. 56, Acc.13).

designated *panch* of the village, they were expected to act in concert (*sab panchan milikare*).[20] In yet another sale deed of land of a village of Vrindāban, the number is still larger: twelve are named, and there are others making up "all *panch*, small and big, of village Haidu". All of them severally and individually, were to be held answerable, should any other claimant come forward to assert his right to the land sold.[21]

We are thus led to see the *panch* as forming a collective body or assemblage, the *panchāyat* of tradition. The latter word duly makes its appearance in two documents of 1599. Five named persons "and others" there form "the *panchāyat* of the village" of the Gopīnāth temple in Vrindāban, selling plots of land.[22] We are reminded of the occurrence of the same term in a Panjab document of 1732 where it clearly refers to an assemblage of shopkeepers, where decisions were taken on behalf of all of them.[23]

The composition of the *panchāyat* or village oligarchy does not seem to have been necessarily confined to a single family or caste. The Aritha documents of Akbar's reign show that the fathers of all the seven *panch* are different persons. The thirteen sellers, merely styled "inhabitants of village" in the Persian version, but *panch* in the Braj, who sell land in hamlet Nagu (Vrindāban) in 1594, are even more heterogeneously composed, for three of them bear Muslim names.[24] In 1641, the *muqaddams* of Aritha, who confirm the sale of land by their "ancestors" (*buzurgān*) of Akbar's time, are now headed by Bārī Khān, a Muslim.[25] One assumes that, despite the heterogeneity, hereditary succession had much to do with one's obtaining the status of *panch*; for only then could the *muqaddams* of a later time speak of the earlier *panch* as their

[20] Wright 6 (Govind-dev collection). Dosāich (Dosait) is now a part of Vrindaban.

[21] Wright 9 (collection not indicated).

[22] IVS, 156, 157. IVS 156 is dated; IVS 157 undated, belongs to about the same time.

[23] "The whole *panchāyat* of the market of the township of Muhiuddinpur [Madhinpur, Dist. Gurdaspur] has determined that every person shall pay one *tanka* upon each shop [to a religious divine]. None should excuse himself, we have agreed of our own free will" (document reproduced in Goswamy and Grewal, eds, *The Mughals and the Jogis of Jakhbar*, 157-8).

[24] Both versions (originals) in Govind-dev collection (the Braj version is Wright 6). The three Muslims are Niẓām, Hamyān (Braj: Hamāū) and Naṣṣo. The latter two are obvious corruptions of Humāyūn and Naṣīr.

[25] Rādhādāmodar 9. Here his name is given as Bārī; but it is Bārī Khān in the bilingual Madan Mohan 4, of 1642, in both the Persian and Braj versions.

ancestors. But other factors, such as caste or community, money, influence or factious behaviour, might also have played a part–factors about which we have now little information.[26]

By chance, owing to the practice in the documents of giving the name of the father and sometimes grandfather of a deponent or party in a transaction, it is possible to reconstruct the genealogical tree of a family, descended from Jadū of the Gaurawa caste[27] who was one of the *panch* alienating land at Vrindāban in 1600.

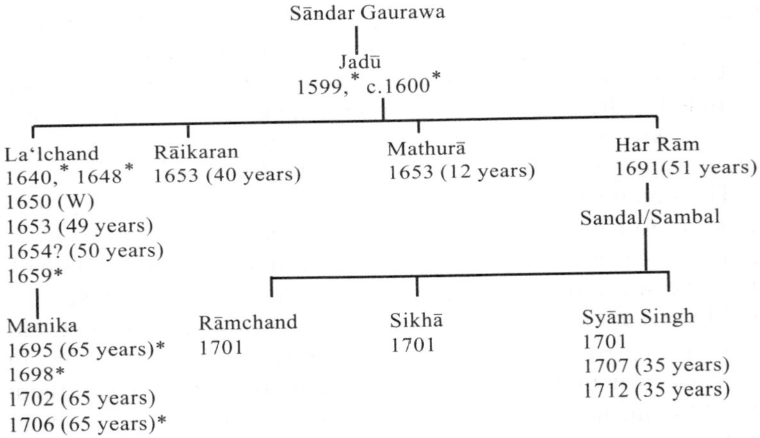

Note: The dates are those of transactions in which the members of this family appear as sellers; where the appearance is only as witness (a single case), the date is followed by '(W)'; where the *ḥuliya* (description) of the person is given and, therefore, his approximate age is recorded, it is given within brackets; and transactions on behalf of the *panch* are asterisked.

From this chart one can see that the right to participate in the *panch* was duly inherited. But the documented succession, Jadu-La'lchand-Manika, and dates of transactions, show that at any one time only one member of the family acted as a *panch* representative. The transaction of 1653, in which La'lchand and two of his

[26] One could conjecture that Bārī Khān may have owed his position among the *panch* of Aritha in 1640-42 to his community; on the other hand, he could just have been a *panch* who had turned Muslim. We find a village notable of hamlet Gopa in Dosāich-Vrindaban, called 'Alī Khān, son of Angad, son of Rāgho Gaurawa, in a deed of AH 1064/1654 in the Govind-dev collection. He was obviously a convert.

[27] For the Gaurawas, a low-ranking cultivating Rājpūt caste, who practised widow remarriage (*karewa*), a hallmark of such other agricultural communities, see Elliot, *Memoirs*, I, 115, and *Gazetteer of the Delhi District, 1883-84*, 76.

brothers appear as sellers of their own agricultural land, further shows that the right to perquisites (*biswa muqaddamī*) was not monopolized by the senior member, as *panch*, but shared among the brothers, for this right too is here sold away along with the land.[28] What the position of the buyer, a priest of the Govind-dev temple, now was vis-á-vis the *panch* does not, however, appear from our documents.

We can draw some inferences from the documents about the extent and nature of authority that the *panch* or *panchāyat* exercised. As we have seen from the Aritha documents, they could sell "village land", which happened to be "wasteland". From a deed of 1594, relating to the immediate proximity of Vrindāban, it transpires that the thirteen *panch* of the village had authority to lease or allow the use of the wasteland (*vīthalvārī*), for they had given 4 *biswas* of it to a *bairāgī* (recluse) to set up some structures. The latter's use of the land gave him a voice in its ultimate disposal by sale by the *panch*, for now the agreement of the *bairāgī's* disciple to the transaction was required, he himself being dead.[29] One should infer, then, that if the land was cultivated by individual members of the peasant community, or Nainsī's *lok*, the authority of the *panch* to dispose of it ceased, and an individual right was created. When a *bīgha* and a half of "cultivated land" (*zamīn-i zirā'atī*) were sold in the same locality the same year (1594), the sellers are not the village *panch*, but two individual peasants who must have inherited the land from their fathers.[30] There thus existed individual peasant right over the arable side by side with community right over the waste. One may presume that when outside peasants, the *pāi-kāsht* were allowed to cultivate the wasteland, the arrangement had to be approved by the *panch*, in the name of the village, though of this there is no direct evidence.

One must ask the question as to what the *panch* did when they obtained money on alienating wasteland on behalf of the village or on giving lease to non-resident peasants. In an early eighteenth-century Vrindāban document, Benī Rām, son of Dūndī, who appears as a *muqaddam* in 1691, and as a *panch* in 1698, says that

[28] Govind-dev 39.

[29] Persian and Braj versions in the Govind-dev documents (Braj:Wright 6). Curiously no reference is made to the *bairāgī* in the Braj version. The Persian version does not designate the land sold as waste, but says it was bounded on two sides by the road, and on the other two, by wasteland.

[30] IVS 208.

Dūndī and Manika, the latter of whom we have already met as a *panch*, had sold seven *biswas* of land for Rs 72, of which Rs 61 were taken by "the body of the *panch* of the said village", and the remaining Rs 11 by Benī Rām, apparently on behalf of his father. This suggests that the individual *panch* members took their share out of the proceeds of the sale, the bulk of which went to some financial pool of the *panch*. This helps to explain a statement that occurs in the Persian version of the sale of land by the *panch* of Vrindāban to Rāja Mān Singh in 1594, where the *panch* say that they had received the price (Rs 20½) "in the presence of Muslims and Hindus, taking it, after distributing the apportioned share (*ḥiṣṣa-rasad*) among ourselves".[31] Presumably, after the *panch* had taken their shares, there remained a balance to be put into the common fund. That such a fund existed is proved by the claim made in the same document by the thirteen *panch* acting jointly, that one Pathal *bairāgī* had borrowed Rs 150 from them.[32] Elsewhere, we have a still more precise reference to a common village pool in a petition of "peasants (*ri'āyā*) of a village", three of whom are named, complaining of the excessive exactions of a *chaudhurī* who had taken the village on farm (*ijāra*). The *chaudhurī* had not only exacted large sums as revenue at the harvest, but seized a large amount from "the fund" (*foṭa*) of the villagers, and taken away the village accounts (*kāghaz-i khām*) apparently to conceal the seizure.[33]

Fortunately, Mughal official literature lets us have a more tangible picture of what the village financial pool comprised. The *Ā'īn* says that the *paṭwārī* "is an accountant on behalf of the peasants;[34] he records the expenditure and income; and there is no

[31] Govind-dev, unnumbered. For *rasad,* meaning share (*ḥiṣṣa*), and *ḥiṣṣa-i rasad* bearing the same sense, see "Ārzū", *Chirāgh-i Hidāyat* (*c*.1740), s.v. Cf. Fallon, s.v. *rasad*: *ḥiṣṣa-i rasadī* ("proportionate share"). In Todar Mal's original Memorandum, Art. 9 (Add. 27,247, f.331a), the word *rasad* is clearly used in the sense of apportioned share. Abū-l Faẓl substitutes for it the Arabic word *qismat* in his polished summary of that document in the final version (*A.N.*, III, 382). Cf. Moosvi *People, Taxation and Trade in Mughal India*, 171, for the rendering of *rasad* in Todar Mal's memorandum. The other meaning of *rasad* as grain supplies to the army and the court, is noted in Ārzū, op.cit., as peculiar to late Mughal court usage.

[32] The Braj version (Wright 6) contains no reference to this transaction.

[33] *Durru-l 'Ulūm*, f. 65a-b. The petitioners were "Sondhī, Shyām, Pahlād, etc., *ri'āyā* of village Jasapur, *pargana* Palwal [near Dehli]". The document from which we learn of the petition is itself a *ḥasbu-l ḥukm*.

[34] *Az ṭarf-i barzgarān*, rather in the sense of "on the side of (or employed by) the peasants".

village without him".[35] Here we see the villagers in a collective capacity as employers of a functionary whose modern successor was to become unequivocally a government servant. The description of what the *paṭwārī* recorded is also significant because we learn that every village had its own "expenditure and income", that is its common finances. Although the *paṭwārī's* papers were not regarded as part of the administrative records of the Mughal government, they were drawn upon for purposes of audit (*barāmad*) of the accounts of the revenue officials.[36] Specimen summaries of the village accounts prepared by the auditors from the *paṭwārīs'* papers, are reproduced in three accountancy manuals of Aurangzeb's reign, and we can duly see here the major items of village income and expenditure.[37]

The income of the village is made up of payments from individual peasants.[38] It is such payments, probably, to which Aurangzeb's *farmān* to Rasikdās refers, when in its Art. 11, it requires the revenue officials to "discover, for auditing the Hindwī accounts in Persian, the real amounts of *bāchh* and *behrī-māl* and the fees and perquisites taken from each individual – everything, that is, which comes out of the house of the peasant on any account". *Bāchh* is a term peculiar to the joint (*bhaiyāchāra*) village and has meant even in recent times the rate paid by individual members of the fraternity into the common pool. The term *behrī* is generally used for a subscription or instalment of rent, but in *bhaiyāchāra* villages had the special sense of a subdivision or fraction of the total landholding, so that *behrī-māl* would be revenue (*māl*) paid on their shares of the land by members of the fraternity.[39]

[35] *Ā'īn*, I, 300.

[36] *Akbarnāma*, III, 457; *Ā'īn*, I, 288-9; *Farmān* to Rasikdās, Art. 11; *Siyāqnāma*, 75-76; *Khulāṣatu-s Siyāq*, f.91b (Or. 2026, 59a).

[37] *Dastūru-l 'Amal-i 'Ālamgīrī*, ff.41b-42b; *Siyāqnāma*, 77-79; *Khulāṣatu-s Siyāq*, ff.92a-94a (Or. 2026, ff.59b-64a). The first manual was written in Bihar, the second in Ilahabad province, and the third in the Panjab.

[38] This is clearly indicated in the *Khulāṣatu-s Siyāq*. Cf. also *Ā'īn*, I, 287.

[39] See for the significance of *bāchh* and *behrī*, Elliot, *Memoirs*, II, 23, 38; Wilson, *Glossary*, 42, 70-71. For *behrī* in *bhaiyāchāra* (and *paṭṭīdārī*) villages, see also *Revenue Selections*, 200, 219-20, 224. Add. 6603, f.50a, defines *behrī* as "an amount apart from the revenue and cesses that is demanded from each individual peasant"; it adds that in Dehli this was known as *bāchh*. This meaning of *bāchh* accords with the way this term is sometimes employed in Mughal documents, e.g., in *Nigārnāma-i Munshī*, ed., 91, where the *qānūngo* is advised never to "go near oppression, violence and (extortion of) *bāchh*". But the language of the *farmān* to Rasikdās implies clearly that *bāchh* and *behrī-māl*, together with the "fees and

The village income thus obtained was set off against a number of items of expenditure. The amount paid into the treasury to meet the revenue demand appears as the first and largest item.[40] This is followed by the fees and perquisites of the various officials and their agents along with payments made to cover certain special demands of the authorities. At the bottom we have the interesting item of *kharj-i deh* or *deh-kharj*, "expenses of the village".[41] These include allowances drawn by the headman and the *paṭwārī*, the perquisites of the *qānūngo* and the land surveyor,[42] the amount spent on entertaining the *chaudhurī*, etc. In one manual a large figure is shown under this head as having been paid to the *mahājan* (money-lender) in repayment of a loan.[43] The amount involved in this particular case is three-fourths of the revenue paid that year, and we may imagine that it had been borrowed in some previous year on behalf of the village to pay part of the revenue demand or help tide over the effects of natural calamities. Where the village

---

perquisites", comprised everything that the peasant had to pay. In the same article, moreover, the *farmān* prescribes the deduction of the amount paid to the treasury (*wāṣilāt-i foṭakhāna*) from the total made up of the above four items. *Bāchh* and *behrī-māl*, therefore, must, between them, have provided the full amount of the revenue demand.

[40] In the *Dastūru-l 'Amal-i 'Ālamgīrī*, the payment to the treasury amounts to Rs 4,427 out of a total village expenditure of Rs 4,655; in the *Siyāqnāma*, to Rs 109 out of Rs 218; and in the *Khulāṣatu-s Siyāq*, to Rs 1,011 out of Rs 1282.

[41] The Hindi word for all payments from the village fund, apart from the land-revenue and so including the perquisites of the various officials and the "village expenses", is *malba*. (See Wilson, *Glossary*, 324; *Meerut District Gazetteer*, 1922, 108.) This term frequently occurs in Mughal documents, e.g. Todar Mal's Recommendations in *Akbarnāma*, Add. 27,247, ff.331b, 332b; Fatḥullāh Shīrāzī's Memorandum, *Akbarnāma*, III, 458 (Add. 26,207, ff.194b-195a); *Farmān* to Rasikdās, Art.10; and *Nigārnāma-i Munshī*, ed., 136, 145, as signifying, in general, the officials' private exactions from the villages. See also Chapter VI, Section 7.

[42] Called *mīrdeh*, lit. chief of the village. The position and functions of this official are described in Malcolm, *Memoir of Central India*, II, 13-14. In the specimen village accounts in the *Dastūru-l 'Amal-i 'Ālamgīrī*, the perquisites of the *mīrdeh* are not included in the *kharj-i deh*, but classed with the exactions of revenue officials and their agents.

[43] *Siyāqnāma*, 79. The total amount of loan repaid is put at Rs 80 against the total village income of Rs 218, and tax-payment of Rs 109.

For later evidence of such loans contracted by *paṭels* (headmen) on behalf of the village when assessed beyond its capacities, see George Perott's report from Broach, 1776, in *Selections from the Bombay Secretariat, Home* II, 183. Thomas Coats, 'Account of the present state of the township of Lony [near Poona]', 1820, in *Transactions of the Literary Society of Bombay*, III (London, 1823), 212, found that "the debt owing by the community" amounted to Rs 3,075, while the total of debts owed by individual cultivators was Rs 14,532.

had a surplus, as must have been rare, the *panch* could also lend out of the pool, as they apparently did at Dosaich some time before 1594. The "village expenses" also covered the cost of some productive enterprise, such as the amount spent in damming water channels (*nālas*) or in buying musk-melon seeds.[44] Some expenses too were incurred for providing general entertainment or towards meeting the moral responsibilities of the village. So we find entries concerning payments made to jugglers and minstrels and expenditure on hospitality to strangers and charity to beggars.[45]

The financial pool, as suggested by the Dosaich deed of 1594, was in the hands of the *panch*, or the *panchāyat*, the bulk of the peasantry being clearly not involved in the mechanism of control. This conforms to Baden-Powell's observation that "the most surviving occasion of the *panchayat's* action", in the "joint villages", where the members of the *panchāyat* would be the joint owners, was the adjustment of accounts, taking place in some villages annually, in others at each harvest, with the object of fixing the proportion of revenue dues to be paid on each holding and of sanctioning the "common expenses" of the village.[46]

We thus have for northern India a picture of the control by a village oligarchy over tax collection that is very close to the one furnished to us in an exceptionally clear report from the Konkan in 1579. Speaking of the "Island" of Salsette (Goa), Monserrate tells us:

> It has 66 aldeas (villages), which are reduced to 12 which are their capitals and are called the General Chamber. It has this name because they are the ones who alone govern the whole island and the whole of the Conchan (Konkan) in this manner: Two men from each of these 12 aldeas assemble in a certain place with their scrivener and there, as in a meeting, they settle what has to be done for the common weal and to obtain the quit-rent and revenue of His Highness (the King of Portugal). When they have settled what has to be done, the scrivener gives a shout, like a crier at an auction (and they call this *nemo*), which is their common agreement. And if only one should fail, and he should not approve of it, nothing can be done; and the scrivener alone testifies to what is settled, none of them

[44] These items are given in the *Dasturu-l 'Amal-i 'Ālamgīrī*.

[45] See *Khulāṣatu-s Siyāq*. Cf. Thomas Marshall, 'A Statistical Account of the Pergunna of Jumboosur [Gujarat]', 1820, in *Transactions of the Literary Society of Bombay*, III, 377-83. For references to "Khurch Deha" (=*kharj-i deh*), see *Revenue Selections*, 170, 299. Also see *Meerut Dist. Gaz.*, 108; Baden-Powell, *Indian Village Community*, 25.

[46] Baden-Powell, *Indian Village Community*, 24-25.

affixing his signature, even though it be in most important matters. His Highness' revenue is limited in such a way that that amount is always given him, whether the lands yield much or little. And if an aldea was lost and had no harvest, the others pay for it; and if anything remains over, it is divided among the same. The dominion and administration of this island is in the hands of these men who are called Gancares.[47]

In disposing of the untilled land, or distributing the tax burden and remitting it through the financial pool, the village oligarchs acted on behalf of the peasants. But there were people other than peasants too in the village, namely the labourers and artisans, whose presence was essential for agricultural work and for meeting the very elementary needs of the villagers. The maintenance of such a population could be secured partly at least by allotments of lands and house sites out of village lands and by distribution of customary shares in harvests.

When Broach (Gujarat) was administered by an English collector in 1776, he reported: "That a certain proportion of land of each village is requisite to be set apart [tax-free] for the maintenance of such artificers and labourers as are absolutely necessary for the common services of the village is according to the custom of the country true."[48] In 1800 Buchanan observed in Karnataka how petty shares from harvest heaps were set aside for the priest and mendicant, astrologer, barber, pot-maker, carpenter and blacksmith, washerman, measurer, beadle, watchman and conductor of water, besides the village headman and accountant. The rates of the shares varied with the size of the individual peasant family.[49] In 1811-12, in his survey of the district of Bihar and Patna, the same author noted that carpenters and blacksmiths in the villages "usually belong to the manorial establishment and the payment for the implements of agriculture arises from a share of the crop".[50] There is an echo of this from Sind, where a report (1847), soon after its annexation, speaks of a "strong bond of union between

[47] Monserrate, 'Informacion', transl. Hosten, *JASB*, NS, XVIII, 1922, pp.351-2. He adds that villages were administered on similar lines in the Chovar and Divar islands near Goa (ibid., 365). He was writing in 1579. "Ganacare" is a corruption of *gāonkār*, meaning a villager in Marathi, a village headman in Kannada.

[48] *Selections from the Bombay Secretariat, Home*, II, 181. See aslo a Goa document of 1526 to the same effect (transl. B.H. Baden-Powell, *JRAS*, 1900, p.268).

[49] *Journey from Madras*, I, 65-8, 299-300, 337.

[50] *Patna-Gaya Report*, II, 639. By "manorial" Buchanan obviously means the village establishment, for which see his description, ibid., 566-68.

all members" of the village, and of the carpenter receiving "his fee for the annual repair of the Persian wheels, and the potter for the supply of the earthen vessels attached to them".[51] Evidence like this reinforces the classic description of the village community in the *Fifth Report* (1812), professedly concerned with the Northern Circars (coastal Andhra), but drawing upon material from a wider area.[52] This served as the basis of theoretical speculations by James Mill, Hegel and Marx.[53] Towards the end of the century, Baden-Powell, with his massive command of official literature, gave a brief, but identical, description of the attachment of the village servants and artisans to the village community.[54]

A major modification of the standard view was urged by W.H. Wiser (1936) whose finding was that the customary attachments tied the village servants and artisans not to the whole village but to groups of client families, their *jajmāns*, within it.[55] To Louis Dumont this is not simply analogous to, but is really an extension of, the relationship between the priest and his clients: "the hypothesis deduces interdependence from religion."[56] This theory seems to disregard the allotment of land to village servants and artisans which were not out of individual holdings but out of village lands. If they were made tax-free, it meant that the entire peasant body had to make up the resulting shortfall in tax collection. Similarly, the shares from harvests appear to have been taken from all villagers. Fukazawa has shown from eighteenth-century records from Maharashtra how the servants and artisans claimed their *waṭan* or *mīrāṣ*, that is hereditary land allotment, from the village as a

[51] Thomas, *Memoirs on Sind*, III, 728.

[52] *Fifth Report*, 80-81.

[53] Part of the passage in the *Fifth Report* was quoted by James Mill, *History of British India*, I, 140-41, and, through Mill, was apparently the source of Hegel's description of the Indian village community in *Philosophy of History*, [1830], transl. J. Sibree, 154. Marx quoted the *Fifth Report* in an article of 1853 (Marx and Engels, *On Colonialism*, 39-40); but in *Capital* I, 350-52, he appeals to a similar account in Mark Wilks, *Historical Sketches of South India*, I (London, 1810), 118-20; reprinted (Mysore, 1930), I, 137.

[54] Baden-Powell, *Indian Village Community*, 16-17. He not only recognizes the prevalence of these arrangements in the "raiyatwari" (ryotwari) villages but says they are to be found "naturally" in the joint-villages, the other principal type of villages that he distinguishes.

[55] Wiser, *The Hindu Jajmani System*, Lucknow, 1936. For a convenient summary of the view of sociologists and historians on this matter, from Marx and Weber to contemporary times, see Hiroshi Fukazawa, *Medieval Deccan*, 199-209. Since this essay was originally published in 1972, Fukazawa was just too early for taking note of Dumont's work (1972).

[56] *Homo Hierarchicus*, 150.

whole, and how they exacted their *balūta*, or remuneration at harvest, from the fields of all villagers.[57] It is possible to argue that the kind of situation Wiser detected in his fieldwork was a result of the disappearance of the village community and the complete triumph of individual private landownership, when the menials and artisans could perforce seek the patronage only of individual families.

The attachment of lower servants, labourers and artisans, to the village community was by no means a relationship between equals. We have seen that in Nainsī's survey artisan castes seldom win recognition as village "folk" (*lok*), and the menial castes never. Presumably, the *panch* seldom or never came from these castes. It is also possible that the *panch* obtained much more than their proportionate share of the labour of the families attached to the village; and that the community framework was thus also an instrument of exploitation of the artisan and menial population by the village oligarchs.

The *panchāyat* did probably have an element of consultation and public deliberation, which made its members witnesses to transactions.[58] But there was otherwise little in the village community to justify any vision of "a communal life shared together, a sense of equality, and democratic methods".[59] Composed in the early centuries of the Christian era, the *Milindapañho* tells us that when the village headman summoned

[57] Fukazawa, *Medieval Deccan*, 209-34. Where the *yejmāns* (*jajmāns*) are mentioned, they are families of different castes (including *kuṁbīs* or peasants) appearing as clients of families of Brahmans. They are not confined to particular villages; as Fukuzawa points out, caste here overrides territoriality (ibid., 234-41).

On land allotment made collectively to a set of village servants or labourers there is the interesting evidence of a *chaknāma*, or boundary-demarcation document of village Rajpur, near Vrindāban, 1692 (Rādhādāmodar 158). Here the northern boundary of plot no.7 is shown as running along "the field (*kisht*) of the *chamārs* of the village of Rājpūr". Thus not an individual, but the *chamārs* of the village as a group appear as occupants of the field, assigned to them presumably by the village for subsistence. As tanners, skinners of dead animals and field labourers, they were, of course, indispensable to the village.

[58] In Govind-dev documents (unnumbered) there is a deed of gift of 1696, where the person making the gift says he was pronouncing the words "by way of *hibā* [rect. *hiba*]-*nama-i panchāyati*", where he meant a public act in front of witnesses. In 1734, the testimony of "*panchai* [*panchāyat*] of *zamīndārs* and inhabitants" was invoked to counter a claim on land near Gopīnāth temple, Vrindāban (IVS 167). For the sense of *panchāyatī* as "common, public, open to all", see Fallon, s.v. *panchāyatī: panchā'etī*. 2.

[59] Jawaharlal Nehru, *Discovery of India*, 4th edition, (London, 1956), 251.

the villagers (*gāmikas*) through the crier for consultation, only the notables (*kutipurise*) responded, not the ordinary peasants and labourers and women: they "do not count".[60] Some fifteen hundred years later conditions were not in this respect very different. If anything, commodity production having intensified internal differentiation, the oligarchs were now probably more powerful in respect of their weaker brethren. Whether they were styled *panch*, or "big men" (*kalāntarān*), or "dominant ones" (*mutaghallibān*), or *muqaddams*,[61] it was they who spoke in the name of the village and controlled the community. Their principal gain lay in manipulation of the village finances so as to impose a proportionately higher burden on the small peasantry (*reza ri'āyā*) and to let themselves off lightly. Todar Mal in his uninhibited language, spoke, in his memorial to the emperor, of "the bastards and headstrong" of the village, who "do not pay their own share [of the revenue-demand on the village], transferring it to the *reza-ri'āyā*".[62] The *A'īn*, therefore, warned the revenue officials against "making a *nasaq* [summary assessment] with the 'big men' (*kalāntarān*) of the village", for "it gives strength to dominant men of oppressive bent".[63] In Aurangzeb's *farmān* to Rasikdās, Art. 6, the same view is taken, it being stated that, unless care was exercised, individual peasants would suffer in the process of distribution of the revenue demand (*tafrīq-i jama'*) on the village at the hands of the "dominant ones" (*mutaghallibān*), colluding with the local and village officials (*chaudhurī*, *muqaddam*, *paṭwārī*).

These expressions of official irritation at such inequities, should not obscure the fact that once community mechanism was used by the revenue authorities for collection of revenue, they inescapably provided the umbrella for the sub-exploitation of the lower peasantry and the non-peasant rural population by the village oligarchs. The community, by sustaining village self-sufficiency, enlarged the surplus, and made its realization easier; the oligarchs as controllers of the community mechanism became petty sharers

[60] "Women and men, slave girls and [male] slaves, hired workmen, servants, [ordinary] villagers (*gāmika*), sick people, oxen, buffaloes, sheep and goats and dogs – but all those do not count" (*Milindapañho*, text, 167; transl. Rhys Davids, I, 208-9).

[61] According to the *Bahār-i 'Ajam*, s.v. *kalāntar*, the word *kalāntar* meant *muqaddam* in Hindustān.

[62] Original text of Todar Mal's recommendations in *Akbarnāma*, Add. 27, 247, f.232b.

[63] *Ā'īn*, I, 286.

in the surplus; but it was the Mughal ruling class, to which the major share of the surplus went in the form of tax, that was the ultimate beneficiary. All the three elements formed in normal times a cohesive exploitative whole.[64]

4. VILLAGE OFFICIALS

In the official documents it is ordinarily not the village community, but the headman, usually called *muqaddam* in northern India and *paṭel* in the Dakhin, who appears as the principal person in authority in the village, side by side with the *paṭwārī* or village accountant.[1] A village could have more than one headman and as many as seven are named in documents.[2] They came from the ranks of the village oligarchs. In Jahāngīr's reign in *pargana* Navsari (southern Gujarat) "there were many Brahmans, who carried on cultivation like peasants (*ra'īyat*); those from amongst them who are big men (*kalān*), came to be *muqaddams* in those villages".[3] The Vrindāban documents illustrate a similar origin of *muqaddams* in that area. In a transaction of 1558 or 1569, the four sellers of land in the village of Vrindāban designate themselves

[64] I would, therefore, not argue any longer, as I did in the first edition of this book, 128-9, that the growth of differentiation and the existence of an internal oligarchy were signs of the disruption and decline of the village community. My present position was first set forth in detail in V.K. Thakur and A. Aounshuman, eds, *Peasants in Indian History*, (Patna, 1996), 355-71.

[1] *Muqaddam* is an Arabic word, meaning one who is placed first. It came to be used in the specific sense of a village headman very early in medieval India. (Baranī, *Tārīkh-i Fīrūzshāhī*, 288, 291, 430. Cf. Moreland, *Agrarian System*, 19 & n). For the identification of *muqaddam* with *paṭel* in the Dakhin, see *A'īn*, I, 476. It is curious that these are the only two terms which won official recognition, for there seems to have been a number of others in local use. The author of Add. 6603, who was familiar with the nomenclature of Dehli and Bengal, mentions *manḍal*, *jeṭh-i ra'īyat*, and *mahtaun*, besides *muqaddam* (f.81a-b). The term *mahtaun* for the village headman occurs in Kabīr's verses (*Gurū Granth Sāhib*, Nagari text. 1104; *mahta* is used in another version of the same verses, *Kabīr Granthāvalī*, 163). In Orissa in the 16th century he was styled *padhāna* (Chakravarti in *JASB*, NS, XII [1916], 30). Abū-l Fazl at one place employs the word *ra'īs-i deh* for the same worthy (*A'īn*, I, 285), and in this he is followed by a late 18th century work, the *Dastūru-l 'Amal-i Khāliṣa Sharīfa*, Edinburgh 230, f.33a, where it is used to explain the significance of the term *manḍal*.

[2] See the sale deed of the *muqaddamī* of a village in Awadh, AD 1653 (Allahabad 1183). Five named persons and others, issue a document in the capacity of *muqaddams* of village Aritha in *pargana* Sahar (same *sarkār*, *ṣūba* Agra) in 1641 (Rādhādāmodar 9). Three petitioners jointly claimed the office of *muqaddamī* in a village in Awadh, *Durru-l 'Ulūm*, f. 55b. For two *muqaddams* in one village, see Allahabad, 329 & 1198; *Siyāqnāma*, 29, &c.

[3] *Dastūr Kaikobād Mahyār's Petition and Laudatory Poem Addressed to Jahāngīr*

panch in the Braj version, but *muqaddams* in the Persian.[4] In village Aritha, in a series of Persian versions, the seven sellers are merely designated "resident villagers" but they are styled *panch* and once even *panch mukadams* in the Braj versions; they turn into simple *muqaddams* in the comprehensive Persian statement of all plots transferred, written in 1588; and their successors claim the same designation in 1641.[5] The office was hereditary,[6] and could also be bought and sold, testifying to the growth of money relations.[7] The headman was normally a peasant himself; but sometimes, since the office could be purchased, an outsider, even a townsman, could hold the office.[8] He was never, properly speaking, a government servant. But the revenue authorities could at times depose a headman for failing in his obligations;[9] and they exercised

and Shāh Jahān, ed. & transl. Jivanji Jamshedji Modi, (Bombay, 1930), 12-13.

4 Rādhādāmodar Ser. 5, Acc. 33 & Ser. 21, Acc. 37, two copies of Wright 3, dated 1558; same coll., Ser. 56, Acc. 13 (Persian version, original of 1569).

5 The source-documents have been individually cited in the preceding section.

6 The seven *muqaddams* of a village, referred to above, claim that they had received their office from their forefathers (Allahabad 1183). A petitioner praying for the restoration of his office from the hands of a usurper, speaks of "the *muqaddamī* of that village which, from his ancestors, has belonged to the petitioner" (*Nigārnāma-i Munshī*, ed., 98). The hereditary nature of the office of *paṭel* is recognized in an 'Ādil Shāhī order of 1566 (*IHRC*, XXII [1945], 11). The principle is assumed in Khāfī Khān, I, 733 n., Add. 6573, f.261, in his reference to villages being left without *muqaddams* in case of failure of heirs.

7 A document of 1578 from Bihar, photograph published in K.K. Datta, ed., *Some Firmans, Sanads and Parwanas (1578-1802 A.D.)*, facing, p.104, records the sale of the office of *muqaddams* of a village, together with its land. Allahabad 1183 is a deed of sale of "the profits of *muqaddamī*" of a village in Awadh, dated 1653. See also *Durru-l 'Ulūm*, f.55a-b, for what is described as a voluntary transfer of the office by its previous incumbents, but was probably a sale.

8 In Allahahabd 329 (AD 1677), two *muqaddams* expressly call themselves "cultivators" (*muzāri'ān*). One may infer from the reference to the *muqaddam* of Palam and the conversion of his land into *madad-i ma'āsh* (revenue grant) at the orders of Akbar, that he was otherwise an ordinary revenue-payer (*Ṭabaqāt-i Akbarī*, II, 336). The *Dastūru-l 'Amal-i Navīsindagī*, ff.182a, 185a, shows land-revenue being assessed on the *muqaddams'* fields alongside those of other peasants (*āsāmī*). Manucci, II, 450, also speaks of "principal husbandmen", while obviously referring to the headmen.

On the other hand, it transpires from an order on a petition in the *Durru-l 'Ulūm*, f.55a-b, that the *muqaddamī* of a village had been sold by a group of persons belonging to a *qaṣba* or township to three other persons of the same *qaṣba*. In a Bihar document of 1578 (Datta, op.cit.) the seller is a non-Muslim, the buyer a Saiyid, and presumably an outsider. We may make the same presumption about the buyer when we find seven *muqaddams* bearing non-Muslim names, selling the *muqaddamī* of their village to a single person, a Muslim, for as much as Rs 230 (Allahabad 1183).

9 A *parwāna* issued on a petition claiming the *muqaddamī* of a village for the

the power of nominating headmen for villages that were newly settled or were due to be settled, and for old villages where the office was vacant owing to the absence of natural heirs.[10]

The authorities held the *muqaddams* to be primarily responsible for the payment of revenue assessed on the village.[11] It, therefore, became their duty to collect the revenue share of each individual peasant.[12] For this service they were remunerated either through being assigned 2½ per cent of the assessed land of the village, to be held by them revenue-free, or through a deduction of the same percentage from the total revenue collected by them.[13] Alternatively, they could impose a cess over and above land revenue, called *dah-nīm* (five per cent).[14] But the suspicion was always entertained that the *muqaddams*, if left to themselves, would make large unauthorized collections from the weaker peasants, under the pretence of realizing money to meet the revenue demand or pay the

---

petitioner on the basis of hereditary possession, ordered it to be secured for him, provided that "it had not been transferred to anyone else by former officials (*ḥukkām*) owing to the refractoriness or incapacity of the complainant" (*Nigārnāma-i Munshī*, ed., 98). It seems, however, that *jāgīrdārs* were not free to depose *muqaddams* at will. See, for instance, the report on a quarrel between the *muqaddam* of Alhanpur and the *jāgīrdār* of that place, in which the former secured imperial protection for himself (*Waqā'i' Ajmer*, 64-65). It is probable that the right to depose or nominate headmen lay only with the imperial administration.

[10] Murshid Qulī K͟hān, *dīwān* of the Dakhin during the last years of Shāhjahān, "assigned the land that had not come under the plough to men who had the ability to settle it and look after the peasants; having given them robes of honour and the title of *muqaddam*, he caused them to attend to (the business of) cultivation". (Ṣādiq K͟hān, Or.174, f.185b, Or. 1671, f.91a). K͟hāfī K͟hān, I, 733 n, who otherwise follows Ṣādiq K͟hān in this passage, here reads differently. Murshid Qulī K͟hān, he says, appointed new *muqaddams* in "villages which had no *muqaddams*, the heirs of the former *muqaddams* of these places having disappeared through the adversity of fate".

[11] Cf. *Ā'īn*, I, 285, where he is designated *ra'īs-i deh*. *Qabūliyats* or papers accepting the revenue demand and affirming their duty to pay it, signed by the *muqaddams*, are reproduced in *Farhang-i Kārdānī*, f.34a-b; *Siyāqnāma*, 29; and *K͟hulāṣatu-s Siyāq*, ff.74a-75a. Or. 2026, ff.23a-24b. Cf. also *Factories, 1622-23*, 253-4.

[12] *Ā'īn*, I, 288 (under "*Ā'īn-i Bitikchī*"). Cf. Manucci, II, 405, who says that to collect the revenue "it is necessary to tie up the principal husbandmen", who "collect with equally severe measures from the peasants".

[13] *Ā'īn*, I, 285; *Mir'āt*, I, 173. The words of the *Ā'īn* suggest that the former mode of remuneration was the more usual. In the records of the Papal *pargana*, *ṣūba* Berar, the *muqaddams* like other officials are shown as holding certain lands revenue-free (*IHRC* [1929], 85-86).

[14] *Ā'īn*, I, 300, where this is said to have replaced, upon Akbar's orders, a higher cess, called *dah-yak*, "ten per cent"). *Mir'āt*, I, 173, says orders were issued in

revenue officials' perquisites.[15] When the authorities advanced *taqāvī* loans to encourage cultivation, these too were distributed among the peasants through the headmen, who doubtless took their share before passing the money on to the peasants.[16] In addition to the financial advantages accruing from, or made possible by, these functions, the *muqaddams* exacted certain customary perquisites such as their *khwurāk* or board from the village fund[17] and a rate known as *muqaddamī* from the villagers individually.[18]

The *muqaddam's* jurisdiction over the village was not purely financial. He was held answerable for any crime committed within or near his village. In cases of robbery or murder of travellers, especially, he was obliged to produce the culprits and the goods

---

1588-92 for *desāīs* and *muqaddams* in Gujarat to share the 5-percent charge equally. *Mazhar-i Shāhjahānī*, 185, mentions *dah-nīmī*, and explains it as a five-per cent charge on revenue, in cash and kind, collected by *arbābs* and *muqaddams*; but here, in Sehwan (Sind), it used to be paid out of the revenue collected, and was thus an allowance and not a cess. The earliest occurrence of *dah-nīm* (under that spelling) is in a *farmān* of Akbar of 1565 (Vrindāban: Madan Mohan, 50), which lists it among cesses remitted the revenue-grantee. Henceforth it appears as *dah-nīmī*, often alone, but sometimes paired with, or replaced by, *muqaddamī*, in the *farmāns* of *madad-i ma'āsh* grants down to Aurangzeb's reign. Add.6603, f.61b, defines *dah-nīmī* as the share of the *muqaddams*, amounting to 5 per cent, out of what is collected from the village. This percentage explains the *muqaddam's* right in respect of a plot of land sold in Vrindāban in 1653 being designated *biswa muqaddamī*, "the *muqaddam's* right to one-twentieth" (Govind-dev, 39). In the specimen accounts given by the *Khulāṣatu-s Siyāq*, ff. 40b, 40a, a deduction (*mujrā*) for the *muqaddam's* remuneration (*in'ām-i muqaddamī*) is allowed at the rate of Rs 16, as. 14, for every thousand of rupees collected in revenue (*ḥasbu-l huṣūl*). It would then seem that the rate of 5 per cent, of which the *muqaddam* got a half, was only the nominal or maximum rate, and the actual rate probably varied with the locality.

15 'Abbās Khān, ff.11b-12a, 106a; Aurangzeb's *farmān* to Rasikdās, Art. 6. Remissions of revenue in lump sum for villages were discouraged for the similar reason that the headmen would not then pass the remissions on to the individual peasants. See Chapter VI, Section 4.

16 See Chapter VI, Section 8.

17 *Khwurāk-i muqaddamān* is entered as a charge under *kharj-i deh* in all the three village accounts studied in the previous section. In two of them the charge under this head is very small, amounting to less than a third of one per cent of the revenue paid. In the *Siyāqnāma* it exceeds 3 per cent, but might well include other charges, such as the allowance of the *paṭwārī*, for which no provision has been made in its accounts. *Khwurāk* means food or diet and it is possible that the charge under this name was supposed to provide board to the headman, when he went outside the village on the village's business.

18 As mentioned in note 14 above, *muqaddamī* is paired with *dah-nīmī* (the formula being *dah-nīmī o muqaddamī*) in the list of cesses remitted to *madad-i ma'āsh* holders in 17th-century *farmāns*.

stolen.[19] Put in this position, the temptation must often have been irresistible for him to "father yet uppon some poore man that hee [himself] may be cleare".[20] Here was another weapon which the *muqaddam* could use to intimidate his fellow villagers.

Finally, the *muqaddams* possessed the right of allotting the uncultivated land of the village to such as wished to till it.[21] This right was implicitly recognized by the authorities when they entrusted the task of settling new villages to certain persons as *muqaddams*.[22] The headman could not probably interfere with the land already occupied, though in one case at least we find him arbitrating in a boundary dispute between two landholders.[23]

In any village not utterly ruined by the burden of land revenue, the position of the *muqaddam* was a profitable one. There is evidence that moneyed persons were sometimes tempted to buy this office as a good investment for their money. Thus in one transaction (from Awadh, 1653), we find an evident outsider, buying out the old hereditary *muqaddams* of a village for Rs 230, a considerable sum for those times.[24] In another document, three

19 Sher Shāh's rough and ready system of maintaining law and order by this means is described most fully in 'Abbās Khān, ff.110-111a, ed., 220-22. It was continued in all its essentials by the Mughal administration. See, for example, the report in *Factories, 1622-23*, 250-52, 253-54, of the pillage of the wreckage of an English ship: the *muqaddam* of the village suspected was immediately summoned to find out the culprits and recover the plunder. A letter in Bālkrishan Brahman, f.33a-b, asks an undesignated officer to punish the *muqaddam* of a village from which certain persons had trespassed into another village and assaulted revenue guards posted there. Finally, the *Siyāqnāma*, 69, gives the draft of the undertaking (*muchalka*) taken from the *muqaddams* of a village situated on the highway (*shāhrāh*). They declare that if any theft or robbery occurred within their jurisdiction, they should be held guilty thereof. They also pledge themselves to either produce the stolen goods or pay compensation.

20 This is said of the *muqaddam* suspected of having had a hand in the pillage of an English ship (*Factories, 1622-23*, 254).

21 "Anyone who wants to cultivate any land goes to the headmen of the village, who are called *mukaddams* and asks for as much land as he wants at the place which suits him. This is rarely refused, but always granted" (Geleynssen, *JIH*, IV, 78-79; the sense of this passage is much distorted in De Laet, 95). Geleynssen's statement refers specifically to Gujarat. The *Dīwān Pasand* (Or. 2011, f.7b), written in the Doab early in the 19th century, says each village contains a few headmen and hundreds of peasant cultivators (*āsāmī-i bazrgar*), who till the land, marking out their individual fields, with the consent of the headmen and of the revenue authorities.

22 See note 10 above on Murshid Qulī Khān's appointment of *muqaddams* for settling new villages.

23 Allahabad 1197. The *muqaddam* here arbitrated not *ex-officio* but because he was nominated as *ṣāliṣ* (arbitrator) by both parties.

24 Allahabad 1183. The contents of this document have been commented upon

persons of a township declare that after obtaining the office of *muqaddam* of a ruined village, they had spent "a large amount" to resettle it and advanced Rs 400 in *taqāvī* loans to the cultivators out of their own resources.[25]

The distance that grew up between the headman and the ordinary peasants must have led to a visible conflict of interest between them. Kabīr presents one side of it when he shows the soul as *mahtaun* (headman) grieving that the five senses, being the *kirsāns* (peasants), had fled the village, leaving the soul to face the authorities and answer for the arrears of revenue.[26] Gurū Arjan shows us the other, when he presents the soul as rejoicing that the five peasants had been held captive and had become the headman's *mujere* (*muzāri'*), or cultivators.[27] The considerable power that the headmen came to wield over the village, also sometimes led to their claiming or acquiring certain rights identical with those of the *zamīndārs*. Indeed, in two adjoining localities of the Doab and Awadh the term *muqaddamī* (and, during the earlier part of the sixteenth century, the synonymous term *khoṭī*) was employed to designate a right that was alternatively, or additionally, described as *milk* (proprietary right), and was in later days assumed to be identical with *zamīndārī*.[28] In a Vrindāban document of 1653, a plot of land is first declared to be held in proprietary possession (*taṣarruf-i mālikāna*) of the seller, who then proceeds to transfer "the whole of the *biswa* (share) of the *muqaddamī* of (the plot of) one *bīgha* of cultivated land".[29] In two documents from Awadh of

---

in notes 6-8 of this Section.

[25] *Durru-l 'Ulūm*, f. 55a-b. [26] *Gurū Granth Sāhib*, Nagari text, 1104.

[27] Ibid., 73. I am indebted to Dr Bhai Jodh Singh for very kindly clarifying the sense of these verses in a personal letter to me.

[28] The localities are the *pargana* of Shamsabad (in District Fatehpur) and Bilgram (District Hardoi). Shamsabad Docs. No.1, dated 1530, records the sale of "20 *biswas*" of the *ḥaqq-o-milk-i khoṭī* (right over the entire village). In sale deeds from *pargana* Bilgram, dated 1531, 1542-43, 1556 and 1557, copied in the *Sharā'if-i 'Uṣmānī*, ff.55a-b, 63a-65b, the right sold is termed *milk-o-khoṭī*. Subsequent documents from both these localities replace *khoṭī* by *muqaddamī*. In Shamsabad Docs. 2, dated 1545, the right transferred by Doc.1, is described as the *ḥaqq-o-milk* of *muqaddamī*, and in Shamsabad Docs. 5, the original possessors of the right are simply styled *māliks*. Similarly what is designated *muqaddamī* in Bilgram Docs. 8 appears as a superior private right in Bilgram Docs. 9, both the documents being dated 1570. More explicitly, in Shamsabad Docs. 8, dated 1705, the *ḥaqq-o-milk* of the sellers, who style themselves as the heirs of a *zamīndār*, is stated to comprise *muqaddamī* plus (possession of) a well, pond, tank, orchards, trees, fruit-trees, ruins, etc.

[29] Vrindāban Docs. (collection not stated = Wright 11).

Aurangzeb reign we find *muqaddamī* being coupled with *satārahī* and *biswī* or *biswa-hā*, which were the hallmarks of *zamīndārī* right.[30] It is not suprising, therefore, that a late eighteenth-century glossary should define the *muqaddam* as "the proprietor (*mālik*) of one village", different, perhaps, from the *zamīndār* only in that the latter could also have more than one village in his possession.[31]

Thus in *ra'īyatī* areas, a *muqaddam* might in time acquire the substance of the right of *zamīndār*. His position, however, was very different in such villages as lay in the absolute possession of *zamīndārs*. In the record of a dispute over the *zamīndārī* of a village in 1662, one party accused the other of expelling the "old *muqaddam*" of the village, while the defendant styled the person so treated as his *kārinda* (agent), whom he, as the ancestral *zamīndār* of the village, was fully entitled to remove.[32] The defendant's position was upheld by the revenue and judicial officials, and we may infer from this that the headman's position was regarded here as that of a servant of the *zamīndār*, holding his office at the latter's pleasure. The conversion of *zamīndārī* into full landownership under British rule accordingly served to depress the position of the headman very greatly, and he shrank in many parts of the country to a mere name.[33]

We have already referred more than once to the village accountant or *paṭwārī*.[34] His office was an old one and his name appears in the description of 'Alā'uddīn K͟haljī's administrative measures (1296-1316).[35] As Abū-l Faẓl tells us, the duty of the *paṭwārī* was to keep an account of "the expenditure and income" of the village.[36] When the authorities had worked out the total revenue assessment on the village, the *paṭwārī* was to record the tax-share (*rasad*) of "each cultivator (*kārinda*), name by name"; and the revenue collectors were to take bonds (*muchalka*) from the *paṭwārīs* and

[30] Allahabad 295; *Nigārnāma-i Munshī*, ed., 98. (In the Bodl. MS. f.98b, the document is introduced with the heading: "Complaint concerning *muqaddamī* and *zamīndārī*").

[31] Add. 6003, f. 81a. On the same folio it also describes the *muqaddam* as "a leading man amongst the peasantry".

[32] Allahabad 375. The village lay in *pargana* Sandila in Awadh.

[33] Cf. W.C. Benett, *Chief Clans of the Roy Bareilly District*, 66-7.

[34] The term *paṭwārī* was invariably employed in northern India. The equivalent in the Dakhin was *kulkarnī* (*Ā'īn*, I, 476), and in Orissa, *bhoi* (*JASB*, NS, XII [1916], 30).

[35] Baranī, *Tārīk͟h-i Fīrūzshāhī*, 288-89.

[36] *Ā'īn*, I, 300.

muqaddams to ensure the realization of the revenue so determined.[37] The revenue officials were required to insist that the *paṭwārī* give to each peasant an accurate memorandum or *sarkhaṭ* of the payment made by him, and submit a record of these receipts, "name by name", as well as the balance (*bāqī*), "with the marks of the [village] oligarchs (*'aiyān*)."[38] The *paṭwārī's* own name probably came from his concern with the *paṭṭas* or documents stating the revenue-demand assessed upon a village or individual cultivators;[39] and he usually maintained his records, known as *bahī* or *kāghaz-i khām*, in "Hindwī" or the local language;[40] in its original garb (*kāghaz-i khām-i aṣl*), this record was to be regarded by revenue and financial officials as the authentic evidence for actual payments.[41] Abū-l Fazl is again our authority for the statement that the *paṭwārī* was an employee of the villagers,[42] and we must assume that wherever the village community existed, he functioned as its servant. In the specimen village accounts available to us, the allowance given to him is made a charge on the village fund under the head of "village expenses".[43] But the administration also remunerated him for his services: under Akbar he was assigned a commission of one per cent of the revenues of his village, to be realized through an additional cess.[44]

[37] Todar Mal's Memorandum, Art.9, Add.27,247, f.332a (summary in *AN*, III, 382-3); Moosvi's transl. in her *People, Taxation and Trade in Mughal India*, 171.

[38] *Ā'īn*, I, 232.

[39] *Khulāṣatu-s Siyāq*, ff.73b, 75a, Or. 2026, ff.22b-23a; *Durru-l 'Ulūm*, f.62a; *Farhang-i Kārdānī*, f. 35a; Allahabad 177, 897, 1206. See also the definition of *paṭṭa* in Wilson, *Glossary*, 408. Wilson, ibid., 406, seeks to derive the term *paṭwārī* from the Marathi *paṭ*, meaning 'a register or record', but admits that the word *paṭ* in this sense is not found in Hindi and the term *paṭwārī* is unknown in Maharashtra.

[40] *Akbarnāma*, III, 457; *Ā'īn*, I, 289; Aurangzeb's *farmān* to Rasikās, Art. 11; *Khulāṣatu-s Siyāq*, f.91b, Or. 2026.

[41] Todar Mal's Memorandum, Art.9, Add.27,247, f.332b (this portion is omitted in Abū-l Fazl's summary in the final version of *A.N.*).

[42] *Ā'īn*, I, 300.

[43] In the *Dastūru-l 'Amal-i 'Ālamgīrī*, ff.41b-42b, this allowance appears under the name *kāghaz-i paṭwārī* as if it was meant to cover the cost of paper (*kāghaz*) needed by that official. In the *Khulāṣatu-s Siyāq* provision is made for two separate allowances, viz. *faṣlāna* (from *faṣl*, harvest) and *khwurāk* (lit. food), for the *paṭwārī*. Cf. *Revenue Selections*, 170, 299.

[44] He was entitled to a half-share in the cess called *ṣad-doī-i qānūngoī* ("the *qānūngo*'s charge of 2 per cent"), *Ā'īn*, I, 300. Probably what is the earliest mention of this cess occurs in Akbar's *farmān* of December 1559 (photograph, CAS in History, Aligarh); it then continues to be listed among exactions from which *madad-i ma'āsh* grantees were exempt.

It is difficult to say how the *paṭwārī* was affected by the growth of power of the dominant elements in the village community, especially the *muqaddams*. In some cases, at least, the *paṭwārī* also obtained sufficient strength to oppress the smaller peasants.[45] And so the cry of the peasant, who has not sown the land, but is yet taxed: "O God's people, the *paṭwārī* constantly harasses me."[46]

[45] See Aurangzeb's *farmān* to Rasikdās, Art. 6. In Art. 9 he is put alongside the *chaudhurī*, *qānūngo* and *muqaddam* in opposition to the *reza ri'āyā*, the small peasantry.

[46] Kabīr in *Gurū Granth Sāhib*, Nagari text, 793.

CHAPTER V

THE ZAMĪNDĀRS

1. NATURE OF ZAMĪNDĀRĪ RIGHT

"Zamīndār" in modern Indian usage means a landlord. Much controversy has centred around the question whether he is wholly a creation of British rule. The controversy has involved the further question whether the word *zamīndār* when used in the literature of the Mughal period bore the same sense that it now has. There appeared to be no direct explanation of what it then signified in the *Ā'īn-i Akbarī* or in any of the more easily accessible historical sources. Some of the earlier modern interpretations, therefore, tended perforce to be inferences drawn from rather scanty materials. At the time the first edition of this book appeared (1963), the generally accepted view seemed to be that the *zamīndār* in Mughal times was really a "vassal chief" and could not exist in the directly administered territories of the empire.[1]

The word *zamīndār* is a Persian compound, meaning literally the controller or holder of *zamīn* or land. Its use originated in India, the word being practically unknown in Persia.[2] In India, however, it occurs quite early; an early fourteenth-century dictionary uses it as a synonym of *marzbān*, explained as "overseer (*shaḥna*) of a territory".[3] In 'Iṣāmī (1350) it appears as a designation of the holder of an *iqṭā*' (territorial assignment) or controller of a territory

[1] Moreland put forward this view in *Agrarian System*, 122, 279, in apparent modification of his earlier statements in *India at the Death of Akbar*, 3-4. He admitted, however, that it was possible for the term *zamīndār* to have a wider connotation in Bengal (*Agrarian System*, 191-4); and he also found it hard to reconcile the local traditions of chiefs, their clans and martial exploits in parts of Awadh with his own reading of the *Ā'īn* (ibid., 123). Saran was not assailed by any doubts of this kind. After defining *zamīndār* in the same manner as Moreland ("vassal chief"), he dismisses as an "absurdity" the suggestion that *zamīndārs* could have been found in all parts of the empire (*Provincial Government*, 111 & *n*).

[2] The word is not listed in the glossary of terms of "land tenure and revenue administration" in A.K.S. Lambton, *Landlord and Peasant in Persia*, 422ff. It does not appear in its own place in the *Farhang-i-Rashīdī*, the standard 17th-century lexicon for purely Persian words. It is used to explain the word *marzbān*; but, then, this dictionary was, after all, written in India. In the *Bahār-i 'Ajam* the word is indeed admitted, but only the verses of poets who had composed in India are quoted to illustrate its use.

[3] *Farhang-i Qawwās*, ed. Nazir Ahmad, 33, 88. The author, Fakhr Qawwās, was

(*ẓābiṭ-i zamīn*).[4] As Moreland points out, two other fourteenth-century historians, Baranī and 'Afīf, employ the term for any chief found outside, as well as inside, the Sultanate.[5] But a different sense, that of the holder of any superior right over land, and so not necessarily implying possession of political authority, was already developing. In 1353 Fīrūz Shāh Tughluq speaks of *zamīndārs* as comprising "headmen (*muqaddamān*), government-appointed land-holders (*mafroziān*) and landowners (*mālikān*)".[6]

That the word *zamīndār* still continued to be applied in the Mughal period to chiefs in general is beyond dispute.[7] But it was not by any means confined to such use. There is no easier way of refuting an exclusive identification with vassal chiefs than by showing that the *zamīndārs*, so called, existed everywhere in the regularly administered territories and not only in the tributary states. It happens that the evidence of the *Ā'īn-i Akbarī* is alone sufficient to establish this fact. Why this was not obvious for so long, has been owing to a single long undetected error in Blochmann's standard edition of the *Ā'īn*, an error that resulted in a serious misrepresentation of its statistical information.[8]

Presumably for convenience of printing, Blochmann did not reproduce the statistics under the "Account of the Twelve Provinces" in their original tabular form. He not only dispensed with the columns of the original tables, but also dropped, without any

---

a notable poet of the time of 'Alā'uddīn Khaljī (1296-1316) and was mentioned as living in 1342-3 (ed.'s introd., ibid., 2-3, 12).

4 *Futūḥu-s Salāṭīn*, ed. S.A. Usha, 398, 597.

5 Cf. *Agrarian System*, 18 & *n*.

6 'Ainu-l Mulk 'Māhrū, *Inshā-i Māhrū*, 17. Cf. *Cambridge Economic History of India*, I, 58-9, for *mafrozī and mālik*.

7 See Section 4 of this chapter. Two standard Persian dictionaries written in India in the 17th and 18th centuries, the *Farhang-i Rashīdī*, s.v. *marzbān*, and the *Bahār-i Ajam*, s.v. *zamīndār*, consider the terms *marzbān* and *zamīndār* to be synonyms; and *marzbān* usually meant a governor or chief. But in the *Miftāḥu-l Fuẓalā*, Or. 3299, f.270a, written in 1468-9, the word is given a wider meaning: "*zamīndār*, overseer and owner (*mālik*) of land". Moreover, among the verses quoted in the *Bahār-i Ajam*, to illustrate the use of the word *zamīndār*, there is one which expresses contempt for Farhād and Majnūn, because the former was only a labourer and the latter only a *zamīndār*. Surely here it must mean someone of a much lower station than a chief.

8 Blochmann's edition, Bib. Ind., Calcutta, 1867-77. The two editions of 1882 and 1893 issued by the Nawal Kishor Press, which probably have had a wider public, follow Blochmann in dispensing with the original tabular form. Saiyid Ahmad's edition of the *Ā'īn* (1855), lacked Vol. II, which would have contained the statistics.

explanation, the column headings. His reader, therefore, has no means of knowing that the names of castes entered against each *pargana* in these tables, belong really to a column headed "*zamīndār*", or, occasionally, "*būmī*" (for which see below), in the manuscripts.[9] The entries under this column are provided for practically every *pargana* in the directly administered territory in all but the five provinces of Bengal, Orissa, Bihar, Berar and Khandesh. In these five provinces and in the tracts ruled by tributary chiefs in other provinces, no entries in this column are put against *parganas*, the *zamīndār* castes being usually specified, if at all, for whole *sarkārs*.[10]

The testimony of the *Ā'īn* is backed by extensive documentary evidence in the form of sale deeds, official papers and other records of the sixteenth and seventeenth centuries. Here also we come across *zamīndārī* rights in almost all parts of the Mughal empire, in the provinces of Agra, Dehli, Lahor, Ajmer (imperial territories) and, especially, Awadh, not to speak of the more distant provinces of Bengal, Bihar and Gujarat.[11] It may be said with assurance that wherever the surviving records are extensively surveyed, the existence of *zamīndārs* is bound to be detected.

In the light of this evidence, let us return to the question of definition. While our sixteenth- and seventeenth-century records and histories contain no definition of *zamīndārī* nor a description

[9] In the original tables we have eight columns with the following headings: *Parganāt* (*parganas*), *Qilā'* (forts), *Ārāẓī* (measured area), *Naqdī* (revenue stated in cash), *Suyurg͟hāl* (revenue grants), *Zamīndār* (or *Būmī*), *Sawār* (cavalry) and *Piyāda* (infantry). In Blochmann's edition all the headings are omitted, except for *suyurghāl*, *sawār* and *piyāda*, which, abbreviated to their initial letters, are put with the respective figures against each *pargana*.

The confusion introduced by Blochmann's handling of the original tables has been increased further by the eccentric restoration of the columns and headings in Jarrett's translation of the *Ā'īn*, Vol. II, ed. Sarkar, 129ff. He substitutes the heading "Castes" for "*Zamīndār*" and pushes its column from the sixth position in the original tables to the last one. At the same time he puts the columns of cavalry and infantry figures immediately after "Revenue".

[10] See Irfan Habib, "Zamīndārs in the *Ā'īn*", in *PIHC*, 21st Session, 1958 Trivandarum, 320-3.

[11] The evidence is far too extensive for specific references here. Nor are they necessary, for documents relating to *zamīndārs* in all the regions mentioned will be cited in this section in various contexts. I have put the word "especially" before Awadh simply because there are a very large number of *zamīndārī* documents from that area in the U.P. Record Office, Allahabad, which I have seen. It is not intended to imply that the *zamīndārs* were more numerous or the institution of *zamīndārī* more strongly established in Awadh than elsewhere.

of its essentials, they do provide substitute terms. A Persian word used as a synonym for *zamīndār*, quite often by Abū-l Faẓl, and occasionally by other writers, is *būmī*. Its literal meaning (from *būm*, land) is the same as that of *zamīndār*, and it too does not seem to have been used in any technical sense in Persia.[12] While these two Persian terms in time gained currency, *zamīndār* becoming the standard official term, there still survived local names which were considered to represent the same right as *zamīndārī*. There were *satārahī* and *biswī* or *bis'ī* in Awadh;[13] and *bhūmīa* is said to have been the real counterpart of *zamīndār* in Rajasthan.[14] The literal sense of the first of these three terms is one-seventeenth, while the second means one-twentieth, neither of which senses for the moment brings us much enlightenment.[15] The third word goes back etymologically to the same Indo-Iranian root as the Persian word *būmī* and means the same thing.[16] In the

[12] The word *būmī* does not seem to have been used in classical Persian and in the mouth of Abū-l Faẓl was undoubtedly a contrived archaism. It is not found in *Farhang-i Rashīdī* or *Bahār-i 'Ajam*; nor in Lambton's Glossary. op.cit.

[13] Both these terms are found in a sale deed of Akbar's reign (Allahabad 317 of 1586). A document of 1650 employing the formula, "*biswī*, known as *satārahī*", shows that they were synonymous. *Satārahī* occurs much more often than *bisī* or *biswī*, but both are used only in records belonging to the neighbourhood of Lakhnau, especially Sandila. They are not found in the records of Bahraich *sarkār*. There is no direct identification of *biswī* with *zamīndārī*, but *satārahī* is expressly identified with *zamīndārī* in the formula "*milkiyat-i zamīndārī*, known as *satārahī*", found in two 18th-century documents (Allahabad 457 of AD 1764; and Allahabad 362). An earlier document, a sale deed of 1698, uses a shorter formula, "*milkiyat*, known as *satārahī*", which serves as well, since the terms *zamīndārī* and *milkiyat* in these records are almost interchangeable.

[14] Cf. James Tod, *Annals and Antiquities*, I, 133, 136; S.P. Gupta, *Agrarian System of Eastern Rajasthan*, 134-40; B.L. Bhadani, "The Allodial Proprietors (?) – the Bhumias of Marwar", *IHR*, VI (1-2), 141-53.

The term also occurred outside Rajasthan. In 1583 a Gujarat rebel sent letters to "*bhūmīas* and *zamīndārs* possessing retainers" (Abū Turāb Walī, *Tārīkh-i Gujarāt*, 103). The *Tārīkh-i Ṭāhirī*, f. 25a, written in Jahāngīr's reign, refers to "*zamīndārs* and *bhūmīas*" in Sind. In the Punjab, Gurū Arjan tells us that "the *bhūmīa* ever strives for land (*bhūmī*)" (*Gurū Granth Sāhib*, Nagari text, I, 188).

[15] The term *satārahī*, from *satara* or seventeen, seems to have disappeared altogether. It was formed on the analogy of *bis'ī* or *biswī* (with *bīs* or twenty as the root); and S. Zaheer Husain Jafri cites Allahabad 199, where *satārahī* is explained in Persian as *haftdahī*, one-seventeenth ('Agrarian Conditions of Awadh under the Mughals and Nawab Wazirs: 1595-1856', Ph.D. thesis [unpublished], Aligarh, p.122).

[16] *Bhūmīa* is derived from the Sanskrit *bhūmi*, which like the Persian *būm*, means "earth, land". The words are closely related, being just slightly altered forms of a common Aryan parent word. Indeed, it is quite possible that the term *būmī* in Persian was coined in India (by Abū-l Faẓl?) under the influence of the indigenous *bhūmīa*.

latter part of the seventeenth century, we come across a new set of terms used practically all over the country, *ta'alluqa* and *ta'alluqdār*, as substitutes in certain cases for *zamīndārī* and *zamīndār*. Their exact significance will be discussed in Section 3 of this chapter; at present, it is enough to say that they are derived from the word *ta'alluq*, which simply means "connexion"; and these terms too, therefore, do not bear their real meaning on their face.

The synonym for *zamīndār* used most often was *mālik*. In some documents, a *zamīndār* is alternatively termed *mālik*.[17] In two seventeenth-century documents, *mālikiyat* (i.e. the right of a *mālik*) and *zamīndārī* are used indifferently for the same right;[18] and in a large number of documents, we find "*milkiyat* and *zamīndārī*" coupled together as names of a single right.[19] Now, while the significance of the other synonyms is obscure, *mālik* is an Arabic term which has its own distinct sense in Muslim law, namely that of "proprietor". *Milkiyat* is, therefore, what in English would be called "private property".

It is, however, one thing to say that *zamīndārī* was a form of *milkiyat*, and quite another to assume that all rights designated *milkiyat* were *zamīndārī* rights. As a property right, *zamīndārī* had, in the first place, specifically rural and agrarian associations. This seems to be the one element in a definition of the word *zamīndār* offered by Ānand Rām Mukhliṣ, an official at the Dehli court, writing in 1745. "*Zamīndār*", he says, "etymologically (*dar aṣl*) means a person who is a master of land (*ṣāḥib-i zamīn*), but now signifies a person who is the *mālik* of the land of a village or township and carries on cultivation."[20] The second element in this definition relates to the superior nature of *zamīndārī* right: it is seen as being possessed over the village, rather than over any particular plot of land. It was thus mainly to the holder of a share of the village that the term *zamīndār* was applicable. We have seen

17 In a *ḥasbu-l ḥukm* issued by Rāja Raghunāth, Aurangzeb's finance minister, 9 September 1660, the holders of the *zamīndārī* of a village are styled its *māliks* (Sihunda Docs. 17). The phrase "*mālik* and *zamīndār* and *chaudhurī*" occurs in Allahabad 1192 of AD 1669. Add. 6603, f.79a, speaks of the *mālikiyat*, i.e. position as *mālik*, of *zamīndārs*.

18 Allahabad 375 (AD 1662) and Allahabad 323 (AD 1675).

19 Allahabad 891, 1192, 1196, 1205, 1216, 1219, 1221, 1222, 1224, 1227, etc. (all seventeenth-century documents).

20 *Mir'ātu-l Iṣṭilāḥ*, f.153a.

in the previous chapter that the peasants too were often described as *māliks*; but in terms of Mukhliṣ's definition, they could not be called *zamīndārs*. The association of *zamīndārī* with the village, rather than the field, is borne out by the manner in which the size of the area held under *zamīndārī* rights is specified in the documents of the period. A *zamīndārī* is nearly always said to comprise a village or a certain fractional part of it, seldom so many *bīghas* or definite units of area. The word *biswa* which is sometimes employed in stating the area of *zamīndārī* does not mean, in this context, the actual unit of area of that name, equal to one-twentieth of a *bīgha*, but represents a twentieth part of a village.[21]

Zamīndārī was, therefore, a right which belonged to a rural class other than, and standing above, the peasantry. Before we enquire into the actual relationship between the peasantry and this class, it is important to note that the sway of the *zamīndārs* did not necessarily extend over the entire countryside. On the other hand, there seem to have been large numbers of villages where no *zamīndārī* right existed and which, therefore, were known as *ra'īyatī*, or "peasant-held", as distinct from the villages of the *zamīndārs*.

This division between *ra'īyatī* and *zamīndārī* villages was well established, if not always equally well marked, throughout the empire. An administrative manual written in Dehli province divides the land of a village into *khwud-kāshta-i zamīndārān* ("self-cultivated land of the *zamīndārs*") and *ra'īyatī*.[22] Another, written in Ilahabad province, similarly classifies villages of a *pargana* as *ta'alluqa* (i.e. under *ta'alluqdārs*) and *ra'īyatī*.[23]

The British regime in this region (plains of the present Uttar Pradesh) inherited the division. In the early nineteenth century, its officials spoke of the "village *zamīndārs*", who held "at least four-fifths" of the villages, while the remainder were held by big *zamīndārs* and chiefs.[24] But the "village *zamīndārs*" themselves

21 For example, a sale-deed of Akbar's reign, transferring *satārahī* and *bis'ī* rights, describes them as covering "the whole village", which assertion after a few lines, is restated as "twenty *biswas* of the said village" (Allahabad 317 of AD 1586).

The word *biswa* also came to mean simply a share in the *zamīndārī* of any village. Thus we a have reference to "the *biswas* ("*biswa-hā*") of the *zamīndārī* of half the village" in Allahabad 1191 (AD 1667). See also *Nigārnama-i Munshī*, ed., 98; *Durru-l 'Ulūm*, ff.48a (Bengal), 53a (Bihar), and 61b-62a.

22 *Dastūru-l 'Amal-i Navīsindagī*, f.183a.

23 *Siyāqnāma*, 35, 36, 38, 39, 53, etc.

24 Colebrooke's minute of 20 July 1820, *Revenue Selections*, 205-6.

belonged to two classes, the superior non-peasant right-holders, or *zamīndārs* proper;[25] and others, who were simply peasants. The latter were known to local officials not as *zamīndārs*, but as "Ryot and Assamee" (*ra'īyat* and *āsāmī*), terms which were applied as well to "cultivators of the lands of others".[26] These in various villages acknowledged no superiors, though they might have bodies of subordinate cultivators under them, such as the *pāikāsht*.[27]

In respect of Gujarat, we have an account of this division, which comes from the *Mir'āt-i Aḥmadī*, the celebrated history of the province, completed in 1761. There are other things of interest in its account as well and it deserves to be quoted at length.

During the viceroyalty of the Khān-i A'ẓam [1588-92, during the reign of Akbar], the *desā'īs*, *muqaddams* and peasants of most of the *parganas* complained to the imperial court that the agents of the governors and *jāgīrdārs* were seizing all the revenue (or produce, *ḥāṣilāt*) through (various) cesses (*abwāb*); and after their taking it away, the Rājpūts, Kolīs and Musalmāns raised a tumult, laying waste the produce (*ḥāṣil*) and fields of the petitioners. This way lay the ruin of the peasantry and a cause of fall in the revenues of the government. It was, therefore, ordered that ... one-fourth of the land of the Kolīs and others be set apart, no revenue demanded therefrom, and trustworthy sureties taken for their good conduct. The *zamīndārs* of entire villages (*dehāt-i dar-o-bast*) and principalities (*makānāt-i 'umda*) should have their horses branded, so that presenting themselves before the Governor, they might perform services for the government; and from the land they might have sold, which is called *bechān*, they ought to take half the revenue (*maḥṣūl*). The order was put into effect and the province at that time prospered with each passing day.

Let it not be hidden ... that in olden times the country of Gujarat was in the possession of the Rājpūts and Kolīs, as has been mentioned earlier.[28] During the time of the Sultans of Gujarat, when the power and strength of the Muslims was fully established, owing to the rebelliousness of these people (the Rājpūts and Kolīs), they (the Sultans) devoted themselves to punishing and chastising them. Helpless, they had no choice but to offer submission and obedience. Entreating (to be forgiven), they accepted (the

[25] Holt Mackenzie, Memorandum of 1 July 1891, para 349 n. (*Revenue Selections*, 88 & *n.*).

[26] Ibid., para. 265 (*Revenue Selections*, 132).

[27] Cf. Wauchope's letter of 12 August 1809, para 10 (*Revenue Selections*, 219). There are hints of application of the term *zamīndār* to such peasants in seventeenth-century documents as well. Two peasants of a hamlet of Vrindaban belonging to families of the village *panch*, as established from other Vrindaban documents, are designated *zamīndārs* in a deed of 1691 recording the sale of 880 square *gaz* of wasteland by them to a Brahman (Govind-dev Docs.).

[28] The words here are jumbled up in the printed edition.

obligations of) service and payment of revenue. A fourth part of their native places and villages, which (part) was called *bānṭh* in the dialect of Gujarat, was settled upon them, while the (other) three-fourths of it (their land), called *talpad*, was attached to the Imperial government. The big *zamīndārs* who held many (lit. most) *parganas* had their *ta'alluqa* settled upon them on condition of their joining service and maintaining troops, in the same way as by *jāgīr*, that is, everyone was to be present with his troops of horse and foot, according to his resources and strength. So that for a long time, the Kolīs and Rājpūts who held *bānṭh* in various villages performed watch and ward duty (*chaukī o pahra*) in their respective places and enjoyed the possession of their *bānṭh*, giving on each crop something by way of *salāmī* (offering) to the *jāgīrdār*. In course of time, some of the Rājpūts and Kolīs and others who had acquired a little strength, raised disturbances in the *ra'īyatī* villages far and near, lifting cattle and killing the cultivators. The peasants of those places were thus compelled to gratify them by giving them, in some places, a fixed amount of money every year, or one or two cultivable fields. This exaction is known as *girās* and *va'dal*. This custom has become well established in this country and, owing to the weakness of the governors, has become universal (lit. reached perfection). There is hardly a place in the *parganas* where a group of Rājpūts, Kolīs and Musalmāns have not got their home or *girās* and *va'dal*.

The passage goes on to describe the conditions at the time the work was written: Now, "owing to the absence of (imperial) control," these people "have settled in certain places and are seizing (not only) the whole of the *talpad* or the part under the government, but in addition many (other) villages to meet their (claim of) *girās*".[29]

What emerges chiefly from this passage is that in Gujarat the land was divided between *ra'īyatī* villages and the *ta'alluqa* of *zamīndārs*,[30] a division that we know to have continued under British rule.[31] Of the *zamīndārī* villages a large number were left entirely in the possession of *zamīndārs*, but others were divided

[29] *Mir'āt*, I, 173-4; see also Supp., 228-9. "Manjhū" (AD 1613), *Mir'āt-i Sikandarī*, 363-4, says one-fourth of Gujarat was held in *bānṭh* by *girāsya* Rajputs under Maḥmūd II (1537-54). The tradition about a contract entered into by "Ecbar, the then Emperor of Mogul" and the "Gracias" of Gujarat over the "Ground Rents paid to them and their Posterity" is also recorded by Hamilton, I, 88.

[30] A similar division is implied in *Mir'āt*, Supp. 215-17, where the villages of certain *maḥals* of *sarkār* Sorath are shown as *ra'īyatī*, obviously to distinguish them from the remainder which were held by *zamīndārs* or were under tributary chiefs.

[31] The two categories appear in Mountstuart Elphinstone's minute of 6 April 1821 as "Khalsa" and "grassia"; Rogers designates them "rasti" and "mewasi" (A. Rogers, *Land Revenue of Bombay*, I, 13-15).

into two portions, the revenues of one of which, the *bānṭh* or *vanta*, were to be retained by the *zamīndārs*, and of the other, the *talpad* or modern Gujarati *talpat*, were to be collected by the administration.[32] In the later period, the *zamīndārs* not only tended to seize the *talpad*, but also to levy exactions called *girās* on *ra'īyatī* villages.[33] This statement alone is enough to prove that the *ra'īyatī* areas were distinct from *talpad* and were not even originally under the possession of the Rājpūts, Kolīs and others.

Similarly, even in the earlier part of the nineteenth century, Tod was able to find traces in Mewar of two distinct categories of villages. The *bhūmīas*, "the allodial proprietors", whom he identifies with the *zamīndārs*, held only a limited number of villages in the country; the rest were under *paṭṭāwats*, whom he also calls *girāsyas*. The position of the latter had by then become almost indistinguishable from that of *bhūmīas*, but tradition suggested that in an earlier period they had been servants of the state, holding revenue assignments similar to the *jāgīrs* of the Mughal empire.[34]

If, then, all villages were either *zamīndārī* or *ra'īyatī*, it might be supposed that the *milkiyat* rights of the *zamīndārs* and peasants were mutually exclusive. Where one existed, the other could not. Thus Qāẓī Muḥammad A'lā, writing in the earlier part of the eighteenth century, tells us that the peasants (*ri'āyā*)

[32] Giving an account of the history of the chiefs of Navanagar, *Mir'āt*, I, 285, tells us that in the time of Muẓaffar, the last Sultan of Gujarat, "the *zamīndār* (i.e. ruler) of Navanagar had within his *zamīṇdārī* 400 entire (*dar o bast*) villages and a fourth part of 400 villages". This probably means that in 400 villages he was only allowed to collect revenue from the *bānṭh*. See Rogers, *Land Revenue of Bombay*, I, 27, for "a division of village lands [in Gujarat] into *talpat* or state property, and *vanta* or 'divided' land held by the original Grassia proprietors ousted by the Mussulmans in former days".

[33] The report by George Perrott, Revenue-Collector of Broach, 16 May 1776, amply confirms the picture that the *Mir'āt* draws of later developments, though with some difference in the terminology employed. There were, says the report, a total of 431,329 *bīghas* of land in *pargana* Broach, of which 218,465 were cultivated. Of the cultivated area, 108,826 *bīghas* "appertain to the Sircar" or government, without any co-sharer in revenue. Of the other part, the "Grashias" held 56,404 *bīghas*, of which 46,918 being cultivated, their revenues were exclusively appropriated by them. Outside of these lands, the "Grashias" levied "Toda Gras", a "ready-money tribute" on several villages (*Selections from the Bombay Secretariat*, Home Series, II, 179-89). The "Grashias" of this report seem to be identical with the holders of *bānṭh* in the *Mir'āt*; and "Toda Gras" with the *girās* of the latter. For *girās*, see also below in this section.

[34] Tod, *Annals and Antiquities*, I, 132-8. For *paṭṭāwats*, see Section 4 of this chapter.

recognized the *zamīndārs* to be proprietors and acknowledged their right to evict them and give their land to others for cultivation.[35] Such a right was, in fact, claimed by the *zamīndārs* in the early period of the British regime, though in conditions of land abundance it might have had little practical significance.[36] The claim seems to have been based on the admitted right of a *zamīndār* to assign wasteland to cultivators of his choice. A *farmān* of Akbar (1563-4) acknowledges the right of *māliks* of virgin lands (*ārāẓī-i iḥyāī*) to give these out for cultivation (on lease) (*ba-muzāri'a*), obtaining thereby their share of the produce (*ḥiṣṣa-i mālikāna*).[37] A letter included in a collection of Aurangzeb's reign refers to the distribution (*taqsīm*) of the land of a village among revenue-paying cultivators (termed *chhappar-banḍī,* "putting up straw-huts") by a person who had obtained a grant of the *zamīndārī* of that village.[38] It could follow that what was given by choice could also be resumed. In 1677, in a document from Awadh, two headmen (*muqaddams*) declare that the *milkiyat* of two villages (one their own) was in "the ancestral *zamīndārī*" of a certain *chaudhurī*; and they acknowledge "that we are his cultivators (*muzāri'ān*) and till the land by his leave (*raẓāmandī*)".[39] The right of eviction is almost explicitly conceded here.

Yet the evidence is not extensive or unqualified enough to prove that *zamīndārs* everywhere without exception possessed the right to dispose of land cultivated by the peasants. They might not indeed in many cases have been seeking it. In the previous chapter we have argued that the right to evict peasants was a right worth claiming or exercising only in a very few areas. With large wastes still unploughed, the chief object of a *zamīndār* in normal circumstances would have been to keep his peasants rather than to lose them. It is not certain that the *zamīndārs* could legally keep the peasants on their lands by force, as could the imperial authorities (including the *jāgīrdārs* and their officials). The only

[35] *Risāla Aḥkām al-Ārāẓī*, f.44a.

[36] See Colebrooke's summing up in 1819 of the responses to queries sent in 1815 to Collectors of all districts of the Conquered and Ceded Provinces; and Holt Mackenzie's memorandum of July 1819, paras 431-41 (*Revenue Selections*, 95-97, 253). See also John Shore's minute of June 1789, paras 406-7, in *Fifth Report*, 206-7, for the ryot's "right of occupancy".

[37] Bilgram Docs. 7.

[38] *Durru-l 'Ulūm'*, f. 90a. The locality is not indicated.

[39] Allahabad 329. The word *zamīndārī* is not very clear. Though the *pargana* is not mentioned in this document, it is Sandila in *sarkār* Lakhnau.

evidence we have about this is provided by the draft of a *muchalka* (bond), where along with the *muqaddams* and *paṭwārīs*, the *zamīndārs* bind themselves "not to allow any cultivator to leave his place".[40] Even here it is open to question whether their authority to restrain the peasants derived from their own right or was only delegated to them by the administration, for it is equally shared by the two village officials mentioned beside them.

The purpose of *zamīndārī* right was naturally to provide its possessor with an income. Since it was a right primarily associated with land, we may expect that it gave its possessor a share in the land's produce. This share bears in our records a variety of names, and it is possible that it varied considerably in magnitude according to localities.

Certain documents from Awadh introduce us to the terms, *rusūm-i zamīndārī* (customary exactions of *zamīndārs*) and *ḥuqūq-i zamīndārī* (fiscal rights of *zamīndārs*).[41] In a reference to a complaint made by the *zamīndārs* of a village, it is stated that a certain *qāẓī* (judge) forcibly took the *rusūm-i zamīndārī* of the village and also seized its land revenue (*maḥsūl*, *ḥāṣil*) of a whole year.[42] This may be read with a passage in another document, where the holder of a *madad-i ma'āsh* grant, which entitled the grantee to the whole land revenue, is required "to pay the *ḥaqq-i milkiyat* (claim based on *milkiyat*)" on the land of his grant to the *māliks*.[43] These documents, coming from the same part of Awadh (Bahraich *sarkār*), therefore, show that the *zamīndār* had a claim to a rate or cess upon the land, distinct from the authorized land revenue.

A *farmān* of Akbar (known to us only through an English translation) recognizes the existence of such a cess when it confirms the right of the holder of a *zamīndārī* of 95 villages in *pargana* Bithur (in *ṣūba* Agra, but bordering upon Awadh) to levy a *tanka* (double-*dām*) per *bīgha* "by right of seigniory".[44] From the neighbourhood of Lakhnau (Lucknow), inside Awadh, we have evidence of a rate of this kind being levied under the name of *satārahī*, the local term for *zamīndārī*. In a paper given by certain village officials (*kārindas*) in 1746, the *satārahī* is defined as a

40 Bekas, f. 67b.

41 Allahabad 782 (14th year of Aurangzeb) and 1214 for the former term, and Allahabad 375 (AD 1662) for the latter.

42 Allahabad 782.

43 Allahabad 1203 (19th year of Aurangzeb).

44 J. N. Wright's translation in *Indian Antiquary*, II (1873), 36.

rate of ten *sers* of grain per *bīgha* and is coupled with *dāmī*, a rate of one copper coin (*fulūs*) per *bīgha*. The *kārindas* bound themselves to deliver to the holder of these rights a quantity of grain as *satārahī* and an amount in cash in payment of the *dāmī*, both presumably based on the rates stated.[45]

Similar cesses were imposed by *bhūmīas* (the local version of *zamīndārs*) in Rajasthan. In 1687 the *bhūmīa's* customary imposition in Amber is reported to be a *ṭaka* (copper coin) per *bīgha*, but a *ser* per *man* (2.5 per cent) when the revenue was collected through crop-sharing (*jinsī*).[46] In Marwar, the *bhūmīas* imposed levies in kind on produce, ploughs (or pairs of bullocks) and wells, and thus essentially on cultivation, at various, though seemingly modest, rates.[47]

Besides these claims to a share in the produce of agricultural land, the *zamīndārs* included other sources of income within their rights. The sale of *milk* and *khoṭī* of a share in a village in Bilgram (Awadh) as early as 1531 lists, among the appurtenances (*marāfiq*) transferred, the "trees, ruins, channels, tanks, and *takāb* (inundated land)";[48] and when *satārahī* and *bisī* rights were sold in the neighbouring locality of Sandila in 1586, a similar list appears, with the addition of orchards, wells and wild rice.[49] At the other limit of our period, when the *zamīndārī* of a part of the village was sold in the same locality, but on the western side of the Ganga, the list appears practically unchanged.[50] When we pass on to another locality (Bahraich in Awadh) for which our documentation is relatively abundant, we have residential land or houses almost

45 Allahabad 299. The total amount of grain to be delivered was fixed at 50 *mans* for the year. For the kharif crop, it came to 25 *mans*: rice, 10 *mans*; millets (*kūdrum* and *shāmākh*), 6; and *māsh*, 5. A note is made here in the document which seems to suggest that the deficit of 4 *mans* was to be made up from the cultivation of sugarcane and cotton. The 25 *mans* to be delivered from the rabi harvest were to comprise wheat, 8 *mans*; gram, 8; and barley, 9. As for cash, Rs 7 were to be paid in the year, half at each harvest.

46 Cf. S.P. Gupta, *Agrarian System of Eastern Rajasthan*, 137. The rate was quoted when the ruler of Amber himself claimed the right (*bhom*). The *ṭaka* could by now have been representing the half-*ṭanka* or the original *dām*.

47 Bhadani, in *IHR*, VI, 1-2 (1979-80), 147-8. Some of the rates quoted are: 5 *sers* per *man* of produce (12.5%); one *ser* (also 10 *sers*) per plough; one rupee on a shallow well, and half a *man* on a Persian-wheel well.

48 *Sharā'if 'Uṣmānī*, f.55a; see also ibid., f.64a, for a sale-deed of 1542-3. For *takāb*, see *Burhān-i Qāṭi'*, s.v.

49 Allahabad 317. The word used here for inundated lands is *jor-hā*. See Elliot, *Memoirs*, II, 358, s.v. *johar*.

50 Shamsabad Docs. 8. The word *khaiṛa* in its list means mounds or ruins.

invariably listed among the appurtenances of *milkiyat* and *zamīndārī*, besides orchards, trees, tanks and ruins.[51] In the sale deed of the Calcutta *zamīndārī*, of 1698, "jungle" too is included among the items over which the transferred right extended.[52]

With such claims advanced above and beyond those on the produce of the fields, it is not surprising that the *zamīndārs* could consider themselves entitled to levy a number of miscellaneous cesses. Such were the *jalkar* and *bankar*, or levies on water and forest produce, mentioned among "the appurtenances" in a sale deed of 1578 or 1618 from Bihar,[53] and in the sale deed of the Calcutta *zamīndārī*.[54] From Rapri (*ṣūba* Agra) comes the complaint that the *zamīndārs* of the township were collecting a house tax (*khāna-shumārī*);[55] according to another complaint made earlier in the same reign (Aurangzeb's), *zamīndārs* of a village in *pargana* Kaithal (Haryana) levied a poll-tax on men (*dastār-shumārī*, "tax on turbans") besides taxes on marriages and births.[56] The *zamīndārs* also claimed the right to levy a tax on the craft professions, called *muḥtarifa*, which is documented for Bihar and Bengal.[57] In addition to collections in kind and money, the *zamīndār* could also lay claim to certain services. In seventeenth-century Marwar, for example, the *bhūmīa* could apparently demand a plough from each house (for a day?) for use in his field.[58] The 'menial' castes were particularly subjected to forced and largely unpaid rendering of labour (*begār*). Balāhars, Thorīs, Dhānuks and Chamārs in northern India had to act as guides and porters for their *zamīndārs* and also, apparently, for all men of *zamīndār* castes who happened to pass through their locality.[59]

[51] See Allahabad 1180 (of 1642), 891 and 1205 (both of 1677) and 1092 (of 1681).

[52] Add. 24,039, f.39a.

[53] Datta, *Some Firmans*, reproductions facing p. 104. [54] Add. 24,039, f. 39a.

[55] The tax was at the rate of 9 *tankas* on each house, and 900 *tankas* had been collected in what was declared to be an "innovation" (*bid'at*) (*Durru-l 'Ulūm*, f. 51a-b).

[56] A tax of Rs 4 on marriage and Rs 2 on a birth (Bālkrishan Brahman, f. 52a-b). See also *Revenue Selections*, 154, for such "zemindaree perquisites".

[57] Datta, *Some Firmans*, reproduction of sale deed of 1578 or 1618, facing p. 104; Add. 24,039, f.39a.

[58] See Bhadani, in *IHR*, VI, 1-2, 148.

[59] See *Waqā'i' Ajmer*, 131, where there is a report of the flight of a party of Rājpūts with a wounded comrade. In each village they requisitioned the services of the Thorīs of the local *zamīndārs*, who carried the *chahārpāī* (cot) of the wounded man to the boundary of the next village, where the Thorīs of that village took over.

The *zamīndār's* income from these varied sources rested on his proprietary right, his *ḥaqq-i milkiyat*. So long as he enjoyed his original right, it was for him to collect his dues. But if he was to be divested of his authority by the administration, then he became entitled to some recompense for his lost income. This was called *mālikāna*. An eighteenth-century glossary of revenue terms, compiled by an official familiar with the practice of both Dehli and Bengal, tells us that "the *mālikāna* is a right (*ḥaqq*) of the *zamīndār*: when they (the authorities) convert the *zamīndār's* land into *sīr* [i.e. impose direct assessment and collection of revenue from the peasantry], they give him (the *zamīndār*), on account of his being the *mālik* (*mālikiyat*), something out of every hundred *bīghas* or every hundred *mans* of grain".[60] It reiterates elsewhere that this was given only when the *zamīndār's* land was, or had been made, *sīr*: when "he was himself the revenue-payer, he would not get the *mālikāna*, but only *nānkār* (an allowance for service)."[61] *Mālikāna* was, therefore, allowed only when the state directly assessed and collected the land revenue, by-passing the *zamīndār*.

The normal rate of *mālikāna* is defined in the same glossary as ten per cent of the total revenue collected.[62] This was true of cases where it was granted to the *zamīndārs* as an annual allowance in cash. But, as implied in the definition quoted above, *mālikāna* could also be given in the form of revenue-free land, set as a small proportion of the total revenue-paying land ("something out of every hundred *bīghas*"). Our earliest reference (1595) to *mālikāna*

See also Add. 6603, ff.51b-52a, and *Tashrīḥu-l Aqwām*, ff.181b-182a, 188a. Caste seems to have usually determined whether a person was liable to render *begār*. The Chamārs were known as Begārīs because they had to work as porters without payment (*Tashrīḥu-l Aqwām*, ff.181b-182a). On the other hand, we read of a Gūjar who refused to render *begār* to some Rājpūts, apparently because he felt he was not liable to it; he was thereupon beaten to death (*Waqā'i' Ajmer*, 187).

60 Add. 6603, f.79a; also f. 66a-b. This sense of *sīr* in these two passages should not be confused with its other one, now far more common, of the special lands of the *zamīndārs*, cultivated by themselves, or by their labourers or tenants-at-will. Wilson, *Glossary*, 818, gives this meaning precedence, but notes that "the term is also sometimes applied to lands cultivated on account of the state, or to those in which the revenue is paid by the cultivators without any intermediate agent".

61 Add. 6603, f. 61b. At another place, f. 58b, it says the same thing while speaking of the *chaudhurī*: he gets his *mālikāna*, when his land is made *sīr*. "If he himself is the revenue-payer for his land, he does not get the *mālikāna*." Cf. Ballab Bahādur's answers to John Shore's queries (1786), Q. no.15, Add. 19,503, f.55a.

62 Add. 6603, f.61b. John Shore in his minute of 18 June 1789, paras 353-4, *Fifth Report*, 202, considers *mālikāna* to have amounted to one-tenth of the revenue in Bihar, for which, see his minute of 2 April 1788 in Firminger's edition of the

reveals it, indeed, as a landholding.[63] A later source, Yāsīn's glossary, tells us that *do-biswī*, or two *biswas* of land in every *bīgha*, i.e. a tenth part, was the right (*ḥaqq*) of the *zamīndār* and was the same thing as *mālikāna*.[64] An early nineteenth-century memoir on Gorakhpur contains a reference to *zamīndārs* known as *birtyas*, who, when the revenue was assessed directly upon the peasants (*hangām-i khām*), "got one-tenth or *do-biswī*".[65]

A broadly similar arrangement seems to have been made by the authorities with *zamīndārs* in Gujarat. The central point in the long passage quoted above from the *Mir'āt-i Aḥmadī* is that the *zamīndārs'* land was divided into two parts, the *talpad*, which was three-fourths of it, and the *bānṭh*, which was one-fourth, the revenue from the former being taken by the authorities and that from the latter by *zamīndārs*. The *bānṭh*, being one-fourth, represented a higher proportion of the land than *mālikāna*, which amounted usually to one-tenth of the land. But both were identical in nature. Thus *bānṭh*, like *mālikāna*, could also take a money form. This was obviously what happened when the *zamīndār* of Porbandar in Gujarat was paid one-fourth of the total revenues of the port of Porbandar by the Mughal authorities.[66] In such cases presumably

---

Fifth Report, II, 747. According to *Revenue Selections*, 8, "the British government set 10 per cent [of the land revenue] as the highest allowable rate of *mālikāna*". See also ibid., 5, 8-9, for *mālikāna* in general.

[63] Allahabad 294 (of AD 1595). This document was issued in the name of a group of persons. They grant two plots of 20 and 9 *bīghas* respectively, as *mālikāna*. The formula used is: "We grant *mālikāna* to X. We made ... *bīghas* of land [tax] exempt (*ma'āf*)." It is not clear who the grantors were; they were probably *madad-i ma'āsh* holders.

[64] Add. 6603, f.61b.

[65] Ghulām Ḥazarat, *Kawā'if-i Ẓila'i Gorakhpūr* (1810), Aligarh MS, f.14a-b. The author classifies the *zamīndārs* of that district into three categories: *Zamīndārs*, who were complete proprietors not sharing their right with any other; *Ta'alluqdārs*, who paid the revenue for lands which were held in proprietorship by *birtyas*; and *Birtyas*, whose lands were included in the *ta'alluqas* of the *ta'alluqdārs*. The meaning of *ta'alluqdār* will be discussed later, but, to anticipate our findings, we may say that he was usually a *zamīndār* who also paid revenue on land not included within his *zamīndārī*. When he paid revenue on his own *zamīndārī*, he would be an ordinary *zamīndār* falling into the first category. The *birtyas*, then, were *zamīndārs* who did not directly pay the revenue to the authorities, but paid through a *ta'alluqdār*.

The use of the term *birt* in a 17th-century document also suggests that it was simply a term for *zamīndārī* created out of gift. The author of a transfer deed of 1669 declares that he gave away his "*milkiyat*, *zamīndārī* and *chaudhurāī*" of a village "in the form of *birt*" (Allahabad 1192).

[66] *Mir'āt*, I, p. 288. The port was then (1677-8) placed in the *khāliṣa*.

the revenue of the entire land of the *zamīndār* was collected by the administration, which then paid him a fourth of the collections.

It is significant that the *Mir'āt* clearly distinguishes between *bānṭh* and *girās* (and *va'dal*).[67] *Bānṭh* was a portion of land within the *zamīndārī* of its possessor; *girās* was an exaction, whether in the form of money or land, from *ra'īyatī* or peasant-held villages outside the exactor's *zamīndārī*. *Bānṭh* thus derived from an earlier, legally recognized right, *girās* from the threat or actual exercise of force.[68] An imperial order of 1672, relating to Gujarat, speaks of *girāsyas* and *zamīndārs* together (compare Tod's *girāsya ṭhākurs* and *bhūmīas* in Mewar), probably implying general similarity but also a shade of distinction in the sense of the two terms.[69]

An appreciation of the significance of the terms *bānṭh* and *girās* may provide us with a fresh insight into the origins of the *chauth*, the imposition made notorious by the Marathas. Some historians have compared Shivājī's *chauth* to Wellesley's demand for subsidy from the "native states"; others have more bluntly described it as "blackmail money".[70] With him and his successors, it was really a demand for the payment of a fourth of the revenues of a district as the price of its immunity from their depredations.[71] Studies of Portuguese records have established that neither as an imposition

67 "Gras, 'a subsistence' literally and familiarly, 'a mouthful'" (Tod, *Annals and Antiquities*, I, p. 33).

68 Cf. Rogers, *Land Revenue of Bombay*, I, 137, for a corroboration of this distinction between the origin "of Vanta, land divided off to old proprietors by the Mahomedans on assuming direct revenue management of the country, and of Gras, land extorted from villagers in Bharuch and Surat as blackmail by Rajpoots from Rajpipla and other neighbouring territories".

69 For the Mughal order, see *Mir'āt*, I, p. 279. For Tod's "Grasya Thacoor" and "Bhoomia", see his *Annals and Antiquities*, I, 133.

70 Ranade apparently meant it as a compliment to Shivājī when he compared his *chauth* to Wellesley's "Subsidy". He lauds it as an "idea"originally worked out by Shivājī, which in Wellesley's hands "bore such fruit" (quoted in S.N. Sen, *Military System of the Marathas*, 37-8). "Blackmail" is a word freely used by Sarkar for the extortion of *chauth* by the Marathas (e.g. in *Shivājī and His Times*, 353, 357-8, 373).

71 *Chauth* meant, literally, "one-fourth". The earliest reference to Shivājī's extortion of *chauth* is in a letter of the English factors at Surat to the Company, 26 November 1664: "Sevagee(s)... dayly threatens heartily to visitt this towne once more, except the King will give him peacible(y) the fourths of what hee receives of the towne and country yearely" (*Factories, 1661-64*, 312). The best discussion of the *chauth* demanded by the Marathas will be found in Sen, *Military System of the Marathas*, 37-9, where it is rightly stressed that the Marathas offered to those paying *chauth* protection from none but themselves; they made no pretensions to taking over duties of a protective power.

nor as a name was the *chauth* an invention of Shivājī. The Portuguese of Daman had been paying "a fourth" of the revenues under this name to petty neighbouring *rājas* from the sixteenth century onwards.[72] It would seem to be a mistake to assume that the arrangements at Daman were unique and the sole prototype of Shivājī's *chauth*.[73] That there was nothing unique about them is shown by the fact, already mentioned, that the Mughal authorities used to pay a fourth of the revenues of Porbandar, on the Saurashtra coast, to its *zamīndār*. This again, as we have seen, was almost certainly a derivation from the *zamīndār's* right to *bānṭh*, or a fourth of the land of his *zamīndārī*. Analogy would suggest that the *chauth* paid at Daman arose out of a similar right held by *zamīndārs* in Gujarat and possibly some parts of the Konkan. There is evidence that *bānṭh* (Gujarati form, *vanṭh*) existed also in Maharashtra, where an 'Ādil-shāhī *farmān* of 1665 refers to *vartana* or lands and allowances of "*desāīs*, *deskulkarnī*, *nārgonda*, *paṭel*, *kulkarnī* and the twelve *balūtas*".[74] There is, indeed, a strong possibility that the term *vatan* for such lands, coming into use in Maharashtra later, was an Arabicization of *vanṭh/vartana*, under the influence of a confusion with the *waṭan* ("home") *jāgīrs* of the Rājpūt chiefs.[75] It is also noteworthy that the *chauth* at Daman was similar to the *bānṭh*, but essentially dissimilar to Shivājī's *chauth*, in being a payment or allowance made by a superior to an inferior, even a subordinate, power.[76] Although the origin of Shivājī's *chauth* lay

[72] For Sen's interpretation of this evidence, accompanied by translations of some long extracts, see his *Military System of the Marathas*, 20-9. Cf. Sarkar, *Shivājī and His Times*, 350-54. See also *Hobson-Jobson*, 215 (s.v. *chowt*), for quotations of 1559 and 1664. There are references to this arrangement in the printed English records as well. Early in 1639, two Portuguese envoys came from Daman to Surat and asked its Governor to intercede on their behalf with Aurangzeb, viceroy of the Dakhin. As the price of the withdrawal of Mughal troops, then "vex[ing] and destroy[ing]" the country around Daman, the Portuguese "willingly submitted to pay what they were accustomed annually to give the Rāja Rammugar [Ramnagar], the haereditary prince of the country, vizt. the quarter of its provenue" (Foster, *Suppl. Cal.*, 141; also see ibid., 147, and *Factories, 1637-41*, 214).

[73] Cf. Sen, *Military System of the Marathas*, 29, 32, 43, who takes precisely this view.

[74] Khare, *PSIH*, V(i), 187. Also a *farmān* of 1671 in *Ādilshāhī Pharmāne*, 78-85.

[75] If suspicions of a forger's hand in Shāhjahān's *farmān* of 1628, facsimile pub. with translation by G.T. Kulkarni, *PIHC*, 53rd Session, 1992-93, Warangal, 199-204, prove unfounded, the use of the Arabic form *waṭan* for *vartana* would be established for early 17th century. But the suspicions are strong (see Bibliography No.74) and by no means quieted by the occurrence in it of *waṭan* in a sense otherwise only rarely documented (if at all) from the 17th century.

[76] Evidence has yet to be found of the term *chauth* in the Konkan or the Dakhin

in a right claimed by *zamīndārs*, yet, as his power grew, his claim shed all semblance of a legal claim based on actual *zamīndārī* right and became an extortion imposed simply by force. There are, however, some indications that even at Daman the *chauth* had begun to acquire predatory associations. In 1638 it was defined as "a kind of impost which obliges the said King [the Rāja of "Sarceta"] not to harbour robbers in his dominions and to refrain from capturing men and cattle belonging to the farmers of the province of Daman".[77] In other words, it was here conceived of as an exaction similar to what the *Mir'āt-i Aḥmadī* knew as *girās*. In 1617 this term, in the Portuguese garb of "grasso" was actually used to designate the vartana or *chauth* paid on a part of Daman.[78]

To sum up, there existed almost throughout the Mughal empire, fiscal claims of the *zamīndār* upon land lying within his *zamīndārī*, the claims being met either through cesses or levies on the peasants and others or through the holding of a portion of the land revenue-free or through a cash allowance out of the revenue collected from the entire land by the authorities. In the last two forms, it was known by the names of *mālikāna* and *do-biswī* in northern India and Bengal, and as *bānṭh* (=*vanth*) in Gujarat and *vartana* or *chauth* in the Dakhin.

This represented a large part of the income that the *zamīndār* obtained out of his proprietary right. There was another source of income too; and this arose out of his position as a servant of the state, a cog in the machinery of revenue collection. As we shall see in Section 3 of this chapter, for his services the *zamīndār* received a "subsistence" allowance, called *nānkār*, ranging from 5 to 10 per cent of the revenue, paid in money (as deduction from the gross revenue collection) or in the form of revenue-exempt land.

To measure the magnitude of the *zamīndār's* income from such varied evidence as we have, the best way seems to be to compare it with the size of the land revenue. It certainly was much

before Shivājī. A. Wink, *Land and Sovereignty in India*, 45 n., cites an alleged Bahmanī document of 1426, promising the grant of *chauthāī* along with *deshmukhī*. But the promised grant is not of *chauth*, but of *chauthāī 'amal deshmukhī*, or of a quarter of the jurisdiction of the *deshmukh* (see text in *Selections from the Peshwa Daftar*, Vol. 31, ed. G.S. Sardesai [Bombay, 1933], 1, No.1). Moreover, what we have is only a Marathi part-transcription, part-translation of a supposedly original Persian document of AH 827 or AD 1423 (not 1426). The use of the phrase "*sarkār* Junnar, *ṣūba* Bedar" proclaims even the supposed Persian original (if there ever was one) to be a late Mughal-period concoction.

[77] Sen, *Military System of the Marathas*, 28-29.

[78] Ibid., 26-27.

less, and set on a different range altogether. If the term *satārahī*, a synonym of *zamīndārī*, originated from its being a claim to a seventeenth part of the produce (and so, by analogy, *bisī*, another such synonym, to a twentieth), this would hardly be in the same class as land revenue, which ranged from a third to a half of the produce. When the *satārahī* rate is given in absolute quantities (ten *sers* of grain and one *tanka* per *bīgha*),[79] this too suggests a petty share, when compared with the land revenue rates in money, as given, for example, in the *Ā'īn-i Akbarī*.[80]

A more precise way to relate the *zamīndār's* total income to land revenue could be by assuming the *mālikāna* at 10 per cent of the revenue (25 per cent in Gujarat) to represent the minimum level of the *zamīndār's* income from his "proprietary" claims; to this must be added the *nānkār* (5 to 10 per cent) that he received from the revenue authorities. In all, then, his income should not have been less than 15 to 20 per cent of the revenue in northern India, and 30 to 35 per cent in Gujarat.[81]

The fact that in the territories under direct imperial administration, the *zamīndārs'* share of the surplus produce was much smaller than that appropriated in land revenue is confirmed by a study of the sale prices of the *zamīndārīs* of some villages, set beside the land revenue paid by the same villages. Anyone familiar with transactions in modern real estate would be surprised to find that the price of a *zamīndārī* in Mughal times was seldom more than double, and in a few cases only barely in excess of the land-revenue demand for one year, although the price should have been the capitalized value of the annual income expected from possession of the right.

We have for a locality (Shamsabad) in the Doab, bordering upon Awadh, a document of 1530 by which, while the "proprietary" right (*ḥaqq-o-milk*) of khoṭī over a village was sold for 700 *tankas*, the right to levy revenue (*kharāj-in'ām*) was leased for 300 *tankas* per annum.[82] Though khoṭī was nominally identical with

[79] As mentioned above, the rates of *satārahī* are given in Allahabad 299 of AD 1746.

[80] Crop rates (*rai'*), presumably those promulgated by Sher Shāh, and forming the floor for calculation of Akbar's cash revenue rates (*dastūrs*), are given in the *Ā'īn*, I, 297-300. On wheat, the revenue demand per *bīgha* is set at 4 *mans*, 12.75 *sers*; on gram 3 *mans*, 8 *sers* (1*man* = 40 *sers*). The values of these units of area and weight varied (see Appendices A and B), but the difference in magnitude from the *satārahī* rate is sufficiently suggested by these figures.

[81] Cf. Moosvi, 175. [82] Shamsabad Docs. 1. Summary in *IESHR*, IV(3), 220-1.

muqaddamī, we have shown elsewhere that in the sixteenth-century documents from this area it meant superior right in general, being a precursor of *zamīndārī*.[83] If, then, 700 *tankas* represented the value of the proto-*zamīndārī* right, and 300 the annual land revenue, the one to the other would be in the ratio of about 100:43.

A series of documents concerning a group of adjoining villages in a *pargana* of Awadh provide us with particulars of the prices at which the *milkiyat* and *zamīndārī* rights of these villages were sold in the middle years of Aurangzeb's reign; two other documents give figures of the annual land revenue imposed on the same villages in four years. The details are set out in Table 5.1.

Table 5.1

Village	Year of Sale (AD)	Sale Price of *Milkiyat* & *Zamīndārī* (Rs)	Land Revenue	
			Year (AD)	Amount (Rs)
Baidaura-Baidauri (2 villages)	1672[84]	301[85]	1676-7	239
			1677-8	239
			1684-5	226
			1685-6	126
			Average	207, as.8
Pasnajat (half of the village)[86]	1672(1/3)	589	1676-7	271, as.8
	1688 (1/9)		1677-8	224, as.8
	?(1/18)		1684-5	194, as.11
			1685-6	209, as.(11)
			Average	225, as.1½
Anchhapur	1677	136[87]	1684-5	44, as.9
			1685-6	34, as.9
			Average	39, as.9
Debidaspur	1682	175	1684-5	54, as.12
			1685-6	54, as.12
			Average	54, as.12

[83] *IESHR*, IV(3), 213-14.

[84] The documents relating to the sales are Allahabad 891, 1195, 1196, 1205, 1215, 1216, 1221, 1222 and 1224; and to the revenue, Allahabad 1206 and 897. The sale deeds are dated according to the Hijri calendar, while the revenue demand was levied for Fasli years. In Allahabad 897, the Fasli year cannot be properly read, but luckily the document also carries a Hijri date. In this and the other revenue documents, the revenue of the previous year is also stated under the term *aṣl*; every change, whether a reduction or an increase, from that figure in the revenue of the current year is then indicated. Each document thus gives us revenue figures for two years.

It will be seen from the table that if A is the total sale price of the villages, Rs 1,201, and B, the total of the averages of land revenue, Rs 526.as.14½, then A:B = 100:44.

The price of *zamīndārī* was thus less than two and a half times the annual land revenue in this part of Awadh in the 1670s and 1680s – a ratio practically the same as in 1530 in the Doab. If the buyer of the superior right expected to recover his principal in ten years, the *zamīndār's* net income could not have been more than a quarter of the land revenue. One would, of course, have felt easier if one could have compared price with price rather than with income. Since in the classic period of the Mughal Empire, the right to revenue (in forms of *jāgīr* or *madad-i ma'āsh*) could not be sold, such a comparison is not possible. But from the middle of the eighteenth century such sales begin to be documented. Zaheer Jafri has drawn attention to three documents of 1759 and 1763 from

---

All the villages belonged to the *tappa* of Chaurasi in *pargana* Hisampur, Bahraich *sarkār*. The *zamīndārī* of the villages had been gradually purchased by Saiyid Muḥammad 'Ārif, and the sale prices are in all cases, except one, those which he paid. In the revenue documents, he is made responsible for payment of the revenue of these villages. We know for certain that while he purchased one-third of Pasnajat, three-fourths of Anchhapur and the whole of Debidaspur before the years for which we have revenue figures, he purchased half of Baidauri and one-ninth of Pasnajat only later. It should, however, be remembered that in the two revenue documents, 'Ārif is described as *ta'alluqdār,* so that assuming its sense to be the one established in Section 3 of this chapter, we should not be disconcerted by his paying revenue on land which he did not entirely hold in his *zamīndārī*.

[85] The price and year are not those of sale, but of sale first agreed upon at a given price and then cancelled at the request of the intending purchaser (Allahabad 1195).

The two villages passed later on to Muḥammad 'Ārif and the sale deed of a half portion of the village Baidauri, executed in 1686, is extant (Allahabad 1219).

[86] Allahabad 1206, the first of the two revenue documents, fixes the revenue on "the *paṭṭī* of Pasnajat"; the later one, Allahabad 897, fixes it on "the two *paṭṭīs* (that is) half of the village of Pasnajat". In 1672, Saiyid 'Ārif's father, Saiyid Aḥmad, had purchased the whole of a third portion of the village (Allahabad 1196). The next dated purchase (of a ninth portion of the village) was made in 1688 and a sale deed whose date is lost concerns the purchase of one-eighteenth of the village out of the second *paṭṭī*, to which the one-ninth also belonged (Allahabad 1221, 1222). These two acquisitions are demarcated in a *qismat-nāma* (Allahabad 1186). The total price given in the table is made up of the sale prices of all these three portions. But it is possible that since the acquisitions in the second *paṭṭī* were made later, the revenue shown for 1676-7 and 1677-8 was assessed only on one *paṭṭī*, or one-third of the village. In that case the ratio would be still more favourable to land revenue.

It may be noted incidentally that 'Ārif purchased an additional 1/18 share in the village in 1689 for Rs 61 (Allahabad 1224).

[87] We have two sale deeds both executed in 1677, one for a half-portion (price,

pargana Sandila in Awadh, from which he ingeniously adduces that the sale price of *zamīndārī* was two-fifths of that of the right to levy the land tax.[88] In other words, the *zamīndār's* net annual income was expected here to be 40 per cent of the net annual revenue realized. It is probable, from the circumstances of the time, that the *zamīndār's* income was generally higher then than in the preceding century; but it still amounted to much less than a half of the land revenue.

Little evidence of this sort from other regions has yet been brought to light. From Bengal, however, we can cite particulars of the sale of the *zamīndārī* of what later became the core of Calcutta, but then comprised Dahi Kalkatta and two other villages. In 1698 the English Company purchased the *zamīndārī* of the villages for Rs 1,300 while undertaking to pay a *jama'* or annual land revenue of Rs 1,194, as.14.[89] If there was not more than a suggestion that the price of *zamīndārī* was lower than normal owing to administrative pressure exercised on behalf of the English,[90] one might entertain the notion from the two figures here that the *zamīndār's* income in Bengal was substantially smaller in relation to the land revenue, than in parts closer to the centre of the empire.

Given the distinctly subordinate share in the surplus that the *zamīndār* could claim, it is obviously difficult to see him as a true proprietor of the soil. He might formally be known as *mālik*, and his right termed *milkiyat*, but there was little in him of the landed proprietor of the later phase of the colonial era, who made his income by paying a more or less fixed land tax and collecting variable rents fixed by himself from his tenants. At the same time, already in Mughal India, *zamīndārī* in itself (not the land under

Rs 70) and the other for one-fourth (price, Rs 32) (Allahabad 891, 1205). The price for the whole village has been worked out on the basis of what is thus known to have been paid for three-quarters of the village.

88 'Agrarian Conditions of Awadh Under the Mughals and Nawab Wazirs, 1595-1856', Ph.D thesis, Aligarh, 123. The documents he cites are Allahabad 355, 439, and 443.

89 Add. 24,039, f.36a-b, contains a copy of the *parwāna* issued by the dīwān recognizing the sale. On the back (*ẓimn*), along with endorsements three other documents have been copied: the sale deed, an earlier *nishān* in favour of the English, and a *muchalka* of the Company's *vakīl* (agent), pledging himself on behalf of his client to pay the specified amount of revenue annually. The sale deed is given separately on f.39a.

90 Cf. extracts from Consultations at Chuttanutte, 1697 and 1698, in *Hobson-Jobson*, 980, s.v. *Zemindar*.

zamīndārī) had all the hallmarks of an article of private property. It was inheritable and could be freely bought and sold. Hereditary succession to *zamīndārī* was a general law in the Mughal Empire. We find partisans of the sons of Jaswant Singh (d.1678) appealing to this law in the reign of Aurangzeb. "The *zamīndārī* of the country of Marwar", they declared before the *qāẓī* of Jodhpur, "was the property (*milk*) of Rāja Jaswant Singh, which should pass upon his death, by inheritance and of right, to his sons."[91] In contemporary records of sales or disputes we often find one party or another claiming a *zamīndārī* on the basis of hereditary possession as if this gave them the primary right.[92] A deed of transfer contains a specific provision debarring any "heirs" of the transferor from laying claim to the *zamīndārī*.[93] In some sale deeds the sellers bind themselves to compensate the purchasers, if "heirs" (presumably with greater claim to the *zamīndārī* than the sellers) appeared and proved their claim.[94] It is not necessary, and in any case space would hardly permit us, to cite the numerous cases known through our records where sons or relations of a *zamīndār* actually inherited his right. Of particular interest is the fact that the Hindu and Muslim laws of succession to property were fully applied. Since both laws provide for the sons' inheriting equal shares in the father's property, the *zamīndārī* was invariably divided among the sons – a practice which is illustrated by some specific instances given below. Moreover, the claims of female heirs, as prescribed under Hindu and Muslim laws, were also honoured, and in our records from Awadh, we actually find women, Hindu and Muslim, inheriting, selling and otherwise disposing of their *zamīndārī* or *milkiyat* rights.[95]

[91] They add: "And when his sons are there, what business has Indar Singh to become the possessor (*mālik)* of the *waṭan* and *zamīndārī*?" Jaswant Singh died in December 1678 and Aurangzeb overruled the claims of his two sons, born posthumously, in favour of Indar Singh. This protest was delivered, after the emperor's decision, to the *qāẓī* by two officers of the dead king, who wanted the *qāẓī* to tell them what the *Sharī'at* had to say on their case (*Waqā'i' Ajmer*, 245-6).

[92] A large number of persons selling the *satārahī* of a village in Awadh declare that it had been in "the power and possession of us proprietors, by way of inheritance, from our fathers and forefathers" (Allahabad 435 of 1698). Some petitioners, complaining to the imperial court against the usurpation by some Afghans of their "*biswas* and *zamīndārī*" in Bihar, claim that the right had been in their possession "from fathers and forefathers" (*Durru-l 'Ulūm*, ff.52b-53a). Similar assertions made in cases of dispute are found in Allahabad 375 and 1214, both from Awadh and belonging to Aurangzeb's reign.

[93] Allahabad 1192 (AD 1669). [94] Allahabad 891, 1196, 1205, etc.

[95] In Allahabad 1215 (of 1681), "Sabhānū, the sister and heir of Mahāsingh",

A *zamīndārī* does not seem to have been regarded as an indivisible unit, for, as we have just said, it could always be divided to meet the claims of the heirs. We have one case where a big *zamīndārī*, consisting of a *pargana* in Sambhal territory, was divided up among "cousins descended from the same grandfather", a number of villages being allotted to each heir for his share.[96] By constant division a stage could conceivably be reached when a share in the old *zamīndārī* consisted of no more than a village; this is apart from the fact that a *zamīndārī* when originally founded might have comprised only one village. In either case, at the next succession, the village itself would have to be divided up among the heirs. A *zamīndārī*-share would henceforth appear as a particular fractional part of the village. In seventeenth-century documents from Awadh we are able to trace in some detail a process of such division and subdivision of the *zamīndārī* of a village called Pasnajat in *sarkār* Bahraich.[97] This was apparently a big village and belonged originally to a family of Brahmans. At first it was

confirms through an agent (*vakīl*) the sale of two-thirds of the village Debidaspur made earlier by Mahāsingh and assures the purchaser that if some named persons succeed in proving their claims to this village, she would give him an equal area of land from another village held by her. Later in the same year, she sold to the same purchaser the rest of the village (Allahabad 1216). She belonged to a Khatrī family, as appears from the caste of Mahāsingh mentioned in Allahabad 1205. From Allahabad 1195 (of 1672), it appears that a certain "*musammāt* (lady) Bhīkan, daughter of Harīrām" was then the proprietress (*mālika*) of two villages, Baidaura and Baidauri, lying near Debidaspur. A half-share of Baidauri was sold in 1686. The two sellers, who described themselves as Brahmans, add after their father's name that of their mother, which is not clear but is probably Bhīkan (Allahabad 1219). The giving of one's mother's name was unusual and it has been done here presumably because the sellers derived their right to the village not from their father, but from their mother. In 1688 Zorāwar Kūar, a Hindu woman, sought the authorities' assistance to recover proprietary possession over a village in *sarkār* Saran, her right having been usurped by two persons (Datta, *Some Firmāns*, 50, no.168).

References to Muslim women holding *zamīndārī* rights are quite numerous. See Allahabad 359, 810, 1191, 1203, etc. (all from the 17th century). A number of Muslims (Shaikhs) and a Hindu carpenter, selling the *satārahī* of a village, declare that they were acting "for themselves and on behalf of their mothers and sisters", who must therefore have been co-proprietors (Allahabad 435, of 1698). Muslim women often obtained their shares in *zamīndārī* in satisfaction of their *mihr* or dowry claims upon their husbands (see Bilgram Docs. 6; *Sharā'if-i 'Uṣmānī*, f.63a-b; *Nāma-i Muẓaffarī*, I, 339-42).

[96] *Durru-l 'Ulūm*, ff.43a-44a.

[97] The documents are Allahabad 1186, 1196, 1221, 1222, 1224. All except 1186 are sale deeds. This is the same Pasnajat that has appeared earlier in this section, in Table 5.1 on p.188.

divided into three supposedly equal parts, called *paṭṭīs*, probably among three brothers. The boundaries of these *paṭṭīs* were at some stage demarcated.[98] The surviving sale deeds relate to two of the three *paṭṭīs*. These show that at least three generations had passed since the initial division; and each *paṭṭī* had been further divided and subdivided among heirs. The following family tree showing the holdings possessed by the heirs, will show exactly how each fraction represented the heir's share in the inheritance of the whole village, according to the law of equal division among brothers. The shares shown within brackets are inferred.

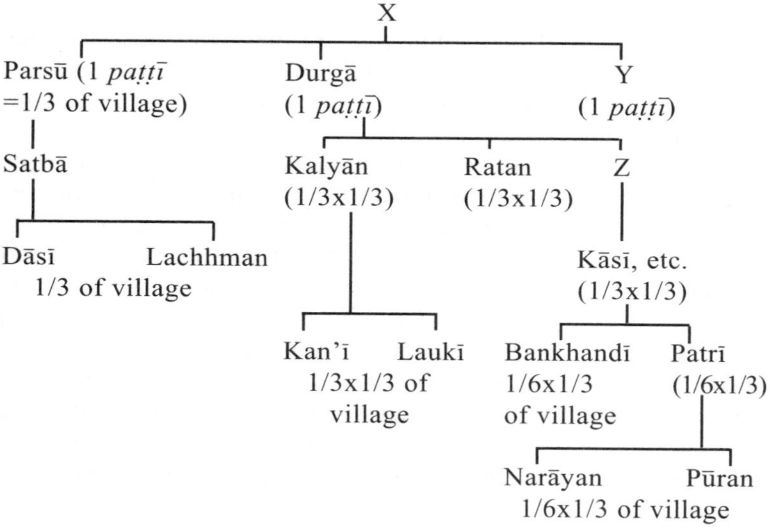

Though the village had been divided into three *paṭṭīs*, each heir's share has been defined as a fractional part of the whole village as well as of the *paṭṭī*, in words such as "the full sixth part of one-third (i.e. 1/6 *paṭṭī*) of the village of Pasnājat, that is, one-eighteenth of the whole village". The prices at which the various shares were sold – all within a period of two decades – also correspond fairly closely to their fractional values.[99]

[98] This is clear from Allahabad 1196, the earliest of the Pasnajat documents. The sellers declare that they hold one-third of the village and "the *paṭṭī*, consisting of the third part belonging to us, is set apart and bounded on all sides as follows", etc. Allahabad 1186 also shows that the boundaries of the three *paṭṭīs* had been marked on the ground.

[99] The following are the sale prices of various shares in the *zamīndārī* of Pasnajat specified in the surviving deeds:

Although the *zamīndārī* was always divisible, the definition of the rights of the heirs as fractional parts of the original *zamīndārī* implies that some kind of recognition of its unity survived. In some cases, *zamīndārīs* divided up among heirs are described as *mushtarik*, i.e. held in common.[100] There is evidence that while the share of each heir in the *zamīndārī* was recognized, the land was not actually divided and continued for some time, at least, to be regarded as a joint-family holding. The income was probably distributed among the heirs according to the size of their shares. This is the inference to be drawn most naturally from a Pasnajat document which shows that despite numerous co-sharers, the land of the middle *paṭṭī* of the village had not been divided until an outsider purchased two shares, amounting to a half of it, the boundaries of the land corresponding to these shares being then demarcated.[101]

When so much of our information about *zamīndārī* in its various aspects comes from contemporary sale deeds, we run the risk of labouring the obvious if we try to prove that *zamīndārī* was in fact salable. We may recall the statement made by Qāẓī Muḥammad A'lā early in the eighteenth century that *zamīndārs* presumed to claim proprietary right (*tamalluk*) and so bought and sold their land (*ārāẓī*).[102] But the imperial recognition of this right can be traced to a much earlier time: as early as 1563-4, Akbar in a *farmān* acknowledged the right of *māliks* of newly cultivated lands in Awadh to sell the land.[103] In a very interesting long document of dispute over possession of a village in *pargana* Bilgram

Paṭṭī I (1/3rd of the village):
Rs 405, AD 1672 (Allahabad 1196)
1/3rd of 1/3rd part (*Paṭṭī* II) of the village:
Rs 127, AD 1688 (Allahabad 1922)
1/6th of 1/3rd part (*Paṭṭī* II):
Rs 57, – (Allahabad 1221)
1/18th part of the village (in *Paṭṭī* II):
Rs 61, AD 1689 (Allahabad 1224)

100 *Durru-l 'Ulūm*, f.44a; also f.47b.

101 Allahabad 1186: a *qismat-nāma*. The land was measured and divided into two plots (*takhtas*). Then equal portions were assigned to the purchaser and the remaining holders. The length and breadth of each portion with its boundaries are set out in great detail. I failed to note the date of the document, but it probably belongs to 1688 or 1689.

102 *Risāla Aḥkām al-Ārāẓī*, ff.1b-2a, 49a. See also Yāsīn's glossary, Add. 6603, f.65a, a later, 18th-century text.

103 Bilgram Docs. 7, summary in *IESHR*, IV (3), 225. In the first edition (158, n.73) I had cited Jhaveri IV (a *farmān* of Akbar of 1593) for recognition of "the

(Awadh) in 1570, the imperial officials decided the issue on receiving evidence about purchase by the rightful party.[104]

Orders issued from Aurangzeb's court about a hundred years later require that in judging conflicting claims to *zamīndārī* rights, cognizance be taken of any sale that might have been effected.[105]

The actual evidence of sale, preeminently in the form of sale deeds, predates both the surviving statements of official recognition and the universalization of the designation *zamīndārī* for the right sold. The series of sale deeds in the Shamsabad-Bilgram area in the Doab and Awadh begin with 1530.[106] In the vicinity of Mathura, numerous sale deeds attest to purchases of village lands from early in Akbar's reign, if not earlier.[107] In the seventeenth century, sales of *zamīndārī* right, under that designation, begin to be found in great profusion.[108] In this book much use has been made of such documents coming from Awadh.[109] In Bengal, the English in 1681 purchased land from a *zamīndār* in Malda[110] and in 1698 the *zamīndārī* of the three villages of Dahi Kalkatta, etc.[111] In Gujarat the sale of land by *zamīndārs* was so established a practice

---

purchase of land from *zamīndārs*" in a *pargana* near Mathura by a religious divine; but a close examination of the format, writing and style has proved the document to be a late-17th or 18th-century forgery.

104 Bilgram Docs. 9, summary in *IESHR*, IV (3), 226-8. See also a document in *Sharā'if-i 'Uṣmānī*, ff. 64b-65b, where claim to the *milk* and *khoṭī* of part of the village was recognized by the *qāẓī* of Bilgram on the basis of inspection of sale deeds (*IESHR*, IV(3), 223-4).

105 *Durru-l 'Ulūm*, ff.48a, 62a.

106 See calendar of these documents in *IESHR*, IV(3), 219-32, the earliest sale deeds being of 1530 (Shamsabad Docs.1), 1531 (*Sharā'if-i 'Uṣmānī*, f.55a-b) and of 1542 (ibid., ff.63b-64b).

107 These survive in the rich Vrindaban collections of documents. Sales of village lands in Aritha (*pargana* Sahar) begin, to go by the dates on the documents, in 1538, but there is good reason to believe that all the Aritha sale deeds that we have were in fact drawn up in 1579 if not in 1588 (cf. Rādhādāmodar 11 of 1579 and Govinddev 8 of 1588). In Vrindaban itself the earliest sale deed (Rādhādāmodar; Ser.5, Acc.3, and Ser.21, Acc.37) is of 1558 (its Persian version, Rādhādāmodar 13, being dated 1569).

108 Sellers of land at Vrindaban are designated *zamīndārs* for the first time in 1601(Rādhādāmodar 136).

109 Allahabad 891, 1180, 1194, 1196, 1205, 1215, 1219, 1221, 1222, 1224, 1227 are sale deeds from *sarkār* Bahraich; Allahabad 317, 435, 464, from *pargana* Sandila, *sarkār* Lakhnau. They date from Akbar's time and come down to the time of Aurangzeb. Allahabad 1192 (of AD 1669) is a simple deed of transfer.

110 Malda Diary and Consultations, *JASB*, NS, XIV (1918), ff.81-2, 122-3. The land was purchased from one "Rajaray" here described as *chaudhurī*, but subsequently (174, 182, 196, 202) as "jimmedar", an obvious corruption of *zamīndār*.

111 Add. 24,039, ff.36a-b, 39a.

in the sixteenth century that Akbar is said to have laid down the obligation of the buyer in respect of revenue on such land, termed *bechān* ("sold").[112]

It seems that there were usually no official restrictions on the sale of *zamīndārī* right. Although the purchase by the English of Kalkatta and other villages was recognized in a *parwāna* from the provincial dīwān, this was a patently special case, involving a foreign company, and even here, as elsewhere, there is no indication that the prior permission of the authorities had to be obtained before the transaction could be effected. Nor does custom seem to have offered an impenetrable barrier. A *zamīndārī* could be divided for sale just as for inheritance: its possessor might sell one portion while retaining the other.[113] We also find, in the case of Pasnajat, members of a family to which the *zamīndārī* of the entire village had originally belonged, selling away their individual shares without reference to their co-sharers. Elsewhere, however, we have instances of the existing holder of one share claiming the right of preemption in respect of the purchase of another share.[114]

If the *zamīndārī* could be sold, it could also be transferred on lease. One deed of lease (*ijāra*) sets down in detail the amounts payable by the lessee for each of the two harvests in the year, for three years.[115] Another allows the lessee to recover in instalments any *taqāvī* (taccavi) loans given by him to the peasants and still outstanding at the time of his surrendering the lease.[116] It is also stressed in two of our documents that taking a *zamīndārī* on lease did not confer on the lessee any *milkiyat* rights.[117]

2. GENESIS, COMPOSITION AND STRENGTH OF THE ZAMĪNDĀR CLASS

We have till now concerned ourselves only with the legal and economic nature and substance of *zamīndārī* right. We have excluded

[112] *Mir'āt*, I, 173. For "vechania" (*bechān*) land, see Rogers, *Land Revenue of Bombay*, I, 175.

[113] Mahāsingh, for example, sold 2/3 of the village of Debidaspur, while it was only later that his heiress Sabhānū sold the remaining one-third of the village (Allahabad 1215, 1216).

[114] Bilgram Docs. no.9 of 1570 (cf. *IESHR* IV(3), 227); Allahabad 1200 (of 1676); and Shamsabad Docs. 7 (Aurangzeb's reign).

[115] Allahabad 1230. The holder of "*milkiyat* and *zamīndārī*" of the village also held it in *madad-i ma'āsh*, so that the lease also covered the right to collect its revenue.

[116] Allahabad 323.

[117] Allahabad 323, 421. All the *ijāra* documents cited in this paragraph belong to the reign of Aurangzeb.

from our consideration the historical context in which the right must be placed. To this we must now turn.

Our documents suggest that *zamīndārī* right might arise when a village was settled by a person who had its virgin land brought under cultivation by client peasantry.[1] Or it might arise out of a subversion of peasant right when persons of superior non-peasant status imposed their control over the village by buying out the rights of the peasants.[2] But both these modes of creation of *zamīndārī* right in particular villages presuppose the previous existence of the *zamīndār* class, or, at any rate, of a class of persons with resources and power enough to settle and purchase land. We must, therefore, consider how this class itself originated.

Eighteenth-century texts recognize clearly that the origins of the class went back to the time that the Muslim kings made their arrangements with partially subjugated potentates.[3] We can indeed trace the process by which the pre-Sultanate rural potentates were transformed into *zamīndārs* by the sixteenth century, under the increasing pressure that the conquering ruling class exerted upon them.[4] But one ought perhaps also to recognize the continued influence of the factors of caste and force which had earlier so greatly helped to mould the dominant classes of "Indian feudalism".[5] For this our major source remains tradition.

Such tradition usually reveals a long process according to a set pattern: there is, first, a settlement by members of a caste or clan, perhaps, dominating over peasants settled earlier, or, perhaps, peasants themselves. Then another clan appears, drives them out or establishes its dominion over them; and then still another. At some stage, if not from the beginning, the dominion of the victorious caste crystallizes into *zamīndārī* right, held by various

[1] See Bilgram Docs. 9, of 1570, for the claim of *muqaddams* to the possession of a village on the ground that it was their "revenue-paying, newly-broken land" (*zamīn-i kharājī-i iḥyāī*); the same claim is implicit in Akbar's *farmān* of 1563-64 (Bilgram Docs. 7), permitting *māliks* of newly broken lands (*ārāẓī-i iḥyāī*) to sell or lease the land. For summaries of the documents see *IESHR*, IV(3), 225, 226-28.

[2] In Shamsabad Docs. 4, of 1611, the original *māliks* of the village are said to have been Kāchhīs and Chamārs, from whom the existing superior proprietors, who were Muslims, claim to have derived their right by purchase (summary in *IESHR*, IV(3), 230-32).

[3] The classic statement is in Qāẓī Muḥammad A'lā, *Risāla Aḥkām al-Ārāẓī*. It is implicit in the passage about the origins of *bānṭh* in the *Mir'āt*, I, 173-5; see also Add. 6603, f.65a.

[4] Cf. Irfan Habib, in *Cambridge Economic History of India*, I, 53-60.

[5] Cf. I. Habib, *Essays*, 75-80, 138-40.

leading members of it over different portions of the subjugated territory. What we can be certain about is that such changes continued down to the Mughal times, and we have other sources besides tradition to tell us that they did not end there.[6]

This summary of the typical traditional account of the establishment of *zamīndārī* rights makes it obvious that these accounts treat the *zamīndār* class as consisting of a number of castes which monopolized *zamīndārī* holdings in different areas. With this association of *zamīndārī* with caste the testimony of the *Ā'īn-i Akbarī* is in full accord. When in its detailed census of the "Twelve Provinces", the *Ā'īn* puts a column for *zamīndārs* or *būmīs*, the sole information it provides under it is about the castes (*qaum*, plural *aqwām*) of the *zamīndārs*. As noticed at the beginning of this chapter, separate entries are made in this column for each *pargana* under most of the provinces. Usually, there is only one caste named against a *pargana*, but sometimes there are two or three; and it is only rarely that the words "various castes", or simply "various", are entered.[7] We must suppose, therefore, that there were well-marked blocks of territory, each consisting of a single *pargana* or group of *parganas*, under the *zamīndārī* of members of the same caste.[8]

[6] A short passage from an early 19th-century Persian memoir of the district of Gorakhpur can serve as a typical example of the traditional testimony: "In ancient times the dominion (*riyāsat*) and *rāj* of the neighbourhood of this city [Gorakhpur] belonged to the caste (*qaum*) of Ḍoms. Thus remains of their forts at Batyalgarh, Ramgarh, Bhindiagarh, Domangarh, etc., in the areas adjoining the city are found to this day. And in the villages the caste (*qaum*) of Thārūs, i.e. the hill-men, of the race (*qism*) of those who are now settled at the foot of the hills, had their settlements. The market of Butwal for the sale of goods from the hills was held in Gorakhpur. From the time of the establishment of the rule of the Muslims, the market and settlements of the Thārūs gradually disappeared and exist now only in the Tarai. Some Sarnet Rājpūts, natives of Srinagar, having extirpated them, established their power and are uptill now known as Rāja Gorakhpūrī. Thus their descendants hold the *zamīndārī* of some of the villages of Silhat and of the *pargana* of the environs of Gorakhpur. Many *birtyas* in the *pargana* of the environs of Gorakhpur and Silhat hold (their lands) in accordance with the *sanads* (deeds) of the Rāja Gorakhpūrīs. Afterwards, in the time of Akbar, the ancestors of the *ta'alluqdār* of Kachhwa, formerly residing in the *pargana* of Bhauwapara, with their kinsmen (lit. brothers) seized the *zamīndārī* of the environs of Gorakhpur and Silhat, which, till now, is in the hands of their descendants" (Ghulām Ḥaẓarat, *Kawā'if-i Gorakhpūr* (AD1810), I.0.4540, ff.5b-6a; Aligarh MS f.7a-b).

The two classic studies of local *zamīndārī* traditions in Awadh are C.A. Elliott, *The Chronicles of Oonao*, and W.C. Benett, *A Report on the Family History of the Chief Clans of Roy Bareilly District*.

[7] *Aqwām-i mukhtalifa* or just *mukhtalifa* in the original. Cf. Elliot, *Memoirs*, II, 204.

[8] In Elliot, *Memoirs*, II, between pages 202 and 203, there is a very interesting

The testimony of the *Ā'īn* may be supplemented by individual references to the *zamīndār* castes in certain territories. We know from Bābur that the Salt Range was divided into three portions, in the possession, respectively, of the Jūd, Janjūha and Ghakkar tribes who exacted from all other inhabitants certain customary dues (which we may suppose to be *zamīndārī* cesses) upon every yoke of oxen and household.[9] Similarly, in Ajmer province we find Rājpūt clans referred to, collectively, as holding the *zamīndārī* of some areas.[10] Out of contiguous areas in the provinces of Awadh and Ilahabad, a district was officially constituted under the name Baiswāra; it consisted, we are told, of "the many *maḥals* that are the home of the seditious *zamīndārs* of the clan (*qaum*) of Bais".[11]

One of the best students of local history, Charles Elliott, seems to have been forcefully struck by this division of land among *zamīndār* clans. He remarks that "the limits of a Pergunnah hardly ever coincide with physical or geographical boundaries, and the only other cause for their irregular tracing seems to be proprietary right." And then, following a line of argument of no concern to us at the moment, he suggests that the *pargana* may be "defined as a tract of land in the possession of one undivided clan".[12]

The territorial division of *zamīndārī* possession among clans and castes was the result of the way the *zamīndārī* right had come into existence: it was historically created. One would be mistaking the nature of its creation, if one supposed that it was

---

set of maps. The first is of the old North-Western Provinces (excluding "Oudh"), showing "Zameendaree Possession according to the Ayeen-i Akbaree", while the second shows the "Zameendaree Possession in AD 1844". The maps, owing to their small scale, do not show certain details. For example, the various Rājpūt clans named in the *Ā'īn* are not distinguished and the "possessions" of all of them are shown under one colour. Nevertheless, the maps indicate fairly well the broad changes which occurred in the areas held under *zamīndārī* by the big castes between the time of the *Ā'īn* and the period before the 1857 Rebellion.

[9] *Bāburnāma*, ed. 351-2, 359; Bev., I, 379-80, 387. See also *Ṭabaqāt-i Akbarī*, II, 159-60.

[10] See references to the clans (*qaum*) of Saindhal and Dewal in *Waqā'i' Ajmer*, 364-5.

[11] *Inshā'-i Roshan Kalām*, ff. 6b-7a. Baiswāra included parts of the *sarkārs* of Lakhnau, Awadh, Manikpur and Korra. The Bais survive as an important *zamīndār* clan in the region. It is interesting to compare the list of *maḥals* against which the *Ā'īn* has entered the name of the Bais as *zamīndārs*, with that of the *maḥals* of Baiswāra given in Elliott's *Chronicles of Oonao*, 67. Most *maḥals* are common to both lists, but there have been important changes.

[12] *Chronicles of Oonao*, 149 n.

systematic. A clan might seize a piece of territory, but might not be able to entirely drive away the clan previously dominant, and some members of the latter might continue to hold their own in enclaves and corners.[13] A still greater irregularity would be introduced whenever the *zamīndārī* right became a full-fledged article of property and so became subject to sale and purchase, as it was throughout Mughal times. Then money might erode the old caste bastions and open the gates to outsiders.

The *zamīndārī* sale deeds from Awadh provide us with ample evidence of how the rights were sold to men of different castes and, in many cases, of different religions, from those of the sellers. The group of five villages in Hisampur, which we have already referred to as illustrating some aspects of *zamīndārī* right, may again serve as an example. Even originally, these five villages, adjoining each other, did not belong to men of one caste: three belonged to Brahmans and two to Khatrīs. But over a period of twenty years two Saiyids, father and son, through successive purchases, bought out all the old *zamīndārs*.[14] In the *pargana* of Sandila, the Bāchhal and Gahlot clans of the Rājpūts were recorded as *zamīndārs* in the *Ā'īn*.[15] But a document of Akbar's reign itself shows a number of Brahmans and others selling *satārahī* and *bīsī* rights in a village in this *pargana* to a Muslim.[16] And in Aurangzeb's reign, a number of Muslims (Shaikhs) and a Hindu carpenter band together to sell "the *milkiyat*, that is, the *satārahī*" of a village in the same *pargana* to two Hindus belonging to the caste (*qaum*) of Kalwārs (distillers).[17] One could go on multiplying such instances from the documents. In course of time such transactions could modify the dominance of particular castes over the *zamīndārī* in particular localities: in *pargana* Bilgram, for example, we are told that the Rājpūts had been the ancient *zamīndārs*, but then Muslims acquired a large share of it, mostly by purchase.[18]

[13] From the passage we have quoted from Ghulām Ḥaẓarat's memoir of Gorakhpur in n.6, it clearly appears that while the ancestors of the *ta'alluqdār* at Kachhwa and his kinsmen seized the *zamīndārī* of the *parganas* of Silhat and the environs of Gorakhpur, the older clan of Sarnet Rājpūts continued to enjoy the *zamīndārī* of "some villages" in both *parganas*.

[14] Allahabad 891, 1196, 1205, 1215, 1216, 1219, 1221, 1222, 1224. The *Ā'īn* has the following entry under "*zamīndār*" against the *pargana* of Hisampur: "Rekwār, Bhāle and some Basīn". Neither Brahmans nor Saiyids are mentioned.

[15] *Ā'īn*, I, 439. [16] Allahabad 317. [17] Allahabad 435.

[18] *Sharā'if-i 'Uṣmānī*, f.66 b. This work was written in 1765-66. Muslim acquisitions of *zamīndārīs* in Bilgram seem to have begun quite early, for the *Ā'īn*

These changes in caste composition might have often represented only the gain of one *zamīndār* caste over another in a particular area. But it is possible that salability of *zamīndārīs* sometimes enabled true outsiders to enter the ranks of that class. A few such groups can be identified.

First, there were members of the families of the nobility, or *jāgīrdārs*. An Afghan noble of Aurangzeb and his descendants, who established *zamīndārīs* largely by purchase in *pargana* Pali, had initially obtained *the pargana* in permanent (*āl-tamghā*) *jāgīr*.[19] Lower officers in the imperial service similarly acquired *zamīndārīs*: witness the dispute over the purchase of "two *biswas*" (one-tenth) of a village in *pargana* Shamsabad (Doab) between two Afghans, one "an imperial servant" (*naukar-i pādshāhī*) posted to *ṣūba* Bengal; and the other "in service at the imperial court."[20] Excluding the Afghans, such *zamīndārī* acquisitions by nobles and officers seem, however, to have been exceptional. More common were those made by revenue grantees, who invested their savings in *zamīndārī* purchase. Evidence from Awadh documents such purchases by grantees in both the sixteenth and seventeenth centuries.[21]

According to an English report from Surat in 1669, the great merchants found "noe firm estates in land" in which to invest their money.[22] But if town merchants were not investing in *zamīndārī* acquisition this was not entirely true of rural merchants and usurers. A document of 1611 refers to earlier Muslim *māliks* of a

---

enters Saiyids and Bais as the *zamīndārs* of the *pargana*.

[19] Diler Khān was given the *al-tamghā jāgīr* in 1662. In 1689 his son Kamāluddīn Khān is found speaking of "the villages of *pargana* Pali that are in this person's *zamīndārī* and *ijāra* (revenue-farm)". In 1732 Kamāluddīn Khān's son gave away the entire *zamīndārī* of a village in the same *pargana*, claiming that it belonged to him "by purchase and inheritance". See *Nāma-i Muẓaffarī*, I, 315, and II, 163.

[20] Shamsabad Docs.7 (undated, but Aurangzeb's reign, to judge from dates on seals).

[21] In 1527 Bābur confirmed the grant of a village and 250 *bīghas* in Fathpur Sandi held by Qāẓī 'Abdu-l Dā'im. In 1531 the latter purchased "*milk* and *khoṭī*" rights over 4/5 of a village in the adjoining *pargana* of Bilgram (*Sharā'if-i 'Uṣmānī*,ff. 50a-b, 55a-b). During the latter half of the 17th century, we find Saiyid Muḥammad 'Ārif holding *madad-i ma'āsh* grants near Bahraich (Allahabad 879, 1202, 1217, 1228-30), and also making extensive purchases of *zamīndārī*, for which see Section 1.

[22] *Factories, 1668-69*, 184. The merchants to whom estates were supposed to be not available were the two principal merchants of Surat ("prodigious moneyd men") and the reason given was the usual one: "the whole country being the Kings and not held by any tenure."

village in the Doab who had mortgaged the village with a *baqqāl*, or a *banya*, and then redeemed it.[23] A mid-eighteenth-century work from Bengal tells us how some *mahājans* (money-lenders) in that province had the ambition of becoming *zamīndārs* themselves, one that they sought to achieve by lending large sums to the *zamīndārs* and then obtaining their lands in repayment.[24]

The extent to which the mercantile classes actually succeeded in turning into *zamīndārs* was, however, limited; the *Ā'īn* records the *baqqāls* or *banyas* as *zamīndārs* in only seven *parganas* (two each in Agra and Lahor provinces and three in Malwa); another mercantile community, the Multānīs, appear jointly with three other castes in *pargana* Hansi in Dehli province. It is possible that the merchants' lack of success in setting up as *zamīndārs* was owing to their lack of armed power: indeed, we see them occasionally as hapless victims of spoliation by *zamīndārs*, from some of whom they had then, perforce, to obtain protection.[25]

A universal element in the traditional accounts of the establishment of particular clan and caste *zamīndārs*, is the employment of armed force, so that possession of armed power seems to have been a necessary attribute of *zamīndārī* right.

"The troops of the *zamīndārs* [of the Empire]", says the *Ā'īn*, "exceed forty-four lakhs."[26] By an additional clause in the same sentence, it tells us that the details of these forces have been provided elsewhere. The reference must be to the columns bearing the headings "Cavalry" and "Infantry" in the statistical tables of

[23] Shamsabad Docs. 4: summary in *IESHR*, IV(3), 230-32.

[24] *Risāla-i zirā'at*, f.15b.

[25] The dual aspect of the relationship can be seen from the following two incidents. In 1653 Qāẓī 'Abdu-r Rasūl sought relief from Prince Dārā Shukoh for certain *mahājans* living in a village in his proprietary possession (*milk*), since they had been forcibly driven away by *zamīndārs* of an adjoining *pargana* (Dārā Shukoh's *nishān* in *IHRC*, XIX, 56-7). In 1680 a Muslim officer serving in the Mughal army in *ṣūba* Ajmer complained that the *mahājans* of his village (named partly after his father and so presumably belonging to his family) in Jalandhar Doab (Panjab) had been plundered by *zamīndārs* of neighbouring villages. He explained his own anxiety by declaring that "the *mahājans* of that place, except in religion and faith, are one with us, being like relatives and brothers" (*Waqa'i' Ajmer*, 555). Thus *zamīndārs* appear as both assailants and protectors.

[26] *Ā'īn*, I, p. 175. Blochmann notes that two of the MSS consulted by him read "the troops and *zamīndārs*", by putting in the word *wa* ("and") before "*zamīndārs*". Though this makes no sense, Saran (*Provincial Government*, 262) accepts this variant, "whatever this alternative reading may mean".

On the entire matter of the local armed men, retainers and mercenaries, see Derek H.A. Kolff, *Naukar, Rājpūt and Sepoy*, Cambridge, 1990.

"The Twelve Provinces".[27] These are placed immediately after the column of *zamīndārs*, and although it is not specifically stated, these give quite obviously the figures of the *zamīndārs'* troops. Wherever the entries for the *zamīndārs* column are filled in for each *pargana*, the cavalry and infantry figures are also given.[28] Similarly, when the *zamīndār* castes are only stated for whole *sarkārs*, we have only *sarkār* figures for the troops. The *pargana* figures also make it clear that the census is not confined to the troops of tributary chiefs, but mainly records those of ordinary *zamīndārs*; the number of troops recorded against *parganas* in the directly administered territories in fact far exceeds that recorded for the areas of the tributary chiefs. The totals of troops are also stated for each of the provinces, and here we find them described usually as *būmī*, the synonym of *zamīndār*. The total of provincial figures only slightly exceeds 44 lakhs, the number given for the whole empire. These figures are interesting also for the composition of the *zamīndārs'* troops in the empire that they reveal: 384,558 cavalry; 4,277,057 infantry; and 1,863 elephants, 4,260 guns and 4,500 boats.[29]

How Akbar's administration obtained information about the military resources of the *zamīndārs* is not known, but the detailed nature of the census invites respect. The immense totals, on the one hand, and the breakdown of the figures by *parganas*, on the other, show that almost every *zamīndār* of any consequence reported possession of armed retainers. Two unpretentious documents relating to villages in the *pargana* of Hisampur provide

[27] There is no separate column in the original tables for elephants. In the comparatively few cases where their number is stated, it has been placed in the column for "Cavalry".

[28] Cases where cavalry and infantry figures are stated for a *pargana*, but the space for *zamīndārs* is left blank, are rare; those where *zamīndārs* are specified, but the figures for troops are omitted, are still rarer. In a few cases of the latter type a note is specially put in, to the effect that the number of troops in that *pargana* is assimilated to the figure given against another (*Ā'īn*, I, 435, 459, 494-5, 541). Sometimes (ibid., 435, 459, 541) the note is made directly below the name of the *zamīndār* caste – a further proof that the troops were really those of the *zamīn dārs*. To appreciate this point, one must look up the corresponding entries in the *Ā'īn* MSS, since Blochmann has dispensed with the columns. Jarrett's restoration of columns in his translation of the *Ā'īn* is misleading since the original arrangement of the columns is not retained: the columns for cavalry, infantry and elephants precede, not follow, as they ought to, that of "Castes" (read "*Zamīndārs*").

[29] Of the last two figures, the first is for Bengal only, and the second represents the total of the figures for Bengal (4,400) and Bihar (100). The largest number of elephants was also recorded for Bengal (1,170).

striking confirmation of this general fact. The first, a complaint of a night attack, shows by a casual reference that even in a *zamīndārī* of five villages, acquired through purchase, it was thought necessary by the *zamīndār* to build a *qil'acha*, "small fort", to protect his possessions.[30] The second is an official order which takes note of a complaint by the *mālik* of only a third part of a village that "the *qil'acha* he had built there for stationing his men" had been razed to the ground by a usurper who had occupied his land: the order directs that the *qil'acha* be rebuilt and restored to him by those responsible for its destruction.[31] These two documents, which are both meant for the eyes of officials, show that not only was it normal for *zamīndārs* to raise *qil'achas*, but the authorities too regarded this as a perfectly legitimate proceeding on their part. The country must have been dotted with innumerable such fortresses. They became obnoxious to the authorities only when the *zamīndārs* used them not for maintaining their rights over the peasants, but for defying the administration. Reports of official action against such forts, described as *qil'achas* and *gaṛhīs*, abound.[32] From these it becomes clear that they were found not only in provinces like Awadh but even in an area as close to the heart of the empire as central Doab.

The forts were the visible symbols of the armed power of the *zamīndārs*. They served them as strongholds, garrison-houses and bases. But their real power must have lain in the large numbers of their armed retainers.

Since caste had played such a role in the formation of *zamīndārī*

[30] Allahabad 1225. The *qil'acha* was built in the biggest of the five villages, Pasnajat. The complaint is made by the *zamīndār* Saiyid Muḥammad 'Ārif himself. The document is not dated, but the date of the raid is given as 12 December 1689. Saiyid 'Ārif's papers show that he held some other villages in his *zamīndārī*, but none of these adjoined the Pasnajat group of villages.

[31] Allahabad 786 (dated January 1684).

[32] A petition to the court by an officer, probably the governor of Akbarabad (Agra), reports the march conducted by a subordinate from Kalpi and Etawa via Kol and Marehra to Agra, destroying *zamīndārs'* forts on the way. A full list (*ṭūmār*) of the *gaṛhīs* destroyed by him is referred to as a testimony to his good service (*Durru-l 'Ulūm*, ff.73a-74a). For operations against such forts in Baiswāra, see *Inshā'-i Roshan Kalām*, esp. ff.2a-4a, 6a-8a. A *faujdār* of Korra in Ilahabad province reported to the court that seditious *zamīndārs* in that area had built "three or four *qil'achas* in every village" (*Akhbārāt* 47/150). References to *zamīndārs'* village forts in the various regions of the Empire are too numerous to be listed, but the following may serve as examples: *Waqā'i' Ajmer*, 236; *Akhbārāt*, 47/56; *Aḥkām-i 'Ālamgīrī*, f.205; Bekas, ff.52b-53a.

right, it is reasonable to suppose that a *zamīndār* usually drew his most loyal retainers from members of his own caste who had come and settled with him. That this was the general practice may be seen from the way in which writers belonging to the seventeenth century used the word *ulūs*. This word came from the Mongols for whom tribes and military contigents were not separate entities.[33]

In India it was not applied to divisions of the imperial army, but was used in the first place to signify *zamīndār* castes: we thus hear of the *ulūs* of the Kachhwāhas, Rāṭhors, Gonds, Balūch, etc.[34] An official report from Ajmer province says that the *ulūs* of Saindhal Rājpūts held their *zamīndārī* somewhere in Mewar.[35] At the same time, the word bore the sense of a body of armed men from one's clan or tribe: a person to be recognized as their *zamīndār* in disturbed territory was generally expected to be in possession of an *ulūs*.[36]

It is, however, quite unlikely that the four and a half million troops recorded in the *Ā'īn's* census all belonged to *zamīndār* castes. Possibly the horsemen, fewer and of a higher status than the infantry, were largely made up of caste retainers. But there is an instance on record where a seditious Bais (Rājpūt) *zamīndār* of a *pargana* in Baiswāra employed an Afghan and placed in his hands the command of a fort he had built.[37] If money could interfere with caste possession of *zamīndārī* right, it is not surprising that some *zamīndārs* were prepared to enlist mercenaries belonging to other castes or communities.

It seems probable, though there is little hard evidence for it, that the foot-troopers of the *zamīndārs* consisted largely of peasants

[33] The *Ghiyāṣu-l Lughāt*, s.v. *ulūs*, is correct in treating the word as of Turkic origin, but the sense of *qaum* (tribe, people) that it gives to it, comes from the meaning the word acquired as a loan-word in Mongol (Clauson, *An Etymological Dictionary of Pre-13th-Century Turkish*, 152-3). Within the 13th-century Mongol empire it came to mean the (armed) tribes, forming the "horde" (which English word is itself derived from the old Turkish-Mongol *ordu*, royal camp) placed under one of the great Mongol princes. Hence *ulūs-i Chaghatāī*, the Chaghatāī clan, in Yazdī's *Ẓafarnāma*, I, 43, the model text for Mughal-Indian historians and secretaries.

[34] *Akbarnāma*, II, 156; *Ā'īn*, I, 477, 486; Sujān Rāi, 63.

[35] *Waqā'i' Ajmer*, 364. It goes on to say that the Saindhals, expelled from Mewar by the Rānā, were to be provided with a *zamīndārī* near Jalor. They came "two thousand and five hundred men, horse and foot, along with their families".

[36] *Inshā'-i Roshan Kalām*, ff.3b-4a; *Kalimāt-i Ṭaiyabāt*, ff.127b-128a.

[37] *Inshā'-i Roshan Kalām*, f.6b. Not only that, he named the fort Salimgarh, after this Afghan.

or villagers, impressed to serve their *zamīndārs* in times of need. We do sometimes hear of large bodies of *ganwārs*, "villagers", used by *zamīndārs* in their own local frays or in resistance to the authorities.[38] In the account of the operations of Farīd (later Sher Shāh) in his father's "*jāgīrs*" in Bihar against *zamīndārs* who had defied his authority, it is stated that on storming their village he killed all the men he found there and, not leaving a trace of the old population, settled new peasants on the land. The assumption behind this action must have been that all the previous peasants were either the retainers of the *zamīndārs*, or, at least, had served them in battle.[39]

The way the *zamīndārs* paid their armed followers probably varied considerably. A *zamīndār* preparing to resist an attack of the revenue collector's troops is shown as first drawing up "the list of his horsemen and foot-soldiers, old and new, and of retainers (*naukarān*) paid by grant of land or in cash".[40] It is quite possible that *zamīndārs* usually gave some of their own lands to their fellow clansmen in return for their pledge to serve them, as was the case with the Rājpūts in the territories of the autonomous chiefs.[41] Whether the ordinary *ganwārs*, called upon to defend the interests of the *zamīndār*, received any pay or rendered their services in the form of *begār* (unpaid labour), remains, from the limitations of our records, an open question.

On the basis of the information assembled in this and the previous section, a few general remarks may be made on the position of the *zamīndārs* as a class. Theirs was, in the first place, an exploiting class in that they claimed a share in the surplus produce of the peasantry. But, though this share varied from place to place, it was on the whole a subordinate share, compared with what was extorted from the peasants in the form of land revenue and other cesses and taxes in the name of the state. Secondly, they represented, in various ways, elements of a despotism or power which

38 For *ganwārs* serving a petty *rāja* in the *pargan*a of Jalesar (Agra) during a battle with a body of troops led by imperial officers in the time of Akbar, see Badāūnī, II, 151. Allahabad 1202, dated May 1676, contains a complaint by Saiyid Aḥmad and others that their *zamīndārī* rights in certain villages had been wrongfully seized by some persons. When they complained to the local officials, some horsemen were sent to their assistance. Their opponents, however, gathered "a large number of sedition-mongers and *ganwārs*" and scared the horsemen away.

39 'Abbās Khān, ff. 14b-15a; ed., 26-29.

40 Bekas, f. 52b.

41 "The Rājpūt practice is that in the *maḥals* of their home territory (*waṭan*), they grant villages to Rājpūts, and the latter offer their lives whenever the time of

was purely local. Their right over any particular land was hereditary and, though clan movements or sales might interfere with *zamīndārī* possession, a *zamīndār* normally would have deep roots in the land belonging for generations to his family. His great advantage must have been his close knowledge of the productivity of the land and the customs and traditions of its inhabitants. Local associations, however, also meant parochialism, and the *zamīndār's* outlook was often narrowly bound by his caste affiliations. We have seen that the *zamīndārs* as a class were really largely made up of a number of castes which had for long been uprooting and subjugating each other. The social heterogeneity of the class must have increased still further with the sale and purchase of *zamīndārīs*. Besides this social division, there was a territorial one as well, for, as shown at the beginning of this chapter, the contiguity of *zamīndārī* possession was broken all over by blocks of *ra'īyatī*, or purely peasant-held, villages.

The strength and weakness of the *zamīndār* class was reflected in the type of armed power it commanded. The *zamīndār's* fort was the symbol of his determination to defend the land inherited from his ancestors. The peasants with their large numbers probably never left him short of foot-soldiers; four million infantry is no mean figure. The numerically dominant infantry too accorded with the *zamīndār's* purely local ambitions and the absence of any great desire on his part for mobility or long-range operations. Accordingly, his strength in cavalry, the arm most necessary for mobile warfare, was usually far weaker. The *Ā'īn's* census shows that the *zamīndārs* had hardly one horseman for ten foot-soldiers. As against this, an official estimate of the time of Shāhjahān put the number of imperial cavalry (excluding such as were employed in the work of revenue collection under *faujdārs* and revenue officials) at 200,000 and infantry at 40,000 – giving five horsemen to one foot-soldier.[42] Since this figure of the imperial cavalry excludes forces employed for revenue collection purposes, it cannot be

battle comes" (Indar Singh Rāṭhor's submission to the court in *Documents of Aurangzeb's Reign*, 121). Cf. Bernier, 39, 208.

[42] Lāhorī, II, p.715. Lāhorī's estimate is not based on an inspection of the brand-rolls of the *manṣabdārs*' contingents: he has apparently arrived at his figures by simply dividing the total number of *sawār* ranks by four (after "the Rule of One-fourth") and then adding the number of *manṣabdārs* and horsemen directly paid from the imperial treasury. In actual fact, however, *manṣabdārs* who had *jāgīrs* in the same province where they were serving had to bring to the brand horsemen

assumed that the total figure fell very far short of the nearly 400,000 horsemen of the *zamīndārs* counted by the *Ā'īn*. Moreover, the latter could hardly have compared with the imperial troops in the breeds of their horses. This apart, the very fact that the *zamīndārs'* forces were not unified but were dispersed and engaged so often in internecine quarrels must often have deprived them of the capacity for effective resistance against imperial armies.

The *zamīndār* class was so fatally divided, so narrowly bound by its caste and local ties (though they were indeed in some respects its real strength and ensured its survival) that it could never form into a united governing class and create an empire. This incapacity on the part of the most powerful indigenous class may provide us with at least one explanation of why the main impetus towards empire building in medieval India came so repeatedly from foreign conquerors and immigrants.[43]

3. IMPERIAL ADMINISTRATION AND THE ZAMĪNDĀRS

Before studying the relationship that was established between the imperial administration and the *zamīndārs*, it will be useful to remember a distinction which we have made in the preceding sections of this chapter. This is the one between the tributary chiefs who were also called *zamīndārs*, and the ordinary *zamīndārs* within territories directly under imperial administration. We shall take up the position of the tributary chiefs in the next section, and for the present concern ourselves with the ordinary *zamīndārs*.

We have seen that within the imperial territories the *zamīndārs* in most provinces held rights over only a portion of the land and there were *ra'īyatī* areas where the peasant's right, such as it was, stood alone. In these areas the authorities normally dealt with the

---

numbering a third of their *sawār* ranks, while, on the other hand, those placed below 6-months in the month-scale brought fewer than the standard (cf. Lāhorī, II, 506-7). Lāhorī's figure may then serve only as a rough estimate. As for infantry, it consisted, he says, of "musketeers, gunners, cannoniers and rocketeers", 10,000 of whom were stationed at the court and the rest (3,000 in the printed text being an obvious error for 30,000) "in the provinces and forts".

[43] The preponderance of elements of foreign birth or origin in the Mughal nobility has been a subject of comment since Bernier, 215. Moreland shows, on the basis of the list of *manṣabdārs* given in the *Ā'īn*, that Akbar's "Service" consisted "predominantly" of foreigners, i.e. mainly Turanis and Persians (*India at the Death of Akbar*, 69-70). The ethnic composition of the Mughal nobility has now received comprehensive treatment in M. Athar Ali, *The Apparatus of Empire: Awards of Ranks, Offices and Titles to the Mughal Nobility, 1574-1658*; see especially his introduction, xx-xxi.

peasants direct, and this left its imprint on the whole machinery of Mughal revenue administration. It is not only that direct contact with the peasants, assessment of the peasants' lands and collection of the land revenue from them individually, is always the ideal recommended in official regulations; many of these regulations, especially those of Todar Mal and Fatḥulāh Shīrāzī, the *Ā'īn*, and Aurangzeb's *farmān* to Rasikdās[1] never refer to the *zamīndār*, though they lay down in detail the procedure for assessing and collecting land revenue. The *zamīndār* thus seems to have had no place in the recognized scheme of revenue administration and his name only creeps in surreptitiously here and there in the administrative manuals of the period. Indeed, it has not yet been possible to trace any document from Akbar's reign in which the *zamīndār* actually appears as the revenue payer for the area of his *zamīndārī*.[2] The only exception is provided by a passage from 'Abbās Sarwānī, where the terms *zamīndār* and *muqaddam* are used interchangeably, and it is alleged in an account of Sher Shāh's proceedings in his father's assignments in Bihar that, unless kept under control, the *zamīndārs* collected more from the land than they paid in revenue, seizing much money from the weak and hapless peasantry (*ra'īyat*).[3]

On the other hand, there is much evidence in our documents from the seventeenth century to prove that the *zamīndār* was normally called upon to pay the revenue for the land over which he claimed his right as *zamīndār*. One may begin by citing a *farmān* of Shāhjahān of his 6th regnal year, which exempts a religious dignitary from paying the revenue and other taxes (*māl o jihāt*) of a village in *pargana* Sahar near Mathura that he had purchased from *zamīndārs*. Clearly, but for the exemption, he would have had to pay the full revenue for the village.[4] There is an exceptionally large amount of such evidence from the reign of Aurangzeb for various parts of the Empire, from Bengal to Rajasthan. A copy has come down to us of an undertaking (*muchalka*) given on behalf of the English Company to pay the land revenue (*māl-i wājib*) of certain villages, including Dahi Kalkatta, ancestor of modern

[1] This does have one reference to *zamīndārs*, but not in connexion with the procedure of either assessment or collection of revenue.

[2] In the first edition of this book Jhaveri Doc. IV, dated 38th *Ilāhī* year, was treated as constituting evidence that the *zamīndārs* were revenue payers for villages they held under their right. I now find this document to be a forgery.

[3] 'Abbās Khān, ff.12a-15b, esp. f.15a.

[4] Jhaveri, Doc. VI, which unlike Doc. IV is genuine.

Calcutta, when they obtained their *zamīndārī* by purchase in 1698.[5] There is a good deal of other evidence for Bengal to the same effect,[6] but we shall be considering it in another context shortly. From Awadh comes a set of documents called *qaul-qarār*, issued by officials fixing the land revenue on *zamīndārs* for particular years.[7] Other documents from the same collection contain references to the *zamīndārs*' obligation to pay the *jama'*, or the amount of revenue assessed on their villages.[8] A letter from the *faujdār* of Baiswara speaks of "the peasants and *zamīndārs*" of a particular locality, who "attending upon the agents of the *jāgīrdārs* duly pay the land revenue".[9] In the two *sarkārs* of Sambhal (Dehli province) and Kalpi (Agra), regular payment of the revenue as *zamīndārs* in the past by the petitioners is made a pre-condition for entertaining their complaints.[10] A *parwāna* recording the grant of a *zamīndārī* of twenty-five villages near Mathura to one Qāsim, who was already holding them in *jāgīr*, informs the new *zamīndār* that "so long as the villages remain in his *jāgīr* he may keep the land revenue and official taxes (*māl-i wājib o ḥuqūq-i dīwānī*). Afterwards when they are assigned in *jāgīr* to someone else, he shall be answerable to the '*āmil* (revenue collector) of that place [on behalf of the new *jāgīrdār*, presumably] for the revenue collected (*ḥāṣil*)."[11] In an official letter we come across a reference to the allegation made by some *zamīndārs* of a *pargana* in *sarkār* Hisar against an '*āmil* who collected the revenue from them at the wrong time.[12] The news-reports from Ajmer province frequently refer to the payment of land revenue by *zamīndārs* either as an established fact or as an obligation on their part that needed to be enforced.[13]

[5] Add. 24,039, f.36b.

[6] Cf. especially *Durru-l 'Ulūm*, ff.47a-48a; Hedges, I, 39.

[7] Allahabad 897, 1206, 1223; also 1220 (which is a deed of acceptance of the assessment). The first two style the assessee *ta'alluqdār*, but we know from sale deeds that in both cases the assessee was the *zamīndār* of the villages (viz. the Pasnajat group of villages, to which we have already referred so often). In the last two documents, the assessees are called *māliks* of the villages. A *parwāna* of 1712 calls upon *zamīndārs* of *pargana* Shāhābād, *sarkār* Khairabad, to pay the land revenue (*māl-i wājib*) to the agents of the *jāgīrdār* (*Nāma-i Muẓaffarī*, I, 317).

[8] See Allahabad 782; also Allahabad 1234.

[9] *Inshā'-i Roshan Kalām*, ff.19b-20a; see also f.7a.

[10] *Durru-l 'Ulūm*, ff.43b, 56b-57a; also ff.61b-62a.

[11] *Nigārnāma-i Munshī*, ed., 152.

[12] Bālkrishan Brahman, ff. 63b-64a. The '*āmil* seized Rs 5,000 by force, selling away the sons and cattle of the plaintiffs at a time "when the fields were green".

[13] *Waqā'i' Ajmer*, 57, 398, et passim.

The evidence that has been set out here is only illustrative, for references to *zamīndārs*' paying revenue that are either general in nature or do not relate to any particular locality, are too numerous to be cited. What we have presented is enough for showing that the collection of land revenue through *zamīndārs* was by no means absent even in provinces which were placed under the *ẓabṭ* system by Akbar. The fact that the evidence belongs so extensively to Aurangzeb's reign is perhaps because from his reign a much larger body of records has survived. It does not necessarily mean that in the sixteenth century conditions were substantially different.

It seems that by the latter half of the seventeenth century, a special term had come into use to designate a *zamīndār* in his aspect as payer of land revenue. *Ta'alluqdār* means the holder of a *ta'alluqa*; the literal meaning of the latter word is 'connexion', but it was used in the sense of land or area over which any kind of right was claimed.[14] In the eighteenth-century definitions of *ta'alluqdār*, two separate statements occur: first, that he was just a kind of revenue farmer;[15] and, second, that he was a small *zamīndār*.[16] Yāsīn's glossary, however, gives an explanation which shows how both these statements could be true at the same time. A *ta'alluqdār*, we are told, was a *zamīndār* who contracted to pay revenue not only for his own *zamīndārī*, but also for the *zamīndārī* of other persons, this arrangement being usually made by the authorities to avoid having to deal with a large number of persons.[17] Thus a *ta'alluqdār* was not necessarily the *zamīndār* of the whole area for which he paid the revenue, but only of a part of it; for the rest he was simply an intermediary.[18] Being a *ta'alluqdār*, therefore, was a smaller thing than being a *zamīndār* of the same area, since the latter would hold the whole and not merely a part of it in *zamīndārī* right. This explains not only the eighteenth-

[14] The word *ta'alluqa* was thus used indifferently for the territories of *jāgīrdārs*, *zamīndārs* and independent rulers. We often come across the formula "the village X, *ta'alluqa-i* (attached to, included in) *jāgīr* of Y" (see, e.g. *Inshā'-i Roshan Kalām*). Thence *ta'alluqa* in the sense of land assigned to a *jāgīrdār* (*Akhbārāt* A, 49). For instances of its use for the area under a *zamīndār*, see *Documents of Aurangzeb's Reign*, 15; Allahabad 1234. Finally, in the *Ma'āṣir-i 'Ālamgīrī*, 206, we read of the *ta'alluqa* or dominion of the "wretched" Sambhājī.

[15] Add. 19,504, f.100a.

[16] *Dastūru-l 'Amal-i Khāliṣa Sharīfa*, ff.9b, 19a; Add. 19,503, ff.55b-56a.

[17] Add. 6603, ff.54b-55a. See also *Risāla-i Zirā'at*, f.9a.

[18] Cf. Holt Mackenzie, Memorandum of 1 July 1819, paras 406 and 408 (*Revenue Selections*, 91).

century definition of *ta'alluqdār* as a small *zamīndār*, but also a passage in the *Fatḥiya-i 'Ibriya*, where claimants to the throne of Arakan, who sided with the Mughals during Shā'ista Khān's Chatgaon expedition, are said to have hoped for something, at least: "If they could not become *rājas*, they might become *zamīndārs*; if not *zamīndārs*, then *ta'alluqdārs*."[19] It should, however, be stressed that the *ta'alluqdār* was only a particular kind of *zamīndār*, and in many contexts it seems to have been a matter of indifference which of the two terms was used. Thus, when two revenue documents from Awadh style the assessee *ta'alluqdār*, the word *zamīndār* would have done equally well since he was in fact the *mālik* or *zamīndār* of the assessed villages.[20] Similarly, in the provincial Dīwān's *parwāna* recognizing the English Company's purchase of Dahi Kalkatta, etc., the sellers are designated *zamīndārs*, while the English are called "permanent *ta'alluqdārs*" of their acquisition.[21]

Although we have just used the word "assessee" for the *zamīndār* (and also *ta'alluqdār*), when obliged to pay the revenue on the land of his *zamīndārī*, the official view seems to have been that he was always an intermediary, who merely rendered to the authorities the service of collecting the land revenue from the peasants. Aurangzeb's *farmān* to Rasikdās, making its sole reference to the *zamīndārs* (Art. XI), declares it as one of the tasks of the auditors of village accounts to discover how much "the revenue-assessor and collector (*amīn o 'āmil*) and *zamīndārs*, etc.", had taken from the peasants. The bracketing of *zamīndārs* with revenue officials is significant, and suggests that the authorities claimed as much control over the *zamīndārs*' collection of revenue from the peasants as over that of their own officials. It was therefore natural that administrative documents should have laid

19 *Fatḥiya-i 'Ibriya*, ff. 155b-156a.

20 Allahabad 897, 1206 (see note 7 in this Section). In Allahabad 897 the assessee is actually termed "*mālik o ta'alluqdār*".

21 Add. 24,039, f.36a. Moreland, though he refers to the sale deed on f.39a of this collection, seems to have missed this *parwāna* as well as the endorsements entered on the back of it. He believed that the term *ta'alluqdārī* for the Company's rights was used only in Farrukhsiyar's *farmān* of 1717. From this he concluded erroneously that "at this time, then, Calcutta meant by *zamīndārī* what Delhi meant by *taluqdārī*" (*Agrarian System*, 191-2). The use of the two terms in these documents would, however, conform to a definition, in Add. 6603, f.55a, of a subordinate sense for *ta'alluqdār*: it could mean a *zamīndār*, whose rights were not ancient nor derived from royal grant (*ḥuẓūrī*), but obtained only by purchase. Thus the sellers of Kalkatta, etc., were *zamīndārs*, but the English would be *ta'alluqdārs*.

down, in general terms, how the *zamīndārs* were to treat their peasants.[22]

The *zamīndār* is thus seen primarily as an official or tax-gatherer, rather than a tax payer. Qāẓī Muḥammad A'lā, indeed, asserts that "the king's demand of revenue from cultivated land [is] from the cultivators (*muzāri's*), not *zamīndārs*", and that the position of *zamīndārs* was, therefore, in the nature of a *khidmat* (post of service), they being obliged to encourage cultivation and collect land revenue from the peasants on behalf of the king's collectors (*'ummāl*).[23] That the Qāẓī was here repeating an official doctrine is shown by two *farmāns* granting or confirming *zamīndārī*, which speak of the right as a *khidmat*.[24] This was not only a matter of terminology or paper injunctions. The *zamīndārs*' "service" in collecting and remitting the revenue was actually paid for, through an allowance known as *nānkār*. This was in the form either of a deduction from the revenue paid or of land left to the *zamīndār* revenue-free.[25] The *nānkār*, according to what was apparently the standard rate, amounted to 10 per cent of the revenue demand,[26] although a later document which also mentions this percentage allows that it varied and amounted to 5 per cent in some provinces.[27]

This conception of *zamīndārī* as a form of service rendered to

[22] See the dīwān's *parwāna* concerning the English purchase of Kalkatta, etc., Add. 24,039, f.36a, and revenue officials' *qaul-qarārs*, Allahabad 897, 1206, 1223. The shorter formula employed in these *qaul-qarārs* consists of an injunction to the *zamīndār* that he should pay the revenue assessed, and that "he should keep the peasants contented by his good conduct and exert himself in furthering the cultivation and prosperity (or, increase in the numbers) of the peasants." Cf. *hasbu'l ḥukm* of 1722, *Jour. Pat. Hist. Soc.*, LIX (4), 69-72.

[23] *Risāla Aḥkām al-Ārāẓī*, MS 'A', ff.43b-44a, 56a, 56a-b.

[24] See Jahāngīr's (forged) *farmān* issued in his 13th year and published in *IHRC*, XVIII, p.188 (concerning the *zamīndārī* and *chaudhurāī* of some *tappas* in *sarkār* Mungir, Bihar). The formula *khidmat-i zamīndārī* is also used (and the word *khidmat* alone as substitute for *zamīndārī*) in a *farmān* of Shāh 'Ālam II issued in his 15th year, confirming the descendants of Rāja Sālibāhan in the *zamīndārī* of a *pargana* in *sarkār* Kol, Agra province. A photograph of this *farmān* was in the possession of the late Nawab Sahib of Chhatari, Aligarh. Though a late document, it probably preserves the form used in such documents of the 17th century.

[25] Add. 6603, ff.65a, 79b, 82b. Cf. Add.19,503 (of AD 1766), f.55a.

[26] In Bekas, f.52b, a *zamīndār* addressing a revenue official declares that "if the *jama'* (revenue) of the *ta'alluqa* was assessed according to the statement of the last ten years (*muwāzana-i dah-sāla*), with the deduction of one-tenth as *nānkār*," he was ready to render the official proper service.

[27] Add. 19,504, f.100a. In Add. 19,503, f.55a, the rate of deduction (*dastūr*) allowed on revenue on account of *nānkār* is put at 2 or 3% only.

the authorities brought it very close, in essentials, to the office of the *chaudhurī*. The *chaudhurī*, who was usually a *zamīndār* himself, occupied a crucial position in the machinery of revenue collection and received for his services an allowance, which too was called *nānkār*.[28] Since *zamīndārī* was also treated as implying a duty to collect revenue, it is not surprising that *zamīndārī* and *chaudhurā'ī* are sometimes paired together in Mughal documents.[29]

The established principle, then, which emerges from our evidence, was that the land revenue was a direct imposition on the peasant and that even when the *zamīndār* might be the one who remitted it to the imperial treasury, the peasant was the real assessee. This may be one reason why the standard revenue regulations of the time of Akbar as well as Aurangzeb tend to ignore the *zamīndārs* altogether. The pitch of the revenue demand and the mode of assessment might well remain the same within a locality, irrespective of whether a particular village was *zamīndārī* or *ra'īyatī*. This was, indeed, implicit in the right of the authorities, acknowledged in the eighteenth century, to convert *zamīndārī* land into *sīr*, i.e., impose direct assessment and collection on the peasant, bypassing the *zamīndār* altogether, though giving him an allowance on account of his proprietary right or *mālikāna*.[30] Two specific instances where the revenue demand on *zamīndārī* land was at the same pitch and assessed by the same method as that on the *ra'īyatī*, come from the seventeenth century. In a manual of Shāhjahān's reign, a specimen account shows the *kankūt* method of assessment being applied, at the same time, to the *k͟hwud-kāshta* lands of the *zamīndārs* and the *ra'īyatī* lands within the same village.[31] In the collection of official documents of Aurangzeb's reign we find an order to the effect that the revenue from a village of a *zamīndār*, who had protested against heavy assessment, be realized through crop-sharing, with the state's share amounting to half the produce, which was in fact the standard, if not the maximum rate of land revenue authorized under Aurangzeb.[32] It is

[28] The duties and significance of this official will be discussed in some detail in Chapter VII, Section 2.

[29] Jahāngīr's *farmān* (forged), *IHRC*, XVIII, 188; Allahabad 1192 (AD 1669).

[30] *Risāla Aḥkām al-Arāẓī*, MS 'A', f.47a-b, MS 'B', f.59b, where this practice is said to have been "usual and customary as of old". See also Yāsīn's Glossary, Add. 6603, ff.61b, 66a-b. Yāsīn had experience of revenue administration in both Dehli and Bengal.

[31] *Dastūru-l 'Amal-i Navīsindagī*, f.183a.

[32] *Nigārnāma-i Munshī*, ed. 98. For half-share of the produce as the revenue rate under Aurangzeb, see Chapter 6, Section 1.

possible that in princely states the *zamīndārs* obtained concessional rates on their villages as compared with peasant-held villages; but, in the case of Marwar, this is not definitely proved.[33]

The assessments on *zamīndārs* do not seem, however, to have been exempt from constant change. Two documents from Awadh, stating the revenue assessed on a *zamīndār*, show that the revenue demand was revised every harvest, so that there must have been a fresh assessment during each season, in the same way as was prescribed in the imperial regulations for ordinary land.[34]

There, nevertheless, seem to have been cases where the assessment once made was continued for some time. In two documents, again from nearly the same area of Awadh, the revenue is fixed *bi-l maqṭa'*, i.e., at the same figures permanently, upon the 'proprietors' (*māliks*) of a number of villages.[35] Similar arrangements are also found in Bihar, where the *māliks* of particular villages were, as a concession, required to pay a fixed sum in revenue year after year, under the designations *muqarrarī* (settlement) and *muqarrarī-i istimrārī* (permanent settlement).[36] But since the concessions were given only by the *jāgīrdārs* or their agents, the fixed amount of assessment could be valid only during their own terms of assignment which were by no means of long duration.

The system was different mainly in Bengal, where the *zamīndār* seems to have paid his land revenue according to a figure fixed by the administration for long, though unspecified, periods. The evidence for this system goes back to the *Ā'īn-i Akbarī*, which declares that the *jama'* of Bengal was "wholly *naqdī*".[37] Now, since *naqd* means cash, the phrase standing by itself may be taken to mean simply that the land revenue in Bengal was collected in

[33] *Contra* Bhadani in *IHR*, VI, 151-2, where *Vigat*, I, 409-15, is cited. He should have mentioned that Nainsī here separately lists *raitī* (*ra'īyatī*) villages and those villages which, abandoned by peasants, are available for settlement (*basī lāyak*). The *rekh* (*jama'*) on them might, on average, have been lower simply because they were in a ruinous state.

[34] Allahabad 1206 and 897 (of 1677, 1685). Under each harvest there is a figure under *aṣl*, the previous year's assessment for the corresponding harvest; followed by *iẓāfa* (increase) or *kamī* (reduction), as the case might be; and, then, the total now due.

[35] Allahabad 1220 and 1223 (of 1687). The figures for the two successive years show no change in respect of any village. See also Chapter VI, Section 4, for *muqṭa'ī*.

[36] Datta, 93 (No.413, of 1662) and 103 (No.467, of 1664); also 122 (No. 561, of 1718) and 126 (No.581, of 1712).

[37] *Ā'īn*, I, 393.

money.[38] But this interpretation fails when we find the *jama'* of the *zabṭī parganas* in Bihar and Ilahabad being distinguished from that of the *naqdī parganas*.[39] The imposition of cash revenue rates was essential to the *zabṭ* system, and if it could still be regarded as different from *naqdī*, the latter must mean something other than mere cash payment. Some indication of its sense may be obtained by turning to the other places in the *Ā 'īn's* statistics where the *jama'* figures are preceded by the word *naqdī* or *az-qarār-i naqdī* ("as settled in money").[40] All the *mahals* against which these words are put uniformly lack measured-area statistics.[41] Furthermore, the *sarkār* of Sorath (Saurashtra) in Gujarat is declared to be *naqdī*,[42] and we know from the *Ā 'īn* as well as the *Mir'āt-i Ahmadī* that this consisted entirely of the territories of tributary chiefs. At first sight, the fact that only a few *mahals* in Ajmer province, the homeland of the Rājpūt chiefs, are specifically described as *naqdī* may appear to militate against any connexion between *naqdī* and tribute. But actually the great Rājpūt chiefs did not pay any tribute: they became *jāgīrdārs*, holding their ancestral domains as *waṭan* and keeping their revenues for themselves. The *naqdī mahals* of

---

[38] Abū-l Faẓl, in fact, uses the word *naqdī* to mean "stated in money" when he puts it as a heading over his column of *jama'* figures in the tables of statistics for the "Twelve Provinces".

[39] *Ā 'īn*, I, 417, 424. In respect of the *sarkār* of Ilāhābās (Ilahabad), Blochmann's text is very misleading. Where the MSS read: "Consisting of *Zabṭī*, 9 *mahals*: 2,08,38,384 *dāms*; and *Naqdī*, 6 *mahals*: 19,93,615 *dāms*", Blochmann has: "Consisting of 9 *mahals*: 2,08,33,374 ½ *dams* and *naqdī*".

[40] A reader of Blochmann's text is, again, likely to be led astray here. Blochmann, dispensing with the columns, had no place to put the word *naqdī* used as the heading for the *jama'* column. He put it here and there alongside the *jama'* figures of certain *sarkārs* and *parganas*, which in the original appear without this distinction. Without consulting the MSS, one has no means of knowing whether the term *naqdī* qualifying a *jama'* figure at any place is the result of Blochmann's interpolation or was intended to be placed there by Abū-l Faẓl himself.

Saran, 315, makes a distinction between *naqdī* and *az qarār-i naqdī*, which is unwarranted. The former term is used for part of the *jama'* of the province of Bihar, and the latter (in the formula, *az qarār-i zabṭī o naqdī*) for the corresponding portion within the *jama'* of Bihar *sarkār* (*Ā 'īn*, I, 417-18).

[41] The *mahals* are Ajaigarh in *sarkār* Kalinjar (Ilahabad); Khandela in *sarkār* Narnaul (Agra); Udaipur, Islampur (Mohan), Bainsarur, Sanwar Ghati, Saimbal "with cultivated land", Mandalgarh and Madaria in *sarkār* Chittor, and Amkhora and Dablana in *sarkār* Ranthambhor (Ajmer); Seoni in *sarkār* Handiya and Uparmal and Gagraun "with the city" in *sarkār* Gagraun (Malwa); Bandar Sola (Ghogha) in *sarkār* Ahmadabad (Gujarat); and Darband in *sarkār* Sindhsagar (Lahor). Blochmann also puts *az qarār-i naqdī* against Singhana-Udaipur in *sarkār* Narnaul and Thamna in *sarkār* Ahmadabad, though this is not supported by either Add. 7652 or Add. 6552.

[42] *Ā 'īn*, I, p.493.

Ajmer province were probably the few areas whose chiefs had not joined imperial service as *jāgīrdārs*, but paid tribute in cash. If then we apply this sense of *naqdī*[43] to Bengal, we may suppose that the land revenue there was taken in fixed amounts of money from the *zamīndārs*, as if it were tribute rather than a variable tax on the produce of the land.

That such was in fact the system in force in Bengal is borne out by two documents of the reign of Aurangzeb. The first, a *ḥasbu-l ḥukm*, recites that the *jama'* upon the co-sharers of a *zamīndārī* of two *parganas* was arbitrarily increased by Mīr Jumla, not after an assessment of the revenue-paying capacity of the land, but as a punishment for some fault of the *zamīndārs*. The increased *jama'*, moreover, was not for any particular year, but obviously a per-manent imposition.[44] The second is the Dīwān's *parwāna* of February 1699 recognizing the sale of Dahi Kalkatta and two other villages to the English Company: it gives a fixed amount of *jama'* as the land revenue payable on these villages, and this, in the undertaking given by the Company's *vakīl* (agent) and copied on the back of the *parwāna*, is broken up into figures fixed for each of the villages.[45] Contrary to the specifications in similar revenue documents from Awadh, the *jama'* is not laid down for any parti- cular year; and one learns from the English records that the same amount continued to be paid year after year.[46] Indeed,in a *nishān* of May 1698 issued to the Company, it is asked to pay the revenue (*ḥāṣil*) in accordance with the *jama'-i ṭūmār*.[47] This last was the name given in Bengal to the *jama'* on the basis of which *jāgīrs* were assigned;[48] and we must, therefore, suppose that the same set of figures was in use in Bengal to obtain revenue from the *zamīndārs* as well as to assign *jāgīrs*.[49]

[43] A similar interpretation is suggested, but not fully developed, by Moreland and Yusuf Ali in *JRAS* (1918), 33.

[44] *Durru-l 'Ulūm*, ff, 47a-48a. To meet the *jama'*, they were required to provide boats whose number was increased from 20 to 29.

[45] Add. 24,039, f.36a-b.

[46] "The rent ... according to the King's books amounts to 1194.14, and something more which is yearly paid into the Treasury." (Wilson, *Early Annals*, II, (2) 60; cf. *Agrarian System*, 192 *n*.). The same amount as mentioned here is stated to be the *jama'* in the *dīwān's parwāna* and the undertaking of the Company's *vakīl*. By 1714, the *jama'* payable annually was still the same in respect of all the three villages, except for the "Paican" portion of village Gobindpur, whose *jama'* had been increased from Rs 123.15.13 to Rs 210.9.0 (Wilson, *Early Annals*, II(1), 174).

[47] Add. 24,039, ff.36n, 37a.

[48] Add. 6586, f.22b.

[49] This is also suggested by the fact that while *ḥāṣil* (as distinct from *ḥāṣil-i*

The general picture of the system in Bengal, which we have reconstructed exclusively from sources of the period before the death of Aurangzeb, is confirmed by the whole body of eighteenth-century literature.[50] This consistency in our evidence needs to be stressed the more strongly, since doubts have been raised about the historical accuracy of the later literature, which grew up very largely for the benefit of the early English administrators.[51] The idea so firmly entertained by the English of a "land-revenue settlement", whether permanent or for long periods, was thus at least partly derived from the conditions in Bengal and was not entirely exotic.[52] What was novel was that it was made into a

kāmil) statistics are available for all other provinces of the Mughal Empire, none have been provided for Bengal and Orissa (see Appendix D).

[50] Two or three detailed reference, may serve to illustrate this. We are told in Add. 6586, f.22b, that it was in accordance with the *jama'-i ṭūmāri* that "the *zamīndārs* obtain their *sanads* [deeds of recognition] till now, and it was on the basis of it also that the *jāgīrdārs* obtained their pay-assignments (*tankhwāh*)". It adds that since the *jama'-i ṭūmārī* was much less than what the land could afford, the country (so in our text; but we should, perhaps, say, the *zamīndārs*) became more prosperous. The *Risāla-i Zirā'at*, f.12b, a work written *c*.1750, says that the *jama'-i ṭūmārī* was instituted by Todar Mal in the time of Akbar, that it was never revised by actual assessment and that while "men" (i.e. *zamīndārs*) paid the revenue to the authorities according to the *jama'-i ṭūmārī*, they realized the income from their estate (*jā'idād*) and collected the land revenue (*ḥāl-i ḥāṣil*) by actual assessment. The amount actually assessed on land was called the *jama'-i tashkhīṣ*. Our work goes on to add that the *jama'-i tashkhīṣ* usually exceeded the *jama'-i ṭūmārī* many times over, and there was scarcely a place in Bengal where it was less than the latter. A report on the revenue system of the pre-British regime, prepared by the Rāi Rāyān and the *qānūngos* at the instance of the Governor-General and Council (25 January 1775) also declares that the *zamīndārs* used to pay the revenue (*māl-guzārī*) according to Todar Mal's *jama'-i ṭūmārī* (Add. 6592, f.77a; Add. 6586, f.53a). See also Shore's minute of June 1789, especially paras 379 and 380 (*Fifth Report*, 204).

Ghulām Ḥusain says in his history of Bengal, the *Riyāẓu-s Salāṭīn*, completed in 1787-8, that Murshid Qulī Khān during his tenure of office as deputy governor in the last years of Aurangzeb, tried to abolish or, at any rate, overhaul the old system. He brought under control the exactions of the *zamīndārs*, allowing them only *nānkār*; he assessed the revenue and collected it directly from the peasants, employing measurement; and, for this, he appointed his own revenue collectors (*'āmils*) and placed *shiqqdārs* and *amīns* under them (Bib. Ind., 252). It is obvious from our later evidence that Murshid Qulī Khān's measures could have had only limited success. The account is more significant for its revelation, by implication, of what the system was before Murshid Qulī Khān.

[51] Moreland suspected that the whole of this evidence had been cooked up to mislead the English (*JRAS*, [1926], 51-2). In his *Akbar to Aurangzeb*, 325, he suggests that the figures for Bengal in the Mughal statistics were also falsified with the same intent. Truly, a case of Omichand out-deceiving Clive!

[52] One must distinguish between the attempt to create formal private property

universal element of every major land-tax system in India (Permanent, Ryotwari, Mahalwari, etc.) and so into the one great instrument employed to mould freebooter and moneylender alike into that "pukka" loyalist of British raj, the modern Indian landlord.

We have seen earlier that the *zamīndārī* right was regarded in our period as an article of private property. This appears clearly in the way the Mughal administration dealt with disputes among *zamīndārs*. Our documents show that the possession of a *zamīndārī*, when disputed, was established usually by judicial means, that is by or in collaboration with the *qāẓī*. When the right had been so established, or when it was not judicially contested by others, it was enforced by the *faujdār*, the commandant of the area.[53] Disputes over possession of *zamīndārī* could go right up to the imperial court, from which orders, known as *ḥasbu-l ḥukms*, were usually issued, directing local officials to take appropriate action.[54] This was probably the normal way the *zamīndārī* right was treated: it had its sanctity as private property. But there were associated

out of the *zamīndār's* existing rights and the idea of a fixed assessment. The former notion was certainly exotic (cf. Ranajit Guha, *A Rule of Property for Bengal*); the latter was designed to enable England to continue to extract its tribute on the existing scale, by being able to collect what was fixed permanently and to levy taxes on commerce contingent on future prosperity based on prosperous agriculture (cf. Cornwallis's minute of 3 February 1790 in *Fifth Report*, 483-93). That such prosperity did not actually come about was due not to any deformity of "colonial knowledge", but to the pressures of colonial circumstance.

[53] From Akbar's reign we have two decisions over disputes about *milkiyat* rights from the same locality. In 1557 the *qāẓī* of Bilgram gave such a decision (*Sharā'if-i 'Uṣmānī*, ff.64b-65b); in 1570 two imperial officials (possibly *jāgīrdārs*) did so, when asked to settle another dispute by an imperial *farmān* (Bilgram Docs. no.9). For summaries of the two documents, see *IESHR*, IV (1-2), 223-4, 226-9.

From the reign of Aurangzeb comes a much larger body of such evidence. For a dispute over possession of *zamīndārī*, taken directly before a *qāẓī*, see Allahabad 421; a dispute heard by the *faujdār* and *qāẓī* together, the judgment being given by the *qāẓī* alone, Allahabad 359; a complaint of usurpation of *zamīndārī*, contested on grounds of right, was referred by the *amīn-o-faujdār* to the *qāẓī* and *mutawallī* (trustee of *madad-i ma'āsh* lands) for judgment (Allahabad 375). When the *faujdār* appears to be acting on his own in judging a dispute, he might in fact have had before him the judgments of some *qāẓīs* given on it previously (Allahabad 370, 1201). In Sihunda Docs. 26, we have a dispute heard and settled by an *aḥadī* (cavalry trooper) from the headquarters, together with the *amīn* and *qāẓī*. For official action restoring *zamīndārī* rights to legitimate claimants, see Allahabad 1202, 1203, 1225.

[54] Two such *ḥasbu-l ḥukms* have survived in the original, Sihunda Docs. 17 and Allahabad 1214. See also *Durru-l 'Ulūm*, ff.43a-44a, 49a-b, 52b-53-a, 56b-57a, 61b-62a.

with it two important features which inspired in the administration a different view towards it. We have seen above that since the *zamīndār* was usually expected to collect and remit land revenue, his right came to be described, in the formal language of official documents, as a form of *khidmat* or service. If he did not perform the service well and did not pay the land revenue, he could be deposed and replaced by someone else. Secondly, the *zamīndārs* usually kept armed retainers: they were, therefore, a possible source of sedition as well as potentially effective allies in suppressing sedition. A disloyal *zamīndār* naturally lost all claim to his right, and the administration would then attempt to install a loyal man in his stead.

From the necessity for such interference arose the doctrine that the imperial government could resume or confer any *zamīndārī* at its will, a doctrine stated in its most uncompromising terms by Qāẓī Muḥammad A'lā.[55] We are also told elsewhere of a saying that "an assignee (*ḥākim*) of a day could in a moment remove a *zamīndār* of five hundred years and put in his stead a man who had been without a place for a whole life-time".[56] A later work stated the same principle in less drastic terms: the emperor could transfer the *zamīndārī* of any person, if a fault had been committed; the governor or any assignee (*ṣūba o ḥākim*) did not have the power to do this.[57] This is confirmed by our seventeenth-century evidence, which shows that all changes in *zamīndārīs* were in fact made only on imperial orders, the powers of the local officials being limited to sending their recommendations (*tajwīz*) to the court.[58]

A forged order of conferment of *zamīndārī* is attributed to Jahāngīr.[59] But for the rest, our material comes almost exclusively from the reign of Aurangzeb, during which numerous transfers, depositions and appointments of *zamīndārs* are recorded. Wherever the reasons for deposing the old *zamīndārs* are stated, they are usually non-payment of revenue and rebellious conduct, the two being normally combined.[60] If the *zamīndārs* paid their revenue, no

[55] *Risāla Aḥkām al-Ārāẓī*, MS 'A', ff.44a, 47b; MS 'B' ff.55a, 70a.

[56] Bekas, f.51a. *Ḥākim* in these documents is usually employed for *jāgīrdār*, but also for the imperial revenue collector, the *karorī*.

[57] Add. 6603, f.65a.

[58] See *Waqā'i' Ajmer*, 396-8, *Akhbārāt* 38/137, etc.; *Nigārnāma-i Munshī*, ed., 152; *Inshā'-i Roshan Kalām*, ff.3b-4a, etc.

[59] *IHRC*, XVIII (1942), 188-9. It confers *zamīndārī* and *chaudhurā'ī* of some *tappas* in *sarkār* Mungir, Bihar. See Bibliography, No.70.

[60] *Waqā'i' Ajmer*, 365, 396-8; *Inshā'-i Roshan Kalām*, ff.7b-8a, etc.; Bekas, ff.50a-53a.

case for their deposition existed.[61] Conversely, the persons appointed to *zamīndārīs* were given the responsibility of paying the revenue as well as suppressing sedition. An administrative manual has set out the rules for newly appointed *zamīndārs*: a *manṣab* (or rank, including *sawār* rank, imposing military obligations) could be given against the income expected from the right conferred; and the *zamīndār* had to accept the duty of controlling the seditious elements in his *zamīndārī*.[62] The "expulsion of evil-mannered sedition-mongers" takes pride of place among duties prescribed for the recipient of a *zamīndārī* granted near Mathura.[63] Clearly for this reason, other documents make possession of an *ulūs* (a body of armed followers) a prerequisite for such a grant.[64] We should not be surprised, therefore, when we find the duties of *faujdār* (local commandant) and *zamīndār* of a *pargana* conferred together on the same person.[65] But money too had a role to play in the appointments: the aspirants usually had to promise a substantial cash offering or *peshkash* to the court before they could obtain the *zamīndārīs* they sought.[66] Some of our records also suggest that the imperial grants were not always hereditary,[67] nor in some cases, at least, even for life since they refer to the transfer (*taghaiyur*) of such *zamīndārīs* in the same terms as used for *jāgīrs*.[68]

From the seventeenth-century evidence just set out it is obvious that the person holding a *zamīndārī* grant was usually an instrument of imperial administration rather than, as frequently in the

61 *Inshā'-i Roshan Kalām*, f.20b.

62 Fraser 86, f.62a-b. Cf. *Inshā'-i Roshan Kalām*, f.3b, where a candidate for a *zamīndārī* grant is put forward and the grant to him of a *manṣab*, "conditional on *zamīndārī*", is recommended. See also *Akhbārāt*, 44/142.

63 *Nigārnāma-i Munshī*, ed., 152. Cf. Or. 1779, ff.220b-221a.

64 *Inshā'-i Roshan Kalām*, ff.3b-4a; *Kalimāt-i Ṭaiyabāt*, ff.127b-128a.

65 *Waqā'i' Ajmer*, 218-19. An official, Mān Singh, was deprived of his "*faujdārī* and *zamīndārī*" at the same time.

66 *Akhbārāt* 38/137 (*zamīndārī* of *pargana* Baran, Dehli province), 44/142 (Jahangirabad, Awadh); *Inshā'-i Roshan Kalām*, f.8a.

67 As shown by the grant of the *zamīndārī* of Baran to another officer on the death of the former incumbent (*Akhbārāt* 38/137). But see *Akhbārāt* 48/148, where, on the death of a *zamīndār* in *sarkār* Sambhal, who held a *manṣab*, the *zamīndārī* was conferred on his two sons, and his *manṣab*, held against the *zamīndārī*, was equally divided between them. In Jahāngīr's (forged) grant of *zamīndārī* and *chaudhurāī*, the passing on of the grant to the sons of the grantee is specifically provided for by the phrase *bā farzindān* ("with sons") in the text (*IHRC*, XVIII, 188-9). Possibly, if a *zamīndārī* grant was to be hereditary, this had to be explicitly laid down in the imperial order.

68 *Waqā'i' Ajmer* 219; *Akhbārāt* 38/283, 44/142, 48/106; *Ma'āṣir-i 'Ālamgīrī*, 514.

next century, one who had obtained power first and then got it recognized by the imperial court. The imperial power to expel and appoint *zamīndārs*, though not normally exercised, was an important weapon for keeping them in order. It introduced here and there, among their ranks, elements loyal to the government simply because they were controlling, under its dispensation, land to which the dispossessed would continue to lay claim for a long time. Sometimes, it seems, the grantees were chosen so as to break a caste monopoly over the *zamīndārīs* in certain areas: we find local Muslims being granted big *zamīndārīs* in the midst of Bais Rājpūt territories in Baiswāra.[69] Or, we find a Rājpūt clan being brought in as *zamīndārs* expressly to dispossess another whose loyalty was suspected.[70] It is possible that the *zamīndārī* grants of this period have been one factor amongst others in the altering of the boundaries of *zamīndārī* possession of various castes since the time of the *Ā'īn*. It is also possible that the changes made in Aurangzeb's reign were in favour of certain sections of Muslims: a number of the *zamīndārs* appointed by the court whose names occur in our records are certainly Muslims. This would have been in conformity with Aurangzeb's general religious policy, but the available evidence on the point is not such as to allow us to make an unqualified assertion.

4. AUTONOMOUS CHIEFS

Hitherto in this chapter we have restricted our treatment to those *zamīndārs* who existed within the territories under direct imperial administration. We have found that a person who was not a peasant was called *zamīndār* when he possessed a particular right to the land, normally designated "proprietary" in our records but known by various names locally. The right was not often, in fact, proprietary, but was distinguished by three essential features: it was superior to that of the peasant; it had originated independently of the existing imperial power; and it implied a claim to a share in the produce of the soil, which was distinct from, though it might be laid side by side with, the land revenue demand of the state. In addition, the right was usually accompanied by possession of armed force, the instrument for establishing and enforcing the right. The *zamīndār* in the imperial territories was held to be entirely subordinate to the administration, whose constant endeavour it

69 *Inshā'-i Roshan Kalām*, ff. 3b-4a, 8a.

70 *Waqā'i' Ajmer*, 364-5.

was to convert him into a mere tax-gatherer. But there were features which he had in common with men of greater power, with chiefs and, kinglets, the so-called *rājas*, *rānas*, *rāos*, *rāwats*, etc.[1] Like them, he held some territory which he could call his own; like them he was no creature, normally, of the imperial government; and, like them, he had armed men to defend his possessions. Sometimes the lines between the two could not be rigidly drawn. We may find a person calling himself *rāja* selling his right to a village like any other *zamīndār*.[2] And in the Dakhin, a *deshmukh* (equivalent to the north Indian *chaudhurī*) could grow into a chief,[3] while the descendants of a powerful chief might shrink into *deshmukhs*.[4] For an imperial chancery, anxious to depress the status of all subordinate rulers in the empire, the similarities were enough to suggest identity; and so the master of a large kingdom and a petty claimant to a share in the possession of a village could alike be designated *zamīndār* or *būmī*.[5]

[1] These traditional titles were generally confirmed by the Mughal emperor on the submission of a chief. But they were also granted to men who had no pretensions to being chiefs, e.g. Todar Mal and Bīrbal under Akbar.

[2] Allahabad 1227 (dated 12 December 1695). The seller styles himself "Rāja Barthun Singh, son of Rāja Pratāp Narāyan, son of Rāja Murār Singh, *zamīndār* of the village Nahaska". The village sold was a different one. Both lay in the *sarkār* of Bahraich, Awadh.

[3] Chanānerī *Deshmukh*, chief of Indur in Telangana, is mentioned in the *Ā'īn*, I, 477, as one of the chiefs of Berar. The financial obligations of his descendants, all called Chanānerī *Deshmukhs*, form the subject of a letter from Aurangzeb, when viceroy of the Dakhin (*Ādāb-i 'Ālamgīrī*, I, 636-9).

[4] This happened to the descendants of Udājī Rām, chief of Mahur (*Ma'āṣiru-l Umarā*, I, 42-45).

[5] For the use of the terms *zamīndār* and *būmī* for autonomous chiefs, see *Ā'īn*, I, 477-82, 486, 492; *Akbarnāma*, III, 533; *'Ālamgīrnāma*, 677, etc. The term *zamīndār* was applied to chiefs even in the period of the Dehli Sultanate. See Baranī, *Tārīkh-i Fīrūz-Shāhī*, Bib. Ind., 326, 539, and Shams Sirāj 'Afīf, *Tārīkh-i Fīrūz-Shāhī*, Bib. Ind., 170.

The tendency of the Mughal chancery to be liberal with the designation *zamīndār*, and very sparing with any title suggestive of sovereignty, caused much "shame" to the English factors. The Bombay Council in 1678 was indignant that in their conversations with the Mughal officials, the Company's "Banyans ... dare not owne his Majestie of England to be a King, but when they discourse of him call him Simindar [*zamīndār*], which in effect is no more than a Desy [*desāī*]" (*English Records on Shivājī*, II, 170).

Incidentally, Abū-l Faẓl does not speak of any contemporary Indian ruler as "king", but usually only as *marzbān*, "chief over a territory". The Mughals insisted on calling 'Ādil Shāh "'Ādil Khān" and Quṭb Shāh "Quṭb-l Mulk"; and from Akbar's time onwards both of them were styled *dunyādārs* ("men of the world"), a term suggesting, first, that the persons so styled were only glorified *zamīndārs*

The use of the same term for chiefs and ordinary *zamīndārs* may cause confusion sometimes when the term is employed in a general sense. Its virtue lies in reminding us that from the point of view of the Mughal government there was a chain of local despotisms, covering the whole empire, here semi-independent, there fully subdued, here represented by chiefs, there by ordinary *zamīndārs*. In various contexts the two categories could appear as forming a single class.

But the difference between the two should not be lost sight of. This did not lie simply in the superiority that the chiefs enjoyed over ordinary *zamīndārs* in military power and territory. A distinction was made between the two by custom also, which prescribed different principles of succession in respect of their possessions.[6] But the difference lay most clearly in the relationship with the imperial power which allowed autonomy to the chiefs, while it made ordinary *zamīndārs* mere propertied subjects of the emperor.

The relations between the chiefs and the Mughal government were not, by any means, of a single kind. Some, like the great Rājpūt chiefs, entered imperial service and obtained *manṣabs* or ranks. Their ancestral domains were considered a special type of *jāgīr*, untransferable and hereditary, known in official terminology as *waṭan*. The practice was to assess summarily the total revenue of a territory at some figure and then assign to its ruler a rank for which the sanctioned pay would be equal to that figure.[7] From some of these and from almost all the other chiefs (outside the imperial

(*zamīn* also meaning earth) and, secondly, that the men so styled were really not firm of faith, being worldly men.

[6] In the ordinary *zamīndārīs*, as we have seen, the patrimony was equally divided among the sons; but a chief was succeeded by only one of his sons. We are told that among the Rājpūts generally, the practice of primogeniture was followed, but among the Rāṭhors, it was the son born of the mother for whom the father had the greatest affection who succeeded (Lāhorī, II, 98).

[7] This principle is cited in a representation made to Aurangzeb on behalf of Rāja Indar Singh: "After the death of holders of *waṭan*, *manṣabs* are given [to their heirs] according to the assessed revenue (*dām-hā*) of their *waṭan*." The *jama'* figure for his own *waṭan* showed an excess of Rs 40 lakh over his pay and he prayed that either his rank should be increased to cover this excess, or the *jama'* figure be reduced (so that no part of it might be assigned to anyone else in *jāgīr*). His *manṣab* was increased (*Documents of Aurangzeb's Reign*, 121). The same practice is well illustrated, as pointed out by Moreland in *Agrarian System*, 267, by a passage in Lāhorī, II, 360-1, relating to the submission and entry into imperial service of Partāb, the *zamīndār* of Palamau in Bihar. See also *T.J.*, 192, 336; Lāhorī, I, 161, I, ii, 95; *Ādāb-i 'Ālamgīrī*, Or. 177, f.56a, *Ruq'āt-i 'Ālamgīr*, 167-8; *Documents of Aurangzeb's Reign*, 84, 121.

service) it was usual to demand a fixed annual "offering", or *peshkash*, which was regarded as both the hallmark and substance of submission.[8] The territories of many chiefs were also assessed at different amounts of *jama*', to be paid annually to whomsoever it was assigned in *jāgīr* (or, to the imperial treasury when assigned to the *khāliṣa*).[9] It was therefore, different from *peshkash*, which was paid into the imperial treasury alone and, so far as our knowledge goes, was never assigned in *jāgīr*. It was, indeed, possible to require a chief to pay both, one amount as *jama*' and an additional amount as *peshkash*.[10]

Once the imperial government had exacted military service or money from the chiefs, it left them free to manage their internal affairs as they wished. For example, complaints made to the court by the subjects of chiefs are rather rare. They were free to levy cesses and duties on trade passing through their territories at rates fixed by themselves.[11] Their methods of revenue administration did not necessarily follow the regulations laid down by the imperial government. With the few exceptions noticed below, the *Ā'īn* does not set out any revenue rates or measured-area statistics for the chiefs' territories. Two of our authorities, however, offer more positive evidence on this point when, speaking of a popular uprising in favour of the deposed ruler of Kuch Bihar, they declare that the *zamīndārs* as a rule practised more flexible methods of

[8] See, for example, *Akbarnāma*, III, 533 (Kumaun), II, 360 (Palamau); *Ādāb-i 'Ālamgīrī*, I, 226-7, 231, 234-5, *Ruq'āt-i 'Ālamgīr*, 109 (Deogarh); *Ma'mūrī*, f. 179a, Khāfī Khān, II, 377; *Dilkushā*, f.139b; *Mir'āt*, I, p.25.

[9] See the detailed account of the *jama*' assessed upon Chanānerī *Deshmukh*, the ruler of Indur, as paid in different years to the *jāgīrdārs* and the *khāliṣa*, (*Ādāb-i 'Ālamgīrī*, I, 636-9). An interesting 19th-century history of the Rājas of Azamgarh declares that Rāja Harbans Singh obtained a *farmān* from Akbar, whereby the *pargana* of Nizamabad and the *tappa* of Daulatabad were granted to him in *zamīndārī* at a fixed *jama*' of Rs 60,000, which he first paid to the Khān-i Khānān ('Abdur Raḥīm), who held them in *jāgīr*; later on he and his descendants kept on paying the amount to whomsoever the territory was assigned in *jāgīr* (Edinburgh 238, folio numbers unmarked).

[10] The terms arranged with the Rāja of Nagarkot in 1573-4 ran as follows: "... Second, that he should pay a suitable *peshkash*;... Fourth, since this territory is conferred in *jāgīr* upon Rāja Bīrbar, he should be answerable to him for a large amount ..." (*Akbarnāma*, III, 36-7). When the *jama*' imposed upon him was raised substantially, Chanānerī of Indur asked to be allowed to pay the increase separately as *peshkash* and not as part of the *jama*' (*Ādāb-i 'Ālamgīrī*, I, 636-9).

[11] See *Factories, 1624-29*, 176, for Baglana; Mundy, 5, for Handiya (Malwa); ibid., 260, and *Factories, 1646-50*, 193, for Ajmer province; and *Factories, 1637-41*, 138, for Jaisalmer.

revenue collection than the imperial government.[12]

Some of the Rājpūt states seem to have been influenced considerably by the general pattern of Mughal administration. In the kingdom of Jodhpur, for example, a kind of *jāgīr* system existed. The rāja held a few villages in each *pargana* for his own treasury, while he assigned the rest in *paṭṭas*, equivalent to *jāgīrs*, to his officers in lieu of their pay.[13] Tod's account suggests that a similar system was in vogue in Mewar.[14] It even appears from the *Ā'īn* that in some Rājpūt states, especially Amber and Jodhpur, an attempt was made to copy the *ẓabṭ* method of revenue assessment established in the imperial territories.[15] But if these states copied the Mughal system, they presumably did so of their own volition. Nor was the copying ever total. Jodhpur, for example, did not have *qānūngos*, officials whose functions were vital for the working of the *jāgīr* system.[16] Nor did it enforce the *ẓabṭ*, for though it had established cash revenue rates it did not apparently come round to measuring the land, and the *Ā'īn* fails to provide area statistics for its territory.[17]

In its account of the different provinces, the *Ā'īn* often specifies the areas which were under the control of the great *zamīndārs* or *būmīs*. This can be supplemented with information derived from other sources, but the *Ā'īn's* own statistics provide us with a tool for detecting the presence of such chiefs in the various *maḥals*.[18] Where the revenue is given in round figures, it implies strongly that the *jama'* had been assessed not upon the peasants, but upon some intermediary.[19] Where, in addition, the measured area and

[12] *Fatḥiya-i 'Ibriya*, ff.47b-48a, 90; *'Ālamgīrnāma*, 781-2.

[13] See G.D. Sharma's study of the *paṭṭa* system in Marwar in his *Rājpūt Polity* (New Delhi, 1977), 118-23. Apparently the *rekh*, which Nainsī in his *Vigat* provides for practically every village, was the set of figures established by the Marwar court to enable it to assign *paṭṭas* and determine the size of contingents and service expected from the assignees. See also *Waqā'i' Ajmer*, 82, 114, where references are made to the assignment of *jāgīrs* or *paṭṭas* by Rāja Jaswant Singh. In 1690-1, in a phase of Mughal occupation of Marwar, Shujā'at Khān found it politic to give "*paṭṭas* in lieu of *jāgīrs* to most Rājpūts and *paṭṭāwats* in accordance with the ancient practice of their ancestors" (*Mir'āt*, I, 325).

[14] Tod, *Annals and Antiquities*, I, 133 and *n*.

[15] The *Ā'īn* sets out *dastūrs* or cash revenue rates under *ẓabṭ* for both Amber and Jodhpur. But in its statistical tables, measured area statistics are given for Amber, while they are omitted for Jodhpur. For Mughal influence on the revenue system in Amber, see S.P. Gupta, *Agrarian System of Eastern Rajasthan*, 163ff.

[16] *Waqā'i' Ajmer*, 163, 171. [17] See note 15.

[18] Cf. Moreland, *Agrarian System*, 268-9.

[19] It may be noted that many *maḥals* expressly stated to be under the rule of

suyurghāl figures are also omitted, it may be regarded as practically certain that the *maḥal* concerned was part of the territory of a chief.

It is not possible to give the results of our study on these lines in any detail, but the main conclusions may be stated.[20] In the great belt of the *ẓabṭī* provinces from Lahor to Bihar there is little sign of such chiefs except on the periphery. A series of petty kingdoms stretched in and along the Himalayas from Jammu to Kumaun[21] and then here and there in the Tarai further eastwards.[22] There were Balūch chiefs west of the Chenab in Multan province.[23] On the southern fringe of the plains, parts of Haryana lay under Rājpūt chiefs.[24] The southern parts of Agra, Ilahabad and Bihar provinces, where they approached the spurs of the Vindhyas, were similarly outside the sphere of direct imperial administration.[25] Speaking in general and allowing for exceptions,[26] we may, therefore, say with Pelsaert

---

chiefs, do not carry round figures for their *jama*'. This might be the result of small adjustments of which we have no knowledge.

[20] These may be compared with the findings in Ahsan Raza Khan, *Chieftains in the Mughal Empire During the Reign of Akbar,* Simla, 1977.

[21] See *Akbarnāma*, III, 533, 588. The *sarkār* of Kumaun is included in Dehli province in the *Ā'īn*: only *jama*' figures are supplied for it, all in round numbers and all palpably nominal. Cf. also Manucci, II, 438.

[22] The *sarkār* of Sambhal and *maḥals* of Kant and Gola were especially notorious for their powerful and refractory *zamīndārs* ('Abbās Khān, ff.107b-108a; Ṣādiq Khān, Or. 174, f.183b; Or. 1671, f.90a). But in the *Ā'īn* all the statistics are fully provided for this region, and it is possible that the local *zamīndārs* were not recognized as vassal chiefs. A few *maḥals* in the *sarkār* of Gorakhpur appear to belong to tributary chieftains. For the chieftaincy of Champāran in Bihar, see *Akbarnāma*, II, 136 (where the misprint "Jaitāran" is to be corrected) and Desideri, 320 ("king of Bitia").

[23] Sujān Rāi, 63; Manucci, II, 426.

[24] Some *maḥals* in Hisar *sarkār* seem, from their statistical peculiarities, to fall under this category.

[25] The *Ā'īn* ignores the Bundel kingdom of Orchha. The *sarkār* of Bath Ghora was really a kingdom in its own right (cf. Saran, *Provincial Government*, 123-4). The entries for a number of *maḥals* in the *sarkārs* of Rohtas and Bihar show that the whole country south of the plains was ruled by chiefs (see Beames in *JASB*, LIV [1885], 168, 181; for Rohtas itself, see Mundy, 167, and for Palamau, Lāhorī, II, 360-1). The *sarkār* of Mongir which, stretching from the Rajmahal Hills northward across the Ganga had a very high proportion of summarily assessed *maḥals*; Hamilton, II, 13, refers to "some impertinent troublesom Rajahs whose Territories ly on the Banks of the Ganges between Patana and Cassembuzaar".

[26] It is possible that a *maḥal* might show both area and *suyūrghāl* figures and yet have a part of it ruled by a petty *rāja* paying a fixed tribute. By a tradition already referred to, which there is no particular reason to doubt, Rāja Harbans Singh is said to have been granted the *pargana* of Nizamabad and the *tappa* of Daulatabad (in the *sarkār* of Jaunpur) at the *jama*' of Rs 60,000 (Edinburgh 238). He was a Gautamī Rājpūt and the Gautamīs are entered in the *zamīndār* column

and Manuchy that in Hindustan proper, the tracts ruled by the *rājas* and princely *zamīndārs* were usually to be found only behind mountains and forests.[27]

The statistics for Bengal in the *Āʼīn* are not given in such a form as to allow a distinction to be made between the *maḥals* under ordinary *zamīndārs* and those under real princes or kinglets. But we know that large portions of the province must have been covered by petty kingdoms.[28] To the north was Kuch Bihar,[29] to the east Kamrup and Assam;[30] the Gangetic delta contained two kingdoms[31] and beyond, to the south-east, lay the pirate-infested kingdom of Arakan.[32] It is also clear from the *maḥal* lists of the *Āʼīn* that the imperial territory extended in Orissa only to a narrow belt along the coast and a part of the Mahanadi delta.[33]

A number of *maḥals* in Ajmer province were under imperial administration, but the bulk of it was covered by the dominions of the great Rājpūt princes.[34] Tributary states also covered the entire *sarkārs* of Mandsur in Malwa and Sorath (Saurashtra) in Gujarat. The imperial territories in the latter province were ringed by a belt of states which included in the south the chieftaincy of Baglana.[35]

There was, finally, a large block of states in central India, extending from Garh with its centre near Jabalpur down to Indur

---

against Nizamabad in the *Āʼīn*. But Brahmans and "Raḥmatullāhs" are also entered as *zamīndārs* and (converting *dāms* into rupees) the *jama*ʻ of the *maḥal* is put at no less than Rs 150,515. Harbans Singh, therefore, could only have controlled a small portion of the *maḥal*.

27 Pelsaert, 58-9; Manucci, II, 444.

28 Cf. Raychaudhuri, *Bengal Under Akbar and Jahāngīr*, 17-24.

29 *Āʼīn*, I, 387. It was annexed to the Empire in 1661.

30 Ibid. Kamrup was also annexed as a result of Mīr Jumla's campaign.

31 Ibid. Also see Fitch: Ryley, 118, *Early Travels*, 27-8.

32 *Āʼīn*, I, 368. The name given to Arakan in the Persian sources is Rakhang. Chatgāon (Chittagong) was its principal port. The *sarkār* of Chatgāon appears in the statistical tables of the *Āʼīn* as if under regular imperial administration. This is explained by a passage in the *Fatḥiya-i ʻIbriya*, f.164a, where it is stated that the Sultans of Bengal had once subjugated this tract and from then on its revenue figures continued to be shown on the *qanūngos'* lists. Its *maḥals* were technically known as *pāʼibāqī-i ghair ʻamalī*, i.e. "non-revenue-paying territory, not assigned in *jāgīr*". Chatgāon was finally conquered by Shāista Khān in 1666.

33 The *Āʼīn* does not give *maḥal*-wise statistics under the *sarkārs* of Kaling Dandpat and Rajmahindra, and these were probably then claimed for the empire on paper only. Most of the other three *sarkārs*, Jalesar, Bhadrak and Katak, carry round figures for their *jama*ʻ and there are many entries under "Forts". Cf. Manucci, II, 427. See also Saran, 152-3.

34 Cf. Saran, 126-47.

35 *Āʼīn*, I, 486-93; *Mirʼāt*, Supp., 188 ff., especially 211-21 and 224-36. Kachh

in Telangana.[36] But so far as we can judge from the available records of Shāhjahān's reign,[37] western Berar and Khandesh and Aurangabad provinces did not contain any large or important tributary states.

It would appear from this outline that while the richest and most populous lands lay generally under imperial administration, the extent of the territory ruled by chiefs and princelings was not by any means negligible. Geographical barriers such as hills, forests, rivers and deserts helped to maintain whole regions under their rule. The existence of these states meant not only that there were limits to the centralized administration that the Mughal empire could impose, but also that a potential challenge to the imperial regime still remained. Moreover, the numerous *zamīndārs* within, whom the imperial government sought to reduce to the status of its servants, could, by casting a glance at the surviving princelings, still recall or imagine their own past and nurse ambitions for the future.

was also a separate kingdom. Baglana was annexed in 1638.

[36] *Ā'īn*, I, 477-82.

[37] The sources I have specially in mind here are the *Ādāb-i 'Ālamgīrī* and *Selected Documents of Shāh Jahān's Reign*, besides the chronicles.

CHAPTER VI

THE LAND REVENUE

1. MAGNITUDE OF THE LAND-REVENUE DEMAND

In Chapter III we dwelt on the fact that the conditions of life of the peasant generally approximated to the lowest possible levels of subsistence. The central feature of the agrarian system of Mughal India was that the transfer from the peasant of his surplus produce (i.e. produce above what was required for his and his family's subsistence) was largely by way of exaction of land revenue.[1] Geleynssen attributed it to the high pitch of the revenue demand that "the peasants cannot earn more than their subsistence." They are left so little, he adds, that "their share is usually consumed before it is gathered".[2] Pelsaert, while speaking of the land-revenue assignments, declared that "so much is wrung from the peasants that even dry bread is scarcely left to fill their stomachs".[3] The equation of land revenue with surplus produce, it is true, is no part of the official doctrine as expressed in the administrative documents.[4] But Abū-l Faẓl, who may well be regarded as the most authoritative exponent of imperial outlook on such matters, says frankly that no moral limits could be set to the fiscal obligation owed by the subject to the ruler: the subject ought to be thankful even if he were made to part with all his possessions by the protector of his life and honour.[5] If, then, the revenue imposed did not usually exceed the surplus produce, this was only because such a course, leading to a wholesale extermination of the revenue-payers, would have reduced, not increased, the total revenues in the longer run and thus defeated its own purpose.[6]

[1] *Ā'īn*, I, 294.

[2] Geleynssen, transl. Moreland, *JIH*, IV, 78-9. The statement refers particularly to Gujarat.

[3] Pelsaert, 54.

[4] But the equation was certainly recognized by early British administrators. Thus Holt Mackenzie, 1819, speaks of "the property (vested in government by imme-morial usage) of 10/11 of the net rental of the country" *(Revenue Selections*, 62n.).

[5] *Ā'īn*, I, 291. He adds, though, that "just sovereigns" do not exact more than what is required for their purposes, which, of course, they would themselves determine.

[6] This warning is put in the mouth of Timūr in Abū Ṭālib al-Ḥusainī's Persian translation of the so-called *Tūzuk-i Timūrī*, presented to Shāhjahān in 1637, portion

We have no means of knowing what the average size of surplus produce as a portion of the total produce was in Mughal India. Owing to the differences in the productivity of the soil and also in climatic and social conditions that determined the minimum levels of subsistence, the size must have varied from tract to tract.[7] The share that could be taken out of the peasant's produce without destroying his chances of survival must have been established by experience in each locality. If we are right in assuming that the land revenue did not normally exceed the surplus produce, its rates should have been so formulated as either to approximate to these established local rates or to remain below them. Numerous statements are found in our sources which define the land revenue as amounting to a particular portion of the total produce. Not everything, however, is straightforward in this evidence, especially when it relates to cases where, as in the *ẓabṭ* system, there was no direct relationship between the magnitude of the land-revenue demand and the actual harvest. On such points as this the findings set out in the next two sections have been freely anticipated in the following paragraphs so as to avoid here any lengthy digressions on problems connected with the various systems of revenue assessment and collection.

Abū-l Faẓl tells us that Sher Shāh framed three crop rates, and the principle he adopted was to fix the demand at one-third of the average of these rates for each crop.[8] This process was a part of

printed in *Institutes, etc., by the great Timour*, ed. and transl. Major Davy and Joseph White, 360. The heavy toll of life during famines (see Chapter III, Section 2) suggests that the contemporary idea of the part of the produce necessary for the peasant's subsistence took into account only normal times and did not allow for savings (in the form of reserve stocks of foodgrains) to provide sustenance to the peasant and his family in times of famine.

[7] It is interesting to recall here Bhīmsen's remarks about the low level of subsistence in "Karnātak" (Tamilnadu) in contrast to the extreme fertility of the soil, a state of affairs that made it possible for the *rājas* to accumulate enough wealth for building the magnificent temples he found there (*Dilkushā*, ff. 112b-113b).

[8] *Ā'īn*, I, 297-300. As Moreland has shown in a comprehensive discussion of the subject, there is the strongest presumption that the proportion of one-third for the revenue demand was inherited by Akbar from Sher Shāh's administration (*JRAS*, 1926, 452-4). Ishtiaq Husain Qureshi had insisted in his *Administration of the Sultanate of Dehli*, 2nd edn., 118-9, that Akbar raised the revenue demand from one-fourth of the produce to a third. However, in his later work, *The Administration of the Mughal Empire*, 166-7, he no longer repeats this assertion and follows Moreland's conclusions regarding the continuance of Sher Shah's "schedules" under Akbar. It therefore seems necessary no longer to repeat what was said in regard to Qureshi's earlier views in this book's first edition (191-2, n. 7).

the *ẓabṭ* system of assessment and accordingly could have been applied only in the provinces of Hindustan, i.e. the territory from Lahor to Awadh. These crop rates themselves seem, at the beginning of Akbar's reign, to have been fixed arbitrarily. They became more realistic subsequently, varying with localities, and ultimately came to be framed on the basis of the average yield worked out separately for each locality.[9] But the revenue was now fixed in cash, not kind. It is very unlikely that the prices which formed the basis for commuting the demand into cash were identical with those at which the peasant parted with his crop at the time of the harvest, when there was a glut in the market. If so, the actual imposition even on an average must have considerably exceeded one-third of the produce.[10] Furthermore, since the demand under *ẓabṭ* was based, first, on one unvaried crop rate and, then, on unvaried cash rates, the peasant was left to bear practically all the risks from the inconstancy of the harvests. Manifestly, then, the proportion of produce to be claimed as tax under *ẓabṭ* could not have been set as high as under simple crop-sharing, where the risks were evenly shared between the peasant and the state. There is nothing to show in Abū-l Faẓl's statements that the proportion of one-third also obtained under crop-sharing and *kankūt*, whenever these methods were applied within the *ẓabṭi* provinces.

Outside these provinces conditions varied considerably during Akbar's reign. In Kashmir his administration found the demand to be set in theory at one-third of the produce, but amounting in reality to two-thirds: Akbar ordered that one-half should be demanded.[11] In the province of Thatta a third was realized through crop-sharing.[12] But according to the *Maẓhar-i Shāhjahānī*, a memoir on the administration of Sind written in 1634, the Tarkhāns, who held Thatta in *jāgīr* when the *Āʾīn* was written, "did not take more than a half of the yield of the harvest from the peasantry and also took in some places a third or a fourth part," so

[9] As we shall see in the next section the revenue rates on the cash crops were determined generally in a much more arbitrary fashion.

[10] See Moosvi, 108-9, for an ingenious statistical demonstration. Khāfī Khān, I, 156, declares that Todar Mal set the demand at half the produce in the case of crops dependent upon rainfall; from fields irrigated by artificial means he took a third, if sown with foodgrains; still lower proportions were taken if the fields were sown with cash crops. But, as Moreland explains, this is apparently a late legend (*Agrarian System*, 255-8).

[11] *Āʾīn*, I, 570. Cf. also *T.J.*, 315.

[12] *Āʾīn*, I, 556.

that half the produce would really seem to have been the standard.[13] In Ajmer province, presumably in the desert regions only,[14] the proportion taken amounted to just one-seventh or one-eighth of the crop.[15]

For the next century, we have first the evidence of an accountancy manual written probably in Dehli province in the later years of Shāhjahān's reign. In the specimen assessment accounts that it contains, the rate of one-half of the produce is adopted, under *kankūt*, for all crops of the rabi harvest (e.g. cotton, barley, gram, mustard seed) excepting wheat, the rate for which is put at one-third. Under crop-sharing, applied to kharif crops (rice, pulses, rapeseed, moṭh), the rate is uniformly a third of the produce.[16] Aurangzeb's *farmān* to Rasikdās, which presumably has relevance to conditions in the central regions of the empire, recites in its preamble that when the authorities had recourse to crop-sharing, usually in the case of distressed and indigent peasantry, the proportions levied were "a half or a third or two-fifths or more or less". Towards the end of Aurangzeb's reign a manual reproducing the assessment accounts from the records of a *pargana* near Lahor shows that the proportion of one-half was there applied to wheat and barley under both *kankūt* and crop-sharing. This work also gives the *dastūrs* (revenue rates) for these two crops as well as gram.[17] These may be compared with the *dastūrs* given in the *Ā'īn* for the same circle, and the result is that, allowing for the change in the size of the *bīgha*,[18] the rates for the respective crops now

[13] *Maẓhar-i Shāhjahānī*, 51-2. In *sarkār* Sehwan Ba<u>kh</u>tyār Beg, who held it in *jāgīr* (1593-99) under Akbar, is said to have "exacted one-half of the harvest and in some parts also one-third and one-fourth and two-fifths only" (ibid., 101; see also p.121 for similar arrangements by another *jāgīrdār*, the author's own father).

[14] Most of the fertile portions of this province lay under *ẓabṭ*: the *dastūrs*, or revenue rates, given for them in the *Ā'īn* are generally as high as those elsewhere.

[15] *Ā'īn*, I, 505. [16] *Dastūru-l 'Amal-i Navīsindagī*, ff.183b-185a.

[17] *<u>Kh</u>ulāṣatu-s Siyāq*, ff.75a-76b, Or.2026, ff.24b-28a. The cash *dastūrs* in this manual are particularly deserving of confidence because they are precisely dated (rabi harvest, the 41st regnal year of Aurangzeb or 1697), and the village and *pargana* to which they relate are named. This cannot be said of the *dastūrs* given in the *Dastūru-l 'Amal-i Navīsindagī*, where the model assessment papers are purely hypothetical and bear neither a date nor an indication of their locality: the rates given are for sugarcane, tobacco and brinjal, and are patently nominal.

[18] The *bīgha* used in the *<u>Kh</u>ulāṣatu-s Siyāq* is neither the *bīgha-i Ilāhī* nor the *bīgha-i daftarī*, but one based on a *dir'a* of 48 digits (f.75a; Or. 2026, f.24b). It should therefore have been larger than the *bīgha-i Ilāhī* by 37 per cent (see Appendix A).

were 2.6, 3.2 and 1.9 times higher than in the *Ā'īn*. But since there was a general rise in agricultural prices in the interval, amounting, as indicated by another document in the same manual, to about 2.9 times in respect of wheat at Lahor,[19] no real change in the pitch of the demand would seem to have taken place.

From *ṣūba* Ajmer, Nainsī (1664) reported the land-tax to be set at half the produce under crop-sharing (*bhog ādh banṭāī*) in *pargana* Merta;[20] and it has been inferred mainly from early eighteenth-century records of the Amber rulers' *jāgīrs* that the state's share ordinarily came to 40-45 per cent of the total produce in normal years.[21]

The author of the *Maẕhar-i Shāhjahānī* says that in his time (1634) the country of Thatta could be populous if, under crop-sharing, "the *jāgīrdārs* did not take more than half ".[22] For parts of the *sarkār* of Sehwan he recommended still lower rates, but allowed half where the peasants were submissive and not exposed to raids from the hills.[23]

The other regions for which we have similar information are Gujarat and the Dakhin. Writing in 1629 Geleynssen says that the peasant in Gujarat was made to part with three-fourths of his crops.[24] Two authorities following him in the next decade modify his statement a little,[25] but in the eighth regnal year of Aurangzeb an imperial order describes the *jāgīrdārs* as demanding in theory only half, and in practice actually more than even the total yield.[26] And a little later Fryer found the peasants near Surat able to keep only a fourth of the produce for themselves.[27]

In the Dakhin, when Murshid Qulī Khān established the system of crop-sharing in the closing years of Shāhjahān's reign, he took half the produce from ordinary lands, but one-third from those irrigated by wells and still lower proportions (down to one-fourth) from high-grade crops.[28]

[19] See Chapter II, Section 3. [20] Nainsī, *Vigat*, II, 89.

[21] S.P. Gupta, *Agrarian System of Eastern Rajasthan*, 148. Gupta offers much relevant evidence on pp.59-60, 146-9, 154. Unfortunately, he omits to give the year and territory to which his Table II on p.149 relates.

[22] *Maẕhar-i Shāhjahānī*, 51.

[23] Ibid., 204, 207, 214-16, 219, 225, 229, 230 for lower rates, and 209-10, 220, 223, 227, 229 for one-half of the harvest.

[24] *JIH*, IV, 78-9.

[25] "Nearly three-quarters" (De Laet); "one half or sometimes three-quarters" (van Twist). Cf. Moreland in *JIH*, XIV, 64.

[26] *Mir'āt*, I, 263. [27] Fryer, I, 300-301. Also Hamilton, I, 148.

[28] See Section 3 of this chapter.

It is in the light of these specific instances from actual practice that we should view the dictum which becomes all-pervasive in the revenue literature of Aurangzeb's reign, in general instructions as well as orders passed on particular cases, that the land revenue should everywhere amount to half the produce. This is sometimes stated to be the maximum permissible, but most often as representing the exact amount, neither more nor less, of what was to be exacted.[29] It is probable that this repeated emphasis on the proportion of one-half was partly partly inspired, as is explicitly made clear in some of the documents themselves,[30] by a formal regard for the *Sharīat* (Muslim law), which prescribes this as the maximum for *kharāj* (land tax).[31]

It is difficult to say how far this meant a change from previous conditions. We know that in parts of Gujarat where the land was exceptionally fertile, the revenue continued to exceed the newly fixed maximum despite imperial strictures. In Kashmir, Sind and the Dakhin, ordinary lands were paying half the produce in revenue before Aurangzeb's accession, so that there the new rate simply recognized the existing practice. The real question is whether in the central provinces it implied any increase in the revenue demand. Moreland was firmly of the opinion that such an increase did occur, taking the revenue from one-third of the produce to a half.[32] But he assumed that the demand under *ẓabṭ* during Akbar's reign did not exceed one-third of the actual produce. We have

[29] *Mir'āt*, I, 263; *Farmān* to Muḥammad Hāshim, Arts 4, 6, 9 and 16; *Nigār-nāma-i Munshī*, ed., 62, 80, 92, 98, 144-5; *Durru-l 'Ulūm*, ff.42b-43a, 51a, 55a; *Khulāṣatu-l Inshā*, Or.1750, f.111a-b; *Dastūru-l 'Amal-i Āgahī*, f.28a; *Aḥkām-i 'Ālamgīrī*, f.244a-b; *Khulāṣatu-s Siyāq*, f.73b, Or.2026, f.21b; Or. 1779, ff.216a, 228a. See also Ovington, 120, speaking generally of "*Indostan*".

[30] *Nigārnāma-i Munshī*, 80, and *Khulāṣatu-l Inshā*', op. cit. The *farmān* to Muḥammad Hāshim (see especially its preamble) shows that Aurangzeb was trying to reconcile the realities of his revenue administration with the formal laws of the *Sharī'at*. Abū-l Faẓl also might have a particular injunction of the Muslim law in mind, when, speaking of "Iran and Tūrān", he says that "from ancient times they used to take one-tenth (of the produce), but often it happens that it exceeds one-half, and out of cruel-mindedness this does not appear bad to them" (*Ā'īn*, I, 293).

[31] Qāẓī Muḥammad A'lā, in early 18th century, argues that since "the kings past and present in most parts (of India) have been exacting half the produce of the land from *zimmīs* (non-Muslims)," and, taking the collection-cess and other cesses in addition thereto, the land revenue in India could not be designated *kharāj* at all, "it being forbidden to take more than half in *kharāj*" (*Risāla Aḥkām al-Arāẓī*, MSS: 'A', f.47a, 'B', f.59a).

[32] *Agrarian System*, 135. He suggests in *Akbar to Aurangzeb*, 260-61, that the revenue burden might have also increased if the demand continued to be made in

seen above that this was really not the case in practice, and the real rate came probably to much above one-third. On the other hand, there is no proof that Aurangzeb set about reformulating the *ẓabṭ* revenue rates on the basis of half of the estimated crop. The *Sharī'at* was concerned with the actual produce and not the average, or arbitrarily fixed yield on paper. Moreover, when in one instance we are able to compare cash rates from the later years of Aurangzeb with the corresponding rates in the *Ā'īn* for the same locality (Lahor), no real increase can be discerned once allowance has been made for the rise in prices during the intervening period. The proportions fixed for *kankūt* and crop-sharing under Akbar are not known, but a manual of Shāhjahān's reign sets the state's share at half in all crops, except wheat, when assessed by *kankūt*.[33] Under crop-sharing, it shows a third as the state's share,[34] but this proportion is also allowed, for crop-sharing, by Aurangzeb's *farmān* to Rasikdās. In other words, the increase postulated by Moreland is more apparent than real. It seems that from the beginning the demand was set so high that it could hardly have been increased any further. If we also take into account the other taxes imposed on the peasants and the regular and irregular exactions of officials and others, we can visualize what a heavy burden was borne by the peasantry. If the authorities were simply to insist on all their rights, to collect the full authorized demand and arrears and to refuse to offer relief at proper times, the amount realized by them could even cross the danger mark and encroach upon what was essential for the peasant's subsistence. But with this we are not immediately concerned, and the question whether there was an increase in extreme oppression of this kind may be deferred to the last chapter.

2. METHODS OF LAND-REVENUE ASSESSMENT

Like any organized system of taxation, the land-revenue arrangements of the Mughal administration consisted mainly of two stages: first, assessment (*tashkhīṣ*) and, then, the actual collection (*taḥṣīl*). The term *jama'* signified the amount assessed as opposed to *ḥāṣil*, the amount collected.[1] In accordance with the great seasonal division

---

dāms which greatly appreciated in value in relation to silver in the 17th century. This point is discussed in Section 5 of this chapter.

[33] *D. Navīsindagi*, ff.182a-184b. [34] Ibid., f.185a.

[1] In accountancy *jama'* is also used for "receipts" and thus stands opposite to *kharj* or *kharch*, expenditure. Cf. Moreland, *Agrarian System*, 212-15.

of the agricultural year in India, the assessment was separately made for the kharif (autumn) and rabi (spring) harvests. When the revenue had been assessed, the authorities issued a written document called *paṭṭa, qaul* or *qaul-qarār,* setting out the amount or rate of the revenue demand. At the same time, the assessee gave, in acknow-ledgement, his *qabūliyat,* or "acceptance", of the obligation imposed upon him, stating when and how he would pay the tax.[2]

The assessment was made by various methods, which deserve careful study. This section will be devoted to defining and describing the main features of these methods separately, leaving to the next a survey of their application in the different territories of the empire.

To begin rather negatively, the practice we consider first is not really a method of assessment, but of collection in such a manner as to dispense with assessment. This is crop-sharing, in Persian termed *g͟halla-bak͟hshī*, and in Hindī and allied languages *baṭāī* and *bhāolī*. The *Ā'īn* distinguishes three types of sharing. The first consisted of the division of the crop at the threshing floor "in the presence of both the parties, in accordance with the agreement (*qarār-dād*)". This seems to have been regarded as the proper form of *baṭāī*. The second was *khet baṭāī,* the division of the field or the standing crops; and the third, *lāng baṭāī*, where the crop after being cut was stacked in heaps, which were then divided.[3] Crop-sharing is described in an official document as the "best method of revenue collection";[4] it was, perhaps, generally preferred by the peasants because they were enabled to share the risks of the season with the authorities. It was regarded as best suited to such villages

[2] *Farhang-i Kārdānī*, ff.34a-35a; *Durru-l 'Ulūm*, f.62a; *Siyāqnāma*, 29-30; *K͟hulāṣatu-s Siyāq*, ff.73b-75a, Or.2026, ff.22b-24b. The *Farhang-i Kārdānī*, *Siyāqnāma* and *K͟hulāṣatu-s Siyāq* also reproduce specimens of these documents. Allahabad 177, 897, 1206 and 1223 are *paṭṭas* or *qaul-qarārs* and are so described in their headings. Allahabad 1220 has no heading but is a *qabūliyat*. All of these belong to the reign of Aurangzeb.

The *Ā'īn*, I, 286, refers to the '*amalguzār* (revenue official) exchanging papers with the peasants on making his assessment, but does not enter into any particulars.

[3] *Ā'īn*, I, 286. What is meant by the last method is probably that the crop was stacked by the peasants in equal heaps, and the revenue collector chose a number of these, proportionate to the state's share.

The *Farhang-i Kārdānī*, f.33a (Edinburgh 83, f.55a), distinguishes *g͟halla-bak͟hshī* from a practice which it calls *pola-bandī*. But it seems to have been only a particular form of crop-sharing in which the authorities arranged for the reaping and threshing of the harvest and took the state's share out of the threshed grain.

[4] *Nigārnāma-i Munshī*, ed., 76.

or peasants as were suffering from exceptional distress.[5] For the administration it was a good method of checking the productive capacity of a village where the standing assessment gave cause for doubt.[6] It was also profitable when grain fetched high prices in the market.[7] The main objection from the official point of view, as stated by Abū-l Faẓl, was that "this requires a large number of alert watchmen, otherwise the ill-starred ones soil their dishonest hands with misappropriation".[8] It was, therefore, an expensive method; and Aurangzeb declared that when it was introduced in the Dakhin the costs of revenue collection doubled simply from the necessity of organizing a watch on the crops.[9]

Among the methods of assessment, the most summary one was known as *hast-o-būd*: the assessor inspected the village and viewing good and bad lands together made an estimate of the total produce, on the basis of which he fixed the revenue.[10] Another method, nearly as summary, was simply to count the ploughs and assess the revenue by applying to them rates fixed according to localities.[11]

The defects in these two practices are obvious. In the first, all would depend on the personal capacity and integrity of the assessor, and the second would have resulted in an extremely uneven distribution of the revenue demand. To some extent these defects were mitigated in a more developed system known as *kankūt* or *dānabandī*.[12] It is very clearly described in the *Ā'īn* and other authorities and seems to have consisted of two stages. In the

[5] Aurangzeb's *Farmān* to Rasikdās, Preamble.

[6] Both when it was too heavy (*Nigārnāma-i Munshī*, ed., 76, 98) or too light (*Aḥkām-i 'Ālamgīrī*, ff.244a-b).

[7] *Farhang-i Kārdānī*, f.32b; Edinburgh 83, f.35a.

[8] *Ā'īn*, I, 28b, Cf. *Nigārnāma-i Munshī*, ed., 76, 98, *Farhang-i Kārdānī*, op. cit. Bekas, f.71b, quotes a Hindī proverb, "*baṭāī* is *luṭāī*", crop-sharing is loot.

[9] *Ādāb-i 'Ālamgīrī*, Or.177, f.118a. This letter is missing in the printed ed.

[10] *Farhang-i Kārdānī*, f.32b, Edinburgh 83, f.35a. Add.6603, f.84a, defines *hast-o-būd* as "what is being currently cultivated and grown: when the *ḥākim* [claimant to revenue] is capable, the *zamīndār* says: 'Assess my place according to *hast-o-būd*'." For the meaning of *hast-o-būd* as whatever is actually available, see *Bahār-i 'Ajam*, s.v. *hast-o-būd kardan*.

[11] This prevailed in the Dakhin and has been described by Ṣādiq Khān, Or.174, f.185a-b, Or.1671, f.90b; Khāfī Khān, I, 732n.

[12] Abū-l Faẓl explains, with a careful spelling of the term, that *kan* means grain and *kūt*, appraisal or estimate (*Ā'īn*, I, 285; cf. Fallon, s.v. *kan*, *kūt*; also Maya Singh, *Panjabi Dictionary*, s.v. *kan*, *kankūt*, *kanoī*). That is, a system where the grain yield (or more properly, the crop rate) was estimated. *Dāna* means grain and *bandī*, when forming part of compounds, is used in revenue literature in the general sense of fixing or determining anything, as in *jama'bandī*.

first, the land was measured either by means of a rope (*jarīb*) or by pacing.[13] After this the yield of each crop per unit of area, i.e. the crop rate, was estimated and applied to the whole area under the crop. If the assessor found it difficult to fix the crop rate on the basis of observation only, he was required to make three sample cuttings, from good, middling and bad lands, and on the basis of these make his estimate.[14] As Abū-l Faẕl tells us, an important feature of *kankūt* was that the demand was primarily assessed not in cash, but in kind.[15] Thus in the specimen *kankūt* papers we find, first, the assessment of the full crop (on the basis of the crop rates); then from this the "share of the peasantry" is deducted. Finally, the remaining portion, representing the revenue, is commuted into cash by applying a schedule of prices for the various crops.[16]

[13] *Ā'īn*, I, 285; *Khulāṣatu-s Siyāq*, f.76a, Or.2026, f.27a; Bekas, f.70a-b. Cf. Add. 6603, f.71b. The fact that measurement of the area was an essential part of this system appears also from the specimen tables in *Dastūru-l 'Amal-i Navīsindagī*, ff.182a-185a, and *Khulāṣatu-s Siyāq*, ff.75a-76b; Or.2026, ff.24b-28a. In the former the area is given in terms of *bīghas*; the *Khulāṣatu-s Siyāq* prescribes *kanāls*, being units of "the Indian scale of measures" (*ẕabṯ-i Hindī*), but these were used only in the Panjab.

[14] *Ā'īn*, I, 285-6. It says that with practised eyes the estimate on sight used to be quite accurate. Cf. *Khulāṣatu-s Siyāq*, f.76a, Or.2026, f.27a. Bekas, ff.70b-71a, prescribes two methods for estimating the crop rate: one involved sample cuttings in two plots chosen respectively by the assessor and the peasants; the other called for weighing the grain in one corn heap (and setting it against the area of the field from which it had been cut?).

How the crop rates were applied to the area under each crop is illustrated by the *kankūt* tables in the *Dastūru-l 'Amal-i Navīsindagī*, ff.182a-185a, the *Khulāṣatu-s Siyāq*, ff.75a-76b, Or.2026. ff.24b-28a. No crop is listed twice in the table in the *Dastūru-l 'Amal-i Navīsindagī*, but in the *Khulāṣatu-s Siyāq* table we have two wheat fields assessed according to different crop rates, 4 and 4.3 *mans* per *kanāl*. The implication obviously is that it was necessary to fix different rates if in a village some fields happened to be more fertile or better irrigated than others.

Another interesting point about these *kankūt* tables is that they do not carry a column for *nābūd*, the deduction from the total measured area on account of crop failure, which is found in all *ẕabṯ* tables. This is probably because the crop rates under *kankūṭ* were fixed at the time of the harvest for each village (or even field) and it was expected that an allowance for crop failure would have been made in the crop rates themselves.

[15] *Ā'īn*, I, 285-6: The '*amalguzār* "should not make it a habit to take cash only and should collect grain also. And that consists of various methods (*bar chand gūna buwad*): *kankūt* ... *baṭāī*...".

[16] See the tables in *Dastūru-l 'Amal-i Navīsindagī*, ff.182a-185a, and *Khulāṣatu-s Siyāq*, ff.75a-76b, Or.2026, ff.24b-28a. The prices were (or were supposed to be) those prevailing in the market. Cf. *Ā'īn*, I, 286: "If it is not burdensome to the peasantry, let him (the '*amalguzār*) commute the share of the crop into cash at

It will be seen that the *kankūt* system resembled crop-sharing in being based upon the actual yield of the harvest, but was far less expensive since it required no watch to be kept on the reaping and threshing of the crop. It was also obviously far more efficient and accurate than either of the other two practices we have considered. Nevertheless, in requiring the assessor himself to determine the crop rates, it allowed him a very high degree of latitude. It was perhaps a wish to divest him of this power that induced the governor of Bhakkar in 1575-76 to fix "the revenue, under the system of *kankūt*, uniformly at five *mans* per *bīgha*".[17] Here the element of local seasonal appraisement disappears altogether and we are on the borderline of the sphere of *ẓabṭ*.

The word *ẓabṭ* is assigned a technical meaning in Indian revenue literature which is not to be found in the dictionaries.[18] It is taken to be synonymous with *jarīb* or *'amal-i-jarīb* and to signify measurement as well as the assessment based upon it.[19] We thus hear of *kankūt* as *ẓabṭ-i kankūt* since it took account of the area of the assessed land.[20] But the *ẓabṭ* was in its own right a distinct mode of assessment.[21]

The evolution of the main features of this system can be traced best in the *Ā'īn*. Sher Shāh and Islām Shāh are said to have brought Hindustan under *ẓabṭ*.[22] We are told that Sher Shāh established a *rai'*, or crop rate,[23] for lands which were under continuous cultivation (*polaj*) or were only very rarely allowed to lie fallow (*parauṭī*).

market prices". From the context it would seem that this statement applies to crop-sharing (*baṭāī*) as well as *kankūṭ*.

[17] Ma'ṣūm, *Tārīkh-i Sind*, 245.

[18] Cf. *Agrarian System*, 235. *Ẓabṭ* is not listed in the glossary of revenue terms in Lambton's *Landlord and Peasant in Persia*. *Ẓābiṭ* is there (443) defined as "revenue collector, controller; bailiff", which sense is probably derived from the literal meaning of *ẓabṭ*, "confiscation, sequestration".

[19] This sense is established from Abū-l Faẓl's use of the word in many contexts. Cf. Moreland, *Agrarian System*, 235 and *passim*. It is invariably used with the narrow connotation of measurement in a passage about the calculation of the area of the fields of many sizes in *Khulāṣatu-s Siyāq*, f.75a, Or.2026, f.24b. Add.6603, f.71b, defines *ẓabṭ* as "the measurement of the area (*muḥīṭ-bandī*) of anything".

[20] *Dastūru-l 'Amal-i Navīsindagī*, f.182a; *Dastūru-l 'Amal-i 'Ālamgīrī*, f.105b; Bekas, f.70a. See also the definition of *kankūt* in the *Khulāṣatu-s Siyāq*, f.76a, Or.2026, f.27a, where the assessor is asked to "(first) bring the land under *ẓabṭ*".

[21] For reference to *ẓabṭ* and *kankūt* as separate systems, *Ā'īn*, I, 285, *Khulāṣatu-s Siyāq*, f.74a, Or.2026, f.22b; *Farhang-i Kārdānī*, f.32b, Edinburgh 83, f.35a. In Aurangzeb's *farmān* to Rasikdās (Preamble) the distinction is duly made between *'amal-i jarīb* and *kankūt*.

[22] *Ā'īn*, I, 296.

[23] The dictionary definition of the word *rai'* as given in the *Ghiyāṣu-l Lughāt*,

The *rai'* was based on three rates, representing good, middling and low yields. These were averaged to obtain a general rate for the produce, and a third of this was recognized as the "remuneration of sovereignty", i.e. land revenue. We are provided with a long table of rates per *bīgha* for the various crops of the rabi and kharif harvests,[24] which may be assumed to represent the *rai's* of Sher Shāh.[25] Akbar accepted and sanctioned these rates apparently for the whole of his dominions at the beginning of his reign; and in a statement made later on in the *Ā'īn* it seems implied that not only the crop rates, but also the proportion thereof assigned to revenue, was inherited by him from the Sūr administration.[26]

The rate in kind however did not directly express the revenue demand but had to be commuted into cash for "the benefit of the army", i.e. the *jāgīrdārs*.[27] Abū-l Faẓl says that it was the practice from the early years of Akbar's reign for the details of the prices to be reported each year from every region of the Empire; these were then examined and approved by the court, the *rai's* being thereupon converted at the sanctioned prices into cash rates, known as *dastūru-l 'amals* or simply *dastūrs*.[28] The annual *dastūrs* for the

---

s.v., is: "... whatever is obtained from cultivation; the revenue (*maḥṣūl*) from cultivation for the sovereign; the rate on taxable possessions." It might thus mean the rate of both produce and revenue. Abū-l Faẓl seems to have used it in the sense of both the crop rate and the revenue rate in kind. It is clearly the first sense he has in mind, when he says of the Iranian emperor Nausherwān that, having fixed a certain area as equivalent to a *jarīb*, he "determined the *rai'* thereof to be one *qafīz* (measure of bulk) at the value of three *dirhams*. And he took one-third of it as revenue" (*Ā'īn*, I, 292-3). Elsewhere, however, in defining *māl* or land revenue, he explains that it is "fixed on the cultivated area by way of *rai'*" (*Ā'īn*, I, 294), and here the sense of revenue rate in kind would better suit the context. At another place still he speaks of the "formulation of the *rai'* of Kashmir", by which he means the rate of revenue in kind taken from each *paṭṭa* of land under different crops (*A.N.*, III, 548-9).

[24] *Ā'īn*, I, 497-300. [25] Cf. Moreland in *JRAS*, 1926, 454ff.

[26] *Ā'īn*, I, 300. It is stated at the end of the *rai'* schedules that "the enlightened emperor sanctioned the *māl* (revenue) as set out above".

[27] *Ā'īn*, I, 297.

[28] *Ā'īn*, I, 303, 347; *A.N.*, 282-3. For certain crops like muskmelon, *ajwā'in*, onion and other vegetables in the rabi harvest, and indigo, poppy, *pān*, turmeric, *singhāṛa*, hemp, etc., among the kharif crops, no *rai'* had been prepared, the *dastūru-l 'amals* being directly fixed in cash (*Ā'īn*, I, 298, 300).

Dastūru-l 'amal should, as a word, mean regulation for guiding executive work (cf. Add.6603, ff.61b-62a), and thus many administrative manuals are styled *dastūru-l 'amals*. But *'amal* also bore the sense of revenue collection (whence *'āmil*, revenue collector), so that the use of this term for revenue rates was not inappropriate.

various crops in each of the *ẓabṭī* provinces (except Ajmer and Bihar), for "Nineteen Years", running from the 6th to 24th regnal years (1561-80), have been tabulated in the *Ā'īn*.[29] In these extensive tables, the figures for regnal years 6 to 9 in all provinces (except Malwa) are, for each crop, either identical or nearly so; moreover, there is no, or only a very slight, change in the *dastūrs* from year to year.[30] We must, therefore, assume that in the beginning there was not only a single *rai'* for the empire, but also, for all practical purposes, a single price schedule applied each year in all the regions with only small modifications.

It is difficult to imagine how these uniform rates could at any time have been imposed upon the peasants of such a large area as that extending from Lahor to Awadh. One can only regard them as essentially paper rates. Abū-l Faẓl recognizes that "much distress used to occur" from the promulgation of the *dastūrs* in the early years of the reign and immediately goes on to explain that the *jama'* or general assessment at that time, known as the *jama'-i raqamī*, was greatly inflated, and in individual cases the assignments were either greatly over- or under-assessed.[31] Moreland, who is fundamentally correct in his appreciation of the nature of this *jama'*, does not appear to see any direct connexion between it and the *dastūrs*.[32] But unless Abū-l Faẓl's reference to it in the context of the *dastūrs* is an irrelevant digression, it would be natural to suppose that the *jama'* was inflated to some extent precisely because it was derived from an estimate of total revenue collection based upon these unreal cash rates. Akbar's administration must have inherited some record of measured areas from the archives of the Sūrs and the *dastūrs* could have easily been multiplied by these to yield the *jama'* for each locality. But since the *dastūrs* themselves were uniform and bore little relation to local productivity or price fluctuations, the widest discrepancies must have existed between the actual revenue-paying capacity of the peasants of an area and the *jama'* at which the area was assigned

[29] "*Ā'īn-i Nuwazdah-sāla*" in *Ā'īn*, I, 303-47. The provinces covered are Agra, Ilahabad, Awadh, Dehli, Lahor, Multan and Malwa. The tables under Ajmer are left blank. Nothing is said about the *dastūrs* of Bihar in the *Ā'īn*, though much of the province is stated to have been under *ẓabṭ*.

[30] The uniformity of the figures appears even greater in the tables as given in MSS Add. 7652 and Add. 6552 than in Blochmann's edition.

[31] *Ā'īn*, I, 347. For *jama'i raqamī* see Chapter VII, Section 1.

[32] *Agrarian System*, 242.

to the *jāgīrdārs*. Moreover, it seems, the area statistics could be manipulated, for Abū-l Faẓl says that the *jama'* could be increased by a stroke of the pen in order to meet salary claims.[33]

The absence alike of enforceable revenue rates and reliable area statistics may explain the nature of the measures taken in the 11th year of the reign (1566-7) under the direction of Muẓaffar Khān and Todar Mal.[34] "They obtained the local area and revenue statistics (*taqsīms*) of the country[35] from the *qānūngos*. Leaving the

[33] *Ā'īn*, I, 347.

[34] In the *Ā'īn*, I, 347, the year given is the 15th and this reading is supported by the best MSS. But *pānzdahum* (15th) in Persian writing is easily interchangeable with *yāzdahum* (11th) and it is possible that the confusion took place at an early stage in the transcription of the work. The testimony of the *Akbarnāma* on this point must be regarded as decisive since it follows a strictly chronological arrangement and places this event under the 11th year (*A.N.*, II, 270). Moreland in *Agrarian System*, 246-7, tries to reconcile the two dates by suggesting that the work began in the 11th year and finished in the 15th, a view supported by neither text.

[35] "*Taqsīmat-i mulk*". The papers known by the name *taqsīm* (plural, *taqsīmāt*) are referred to in the manuals of the 17th century. They are stated to be the same as the *muwāzana-i dah-sāla* papers (*Dastūru-l 'Amal-i 'Ālamgīrī*, f.36b; *Siyāqnāma*, 100; and *Khulāṣatu-s Siyāq*, f.74a, Or.2026, f.23a). Under the heading "*Muwāzana-i dah-sāla*, which they also call *taqsīm-i sanwāt* ('*taqsīm* of [past] years')," the *Dastūru-l 'Amal-i 'Ālamgīrī* sets out the main items of information which these papers contained. The contents included the *mujmil*, the summary account of revenue realized and local expenditure (cf. *Khulāṣatu-s Siyāq*, f.82b. Or.2026, f.38b); particulars of the land revenue and other taxes (*māl-o-sā'ir*); details of the number of villages in the *pargana*; and, finally, area statistics. The last gave the area of uncultivated land (specifying separately what lay under habitation, tanks, gardens, nullahs and forest) and, then, the area of cultivated land. This is followed by a heading giving the title of another document, *taqsīm-i yak-sāla*, "the *taqsīm* of one [the immediately preceding?] year". This provided information about the land revenue levied on the area cultivated by the peasantry, the taxes on gardens and trades, the *nānkār* and *madad-i ma'āsh* lands, etc. The *Hidāyatu-l Qawā'id*, f.10a-b, Aligarh MS. ff.27b-28a, confirms that revenue and area, and certainly the latter, were the main items of information which the *taqsīm* or *muwāzana-i dah-sāla* (terms which it uses interchangeably) contained. The *amīn* or revenue assessor, it says, ought to "compare the actual area with that recorded in the papers of the *qānūngo*. If the area corresponds with it, it is all right; but if it exceeds that of the *taqsīm*, let him demand an explanation from the *qānūngo*, etc." The sense of *taqsīm(āt)* thus brought out in revenue literature is confirmed by the endorsement on the reverse of a *farmān* of Jahāngīr (1610). Here the given area of the village whose revenues were granted away, is stated to be derived from the *qānūngo's taqsīm* (*az-qarār-i taqsīm-i qānūngoī*) (*Asnādu-ṣ Ṣanādīd*, 32). See also the actual sheets of *taksīm daih-sālā* papers in Rajasthani, for *pargana* Udehi, giving data of area and revenue for years 1650-5 to 1664-6 village-wise, reproduced in Gupta and Khan, 308-20. Moreland, who was not aware of the use of *taqsīm* in 17th-century revenue literature, interpreted it to mean "local schedules" or revenue

maḥṣūl (produce or revenue)[36] to appraisement and estimate, a fresh *jama'* was brought into being."[37] It seems that it was this summary way of determining the yield or crop rates that was responsible for the defects of the new *jama'*, which is said to have been still "far away" from the actual revenue received (*ḥāṣil*). But a change is at the same time noticeable from the tenth year (1565-66) onwards in the "Nineteen-Years" tables of the *Ā'īn*. The differences among the rates of different provinces, and among the rates of each province in different years, now become very pronounced. Moreover, the rates are often expressed in two, maximum and minimum, figures, representing the range of divergence in the rates for each crop promulgated within the province for different localities. It seems certain that new local crop rates had now been worked out and that henceforth the price schedules were drawn up afresh every year, separately for each locality. It may be assumed that these changes were the result of the measure undertaken by Muẓaffar Khān and Todar Mal to work out new revenue rates with a view to instituting a new *jama'*.[38]

As the *dastūrs* approached closer to actual conditions, the administration was probably able to enforce them to some extent for determining the revenue demand upon the peasants. Abū-l Faẓl now comments on the distress caused by the annual commutation

---

rates, deriving it from the term *qismat* which meant the apportionment of the produce between the state and the peasants (*Agrarian System*, 244-5) I.H. Qureshi seems sure that *taqsīm* meant "schedules of produce" and he refers us to Baranī's phrase *qismāt-i būd o nābūd*, of which, he thinks, *taqsīm* is "another version". (*Journal of Pakistan Historical Society*, I, iii, 212; *Administration of the Mughal Empire*, 269-71). But *qismāt* meant taxes or cesses (see I. Habib in *Cambridge Economic History of India*, I, 63 and n., where the evidence is cited), and not documents or records of any kind.

36 The word *maḥṣūl* is used by Abū-l Faẓl as well as other authorities in two senses. First, in that of produce as, for instance, in the reference to the "carrying away of the *maḥṣūl*" by the peasants in *Ā'īn*, I, 286, or even more clearly in the passage concerning Sher Shāh's *rai'* (ibid., 297-8). It is also used with the same significance in Aurangzeb's *farmān* to Muḥammad Hāshim, Arts. 11 and 14. We have the second sense of revenue clearly indicated, however, when the *bitikchī* is asked to record the *jama'* on each peasant and, having totalled the amounts, to arrive at the *maḥṣūl* of the village (*Ā'īn*, I, 288). See also Todar Mal's recommendations (*A.N.*, III, 382). It is similarly used in 'Abbās Khān, f.10b; Aurangzeb's *farmān* to Rasikdās, Preamble; and Khāfī Khān, I, 156.

37 *Ā'īn*, I, 347.

38 The interpretation offered here is in some respects materially different from that of Moreland, *Agrarian System*, 86-7, 245-7. He links this measure with the change discernible in the rates in the 15th year and calls the rates from this year onwards "Qanungo Rates".

of the *rai'* into cash rates. The empire had greatly expanded, he says, and long delays used to occur in the communication of the local price reports to the court and the sanctioning of the revenue rates thereafter. As a result sometimes the peasants complained that more had been taken from them (in the interval) than was ultimately sanctioned and sometimes the *jāgīrdārs* protested about the balances of revenues left unrealized, owing presumably to the delay in receiving the approved rates.[39] "Moreover, it became notorious that some of the price-reporters had deviated from the path of uprightness."[40]

The remedy which was finally adopted for this state of affairs is linked up in both the *Ā'īn* and the *Akbarnāma* with the preparation, in the 24th year (1579-80), of the *Jama'-i Dah-sāla*, "the *Jama'* of Ten Years". Although the discussion of this general assessment should be left properly to Chapter VII, it is so intimately connected with the evolution of the final *dastūrs* that it seems necessary to enter some remarks upon it here. Moreland believed that the *Jama'-i Dah-sāla* was instituted simply by averaging the total revenue demand actually levied upon the peasants in the preceding ten years.[41] But it is difficult to see how this can be maintained when we are distinctly told by Abū-l Faẓl that "the essence of this innovation is that having ascertained the ten years' state (*ḥāl-i dah-sāla*) of every *pargana* in regard to the categories of cultivation and the levels of prices, they fixed the tenth part thereof as the annual revenue (*māl-i har-sāla*)".[42] It would have been entirely irrelevant to obtain information about the produce and prices if the object was only to discover the actual revenue receipts of the previous decade. Ordinary revenue accounts, like the *taqsīms*, should have sufficed. Moreland seems to rely mainly upon the passage in the *Ā'īn*, where it is declared that the process consisted first of ascertaining the *maḥṣūl-i dah-sāla* and then striking an average to obtain the (*maḥṣūl-i*?) *har-sāla*.[43] *Maḥṣūl* is however used by Abū-l Faẓl in the sense of both revenue and produce.[44] From a later administrative manual we learn that the papers called *dah-sāla* contained area statistics of each *maḥal* and

[39] *Ā'īn*, I, 348; *A.N.*, III, 282. In the *Ā'īn* the peasants are said to have "demanded justice" against *afzūn khwāhī*, i.e. collection in excess of the authorized demand. The corresponding word in the *Akbarnāma* is *fāẓil* (surplus collection). The *jāgīrdārs* (called here *iqṭā'dārs*) conversely complained against *baqāyā*, or revenue lying in arrears.

[40] *A.N.*, op. cit. [41] *Agrarian System*, 96-7, 249-54. [42] *A.N.*, III, 282-3.

[43] *Ā'īn*, I, 348. [44] See note 36 on the word *maḥṣūl*.

the areas given in the *har-sāla* papers were based on this record.[45] It is, therefore, probable that the investigations were not confined to ascertaining what had been exacted before, but were also aimed at establishing the area as well as the productivity of the different districts. Since information for prices was also called for, what seems to have been done was to work out the crop rates retrospectively for a locality for each year and then simultaneously prepare a parallel schedule of prices, so that the cash revenue rate for each of the previous years could be determined. These data were doubtless far more difficult to collect than records of revenue realization. We are told that information for "the twentieth year to the twenty-fourth [1575-6 to 1579-80], they obtained by way of actual knowledge (*taḥqīq*) and (of) the five preceding (years) (15th-19th) from the representations of truthful men".[46] This has obvious reference to the changes brought about in the 19th year (1574-75) when the whole of Hindustan (excluding Bihar) was resumed to the *khāliṣa* (where the revenue was collected directly for the imperial treasury) and placed fully under *ẓabṭ*. The new revenue collectors (*kaṛoṛīs*) were reputed to be charged especially with the task of extending cultivation;[47] and it is not improbable that this was associated with the detailed agricultural information they were required to supply. To sum up, our evidence suggests that a new crop rate or *rai'*, averaged from the actual rates for the harvests of the previous ten years, was first instituted for each locality.[48] The average of the cash rates of the previous ten years, based upon this and the known prices, produced the final or permanent *dastūru-l'amals*. This offers the best explanation of why Abū-l Faẓl should put on the chapter introducing the tables of the final *dastūrs,* the title *Ā'īn-i Dah-sāla*, "the *Ā'īn* of Ten Years".

[45] *Hidāyatu-l Qawā'id*, f.10b. Aligarh MS, ff.27b-28a. The *dah-sāla* and *har-sāla* papers of this manual are apparently identical with the *muwāzana-i dah-sāla* (*taqsīm-i sanwāt*) and *taqsīm-i yak-sāla*, respectively. The work itself once mentions *taqsīm* in place of *dah-sāla*. See note 35 above, where the synonymity of *taqsīm* with *muwāzana-i dah-sāla*, as revenue and area record, is discussed.

The *Ā'īn*, I, 288, speaks of *muwāzana-i dah-sāla-i naqdī o jinsī*. This shows at least that in addition to carrying information about revenue in cash (*naqdī*), it also gave some data on produce (*jinsī*). It is also quite possible that, by the latter, information on the areas under various crops is meant.

[46] *Ā'īn*, I, 348.

[47] 'Ārif Qandahārī, 177; *Ṭabaqāt-i Akbarī*, II 300-1; Badāūnī, II, 189.

[48] Abū-l Faẓl probably has in mind the crop rates thus established in the various regions, when he says, with reference to Sher Shāh's *rai'*, that "today they do not indicate any [*rai'*] lower than that in any of the provinces" (*Ā'īn*, I, 297).

The multiplication of the average area figures by these *dastūrs* could provide the figures for the *Jama'-i Dah-sāla*.[49]

The closing passage of the chapter *Ā'īn-i Dah-sāla* shows that in determining the final *dastūrs* for some crops an exception was made from the general rule. This passage has been variously interpreted, but the following rendering, for reasons given in the footnote, seems to be the most plausible: "And, further, the revenue [rate] on the high-grade crops exhibited reliability; they selected [lit., 'took up'] the year when it was greater. It is accordingly shown in the table."[50] The last sentence must refer to

[49] Moreland (*Agrarian System*, 87-9, 251-4) believes that while the *Jama'-i Dah-sāla* was averaged from the actual revenue receipts of the previous ten years, the *dastūrs* were probably averaged from the cash rates as actually promulgated in the previous decade. But should we accept his interpretation of the text of the "*Ā'īn-i Dah-sāla*", Abū-l Faẓl would be guilty here of speaking incoherently and irrelevantly to a surprising degree. We see that he repeatedly describs evils the cure for which was the formulation of permanent cash rates; and yet when he comes to the point of describing the remedy, he is supposed by Moreland to speak of something completely different, viz. the *Jama'-i Dah-sāla*.

[50] *Ā'īn*, I, 348. Blochmann's text was amended by Moreland, after collating several MSS, to read as follows: "*Wa nez māl-i jins-i kāmil i'tibār namūd. Sāle ki afzūn būd bar-giriftand. Chunānchi jadwal ān-rā barguzārad.*" Blochmann had read the first three words as *wa bar sāl* . The MSS are by no means in agreement here; but the best of them support Moreland's reading. Add.6552 agrees with it completely and so does Berlin MS Hamilton 1, which is of an equally early date (information about the latter MS kindly supplied to me by Mr. B.R. Grover). Add. 7652 and its copy I.O. 6 read *wa har māl-i*, etc., which means that the presence of the word *māl* is at least definitely established. *Jins-i kāmil* is used by Abū-l Faẓl and by all other authorities in the sense of high-grade crops (e.g. *Ā'īn*, I, 286; Aurangzeb's *farmān* to Rasikdās, Preamble; Add.6603, f.57a). The phrase *i'tibār namūd* looks awkward at first sight and the *Bahār-i 'Ajam* (s.v. *i'tibār*), despite five quotations, does not supply any example of the use of the verb *namūdan* with *i'tibār*. But the rendering given by us is justified by the literal senses of the two words and by a similar phrase found in the *Ā'īn*, I, 26, when it is stated that though the rate of *dāms* to the rupee "gets sometimes above and sometimes below forty *dāms*, yet in payment of salaries this value is given credit (*īn qīmat i'tibār rawad*)".

Leaving aside Jarrett's translation, which in any case must be entirely superseded, we have Moreland's translation of the three sentences: "And also taking into account the (figures known as) *māl-i jins-i kāmil* 'they' took the year which was greatest, as the table shows" (*Agrarian System*, 249). The expression *māl-i jins-i kāmil* he interprets as meaning "Demand" on high-grade crops, i.e. not the revenue rate applied to the crops, but the total amount of revenue levied on the area under them. *Māl* is admittedly open to both the meanings of revenue and revenue rate, but the rendering of *afzūn* in the sense of "greatest" and the explanation of the "greatest" as the year of the maximum revenue, for which in fact there was a definite technical term, *sāl-i kāmil* or *sāl-i ḥāṣil-i kāmil*, seems a little strained. Moreover, if what Abū-l Faẓl is here speaking about relates to *jama'* and

the tables of the *dastūrs* which now follow. The whole passage may be read with the statement made earlier in the *Ā'īn* that no *rai's* had been prepared for such crops as indigo, poppy, *pān* (betel leaf), turmeric, hemp, etc., for which the revenue rates had been directly formulated in terms of cash.[51] In addition, the thick or *paunḍa* sugarcane seems to have been omitted from the *rai'* list.[52] Perhaps the yield of these crops was liable to such fluctuations every harvest[53] that no crop rate could be fixed that might be of any practical use. What Abū-l Faẓl means is, then, probably, that

---

not the *dastūrs*, the reference to the "table" become pointless, for the tables that follow are not of *jama'*, but of *dastūrs*. This Moreland counters by supposing that a great editorial reshuffling of materials took place after the first draft of the *Ā'īn* had been prepared: there were originally *jama'* tables here, but they were later on removed (ibid., 251-3). But there are no "signs of hasty editing" in the *Ā'īn*; and an error of the magnitude, with which Moreland would credit it, cannot be lightly assumed.

We have, then, the interpretation originally given by Ishtiaq Husain Qureshi in *Jour. Pak. Hist. Soc.*, I, 215-6 with a revised version in his *Administration of the Mughal Empire*, 269-79, the latter partly in response to my criticisms of the former made in this note in the first edition (208-9n.). He takes *jins-i kāmil* to mean "the full produce which has not been affected by calamity or loss", a meaning never heard of in revenue literature; and he takes *afzūn* to mean "superfluous", not greater. From this he infers that *maḥṣūl*, or "medium" produce (this being the meaning he adopts for it), was averaged every year from the total produce harvested during the previous ten years. So that, as each new year came round, one year at the other end (the eleventh, counting backwards) became "superfluous" and was taken out. In support of this he cites the *Farhang-i Kārdānī*, Aligarh MS. But this manual (f.32b) makes this statement with reference to the assessment of the *jama'* under *nasaq*, while for *ẓabṭ* it prescribes the usual survey and application of the *dastūru-l 'amal* (revenue rate). In respect of *jins-i kāmil*, which Qureshi continues to insist means produce up to the standard, the preamble to Aurangzeb's *farmān* to Rasikdās may especially be seen. Here information is annually demanded on *ajnās-i kāmil o nāqiṣ*, which, the word *ajnās* being the plural of *jins*, can only signify "kinds of superior (*kāmil*) and inferior (*nāqiṣ*) crops", and *not* "full and insufficient produce", which would require *jins* to be in the singular. Finally, the sense of "taking out" or "discarding" attributed to *bar-giriftan* by Qureshi is not justified by the definition and citations in *Bahār-i 'Ajam*, s.v. *bar-giriftan*, nor indeed by the two couplets from Ḥāfiẓ quoted by Qureshi himself. The *Bahār-i 'Ajam* admits only the following meanings: "To lift, to reach the bearing-age for plant and animal, to patronise, to bring up (nurse)."

51 *Ā'īn*, I, 298, 300.

52 Sugarcane appears in this list under the name *qand-i siyāh* which actually means *guṛ* (*Ā'īn*, I, 299). It may be a mistake for *neshkar-i siyāh*, or the thick or paunda sugarcane, but in that case the ordinary sugarcane would have no place on the list.

53 The uncertainty of yield is one of the principal reasons for the high prices of certain cash crops. Thus indigo cropping was "liable to many more accidents and misfortunes than other crops or products" (Pelsaert, 13).

in determining the permanent *dastūrs* for such crops no attempt was made to fix the local crop rates by the process of averages, the method adopted being simply to choose certain good seasons and accept the revenue rates determined for them.

It is not absolutely clear whether the figures under the years 15th to 24th in the "Nineteen Years" tables are the actual *dastūrs* promulgated from year to year or those determined retrospectively in connexion with the preparation of the *Jama'-i Dah-sāla*. There are some indications that favour the latter possibility. From the 15th (and in some cases the 14th) year the variations between rates in the different provinces, and between the annual rates within each province, become much more pronounced, and many new crops appear on the schedules. The introduction of the bamboo measuring rod in the 19th year was officially assumed to have increased the size of the *bīgha* by 15 per cent,[54] but there is no hint of a proportionate rise in the rates under the 19th or 20th year.[55] This can be explained best if we conceive the figures to have been those retrospectively worked out in the 24th year, when a uniform size for the area unit for all the years from the 15th onwards would have been assumed.

The final *dastūrs*, which are reproduced at length in the *Ā'īn*,[56] preserve the same tabular form as the "Nineteen Years" rates, with this difference that at the head of the columns the years are replaced by groups of *maḥals* and the entries now carry single figures only. Thus each group of *maḥals* constituting an assessment circle has a single rate or *dastūr* for each crop. The *Ā'īn* contains full lists of the *maḥals* grouped in these circles.[57] As Moreland observes, each

[54] The *Ā'īn*, I, 296, says that the *bīgha* formerly used to be 13 per cent shorter than its real size. A *farmān* of Akbar of 1580 actually deals with the reduction in the area of grant in Sandīla (Awadh) on account of the bamboo rod, that amounts to 13.03 per cent precisely (National Archives of India: Acquired Documents no.1441: copy). A *parwāna* of 1757 in the Batala series of *madad-i ma'āsh* documents, while confirming a grant of 1569, reproduces its endorsements, which show a reduction of 13.03 per cent in the area of the grant "on account of the rod" (I.O. 4438: 55). Such a reduction in grants implies that the *bīgha* measured by the bamboo-rod was nearly 15 per cent larger than the former *bīgha* (13.03:86.97). See also Appendix A.

[55] This is most obvious in the case of crops carrying flat, or nearly flat, rates, such as poppy, musk-melons (Central Asian and Indian), onion, *paunḍa* sugarcane, turmeric and *singhāṛa*.

[56] *Ā'īn*, I, 348-85.

[57] Owing to this Elliot was misled into regarding the *dastūr* as a territorial unit between the *sarkār* and the *pargana* (*Memoirs*, II, 201). Cf. Moreland in *JRAS*, 1918, 12,13.

of these circles usually forms a homogeneous block from the point of view of agricultural conditions.[58]

It is implicit, rather than explicit, in Abū-l Faẓl's account and the nature of the tables, that the final *dastūrs* were permanent and were to be applied each year without any reference necessarily to the current yield or prices, so that the element of confusion and hardship complained of in connexion with the annual commutation of the revenue rates into cash was now removed.[59] It is, however, probable that revisions took place from time to time and that the final *dastūrs* as preserved in the *Ā'īn* are not exactly those established in the 24th year, but as they stood in or about the 40th year (1595-96). The *dastūrs* for *singhāṛa* and turmeric, which are practically uniform in the final schedules, show in comparison to the figures under the "Nineteen-Year" rates an increase corresponding to the enhancement in the size of the *bīgha* brought about by the introduction of the *gaz-i Ilāhī* in the 31st year (1586-87).[60] Moosvi has now conclusively shown that almost in each case the present rates in *dāms* and *jītals* can be restored to the original rates in complete *dāms*, once one allows for the changes brought about to adjust each of the rates to the *gaz-i Ilāhī*.[61] One can infer then that the rates as we have them are those in force about or after 1586-87. This still leaves the question open whether, if, after we have allowed for the adjustment to the new measure, there is any means of checking whether these final *dastūrs* were averaged from the rates for R.Ys.15-24, the difficulty arising, as Moreland pointed out, owing to the difference in the presentation of the rates in the two tables.[62] There are, however, some simple ways still in which such a check can be made. It seems that even after allowing for the increase in the size of the *bīgha*, at least some of the final *dastūrs* for cash crops, which were not determined by

[58] *Agrarian System*, 88. For certain exceptions, see Moosvi, 117-8.

[59] *Agrarian System*, 88.

[60] The reduction in specification of the area of the older *bīgha* after the introduction of *bīgha-i Ilāhī* is put at 10.54 per cent in the *Ā'īn*, I, 297. In the *madad-i ma'āsh* grants of the Batala series (I.O.4438: 7, 25 and 55) and in Allahabad 879 and 1177, the reduction in area of the former grants on account of the new *gaz* is calculated at 10.5 per cent. This implies an increase in the size of the *bīgha* by about 11.78 per cent. (See also Appendix A.) *Singhāṛa* and turmeric are uniformly rated in the "19-years" rates at 100 *dāms*, but in the final *dastūrs* the figure is increased, with only a few exceptions, to 111 *dāms*, 20 *jītals*.

[61] See Moosvi, 97-100. Her reconstruction of the conversion table for change in the rates (pp.119-20) is particularly ingenious.

[62] *Agrarian System*, 89.

the mechanism of averages, could not possibly have been based upon any of the rates given under the ten years from the 15th to the 24th;[63] while in the case of other crops a number of the final *dastūrs* could not just have been averaged from the rates of these years.[64] It is thus difficult to agree with the view that the final *dastūrs* were simply averaged from the retrospective rates for these

[63] The *paunḍa* or thick sugarcane has an unvaried rate of 200 *dāms* under the regnal years 15-24 in Awadh, Lahor and Multan, yet the final *dastūrs* range from 230 d. 8j. to 240 d. 9j. in Awadh, and from 180 d. 12½ j. (one *dastūr*) to 240 d. 12 j. (in six, including one giving 240 d. 12½ j. in Lahor). In Multan also the figure is 240 d. 12½ j. (two *dastūrs)*. In Lahor and Multan the highest figure against indigo in the rates of the ten years is 136 *dāms*, but the permanent *dastūrs* in the two provinces rise respectively to 158 d. 19 j. and 159 d. 22 j.

[64] The test applied is based on the assumption that if the final *dastūrs* have been averaged from the rates under the 15th-24th years, none of them should exceed the average of the maximum annual rates for the same province, or fall below that of the minimum rates, after allowing for the increase of over 11 per cent consequent upon the change in the length of the *gaz.* The following tables will perhaps speak for themselves.

TABLE I

Province	Crop	A Average of the Maximum Rates	B Maximum among the Final *Dastūrs*	B:A %
Ilahabad:	Kabuli gram	56.40 d	71 d 14 j (5 *dastūrs*)	126
do	Safflower	70.00 d	83 d 21 j (4 *dastūrs*)	119.6
do	Rapessed	47.00 d	101 d (1 *dastūr*)	215
Awadh	Lentils (*masūr*)	22.70 d	35 d 20 j (1 *dastūr*)	156
do	Peas (*matar*)	27.35 d	38 d (1 *dastūr*)	135
Dehli	Ajwa'in	71.20 d	89 d 15 j (1 *dastūr*)	122

TABLE II

Province	Crop	A Average of the Minimum Rates	B A x 11/100	C Minimum among the Final *Dastūrs*
Ilahabad	Chīna (*arzan*) (Rabi)	15.20 d	16.87 d	15 d 19 j (one *dastūr*)
Awadh	do	15.10 d	16.76 d	7d 22j (one *dastūr*) 15 d 3 j (one *dastūr*)

These figures have been used after collating Blochmann's text with MSS. Add. 7652 and 6552, and doubtful entries have been ignored. All the crops except Kabuli gram and *ajwā'in* are listed in Sher Shāh's *rai*ʻ schedule. See also Moosvi, 100-5, for a more extensive check on similar lines, leading to similar conclusions.

years. Moreover, it is possible that considerable revision continued to be made in the *dastūrs* from time to time after the initial formulation of the permanent or standing rates.[65]

The imposition of the permanent *dastūrs* meant that the revenue rates were to be largely divorced from the quality of the actual harvest in any year. If the crops failed, relief was not given by lowering the rates but by making a reduction in the measured area under the heading *nābūd* ("destroyed").[66] There was, however, no such device available to meet the contingency caused by a fall in prices, and special remissions had to be ordered from the court in cases of exceptionally abundant harvests.[67] On the other hand, there is also an instance of the revenue demand being raised to correspond with a rise in prices.[68]

The *ẓabṭ* system continued to function in the seventeenth century on fundamentally similar lines. It is defined in a manual written in 1679 as a method of assessment under which the area was measured at each harvest, the *dastūru-l 'amal* being then applied to it to yield the *jama'*.[69] More significant still are the specimen

[65] The *Munshāt-i Namkīn*, ff.75a-76a, contains an order which owing to its use of the term *ṣūba* must have been issued between 1580 and 1594, the year of the compilation of the collection. This required that *qānūngos* from each *maḥal* (*pargana*) were to be sent by turns to the court to give information about the local *rai'* (crop rate) and *hāṣil* (revenue collection). Local officials were also to supply through the *dīwān* of the *ṣūba* information about "the *rai'*, the (state of) prosperity and contentment of the peasantry, the prices of commodities and the enforcement of the *dastūru-l 'amals* framed by orders sent from the imperial court". The concern with the *rai'* and prices shows that the administration was, even after Akbar's 24th regnal year, still gathering data, the purpose of which could only be a modification of the *dastūru-l 'amals* whenever necessary.

[66] If crop failure was reported after the measurement had been completed, the revenue officials were required to fix the *nābūd* after inspecting the standing crops. If the reports came after the crops had been cut, the reduction in the area was to be made on the basis of the evidence of neighbours and the *paṭwārī's* papers (*Ā'īn*, I, 286-8). In his recommendations of the 27th year, Todar Mal fixed 2.5 *biswas* per *bīgha* (or 12.5 per cent of the measured area) as the allowable maximum for *nābūd* in infertile regions during seasons of abundant rain. For jungle and desert land a maximum of 3 *biswas*, or 15 per cent, was allowed (*A.N.*, III, 382; see the original text of the recommendations in Add. 27,247, f.332a).

[67] *A.N.*, III, 463, 494, 533-4, 577-8. These were made in the 30th, 31st, 33rd and 35th years and applied to the Ilahabad, Awadh, Agra and Dehli provinces, and ranged from ¼ to 1/10 of the total demand.

[68] When Akbar took his court to Lahor, the revenue demand in the Panjab was raised "as from ten to twelve", in order to keep up with the consequential rise in the local prices; when Akbar left Lahor in 1598, this enhancement was withdrawn (*A.N.*, III, 747).

[69] *Farhang-i Kārdānī*, f.32b; Edinburgh 83, f.34b. See also *Maẓhar-i Shāhjahānī*,

assessment papers preserved in this and other manuals of the same period. Here we have first the <u>kh</u>*asra-i ẓabṭ*, the paper giving the details of measurement.[70] It contains six columns giving (1) the name of the cultivator (*āsāmī*) and specifying his crop; (2) the width and (3) the length of his field; (4) the *ārāẓī* or area calculated therefrom; (5) the *nābūd*; and (6) *bāqī*, the area remaining after deducting the *nābūd* from the *ārāẓī*. The net area figures, separately for each crop, are carried over to another document where cash rates per *bīgha* for the respective crops are applied to them for determining the total amount of revenue assessed (the *jama*').[71]

From an administrative point of view, the *ẓabṭ* had some obvious merits. Measurement could always be rechecked, and the fixed *dastūrs* deprived local officials of much of the discretion that they could have otherwise abused. With the promulgation of the permanent *dastūrs* the uncertainties and fluctuations in levying the annual demand were to a great extent eliminated. At the same time the system was not without its limitations. It could not probably be easily applied in places where the soil was not homogeneous in quality; nor, since it left the peasant to shoulder practically all the risks, where the yield was very uncertain.[72] Moreover the method was by no means inexpensive. It required a cess of one *dām* per *bīgha*, called *ẓābiṭāna*, to meet the costs of maintenance

---

13-14, for application of *dastūrs* to crops of *safed-barī* (autumn) and *sabz-barī* (spring harvest) under the "*ẓabṭī*" system of levying revenue ('*amal*).

70 Cf. *Ā'īn*, I, 288: "...the record of *ẓabṭ* (*nus<u>kh</u>a-i ẓabṭ*), which in Hindī they call <u>kh</u>*asra*."

71 *Dastūru-l 'Amal-i Navīsindagī*, ff.182a-185a; *Farhang-i Kārdānī*, f.33b; *Siyāqnāma*, 32-34; <u>Kh</u>*ulāṣatu-s Siyāq*, ff.75a-76b, Or.2026, ff.24b-28a. In the specimen <u>kh</u>*asras* in *Farhang-i Kārdānī* and *Siyāqnāma* there are seven columns, the first (*āsāmī*) giving only the names of the cultivators, the crops being specified in the seventh (*jins*). The *Dastūru-l 'Amal-i Navīsindagī* belongs to the reign of Shāhjahān and was probably written in the *sarkār* of Sambhal. It shows three crops under *ẓabṭ*, viz., tobacco, sugarcane and brinjal. That the high-grade or cash crops were liable to *ẓabṭ* assessment, even when sown in land formerly taxed under other methods, is implied in the *Ā'īn*, I, 286, when it is stated that if land previously under crop-sharing was sown with high-grade crops, the revenue was to be levied at a rate one-fourth less than the usual *dastūr* in the first year.

It is interesting to find that the *ẓabṭī* rents, the sole survival of the Mughal *ẓabṭ* system, found in the Panjab, Upper Doab and Rohilkhand have been described as cash rents levied, according to the area, on cash crops, as well as on fodder and on such other crops as are gathered from day to day (Prinsep, *History of the Panjab*, 167; *Meerut District Gazetteer*, [1922], 109; *Saharanpur District Gazetteer*, [1921], 132; *JRAS*, 1918, 26; and *Agrarian System*, 169n).

72 This is tacitly recognized by Abū-l Faẓl, when he says in his chapter on

of the measuring parties.[73] But there were still greater loopholes in the practical working of the system. Much fraud could be practised in recording the measurements.[74] Thus the *ẓabṭ-i har-sāla*, or annual measurement, in force up to the 13th regnal year (1568-9), is said to have "necessitated great expenditure and caused misappropriation by men" in the *k͟hāliṣa*.[75] A major aspect of the so-called "*Karorī* Experiment" initiated in the 19th year (1574-75) was to bring all the provinces of Hindustan under measurement. As a precautionary step, the hempen rope, which could be fraudulently used, was replaced by the more accurate bamboo rod with iron rings.[76] Nevertheless the peasants were grievously oppressed by the *karorīs*, the new revenue collectors, as Badāūnī tells us;[77] and it seems natural to associate this oppression with the sudden imposition of measurement over such a vast region. One may well imagine how many a village must have stirred anxiously when a measuring party of petty officials thrust themselves upon it, demanding their perquisites and extorting money for putting in correct, as well as false, entries.[78]

Much controversy has centered round the exact nature of the system of assessment known as *nasaq*, literally meaning "good

---

Qandahar that "if the peasant does not have the strength to bear *ẓabṭ*, the practice of taking a third of the crop as revenue (*sih-toda 'amal*) is followed" (*Ā'īn*, I, 587).

73 The *Ā'īn*, I, 300-301, tells us that formerly the measuring parties used to get 58 *dāms* daily as *ẓābiṭāna* (from the treasury or the village?). This was converted into a cess of one *dām* per *bīgha*. In Todar Mal's regulations it is explicitly stated that the daily allowances in cash and kind for the survey staff were to be provided out of this cess (*A.N.*, III, 383). The scales of allowances for the survey officials appear in a revised form in the *Ā'īn*, I, 286. Todar Mal's regulations provided for a minimum area to be measured every day by the staff. The text in *A.N.*, however, interchanges the harvests, and *Ā'īn*, I, 301, supplies the correct reading: 250 *bīghas* were to be measured in the kharif season when the day was longer, and 200 in the *rabi*, the day being shorter. This passage in the text of the original version of the recommendations of Todar Mal, Add. 27,247, f.332b, is unluckily very corrupt.

74 Cf. Mukundarāma's reference to the oppressive acts of the revenue official of a *jāgīrdār*. "The lengths of areas were measured diagonally; a *bīgha* was computed at 15 *kathas* (not twenty); and people's protests were not heeded". (Sukumar Sen, *History of Bengali Literature*, 124, 393; cf. J.N. Dasgupta, *Bengal in the Sixteenth Century A.D.*, 61-63.)

75 *A.N.*, II, 333.

76 Ibid., III, 117-18; *Ā'īn*, I, 296. The hempen rope shrank, when wet, and lengthened, when dry: so the officials would keep it wet on all sorts of pretexts. Badāūnī, II, 189, quotes a verse: "In the warning-laden eyes of the cheated man, the double-headed snake is better than the measuring rope."

77 Badāūnī, II, 187.

78 The dread of such a visit is reflected in Kabīr's verses in the *Guru Granth Sāhib*

order, administration".[79] Abū-l Faẓl refers to it at a number of places, but without anywhere defining it; and none of the interpretations of the term given so far seems to carry conviction.[80] It would surely be tedious to take up the various arguments put on behalf of one or the other of the theories advanced, and we have thought it best to proceed directly to Abū-l Faẓl's own statements.

When we put all his references to *nasaq* together, it strikes us that *nasaq* is often not treated as an independent method of assessment at all but only as a handmaid of other methods. In Hindustan, for example, it appears as a subordinate of *ẓabṭ;* in Kashmir, of crop-sharing. We may expect, therefore, that it was a method or procedure which could be adopted, whatever was the basic method of revenue assessment and collection that was in force.

It appears that we are in a pretty good position to judge what the *nasaq* signified when it was applied under *ẓabṭ*. We are told in what is the earliest reference to it, that in the 13th regnal year

---

(Nagari ed., 793): "Nine surveyors (*ḍāḍī*) and ten assessors (*munsaf*) have invaded the village and do not allow the peasants (*raīat*) (any peace) to settle. They do not measure with the whole rope and take a large amount of maintenance-money (*bistāla*)."

[79] Cf. *Bahār-i 'Ajam*, s.v. *nasaq*, giving many 17th- and 18th-century quotations. One of the verses the author quotes from Shafi' "Aṣar" uses the word in the sense of "decree"; the author's own synonyms for *nasaq* include *band-o-bast*; and under this latter word he quotes a verse from Ẕuhūrī (d.1616), where the poet clearly assigns the sense of a fixed tax demand to *band-o-bast*. As will be seen from the ensuing discussion in the main text, all these could be significant pointers to the technical sense of *nasaq* in Mughal revenue literature.

[80] The following is a summary (probably not exhaustive) of the views on *nasaq* advanced within the last hundred and fifty years or so. Najaf 'Alī Khān, commenting on the *Ā'īn* in 1851, took it to mean revenue farming (*Sharḥ-i Ā'īn-i Akbarī*, Or.1667, ff.177a-178a, 193a-b). Blochmann rendered it as a method whereby "the land tax is settled by the collector and the ryot" (*JASB*, XLII [1873], 219n.). Moreland, writing in collaboration with Yusuf Alī, admitted his inability to define it satisfactorily but thought "it was ordinarily a *zamīndārī* rather than a ryotwari arrangement" (*JRAS*, 1918, 29-30). Subsequently, he took it to mean a "summary assessment on the village or some large area as a unit" (*JRAS*, 1926, 47), and finally, as equivalent to what he termed "Group Assessment" (*Agrarian System*, 234-37). R.P. Tripathi was not satisfied with the rendering "summary assessment" but confessed himself unable to say what *nasaq* really was (*Some Aspects of Muslim Administration*, 357-60). S.R. Sharma suggested that it was a method of assessing the revenue by averaging previous demand (*Indian Culture*, III, 543-5); P. Saran identified it with *kankūt* (*Provincial Government*, 301-9, 453-7). Finally, Ishtiaq Husain Qureshi believes it was an arrangement by way of "contract... between the state and the peasant" (*Administration of the Mughal Empire*, 170).

(1568-69), Shihābuddīn Khān, "having set aside the *ẓabṭ-i har-sāla*... established a (system or form of) *nasaq* (*nasaqe*)" in the *khāliṣa* lands.[81] It may be noted that the form of *nasaq* promulgated did not replace the *ẓabṭ* as such but only "annual *ẓabṭ*". The *ẓabṭ*, as we have seen, consisted of two elements: the fixed cash revenue rates and the measurement of land. We know definitely that the revenue rates continued to be fixed annually up to the 24th year (1583-84) and so what was replaced by *nasaq* in (1568-69) could only have been annual measurement. We may remember that land measurement was after all the real technical meaning of *ẓabṭ*; and in *madad-i ma'āsh* documents the words *ẓabṭ-i har-sāla* are actually used to denote annual measurement of the land.[82] What Shihābuddīn Khān is supposed to have done in 1568-69, Todar Mal recommended again in the 27th year (1582-83). "It is known," he says, "that in the *parganas* of the *khāliṣa* the area (recorded) (*ārāẓī*) is less every year. (Therefore), when the cultivated land has been once measured, they should, increasing it (the area) from year to year," establish a partial *nasaq* (*nasaq-i juzv*).[83] Here it is made quite clear that while the *nasaq* meant the supersession of annual measurement, the record of area measured in any one previous year continued to be used for assessment purposes. The final position as described in the *Ā'īn* was not much different. The revenue-collector was to "keep far-sightedness and justice before him in undertaking measurement. Let him add to the capacity (*nīrū*) of the cultivator everywhere; and, honouring the settlement (*qarār-dād*), let him not demand anything from (the area) cultivated in excess (of it) (*fuzūn kāshta*).[84] If some desire measurement (*paimā'ish*) and others *nasaq*, let him agree."[85] This passage can be interpreted only in one way: the revenue official was to accept the previously fixed area, increasing it presumably

[81] *A.N.*, II, 333.

[82] It is used in the standard injunction to revenue officials: "The *ẓabṭ-i har-sāla* should not be insisted upon, once the boundaries of the area of the grant have been laid down" (*ẓabṭ-i har-sāla ba'd az tashkhīṣ-i chak* Akbar's *farmān*, 1592, in *Sharā'if-i 'Uṣmānī*, f58a; see also I.O. 4438: 3 and I.O. 4435).

[83] *A.N.*, III, 381-2. The corresponding passage in the original version of Todar Mal's recommendations (Add. 27,247, f. 331b) is in sense practically identical, except that it reads just "*nasaq*" for "*nasaq-i juzv*".

[84] There could not, of course, have been any area "cultivated in excess" under actual measurement made between sowing and harvest. Such excess could have arisen only if the area on which the revenue was assessed had simply been fixed on paper on the basis of some previous measurement.

[85] *Ā'īn*, I, 285.

by estimate. If some peasants did not accept this and demanded fresh measurement, he was to agree; but otherwise the *nasaq* was to be enforced. In other words, the *nasaq*, standing in these passages as an alternative to annual measurement under *ẓabṭ*, signified the continuous use in successive years of the same area figures previously determined by actual measurement, but modified from time to time.

This association of *nasaq* with repetition of area figures pro-bably best explains the use of *nuskha-i nasaq*, "document of *nasaq*", in the unmistakable sense of record of area, from which the *nābūd*, or the area allowed for crop failure, was to be deducted.[86] There is still another reference to *nasaq* in the same chapter of the *Āʼīn*. This is in an injunction to the *ʻamalguzār* not "to make *nasaq* with the big men of the village".[87] Far from proving that *nasaq* was identical with "Group Assessment" it shows that, in its authorized form, the contrary was the case. Probably, the specific sense of this prohibition, in the light of our other information about *nasaq* under *ẓabṭ*, is that the revenue officials were not to make modifications or enhancements in the standard area figures by bargaining with the leading villagers.

Nasaq under *ẓabṭ* was only one form of *nasaq*. Thus Abū-l Faẓl can speak of it as *nasaqe*, "a (form of) *nasaq*" and *nasaq-i juzv*, "partial *nasaq*". Gujarat, though it was not, exactly speaking, a *ẓabṭī* province, had probably a similar form of *nasaq*. The *Āʼīn* declares it to be "mostly *nasaqī* (under *nasaq*)", "measurement" being rarely practised.[88] As we shall see in the next section, the measurement to which it is counterposed seems to be annual measurement, which only, and not the use of area statistics for assessment, seems to have been rare in Gujarat.

But in Berar, Bengal and Kashmir, *nasaq* must have existed in very different forms. Berar, we are told, was "*nasaqī* " from ancient times,[89] so that the term *nasaq* is here applied to a system untouched by Mughal innovations. It must then be identical with the time-honoured method of levying revenue in Mughal Dakhin, described by Ṣādiq Khān. This consisted of applying customary rates to the number of ploughs in a village, without reference to the land cultivated or the size of the actual harvest.[90] In Bengal, where crop-

86 "If a calamity befalls cultivation after the *nuskha-i nasaq* has been despatched to the court, let him at once enquire into it and make an estimate of the *nābūd*" (*Āʼīn*, I, 286-7).

87 *Āʼīn*, I, 286. 88 Ibid., 485. 89 Ibid., 478.

90 Ṣādiq Khān, Or.174, f.185a, Or.1671, f.90b: Khāfī Khān, I, 132 n. Incidentally,

sharing was not practised and measurement was the exception, the revenue demand is said to have been based upon *nasaq*.[91] We have already discussed the nature of the revenue system of Bengal in another context, and the conclusion that was reached is that the revenue assessment (*jama*ʻ) on the *zamīndārs* in Bengal had a semi-permanent basis, though it could sometimes be arbitrarily increased.[92] Such absence of annual assessment, then, explains why the term *nasaq* has been used for the revenue arrangement in Bengal.

It is in respect of Kashmir that Abū-l Faẓl offers us the most detailed description of the working of a particular form of *nasaq*. The province is stated to be *nasaqī-i g͟halla-bak͟hsh*, "under a *nasaq* of crop-sharing".[93] The main feature of its revenue system was that the *rai's* (crop rates) on the different crops were fixed and applied to the area of each village, "in accordance wherewith they have estimated some *k͟harwārs* (ass-loads) of rice upon each village and go on demanding that same number of *k͟harwārs* without obtaining information afresh".[94] Here, therefore, we have crop-sharing with this peculiarity that the quantity of produce appropriated as revenue remained fixed or constant from year to year.

By putting together all the information we have of the systems to which Abū-l Faẓl applies the term *nasaq*, we can see that the diversity of form really conceals one essential feature that is common to them all: the whole, or a part, of the assessment was not made afresh every year, the results of assessment once made being (sometimes with summary modifications) repeated year after year. It did not matter how the initial assessment had been made or what was repeated – area figures, amounts of cash, quantities of grain, or numbers of ploughs. Any avoidance whatsoever of the process of actual assessment, by acceptance of something previously worked out or determined, was *nasaq*.

Lambton in her *Landlord and Peasant Persia*, 436, glosses *nasaq* as a technical term in use in Arak for the "capacity of a village in plough-lands".

[91] *Āʼīn*, I, 389. [92] See Chapter V, Section 3.

[93] *Āʼīn*, I, 570. Blochmann puts a dash for stop between *nasaqī* and *g͟hallabak͟hsh*, but a glance at the text would show that the second word could have belonged to the next sentence only if it had been followed by the conjunction *wa* ("and"), which is not the case. Moreland and Yusuf Alī questioned the reading of *nasaqī* on the basis of one MS, I.O.265, which reads *niṣfī* instead (*JRAS*, 1918, 9-10). But there is no doubt that *niṣfī* is a scribe's misreading of *nasaqī*, for the best and earliest of our MSS, Add.7652, Add.6552 and I.O.6, support Blochmann's text (without his punctuation, of course).

[94] *A.N.*, III, 548.

It may have been observed that we have so far relied for our enquiry on the references to *nasaq* contained in the writings of Abū-l Faẓl only. This has been done partly to meet the argument that, in view of the possibility of a change in its significance in the intervening period, later evidence is not admissible for determining what the *nasaq* really signified under Akbar.[95] However, such later evidence as is available is wholly consistent with the conclusion stated in the preceding paragraph. A manual written in Aurangzeb's reign directly defines *nasaq* as follows: "The assessor, keeping in view the *muwāzana-i dah-sāla* (record of the revenue and area of the last ten years) and (the record of) the year immediately preceding or by averaging the *jama*ʻ of the ten or twelve years, assesses the *jama*ʻ."[96] Thus it is the past assessment which determines the present. In another manual prepared near the close of the same reign, *nasaq* appears in exactly the form it had when associated with *ẓabṭ* in the sixteenth century: that is, it signifies the area fixed on paper by the revenue officials for purposes of assessment.[97]

3. THE SYSTEMS OF REVENUE ASSESSMENT IN THE DIFFERENT REGIONS

Abū-l Faẓl tells us that under Sher Shāh and his son Islām Shāh the system of *ẓabṭ* replaced crop-sharing and *muqṭaʻī* (imposition of fixed revenue demand) in Hindustan.[1] This is supported by ʻAbbās Khān, who says that Sher Shāh introduced the method of assessment by the *jarīb* (measuring rope), which had never been practised before him.[2] In his earlier days, in his father's assignments

[95] Saran, 453-57.

[96] *Farhang-i Kārdānī*, f.32b. In Edinburgh 83, f.34b, this definition is reproduced, but its compiler or scribe was obviously unable to recognize the word *nasaq* at all. It also omits the word "or" before "averaging". S.R. Sharma in *Indian Culture*, III, 544-5, refers to a definition of *nasaq* found in a manual in the State Library, Rampur. From his paraphrase of it, it seems almost certain that it is couched in the same terms as the one in *Farhang-i Kārdānī* and might not contain the exclusive emphasis on the principle of averages that Sharma attributes to it.

[97] *Khulāṣatu-s Siyāq*, ff.79b-80a; Or.2026, f34a-b: The *karorī* "having endeavoured to encourage cultivation (and) having fixed the *nasaq*, which in the dialect is known as *sar* (or *sī*), in accordance with the state of the peasantry, should post horse and foot, so that the cultivators may do the sowing according to what has been fixed and allow not a (single) cultivable *bīgha* or *biswa* to remain uncultivated". I cannot identify the Hindi synonym for *nasaq*; cf. the phrase, *nuskha-i nasaq*, in Abū-l Faẓl in precisely the same sense.

[1] *Āʼīn*, I, 296. For *muqṭaʻī*, see the next section.

[2] ʻAbbās Khān, f.106a, ed., 210. The *ẓabṭ* system was possibly an innovation of

in Bihar, he had allowed the peasants the choice between *jarīb* and crop-sharing;[3] but as king he seems to have attempted to make *ẓabṭ* the sole method of assessment. The chronicler declares that revenue was exacted from even the people of the Panjab hills (Nagarkot, etc.) by the use of the *jarīb*,[4] and the people around the city of Sambhal were also compelled to pay revenue assessed by the same means.[5] *Ẓabṭ* was probably extended to Malwa as well, since *dastūrs* for this province, promulgated in the early years of Akbar's reign, are given in the "Nineteen-Years" tables of the *Ā'īn*. Only Multan was treated as an exception: the methods used by the Langahs were retained by Sher Shāh, the *jarīb* was not applied, and a form of crop-sharing was practised.[6]

As the "Nineteen-Years" rates show, the *ẓabṭ* system continued in most of the provinces of Hindustan (Agra, Ilahabad, Awadh, Dehli, Lahor and Malwa) during the early years of Akbar. But it is possible that it lost some ground during this period. In the 13th regnal year (1568-69) the practice of annual measurement was replaced by a form of *nasaq* in the *khāliṣa* lands.[7] In the 19th year (1574-75), however, all the provinces of Hindustan, apart from Bihar, were resumed to the *khāliṣa* and placed under *ẓabṭ*.[8] It was also extended to Multan[9] and parts of Ajmer province.[10] By the time the *Ā'īn* was compiled, the majority of the *parganas* of Bihar, accounting for over three-fourths of its *jama'*, had come under *ẓabṭ*.[11] It is, however, improbable that the *ẓabṭ* covered the whole of the land in any province.[12] The object of the 'Karorī Experiment'

Sher Shāh, but simple measurement for assessment, as in *kankūt*, must have been an old practice in India. 'Alā'uddīn Khaljī (r.1296-1316) had established a system of assessment by measurement (*ba-ḥukm-i misāḥat o wafā-i biswa*) (Baranī, *Tārīkh-i Fīrūz-shāhī*, 287). This and his system of *dāgh* (horse-branding) provided the grounds for Abū-l Faẓl's sneers that Sher Shāh "put into effect some of the numerous measures of Sultan 'Alā'uddīn that are described in detail in the *Tārīkh-i Fīrūz-shāhī*" (*A.N.*, I, 196).

3 'Abbās Khān, f11b (ed., 23). *Jarīb* here probably means *kankūt*.

4 Ibid., f.107a (ed., 212).

5 Ibid., f.108a (ed., 213-4).

6 Ibid., ff.93b-94a (ed., 186).

7 *A.N.*, III, 333; *Iqbālnāma*, II, Lucknow ed., 233.

8 *A.N.*, III, 117-18; 'Ārif Qandahārī, 177-8; Badāūnī, II, 189-90.

9 In the "19-years" tables the entries for Multan begin only from the 15th year. But since it is probable that the rates for the 15th to 24th years are those fixed retrospectively, it is possible that Multan came under *ẓabṭ* only in the 19th year or later.

10 The tables for Ajmer are left blank in the "19-years" tables, but the final *dastūru-l 'amals* are given for nine groups of *maḥals*.

11 *Ā'īn*, I, 417.

12 We have seen in Chapter I, Section 1, that the measured area statistics of

launched in 1574-5 probably was to make as extensive a measurement as possible just for once, or for a period of years, and then use it as the basis for a workable *nasaq*,[13] and for compiling the new general assessment, the *Jama'-i Dah-sāla*. In the *Ā'īn* the instructions to the '*amalguzār* lay down that he ought to allow the peasants the choice of either *nasaq* or fresh measurement. Furthermore, he is asked not to confine himself only to these two methods, which set the demand in terms of cash, but also to use *kankūt* and crop-sharing, where the demand would be expressed in kind.[14] It is indicated elsewhere in the same work that any of these methods, in so far as they suited the locality, were to be applied in *chachar* land (under fallow for three or four years), while in *banjar*, left untilled for a longer period, the choice was to rest with the peasant.[15] It seems to be assumed on the other hand that land, previously under crop-sharing, would come under *ẕabṯ*, if sown with cash crops.[16]

In its essentials this system seems to have continued unaltered in the seventeenth century. The preamble to Aurangzeb's *farmān* to Rasikdās issued in 1665-66, describes the then current practice as follows:[17]

Aurangzeb's reign show a considerable increase over those of the *Ā'īn* and yet indicate clearly that a very high proportion of the villages was still unmeasured in most of the provinces. A comparison of the *Ā'īn's* area figures with these statistics shows that it was only in respect of the Agra and Dehli provinces that the measured area statistics of the *Ā'īn*, were in any sense complete.

Cf. Moosvi, 46-8, where a similar conclusion is reached by considering the varying *jama'*: *ārāẓī* ratios worked out by her for various areas from the *Ā'īn's* statistics.

[13] Bāyazīd Bayāt was asked to undertake revenue duties in the *sarkār* of Ujjain in Malwa in 1576-77, and he describes his work as consisting of "measurement (*jarīb*), assessment (*jama'-bandī*), and (fixing) the *nasaq*" (Bāyazīd, 353). As we have seen, Todar Mal recommended in 1582-83 that measurement was not to be carried out annually in the *khāliṣa*, and a local *nasaq* was to be instituted (*A.N.*, III, 381-2).

[14] *Ā'īn*, I, 285-6. Moreland does not anywhere offer an interpretation of this passage, which in effect says the same thing as the preamble of Aurangzeb's *farmān* to Rasikdās; yet he did not hesitate in taking the latter as offering "decisive" evidence that Akbar's system by then had become "almost entirely obsolete" (*Agrarian System*, 124).

[15] *Ā'īn*, I, 301, 303.

[16] Ibid., 286. See note 71 in Section 2.

[17] There is only the strongest presumption, but no definite proof, that this *farmān* dealt particularly with conditions in northern India. Nothing is known about the official position of Rasikdās or the province to which he was posted. In the copy of the *farmān* preserved in Add. 19, 503, ff.62a-63b, his name is replaced by that of Mīr Muḥammad Mu'izz, the *dīwān-i khāliṣa* of Bihar. It might therefore have been circulated among a number of officials.

The assessors (*umanā'*) of the *parganas* of the imperial dominions assess the *jama'* of most of the villages of the *parganas* in the beginning of the year, keeping in view the revenue (*ḥāṣil*) of the *sāl-i kāmil* (the year of the maximum revenue)[18] and the previous year and the cultivable area and the capacity of the peasantry and other peculiarities; and if the peasants of some of the villages do not agree to this procedure (*'amal*), they assess the *jama'* at the time of the ripening of the crops by the method of *jarīb* or *kankūt*. And in some of the villages, whose cultivators and peasants they know to be in distress and indigent, they enforce the method of crop-sharing at a half or a third part or two-fifths or more or less (as revenue).

We have thus, first, the form of *nasaq* as established in the *ẓabṭī* regions, then measurement, whether under *ẓabṭ* (*jarīb*) or *kankūt*, and, in special cases, crop-sharing. A similar statement is also made in the *Khulāṣatu-s Siyāq*, written in the Panjab near the close of Aurangzeb's reign.[19] The general prevalence of assessment based upon area, whether actually measured each year or maintained by *nasaq*, is emphasized by the area statistics belonging to Aurangzeb's reign. The area recorded in them is, generally, in excess of that in the *Ā'īn;* and while the number of unmeasured villages given in these statistics constitutes a very high proportion of the total in the provinces of Bihar, Awadh and Multan, the number is relatively unimportant in the Ilahabad, Agra, Dehli and Lahor provinces.[20]

The eighteenth century represented a period of administrative disorganization, but elements of the Mughal system still survived. A report on revenue practices in other provinces prepared for the

[18] The term *sāl-i kāmil* occurs first in the text of Mīr Fatḥullāh Shīrāzī's recommendations of 1585 (*A.N.*, III, 457). *Kāmil* literally means perfect, but is here used in the technical sense of the highest revenue ever realized. See the definition of *jama'-i kāmil* in Add.6603, f.57b. A controversy sprang up on the meaning of this term, used in the Treaty of Surat, 1776, between the Maratha and the English authorities, the former insisting that it should be interpreted strictly in the sense attributed to it in revenue literature (Grant Duff, *A History of the Mahrattas*, 1863 ed., II, 237-38).

[19] The *amīn*, or assessor, was to prepare the *jama'* or *daul* at the beginning of the year, separately for both harvests, on the basis of his knowledge of the capacity of the peasants, village by village. When the crop started to ripen, he was to take a fresh *qabūliyat* (affirmation of agreement with the assessed demand) from the peasants. If some, owing to an accident, were unable to pay the *jama'* fixed by him and requested actual assessment (*'amal*) he was to apply *ẓabṭ* or crop-sharing or *kankūt*, whichever he might think profitable for the authorities and not oppressive to the peasants (*Khulāṣatu-s Siyāq*, ff.73b-74a; Or.2026, f.22b. Cf. also Bekas, f.70a-b).

[20] These statistics have been discussed in Chapter I, Section 1.

English authorities in Bengal, sometime before 1788, says that measurement was generally used by the *zamīndārs* for determining the demand upon the peasants in the Punjab, though some *zamīndārs* employed crop-sharing methods. In the province of Dehli, revenue was paid in some villages by crop-sharing, in others by the *bīgha*. In both Awadh and Ilahabad, measurement, or, at any rate, payment of revenue by the *bīgha*, was the general rule.[21] In Bihar, during the early period of the Nazimate some *maḥals* had fixed assessments, but in others *kankūt* was usually applied.[22]

Passing on to the other regions of the empire, we have first the province of Kashmir. Abū-l Fazl describes the system followed here in some detail, and his information may be summarized as follows. Each village was supposed to contain a fixed area of revenue-paying land. A *rai'* for each *paṭṭa*, the local unit of area, was fixed for the major crops, the revenue-share being regarded as one-third of the produce. The amount thus determined (in terms of *kharwārs* or ass-loads of rice) was levied every year without variation. When Akbar's officers carried out a detailed investigation in the 34th year (1589-90), it was discovered that the *rai's* declared to the administration had no basis in actual fact and the revenue was actually being levied in accordance with much higher *rai's* – four times higher, for example, in respect of wheat and one-half in that of rice.[23] Accordingly, not one-third, but even more than two-thirds, of the produce was being collected in tax. Akbar, therefore, fixed the share of the state at half the produce, but the new *rai's* are nowhere given.[24] The system of fixing the *jama'* on each village in kind continued under Akbar's successors, because a *farmān* of Shāhjahān, issued in 1633, speaks of villages with *jama'* of more than 400 ass-loads (*kharwārs*) of rice that had become subject to an additional impost, now abolished.[25] In late eighteenth century an apparently pure form of crop-sharing prevailed in

[21] Add. 6586, f.164a-b.

[22] Report on the pre-British system of administration in Bengal by the Rāi Rāyān and the *qānūngos*, 1777: Add. 6592, f.112b, Add.6586, f.71b. *Kankūt* is here considered a form of crop-sharing (*bhāolī*) though it is stated distinctly that the *jarīb* was employed.

[23] A.N., III, 548-9.

[24] *Ā'īn*, I, 570; *A.N.*, III, 727.

[25] Shāhjahān's *farmān* inscribed on the gate of Jāmi' Masjid, Srinagar, line xiii, copied personally; there are errors in the text as copied in *Tārīkh-i Ḥasan*, II, 500-01. See also Qazwīnī, Aligarh transcript, 501, where instead of *jama'* one reads of the *ḥāṣil* of over 400 ass-loads of rice in the villages made subject to the impost now abolished.

Kashmir,[26] but there is little information about the intervening period.

Bhakkar formed a *sarkār* of Multan province. We are told that in 1575-6 a uniform *dastūru-l 'āmal* (but expressing the demand in kind, not cash) was grafted upon the previous system of *kankūt*, and great oppression resulted from this innovation.[27] Perhaps, in some modified form, this system was maintained. Thus although this *sarkār* is assigned no *dastūr* in the *Ā'īn*,[28] it is provided with area figures in the provincial statistics. The *Maẓhar-i Shāhjahānī* (1634) declares that all the eight *parganas* of *sarkār* Bhakkar had been under the "*ẓabṭī*" system of revenue assessment, with *dastūrs* fixed on crops of both the autumn and spring harvests.[29] The *Chahār Gulshan* has no area statistics for either this or the *sarkār* of Multan,[30] but assessment by measurement survived here till the regime of the Amirs in the nineteenth century.[31] In *sarkār* Sehwan to the south, "*ẓabṭī*" and crop-sharing existed side by side in the seventeenth century.[32] The *dastūrs* set out in the *Maẓhar-i Shāhjahānī* for the various crops are, however, mostly fixed in kind, not cash, and therefore remind us of the modified form of *kankūt* introduced in Bhakkar in the previous century.[33] The province of Thatta remained throughout under crop-sharing, in the time of Akbar as well as afterwards.[34]

To judge from the *Ā'īn*'s tabulation of *dastūru-l 'amals* and area statistics for the *sarkārs* of Nagaur, Ajmer, Ranthambhor and Chittor in *ṣūba* Ajmer,[35] the eastern half of the *ṣūba* seems to have

26 Add. 6586, f.164a.

27 Ma'ṣūm, *Tārīkh-i Sind*, 245.

28 Bhakkar does not appear either on the lists of *maḥals* carrying *dastūrs* or on the tables of *dastūrs* themselves. For the Multan province, it is stated that three of its *sarkārs* (presumably Multan, Dipalpur, and Bhakkar, and excluding Thatta) were "ẓabṭī" (*Ā'īn*, I, 550). But perhaps *ẓabṭ* is here loosely extended to cover *kankūt*, which also involved measurement.

29 *Maẓhar-i Shāhjahānī*, 13-14.

30 See Chapter I, Section 1.

31 Lieut. Hugh James, 'Report on the Purguna of Chandookah', December 1847, in Thomas, *Memoirs on Sind*, II, 729-32. Chandauka belonged to *sarkār* Bhakkar.

32 *Maẓhar-i Shāhjahānī*, 155, 182-5, 203-30.

33 Ibid., 183-4. Idrākī Tattawī, *Beglārnāma*, ed. Baloch, 182, tells of Qāsim Khān, an officer of the Tarkhān ruler Muḥammad Bāqī (1566-83), who, in three *parganas* that later formed part of *sarkār* Sehwan, carried out a survey (*jarīb-kashī*) of the cultivated lands, whereafter the revenue was collected apparently in grain. We can detect a species of *kankūt* here.

34 *Ā'īn*, I, 556; *Maẓhar-i Shāhjahānī*, 51. For *bhāolī* (crop-sharing) in Halakandi, Thatta province, see *parwānas* of 1716 and 1718, *Jour. Pak. Hist. Soc.*, *LIX*(4), 63-68.

35 *Ā'īn*, I, 364-8, 508-13. The larger proportionate extent of *ẓabṭ* can be grasped

been placed extensively under *ẓabṭ*. The *Ā'īn* provides no area statistics for the western *sarkārs* of Bikaner, Jodhpur and Sirohi;[36] and it must be to this zone to which Abū-l Fazl's statement about the prevalence of crop-sharing and rarity of money payment in the *ṣūba* must therefore apply.[37] In the seventeenth century, crop-sharing seems to have returned to large areas. Nainsī (1664), while reporting measured area for the entire *pargana* of Merta (*sarkār* Nagaur) as well as for its individual villages, describes crop-sharing (*banṭāī*) as the general system of collection, confining *ẓabṭ* to the application of the flat rate of a rupee per *bīgha* to cotton, vegetables, etc.[38] The *Waqā'i' Ajmer* (1679-80) also reported crop-sharing (*ghalla-bakhshī*) from this *pargana*, as well as from Jalor (*sarkār* Sirohi).[39] From the rich documentary material for eastern Rajasthan it appears that by the late seventeenth century, *ẓabṭī* rates were in use mainly for kharif cropping, while crop-sharing (*jinsī*), important also in kharif, was entirely predominant in respect of the rabi harvest.[40]

The position in Gujarat presents certain difficulties. The *Ā'īn* declared that it was "mostly *nasaqī*, and measurement is not much (*kam*) practised".[41] At the same time, excepting Sorath and some *maḥals* elsewhere, the whole province is supplied with detailed

approximately from the conversely lower figure of *jama'* in relation to measured area (*ārāẓī*): the *jama'* is thus only about 5 *dāms* per *bīgha* of the reported area in *sarkār* Nagaur, about 11 in Ajmer, 15 in Ranthambhor and 21 in Chittor. The exceptionally low *jama'* rates per *bīgha* might have been due also to low *jama'* figures being framed with a view to benefiting the assignees in the Rajasthan area.

36 Ibid., I, 511-13. The *Ā'īn*, I, 364-8, does provide *dastūru-l 'amals* for *sarkār* Jodhpur, but the rates seem mere repetitions of those of Nagaur, and must be deemed to have been framed for formal purposes only.

37 Ibid., I, 505.

38 Nainsī, *Vigat*, II, 89. The area (*rakabo*, from Arabic *raqba*) is given for the *pargana* on p.77 and for individual villages, on pp.116-213.

39 *Waqā'i' Ajmer*, 114 (Merta), 451-2 (Jalor).

40 S.P. Gupta, *Agrarian System of Eastern Rajasthan*, 60, 62. On 64-6, he tabulates data from *pargana* Amber and three neighbouring *parganas*. Of these, Chatsu (*sarkār* Ranthambhor) constitutes an exception: in 1708, it had not only 66% of revenue from kharif derived from *ẓabṭ*, but also 41% of rabi. As against this, in 1690 Amber had 41% of kharif and only 3% of rabi taxation, derived from *ẓabṭ*.

41 *Ā'īn*, I, 485. The initial word "mostly" corresponds to *beshtar* in the original. Moreland and Yusuf Alī (*JRAS*, 1918, 29-30), while admitting that the MSS do not show any variant reading, suggest nevertheless that we should read *peshtar* (formerly) instead of *beshtar*, and interpret the sentence to refer to past conditions only. But in that case the words at the end, *kam rawad*, would have to be altered to *kam rafte* to carry the past tense; and this would surely be too extensive an interference with the text.

area statistics. Moreover, Shihābuddīn Aḥmad Khān, the governor of Gujarat (1577-85), is said to have "made a measurement of the cultivable area a second time on the complaints of the peasants of the *pargana* of the environs (*ḥavelī*) of Ahmadabad and other *parganas*".[42] From Navsari, near Surat, comes a document of December 1596 demarcating the area of a revenue grant, which shows the measured area of each field, the crops being as many as seventeen, both rabi and kharif.[43] Yet another document of about the same time (1593-97) directs that in another *pargana* near Surat "the villages having been measured (*ẓabṭ namūda*), the revenue be realized according to the prescribed *dastūru-l 'amal*;" alternatively, it permitted revenue assessment (*jama'bandī*) of each village to be made on the basis of the cultivation and produce (*mazrū'āt o ḥāṣil*) of each village.[44] The latter suggests, perhaps, a species of *nasaq*. Early in the reign of Shāhjahān, Geleynssen speaks of the crop being "measured and valued" for revenue purposes.[45] If, then, Abū-l Faẓl says that measurement was "not much" practised, it must mean only that it was not seasonally undertaken for application of the *dastūru-l 'amal* (cash revenue rate) to the area under each crop, as under *ẓabṭ*. Indeed, the *Ā'īn* has no *dastūru-l 'amals* tabulated for Gujarat. The measured area statistics, kept unaltered for long periods, could yet serve to determine revenue demand upon the application to them of the customary local yield rates and current prices. In this case, the stable area figures and crop rates would justify Abū-l Faẓl's reference to Gujarat being mostly under *nasaq*.

Gujarat suffered grievously from the famine of 1630-32; and in the next decade the court became cognizant of the extreme degree of oppression and distress borne by the peasantry. Mirza 'Īsā Tarkhān was appointed governor (1652-54) to remedy matters; and he "established crop-sharing" and "in a short time brought the country to prosperity".[46] It is probable that measurement was

[42] *Mir'āt*, I, 141.

[43] For a reproduction, analysis and translation of this document, see I. Habib in *PIHC*, 54th session, 1993, Mysore, 246-62.

[44] Blochet, Suppl. Pers.482, ff.170b-171b. The document is a *parwāna* of Ṣādiq Khān (d.1597): he had been assigned Surat in *jāgīr* in 1593 (Badāūnī, II, 387).

[45] *JIH*, IV, 79. A *pawāncha* by Masīḥuzzamān, *mutaṣaddī* of Surat (1635-38), refers to the *desāī* of *pargana* Balsar trying to impose *ẓabṭī* on a peasant who was thereupon forced to migrate to another *pargana* (Blochet, Suppl. Pers.482, f.166a-b).

[46] *Mir'āt*, I, 217-18.

not entirely superseded, for in the statistics of Aurangzeb's reign nearly two-fifths of the villages are shown as measured.[47] Crop-sharing itself did not prove a lasting boon to the peasants. An imperial order issued in the 8th regnal year of Aurangzeb discloses an extraordinary perversion of this system. It recites that "owing to the high price of corn" in the earlier years of the reign "the *jama*ʿ had reached the maximum (*kamāl*)". Thereafter the prices fell, but *jāgīrdārs* still demanded the same amounts: though formally following crop-sharing, they would assume the produce to be two and a half times the actual, and setting the demand at half of the imaginary figure, they would take away the whole crop and for the balance make the peasants work a whole year to provide it out of their wages.[48] It is doubtful how far the injunction henceforth to base the demand on the actual harvest was successful. In 1674-75 Fryer found that in the Surat region the peasants were not allowed to remove their crops from the fields unless they had surrendered three-fourths of the produce to the authorities.[49]

For Mughal Dakhin, the *Āʾīn* provides us with no relevant information beyond saying that Berar was under *nasaq*.[50] Ṣādiq Khān, however, tells us that in the Dakhin provinces neither measurement nor crop-sharing had been followed "since ancient times". "On the contrary," he says, "the established practice was that each of the villagers and peasants tilled as much land as he could with a plough and pair of oxen, grew what crop he liked, whether foodgrains or pot-herbs, and paid to the authorities (*sarkār*) a little money on each plough varying with the territory and the *parganas*; and there was no (further) enquiry about, or regard paid to, the quantity of the crop."[51] This might have been the general practice, but from a document prepared in 1642-43 it appears that in some *parganas* at least a kind of *nasaq* based upon measurement was being applied.[52] It is probable that this and other practices were introduced by the Mughal administration in various localities in the course of the five or six decades following Akbar's conquests. Writing from the Dakhin in 1653, Aurangzeb concurred with Shāhjahān's view that the "different

[47] See Chapter I, Section 1.

[48] *Mirʾāt*, I, 268. This passage belongs to the *sharḥ-i ẓimn* ("explanation on the back") of a *farmān* expressly directed to prohibiting illegal exactions (*abwāb-i mamnūʿa*) in Ahmadabad province (ibid., 259).

[49] Fryer, I, 300-301.

[50] *Āʾīn*, I, 478.

[51] Ṣādiq Khān, Or.174, f.185a-b, Or.1671, f.90b; Khāfī Khān, I, 732 n.

[52] This is entitled "Memorandum on the Proposal for Land" (*Yāddasht-i Tajwīz-i*

methods" (*ẓawābiṭ-i gūnāgūn*) followed by the revenue authorities were "a cause of the ruin of that country".[53]

When Aurangzeb was sent in 1652 for the second time as Viceroy of the Dakhin, he was specially charged with the task of improving the land-revenue system.[54] This reform was largely carried out by Murshid Qulī Khān, assisted for some time by Multafat Khān.[55] It began with the classic expedient of crop-sharing, and Aurangzeb's letters make it clear that this applied to the entire territory, including the *jāgīrs*.[56] The particular form of sharing which was used is said to have been an innovation of Murshid Qulī Khān himself.[57] The proportions in which the revenue was to be collected were based on a differential scale. Half of the produce was to be taken from crops raised on rainfall alone; and a third from crops irrigated from wells, but in the case of sugarcane, fruits and spices, the share was to range from one-third to one-fourth, keeping in view the cost of irrigation and (with respect to fruits) the years the trees took to bear fruit. Different rates were also promulgated for crops irrigated from streams and canals. Ṣādiq Khān says that the old system of assessing the revenue by the number of ploughs was still retained in certain areas, while the practice of measurement was introduced in others. For the purposes of the latter, Murshid Qulī Khān is said to have determined the *rai'* for every crop and to have fixed the *dastūrs* per *bīgha* after taking account of the prices.[58] Aurangzeb says nothing about

---

Zamīn). It concerns twenty-eight *parganas*, but three of these had not sent the required returns. The total area amounted to 1,90,006 *bīghas*, 13 *biswas*. Each *pargana* was assigned a certain area of land for ordinary cultivation and for *baghāt*, literally gardens, but used in the Dakhin for fields irrigated from wells (cf. Khāfī Khān, I, 735n.). Some figures are prefaced by the phrase, *tajwīz-i ḥāl*, "proposed currently", which means that they were being added to the area assigned previously. It is not clear whether the document relates to lands of the *khāliṣa* or of Aurangzeb's *jāgīrs* (*Selected Documents of Shah Jahan's Reign*, 101-107.)

53 *Ādāb-i 'Ālamgīrī*; f.36a; ed., I, 139; *Ruq'āt-i 'Ālamgīr*, 97.

54 *Ādāb-i 'Ālamgīrī*, f.26b; *Ruq'āt-i 'Ālamgīr*, 69.

55 In the beginning Murshid Qulī Khān was the *dīwān* of Bālāghāṭ and Multafat Khān of Pāinghāṭ. Subsequently, the latter was transferred to other duties and Murshid Qulī Khān became the *dīwān* of the whole of Mughal Dakhin.

56 *Ādāb-i 'Ālamgīrī*, ff.35a, 36a-b, 38b, 43a, 118a; ed., I, 135, 139, 142, 149, 154,167; *Ruq'āt-i 'Ālamgīr*, 97, 99, 102, 113, 117.

57 This significant statement, which occurs in Ṣādiq Khān's account of Murshid Qulī Khān's reforms, is omitted by Khāfī Khān. Moreland, unaware of having been anticipated by Ṣādiq Khān, points out that this type of "differential sharing" was unfamiliar to Indian practice and was probably derived from Murshid Qulī Khān's experience in Persian administration (*Agrarian System*, 186).

58 Ṣādiq Khān, Or.174, ff.185b-186a, Or.1671, f.91a; Khāfī Khān, I, 733-4 n.

measurement, but since he declares that crop-sharing had proved a very expensive method,[59] he could hardly have contemplated its becoming a permanent fixture. Ṣādiq Khān actually says that Murshid Qulī Khān measured the area of most of the *parganas*.[60] The revenue records of *pargana* Papal (Berar), *c.*1679, give detailed particulars concerning its measured area.[61] But the decisive evidence is furnished by the village and area statistics of Aurangzeb's reign. These show that nearly nine-tenths of the villages of Berar and Aurangabad had been measured, and nearly a half of those of Khandesh.[62] It would seem, therefore, that the major result of Murshid Qulī Khān's reform was the introduction of measurement, and that crop-sharing was only employed at the beginning to help in fixing workable *rai 's* for the different crops.[63]

In Bengal, says Abū-l Faẓl, "the peasantry (is) obedient and revenue-paying. In each year during eight months they pay the (revenue) demand in instalments. They take the rupees and *muhrs* to the appointed place themselves. Crop-sharing is not practised. A state of low prices (*arzānī*) always prevails. They do not object to having it measured.[64] The revenue demand is based upon *nasaq*. The world-ruler [Akbar] out of benevolence retained this system (*ā'īn*)."[65] We have seen in the previous chapter that in Bengal the authorities levied the revenue not upon the peasants but upon the

---

Murshid Qulī Khān is said to have devoted so much attention to formulating the *rai 's* that in order to prevent any inaccuracy he would himself pick up one end of the measuring rope. The reference seems to be not to measurement in general for purposes of assessment, but to measurement made of a sample plot, whose total yield could be determined by instant cutting, in order to determine the local rate of yield per *bīgha*, i.e., the *rai'* or crop rate.

59 *Ādāb-i 'Ālamgīrī*, ff.38b, 118a; *Ruq'āt-i 'Ālamgīr*, 117.

60 Ṣādiq Khān, Or.174, f.185b, Or.1671, ff.90b-91a; Khāfī Khān, I, 733 n.

61 See *IHRC*, 1929, 81, 84-86.

62 See Chapter I, Section 1.

63 Essentially, this would be the same procedure as was attributed by Grant Duff to Malik 'Aṁbar, viz. the collection of "a moderate proportion of the actual produce in kind, which, after the experience of several seasons, was commuted for a payment in money settled annually according to cultivation". (*History of the Mahrattas*, 1863 ed., I, 71 and n., citing "the authority of Maharatta MSS").

64 This sentence is not by any means easy to render. In Blochmann's text it reads: *wa dar paimūdan-i ān bāz nagoyand* – "And they do not ask afresh (or insist) in regard to measuring it". But Add.7652 and Add.6552 both agree in omitting the initial *wa* and reading *az* for *dar*, and the rendering in the text above follows this reading. Strictly speaking, the pronoun "it" should stand for *arzānī*, or cheapness, but this would not make sense, and one must assume with Moreland (*JRAS*, 1926, 45) that by "it" here land must be meant.

65 *Ā'īn*, I, 389.

zamīndārs. It is not, however, immediately clear where in this passage Abū-l Fazl is speaking of the payment of revenue by the peasants to the *zamīndārs* and where of the payment by the *zamīndārs* to the state. The initial statements, since they contain an explicit reference to the peasants, would seem to be referring to them only. Even in the early days of the English administration the "ryots" in general paid their "rents" in cash, and crop-sharing was used only in "some places".[66] The sentence relating to measurement, however, raises some difficulty. The *Ā'īn* does not carry any area figures in its statistics for Bengal; and in the statistics of Aurangzeb's reign also the measured villages constitute an infinitesimal proportion of the whole.[67] On the other hand, a sixteenth-century poet of Bengal refers to fraud in measurement by a revenue official.[68] There is also a reference to "survey" as the means of checking the *jama*' of a revenue assignment in the reign of Jahāngīr.[69] In 1708 we find the "tenants" of the English Company's *zamīndārī* in Govindpur (Calcutta) paying their "rents" to the Company in money on each *bīgha* according to the crop raised; but the Company itself paid the revenue to the *khālisa* or *jāgīrdār* without reference to any survey.[70] According to a late account, however, Murshid Qulī Khān as deputy-governor of Bengal and Orissa in the last years of Aurangzeb, overhauled the whole revenue system and sent his revenue officials to measure the land, cultivated as well as waste, of every village.[71]

It seems probable that the resort to measurement took place in Bengal largely when the old *jama*' fixed on *zamīndārs* was thought to be completely obsolete. A mid-eighteenth-century manual describes this as a recognized practice in Bengal.[72] This may really be the meaning also of Abū-l Fazl's rather vague statement that measurement was not objected to. It is possible that since such measurement was so rarely employed, and then with the use of local standards,[73] no regular area statistics could be compiled on its

[66] Shore's minute of June, 1789, para 226, *Fifth Report*, 192.

[67] See Chapter I, Section 1 (Table of Village Statistics of Aurangzeb's Reign).

[68] Mukundarām in *Chandīmangal*, quoted (with transl.) in J.N. Das Gupta, *Bengal in the Sixteenth Century A.D.*, 61-3.

[69] *Bahāristān-i Ghaibī*, transl. Borah, II, 741-2. I regret I have not been able to check this passage with the original MS in the Bibliotheque Nationale, Paris.

[70] *Early Annals*, I, 294, and II (1), 228, for payments by the Company's tenants and measurement; I, 240, and II (1), 15-16, 116, 126, for revenue demanded from the Company.

[71] *Riyāzu-s Salāṭīn*, 252.

[72] *Risāla-i Zirā'at*, ff.9b-10a.

[73] In late 18th century in some localities the *zamīndārs* used to determine the

basis. Abū-l Faẓl's statement that the revenue demand was based on *nasaq* must then refer to the demand on the *zamīndārs* being retained at the same sets of figures for long periods of years.[74]

4. THE BASIC UNIT OF ASSESSMENT: THE INDIVIDUAL PEASANT HOLDING AND THE VILLAGE

As we have noticed already, it is a recurring theme with official pronouncements that the domineering persons in a village would always seek to shift their own burden onto the shoulders of their weaker brethren. The ideal before the Mughal administration, at least in areas where the *ẓabṭ* system predominated, was to deal with each peasant separately, particularly when determining or levying the revenue demand. The '*amalguzār* (revenue collector) should not, says the *Ā'īn*, "make *nasaq* with the big men of the village, since indulgence and ignorance arise therefrom and it gives strength to the dominant men of oppressive bent. On the other hand, he should reach each individual cultivator and graciously give him a written document and take one from him."[1] A manual written a century later gives exactly the same reason for recommending the principle of individual assessment.[2]

The two documents referred to in the *Ā'īn* must respectively be the *paṭṭa* and the *qabūliyat*. A specimen copy of a *paṭṭa* given to an individual peasant has been preserved for us in a manual,[3] and elsewhere we come across orders passed on the petition of a single peasant who had complained that the *paṭṭa* granted to him was not being honoured.[4]

The *Ā'īn* requires of the *bitikchī*, or accountant, that he should record the name of each peasant, together with that of his ancestor, the crop sown by him and the *jama*' assessed upon it, and then put down the total of the individual assessments as the revenue (*maḥṣūl*) of the village.[5] Briefly, but in the same strain, Aurangzeb's *farmān* to Rasikdās, Art. 3, directs that the *jama*' of each village should be fixed after assessing the peasants individually (*āsāmī*-

---

rents payable by the peasants on the basis of measurement, but Shore notes that the local standards differed widely (Minute of June 1789, paras 230 and 231, *Fifth Report*, 192-3).

[74] See Chapter V, Section 3, and the previous section of this chapter.

[1] *Ā'īn*, I, 285. By "big men" (*kalāntarān*) Abū-l Faẓl probably means headmen here, for, as the *Bahār-i 'Ajam*, s.v. *kalāntarī,* informs us, *kalāntar* signified a *muqaddam* in Hindustan.

[2] *Khulāṣatu-s Siyāq*, f.78a, Or.2026, f.30a.

[3] *Farhang-i Kārdānī*, f.35a.

[4] *Durru-l 'Ulūm*, f.62a.

[5] *Ā'īn*, I, 288.

wār). Similarly, in the specimen assessment papers reproduced in two manuals of the period all the particulars are given, or required to be given, separately for each peasant (*āsāmī*).[6]

Aurangzeb's *farmān* also stresses that in making reductions to meet the effects of natural calamities, the assessor should not make a lump-sum remission, leaving it to the *chaudhurīs, qānūngos, muqaddams* and *paṭwārīs* to distribute it among the peasants, but should himself inspect the fields and estimate the amount of remission for each individual cultivator.[7]

Lastly, when the revenue had been collected, the *bitikchī* was to examine the *sarkhaṭs*, i.e. receipts or memoranda, given by the *muqaddams* and *paṭwārīs* to the peasants, in order to see whether the collections had conformed to the assessments.[8] We have already seen how the administration used to have the village accounts, the *kāghaz-i khām*, inspected from time to time in order to detect misappropriation. It was specifically laid down that if it was discovered that more had been taken than was due, the excess was to be recovered and credited against the balance of revenue payable by the respective cultivators.[9]

The real question is whether these regulations were in practice effective. The difficulties involved in assessing each cultivator separately every year can be visualized. Under crop-sharing in its pure form the problem was perhaps automatically solved, since the revenue share would be collected directly from the field or stacks of each peasant. But this was in itself a very cumbersome and expensive method for the authorities. Under any other system it would have been far easier to assess the whole village than each individual holding. In fact one manual implies that, although undesirable, it was the general practice to make collective (*sarbasta*) assessments for the entire villages.[10] Another goes into great detail

[6] *Dastūru-l 'Amal-i Navīsindagī*, ff.182a-185a; *Farhang-i Kārdānī*, f.33b; *Siyāqnāma*, 32-33; *Khulāṣatu-s Siyāq*, ff.75a-76b; Or.2626, ff.24b-28a.

[7] *Farmān* to Rasikdās, Art.9. The *Ā'īn's* instructions to the '*amalguzār* on making allowances for *nābūd*, or land affected by some calamity, also suggest that he was to assess the extent of the damage for each cultivator separately. He was to give his estimate in writing to the "cultivator", and, if the calamity occurred after the crop had been cut, he was to call in the "neighbours" as witnesses (*Ā'īn*, I, 286).

[8] *Ā'īn*, I, 288.

[9] Fatḥullāh Shīrāzī's recommendations: *A.N.*, III, 457-8. If the cultivator concerned had no balance (*baqāyā*) to pay during the current year, the amount was to be deducted from the demand assessed on him the following year.

[10] *Khulāṣatu-s Siyāq*, f.78a, Or.2026, f.90a.

about how a village ought to be assessed and does not make any reference to the need for assessing individual holdings.[11] Although Aurangzeb's *farmān* to Rasikdās prescribes individual assessment, yet in the description, in its preamble, of the current methods of revenue assessment and collection, it is the village, not the peasant, that appears as the primary unit of assessment. Moreover, in its Art. 6 the *diwān* himself, when on tour, is asked to see whether the *jama*ʻ of the village he was visiting conformed to its capacity and whether in the distribution of the *jama*ʻ (*tafrīq-i jama*ʻ) among the individual cultivators, the *chaudhurī*, *muqaddam* or *paṭwārī* had not been guilty of oppression. It is thus assumed that as a general rule the *amīn*, or assessor, contented himself with fixing the assessment on the village, leaving the shares of the peasants to be fixed by the headmen. Todar Mal's own recommendation that in the *k͟hāliṣa* each village should not be measured each year, but its area increased by estimate under a form of *nasaq*, strongly suggests that the increased area was not to be determined by a minute examination of each holding , but simply upon a view of the whole village.[12] It cannot, indeed be ruled out as impossible that where the *āsāmī-wār* entries did appear on the official assessment papers, these often were either fictitious or simply copied or adapted from the papers of the village accountants or headmen.

If this was the case with *raʻīyatī* or peasant-held villages, the presumption would be strong that in villages held by the *zamīndārs*, the revenue officials would merely assess the whole village and require its *zamīndār* to pay the revenue, without bothering to distribute the assessment among individual peasants. Convenience here would prevail over the official view, which, as we have seen in Chapter V, appears to have been that the *zamīndār* was only an intermediary and the peasant was the real assessee.[13]

There existed certain arrangements, however, where even the pretence of dealing with individual peasants could not be maintained on paper. Abū-l Faẓl tells us that a system known as *muqṭaʻī* was abolished by the Sūrs along with crop-sharing.[14] The

[11] *Hidāyatu-l Qawāʻid*, ff.10a-11a.

[12] *A.N.*, III, 381-2. Cf. Kuwait LNS 235 MS, j, a document from *pargana* Dhar, Malwa, of 1655: a village (not any individual) is here required to bring 10 more *bīghas* of taxable land under sugarcane in return for the protection of its rights over an irrigation tank.

[13] See Chapter V, Section 3.

[14] *Ā'īn*, I, 296.

derivations from the Arabic root *qaṭ'* have carried the most varied meanings in revenue literature, inside and outside India.[15] *Muqṭa'ī* is used at a number of places in the *Maẓhar-i Shāhjahānī* in the obvious sense of "fixed amount".[16] *Muqṭa'ī* means a system in which *muqṭa'* prevailed. Now the word *muqṭa'* is not met with alone in seventeenth-century revenue literature, but always in the phrase, *bi-l muqṭa'*. The dictionary meaning of this word is "stipulated, fixed";[17] in our records it appears uniformly in the sense of a fixed amount to be paid periodically. It is used with references to salaries paid to officials at a fixed rate;[18] in Art. 4 of Aurangzeb's *farmān* to Muḥammad Hāshim it is used to describe a fixed rate of revenue per *bīgha*. In other documents, however, it signifies a fixed revenue demand on the whole village, or a larger area.[19] We find it used in *ijāra* (revenue-farming) documents for indicating that the farmer was to pay a fixed amount of cash to the *jāgīrdār* irrespective of the amount collected from the peasants.[20] Similarly, the revenue assessment of a number of villages imposed on the proprietors (*māliks*) is said to be *bi-l muqṭa'*, and the figures given show that the assessed amount remained fixed for two successive years.[21] A passage tacked on to the *farmān* to Muḥammad Hāshim in a collection of documents of Aurangzeb's reign, suggests that there were also peasant-held villages which insisted on paying a fixed amount (*bi-l muqṭa'*) of

[15] E.g., *iqṭā'*, revenue assignment, and *muqāṭa'a*, revenue-farming. Moreland is not sure with which of these to connect Abū-l Faẓl's term (*Agrarian System*, 74). For *muqāṭa'a* in the sense of revenue-farming, see Baranī, *Tārīkh-i Fīrūz-shāhī*, 487-8; Add.7721, f.14b. Cf. Lokkegaard, *Islamic Taxation in the Classic Period*, 102-8; Lambton, *Landlord and Peasant in Persia*, 435.

[16] *Maẓhar-i Shāhjahānī*, 134: "The Balūch of Bārīcha, who live in the hills in the *pargana* of Bubkan, give a certain number of camels and sheep every harvest to the *jāgīrdār* of Sehwan. (Under Shamsher Khān) they started giving less than the *muqṭa'ī*," etc. See also pp.28, 29, 69, 85. The word is used in the same sense in *Zakhīratu-l Khawānīn*, ed., III, 11.

[17] See Steingass, *Persian-English Dictionary*, 151; Elliot, *Memoirs*, II, 24. I am not sure which spelling is the right one: *maqṭa'* (Steingass) or *muqṭa'* (Elliot). I have adopted the latter as being more likely to represent the Indian pronunciation.

[18] *Selected Documents*, 64, 179; *Waqāi'i' Dakhin*, 49.

[19] Cf. Elliot, op. cit. He says that *bi-l muqṭa'* means a fixed rate of "so much per plough or per Bigha"; also "an engagement to pay a fixed money rent for the lands under cultivation". He adds, finally, that "it is often used to mean 'in a lump sum', or 'on the whole'."

[20] Allahabad 884; Add.6603, f.51b, also 49b.

[21] Allahabad 1223. Compare the revenue figures of this document with those of the previous year's assessment in Allahabad 1220.

revenue and no more.[22] It was a method which was normally disapproved of and permitted only in exceptional circumstances. It is most likely, then, that this method is precisely what Abū-l Faẓl meant by *muqṭa'ī*. In late seventeenth century, similar arrangements begin to bear the name *muqarrarī* or *muqarrarī-i istimrārī* ("fixed" or "permanently fixed") in Bihar, the villages or persons paying such fixed *jama'* being deemed to be enjoying a favour, so that the term *muqarrarī-dār*, the holder of such a right, also appears.[23] *Istimrārī* or permanent arrangements of this nature are also attested to by documents fom Ilahabad province and the Panjab.[24]

As a general practice *ijāra* or revenue-farming lay under official disapproval.[25] Yet in actual fact the revenue officials did sometims farm out the revenues of individual villages.[26] Orders passed on this subject insist that only villages which had fallen into ruin, and whose peasants had no resources left, were to be given away on farm on condition that the farmer should restore them to prosperity.[27] In no case was any revenue official, or *chaudhurī* or *qānūngo* or *muqaddam* or a person in league with any of them, to be permitted to take any village on farm.[28] The revenue farmer was moreover not to take anything beyond the equivalent of land revenue from the peasants,[29] though there can be little doubt that the farmers would only have rarely respected this injunction.[30]

It may be remarked that we are here speaking only of the farming of the revenues of individual villages and not of farming,

[22] *Durru-l 'Ulūm*, f.141b. The *muqṭa'ī* arrangements mentioned in the *Maẓhar-i Shāhjahānī*, 23-9, 85, 134, were made with unruly tribesmen or unsubmissive peasants. The inhabitants of the villages around the Manchhar Lake also paid "*muqṭa'ī*" on the fish and grass collected by them (ibid., 69). Here, obviously, the nature of the produce precluded any other kind of arrangement.

[23] See Datta, esp. Docs. Nos.388 (of AD 1688) and 472 (of 1682). See also Doc. nos.166, 419, 476, 561 and 581, ranging in dates from 1712 to 1746.

[24] Sihunda Dos. No.57 of A.D.1699; Goswamy and Grewal (eds.), *The Mughals and the Jogis of Jakhbar*, Docs.IX and IXA (*ẓimn* of IX) of AD1695.

[25] For prohibition of *ijāra* in absolute terms both in respect of the *khāliṣa* and *jāgīrs*, see *Mir'āt*, I, 292 (Gujarat) and *Akhbārāt* 37/38 (Kashmir).

[26] See *Farhang-i Kārdānī*, f.35a-b, for a statement to this effect and for the draft of a pledge from the farmer to pay the amount of revenue promised.

[27] *Nigārnāma-i Munshī*, ed., 97-8, 149.

[28] *Mir'āt*, I, 292; *Nigārnāma-i Munshī*, ed. 149; Fraser 86, f.93b. The *Nigārnāma-i Munshī* also insists on the consent of the *mālik* (proprietor).

[29] *Nigārnāma-i Munshī*, ed., 92, 149.

[30] A specific case of oppression at the hands of a revenue farmer forms the subject matter of a *ḥasbu-l ḥukm* in *Durru-l 'Ulūm*, f.65a-b: "At this time Dasondhī,

whether open or veiled, encountered at higher levels of administration, in the *jāgīrs* and the *khāliṣa*.[31]

It is not easy to say how widespread the practices of *muqṭa'ī* or *muqarrarī* and *ijāra* were during our period.[32] The general regulations for revenue assessment, read with Abū-l Faẓl's express statement that *muqṭa'ī* as a universal system had been superseded, and with the official orders inveighing against revenue-farming, seem to suggest that the practices were probably heavily restricted at least in the *ẓabṭī* provinces and such regions as Gujarat and (after Murshid Qulī Khan's reforms) Mughal Dakhin.[33] But there might have existed a number of intermediate forms of arrangements: *nasaq* "made with the big men of the village" would not really have been very different from giving the revenues on farm to the headmen.

5. THE MEDIUM OF PAYMENT

The peasant of northern India was probably paying his revenue in cash as early as the thirteenth century.[1] In the Mughal period the methods of assessment, chiefly used in northern India, namely the *ẓabṭ* and the form of *nasaq* based upon it, involved the direct statement of the revenue demand in terms of money. When the methods of crop-sharing and *kankūt*, both of which set the demand

Siyām, Phalād, etc., peasants of the village of Hasanpur, in the jurisdiction of the *pargana* of Palwal, having reached the all-protecting court, have complained that Bhaiya, *chaudhurī* of that place, having entered into collusion with the revenue collector (*'āmil*) of that *maḥal*, himself took the *ijāra* of that village, which previously had been in the farm of one Dost Muḥammad. He has seized Rs 800 during the kharif season by force and violence, and having put an embargo (*qurq*) upon the harvesting of the rabi crop, inflicts upon them all kinds of vexation and injury. Apart from this, within five years, he has taken for himself Rs 1,300 out of the possession of the petitioners, besides the authorised revenue (*māl-i wājib*). And he has seized and taken away the village accounts (*kāghaz-i khām*)". This last action, presumably to prevent his extortions being detected.

[31] For this, see Chapter VII, Section 2.

[32] It was a matter on which the Mughal administration itself was not apparently too well informed. Aurangzeb's *farmān* to Rasikdās complains in its preamble that information about the number of cultivators of each village, with "the separate classification (*tafrīq*) of *mustājirs* (revenue farmers) and peasants (*ri'āyā*)" was not supplied to the headquarters.

[33] In the records of the Papal *pargana* in Berar during the reign of Aurangzeb, only 500 *ṭakas* are shown as being derived from the single *hundisārī* (contract) village, as against 25,877 *ṭakas* in net revenue from land under regular administration (*IHRC* [1929] 86).

[1] Cf. *Agrarian System*, 11, 37-8.

in terms of produce, were used, commutation into cash was permitted at market prices "in case it is not burdensome for the peasantry".[2] In fact, the demand levied under *kankūt* is converted into cash in both the specimen accounts preserved in two manuals of the period, while the demand from crop-sharing is commuted in one, though not in the other.[3] It is significant that Akbar issued special orders for collecting ten *sers* of grain from each *bīgha* as part of the revenue, to be stocked against the threats of famine, but more especially, perhaps, to meet the needs of the animals of the imperial stables.[4] This shows that the collection of revenue in kind was so exceptional that the government lacked sufficent stocks of grain, an inadequacy this measure attempted to remedy. Original records from one part of Awadh show the revenue demand being imposed on whole villages in cash.[5] A letter reporting the collection of revenue in three villages belonging to a *jāgīr* assigned in Haryana may well be illustrative of the general conditions in the *ẓabṭī* provinces. In two of the villages the revenue was assessed in terms of money, and required to be paid in it. The third village was under crop-sharing, the revenue being collected in kind. Of the produce thus acquired, *bājra* was to be sold on the spot "after some days at a suitable price", while the remainder, consisting of *moṭh*, rapeseed and cotton, was to be carted to the headquarters at Hisar.[6] It would, therefore, seem that even when the revenue was realized in kind, it was sometimes thought desirable to put it on the market and obtain cash instead.

Kashmir lay under the peculiar system of a *nasaq* of crop-sharing. Land revenue was calculated in terms of "ass-loads" of rice. Even the amount obtained from the cesses was estimated for purposes of assessment in terms of quantities of rice.[7] Great oppression is said to have resulted, when the *jāgīrdārs* began to "demand gold and silver from this land of crop-sharing"; but Akbar firmly forbade this innovation in 1597-8.[8]

[2] *Ā'īn*, 286.

[3] *Dastūru-l 'Amal-i Navīsindagī*, ff.183b-185a; *Khulāṣatu-s Siyāq*, f.76b, Or.2026, f.28a. Add.6603, f.62a, defines the term *damāū* as standing for the process of commutation of the revenue in kind into cash under crop-sharing. It adds that "they always take it [the amount in cash] at more than the market rate".

[4] *Ā'īn*, I, 199-200. Cf. *Afsāna-i Shāhān*, f.135b, for a similar measure attributed to Sher Shāh.

[5] Allahabad 897, 1206, 1220, 1223.

[6] Bālkrishan Brahman, f.63a-b. The villages lay in the *pargana* of Sirsa.

[7] *Ā'īn*, I, 570.

[8] *A.N.*, III, 726.

Crop-sharing also prevailed in Thatta and portions of Ajmer province, and it was probably later extended to the *sarkārs* of Multan and Bhakkar. Here too the usual practice seems to have been to commute the demand in kind into cash at market prices, for only then does the complaint made in 1700-01 by prince Mu'izzuddīn, governor of Multan, become comprehensible: he represented that since, owing to a good harvest, there had been a very great fall in prices, the *jama'* in his *jāgīrs* had fallen considerably.[9]

It may be assumed that in Gujarat, under the older system of measurement and *nasaq*, the demand would have been set in cash, but under crop-sharing, in kind. Yet here again in January 1703 we come across a complaint that the "amount of revenue" (*zar-i maḥṣūl*) could not be collected in the *pargana* of Patlad, because grain was cheap and duties and exactions levied on the routes impeded its export to Ahmadabad.[10]

In Mughal Dakhin, the payment of revenue in cash, based upon a very summary assessment, is described as an old practice.[11] After the brief interval of crop-sharing introduced by Murshid Qulī K͟hān, payment in cash was re-established though it was now founded on assessment by measurement.[12]

In Garh, in central India, the peasant, according to the *Ā'īn*,

[9] *Ak͟hbārāt* 44/162. There is, perhaps, a subtle difference between the problem as stated here and as it would have been in a *ẓabṭī* province. Under *ẓabṭ* the *jama'* itself would have been unaffected by the fall in prices, though it could not then, of course, have been actually collected. In crop-sharing the demand being commuted at market prices into cash by the assessor himself, a fall in the prices would automatically reduce the *jama'*.

The *Waqā'i' Ajmer*, 114, contains a report that 23 villages in the *pargana* of Merta, where imperial officials enforced crop-sharing, yielded about 15,000 *mans* of grain in revenue. But in the *pargana* of Jodhpur in the same region, the land revenue must have been either directly collected in cash or commuted, at some stage, into cash. For here, on 294 villages a total revenue demand of Rs 13,400, as. 13, was assessed (ibid., 184).

In 1836-37 it was reported that in southern Sind the Amirs had their land revenue collected in kind, but had it sold immediately to a "respectable merchant", designated *aṁbārdār* ("umbardar") (T.C. Carless's journal, in Thomas, *Memoirs on Sind*, II, 540).

[10] *Ak͟hbārāt* A 77.

[11] Ṣādiq K͟hān, Or.174, f.185a-b, Or.1671, f.90b: K͟hāfī K͟hān, I, 732 n.

[12] See Section 3 of this chapter. If one is to judge from evidence relating to Bombay and the island of Salsette, the Konkan (which was not included in the Mughal Dakhin in the time of Murshid Qulī K͟hān) formed an exception, the land revenue being paid in "Morais" of rice (*Factories, 1668-9*, 216-7; Careri, 179).

paid the revenue in gold *muhrs* and copper pieces.[13] Eastward in Orissa, however, the villages were unfamiliar with metallic currency and used cowries instead,[14] though we do not definitely know how they paid the revenue.

In Bengal, as we have seen (Section 3 above) the peasants usually paid the revenue in cash, and crop-sharing was but rarely practised. Jahāngīr declares, however, that in Silhat (Sylhet), the peasants used to offer their children as eunuchs in satisfaction of the revenue demand:[15] in view of the great market for them that the harems of the aristocrats provided they were doubtless as good as money for the revenue collectors.

From the above information it may, perhaps, be concluded that apart from such isolated territories as Kashmir and Orissa, or the desolate portions of Rajasthan, the cash nexus was firmly established in almost every part of the Empire. Its prevalence meant simply that the peasant was normally compelled to sell a very large portion of his produce in order to meet the revenue demand. We have already discussed in Chapter II the conditions under which his relations with the market were conducted; and it is clear that the cash nexus reinforced and increased the share of another class in the surplus produce, that of the village money-lender and rural merchant. On the other hand, once agrarian commerce had developed sufficiently to allow the peasant to grow his crop with an eye to the market, it might well become a hardship for him if the authorities insisted upon receiving their share in kind in all the crops raised by him.[16]

Itself the product of a relatively developed commercial or mercantile economy, the cash nexus provided in its turn the real basis on which the structure of the Mughal imperial system, with its

[13] *Ā'īn*, I, 456. The text reads *muhr o pil*, but I take it that *pil* is a mistake for *pul*. Jarrett (ed. Sarkar, II, 207) renders the sentence, apparently without any misgiving as: "The cultivators pay the revenue in muhurs and elephants."

[14] Master, II, 85; Bowrey, 199.

[15] *T.J.*, 71-2. Jahāngīr says he prohibited this practice but it is unlikely to have been eradicated.

[16] Suppose, for instance, that a peasant grew for the kharif, cotton in one part of his land and *juwar* in the other, the former for the market, the latter for his family's consumption. If he was required to pay the revenue in cash, he would pay by simply selling his cotton. But if a share was taken from both the crops, he would have little left to eat and be compelled to buy the grain back from the authorities, who might name their own price. Methods such as these were apparently used to provide yet another means of extorting money from the peasants in Coromandel. Cf. Raychaudhuri, *Jan Company in Coromandel*, 202.

insistence not on the possession of land, but on the transferable right to collect the land revenue, was founded. It may also explain why serfdom and compulsory labour are not found in Mughal India as major elements in agrarian surplus extraction. Agrestic slavery, though extant, was of limited extent only; and when we meet forced labour or *begār*, it is as a rule an exceptional form of labour imposed upon some inhabitants by the authorities, rather than a regular part of productive work.[17]

Before closing this section a few remarks may be made concerning a question raised by Moreland and only half answered by him. This is whether the demand upon the peasant in the seventeenth century was calculated and realized in terms of *dāms* (copper coins) or of rupees.[18] The question is of some interest because the silver price of copper fell and then rose considerably in our period,[19] and if it could be shown that the revenue was still paid in *dāms*, it would signify first a lightened and then an increased burden on the peasantry.[20] In the *Ā'īn* the *dastūrs* are set down in *dāms* and their fractions (*jītals*), but from the evidence of the succeeding period it becomes obvious that when the copper-silver ratio as fixed under Akbar became obsolete, the demand upon the peasant came to be stated, almost without exception, in terms of rupees, the fractions being expressed in annas.[21] This is true equally for the cash rates and calculations of the *jama*ʻ assessed upon the peasants, and for the accounts of receipts and disbursements including even the village accounts.[22] Almost all incidental references, in contemporary records, to the *jama*ʻ fixed upon the peasants, are in terms of rupees.[23] The *farmān* to Rasikdās, Art. 8, when dealing with the actual coins to be accepted from the peasants in payments of revenue, makes no reference to any unit other than the rupee. It is only the *jama*ʻ, used for assigning *jāgīrs*, that is

[17] See Section 7 of this chapter for the forms of *begār* imposed by the authorities.

[18] *Akbar to Aurangzeb*, 260-61. [19] See Appendix C.

[20] Cf. Radhakamal Mukerji in *JUPHS*, XIV (ii), 75.

[21] In Berar, perhaps, the local *ṭakas* or *ṭankas* continued to be used, but this was entirely a money of account. See Appendix C.

[22] These various kinds of documents may be seen in such accountancy manuals of the 17th century as the *K͟hulāṣatu-s Siyāq*, written in the Panjab; the *Dastūru-l ʻAmal-i Navīsindagī*, written in *sarkār* Sambhal (Dehli province); the *Siyāqnāma*, Ilahabad province; the *Dastūru-l ʻAmal-i ʻĀlamgīrī*, Bihar; and the *Farhang-i Kārdānī*, Bengal.

[23] Cf. Bālkrishan Brahman, f.63a-b (Haryana); *Durru-l ʻUlūm*, ff.54b-55a; Add. 24,039, f.36b (Bengal).

expressed in terms of *dāms* (and it was, therefore, called *jama'dāmī*); but this, as we shall see in Chapter VII, was solely because the salaries of *manṣabdārs* were stated in terms of *dāms*, which were used there only as money of account, at the set ratio of 40 to a rupee. In fact whenever the revenue actually realized, termed *ḥāṣil*, is given, even when stated alongside the *jama'dāmī*, it is invariably expressed in rupees showing that this was the real currency used.[24]

6. COLLECTION OF LAND REVENUE

Except under simple crop-sharing, the collection of revenue and its assessment were entirely distinct operations. In crop-sharing the state's share of the grain was directly seized from the field or the threshing floor at the time of division, so that assessment was totally dispensed with. In other systems, assessment could take place between the time of sowing and harvesting, but collection, whether the medium of payment was cash or kind, usually took place at the time of the harvest.

The revenue collector (*'amalguzār*), says Abū-l Fazl, "should begin the collection for the rabi (season) from Holi [the festival day falling in March] and that of kharif from Dasehra [falling in October]." It was also laid down that "he should properly collect the revenue upon the crop which is being harvested and not delay it for another crop".[1] In the kharif season, the harvesting of different crops was done at different times and the revenue had accordingly to be collected in three stages.[2] Collection of revenue in instalments was thus here a necessity, and Art. 4 of Aurangzeb's *farmān* to Rasikdās provides for such spaced payments in general terms.

The rabi harvest was all gathered within a very short period, and the authorities seem to have been usually anxious to get the revenue collected before the harvest was removed from the fields.[3] Out of this anxiety grew the practice of preventing the peasants

[24] Cf. Lāhorī, II, 330, 397; *Ādāb-i 'Ālamgīrī*, ff.31b-32a, 49a-b; *Ruq'āt-i 'Ālamgīr*, 88, 163-4; *Dastūru-l 'Amal-i 'Ālamgīrī*, f.179a-b. The *jama'dāmī* figures are followed by *ḥāṣil* in rupees in the revenue statistics contained in the *Ẓawābiṭ-i 'Ālamgīrī*, Add.6598, ff.131a-132a, Or.1641, ff.44a, 6b; Fraser 86, ff.57b-61b; *Intikhāb-i Dastūru-l 'Amal-i Pādshāhī*, ff.1b-3b, 8a-11b.

[1] *Ā'īn*, I, 287.

[2] First on *sānwān* (*shāmākh*), then on *bājrī* and, finally, on sugarcane (*Siyāqnāma*, 48-9).

[3] *Siyāqnāma*, 49.

from reaping their crops until they had paid their revenue. This method of coercion is actually prescribed in two administrative manuals of Aurangzeb's reign.[4] The practice might indeed have gained ground in the seventeenth century. Mundy, visiting Kol (the present Aligarh) in Agra province in 1631, found that it was regarded as an innovation. "Here now are in this Castle about 200 of them [villagers] prisoners because they cannot pay the Tax imposed on them, which heretofore, was paid when their Corne was sold; but now they must pay for it in the ground. This is the life of Hindoes or Naturals of Hindustan."[5] There come to us through the records of Aurangzeb's reign two complaints against this practice, one against a *chaudhurī*, who "having put an embargo upon the harvesting of the rabi crop, inflicts upon them [the peasants] all kinds of injury,"[6] and the other against a revenue collector, who realized a large amount of money, "selling the sons and cattle of the plaintiffs [who were *zamīndārs*] at a time when the fields were green".[7] These references show how oppressive it was to demand the revenue from the peasant before the harvest, when he would have absolutely nothing left. The practice was at the same time the mark of a well-developed money economy, for it would have been impossible to attempt it unless the officials expected that the peasants would pay up by pledging their crops beforehand to grain merchants or money lenders.[8]

The revenue was paid into the treasury usually through the revenue collector, though Akbar's administration encouraged the peasants to pay directly to the treasury.[9] The peasants,

[4] The *Siyāqnāma*, 49, prescribes this for the rabi harvest only, but the *Khulāṣatu-s Siyāq*, f.80a, Or.2026, f.35a, states without reference to the season that "when the crops ripen, he (the revenue collector) should set horse and foot on guard so that until the peasants paid the revenue of the current year, the *taqāvī* loans and the revenue arrears from the past, they might not be permitted to gather the harvest."

[5] Mundy, 73-4. Since he visited Kol in December, the revenue demand must have been for the rabi crops.

[6] *Durru-l 'Ulūm*, f. 65a-b.

[7] Bālkrishan Brahman, ff.63b-64a.

[8] For which practice see Thomas Marshall, 'A Statistical Account of the Pergunna of Jumboosur [Gujarat]', *Transactions of the Literary Society of Bombay*, III (1823), 367.

[9] Todar Mal's Recommendations, Art. 6: "In the case of the peasants of trusted villages, who are consistent in word and deed, the revenue officials (*'ummāl*) should lay down time-limits for payment of revenue to the treasury, so that they might themselves, within the said time-limits, deposit their revenue in the treasury and obtain receipt. There is no need for a collector (*taḥṣīldār*) [to be sent to such villages]". (*Akbarnāma*, Add.27, 247, f.332b; *A.N.*, III, 382, contains an abridged and polished version.)

or rather their representatives or village officials, were entitled, whether they paid directly or indirectly, to obtain proper receipts for their payments; the treasurer, on the other hand, was also asked to get the *paṭwārī's* endorsement in his register to establish the amount of payment.[10] These regulations were largely in the nature of precautions that the administration took to protect itself, and only incidentally the revenue-payers, from fraud and embezzlement.

7. RURAL TAXES AND EXACTIONS OTHER THAN LAND REVENUE

The fiscal burden borne by each village did not by any means consist entirely of land revenue. Alongside land revenue proper (*māl*) there were other taxes known as *wujūhāt*.[1] Among these were certain cesses termed *jihāt*, being imposed for the remuneration of officials concerned with the assessment and collection of revenue and often fixed as a particular percentage of it.[2] The *jihāt* were so closely associated with land revenue, that these were assimilated to the latter under the designation *māl-o-jihāt*, so that the *jihāt* now appeared as allowances paid out of the gross tax collected.[3] The other taxes levied on the village were grouped under *sā'ir-jihāt*, comprising taxes on various trades, markets and transit dues, fees of officials – in short practically all taxes other

[10] As seen in the preceding note, Art. 8 of the original version (in Add.27,247, f.332a-b) of Todar Mal's Recommendations requires that receipts be given to peasants when they paid directly into the treasury. Art. 9 of the same version prescribes that the *'āmil* (revenue collector) "should deposit the revenue (*māl*) he has collected into the treasury and the treasurer should give the receipt for this to the peasants. If the accountant (*kārkun*) or treasurer fails to give the receipt or the peasants fail to take it, whosesoever be the fault, the responsibility shall be that of the *'āmils*; and if the peasants complain [about the amount of arrears?], the *'āmils* will not be heard". The corresponding passage, much abridged and lacking important particulars, will be found in *A.N.*, III, 382-3. The *Ā'īn*, I, 289, also provides for a receipt to be issued to the peasants and adds a clause about the *paṭwārī's* endorsing the treasurer's register.

[1] *Ā'īn*, I, 294, 301.

[2] Ibid., I, 300-301, for items included in the *jihāt*: *dih-nīm(ī)* "5 percent", for the remuneration of the *muqaddam* and *chaudhurī*; *ṣad-doī*, "2 percent", for the *paṭwārī* and *qānūngo*; and *ẓābiṭāna*, for the measuring party. The *dah-nīmī* and *jarībana* (*ẓābiṭāna*) also appear under the *jīhāt* in *Siyāqnāma*, 34.
The *Ā'īn*, I, 294, defines *jihāt* as taxes on certain trades, but this is stated in the context of Central Asia and Iran.

[3] See *Ā'īn*, I, 300-01, and the specimen accounts and prescriptions in *Siyāqnāma*, 33-34, etc., and *Khulāṣatu-s Siyāq*, f.77a; Or.2026, f.28a-b.

than land revenue.[4] There were, in addition, exactions and perquisites levied by officials personally, as well as by *zamīndārs*, and these were not included in the *jama*'. They were collectively known as *farū'āt*,[5] but more commonly as *ikhrājāt*[6] or *abwāb* and *ḥubūbāt*.[7]

The two major objects of taxation in an ordinary village, apart from the cultivated fields, were cattle and orchards. The *Ā'īn* lays down the rule that if a man kept under pasture such land as was otherwise liable to land revenue (*kharājī*), a tax of 6 *dāms* per buffalo and 3 per cow (or bullock) was to be imposed upon him. But a cultivator having up to four bullocks, two cows and one buffalo to each plough was to be exempted. Moreover, no tax was to be levied upon the *gaushālas*, or herds of cows kept for religious or charitable purposes.[8]

It is curious that *gāu-shumārī* (tax on cows) is yet included among the taxes remitted by Akbar.[9] It is impossible to say whether this was a tax different from the above, or whether Abū-l Fażl thought the exemptions listed by him a sufficient justification for putting it on the list of remitted exactions.[10] The tax was remitted

[4] *Ā'īn*, I, 301; *Dastūru-l 'Amal-i Navīsindagī*, f.185a; and *Dastūru-l 'Amal-i 'Ālamgīrī*, 23b-24a.

[5] *Ā'īn*, I, 294. A proclamation of the *faujdār* of Sorath (Gujarat), 1686, refers to "the forbidden *abwāb* (taxes), such as *farū'iyāt*" (*Epigraphia Indica, Arabic and Pers. Suppl.* [1955 and 1956], 100).

[6] This sense of the word *ikhrājāt* ("expenses") in revenue literature, is established by the standard formula in *madad-i ma'āsh farmāns* containing the phrase "*ikhrājāt*, such as...", the list of exactions which follows consisting entirely of non-fiscal extortions.

See also Todar Mal's Recommendations, Arts.1 and 9 (*malba* and *ikhrājāt*, in excess of *māl-o-jihāt*) and Art.2 (increase in *ikhrājāt* owing to presence of two accountants in a *pargana*) (original version, *Akbarnāma*, Add.27,247, ff.331b, 332b); Mīr Fatḥullāh Shīrāzī's Memorandum ("*malba*, which is called *istiṣwābī* and *ikhrājāt* by men of the pen" being recovered from officials: *A.N.*, III, 458). *Ikhrājāt* is also used in Art.11 of Aurangzeb's *farmān* to Rasikdās. The significance of the term *malba* is discussed in a note in Chapter IV, Section 3. It meant all that was spent by a village apart from the payment of land revenue and so covered the exactions of officials and *zamīndārs* and the "village expenses". The *ikhrājāt* were thus part of *malba*; but an administration, whose eyes were concentrated on exactions of its officials alone, might naturally use *malba* in the restricted sense of *ikhrājāt*.

I owe guidance on this sense of *ikhrājāt* to the late Professor S.A. Rashid.

[7] Cf. Add. 6603, ff.49b-59b. For the use of the term *abwāb-i malba* in the same sense, see *Nigārnāma-i Munshī*, ed., 136, 145; *Khulāṣatu-l Inshā'*, Or.1750, f.111b.

[8] *Ā'īn*, I, 287. [9] Ibid., 301.

[10] A specific order (*ḥukm*) from the Khān-i Khānān, during the 33rd year of Akbar, forbids the imposition of *gāu-shumārī* in the pastoral grounds of the village of Savi, etc., used for "the cows and bulls of Gobardhan" (Jhaveri, Doc. III A).

again by Jahāngīr, and the remission stood at least till 1634.[11] In addition there was a pastoral levy known as *kāh-charā'ī*, which seems to have been imposed upon grazing animals,[12] and might be the same as *ghāsmārī* in western Rajasthan.[13] From some of our authorities it would appear that Aurangzeb abolished both *gāu-shumārī* and *kāh-charā'ī*,[14] but in the case of the latter, at least, we also have a *ḥasbu-l ḥukm* exhorting local officials to collect it according to the regulations.[15]

Jahāngīr declares with the greatest emphasis that all orchards were exempted from taxation, even when these were planted on land previously cultivated (and so paying revenue earlier), and that never had the tax on trees, known as *sardarakhtī*, been levied in "this everlasting State".[16] This tax had been abolished in 1588 by Akbar.[17] Nevertheless, from a number of documents belonging to Aurangzeb's reign it seems clear that it was then being levied on all orchards, except for those containing graves or yielding no profit. The quantity of the crop was assessed per tree: a fifth thereof was taken from the Hindus and a sixth from the Muslims.[18]

The imposition of the *jizya*, or the poll tax on non-Muslims, by Aurangzeb in 1679 meant an important increase in the magnitude of rural taxation. A separate organization of collectors (*umanā'*) was created for this purpose.[19] The tax was directly collected from

[11] *Maẓhar-i Shāhjahānī*, 155, which protests against the imposition of this illegal tax by a *jāgīrdār* of Sehwan in the early years of Shāhjahān.

[12] A very interesting order issued on 14 March 1658, with two *ṭughrās* styling it simultaneously a *farmān* of Shāhjahān and *nishān-i 'ālīshan* of Dārā Shukoh, forbids the exaction of *kāh-charāī* from the herds of cows attached to the *devāla* of Govardhan Nāth, which used to be brought to the pastures in a particular village (Jhaveri, Doc. XII).

[13] Nainsī reports various rates for *ghāsmārī* added to the *aṣl jama'* as of 1634 in *pargana* Merta, *sarkār* Nagaur, on heads of different grazing animals, e.g. cow, 5 *dāms* ("*dugānīs*"); she-buffalo, 10; goat, sheep, 1. Nainsī also helpfully explains that 40 *dugānīs* made a rupee (*Vigat*, II, 88).

[14] *Mir'āt*, I, 275, 286; *Ẓawābiṭ-i 'Ālamgīrī*, Ethe 415, f.181a, Or.1641, f.136a; Add.6589, f.189a; *Waqā'i' Ajmer*, 63-4, 173.

[15] *Durru-l 'Ulūm*, f.53a-b. The *Jodhpur Rājya kī Khyāt* [*c*.1840], ed. Raghubir Singh and Manohar Singh Ramawat, New Delhi, 1988, 261, in fact, says that a tax on heads of all grazing animals was imposed by the emperor (*pātsāh*) in 1667-8; and it relates this tax to *ghāsmārī* and *charāī*.

[16] *T.J.*, 251-2.

[17] Blochet, Suppl. Pers., 69a-71a. Cf. *Ā'īn*, I, 301.

[18] *Mir'āt*, I, 263-4; *Nigārnāma-i Munshī*, ed., 98, 152; *Durru-l 'Ulūm*, ff.55b-56a; Or. 1779, f.239a.

[19] Īsardās, f.74b; *Mir'āt*, I, 296; Manucci, III, 291; *Dilkushā*, f.139b.

individual subjects in the cities. For the villages it was first decreed that a flat rate of Rs 100 upon 100,000 *dāms*, i.e. 4 per cent of the *jama'dāmī*, was to be paid by the officials of the *khāliṣa* and the holders of *jāgīrs*, who were then to collect the tax at the authorized rates from the peasants.[20] A manual compiled in the later years of Aurangzeb shows, however, that detailed censuses of the men liable to pay this tax were prepared in both towns and villages.[21] The specimen accounts reproduced in it show also that the incidence was not light by any means. Out of 280 males in a village, 185 were held assessable, and of these 137 paid the minimum rate of Rs 3, as. 2, per annum.[22] This at the time would have meant a month's wages for an unskilled urban labourer.[23] As a tax, the *jizya* was extremely regressive and bore the hardest on the poorest.[24] A specimen copy of a *sanad* shows that peasants of a particular area could be granted exemption in cases of acute distress.[25] In 1704, in view of the

[20] *Mir'āt*, I, 298; but, especially, *Nigārnāma-i Munshī*, ed., 77. The fact that having paid an amount in lump sum on the *jama'* of their assignment the *jāgīrdārs* were then expected to recover the amount by collecting *jizya* from the non-Muslims within their jurisdiction, perhaps best explains the proceedings reported from Hugli in 1683: "Parmesurdas", agent of Bulchund, the "Chief Customer" or "Governor of Hoogly and Cassumbazar", "calling all men before him demanded 3 years' Gigeea or head money, whom he pretended they are in arrears to him and forced it from them with all the Barbarous Rigour imaginable" (Hedges, I, 136). Thus we have the sight of a Hindu agent of a Hindu *jāgīrdar* extorting *jizya*, a tax the theoretical purpose of which was to show the superiority of the faithful over the infidels.

[21] *Khulāṣatu-s Siyāq*, Aligarh MS. ff.38b-41b; Or.2026, ff.53a-56b. Cf. also *Nigārnāma-i Munshī*, ed., 76.

[22] *Khulāṣatu-s Siyāq*, Aligarh MS. ff.40a, 41b, Or.2026, f.56a-b. The legal texts lay down the three rates for the *jizya* in terms of *dirhams*; and Aurangzeb's administration had to convert them into rupees. The equivalents given in the authorities vary slightly. For example, the minimum rate of Rs 3., as. 2 in the *Khulāṣatu-s Siyāq* may be compared with Rs 3, as.4, in Īsardās, f.74b, and Rs 3, as. 8, in Manucci, II, 234.

[23] Within roughly the same period we have evidence of wages being paid at the rate of Rs 4 a month in Surat (Ovington, 229); Rs 2, as.10, at Ahmadabad (*Mir'āt*, I, 291); and Rs 2, as. 13, to Rs 3, as.12, at Hugli (Master, II, 41).

[24] This may be judged from the fact that the rich who had 10,000 *dirhams* or over were asked to pay no more than 48 *dirhams*, while the poor with no more than 200 had to pay 12 (*Mir'āt*, I, 296-7. Cf. Īsardās, f.74a-b).

[25] *Nigārnāma-i Munshī*, ed., 139. This document was published by S. Sulaiman Nadvi in *Ma'ārif*, XL (1937), no. 4, 294-6, having been extracted from a later collection, the *Nigārnāma* of Munshī La'l Chand. There is a serious error in the first few lines of the *Ma'ārif* text, where it reads *zamīndārān* in place of *zimmī-i nādār*, "the indigent non-Muslim" of the original. The *sanad* is addressed to a *dīwān* and recites that the *jizya* should not be imposed upon destitute persons. Since the poor peasants (*reza rī'āyā*) who had to engage in cultivation were found

famine and the Maratha War, Aurangzeb remitted the *jizya* throughout the Dakhin for the duration of the war.[26] Nevertheless his general policy was to discourage *jizya* remissions.[27] Other authorities emphasize that the collections were accompanied with the greatest oppression and most of the amount actually collected was embezzled by the officials, so that only a very small part of it used really to reach the imperial treasury.[28]

Another source of revenue was the property of those who died without heirs.[29] In Bengal this was given a rather liberal interpretation, and if any peasant or stranger died without leaving a son, all his possessions together with his wife and daughters were seized for the benefit, depending upon the locality, of the *khāliṣa*, the *jāgīrdār* or the "dominant *zamīndār*". This "abominable practice" was called *ankora* and is said to have been abolished by Shā'ista Khān.[30]

The fees and perquisites of the revenue officials were numerous. These officials exacted from the villages their perquisites (*rusūm*) and other cesses in return for some real or pretended services.[31] From a *farmān* of Aurangzeb it appears that the men sent to collect the revenue and guard the crops were paid their daily expenses by the villagers, but these were deducted from the revenue demand.[32] In the case of the measuring party, however, as we have already seen, a levy of one *dām* per *bīgha*, known as *ẕābiṭāna*, used to be separately imposed. But there were, probably, only a very few officials who contented themselves with the allowances granted

to be in debt even for their seeds and cattle (the *Ma'ārif* text reads differently here), the cultivators were to be exempted from paying the *jizya*; but it was nevertheless to be realized from the *ta'alluqdārs, chaudhurīs, qānūngos, ṭarafdārs* and other inhabitants of towns and villages.

[26] *Akhbārāt* 48/36 and A 245. Cf. also *Akhbārāt* 47/323.

[27] Cf. Ma'mūrī, f.179a; Khāfī Khān, II, 377-8.

[28] *Dilkushā*, f.139b; Manucci, II, 291.

[29] *Dastūru-l 'Amal-i 'Ālamgīrī*, f.23b.

[30] *Fatḥiya-i 'Ibriya*, f.131b.

[31] These levies appear in the specimen audited village accounts under the heading *ikhrājāt* (*Dastūru-l 'Amal-i 'Ālamgīrī*, ff.41b-42b, and *Siyāqnāma*, 77-79). Being outside the payments made to the *foṭa-khāna* or treasury, these would not have appeared in the official revenue accounts. If, then, a *shiqqdār* of a *pargana* near Lahor having thus exacted Rs 4,000 besides the *rusūm*, was faced with the possibility of detection, the best course for him was to collude with the *qānūngo*, destroy the old village papers and get fresh ones written by the "village accountants", after paying them back the money to make up the shortfall (*waẓ'e*) (*Tazkira Pīr Ḥassū Telī*, composed 1647, Aligarh MS, ff.109a-113a).

[32] *Mir'āt*, I, 275-6.

by the administration. Illegal exactions from the peasants by officials were, therefore, the subject of repeated imperial prohibitions. Among such forbidden extortions were customary or compulsory gifts like *salāmī*[33] and *bhenṭ*; fines and bribes, collectively called *bālādastī* ("high-handed"); payments expected on the performance of certain definite acts by the officials, e.g. *paṭṭadārī*, on the grant of a *paṭṭa*, *balkaṭī*, when permitting the crop to be cut, and *taḥṣīldārī*, when presumably accepting the payment of revenue; and, finally, *kharj-i ṣādir o wārid*, "expenses on those coming and going" to meet the needs of the officials during their visits.[34] There were other exactions still, but perhaps little can be gained by cataloguing them here.[35] The exact rates set for these cesses cannot be known, and in any case they could hardly have been uniform. But together they could have sometimes amounted to pretty large sums. This may be illustrated by the complaint of the inhabitants of a village that the "*paṭṭa-dārī*, *bhenṭ* and other forbidden *abwāb*" imposed upon them by the revenue officials (*'ummāl*) came in all to nearly a third of the total *jama'* fixed on the village.[36]

[33] *Ā'īn*, I, 287, 301. Abū-l Fazl explains that *salāmī*, lit. salutation money, was the name given to the gift of a *dām*-coin which the *muqaddam* and *paṭwārī* proferred to the *'amalguzār* whenever they came to see him. Besides this, another item on the list of exactions forbidden by Akbar (ibid., 301) is one called *qunalgha*. It also occurs constantly in *madad-i ma'āsh* documents among the taxes and cesses the officials were prohibited from extorting from the grantees. The word is of Turkish origin and its exact sense was unknown when Charles Elliott conducted his investigations (*Chronicles of Oonao*, 119). Add.6603, f.75a-b defines it as a gift made to the *ḥākim* (official), more particularly the pot of yogurt which the *zamīndār* was expected to offer when paying him a visit. See Lambton, *Landlord and Peasant in Persia*, 102, 437, (*qunughla*), and Mohammad Shafi, *Islamic Culture*, 1947, 390-393 (vars. *qonārgha*, *qonālgha*).

[34] All these exactions, with the exception of *salāmī* and *balkaṭī* are prohibited in *Mir'āt*, I, 304; *Nigārnāma-i Munshī*, ed., 80, 136, 145; *Khulāṣatu-l Inshā'*, Or.1750, f.111b. For *balkaṭī*, see *Ā'īn*, I, 287, 301. *Ā'īn*, I, also mentions *taḥṣīldārī*. For the definitions of *bhenṭ* and *paṭṭadārī*, see Elliott, *Chronicles of Ooano*, 120-21; for *bālādastī*, Add.6603, f.57b.

[35] They are listed in *Ā'īn*, I, 287, 301, and *Dastūru-l 'Amal-i Navīsindagī*, f.185a. Two other items, *chiṭṭhīāna* (from *chiṭṭhī*, letter) and *faṣlāna* (from *faṣl*, crop), are added in *Nigārnāma-i Munshī*, f.189a, Bodl. f.150a.

[36] The *jama'* amounted to Rs 1,350 and the illegal exactions to Rs 400 (*Durru-l 'Ulūm*, ff.54a-55a). In the specimen *barāmad* accounts reproduced in the *Dastūru-l 'Amal-i 'Ālamgīrī*, ff.41b-42b, the total receipts of the treasury amounted to Rs 4,427 as against Rs 172 appropriated by the various officials. In the *Khulāṣatu-s Siyāq*, ff.91b-94a, Or.2026, ff.59a-64a, the corresponding figures for the village of Hamidpur are Rs 1,011 and Rs 92, as.12; and in the *Siyāqnāma*, 77-79, Rs 106 and Rs 27.

The imposition of forced labour on certain sections of the rural population was an old-established practice.[37] Abū-l Faẓl tells us with apparent disapproval that in Kashmir according to an old practice the saffron obtained in revenue was redistributed among the peasants who were compelled *gratis* to pick out the seeds; furthermore, they were required to bring wood from distant places. Akbar abolished both these practices,[38] but these were again found prevalent in 1633 when Shāhjahān issued a public proclamation forbidding these and other oppressive practices.[39] The custom of impressing labour to carry the baggage of officials and superiors was quite general in India.[40] In an official document we find the inhabitants of a town complaining of "*begār* and (the task of) carrying bed-cots", which were among the odious burdens imposed upon them by the revenue officials.[41] In 1670 the Kewats (members of a subdivision of the well known peasant caste of Kurmis) of a village in *sarkār* Kalinjar needed to obtain a confirmation of their previous exemption from *begār* from the local officials.[42] In *madad-i ma'āsh* documents, the standard list of impositions remitted to the grantees includes "*begār* and *shikār*".[43] The latter word means a hunt or chase, but it must here refer to the labour required from the peasants when a hunt was organized for the benefit of some potentate or the other: jungles might have to be cut down, paths cleared, the camp baggage carried, animals rounded up, all in the preparation of a single chase.[44]

[37] "Since the august reign of Sultan [Shihābu-ddīn] of Ghaur" (Ḥasan Alī Khān, *Tawārīkh-i Daulat-i Sher Shāhī*, fragment pub. in *Medieval India Quarterly*, I [1], 3). It has, of course, a far more ancient history.

[38] *A.N.*, III, 727, 734. The practice of forced carriage of loads went back to the 9th century in Kashmir (Kalhaṇa, *Rājataraṅgiṇi*, transl. A. Stein, I, 209). Akbar took particular pride in the fact that when he built the fort of Nagarnagar near Srinagar "no one rendered forced labour (*begār*) here; all obtained wages from the treasury" (inscription on the fortress gate, copied in *Tārīkh-i Ḥasan*, I, 387; also seen personally).

[39] Inscription on the gate of Jāmi' Masjid, Srinagar, copy personally made, the one in *Tārīkh-i Ḥasan*, 500-01, being defective and inaccurate. Qazwīnī (Aligarh transcript, 509-10) gives an abridged version. See for transl. (with annotation) of these versions, S. Moosvi in *Aligarh Jour. of Oriental Studies*, III (2), 1986, 141-52.

[40] The *Tashrīḥu-l Aqwām*, ff.181b-182a, tells us that the Chamārs were called *Begārīs*, because they used to be compelled to carry baggage without payment. Cf. Charles Elliott, *Chronicles of Oonao*, 119; Elliot, *Memoirs*, 232.

[41] *Durru-l 'Ulūm*, f.53a-b. The township was Muradabad, which then belonged to *sarkār* Sambhal.

[42] Sihunda Docs. no.66.

[43] Cf. Elliott, *Chronicles of Oonao*, 119.

[44] The subject of *jangal-barī* (jungle clearance) by the *jāgīrdārs* and officials

8. METHODS OF RELIEF AND AGRICULTURAL DEVELOPMENT

The basic object of the Mughal agrarian administration was to obtain land revenue on an ever-ascending scale. However, agricultural production, dependent as it is on a number of natural phenomena, undergoes so many fluctuations every year that the surplus produce, of which land revenue formed the larger part, could not have remained constant in volume, let alone in its rate of increase. The cash nexus, it is true, considerably reduced the fluctuations in terms of money, since, generally speaking, prices should have moved in an inverse direction to the output. But money also introduced problems of its own; and long before the age of capitalist crises and recessions the Mughal administration was being embarrassed from time to time by abnormal falls in prices, so that "low prices" took their due place in official regulations, alongside "the decrease in produce, drought and blight", the natural "calamities".[1] As we have seen in some detail, there was under all methods of revenue assessment some provision for relief in the case of bad harvests. In crop-sharing and *kankūt* this was automatic in that the state's share would rise and fall with the amount of yield obtained in the year concerned. A commutation of the demand at market prices meant that the authorities would also shoulder part of the risk from price fluctuations. In the *ẕabṭ*, and the form of *nasaq* associated with it, there had to be deliberate provision for crop-failure in the form of reduction of *nābūd* from the assessed area.[2] But revenue could be adjusted to drastic changes in price levels only through special action by the court.

Once the final assessment had been made, the duty of the revenue collectors or *'āmils* was to collect it in full, leaving no

---

in connexion with Prince A'ẓam's hunting expedition in Gujarat crops up frequently in the news-letters from his headquarters (*Akhbārāt* A 49 and *passim*). A *parwāna* reproduced in the *Nigārnāma-i Munshī*, f.196a-b, Bodl. f.155b, ed.150, orders all the smaller rivers from Dehli to Khizrabad near the foot of the mountains to be bridged in preparation for the prince's (Mu'aẓẓam's?) hunting tour, and the officials of the *parganas* concerned are asked to provide materials and labour to the official deputed for the task.

[1] Aurangzeb's *farmān* to Rasikdās, Preamble.

[2] In the *khasra* (assessment paper) under *ẕabṭ* there was a special column for the area of *nābūd*, to be deducted from the area originally measured (*ārāẓī*) (see section 2 of this chapter). A pre-1648 document from *sarkār* Surat (Gujarat) concerns inspection by officials of the crops standing on the alleged area of *nābūd*, which the peasants were enjoined not to harvest until the inspection established the extent of crop damage. (Blochet, Suppl. Pers. 482, f.131a).

balance (*bāqī*) behind.[3] Sher Shāh is said to have declared that concessions could be permitted at the time of assessment, but never at the time of collection.[4] The suspicion is expressed in the preamble of Aurangzeb's *farmān* to Rasikdās that the large remissions granted from the assessed figure for pretended losses from calamities were largely fictitious. Another *farmān* of the same emperor lays down that no remissions were to be allowed once the crop had been cut.[5] Nevertheless in practice it could hardly have been possible always to collect the entire amount; and the balance was generally carried forward to be collected along with the demand of the next year. A bad year, therefore, might leave an intolerable burden for the peasant in the shape of arrears.[6] These had a natural tendency to grow and this led to a distinction being made between the arrears from the immediately preceding year, which were scheduled to be collected in full during the current year, and the arrears technically known as *sanwāt bāqī*, which dated from earlier years.[7] A manual recommends that the latter should be recovered gradually in annual instalments, not exceeding five per cent of the current *jama'*.[8] It also seems to have been a common practice to demand the arrears, owed by peasants who had fled or died, from their neighbours. A *ḥasbu-l ḥukm*, issued in 1672-73, from Aurangzeb's court, seeks to check this practice in both the *k͟hāliṣa* and the assignments of the *jāgīrdārs*: no peasant could be held liable for arrears contracted by any other; and only arrears from the year immediately preceding were to be recovered, all older arrears being written off.[9]

In conditions of famine, remissions had sometimes to be granted on a large scale, which in most cases might have amounted to little more than making a virtue of necessity. The most liberal on record are those made in Gujarat and the Dakhin by Shāhjahān during the great famine of 1630-2. Seventy lakhs of rupees were

[3] Todar Mal's Recommendations, *A.N.*, III, 382; *Farmān* to Rasikdās, Art. 4.

[4] 'Abbās K͟hān, f.12a, ed. 23.

[5] *Farmān* to Muḥammad Hāshim, Arts. 10 and 18.

[6] The *karorī* of Navsari, near Surat, pleaded the need for delay in dealing with a *muqaddam* and villagers who had pilfered the wreckage of an English ship, *Whale*, in 1623, alleging: "now was the cheife time of their harvest and that mocaddam had not paid in his last years hassell [*ḥāṣil*]". It is added that "the Karori is afraid to beat these people because they owe him money and would probably run away" (*Factories, 1622-3*, 253-4).

[7] *Farmān* to Rasikdās, Art. 5.

[8] *K͟hulāṣatu-l Inshā'*, Or.1750, f.112a. Cf. Or 1779, ff.216b-217a, 218a, 219b.

[9] *Nigārnāma-i Munshī*, ed., 149; *Mir'āt*, I, 290-91.

remitted in the *khāliṣa* lands whose total *jama*ʻ in the whole empire amounted to 80 crore *dāms*.[10] The *jāgīrdārs* had to award similar remissions, and in this they were helped by a reduction in the *jama*ʻ*dāmī*, amounting for the Dakhin provinces alone, to thirty crore *dāms*.[11] During the same reign when a famine occurred in Kashmir in 1642, it was ordered that the assessments on the peasants be reduced;[12] and in Lahor province the *jama*ʻ in the *khāliṣa* lands was reduced in 1651 as a result of scarcity conditions.[13]

Apart from relief measures of this kind, which were meant to help the peasants tide over situations of exceptional distress, it must have been obvious that steps taken in aid of the development of agriculture could offer an effective means of increasing the revenue. The Mughal conception of development is frequently stated in documents and involves the realization of two major objectives: the extension of the area under cultivation and increase in the cultivation of cash crops (*jins-i kāmil*).[14] The first objective derived its importance from the presence of large areas of land lying untilled; and the second held its attraction because cash crops were taxed at higher rates, and a shift to them would naturally enhance tax revenue.

The collection of such statistical information as the Mughal administration possessed was, at least in part, motivated by a desire to discover the possibilities of extending and improving the cropping, and to judge how far any progress in this direction was taking place. The Karorī Experiment under Akbar (1574), which involved area measurement on an extensive scale, is interpreted by three contemporary authorities as chiefly aimed at bringing

[10] Lāhorī, I, 364. The total *jama*ʻ figure apparently belongs to the *khāliṣa* of the whole Empire. Qazwīnī, Or.173, f.221a-b, gives a lower figure for the remission in the *khāliṣa* (Rs 50 lakh) and none at all for the total *jama*ʻ.

[11] Ṣādiq Khān, Or.171, ff.31b-32a, Or.1671, f.18b. Khāfī Khān I, 449, reads "30 or 40 lakhs". The remissions made by the *jāgīrdārs* are referred to in general terms also in Qazwīnī and Lāhorī, op.cit. The reduction in *jama'dāmī*, known as *takhfīf-i dāmī*, entitled the *jāgīrdārs* to claim additional assignment bearing equivalent amounts of *jama*ʻ.

[12] *Takhfīf-i tashkhīṣ*: Ṣādiq Khān, Or.174, f.99b, Or.1671, f.54a.

[13] Wāriṣ, a: f.445a, b: f.76a-b.

[14] See Akbar's general order (*dastūru-l 'āmal*) to officials in *Inshā'-i Abū-l Faẓl*, 60, and *Mir'āt*, I, 165; *Ā'īn*, I, 285-6; *Farmān* to Rasikdās, Preamble and Art. 2 *Nigārnāma-i Munshī*, ed. 77, 81. Both of these objectives were recognized by Muḥammad bin Tughluq (1324-51) and lay behind his attempt to reorganize the agrarian administration of the Doab country during his last years (Baranī, *Tārīkh-i Fīrūz-shāhī*, 498-9).

the uncultivated land under the plough.[15] Shāhjahān used to be personally provided with information relating to the state of cultivation in both the *khāliṣa* and the *jāgīrs*.[16] And from an extant document it appears that reports about newly settled villages and the number of their peasants were called for by the headquarters.[17] But in Aurangzeb's reign the complaint is officially voiced that the *qānūngos* and *chaudhurīs* provided the administration only with figures for the cultivable area and not with particulars about land under actual cultivation, nor about the cash crops, so that little track could be kept of the pace of development or decay.[18]

Revenue concessions were the chief instrument devised by the Mughal administration to encourage development in the two directions recognized by it. Land which had been out of cultivation for some years was, for example, charged half or less than half the standard rate of revenue in the first year of its being brought under the plough; the rate was thereafter raised annually, till in the fifth year the full amount was reached.[19] If the peasants sowed more land than was fixed for the year by the revenue officials (under *nasaq*), no revenue was to be levied for the additional

[15] 'Ārif Qandahārī, 197; *Ṭabaqāt-i Akbarī*, II, 300-01; Badāūnī, II, 189-90.

[16] *Chār Chaman-i Barhaman*, A: f.32a-b; B: f.26a-b.

[17] *Selected Documents*, 244-5.

[18] *Farmān* to Rasikdās, Preamble; *Nigārnāma-i Munshī*, ed., 77. It is probable that the meticulous distinction in the revenue accounts between *aṣlī* (original), *iẓāfa* (additional, newly settled), and *dākhilī* (new village whose *jama*' was still considered part of the *jama*' of an *aṣlī* village) was also maintained for a similar purpose. (See *Khulāṣatu-s Siyāq*, f.77a, Or.2026, ff.28a-29a; and Add.6603, f.80a.)

[19] After setting out Sher Shāh's *rai*' for the *polaj* and *parauṭī* lands the *Ā'īn* says that in the case of *chachar* (land untilled for three or four years) 2/5 of the standard demand should be realized in the first year, 3/5 in the second, 4/5 in the third and the full amount in the fifth. For the *banjar* land (uncultivated for five years or more) the revenue rates for the different years are given in kind for different crops, but the full amount (as set for *polaj*) is reached in the fifth year. The initial rate is nominal, being one-eighth of that on *polaj* in the case of wheat (*Ā'īn*, I, 301-3). In 1582 Todar Mal recommended that land which had been untilled for three or four years should be charged half the standard rate in the first year, 3/4 in the next and the full rate in the third (*Akbarnāma*, Add. 27,247, f.231b; Bib Ind., III, 282).

In Kashmir one-sixth of the crop was to be demanded in the first year on land unploughed for ten years; one-fifth, on land unploughed for four to ten years; and one-third, on land left fallow for two to four years. The maximum proportion of one-half was to be reached in the fourth, third, and second years respectively (*A.N.*, III, 727.).

In Sind, a *parwāna* of 1716 enjoins that only a seventh part of the produce be taken, under *bhāolī*, from peasants newly cultivating floodland (*Jour. Pak. Hist. Soc.*, LIX(4), 63-64).

area.[20] In the case of a village where the wells had fallen in, a royal order prescribes that the person who offered to repair them should not be asked to pay any land revenue, but only a tax at flat rates per well. This was to be increased annually till the fifth year, whereafter it was to remain constant till the tenth, when the normal land revenue was at last to be imposed.[21] After the 1630-32 famine, extraordinarily low revenue rates are said to have been offered in some of the affected areas so as to encourage resettlement.[22] With regard to cash crops, it was ordered that land newly brought under them should initially be charged lower rates than usual.[23] Thus if land previously under crop-sharing was sown with a high-grade crop, the revenue in the first year was to be one-fourth less than was leviable under the normal *dastūr* for that crop.[24]

A number of non-monetary concessions were also prescribed in order to provide incentives for development. The cultivator of *banjar* land could have his choice concerning the method of assessment.[25] If a village had no *banjar* land left and its peasants had the capacity to cultivate more, the *'amalguzār* or revenue collector was advised to transfer to it land from some other village.[26] If during any year the cultivation of cash crops was extended, but the total area under the plough fell off, the *'amalguzār* was not to raise any objection, so long as the *jama'* remained unaffected.[27] But if the peasants left any area of land untilled without reason, they might still be required to pay the revenue they had been paying before on it.[28]

[20] *Ā'īn*, I, 285; *Hidāyatu-l Qawā'id*, f.10b.

[21] The revenue per well in the first year was to be Rs.10, then rising annually, Rs 15-23-34, to Rs 50 in the fifth (*Nigārnāma-i Munshī*, ed., 144).

[22] Ṣādiq K͟hān tells us that Gangā Rām, the *'āmil* of Saiyid K͟hān-i Jahān Bārha, settled new peasants in the *sarkārs* of Nadurbar and Sultanpur by giving them a *qaul* to charge only 100 or 200 *ṭankas* instead of 1,000 or 2,000 as previously (Or.174, ff.31b-32a, Or.1671, f.18b). An English letter, however, paints a different picture in respect of Gujarat. The famine had passed, yet "the villages fill but slowly" and "if the excessive tiranny and covetousness of the governors of all sorts would give the poor people leave but to lift up their heads in one yeares vacancy from oppression, they would be enabled to keep cattle about them, and so to advance the plenty which the earth produceth" (*Factories, 1634-36*, 65).

[23] *Ā'īn*, I, 285. [24] Ibid., 286. [25] Ibid., 303.

[26] Ibid., 285. [27] Ibid., 286.

[28] As was one Jaswant Nāyak who had been cultivating nearly 30 *bīghas* of land in village Anmalsar near Surat, but had now abandoned its cultivation for no known reason (Doc. of 1638 in Blochet, Suppl. Pers. 482, f.145a-b).

The advancing of *taqāvī* (lit. strength-giving) loans to the peasants was another important method of encouraging cultivation. Abū-l Fazl states simply that the *'amalguzār* should assist the "empty-handed peasants" by advancing them loans.[29] Todar Mal was more specific in his Recommendations and suggested that *taqāvī* should be given to cultivators who were in distressed circumstances and did not have seeds or cattle.[30] A later manual recommends that the assessor (*amīn*) should see whether the ploughs in a village are sufficient for tilling the land belonging to it; if not, he should give *taqāvī* to the cultivators for the purchase of bullocks and seeds.[31] The distribution of *taqāvī* for similar purposes also formed an important part of Murshid Qulī Khān's reforms in the Dakhin.[32] We know that his colleague, Multafat Khān was the author of an ambitious proposal to advance Rs 40,000 to 50,000 "as *taqāvī*" from the imperial treasury for financing the construction of dams (*bands*) in the provinces of Khandesh and Berar (Pāinghāṭ region), to be disbursed in the *jāgīrs* and also, presumably, in the *khāliṣa*.[33]

The *taqāvī* loans were, as a rule, advanced through the *chaudhurīs* (or *deshmukhs*) and *muqaddams* (or *paṭels*), who distributed them among the individual peasants and stood surety for their repayment.[34] Loans given to the peasants by the headmen on their own account were also known as *taqāvī*.[35]

Abū-l Fazl recommends that the loan should be recovered "slowly".[36] On the other hand, Todar Mal laid down that the repayment was to be exacted in part at the first harvest and fully in the next.[37] Later evidence also suggests that it was the general

[29] *Ā'īn*, I, 285. Cf. *Farmān* to Muḥammad Hāshim, Art.2.

[30] See the original version in Add.27, 247, f.231b. In the final text of *A.N.*, III, 382, the details are missing.

[31] *Hidāyatu-l Qawā'id*, f.10b.

[32] "For the purchase of bullocks, buffaloes and other necessaries of cultivation" (Ṣādiq Khān, Or.174, f.185b, Or.1671, f.91a; Khāfī Khān, I, 733n).

[33] *Ādāb-i 'Ālamgīrī*, f.53a-b; *Ruq'āt-i 'Ālamgīr*, 131-2.

[34] Todar Mal's Recommendations, Art.3 (original version, Add.27, 247, f.231b): "and bonds should be taken from the *muqaddams*" for repayment of the *taqāvī* loans. (In the corresponding passage in *A.N.*, III, 382, the words, "*taqāvī*", "bonds" and "*muqaddams*", are omitted and "help", "written paper" and "respectable men" substituted.) See also *Ādāb-i 'Ālamgīrī*, f.123b; Ṣādiq Khān and Khāfī Khān, op. cit.; *Farhang-i Kārdānī*, f.35b; *Hidāyatu-l Qawā'id*, f.10b.

[35] *Durru-l 'Ulūm*, ff.43a,55b.

[36] "*Ba-āhistagī*". *Ā'īn*, I, 285.

[37] Recommendations, Art.3 (*Akbarnāma*, Add.27,247, f.231b; Bib. Ind., III, 382).

practice to try to recover the whole amount at the very first crop, and failing that within at least the same year.[38] Multafat Khān had promised that, if his scheme of financing bunds was accepted, the whole amount advanced could be realized within two years.[39] But sometimes collection in annual instalments was also sanctioned;[40] and a manual declares that the *taqāvī* arrears should be added to the *sanwāt bāqī* and collected as part of these arrears.[41] There is no reference anywhere to interest being charged on *taqāvī* loans, and it is possible that, under theological influences, the authorities considered such a practice disreputable. It is nevertheless quite likely that the *chaudhurīs* and headmen, who offered themselves as sureties on behalf of the peasants, duly exacted their commissions or bribes from them for this favour.

In case any of the peasants died or fled, these two officials, who had stood surety, were required to repay the amounts advanced to them. But in at least one letter of instructions it is ordered that the loan was to be completely written off, if the peasants, though present, were because of extreme distress not in the position to repay it.[42]

It may not perhaps be strictly accurate to say that the Mughal methods of agrarian development were confined solely to the fiscal sphere. The idea that the administration itself should undertake the construction of irrigation works is expressed, for instance, in the instructions issued to revenue officials to repair and dig wells as part of the effort to extend and improve cultivation.[43] In Multan province, the "canal superintendent" was required to dig new channels and build dams.[44] Elsewhere an official in charge of a stream (*jūi-āb*) is enjoined to keep the stream "in repair" with the help of the peasants of villages using its water for their cultivation, and to distribute its water equitably among the different villages.[45] There is, then, the striking memorandum, containing proposals

[38] *Khulāṣatu-l Inshā'*, Or.1750, f.112a; *Farhang-i Kārdānī*, f.35b; *Hidāyatu-l Qawā'id*, f.10b. Murshid Qulī Khān is said to have asked for repayment at the time of the harvest, but in two instalments. (Thus Ṣādiq Khān, op. cit. The latter clause is omitted in Khāfī Khān.)

[39] *Ādāb-i 'Ālamgīrī*, f.53a-b; *Ruq'āt-i 'Ālamgīr*, 131-2.

[40] *Ādāb-i 'Ālamgīrī*, f.123b.

[41] *Khulāṣatu-l Inshā'*, op. cit.

[42] *Ādāb-i 'Ālamgīrī*, f.123b.

[43] *Farmān* to Rasikdās, Preamble.

[44] *Nigārnāma-i Munshī*, ed., 151-2. See also *Maẓhar-i Shāhjahānī*, 17-18, for the need of construction of canals in Bhakkar *sarkār*, either by the peasants themselves or by the *jāgīrdārs*.

[45] Or. 1779, ff.224b-225a.

for deepening the Chutang in order to provide irrigation up to Hansi.[46] Moreover the canals laid out in the reign of Shāhjahān were no mean enterprises. All the same, this was not an aspect on which much attention was really bestowed. The main purpose of Shāhjahān's two great canals was evidently not to provide water for the fields, but, in the case of one, to irrigate his gardens at Lahor and, in that of the other, to supply water to the fort at Shāhjahānābād, his new city at Dehli, although these canals undoubtedly proved beneficial to agriculture along their courses. Yet, though two or three instances can be cited where the administration took some interest in promoting irrigation, silence generally prevails on this subject in the mass of the revenue literature of the period. Despite the view traced to Karl Marx, sufficient evidence does not exist to warrant the belief that the state's construction and control of irrigation works was a prominent factor in the agrarian life of Mughal India.[47]

[46] Bālkrishan Brahman, ff.107a-109b. See Chapter I, Sec.2, for this project.

[47] This is a point which Marx makes in his article 'The British Rule in India', 1853 (reprinted in Marx and Engels, *On Colonialism*, 37). He returns to the theme in *Capital*, I, 523 n., where he says: "One of the material bases of the power of the state over the small disconnected producing organisms in India, was the regulation of the water supply. The Mahomedan rulers of India understood this better than their English successors. It is enough to recall to mind the famine of 1865... of Orissa." It is possible that Marx was misled by information relating to the tank system of south India and the irrigation works in Iran and Central Asia.

CHAPTER VII

REVENUE ASSIGNMENTS

1. *JĀGĪRS* AND *KHĀLIṢA*

The peculiar feature of the state in Mughal India was that it served not merely as the protective arm of the exploiting classes, but was itself the principal instrument of exploitation. We saw in the preceding chapter how closely the revenue demand approximated to the surplus produce, or whatever was produced in excess of the minimum needed for the peasant's subsistence. It formally rested with the Emperor's will to dispose of this enormous tribute. Over the larger portion of the Empire, he transferred his right to the land revenue and other taxes within definite territorial limits to certain of his subjects. The areas whose revenues were thus assigned by the emperor were known in the Mughal empire as *jāgīrs*.[1] *Iqṭā*' and *tuyūl* were established synonyms of *jāgīr*, but

[1] Moreland in *Agrarian System* seems to be the first to have appreciated the essential aspects of the system of *jāgīrs*. He rejected the word "fief" by which *jāgīr* had till then been generally rendered and substituted for it "revenue assignment" or simply "assignment". John Shore seems to have anticipated him here, for in his famous minute of 18 June 1789 he held that "jaghire" under the Mughal government "denoted Assigned lands" *(Fifth Report,* 170).

Jāgīr is really a compound of two Persian words and should strictly be, though was not, spelt *jāi-gīr*. Literally, it means "(one) holding or occupying a place". *Bahār-i 'Ajam*, the great Persian dictionary completed in India in 1739-40, offers the following definition of its sense, s.v. *jāgīr, jāigīr:* "Tract of land, which kings, confer upon [read *ba* for *wa*] *umarā*' (nobles) and *manṣabdārs*, and such like, so that they may appropriate the revenue *(maḥṣūl)* thereof from whatever is produced by cultivation; in the terminology of the clerks of the kings of India, [the same as] *tuyūl* and the portion of country given in pay in lieu of the monthly [salary]. Although it occurs in the verses of some recent poets of Iran it does not belong to their idiom. In Arabic it is called *iqṭā*'." One can hardly improve upon this definition. That the term was of Indian provenance may be confirmed from its absence in the glossary of terms appended to Lambton, *Landlord and Peasant in Persia*. I.H. Siddiqui notes its absence from any document or work written even in India before Akbar's accession (*PIHC*, 24th session, 1961, Delhi, 145, 148n); the word *jāgīr* occurring in Ẓiyā Baranī's *Tārīkh-i Fīrūz-shāhī,* Bib. Ind., 40, is an obvious misreading for *chākar* (retainers). The first known document in which the term appears (*jāigīrdārān*) is a *farmān* of Akbar of December 1559 (a revenue grant in *pargana* Fatehpur, *sarkār* Lakhnau: xerox in CAS in History Library, Aligarh). The first document of assignment to a *jāigīrdār*, so styled, is a *farmān* of April 1561 in favour of Rāmdās (transl. with reprod. in *Akbar and his India*, ed. Irfan Habib, 281, 285); the assignment itself is still called *wajh-i 'alūfa*, salary assignment, and not *jāgīr.* Indeed, the term *jāigīrdār* itself was a replacement of the

not commonly used.[2] The assignees were known as *jāgīrdārs* ("holders of *jāgīrs*"), occasionally also as *tuyūldārs* and *iqṭā'dārs*. The governing class of the Mughal Empire obtained its income mainly from these assignments. The *jāgīrdārs* were usually *manṣabdārs*, holding ranks (*manṣabs*) bestowed upon them by the emperor. These ranks were generally dual, viz. *ẕāt* and *sawār*, the former chiefly meant to indicate personal pay, while the latter determined the size of the contingents which the *manṣab*-holder was obliged to maintain.[3] The pay scales for both ranks were minutely laid down,[4] and the *manṣabdārs* received their emoluments either in cash (*naqd*) from the treasury, or, as was more

---

term *wajhdār*, which still occurs in a *farmān* of 1558 concerning a land dispute in a *pargana* under Sambhal (NA 2719/1, for which see S.Z.H. Jafri in *Akbar and his India*, 266-9). For earlier use of the terms *wajh* and *wajhdār* in this sense, see 'Afīf, *Tārīkh-i Fīrūz-shāhī*, Bib. Ind., 296-7; and *Bāburnāma*, ed. Mano, 553. Cf. Iqtidar A. Khan in *Medieval India-1*, 63-4 & n.

[2] *Iqṭā'* is an Arabic word, almost as old as Islām. It first denoted a piece of landed property received from the state, but gradually came to signify revenue assignments "in which the State has the real rights of property" (F. Lokkegaard, *Islamic Taxation in the Classic Period*, 14 ff.). It was purely in the latter sense that the word was used in the literature of the Dehli Sultanate. But by the Mughal period it was used mostly when a formal style was affected and then deliberately to avoid the more mundane word, *jāgīr*. If *iqṭā'* was thus archaic, *tuyūl* was an exotic. It was a term used in Iran, from the 14th century onwards (Lambton, *Landlord and Peasant in Persia*, 101-2). In Mughal India its use became perhaps more common than of *iqṭā,'* but it still remained a secondary synonym of *jāgīr*.

The author of *Mir'ātu-l Iṣṭilāh*, f.26a, seeks to make a distinction between the senses of *tuyūl* and *jāgīr*. According to him, the former was used for assignments held by princes of the royal blood and the latter for those held by *umarā'* (nobles holding high *manṣabs*) and *manṣabdārs*. There is no evidence for the existence of such a refinement in the literature of the 17th century and both the terms are used there indifferently for all assignments. The princes' assignments are generally indicated by formulas such as *tuyūl-i* (or *jāgīr-i) wuklā'-i sarkār-i a'lā* (or *sarkār-i daulat-madār*, etc.). See especially the documents in *Nigārnāma-i Munshī*, many of which are concerned with Prince Mu'aẕẕam's *jāgīrs*.

[3] Abdul Aziz, *The Mansabdari System and the Mughal Army*, and Moreland, 'Rank (*manṣab*) in the Mugul State Service', *JRAS*, 1936, 641-65, constitute pioneering studies of the *manṣab* system. But there has been much subsequent work: S. Moosvi, 'Evolution of *Manṣab* system under Akbar until 1596-7', *JRAS*, 1981, 173-85; I. Habib, *'Manṣab* System, 1595-1637', *PIHC*, 29th session, 1967, Patiala, I, 221-42, and '*Manṣab* Salary Scales under Jahāngīr and Shāh Jahān', *Islamic Culture* (1985), 203-27; and M. Athar Ali, *Mughal Nobility under Aurangzeb*, 38-73.

[4] The pay scales under Akbar are given in the *Ā'īn*, I, 178-85. In the *Iqbālnāma*, II, Or. 1834, f.233a, we have the scales as they stood at the time of Jahāngīr's accession. The scales as promulgated in the 11th year of Shāhjahān (1638-39) under the signature of Afẓal Khān are reproduced in *Farhang-i Kārdānī*, ff. 21a-24a (Edinburgh 83, ff. 19a-21b); those issued in the 14th year (1641-42) under

common, were assigned particular areas as *jāgīrs*. Territories held on the same basis as *jāgīr*, but not against any rank or without any obligation, were known as *in'ām*.[5] Areas due for assignment, but not yet assigned in *jāgīr*, bore the designation of *pāibāqi*.[6] Finally, the *khāliṣa*, or more properly *khāliṣa-i sharīfa*, comprised territories and sources of revenue reserved for the imperial treasury.[7]

The assignee was entitled to collect the entire revenue due to the state; and though this consisted principally of land revenue, it also embraced various cesses and petty taxes which were exacted even in the remotest rural areas.[8] Generally speaking, the markets of the larger towns and the ports were constituted into separate *maḥals* (as distinct from the *parganas*, or territorial *maḥals*), but

---

the signature of Islām Khān are given in *Selected Documents*, 79-84:and those still later under the signature of Sa'dullāh Khān in *Dastūru-l 'Amal-i 'Ālamgīrī*, ff.121a-123a. Unlike those of the *Ā'īn* and the *Iqbālnāma*, these scales are given in terms of *dāms* instead of rupees. Those belonging to Aurangzeb's reign (as given, for example, in the *Ẓawābiṭ-i 'Ālamgīrī*, Add. 6598, f.149b-152a, Or 1641, ff.43a-47b) are practically identical with the later scales of Shāhjahān's reign.

5 Cf. Lāhorī, II, 397, on the assignment of Surat as *in'ām* to Princess Jahān Ārā; and *'Ālamgīrnāma*, 618, where it is explained that since Jai Singh had been granted the maximum rank permitted to any noble, he could be honoured further only by *in'ām* assignments. The *Mir'ātu-l Iṣṭilāḥ*, f.26a. says that the assignments held by royal princesses were termed *barg-bahā*, but I have not found any instance of the use of this term in the 17th century. The princes usually held large *in'ām* assignments in addition to the *jāgīrs* assigned to them against their ranks.

6 *Pāibāqī* is an accountant's word for the balance shown at the bottom of the account. From this, apparently, it derived the peculiar sense of territory held in reserve for assignment as *jāgīrs*, or, as defined in an administrative manual, of "a *jāgīr*, which has been taken from a person and whose revenues, till its assignment to another person, are appropriated by the imperial government" (*Khulāṣatu-s Siyāq*, f.89a-90a, Or. 2026, f.51a-52b). See *Waqā'i' Ajmer*, 74, 375-6; *Akhbārāt* 47/167; *Dastūru-l 'Amal-i Āgahī*, f.31a; and Ma'mūrī, ff.156b-157a, 182b, Khāfī Khān, Add. 6574, f.107a; Bib. Ind. ed., II, 396-7, for use of the term in this sense.

7 See *Mir'ātu-l Iṣṭilāḥ*, f.26a, for a definition of this well-known term.

8 According to the standard formula employed in the assignment orders, the *chaudhurīs* (or *deshmukhs*), *qānūngos* (or *deshpānḍīas*) and *muqaddams* (or *paṭels*) and the peasants and the cultivators were answerable to the assignee for the whole of the *māl-i wājib* (revenue) and *ḥuqūq-i dīwānī* (fiscal demands). See Har Karan, 53, 54; *Selected Documents*, 4, 5, 17, 18, 21, 23, 147, 151, 158, 171, 175-6; *Nigārnāma-i Munshī*, ed., 91-2; Aurangzeb's *farmān*, 37th year, in *Nāma-i Muẓaffarī*, I, 288. The state's taxes in other documents (see Chapter VI, Section 7) are classified into *māl-o-jihāt* (land revenue and related cesses) and *sā'ir jihāt* (transit and other taxes).

The taxes on the artisans *(muḥtarifa)* and tradesmen and the transit dues, were all comprehended under the general name of *sā'ir* (cf. *Dastūru-l Amal-i 'Ālamgīrī*, ff. 23b-24a).

these again were as frequently assigned in *jāgīrs* as the others.[9]

The *jāgīrs* were constantly transferred after short periods so that a particular assignment was seldom held by the same person for more than three or four years. Akbar seems to have, in his own view, decisively established this practice when in 1568 he dislodged the officers of the Atka family from their *jāgīrs* in the Panjab.[10] From that time to the end of our period the practice continued to be rigorously followed, as is constantly shown by our evidence.[11] Close to the capital Agra, we happen to have especially rich documentation from Vrindaban, near Mathura: during Shāhjahān's reign, there is record of as many as eleven successive *jāgīrdārs* of the *pargana*, giving an average term of 2.7 years.[12] For the more distant areas too we get similar results: the *sarkār* of Bhakkar (Multan province), eleven assignments, 1574-90, average term: 1.7 years;[13] Sehwan (Sind), seventeen assignments, 1592-

[9] From a letter in Bālkrishan Brahman, ff.103b-104b, it appears that the market dues (*maḥṣūl-i sā'ir)* of the *parganas* of Hansi and Hisar were regarded as a separate charge from the general revenue of the *parganas*. They had been retained with the *k͟hāliṣa*, while the *parganas* themselves had been assigned to Prince Mu'aẕẕam. Surat was sometimes assigned in *jāgīr* and sometimes held under the *k͟hāliṣa* (Pelsaert, 42), and so also was Hugli (Master, II, 79-80). Cf. Foster, *Supp. Cal.*, 69, for Cambay.

[10] Bāyazīd, 253; *A.N.*, II, 332-3.

[11] The *tag͟haiyur*, or transfer, of a *jāgīr* after short periods was such a common administrative practice at the time that it is usually assumed, and only rarely explained, in our authorities. Abū-l Faẕl philosophizes about it in one passage and describes it as similar in virtue to the transplantation of plants which a gardener practises for the good of the plants themselves (*A.N.*, II, 332-3). References to transfers of particular *jāgīrs* are so numerous in our sources of all types, chronicles, collections of letters, records, etc., that any attempt to list such references will extend to pages and can never be complete. European travellers were generally struck by this practice and offer descriptions of it. According to Hawkins, "A man cannot continue half a yeere in his living, but it is taken from him" (*Early Travels*, 114). Geleynssen's statement is a little more moderate. "Some" of the assignments, he says, "are transferred yearly or half-yearly, or every two or three years" (*JIH*, IV, 72). There was apparently no fixed period for which a *jāgīr* might be held. If we discount Bernier's statement that the *jāgīrdārs,* whom he calls Ṭimariots, were afraid of being deprived of their *jāgīrs* "in a single moment" (Bernier, 227) as the exaggeration of a foreigner, we have an identical statement from an Indian writer during the last years of Aurangzeb. "The agents of the *jāgīrdārs*," says Bhīmsen, "having apprehension concerning the niggardly behaviour of the clerks of the court, who on every excuse ... effect a transfer, do not have any hope of the confirmation *(baḥālī)* of the *jāgīr* for the following year".

[12] Tarapada Mukerjee and I. Habib, *PIHC*, 49th session, 1988 Dharwad, 292, for a tabulation of the recorded names of successive *jāgīrdārs* in documents calendared on 295-8.

[13] See account of the administrative changes in Ma'ṣūm, 242-51.

1634, average term: 2.6 years;[14] Dhar (Malwa), 1653-85, ten assignments, average term: 3.3 years:[14a] and Indur (Telangana), eight assignments, 1631-58, average term: 3.5 years.[15] The only exceptions to the rule of regular transfers were the *waṭan jāgīrs* of the *zamīndārs*,[16] and the few *al-tamghā* assignments, of which we hear first under Jahāngīr and occasionally afterwards.[17]

Since a *jāgīr* was usually assigned in lieu of pay, it was necessary to determine in each case an area that would yield in net revenue (that is, gross revenue, less cost of collection) an amount equivalent to the sanctioned pay.[18] A standing assessment, or *jama'*, was, therefore, prepared for each unit of territory, the

[14] Based on information in *Maẓhar-i Shāhjahānī*, 90-171.

[14a] Based on Dhar documents, Kuwait, LNS 235, MSa-qq.

[15] Aurangzeb's letter to Fāẓil Khān summarizing the particulars of revenue obtained from the *pargana* under successive *jāgīrdārs*, including terms of *khāliṣa* administration (*Ādāb-i 'Ālamgīrī*, ff.161b-162b; ed., I, 636-9).

[16] See Chapter V, Section 4.

[17] Jahāngīr says that he instituted the *āl-tamghā*, or *altūn-tamghā*, as he named it, with the specific purpose of allowing every noble to have his native place (or family sent) under a permanent assignment (*T.J.*, 10; Hyderabad MS, f.12a-b, for the correct text; cf. transl., I, 23& n.).

For an *āl-tamghā farmān* of Shāhjahān, 2nd year, see copy in Shamsabad Docs., and for one of Aurangzeb, 1662, see *Nama-i Muẓaffarī*, I, 174-9, with subsequent confirmations of 1685, 1688 and 1712 on pp. 280-7, 317. In the former *farmān* the *āl-tamghā* was to be held by the assignee "and his sons"; in the latter it was to be continued with the assignee and his descendants "generation after generation". Aurangzeb's *farmān* also uses the formula, "for his (the assignee's) *waṭan*," suggesting a prospective, rather than the native, family seat of the assignee. Thus later in Aurangzeb's reign we find an officer, stung by suspicions about intrigues of members of his family with the fugitive Prince Akbar in Persia, asking that an assignment of "ten lakh *dāms* in the province of Lahor be granted to him as *āl-tamghā* that he might summon his relatives from Persia and settle them there" (*Matīn-i Inshā'*, ff.99b-100a). For *in'ām-i āl-tamghā*, see Chapter VIII.

The *Farhang-i Rashīdī*, 71, says *āl* is used in Turkish for the red seal which was impressed upon grants remitting revenues (*tamghā*): hence, *āl-tamghā*. Jahāngīr sought to alter the initial word, because he used a golden (*altūn*) seal. Yāsīn's glossary, Add. 6603, ff. 48b-49a, says *āl* meant descent through the daughter(!) and therefore *āl-tamghā* in the beginning was given to women only.

[18] In the earliest *farmān* of assignment to a *jāigīrdār* (under that designation), issued by Akbar, 7 April 1561, the village of Hamīrpur in *pargana* Chanwār (near Agra), "whose *jama'-i raqamī* is twenty-five thousand *ṭankas*," was granted "in assignment (*dar wajh*) of salary (*'alūfa*)" to Rāmdās, his master dyer: we infer that Rāmdās was expected to obtain his annual salary of 25,000 *ṭankas* when he collected the revenues from the village (for this and two other *farmāns* in favour of the same Rāmdās, see I. Habib in *Akbar and his India*, 271-87). After the institution of the *manṣab* system (1574-5), the assignment orders followed a set pattern. First, the *ṭalab* or pay-claim was calculated according to the rank (*manṣab*)

village and, more especially, the *pargana* or *maḥal.*[19] To serve best this *jama'* should have approximated as closely as possible to the actual collection or *ḥāṣil*. As Abū-l Faẓl emphasizes, the working out of such a *jama'* was one of the chief objectives of Akbar's revenue measures.

The *jama'* figures inherited by Akbar from the previous administrations were known as *jama'-i raqamī*, and, though worked out for each village even in Bābur's time, these were grossly inflated, owing to purely arbitrary enhancements.[20] In 1566-67 a

---

of the assignee, and then the territorial units (*parganas* or parts thereof) assigned were listed with the *jama'* of each, which in total had to be the same as the *ṭalab*. See *Vīr Vinod*, II, 239-49, 253-8, 259-64, for Jahāngīr's *farmān* of assignment of *jāgīr* to Kunwar Karan of Mewar, May 1615, and other *farmāns* of 1616 and 1618 of a similar character (all documents translated into Hindī but with Persian terminology retained). For original texts of such orders from Shāhjahān's time, see *Selected Documents*, 4-20, 21-2, 109-13, 147-57, 165-72, 175-7, the earliest of which is of 1635. The *jama'* is invariably given in *dāms* in these documents.

[19] The village-wise *jama'* was known as *deh-ba-dehī* and a record of it was kept at the court (Fraser 86, f. 63a; Manucci, II, 70). It was laid down that a single village should not be assigned to more than one person (Fraser 86, f.63a). But another manual gives the method for calculating the shares of four *jāgīrdārs* in the revenues of a single village, if each had been assigned a portion of its *jama'* (*Dastūru-l 'Amal-i Navīsindagī,* f.179a-b). Where two or more *jāgīrs* were assigned in the same *pargana*, the procedure seems to have been, first, to state the amount of the *jama'* of each *jāgīr* ("so many *dāms* from the *pargana*") and, then, to work out the *qismat* or division of the villages of the *pargana* among the *jāgīrs* to correspond to the *jama'* of each. The paper laying down this division, known as *qismat-nāma* or *chiṭṭhī-i qismat*, was prepared by the office of the provincial dīwān. (*Aḥkām-i 'Ālamgīrī*, f.242a, *Waqā'i' Ajmer*, 470, 637). Allahabad 888, dated 2 March 1653, shows that the *jāgīrdārs* could make adjustments in the villages assigned to them under the official *qismat* through mutual consent. It was, however, generally recognized that the best practice was to assign whole *(dar bast) parganas* to single assignees so far as their total salary claims allowed *(Ādāb-i 'Ālamgīrī*, f.1127a; *Ruq'āt-i 'Ālamgīr*, 126-7; *Fatḥiya-i 'Ibriya*, f.117a-b).

[20] *A.N.*, II, 270 (Add. 27, 247, f. 202a); *Ā'īn*, I, 347; *Iqbālnāma*, Lucknow ed., II, 213. Abū-l Faẓl calls the *jama'* by the name *raqamī-i qalamī* in the *Akbarnāma* [the final version] and *raqam-i raqamī* in Add. 27,247, but, simply, *raqamī* in the *Ā'īn*. In the latter work it is stated that "according to whatever reached their heart, they (the officials of the revenue ministry) used to make an enhancement by a stroke of the pen *(ba-qalam afzūda*) and assigned it in pay *(tan namūdand)"*. *Qalamī* would, therefore, seem to bear an extended sense equivalent to that of 'paper' in English, as in 'paper enhancement'. The *jama'-i qalamī*, that is to say, would be a merely paper assessment.

Raqamī, on the other hand, was a technical term, for a village confirmed in *suyūrghāl* by a *farmān* of Bābur, is assigned a *"jama' raqamī* of 2,000 *ṭankas*" (I.O. 4438), and in another *farmān* of his each of the five villages granted is assigned a *jama'-i raqamī*, totalling 4,500 *ṭanka-i siyāh* (Bhojpur Coll., B:1).

revision was attempted by Akbar's administration by collecting information from the *qānūngos* and "knowledgeable men". But the new *jama'*, though acknowledged to be an improvement, was still "a long distance away from the *ḥāṣil*".[21] Eight years later (1574-75) came perhaps the boldest step of Akbar's career, when he simultaneously undertook a number of important measures.[22] He resumed all *jāgīrs*, except those held in Bengal, Bihar and Gujarat. He then fixed permanent local cash rates for the different crops and worked out a new *jama'* for assignment purposes. We have seen in the preceding chapter how the *jama'-i dah-sāla* was determined by striking the average of the annual revenue, calculated on the basis of retrospectively fixed annual cash rates, and multiplied by measured area figures of the previous ten years (15th to 24th year, 1570-71 to 1579-80). This *jama'* was, however, prepared only for the *ẓabṭī* provinces. Abū-l Faẓl tells us of the repeated attempts to determine an accurate *jama'* for Kashmir, and this involved an enquiry about the real rates at which the revenue was customarily paid, and the prevailing levels of prices at which the assignees sold their stocks.[23] Todar Mal was twice (1574 and 1576-77) deputed to settle the *jama'* of Gujarat, but the methods used by him are obscure.[24] In Bengal the *jama'* seems to

In the first extant *jāgīr*-asignment order (Akbar's *farmān*, 1561), the assigned village carries the *jama'-i raqamī* of 25,000 *ṭanka murādī* (I. Habib in *Akbar and his India*, 271-2, 281). *Raqam* means notation or writing and the use of the term *raqamī* for a particular kind of fiscal record should not be surprising (cf. Moreland, *Agrarian System*, 240-41). In Bodl. Or.390, f.9a & ff. the *jama'dāmī* of the different provinces of Shāhjahān's reign is stated again in terms of rupees at the accountant's rate of 40 *dāms* to a rupee, and these figures are called *jama'-i raqamī*; but this is perhaps a use of the earlier term for another kind of *jama'*.

Sir Richard Burn's explanation of the origin of the word *raqamī* from the term *raya-rekha-mar*, meaning assessment by measurement in the Vijayanagara Empire (*JRAS*, 1943, 260-61) is quite implausible. Equally so is A.L. Srivastava's supposition that *raqamī* means revenue in kind, just because he had heard some cultivators refer to their crop, when ready, as *raqam (Akbar the Great*, III, 171-2 & n.). Surely, Professor Srivastava must have heard wrongly, since *raqam* in Hindustani ordinarily means an amount of money, and not a quantity of goods (cf. Fallon, s.v. *raqam*).

21 *A.N.*, II, 270; III, 117; *Ā'īn*, I, 347-8.

22 That this was the motive in instituting the *jama'-i dah-sāla* is brought out in Moreland, *Agrarian System*, 98.

23 *A.N.*, III, 548-9, 595, 617-8, 620, 626-7; *Ā'īn*, I, 570-71.

24 *A.N.*, III, 65, 67; *Ṭabaqāt-i Akbarī*, II, 275, 330; *Mir'āt*, I, 131-2 134-5. Abū Turāb, 94-95, writing close to the event, says Todar Mal acted very harshly (presumably enhancing the *jama'* considerably, to the disadvantage of the assignees) and greatly embarrassed the governor 'Azīz Koka by his demands. According to

have been directly adapted from the *"qānūngoī"* papers of the previous government,[25] and from what we have already seen of the conditions of this province, its *jama'* probably consisted of fixed annual claims of the administration against local *zamīndārs*. A very summary procedure was apparently adopted in the Dakhin provinces, for Akbar enhanced the *jama'* of Khandesh by fifty per cent, a step hardly to be conceived of if there had been any detailed investigation of actual receipts.[26]

The *Ā'īn-i Akbarī* gives us the *jama'* for each of the *ṣūbas* in *dāms*. But while breaking down the figures for each of the *sarkārs* and *parganas* in its detailed tables, it uses the word *naqdī* ("in money") for the column heading. It has been shown conclusively by Moosvi that these figures include the officially estimated income alienated through revenue grants (*suyūrghāl*), for which a separate column is provided.[27] The *suyūrghāl* figures, then, need to be deducted from the *naqdī/jama'*, to give us the net *jama'* at which *jāgīrs* were assigned.

In the seventeenth century the *jama'*, used for the purposes of assignments came to be known as *jama'-i dāmī* or *jama'dāmī*, from its being expressed in terms of *dāms*. The statistics for it survive in some profusion (see Appendix D); and they show that it was subject to constant revision. We know from the administrative documents of this period that reports of the revenue collection (*ḥāl-i ḥāṣil*) in the *jāgīrs* were called for by the imperial administration, as a matter of routine, and the decennial record of area and revenue (*muwāzana-i dah-sāla*) was maintained at the court for the purpose of checking the standing *jama'*.[28] Record was

---

'Ārif Qandahārī, 210, it was ordered in 1577-8 that Muẓaffar Khān and "some clerks" accompanying him "should check (*muwāzana numāyand)* the amount of the *ḥāṣil* of the country of Gujarat and Mandu"; and presumably on the basis of the figures so established, he was to assign *jāgīrs* in Gujarat.

25 See *Fatḥiya-i 'Ibriya*, f.164a, where the explanation is given of why Chātgāon (Chittagong) continued to appear on the *jama'* records of the Mughal administration, though it was not reconquered till the time of Shā'ista Khān. Cf. also Moreland in *JRAS*, 1926, 48-50, and *Agrarian System*, 196-7.

26 *Ā'īn*, I, 474. From the account of the *jama'* of Berar in ibid., 478, one also gains the impression that the *jama'* figures established under the previous regime served as the basis, and the enhancements made by the Mughal administration were purely arbitrary.

27 Moosvi, 153-5, 169-72. As Moosvi points out, Abū-l Faẓl himself notes, while recording each of the *ṣūba* totals, that the *suyūrghāl* figures "form part" (*az ān miyān*) of the *jama'*.

28 For evidence that the *ḥāṣil* reports were called for, see *Selected Documents*,

kept also of the maximum revenue realized in the different *maḥals*, which was known as *ḥāṣil-i kāmil*.[29] This information was used by Akbar's administration to check the collections of the *karorīs*,[30] and it is possible that it was also borne in mind when a revision was made of the *jama*' of any place.

Neither the *jama'-i dah-sāla* nor the *jama'dāmī* figures could for all time and in all places exactly represent the actual receipts. Moosvi has shown how in the case of a very large number of *parganas*, the real *jama*' (that is *naqdī* less *suyūrghāl*) in the *Ā'īn's* statistics turns out to be in figures rounded to thousands, and sometimes to lakhs, which could only have been due to a resort to rough estimation rather than to a totalling of precisely worked out village-wise revenue figures.[31] As late as 1584 we find the *jama*' of a *jāgīr* in Dehli province subject to bargaining between the administration and the prospective assignee.[32] Early in the next reign (1609), we encounter a record termed *sarāsarī* ("average"), where the income or *ḥāṣil* in rupees was set against the much higher *jama*' in *dāms*, down to villages.[33] It is not, therefore, surprising

88-90, 194-5; *Ādāb-i 'Ālamgīrī*, ff. 31b-32a, 43a, 49a-b, 104b-105a; ed., I, 167, 191-2, etc.; *Ruq'āt-i 'Ālamgīr*, 88, 107, 163-4. From Fraser 86, f.162b, we learn that for the purposes of *jāgīr* assignments "the rigister of the *ḥāṣil* of ten years, together with the maximum revenue received from the beginning of the reign to the current year, was to be maintained" in the central secretariat. The *Siyāqnāma*, 102, lists among the papers maintained by the office of the *dīwān* of the empire "the *muwāzana-i dah-sāla* for ascertaining the *jama*' from year to year so that they might recommend the pay-assignment of every one according (to it)". A register showing "increase and decrease in the *ḥāl-i ḥāṣil*"was also maintained (ibid., 101). We read incidentally in the *Mir'āt*, I, 326-7, that in 1691-92 a *manṣabdār* was deputed to Gujarat from the imperial court to obtain the accounts of the revenue collections (*ḥāl-i ḥāṣil*) of the *parganas* and the *muwāzana-i dah-sāla* of the province from the *desāīs* and *muqaddams*. He, however, complained that the *jāgīrdārs* were preventing the *desāīs* from co-operating with him. From a letter from Aurangzeb to Shāhjahān (*Ādāb-i 'Ālamgīrī*, f. 32b, ed., I, 125-6; *Ruq'āt-i 'Ālamgīr*, 118) it seems that the *ḥāṣil* accounts received from the *jāgīrs* were not always considered reliable. Aurangzeb, believing that such suspicion was entertained at the imperial court concerning the accounts of his *jāgīrs*, offered to place them all under the *khāliṣa*, and accept cash pay instead.

[29] Fraser 86, f.162b. [30] *A.N.*, III, 457.

[31] Moosvi, 153-56, 169-72.

[32] Bāyazīd, 363-4, 372-3. The *pargana* concerned was Sunam in *sarkār* Sirhind, *ṣūba* Dehli. Todar Mal asked Bāyazīd to accept a *jama*' of 16½ lakh *ṭankas* (=33 lakh *dāms*), while Akbar had approved 29 lakh *dāms*. In the *Ā'īn* the real *jama*' of the *pargana* is set at 70 lakh *dāms* (Moosvi, 170, place name misprinted: Suram).

[33] See Jahāngīr's *farmān* of R.Y.4, conferring in *āl-tamghā* two villages in *pargana* Ilahabad, in which the *jama*' is stated to be 1,20,000 *dāms*, but the *ḥāṣil*,

that the low revenue-yielding capacity of Hawkins's *jāgīrs*, as against the pay formally sanctioned, should form the burden of his complaints.[34] Pelsaert, c.1526, found that only half the nominal assessment was generally realized by the assignees.[35]

These grievances might have been rectified to some degree under Shāhjahān in whose reign we come across an ingenious attempt to vary the size and quality of the *manṣabdār's* obligation in accordance with the difference between *jama' dāmī* and the actual receipts in each *jāgīr*. The ratio between the receipts and the standing assessment was now worked out for each *maḥal* and expressed in terms of "month proportions" (*māhwār*): where the current *ḥāṣil* equalled the *jama'*, the *jāgīr* was styled "twelve-monthly" (*doazdah-māha*); where it was half, "six-monthly" (*shash-māha*); and so on.[36] As a natural corollary, the system of

according to the *sarāsarī*, is put at only Rs 1,728, or less than 57.6% of the *jama'* (copy lithographed by Namwar Press, Allahabad, n.d.)

[34] Hawkins, *Early Travels*, 91, 93. [35] Pelsaert, 54.

[36] This interpretation of the "month ratios" was for the first time put forward in the first edition of this book. The administrative literature upon whose evidence it is based is too extensive to be quoted, but the main documents are cited below: *Selected Documents*, 64, 248; *Ādāb-i 'Ālamgīrī*, ff. 8a 31b-32b, 40b, 42b-43a, 49a-b, 51a 52b-53b, 58b, 105a; ed., I. 25,191-2, 446-7, etc.; *Ruq'āt-i 'Ālamgīr*, 10, 88, 88, 107, 118, 121-2, 130-31, 135, 163-4; Wāriṣ, a: f. 497a, b: f. 143b; Allahabad 884, 885; and *Akhbārāt*, 38/145. As for the annual variation in the month-ratio of each *jāgīr* (consequent upon variations in the receipts), see Fraser 86, f.162b, where it is laid down that the record of the month-ratios year by year (*māhwār sāl-ba-sāl*) was to be maintained at the imperial court, along with that of *ḥāṣil-i dah-sāla* and *sāl-i kāmil*. Thus also in *Ādāb-i 'Ālamgīrī*, f.104b: "The *ḥāṣil* of the *pargana* of Bir was nearly eight-monthly (*hasht-māha*) in the 28th regnal year and would be set higher than that in the 29th." Elsewhere in the same collection (ibid, f.8a; ed., I, 25; *Ruq'āt-i 'Ālamgīr*, 10) we read of a *jāgīr*, which "this year" had a *ḥāṣil* no higher than "5-monthly".

The *dām* used in the *jama'* records was only a money of account and as such was reckoned as equal to one-fortieth of a rupee. Thus if the *jāgīr* was "twelve-monthly", a *jama'* of one lakh *dāms* would imply a *ḥāṣil* of Rs 2,500. (See, for instance, Lāhorī, I, ii, 205; *Selected Documents*, 77.) In Allahabad 885 and 884 (both belonging to Aurangzeb's reign) the relation between the *dāms* of the *jama'* of the *jāgīr* and the amount in rupees and annas which the revenue farmer promised to pay annually to the *jāgīrdār* is defined in terms of the month scale: *Dāms* 4,40,000; Rs 7,333, as. 4; Month ratio: "8-monthly". *Dāms* 2,10,000; Rs.3,162; Month ratio: "7 months, 7 days". Both the ratios are arithmetically exact. In the *Ādāb-i 'Ālamgīrī*, f.40b, *Ruq'āt-i 'Ālamgīr*, 121-2, it is said of the provinces of Mughal Dakhin that their *ḥāṣil* of Rs 88 lakh did not amount to "3-monthly" (*sih-māha*) of their *jama'*, which was 1,44,90,00,000 *dāms* and so more than four times the *ḥāṣil* figure.

Although the "month ratios" seem to have come into general use in Mughal administration only in the reign of Shāhjahān, a passage in a history of Sind written

month proportions was instituted for the payment of emoluments in cash as well.[37] Once the month slot of each *jāgīr* was thus determined, one could look up the sanctioned schedules for the number of horses and horsemen laid down separately for the standard *sawār* rank under each month ratio.[38] Thus lower receipts would be compensated by the smaller size of contingent to be maintained.

---

in Jahāngir's reign, suggests that the practice had an earlier history. In 1605-6, local deputies of Mirzā Ghāzī Beg Tarkhān, the governor of Sind, proposed that the pay for his troops be reduced from "8-monthly" to "6-monthly". This greatly annoyed his officers for this would have reduced their *jāgīrs* by a fourth (*Tārīkh-i Ṭāhirī*, Or.1685 ff.118a-119b; ed., 251-2).

[37] Cf. *Selected Documents*, 64, 76-7; *Ādāb-i 'Ālamgīrī*, ff.8a, 32b, 42b-43a, 202b, 328b-329a; ed., I, 25, 125-6, etc.; *Ruq'āt i 'Ālamgīr*, 10, 105-7, 117-8, 228; *Ma'āṣir-i 'Ālamgīrī*, 88. The *Dastūru-l 'Amal-i 'Ilm-i Navīsindagī*, ff.147b-148a; Bodl. O. 390, ff. 40a-41a; Or. 1840, ff. 143b-144b; and the *Farhang-i Kārdānī*, f. 24a-b, contain tables giving *naqdī* (cash) equivalents per lakh *dāms* for each month in rupees, with the express statement that this was to be used for determining the pay for *zāt* ranks. This suggests that there was some other method for determining pay for *sawār* ranks of the *naqdī manṣabdārs*. A suggestion about what this method was is made in the next note. However, a table similar to the one referred to above is given by the *Ẓawābiṭ-i 'Ālamgīrī*, Add.6598, f.149-a-b, Or. 1641, ff.42a-43b, without specifically limiting its application to the pay for *zāt* ranks.

[38] This is to be seen most clearly in the particulars given by Lāhorī, II, 506-7, about the contingents to be provided by the *manṣabdārs*, under the various month scales, for service in the Balkh and Badakhshan campaigns. This, however, was an exceptional service where the so-called "rule of the fifth part" applied, i.e. the *manṣabdārs* had to provide cavalry amounting in number to a fifth of their *sawār* ranks. In the *Intikhāb-i Dastūru-l 'Amal-i Pādshāhī*, ff.7a-9b, and the *Khulāṣatu-s Siyāq*, Aligarh MS, f.54a-b, the contingents to be supplied under all the months, are given for *manṣabdārs* serving in the *rikāb* (outside the province of their *jāgīrs*: the cavalry to come up to a fourth part of their *sawār* ranks) and as *ta'īnāt* (*jāgīrs* and service in the same province: cavalry to be a third of the rank). See also *Selected Documents*, 249; *Farhang-i Kārdānī*, Edinburgh 83, ff. 22a-23a.

In Shāhjahān's *farmān* of 1653 (*Mir'āt*, I, 227-9) and some administrative manuals (Bodl. O. 390. ff.42b-43a; Or. 1840, ff.143b-144b; *Farhang-i Kārdānī*, f.24a-b, Edinburgh 83, ff.21b-22a) the pay of the contingents of the *naqdī manṣabdārs* is given in a peculiar way: Rs 40 per horse (or, horseman) under 12 months; Rs 30 under 8 months; and so on. Shāhjahān's *farmān* of 1653 recites that formerly the *manṣabdārs* of 7-and 6-months also used to get Rs 30 per horse(-man?), which it was the object of the order to change to Rs 27½ and Rs 25 respectively. See also *Ādāb-i 'Ālamgīrī*, ff.38a-b, 45b-56a, 117b-118a; ed., 148-50, 178 (but letter on ff.117b-118a not printed), *Ruq'āt-i 'Ālamgīr*, 116-17, 129, for Aurangzeb's protest against the enforcement of this order in the Dakhin and a modification of its terms by Shāhjahān, apparently to be applied in the Dakhin only. It seems, then, that the *naqdī manṣabdārs* were not paid at the rate of 8.000 *dāms* per unit of *sawār* rank as the *jāgīrdārs* were, but were paid per horseman, the rate falling with each lower step in the month scale in view of the prescribed smaller number of remounts, and lower quality of the horses and their riders.

In normal circumstances the imperial administration seems to have left the *jāgīrdār* to bear the risk of fluctuations in revenue collection and to have neither refunded any loss nor recovered any excess receipts.[39] In certain cases, however, if the *jāgīrdār* complained very strongly of the inflated nature of the *jama' dāmī*, a reduction in it, known as *takhfīf-i dāmī*, was sanctioned by the court. For this amount the *jāgīrdār* was admitted to have a claim (*ṭalab*) that could be satisfied either by a grant from the treasury or the assignment of a *jāgīr* with a *jama'* of an equivalent amount.[40] At the same time if the actual receipts were discovered to be substantially in excess of the *jama' dāmī*, or of the ratio to the *jama'* set by the "month" sanctioned for the *jāgīrdār*, the excess amount could be recovered from the latter directly, or added to the *muṭālaba*, i.e. the state's financial claims against him.[41] Akbar had, however, approved the suggestion that any increase in revenue brought about by the good administration of the assignee was to be left with him through a corresponding increase in his rank.[42]

The system of periodic transfers had its own complications and inconveniences for the *jāgīrdār*. For instance, it was assumed for assignment purposes that, except for Bengal and Orissa, the kharif and rabi crops were of equal value everywhere.[43] This was, however, hardly the case in reality.[44] If a *jāgīrdār* held an assignment during

[39] See, for example, the *Waqā'i' Ajmer*, 199, where a new *jāgīrdār* was reminded by the local Mughal commandant that "whatever revenue is collected belongs to him", and if it was less than what could maintain him and his retainers "this was a matter of fate or luck".

That the excess income from the *jāgīr* was for the *jāgīrdār* to retain or dispose of is shown by an order of Shā'ista Khān that all excess collection over the *jama'-i muqarrarī* of his *jāgīrs* was to be returned to the peasants, a step hardly possible if it belonged to the emperor (see *Fatḥiya-i 'Ibriya*, f.127a-b).

[40] *Selected Documents*, 177; *Ādāb-i 'Ālamgīrī*, ff. 31b-32b, 36a-b, 39a-b, 42b-43a, 47b-48a; 151b 152a; ed., I, 597-8, etc., *Ruq'āt-i 'Ālamgīr*, 88, 95-6, 98, 107, 111-12, 136; *Akhbārāt* 38/30; *Aḥkām-i 'Ālamgīrī*, ff. 92b-93a; *Karnāma*, ff. 208b-209a.

[41] *Ādāb-i 'Ālamgīrī*, ff.52b-53a; *Ruq'āt-i 'Ālamgīr*, 130-31; *Ma'āṣir-i 'Ālamgīrī*, 170; *Akhbārāt* 38/145. Bāyazīd was obviously given a concession when Akbar offered him the *jāgīr* of Sunam with a *jama'* of 29 lakh *dāms* with the permission to keep any excess revenue for himself (Bāyazīd, 363). When, in Bengal, several *jāgīrdārs* were given *jāgīrs* with a *jama'* higher than their sanctioned pay, they were required to pay back the balance to the *khāliṣa* (*Fatḥiya-i 'Ibriya*, f.117a-b)

[42] *A.N.*, III, 459.

[43] Cf. *Selected Documents*, 76-77. For the exception made in the case of Bengal and Orissa, see Or.1840, f.140a-b; Fraser 86, f.60b.

[44] For such variations in proceeds from the two harvests in Amber territory, see

the kharif harvest in one place and during the rabi in another, and neither happened to be the important crops in the respective localities, he might be a heavy loser during that year.[45] Moreover, transfers occurred not only with effect from the beginning of the harvest, but from that of any month of the year. In case the transfer was ordered in the course of the harvest season, the old and the new assignee (one of them being, possibly, the *k͟hāliṣa*) had to share the collections of the whole season according to the number of months the assignment had been in the hands of either.[46] A sudden transfer could also place a *jāgīrdār* in some difficulty, if he had not yet been able to collect the full revenue owed to him.[47] At the same time, an assignee might be required to collect the previous arrears of revenue *(baqāyā)* and hand them over to the previous assignee.[48]

The *jāgīr* did not always pass from one hand to another without discord. The Mughal administration seems to have taken care, as a rule, to assign a particular area in *jāgīr* to only one person at a time.[49] But the transmission of transfer or assignment orders took time, and so the agents of one *jāgīrdār* might collect revenue to which another was entitled.[50] Sometimes even physical force was used by one assignee against another, though it seems usually to have happened when one of them had received the transfer orders, while the other had not.[51]

S.P. Gupta, *Agrarian System of Eastern Rajasthan*, 64-6.

45 *Ādāb-i ʻĀlamgīrī*, f. 58b. Cf. *Nigārnāma-i Munshī*, ed., 29.

46 See especially *K͟hulāṣatu-s Siyāq*, ff.89a-90a, Or. 2026, ff.51a-b; also, *Mir'āt*, I, 305; *Dastūru-l ʻAmal-i Navīsindagī*, f.180a-b; Fraser 86, f.76a-b; *Farhang-i Kārdānī*, f.24b-25a, Edinburgh 83, f.19a; Allahabad 890.

47 *T.J.*, 22.

48 Ibid.; *Fatḥiya-i ʻIbriya*, f.130b; *Mir'āt*, I, 305.

Conversely, a new assignee could claim from the older the revenue that had been collected for the period which belonged to the former's term. Thus *Waqā'i' Ajmer*, 199, records the complaint of an officer assigned a *jāgīr* in *pargana* Siwāna, with effect from the rabi season, that the revenue for that season, amounting to Rs 7,270, had been collected by the *karorī* of the *k͟hāliṣa*, it previously having been in the *k͟hāliṣa*. The *karorī* was ready to pay the amount to the new assignee but only after deducting his allowance and other charges which left in the net only "Rs 5,000 and odd". This sum the complainant declined, as being too small, and he consequently refused to take charge of his assignment as well.

49 The great sin of the Bijapur government, says Ma'mūrī, f.119b, was that it assigned the same *maḥal* in *jāgīr* to more than one person at the same time, leaving the assignees to fight it out among themselves.

50 *Nigārnāma-i Munshī*, ed., 143; *Waqā'i' Ajmer*, 199. cf. Sihunda Docs. 49 & 51.

51 *Arzdāsht-hā-i Muẓaffar*, Add. 16, 859, ff. 3b-4a; Bālkrishan Brahman, ff. 64b-65a; *Waqā'i' Ajmer*, 37,42, 187; *Matīn-i Inshā'*, ff.32b-33a, 44b-45a; *Aḥkām-i ʻĀlamgīrī*, f.169a.

A man would seem to have been exceptionally lucky if he obtained a *jāgīr* with effect from the date of his appointment to a *manṣab* or of his promotion to a higher *manṣab*.[52] Sometimes, again, a *jāgīrdār* might not immediately get a fresh assignment after the one he held previously had been transferred to another.[53] For the period that a *manṣabdār* remained without a *jāgīr* he could submit a claim for his pay (*ṭalab*) to the treasury; but in the later years of Aurangzeb, it was ordered that no claim would be honoured for the period immediately following grant of *manṣab*; and in practice the *ṭalab* even in other cases of interval between assignments was now seldom met.[54]

The assignments were often subject to temporary resumption for the satisfaction of *muṭālaba*, or the claim of the imperial exchequer for amounts owed to it by a *jāgīrdār*.[55] These amounts accumulated in a number of ways: from unrepaid loans (*musā'adat*),[56] from the *jāgīrdār's* failure in discharging his various obligations as *manṣabdār* (e.g. not bringing to the brand the required number of horses of standard breeds,[57] or not bringing them within the stipulated period,[58] or failing to supply provisions for the animals of the imperial stables[59]), from pay reductions enforced with retrospective effect,[60] and, as we have seen, from claim on revenues of his *jāgīrs* through arrears of the previous years due to other assignees, especially the *khāliṣa*.

[52] Bāyazīd, 372-74; *Waqā'i' Ajmer*, 405-6. Mirzā Yār 'Alī, the clerk of Aurangzeb's *bakhshī*, was reputed to have said at the court that a youth at the time of appointment to a *manṣab* would be a greybeard by the time he received *jāgīr* for his pay (Khāfī Khān, II, 379).

[53] *Waqā'i' Ajmer*, 413; Ma'mūrī, f.182b, Khāfī Khān , II, 396; *Nigārnāma-i Munshī*, p.35.

[54] Ma'mūrī, f.182b, Khāfī Khān, II, 396-7. Cf. *Aḥkām-i 'Ālamgīrī*, f.19a.

[55] Wāriṣ, a: f.400a-b; *Ādāb-i 'Ālamgīrī* f. 58b, *Ruq'āt-i 'Ālamgīr*, 122-3; *Dilkushā*, f.139a; *Matīn-i Inshā'*, ff. 48a-b, 50a, 52a, 52b-53b.

[56] *Ā'īn*, I, 196-7; *Waqā'i' Ajmer* 22; *Dilkushā*, f. 139a. Cf. also *Factories, 1655-60*, 67.

[57] *Tafāwat-i dāgh*: *Selected Documents*, 195; *Ādāb-i 'Ālamgīrī*, ff. 38a-b, 118a; ed., I, 148-50; *Ruq'āt-i 'Ālamgīr*, 116-17.

[58] *Der-taṣḥīḥ: Zawābiṭ-i 'Ālamgīrī*, Add. 6598, f.148a, Or.148a, Or. 1641, f. 39b; Fraser 86, f. 68a-b.

[59] *Khwurāk-i dawābb*. For the numbers and species of animals to be supplied with provisions, see *Dastūru-l 'Amal-i Navīsindagī*, ff.146a-147a; Fraser 86, ff. 75b-76a. For an actual case where the supplies were demanded, see *Matīn-i Inshā'*, ff. 71a-b, 74a-b. The demand for supplies in kind was later commuted into a cash levy (*Akhbārāt* 46/267; Khāfī Khān, II, 602-3).

[60] Cf. *Matīn-i Inshā'*, f.55a-b.

The system of assignments, with its rigid and complicated regulations, could only be worked with the aid of an enormous army of scribes and accountants. In the eyes of the *jāgīrdār*, therefore, the petty clerk employed by the imperial administration appeared as the root cause of all his troubles, anxious to wreck his interests, both when allotting him his *jāgīr* and when determining the *muṭālaba* against him.[61] At the same time the bureaucratic method had its counterpart in the almost universal practice of bribery, so that much of the rigorous system of inspection and checks to ensure the fulfilment of their obligations by the assignees appeared to exist on paper only.[62]

A crisis in the assignment system developed in the last years of Aurangzeb. From 1682 to his death Aurangzeb carried on an unending war in the Dakhin, in which the concentration of the entire military power of the Mughal empire failed to give him ultimate success. During these years there was an enormous influx into the ranks of the *manṣabdārs* of the "Dakhinīs" or officers of the Dakhin kingdoms and the Marathas. The number of the *manṣabdārs*, as a result, increased to such an extent that the existing *jāgīrs* could no longer suffice for their pay.[63] In one of his letters, Aurangzeb himself refers to "the scarcity of *pāibāqī* and the crowds of men claiming pay" and declares that everything, "flesh and bone", had been assigned and no further demands for assignments could be entertained by the court.[64] Ma'mūrī and K̲h̲āfī K̲h̲ān make similar statements. "Large numbers (lit. a world)", we are told, "had become *jāgīr*-less (*be-jāgīr*)". Persons appointed to *manṣabs* could not obtain *jāgīrs* for years; and if a *jāgīr* was transferred from the hands of anyone, he might not get another.[65] The older nobility (the so-called *k̲h̲āna-zādān*) were extremely indignant at the way their claims were disregarded to provide for the Dakhinīs.[66] But the real victims of the crisis were the small *manṣabdārs*, who possessed neither the money nor the influence to induce the officers

---

[61] Cf. *Fatḥiya-i 'Ibriya*, ff. 129b-131a; *Dilkushā*, ff. 139a-140b.

[62] *Dilkushā*, f. 140b. For bribery practised in checking the cavalry brought to the brand, see Manucci, II, 377-8; *Matīn-i Inshā'*, ff. 66b-67a, 70a-b, 80a-b.

[63] Ma'mūrī, ff. 156b-157a; K̲h̲āfī K̲h̲ān, Add. 6574, ff. 106b-107a. This striking passage, inveighing against the influx of the Dakhinīs, is omitted in the Bib. Ind. text of K̲h̲āfī K̲h̲ān. On the influx of the Dakhinīs, see M. Athar Ali, *Mughal Nobility under Aurangzeb,* rev. edn., 26-30.

[64] *Dastūru-l 'Amal-i Agahī*, f.31; Add.18, 422, ff.17b-18a.

[65] Ma'mūrī, f.157a; K̲h̲āfī K̲h̲ān, Add. 6574. f. 107a.

[66] Ma'mūrī, f.182b; K̲h̲āfī K̲h̲ān, II, 379, 396-7.

of the court to assign them *jāgīrs*.[67]

The emperor's own revenue domain, the *khāliṣa* ought to be conceived of as a group of assignments held directly by the imperial administration. Quite apart from the areas that remained under *pāibāqī* for short periods pending their re-assignment,[68] we come across constant references to the transfer of various *maḥals* from, or to, the *khāliṣa*. It seems, however, to have been an accepted policy to keep for the *khāliṣa* the most fertile and conveniently administered territories.[69] Certain *parganas* were, therefore, kept almost permanently attached to it.[70]

The extent of the *khāliṣa* varied from time to time. In 1574-75 Akbar brought the whole of his Empire, with the exception of Bengal, Bihar and Gujarat, under the *khāliṣa*.[71] This turned out

[67] Ma'mūrī, ff.156b-157a; Khāfī Khān Add. 6574. ff.106b-107a. Aurangzeb himself admitted that in this situation, "great injustice is done to the small men (*reza-hā*)" (*Dastūru-l 'Amal-i Āgahī*, f.31a; Add. 6574, f. 107a).

J.F. Richards, *Mughal Administration in Golconda,* 158-62, 308-9, expresses some reserve in respect of the pressure on *jāgīrs* developing in the late years of Aurangzeb. But as Athar Ali, *Mughal Nobility under Aurangzeb*, rev. edn., xx-xxii, has demonstrated, Richards has read too much in a document containing what he assumed to be "the 1689-90 settlement" of the conquered kingdom, and overlooked a document of 1706 (printed in *Selected Documents of Aurangzeb's Reign*, 233-5) which gives an entirely contrary picture, at least for the 19 Karnatak *sarkārs* of *ṣūba* Haidarabad. For the contraction in the size of the *khāliṣa* attributable to the crisis over *jāgīrs*, see below, pages 315-16.

[68] *Khulāṣatu-s Siyāq,* f.89a-b; Or. 2026, f. 51a-b, cf. *Waqā'i' Ajmer*, 375-6.

[69] Bāyazīd, deputed to the *sarkār* of Sarangpur in Malwa in 1576, reported that it was not "suitable" for inclusion in the *khāliṣa*, and it was accordingly assigned in *jāgīr* (Bāyazīd, 353). Similarly, Aurangzeb ordered certain *parganas* to be re-assigned in *jāgīr* since they were not "fit" for the *khāliṣa* (*Akhbārāt* 42/14). What the main criterion for the suitability of an area for inclusion in the *khāliṣa* was may be judged from Hawkins's statement that "he [the king] taketh" any land "for himselfe (if it be rich ground and likely to yield much)" (*Early Travels,* 114) and from Qazwīnī's deprecation of the fact that only desolate tracts remained in the *khāliṣa* in Jahāngīr's later years (Or. 20,734, p. 444; Or. 173, f.221a-b). The *Waqā'i' Ajmer*, 4-5, suggests that the *parganas* near the fort of Ranthambhor should be taken into the *khāliṣa*, being easy to keep in order, while another *pargana* being *sair-ḥāṣil*, i.e. yielding revenue fully as assessed, was also considered fit for the *khāliṣa*. *Riyāzu-s Salāṭīn,* 245-6, declares that in the last years of Aurangzeb the *sair-ḥāṣil jāgīrs* in Bengal were resumed to the *Khāliṣa*.

[70] Bernier, 24, When Hindaun was transferred from Prince Mu'azzam's *jāgīrs,* Aurangzeb ordered it to be retained in the *khāliṣa* as it always had been from old times (*Akhbārāt* 42/14). In an earlier *farmān* (35th regnal year) the same *pargana* is described as permanently belonging to the *khāliṣa* (*khāliṣa-i muqarrarī*) (*Nāma-i Muzaffarī,* I, 256).

[71] *A.N.*, III, 117; 'Ārif Qandahārī, 197-8. Akbar probably had a precedent in the

to be a temporary measure, and the *jāgīrs* began to be granted again after a time, the political crisis of 1580-81 speeding up the process.[72] From an incidental reference it may be deduced that in 1596-7 the *jama'* of the *khāliṣa* in the provinces of Dehli, Awadh and Ilahabad amounted to about a fourth of their total *jama'*.[73] During the reign of Jahāngīr the *khāliṣa* is said to have suffered considerable reductions till its *jama'* fell to even below five per cent of that of the whole empire.[74] Shāhjahān, however, embarked upon a deliberate policy of expanding its area and revenues, and by the 4th year of his reign (1631-32) its *jama'* is said to have amounted to a fifteenth of the whole.[75] The proportion rose to one-

---

action of Islām Shāh, who also had put all his dominions under his own direct administration *(khāṣa-i khwud)* and paid his nobles in cash (Badāūnī, I, 384; *Tārīkh-i Dāūdī*, 165).

[72] Cf. Moreland, *Agrarian System*, 96-8. What was done is, perhaps, best illustrated by the case of the *sarkār* of Sarangpur referred to above. Its *jāgīrdār*, Shihābuddīn Aḥmad Khān, was transferred to Gujarat and it was brought under the *khāliṣa*. Bāyazīd was appointed to settle its revenue arrangements and he took charge late in 1576. On his deciding against its retention in the *khāliṣa* it was re-assigned (Bāyazīd, 353). That the restoration of *jāgīrs* was hastened by the events of 1580-81 is supported by explicit evidence. Akbar's position had then become critical owing to a rebellion in all the eastern provinces and Mirzā Ḥakīm's invasion from the north-west. His highest nobles took this opportunity to conspire against Shāh Manṣūr, the *dīwān* at the time and one of the architects of the *karorī* experiment. The unfortunate man was executed during Akbar's march against Mirzā Ḥakīm. In the meantime, according to Badāūnī, II, 296, Shahbāz Khān Kambū, the *Mīr Bakhshī*, who had taken charge of the administration at Agra, "during the absence of the emperor, gave away all the country right from Garhi to the Panjab in *jāgīrs* to men on his own authority... When the emperor (on his return) asked him the reason for his having dared to do this, he answered that if he had not conciliated the troops [i.e. officers, obviously], they would have all rebelled immediately." Badāūnī's statements are corroborated by those of Abū-l Fatḥ Gīlānī in his letters from the imperial camp in 1581 (*Ruq'āt-i Abū-l Fatḥ*, 34, 38-9).

[73] Akbar is said to have remitted one-sixth of the *jama'* in these provinces this year and the remission in the *khāliṣa* is said to have amounted to 4,05,60,596 *dāms* (*A.N.*, III, 494), so that the total *jama'* of the *khāliṣa* in the same provinces must have exceeded 243 million *dāms*. In the provincial statistics given in the *Ā'īn*, the total *jama'* of the three provinces amounts to nearly 1016 million *dāms*. The other cases of revenue remission mentioned in the *Akbarnāma* do not offer such a straightforward opportunity for comparison.

[74] Qazwīnī, Add. 20734, 444-5, Or. 173, f.221a-b, says it was reduced to 28 crore *dāms*. The total *jama'* of the Empire about 1627-29 was 630 crore *dāms* (*Majālisu-s Salāṭīn*, ff.115a-b).

[75] Qazwīnī, Add. 20734, 444, Or. 173, f.221a-b. He makes this statement while referring to the remissions, amounting to Rs 50 lakh, granted during the great famine of 1630-32. He adds that after his accession Shāhjahān ordered the *khāliṣa* to be expanded so as to have a *jama'* of 60 crore *dāms*.

eleventh within, perhaps, the course of the next few years[76] and was nearly one-seventh by the 20th year (1646-47).[77] The assessed revenues of the *khāliṣa* were put at a slightly lower figure in the 31st year (1657-8),[78] but the early years of the next reign saw another increase. By the tenth regnal year of Aurangzeb (1667-8) its *jama‘* amounted to almost one-fifth of the total for the empire.[79] We have also the figure of the *ḥāṣil* (actual revenue receipts) for the *khāliṣa* for the 35th regnal year (1691-2), and this is about 33 per cent higher than that for the 31st year of the previous reign.[80]

Valuable information for the *jama‘* and *ḥāṣil* of the imperial *khāliṣa* comes from statistical tables that are datable to 1701-02.[81] The proportions that they bear to the total *jama‘* and *ḥāṣil (-i kāmil)* in each *ṣūba* are given in the following table:

[76] Lāhorī, I, 364, states this in the same context as Qazwīnī. But he raises the figures of both the remission and the *jama‘* of the *khāliṣa*, respectively, to Rs 70 lakh and to 80 crore *dāms*. The difference between the figures of the two authorities can perhaps be explained by supposing that Lāhorī has also used information relating to later years. Saran, 432-3, has already pointed out that the proportion of one-eleventh in Lāhorī has reference not to the size of the revenue remitted, but to the ratio between the total *jama‘* and the *jama‘* of the *khāliṣa*. In fact, Lāhorī gives the total *jama‘* as 880 crores under the 20th year (II, 710), and this is exactly eleven times the figure given by him for the *jama‘* of the *khāliṣa*.

[77] It now amounted to 120 crore *dāms*, compared with the *jama‘* of the Empire, put at 880 crores (Lāhorī, II, 712-13).

[78] At a little over 118 crore *dāms* in the *Ẓawābiṭ-i ‘Ālamgīrī*, Add. 6598, f. 187b; Or. 1641. f.133a.

[79] *Mir‘ātu-l ‘Ālam,* Add. 7657, f.445b.

[80] *Ẓawābiṭ-i ‘Ālamgīrī,* Add. 6598,f. 187b. Or. 1641, f. 133a. The amount shown is Rs 3,33,12,480, to be compared with Rs 2,48,79,500, the figure for the *ḥāṣil* of the *khāliṣa* in the 31st year of Shāhjahān. In 1670 Aurangzeb issued instructions that the income from the *khāliṣa* should not be less than Rs 4 crore per year (*Ma’āṣir-i ‘Ālamgīrī*, 99-100). Comparative statistics for the *khāliṣa* are given for the reigns of Shāhjahān and Aurangzeb at another place in the *Ẓawābiṭ-i ‘Ālamgīrī* Ethe 415, f. 177a-b, Or. 1641, f. 81a-b, but here the exact years are not indicated:

	Number of *maḥals*	Number of villages	*Jama‘* (*dāms*)	*Ḥāṣil* (Rs.)
Shāhjahān's reign	407	78,000	1,34,46,03,245	2,81,21,227
	478	75,000	1,25,76,60,947	2,47,16,983
Aurangzeb's reign	950	958?	1,31,35,61,364	2,61,18,079
	787	938?	1,24,54,64,650	2,34,51,956

[81] *Dastūr al-‘Amal-i Shāhjahānī*, Add.6588, ff.17a-39a. I have assumed a transcriptional error in the *jama‘dāmī* for Kashmir, where, by reference to other statistics of the same period I have substituted 22,99,11,397 for the figure 27,79,11,397 *dāms* in this MS. The *jama‘* figure for the *khāliṣa* in Bihar and the figure for

	Per cent of *jama*ʻ	Per cent of *ḥāṣil* (-*i kāmil*)		Per cent of *jama*ʻ	Per cent of *ḥāṣil* (-*i kāmil*)
Bihar	5.25	4.87	Ajmer	4.74	17.54
Ilahabad	7.52	7.14	Lahor	19.87	24.38
Awadh	2.42	2.65	Multan	10.00	4.31
Agra	11.72	11.91	Thatta	7.33	6.97
Malwa	2.44	1.67	Kashmir	3.26	11.45
Gujarat	11.28	19.70	Kabul	20.31	8.42
Dehli	9.54*	2.25*			

* Figures for *k͟hāliṣa* incomplete

It is immediately apparent that the *k͟hāliṣa* tended to be most extensive in the central provinces (Agra, Dehli and Lahor) and the economically important province of Gujarat, and tended to be smaller in size in other, perhaps commercially less important, provinces. In aggregate, in all the provinces listed in the above table, excluding Dehli (with incomplete figures), the *k͟hāliṣa* accounted for 10.05 per cent of the *jama*ʻ and 11.57 per cent of the *ḥāṣil*. This suggests a considerable contraction in the size of the *k͟hāliṣa* after 1667-68, a contraction that fairly well corroborates our sources when they speak of a great pressure for *jāgīrs* during precisely these years.

2. THE MACHINERY OF REVENUE ADMINISTRATION

The administrative arrangements, under the *jāgīr*-assignment system, were geared mainly to cope with two problems. The first was that of imperial control: the assignee was entitled to assess and collect the revenue, but in both these matters he was required to conform to imperial regulations. Although certain orders and rules were framed specifically for the *k͟hāliṣa,* most of the fundamental

the *ḥāṣil* of *ṣūba* Malwa have been corrected by reference to the Aligarh MS; the figure for the *ḥāṣil* of the *k͟hāliṣa* in Malwa has been modified by totalling the figures given under individual *sarkārs*. No *k͟hāliṣa* figures are provided in these tables for the Dakhin provinces; but there exists a summary statement of the assignments in the 19 *sarkārs* of the Karnatak (*ṣūba* Haidarabad) in 1705-6 *(Documents of Aurangzeb's Reign,* 233-5). This shows that the *k͟hāliṣa sharīfa* accounted for just 6.3% of the total *jama*ʻ *kāmil;* and the *pāibāqī*, after deducting the share of the *pālīgārs*, accounted for another 4.2%. So in this area, too, the *k͟hāliṣa* was by no means extensive.

regulations were set in general terms, applying, by implication, to both the *khāliṣa* and the *jāgīrs*. Abū-l Faẓl's statements show that even in the early years of Akbar's reign the *jāgīrdārs* were obliged to collect the revenue due to them in accordance with the annual cash rates sanctioned by the court.[1] Todar Mal began his recommendations of the 27th year (1682-83) by an article requiring all collections, whether by the *jāgīrdārs* or the officials of the *khāliṣa*, to be in strict accordance with the authorized rates: everything extorted in excess of these was to be recovered together with such fines as might be imposed.[2] When in the late years of Shāhjahān a reform was undertaken in the revenue system of the Dakhin, the change-over to crop-sharing was enforced not only in the *khāliṣa*, but also in the assignments of the *jāgīrdārs*.[3] The *farmān* of Aurangzeb addressed to Rasikdās directs its recipient to require all "the revenue-collectors (*'āmils*) of the *maḥals* of the *jāgīrdārs*" to follow the regulations published in this edict. There must, then, have been some machinery by which respect for imperial orders could be secured in the assignments.[4]

Secondly, there would be the problem faced by the *jāgīrdār* who had to manage a new assignment after every short interval. Neither he nor his staff could have hoped to be familiar with the details of the revenue-paying capacity and the local customs of each new *jāgīr*. Nor would his short tenure at any one place enable the *jāgīrdār* or his agent to build up a local administration from scratch. The assignment system would therefore have resulted in complete anarchy, had there not been some arrangement for ensuring continuity in local records and revenue practice.

To meet these two ends, the administrative structure consisted of three distinct elements. First, there were the officials and agents of the assignee, whether the assignee was the *khāliṣa* or a *jāgīrdār*. Then, there were the permanent local officials, owing their position partly to birth and partly to imperial authority, but unaffected by the transfers of assignees. Finally, there were the full-fledged officials

[1] *Ā'īn*, I, 348; *A.N.*, III, 282. Cf. also *Agrarian System*, 91-2.

[2] *A.N.*, III, 381 (Add. 27,247, f.331b).

[3] This appears from *Ādāb-i 'Ālamgīrī*, f.118a (letter not traced in printed edn.).

[4] Moreland, recognizes that the imperial regulations concerning land revenue affected the assignees as well, but seems to think that their enforcement mainly depended upon the assignees' fear of "informers and enemies" who might report transgressions of which "Akbar would probably have taken serious notice" (*Agrarian System*, 92). But even Akbar surely needed to have some regular instrument for detecting and preventing irregularities.

of the imperial administration who could be used both to help and to control the assignees.

We possess detailed information in respect of officials of the *khāliṣa*, answering to the first category. But no more than a summary description can be offered here. Under Sher Shāh each *pargana* used to have a *shiqqdār*, who had the charge of revenue collection as well as of maintaining law and order.[5] He had also a colleague known as *munṣif* or *amīn*,[6] whose duties do not appear from the sources, but from the significance attaching to his name later on, it may be conjectured that he was in charge of assessment.

These arrangements probably continued during the early years of Akbar's reign. There are explicit references to *shiqqdārs*;[7] the *munṣif* or *amīn* at the *pargana* level is, however, no longer heard of, and it is possible that his position had declined in importance. A radical change in the organization of the *khāliṣa* administration was brought about in 1574-75, when all but three provinces of the empire were placed under it. The whole land was divided into districts, each of which was expected to yield one crore of *ṭankas*. To each district was appointed an *'āmil* or *amalguzār,* who came to be known as *karorī.*[8] These revenue collectors seem to have been allowed the greatest latitude in action, for they are said to

[5] Mushtāqī, f.49a; 'Abbās Khān, ff.106a, 113b, ed., 210, 227. The *madad-i ma'āsh farmāns* of Sher Shāh, published in the *Oriental College Magazine*, IX, No. 3, (1933), 121-2, 125-8, are addressed to "the present *shiqqdār* and the future *'āmils*" suggesting thereby that *shiqqdār* and *'āmil*, or revenue collector, were synonymous terms. See also Allahabad 318 and 'Abbās Khān, ff. 112b-113a. Kabīr speaks of the oppressive *sikdārs* who demand land revenue (*hālā)* from peasants who have not sown any land (*Gurū Granth* Rāg Sūhī, Kabīr, 5.1; Nagari ed., II, 793). One of the two *farmāns* of Sher Shāh (*Oriental College Magazine*, IX(3), 127) requires the grantees to go to the aid of the *shiqqdār* in case of disorder, thus indicating the military or police aspect of his position.

[6] Mushtāqī, f.49a, reads *munṣif.* while 'Abbās Khān, f.106, ed., 210, has *amīn.* Badāūnī, I, 385, explains that the two terms were synonymous. Cf. *Khulāṣatu-s Siyāq,* f. 79a, Or. 2026, f.33a. That the *munṣif*, under Sher Shāh, was an officer of some importance, appears from *Laṭā'if-i Quddūsī,* extracts tr. S.N. Hasan, *Medieval India Quarterly*, I, No.1, 56. Kabīr tells of *munsafs*, who, with *ḍāḍīs* (surveyors), descend upon a village, harassing peasants (*raiat),* measuring with loose ropes and taking bribes *(Gurū Granth*, Rāg Sūhī, Kabīr 5.2; Nagari ed., II, 793).

[7] Bāyazīd held for some years (from 1561 onwards) the post of the *shiqqdār* of Hisar on behalf of one of Akbar's premier nobles, Mun'im Khān. In this capacity he claims to have increased the revenue considerably and to have once successfully defended Hisar against rebels (Bāyazīd, 278-9, 299, 303).

[8] *A.N.*, III, 117; 'Ārif Qandahārī, 197-8; *Ṭabaqāt-i Akbarī,* II, 300-301; Badāūnī, II, 189.

have been guilty of much oppression.[9] When the *Karorī* Experiment was practically wound up and the assignments began to be granted again, the name *karorī* still stuck to the *'āmil* or *'amalguzār* of the *khāliṣa,* set over a *pargana* or group of of *parganas.*[10] His duties, as described in the *Ā'īn*, show this official to be in charge of both the assessment and collection of revenue.[11] The term *shiqqdār* probably continued to be used synonymously with *'āmil,*[12] but subsequently seems to have been used rather for a subordinate collector under the *karorī.*[13] The *amīn* now appears merely as the head of the survey party sent by the *karorī* to carry out measurement for purposes of assessment.[14] The *karorī* also employed troopers known as *sih-bandīs* for enforcing revenue collection.[15] The next important change came under Shāhjahān. His *dīwān*, Islām Khān (1639-40 to 1645-46) set up an *amīn* in every *maḥal*,

[9] Badāūnī, II, 189.

[10] This is nowhere explicitly stated, but is clear from the numerous references to the *karorī* in the records of the subsequent period.

[11] *Ā'īn*, I, 285-8.

[12] In the *Ā'īn*, the *shiqqdār* seems to have been mentioned in two passages only. At one place (I, 300-01) the reference is probably to the old *shiqqdār* before the installation of the *karorī*. At the other (I, 289) it has obviously been used as an alternative designation for the *'āmil*: the treasurer is required to establish the treasury with the advice of the *shiqqdār* and the *kārkun*; but he should not open its door without the knowledge of the *'āmil* and the *kārkun*. Similarly, he is not to make any disbursements without authority and in an emergency must take written orders from the *shiqqdār* and *kārkun* for any payment; but it is the *'āmil* who is to put his seal on his accounts, which he ought to compare with those of the *kārkun*.

[13] The *shiqqdār* appears with the *kārkun* among the subordinate associates (*muta'alliqān)* of the *karorī* in the specimen *bar-āmad* accounts reproduced in the *Khulāṣatu-s Siyāq,* ff.91b-94a, Or. 2026,ff.59a-64a. In Add. 6603, f.67a, the *shiqqdār* is defined as an agent sent by the *'āmil* to enforce collection.

[14] Cf. *A.N.*, III, 383. In the similar provisions made in the *Ā'īn*, I. 286, the word *amīn* seems to have been omitted out of confusion with the preceding word *ā'īn*, but, he is referred to in the same context in ibid., 300-301. The name *amīn* was also given to the official sent down from the headquarters to check on the *'amalguzār's* report of the damage caused by any natural calamity (*Ā'īn*, I, 286-7; *Khulāṣatu-s Siyāq*, f.79a, Or. 2026, f.33a).

[15] *A.N.*, III, 458; Asad Beg's Memoirs, Or. 1996, f. 4a; *Hidāyatu-l Qawā'id*, f. 11a; Khāfī Khān, Add. 6573, f.83a, Add. 26226, f.60a. The *Khulāṣatu-s Siyāq*, ff.79b-80a, Or. 2026, f.34a-b, requires the *karorī* to post "horse and foot" to enforce the full sowing of the area fixed under *nasaq* and to prevent the grain from being lifted before the revenue was paid in full.

The actual meaning of *sih-bandī* seems to be that of troops hired for the occasion, as distinct from troops permanently employed. See, for example, *Bāburnāma*, ed. Mano, 424; tr. Beveridge, II, 470 ("*b:d-hindī*"). Yāsīn's Glossary in its article on this term (Add. 6603, f.66a) says that *sih-bandī* is the name given to the servants of men in authority, and adds that *"faujdārs* and officials follow the custom of transferring the work of assessment from the *karorī* to his new colleague.[16] The *karorī* henceforward concerned himself chiefly with collecting the amount which the *amīn* had assessed.[17] Islām Khan's successor, Sa'dullāh Khān (1646-7 to 1655-6) is said to have further reduced the powers of the *karorī* by putting an end to the practice of combining the offices of *karorī* and *faujdār* (commandant) in the same person. An old territorial unit, *chakla*, comprising a group of *maḥals*, was revived,[18] and an *amīn-faujdār* was appointed over it, the *karorī* becoming really a subordinate of this official.[19]

The practice of giving the revenue of whole *parganas* or large areas on farm (*ijāra*) seems to have been largely the exception in

---

hiring horse and foot at the harvest season only; they dismiss them on the coming of the rains and re-employ them from the Dasehra day, so that the saying in Dehli is: The koel (Indian cuckoo) sings, 'the *sih-bandī* roams'."

The etymology of the word is obscure. Yāsīn's suggestion (ibid.) that it is derived from *sipah-i Hindī*, "Indian troops", is not convincing.

[16] *Khulāṣatu-s Siyāq*, f.79b, Or.2026, ff.33a-34a.

[17] The duties of the *amīn* and '*āmil* (or *karorī*) after this separation of the two offices are described in various documents. See, e.g. *Dastūru-l 'Amal-i 'Ālamgīrī*, f.33a; *Farmān* to Rasikdās, Preamble; *Dastūru-l 'Amal-i Navīsindagī*, ff.153b-154a; *Nigārnāma-i Munshī* ed., 135-7, 144-5; *Farhang-i Kārdānī*, f.29a-b, Edinburgh 83, ff.39a-40a; *Durru-l 'Ulūm*, ff.136b-137a; *Siyāqnāma*, 26-28, 48-50; *Khulāṣatu-s Siyāq*, ff.73b-74a, Or. 2026, ff.21b-22b; *Hidāyatu-l Qawā'id*, ff. 10a-11a. The concern of the *amīn* with assessment and of the '*āmil* with collection is throughout emphasized.

The separation of the two offices seems to have become a dogma with Mughal administrators. When one Sa'dullāh, who was at once the *faujdār*, *amīn* and *karori* of Merta, was suspected of embezzling large sums of money, the governor of Ajmer remarked that this was to be expected when these three offices were combined in the same person (*Waqā'i'-i Ajmer*, 311).

[18] A *farmān* of Akbar, contained in the *Munshāt-i Namkīn*, f.92a, recites that the *chakla*, "in the language of the present day", was a portion *(qaṭ'a)* of a *sarkār* over which a *faujdār* was sometimes apointed. But the term hardly ever occurs in the histories and documents of the time of Akbar or Jahāngīr. The statement in the *Khulāṣatu-s Siyāq* (see the next note for reference) that Sa'dullāh Khān was responsible for re-establishing the *chaklas* seems borne out by the fact that this territorial division begins to be mentioned in the records of Shāhjahān's reign. The *chaklas* were often identical with the *sarkārs*, as in the case of the *chaklas* of Hisar and Sirhind (as would appear from the geographical information in Bālkrishan Brahman, f.180a-b and passim), but in general a *chakla* was considered a smaller unit than a *sarkār* (Add. 6603, f.65b). In Bengal, however, the area of individual *sarkārs* being often small, a *chakla* consisted usually of a group of *sarkārs* (cf. *Dastūru-l 'Amal-i Khāliṣa Sharīfa*, f. 9a). The *sarkār* of Sātgām, for example, was a part of the *chakla* of Hugli (Add. 24,039,f. 36a).

[19] *Khulāṣatu-s Siyāq*, f.79b, Or. 2026, f.34a-b. Cf. Lāhorī, II, 247, for reference, under the 15th year, to Rāi Todarmal, "the *faujdār* and *amīn* of the *chakla* of Sirhind", who had the charge of the *khāliṣa* lands in that district (*zila'*).

the *khāliṣa*.[20] If two foreign observers nevertheless assert that the whole of the *khāliṣa* was held by farmers,[21] this is probably due to the general impression derived from the system of *ta'ahhud,* which meant a pledge given by a prospective official about the amount he would assess or collect. Thus the *karorīs* were originally expected to collect a crore of *ṭankas* from their charges; and in the 30th year of Akbar (1585-86) the current practice, as officially described, was to hold the *'āmils* answerable for any failure to collect the amount set out in their undertakings *(nuskha-i karor-bandī)* or that of the revenue of the best year *(sāl-i kāmil)*. This was now held to be unfair, and it was laid down that they should be questioned only if there was any decline in the revenue compared with the receipts of the previous year.[22] With the separation of the office of the *amīn* from that of the *karorī,* the latter only promised to collect what the former had assessed,[23] while the *amīn* usually pledged himself to raise the assessment, presumably by claiming to employ more rigorous and efficient

---

The *Dastūru-l 'Amal-i 'Ālamgīrī,* f.33a, declares that the *amīn* was superior in authority to the '*āmil*.

[20] For cases of farming in *khāliṣa* in Gujarat during the reigns of Jahāngīr and Shāhjahān, see Blochet, Suppl. Pers. 482, ff.146a-b and 34b-35a. In *Waqā'i' Ajmer,* 209, 359, we have two instances where *jāgīrdārs,* who lost an assignment, obtained, or sought to obtain, the same areas on farm from the *khāliṣa.* An order issued by Aurangzeb states that the *parganas* of the *khāliṣa* in Bengal were being rented out to revenue farmers it and forbids this practice entirely. (The usual term for farming was *ijāra,* but this document notes that in Bengal it was known as *māl-zamīnī.) (Aḥkāmi-i 'Ālamgīrī,* f.207a-b). For an earlier order (1676) to the same effect relating to Gujarat, see *Mir'āt,* I, 292.

It was probably in the reign of Farruk̲h̲siyar, under the aegis of the Saiyid brothers, that *khāliṣa* was first given out on farm on a large scale (K̲h̲āfī K̲h̲ān, III, 773). This passage is seriously misinterpreted by Muzaffar Alam, *Crisis of Empire in Mughal North India,* 42, who even coins the word *baqqālīat* (rendered by him as "shop-keeping") and attributes it to K̲h̲āfī K̲h̲ān (see I. Habib, in *PIHC,* 56th session, 1995, Calcutta, 361, 374). The very first item of reform in the scheme submitted by Niẓāmu-l Mulk to Muḥammad Shāh was the abolition of "the farming out of the *mahals* of the *khāliṣa* that had brought about devastation and ruin of the country" (K̲h̲āfī K̲h̲ān, III, 948). Cf. Shāh Walīullāh, *Siyāsī Maktūbāt,* 43.

[21] J. Xavier, tr. Hosten, *JASB,* N.S., XXIII (1927), 121; Bernier, 224.

[22] *A.N.,* III, 457 (Mīr Fatḥullāh Shīrāzī's recommendations). Three years earlier Todar Mal took care to lay down that if an *'āmil* was successful in raising the total *jama'* of the territory under his charge, he was not to be held answerable for the decrease of the *jama'* in some individual *mahals* under him (ibid., 383).

[23] See the text of a *karorī's ta'ahhud* in *Siyāqnāma,* 50. See also the authorities cited in note no. 17 for the duties and functions of this official, in most of which there is an explicit statement on this point.

methods.[24] It is said, however, that many *amīns* made heavy assessments initially, simply to fulfil the terms of their pledge, and then made large deductions on all sorts of pretexts.[25] Moreover, one document suggests that, according to the *khāliṣa* regulations, the difference between the amount of the *ta'ahhud* and the actual revenue collected was not recoverable from the *'āmil*, though a failure to live up to his undertaking might result in his removal.[26]

No indication about the pay allowed to the *'amalguzār* is given in the *Ā'īn*, but one learns from a later source that, before a change was introduced during the reign of Shāhjahān, the *karorī* used to be allowed 8 per cent of the total receipts for himself and his staff.[27] After the creation of the separate office of the *amīn*, this was reduced to 5 per cent., subject still to some further deductions.[28] But the rate seems to have varied according to localities.[29] A fifth part of the allowance[30] or, as stated elsewhere, one per cent of the

[24] In the text of the *amīn's ta'ahhud* set out in *Siyāqnāma*, 28, no amount is mentioned, the *amīn* only promising to carry out assessment in conformity with "the actual conditions *(maujūdāt)* and the (established) crop-rates *(rai'-i jins)*".

[25] The preamble to Aurangzeb's *farmān* to Rasikdās states that the officials (*mutaṣaddīyān*) usually made natural calamities an excuse for making heavy deductions from the *jama'*. The *Nigārnāma-i Munshī,* ed., 68-9, contains a letter addressed to 'Ināyat Khān, *dīwān*, complaining against the dismissal of two *amīns* who had fulfilled their pledges. It adds that "no reliance should be placed on the pledges of good service given by men, who make a pledge of enhancement (*iẕāfa)* in the beginning, but by the end of the year turn the accounts upside down."

[26] *Nigārnāma-i Munshī,* ed., 58. This letter protests against the claim made by officials of Prince Mu'aẕẕam's *sarkār* against an *amīn* for the difference between the *ta'ahhud* and the collection. This is denounced as being "no audit"; and it is asserted that "the demand for receipts in accordance with the *ta'ahhud* had not been made upon any '*āmil.*" Finally, it asks that the rules of the *khāliṣa*, along with those of the Prince's *sarkār,* should be followed, and one assumes that the former supported the viewpoint of the writer.

[27] *Khulāṣatu-s Siyāq,* f.79a, reads 20 per cent, which is obviously too high a figure. Or. 2026, f.33a, has 8 per cent instead, and since in Persian writing the words for these two numbers are easily interchangeable, the latter reading has been accepted. The *karorī's* allowance was technically known as *ḥuqūqu-t taḥṣīl.*

[28] *Khulāṣatu-s Siyāq*, ff.79b, 84b, 86b; Or. 2026, ff. 34a-b, 42a, 45b-46b. The principal deduction seems to be one called *sā'ir,* amounting to 17 per cent of the total allowance. This is not so clear from the text of the manual but is plainly shown in the specimen accounts. Cf. also *Nigārnāma-i Munshī,* ed., 94. The accounts in the *Khulāṣatu-s Siyāq* show also that out of the allowance remitted to the *karorī,* one per cent of the revenue was meant for his personal pay (*ẕāt)* and four per cent for the salaried staff (*māhīyān)* employed by him.

[29] Thus the rate, after the *sā'ir* deduction, is put at 7 per cent of the receipts, specifically for a particular *pargana* (*Nigārnāma-i Munshī*, ed., 94). In the *Farhang-i Kārdānī*, Edinburgh 83, f.55a-b, it is put at Rs 3, as. 5½, per Rs 100.

[30] *Khulāṣatu-s Siyāq,* f.86b, Or. 2026, f.46a.

revenue,[31] was withheld pending audit. Under Akbar a fourth part of the *'āmil's* allowance used also to be detained pending the col-lection of revenue arrears,[32] but in the subsequent period it seems to have become the practice to assign the whole allowance to arrears (*baqāyā*) of the previous years.[33] It is not very clear how the *amīn* got his pay. One manual suggests he too drew a small percentage of the revenue receipts,[34] but an earlier document shows that, under the rules of the *k͟hāliṣa,* the *amīn* was given a fixed salary per month.[35]

The accounts of the actual collections of the *'āmils,* and their agents were audited in many cases by the help of the village *paṭwārīs'* papers.[36] This practice was recommended by Mīr Fatḥullāh Shīrāzī under Akbar, chiefly with a view to preventing illegal exactions.[37] Shāhjahān's officials seem to have been concerned, on the other hand, rather with ensuring that all such collections (whether authorized or not) should be brought into the imperial treasury. In any case, they are said to have made this method of audit, known as *bar-āmad,* a part of the routine of administration.[38]

[31] *K͟hulāṣatu-l Inshā'*, f.112a. Cf. *Nigārnāma-i Munshī,* ed., 94, where it is stated to be "in accordance with the regulations of the *sarkār*" of Prince Mu'aẓẓam.

[32] *A.N.*, III, 458: Fatḥullāh Shīrāzī recommended that the payments for the staff of the *'amalguzār* should not be debited to arrears left by previous *'āmils*, which were difficult to collect.

[33] *K͟hulāṣatu-l Inshā'*, f.112a. This merely says "arrears", but the *sanad* in *Nigārnāma-i Munshī,* op. cit., goes further and declares that the allowance was first to be deducted from the arrears of the previous years (*baqāyā-i sanwāt)* and then only from the current arrears. This is explicitly said to be in conformity with the rules of the *k͟hāliṣa*.

[34] *Farhang-i Kārdānī,* Edinburgh 83, f.55a. The rate shown is Rs.1, as. 10½, per Rs.100.

[35] *Selected Documents*, 179. The pay amounted to Rs 120 per month "in accordance with the regulations of the *k͟hāṣa-i sharīfa*". The words *k͟hāṣa* and *k͟hāliṣa* were often used interchangeably, the former embracing the whole establishment, the latter only the revenue-collection machinery.

[36] It is not to be assumed, of course, that the village papers always revealed the true state of affairs. Sher Shāh is said to have recommended that the person sent to audit the *'āmil's* accounts should seize the village papers before the *muqaddam* had any warning of it ('Abbās K͟hān, f.18a-b; ed., 34). Ṣūrat Singh in his *Taẕkira-i Pīr Ḥassū Telī* (AD 1647), MS, CAS in History, Aligarh, ff.102a-113a, tells us how a good *qānūngo* saved an embezzling but repentant *shiqqdār* of a *pargana* near Lahor from the enquiries of an upright *amīn*, by advising him to summon the old village papers (*kāg͟haẕ-i aṣlī, kāg͟haẕ-i k͟hām)*, burn them, get them replaced by new ones, and pay back the difference (*waẓ'e*). The ruse was successfully accomplished. Cf. Elliott, *Chronicles of Oonao*, 108-9 n.

[37] *A.N.*, III, 457-8.

[38] *K͟hulāṣatu-s Siyāq,* ff.79a, 91b, Or. 2026, ff.34a, 59a-b. Cf. also *Farmān* to

The *'āmils'* accounts were always subjected to rigorous auditing after their removal. But it took time, and meanwhile the wretched officials often languished in prison awaiting the settlement of the claims against them.[39] Aurangzeb ordered that if they were found guilty of misappropriation, the whole of their personal allowance, and three-fourths of that of their staff, was to be resumed.[40]

There were, besides the *karorī* and the *amīn,* two other officials who were posted independently of them to each *pargana*, namely the *foṭadār* or *khizāna-dār,* the treasurer,[41] and *kārkun* or *bitikchī,* the accountant.[42] Under Sher Shāh there were two *kārkuns*, one for keeping the records in Hindī and the other for those in Persian.[43] Todar Mal is reputed to have made Persian the sole language of accounts,[44] and to this may well be attributed his action in 1582-83, when he replaced the two *bitikchīs*, associated with the *'āmil*, by a single one.[45]

The *pāibāqī*, consisting of lands earmarked for re-assignment to *jāgīrdārs*, was essentially a part of the *khāliṣa*, though for administrative convenience it was kept a separate charge. Its administration followed the same pattern as that of the *khāliṣa*. The same three principal officials, *amīn, karorī* and *foṭadār*, were appointed, and the regulations of the *khāliṣa* were followed in preparing all

---

Rasikdās, Art.11; *Siyāqnāma,* 75-76; *Waqā'i' Ajmer,* 27-8, 32, 38, 44-5.

39 For the fate of the *karorīs* at the hands of Todar Mal, see Badāūnī, II, 189-90; III, 279-80. Fatḥullāh Shīrāzī reported in the 30th year (1585-86) that many *'āmils* were in prison from failure to collect the maximum revenue or the amount they had undertaken to collect (*A.N.*, III, 457). After the death of Sa'dullāh Khān, Shāhjahān ordered the release of some *karorīs* who had been in prison for more than twenty years *(Chār Chaman-i Barhaman*, Add. 16863, f. 32a). Aurangzeb urged in his orders that the cases of the *'āmils* and others imprisoned on suspicion of having misappropriated the funds of the *khāliṣa* should be speedily settled (*Durru-l 'Ulūm,* ff.58a-59b; *Mir'āt*, I, 264, 282-3).

40 *Mir'āt,* I, 264; *Durru-l 'Ulūm,* f. 83a-b.

41 For his duties see *Ā'īn*, I, 289; Harkaran, 54, 56; *Nigārnāma-i Munshī*, ed. 137; *Durru-l 'Ulūm, f.137b)*

42 *Ā'īn*, I, 288; Harkaran, 56,58; *Durru-l 'Ulūm*, f.137a-b.

43 Mushtāqī, Or. 1929, f.49a; 'Abbās Khān, f.106a-b, ed., 210-11. It is a curious feature of Sher Shāh's *farmāns* granting *madad-i ma'āsh* (*Oriental College Magazine*, IX, [3], 1933), that the Persian text is followed by a transcription of it in Nagari characters, obviously for the convenience of those unable to read the Arabic script.

44 Sujān Rāi, 409; *Khulāṣatu-l Inshā'* f.115a; *Khulāṣatu-s Siyāq,* f.65a, Or. 2026, f.4b.

45 *A.N.*, III, 381 (Add. 27,247, f.331b). The complete shift to Persian is put in the 27th regnal year of Akbar (1582-83) in the *Khulāṣatu-s Siyāq,* op. cit., and the 28th year in the *Khulāṣatu-l Inshā'*, op. cit.

records and accounts.[46] Moreover, the whole administration of the *pāibāqī* was under the control of the central *dīwān-i khālisa*.[47]

Next in size to the *khāliṣa-i sharīfa* were the *jāgīrs* of the princes of royal blood. The princes held the highest *manṣabs*, much higher than the maximum permitted to any of the nobles; and the *jāgīrs* assigned to them were, therefore, naturally very large in extent.[48] In general the administrative structure of a prince's *sarkār* or estab-lishment[49] was closely modelled on that of the *khāliṣa*. Its *'āmils* were generally known as *karorīs*[50] and were accompanied by the same officials, the *amīn*, the *foṭadār* and the *kārkun*.[51] There are also explicit statements in some documents belonging to a prince's secretariat that the rules of the *khāliṣa*, on specific points, were to be applied in his *sarkār*.[52] Nevertheless, certain variations from the practice of the *khāliṣa* can be detected here and there. For

[46] *Khulāṣatu-s Siyāq*, f.89b, Or. 2026, f.51a. Cf. *Waqā'i'-i Ajmer*, 27-28, 32, 401: officials, who are stated on pp. 27-28, 32 to have held the charge of *pāibāqī*, are described indifferently as officials of the *khāliṣa* on pp.27, 38.

[47] The affairs of the revenue officials of certain *maḥals* of *pāibāqī* in Ajmer province were investigated by the auditor *(bar-āmad navīs)* of the accounts of all the officials of the *khāliṣa* in the province. When he found the conduct of the *pāibāqī* officials unsatisfactory, he sent a report to the central *dīwān-i khāliṣa*, who was expected to convey its contents to the emperor *(Waqā'i' Ajmer,* 11, 27-28).

[48] In the 20th regnal year of Shāhjahān, Dārā Shukoh held the *manṣab* of 20,000 *zāt*, 20,000 *sawār*, 10,000 *do-aspa sih-aspa*, and his pay amounted accordingly to 40 crore *dams* (Lāhorī, II, 715), i.e. a third of the *jama'* of the *khāliṣa* at the time. By the 30th regnal year his rank had been raised to 40,000 *zāt*, 20,000 *sawār*, 20,000 *do-aspa sih-aspa*. By then his brothers, Shujā' and Aurangzeb, were both holding the ranks of 20,000/15,000/10,000, while the third brother Murād's rank was 15,000/12,000/8,000(Wāriṣ, a: f. 523b, b: f.200a). The highest rank ordinarily permitted to a noble was 7,000 *zāt*, 7,000 *sawār* (Lāhorī, II, 321; *'Ālamgīrnāma*, 618).

[49] The word *sarkār* was widely used in the literature of our period for the establishment or administration of a prince or noble (cf. *Mir'ātu-l Iṣṭilāh*, f.167b). It ought not to be confused with the territorial unit of *sarkār*.

[50] Cf. *Ādāb-i 'Ālamgīrī*, f.169a; *Selected Documents*, 121; Bilhaur Docs., *chaknama*, AH 1056 (AD1646); *Nigārnāma-i Munshī*, ed., 86-87 and passim. It may be mentioned in passing that the orders issued on behalf of the princes can be identified by the formula *ḥasbu-l amr*, as distinct from imperial orders issued through court officials, which were called *ḥasbu-l ḥukm*.

[51] *Nigārnāma-i Munshī*, ed., 58, 85-6, for the *amīn*; ibid., 87, for the treasurer; and ibid., 90, for the *kārkun*. The combined office of the *amīn* and *faujdār* was established in the princes' *jāgīrs* also. See ibid., ed., 79-80; *Durru-l 'Ulūm*, ff. 138b-139a. For the exaction of *ta'ahhud* in the princes' *jāgīrs*, see *Nigārnāma-i Munshī*, ed., 58; *Matīn-i Inshā'*, ff.38b-39a.

[52] E.g. *Nigārnāma-i Munshī*, ed., 58, 84, 94.

example, we come across an order (*amr*) issued by Prince Mu'aẕẕam requiring that the offices of the *amīn* and *karorī* be combined and held by one person only in his *jāgīrs*.[53]

Out of their assignments, the princes sometimes granted *jāgīrs* to their own officials.[54] There is no reason to believe that such sub-assignments required imperial sanction: they were probably transferred from place to place according as the princes' *jāgīrs* were transferred.

The arrangements made by ordinary assignees for the management of their *jāgīrs* could hardly have followed a uniform pattern. In general, since his assignment was transferred from time to time and he himself could be posted at different places, a *jāgīrdār* usually sent his own agents, or *gumāshtas*, to arrange for the collection of revenue on his behalf.[55] Scattered assignments must naturally have been more difficult and expensive for the assignee to administer, than those concentrated in single or adjacent *maḥals*.[56] Indeed, the apportionment of a *pargana* among several *jāgīrs*, a phenomenon known as *mutafarriqa 'amal*, was held to be ruinous in its results; and the official preference was for granting whole *(dar bast) parganas* to single assignees, as far as possible.[57] This rule was laid down especially for *maḥals* containing refractory elements,[58] and, as a corollary to this, small assignees were not

[53] Ibid., 77.

[54] See *T.J.*, 238, for the assignment of a *pargana* in *in'ām* to Prince Shāhjahān to enable him to assign it in *jāgīr* to "one of his leading servants" *(banda-hā-i 'umda)*, Raja Bikramājīt. Of much interest is Princess Jahān Ārā's detailed order (1644) for the sub-assignment of *maḥals* within *sarkār* Surat (then in her *jāgīr*) to her *khāliṣa* as well as to her *manṣabdārs*. The sub-assignments were made on the basis of *ḥāl-i ḥāṣil* (actual revenue) as recorded by the imperial finance ministry *(diwānīān-i 'uẕẕām)*. The order goes on to lay down what should be done were the *manṣabdārs* to decline acceptance of some *maḥals* on the basis of the given *ḥāl-i ḥāṣil* (Blochet: Suppl. Pers. 482, ff.33a-34a). For orders of assignment and resumption of *jāgīrs* issued in Prince Mu'aẕẕam's *sarkār*, see *Nigārnāma-i Munshī*, ed., 91-93.

[55] Cf. Hawkins, *Early Travels*, 91; Pelsaert, 54.

[56] Cf. *Fatḥiya-i 'Ibriya*, f.117a-b. It says that at the time of Shā'ista Khān's appointment to Bengal, the assignments held by the *jāgīrdārs* were generally distributed over several *maḥals*, so that they were put to great loss from being compelled to employ a large number of *shiqqdārs* and '*āmils*. In a letter in *Jāmi'u-l Inshā'*, Or. 1702, f.53a, one Mukhliṣ Khān expresses the hope that the *jāgīr* granted to him against an increase of pay would not be assigned "at some other place", for this would put him to the trouble of having a number of '*āmils*.

[57] *Ādāb-i 'Ālamgīrī*, f.117a; ed., I, 183; *Ruq'āt-i 'Ālamgīr*, 126-7; *Fatḥiya-i 'Ibriya*, f.117a-b.

[58] The *Kalimāt-i Ṭaiyabāt*, f. 98a, preserves a remark of Aurangzeb to the effect

to be granted *jāgīrs* in disturbed or rebellious areas.[59]

The principal agent employed by the *jāgīrdār* was the *'āmil*, also known as *shiqqdār*.[60] Very few assignees could have been able to imitate the *khāliṣa sharīfa* and the princes in the number of officials maintained by them. The *shiqqdār* was probably often saddled with the work of the *amīn*[61] and/or the treasurer.[62] A specimen *parwāna* goes so far as to show a single person being appointed to "the duties of the *amīn, shiqqdār, kārkun* and *faujdār* of the *maḥals* of the *jāgīr*," leaving only the treasurer as his colleague.[63] His staff could include the *munṣif*, appearing now as a mere head of a party of surveyors.[64]

It is probable that the *jāgīrdārs* exacted pledges from their agents concerning future collections, as was the case in the *khāliṣa*. But they generally took in addition a certain amount termed *qabẓ* in advance, and it was apparently common for one person to displace another as the *'āmil* of a *jāgīrdār*, by offering a bigger *qabẓ* to the

---

that since Merta contained only Rājpūt peasantry, it had always been subjected to *mutafarriqa 'amal*.

59 *Hidāyatu-l Qawā'id*, f.3b. The *jāgīr* of the *nāẓim* or governor should, it says, consist in the fourth part of *zor-ṭalab*, i.e. seditious, *maḥals* and, for the rest, of medium *maḥals*. Half of the *jāgīrs* of the *dīwāns, bakhshīs* and the big *manṣabdārs* was to be granted in medium and half in the *ra'īyatī maḥals* (i.e. apparently those which contained submissive, revenue-paying peasantry). The fourth part of the *jāgīrs* of the small *manṣabdārs* was to be assigned in medium and the rest in *ra'īyatī maḥals*.

60 See Abū-l Faẓl's letter to his *shiqqdār* in *Inshā'-i Abū-l Faẓl*, 214-5; and Lashkar Khān's *parwāna* appointing a *shiqqdār* to certain *parganas* assigned to him, November 1658 (I.O.4434). Cf. Bilhaur Docs: *Taḥqīqnāma*, AH 1030, and *Chaknāmas*, AH 1087 and 1094; also Ḥadīqī, Br.M. Royal 16B XXIII, f. 14a; *Riyāẓu-l Wadād*, f. 11a; *Durru-l 'Ulūm* f.137a. These documents, as well as the evidence already cited for the position of the *shiqqdār* in the *khāliṣa*, show beyond doubt that he was chiefly a revenue official. It is not, therefore, possible to accept Saran's contention that he was an "executive officer... not directly concerned with" revenue collection (Saran, 291).

61 Ḥadīqī, op. cit., ff.15a-16a. The *shiqqdār* or '*āmil* in this case was accompanied by a *kārkun* and *foṭadār*. He applied for an *amīn* to be sent to make the assessment, but was asked to do the work himself. On the other hand, from the *chaknāma* of Docs. AH 1087 (AD 1676-77) in Bilhaur Docs, it appears that the *shiqqdār* and *kārkun* of a *pargana* within a noble's *jāgīr* were subordinate to the *amīn* of (all) the *maḥals* in the *jāgīr* of that noble.

62 See I.O. 4434: its contents suggest that the *shiqqdār* was to act as both the assessor and treasurer.

63 *Dastūru-l 'Amal-i Navīsindagī*, ff.194a-195a.

64 Bilhaur Docs: *Taḥqīqnāma* of AH 1030, and *chaknāmas* of AH 1056, 1087 and 1094. All these documents pertain to ordinary *jāgīrs*, except for the *chaknāma* of AH 1056, issued by officials of Prince Dārā Shukoh's *jāgīr*.

latter.[65] On the other hand, it was sometimes extremely difficult for the *jāgīrdārs,* especially if they were serving in some other province, to keep a check on their *'āmils* and prevent embezzlement of the revenue due to them.[66]

Many of the assignees therefore found it simpler to farm out their assignments.[67] This practice, called *ijāra,* was regarded as the source of great oppression, for the farmers, after giving very high bids to get the contracts, would still seek to make handsome profits by extorting money from the peasants by every means imaginable.[68] It is not easy to determine the extent to which revenue-farming was resorted to in the *jāgīrs.* Instances of it are not very often met with in administrative literature and there could certainly have been nothing like the conditions prevalent in the kingdom of Golkunda.[69] Still some documents relating to farming of *jāgīrs* in Awadh have come down to us.[70] It is possible, moreover, that farming existed in many cases in a concealed form and that in reality, if not in name, many *'āmils* were no better than revenue-farmers.[71] It was probably not prudent for the assignees to

[65] *Dilkushā,* f.139a.

[66] The dishonest behaviour of his *'āmils* is frequently referred to by Īzid Ba<u>kh</u>sh Rasā in his letters, *Riyāẓu-l Wadād,* ff.3b-4a, 5b, 10b, 16b. One specifically mentions his inability to deal with the affairs of his *jāgīrs* since he was posted with the imperial army, presumably in the Dakhin (ff.3b-4a). In another letter he declares that "the boat of his *jāgīr* was floundering in the flood of misappropriation raised by his tempestuous *'āmils"* (f.5b). Cf. *Waqā'i' Ajmer,* 679.

[67] "Some of the grantees [*jāgīrdārs*] send some of their employees to represent them or else hand over their grants to *karorīs* (sic!), who have to take the risk of good or bad harvests" (Pelsaert, 54.). Shāh Walīullāh, recommending that "small *manṣabdārs"* should be paid in cash, points out that such people "could not themselves collect revenue from their *jāgīrs* and were compelled to farm them out" *(Siyāsī Maktūbāt,* 42).

[68] *Maẓhar-i Shāhjahānī,* 52-3, citing the opinion of a good *jāgīrdār* of *sarkār* Bhakkar. Cf. Ṣādiq <u>Kh</u>ān, Or. 174, f.11a; Or. 1671, f6b.

[69] For the prevalence of revenue-farming in Golkunda, see *Relations,* 10-11, 57, 81-82; *Factories, 1665-67,* 245, Master, II, 113. Two documents, relating to revenue farms in the Karnatak, are copied in Br. M. Sloane 4092, ff.5b-6a, 8b-9a, one dated 1653 and the other belonging to years 1677-79.

[70] Allahabad 884-87, 889-90. The terms of the *ijāra* as set out in Allahabad 884 and 885 are that the farmer was to pay a fixed sum annually in two seasonal instalments. If a natural calamity occurred, he was to receive a reduction in his obligation according to the rate sanctioned (by the imperial administration?) for the *pargana (sharḥ-i pargana).* If, on the other hand, the farmer was able to collect more than the amount stipulated, the excess was to remain with him.

[71] In this connexion, it is interesting to read <u>Kh</u>āfī <u>Kh</u>ān's passage on the contrast between the days of Todar Mal and his own (the reign of Muḥammad Shāh) when

call for bids openly, since the practice of *ijāra* was disapproved of at the court. Thus when in 1694 it was reported to the emperor that the *manṣabdārs,* who had *jāgīrs* in Kashmir, were giving them on farm to local men, who were extremely oppressive, he ordered that the *dīwān* of the province should prohibit this practice and insist that the assignees send their own *'āmils* to collect the revenue.[72] In 1676 the same emperor (Aurangzeb) had forbidden the practice of revenue-farming in Gujarat, within both the *k͟hāliṣa* and *jāgīrs*.[73]

There was nothing to prevent a *jāgīrdār* from sub-assigning a part of his *jāgīr* to any of his officials or troopers. In the reign of Jahāngīr, we find the Tark͟hān governor of Sind, who held a considerable part of that province in his own *jāgīr*, granting *jāgīrs* to his officials and resuming them at will.[74] In the same reign, 'Abdur Raḥīm K͟hān-i K͟hānān is said to have usually rewarded his dependants and officials by granting them cash allowances as well as *jāgīrs* out of his own assignments.[75] A document of the reign of Shāhjahān, from Awadh, recites that when a particular village had been assigned in pay (*tank͟hwāh*) to a noble, he in turn assigned it to four of his troopers.[76] Another source, belonging to the next reign, refers to a Rājpūt officer, serving in the Dakhin, who had assigned all the villages of a *pargana*, held by him in *jāgīr*, to his Rājpūt troopers in *tank͟hwāh*. Here it is made quite clear that such sub-assignments lapsed with the transfer of the main *jāgīr*.[77] A *jāgīrdār* could resume or transfer the (sub-) *jāgīrs* of his retainers within his *jāgīr,* and such area of the *jāgīr* as was not so sub-assigned was known as his *k͟hāliṣa*.[78]

---

the land was being laid waste by '*ummāl-i ijāradār,* i.e. '*āmils* who took the land on *ijāra* or farm (K͟hāfī K͟hān, I, 157).

[72] *Ak͟hbārāt,* 37/38.

[73] *Mir'āt,* I, 292: for *jāgīrdārs* it uses here the word *tuyūldārs*.

[74] *Tārīk͟h-i Ṭāhirī,* Or. 1685, ff. 102b-103b, 118a-119b; ed., 222-3,252.

Referring to a *jāgīrdār* of Sehwan (Sind) early in Shāhjahān's reign, the *Maẓhar-i Shāhjahānī*, 164-5, tells us that he "assigned the whole country in *jāgīr* to his troopers, except for a few *maḥals* which he kept in his own *k͟hāliṣa*". *K͟hāliṣa* here obviously means the lands reserved for the *jāgīrdār* himself.

[75] See the notices of the poets, musicians, artists, soldiers, and others patronized and employed by this grandee, in *Ma'āṣir-i Raḥīmī,* III, passim: see p.1634, for example, where it is said of an officer of the K͟hān-i K͟hānān, that "the whole year he obtained large sums, by way of *jāgīr* and allowance, from this *sarkār*".

[76] Allahabad 789.

[77] *Waqā'i' Ajmer,* 359. Mān Singh, the *jāgīrdār,* represented that the resumption of a portion of his *jāgīr* in the *pargana* would cause his men, whom he had assigned all its villages, great distress and suggested that he be allowed to hold the area in *ijāra* (revenue-farm), so that the sub-assignments he had made could continue.

[78] Cf. *Maẓhar-i Shāhjahānī,* 164-5; '*Arzdāsht-hā-i Muẓaffar,* ff.109b-110a.

When the *jāgīrdārs* farmed out their *jāgīrs*, the revenue-farmers seem usually to have been local men.[79] But as a rule the revenue officials employed by the assignees, the *jāgīrdārs* as well as the *khāliṣa*, did not have any local interests or connexions.[80] This was, perhaps, partly because each *jāgīrdār* had his own trusty agents whom he would send to his *jāgīrs,* wherever they might be situated.[81] But in a number of cases it was probably a matter also of deliberate choice. *Āmils* with any local links were more likely to enter into league with *zamīndārs* and others to the detriment of the assignees' interests.[82] Thus Jahāngīr on his accession issued an order, which is clearly designed to prevent these officials ("the *āmils* of the *khāliṣa* and [of] the *jāgīrdārs*") from forming marriage ties with the local gentry.[83]

[79] This can be seen from the Allahabad documents (884-7, 889-90): Muḥammad 'Ārif contracts the *ijāra* of *jāgīrs* in *pargana* Hisampur (Bahraich *sarkār*, Awadh), where he himself possessed a number of villages in *zamīndārī*. Similarly, *Akhbārāt* 37/38 refers to "men of Kashmir", who took the *jāgīrs* in that province on *ijāra*. It is a rather rare case when we have a reference, from Gujarat, to the tax-farm of a village given in a prince's *jāgīr* to a *khwāja*, described as "the prince of revenue-farmers, chief of merchants" (Blochet, Suppl. Pers. 482, f. 12a).

[80] Cf. Elliott, *Chronicles of Oonao*, 106: "The Āmil, the Crorie, the Tehseeldar (revenue-collector)...were hardly ever natives of the Pergunnah." Elliott's statements are generally deserving of respect, since he had examined a very large number of *sanads* and other administrative documents of the Mughal period and was at the same time closely familiar with local history. A study of the Allahabad documents leads to a similar conclusion, for it is very rare that any of the local men whose records have come down to us became agents of any *jāgīrdār.*

[81] We can see this from the personal details in the narrative of Bāyazīd, 248-50, 299. He took service under Mun'im Khān, who appointed him the *shiqqdār* of the *sarkār* of Hisar Firuza which lay in his *jāgīr*. When his *jāgīrs* were transferred to the eastern provinces, he appointed Bāyazīd as *shiqqdār* of Banaras *sarkār*. From Bhīmsen (*Dilkushā*, f. 80a-b) we learn of one Gangārām Nāgar, a native of Gujarat, who rose to the position of *dīwān* (steward) in the *sarkār* of Khān-i Jahān Bahādur. When the latter was posted to the Dakhin in the 14th year of Aurangzeb, he sent Gangārām to manage his *jāgīrs* in Bihar. From the names of revenue officials which appear frequently in the Allahabad documents, it is obvious that they changed with every new *jāgīrdār.*

[82] The *Risāla-i Zirā'at,* written *c.*1750, says, with reference to the practice of "the *nāẓims* of the past" in Bengal, that under them "the officials (*mutaṣaddiyān*) of the *khāliṣa* ... did not possess any *ta'alluqa* or *zamīndārī,* etc. If an official had any *ta'alluqas* or villages, the *nāẓims* of former times, as a further safeguard, never appointed him to any office in the *khāliṣa,* for it is unwise to set up the thief as the watchman. As a matter of fact, they never appointed the natives of Bengal to such posts, for most of them are related to the *zamīndārs...*" (f.19b).

[83] They were not to do so, says the order, without permission (*be-ḥukm*) (*T.J.*, 4). The reading of the printed text of the Memoirs is supported by the very early MS in the Central Record Office, Hyderabad, f.9a, and by Add. 26215, also of the

The local element was therefore largely excluded from the assignees' administration. It was, however, represented by two officials, who were independent of the assignee, but were indispensable for him. These were the *qānūngo* and the *chaudhurī*, constituting the second layer of local revenue administration, of which we have spoken earlier. Despite the fact that these officials were so universally found till the other day, it would seem that their position and functions in Mughal times have not been adequately appreciated in many modern studies.[84]

The *qānūngo* (or, as he was known in the Dakhin, the *desh-pānḍīa)*[85] generally belonged to one of the "accountant castes" (Kāyasths, Khatrīs, etc.).[86] The office usually ran in the family,[87] but an imperial order was necessary for the recognition of the rights of any incumbent.[88] It seems to have been usual for the heir of a

17th century. In the *Ma'āṣir-i Jahāngīrī*, Or. 171, f. 25a, ed., 64, however, the text reads *ba-taḥakkum* ("by force") for *be-ḥukm*. This would alter the whole sense of the order and suggest that the intention of Jahāngīr was to prevent not the '*āmils'* collusion with the local population, but rather their oppression of the latter. The authority of the *Tuzuk* must, however, prevail over the latter work.

[84] Charles Elliott in his *Chronicles of Oonao*, 116, undoubtedly emphasized the contrast between the "Canoongoe and Chowdrie" and the temporary officials, "the Amil, the Crori, the Tehseeldar". But he held the mistaken belief that "no material difference existed between the work done by the Canoongoe and the Chowdrie" and that the only purpose of the double office was for one to be a check on the other (ibid., 112). Moreland adopted this opinion and suggested that the *qānūngo* and *chaudhurī* only rose in importance when "group assessment" (as he thought) replaced the "regulation system" of Akbar (*JRAS*, 1938, 521).

[85] *Ā'īn*, I, 476; *Ma'lūmātu-l Āfāq*, f. 174a.

[86] Cf. Elliott, *Chronicles of Oonao*, 112; *Ma'āṣiru-l Umarā'*, II, 350. Hemūn, the minister of 'Adil Shāh Sūr, is said to have replaced all the *qānūngos* and *chaudhurīs* by new appointees belonging to the caste of Banyas (*Baqqāls*), to which he himself belonged (Mushtāqī, Or. 1929, p. 144 (f.173b); *Tārīkh-i Dāūdī*, 200). For the use of the word *baqqāl* for *banya* or *bānya*, see *Ā'īn*, II, 57; cf. S.H. Hodivala, *Studies in Indo-Muslim History*, 672.

[87] Thus the *qānūngos* of Sahasram in Bihar, deposed during the reign of Farrukhsiyar, successfully sought reinstatement in the 3rd year of Muḥammad Shāh on the ground that the office of the *qānūngo* of the *pargana* "had been the privilege of their ancestors since the time of 'Arsh Āshyānī (Akbar)"; and the new *sanad* conferred the office upon them "in heredity as of old" (documents translated by Qiyamuddin Aḥmad in *IHRC*, XXXI, ii, (1954), 142-47).

Concerning Ikhlāṣ Khān, an official under Aurangzeb, we are told that "his ancestors" had held the *qānūngoī* of the *qaṣba* of Kalanaur (*Ma'āṣiru-l Umarā'*, II, 350).

[88] Shahbāz Khān's *parwāna* of 1575 (copy in H.S. Mathur's Coll., Bikaner, photostats: I, 55); *Chār Chaman-i Barhaman*, Add. 16863, f.23b, 1892, f.13a; *Nigārnāma-i Munshī*, ed., 90, 91; *IHRC*, op. cit. *Akhbārāt* 44/13 records a complaint from a *jāgīrdār* concerning a *qānūngo* who was interfering in the affairs of

deceased *qānūngo* to apply to the court for an order, or *sanad*, confirming him in succession.[89] And once conferred, the office was normally for life.[90] Nevertheless, a *qānūngo* could be removed by an imperial order. This might be done for a number of reasons: first, as a punishment for malpractices or dereliction of duty;[91] or, secondly, in order simply to reduce the number of the incumbents of this office, which owing to the division among heirs seems to have constantly multiplied. Under Sher Shāh and Akbar there used to be only one *qānūngo* for each *pargana*.[92] Aurangzeb ordered that no more than two *qānūngos* could serve in any *pargana*, and if there were more, they were to be dismissed.[93] The same emperor inaugurated the policy of supplanting Hindu *qānūngos* with Muslims.[94] But Mammon also came in, and a large present *(peshkash)* paid into the imperial treasury could often secure the removal of

---

his assignment "without a *sanad*". Cf. also Add. 6603, f. 75b. But see *Nāma-i Muẓaffarī*, I, 269-70, for a *sanad* of 1690, issued on his own by Kamālu-ddīn Khān, appointing one person as *chaudhurī* and *qānūngo* in place of two *chaudhurīs* and *qānūngos* of *pargana* Shahabad. This special privilege might have belonged to him since the *pargana* permanently lay within his *jāgīr* as *waṭan al-tamghā* (see Aurangzeb's *farmān* of 1687 in ibid., I, 284-7).

89 See, e.g. Jahāngīr's *farmān*, printed in Maḥmūd Aḥmad's *Tārīkh-i Amroha*, I, 164A-B, where the office of the *qānūngo* of *pargana* Amroha (along with that of *chaudhurī* and *muqaddam* of 12 villages) is conferred upon the two sons of the deceased incumbent. Cf. *Aḥkām-i 'Ālamgīrī*, f. 216b, where a grandson of the deceased *qānūngo* applies for "the *sanad* for his share of the office of the *qānūngo*".

90 Even when Jogīdās, *qānūngo* ("of old") of *pargana* Chaurasi, *sarkār* Surat (Gujarat), abandoned his post and fled during the famine of 1632, he was reinstated in his office upon his return in 1636 (Ḥakīm Masīḥu-zzamān's *parwāna*, Blochet Suppl. Pers. 482, f. 148a). Such security of tenure is also indicated by a later imperial order which, citing a representation, says that the *qānūngos* were guilty of many malpractices because "they have no fear of being transferred or deposed" *(Nigārnāma-i Munshī*, ed., 140). See also Add. 6603, f. 75b: this glossary, belonging to late 18th century, adds that the office of the *qānūngo* could not, in former times, be sold, though the practice was now prevalent.

91 *Nigārnāma-i Munshī*, ed., 140; *Khulāṣatu-l Inshā'*, ff.111a-112b; *Akhbārāt* 38/113.

92 'Abbās Khān, f. 106a; *Ā'īn*, I, 300.

93 *Mir'āt*, I, 263 ("ten" in the printed text must be a mistake for "two"); *Durru-l 'Ulūm*, f.65b; Sihunda Docs. 22, 23, 41, 58.

In Kashmir, the *qānūngos* had apparently multiplied so much that every village had a number of co-sharing *qānūngos* (*qānūngoyān-i juzv)*. Shāhjahān ordered that only one *qānūngo* was to be recognized in each village and the rest were to be dismissed (Qazwīnī, Aligarh transcript, 510).

94 Cf. *Aḥkām-i 'Ālamgīrī*, ff. 216b-217a. The petition for the restoration of the deposed *qānūngos* of Sahasram declares that the deposition was based on "a false case against Sobhāchand charging him with the destruction and desecration of mosques and tombs" (*IHRC*, op. cit., 143).

one incumbent and the appointment of another.[95]

The *qānūngo* was the permanent repository of information concerning the revenue receipts, area statistics, local revenue rates, and practices and customs of the *pargana*.[96] He provided the imperial administration with the revenue and area figures that were used in determining the standard assessments for purposes of *jāgīr* assignment.[97] His most important function, however, was to place his records (especially the accounts of previous assessments, the *muwāzana-i dah-sāla,* etc.) and personal knowledge at the disposal of the *amīn* (or any other official acting as the assessor) sent by the assignee.[98] When the *amīn* drew up the assessment, the *qānūngo* put his signature on it[99] and signed a *qabūliyat* or acceptance, along with the *chaudhurī* and the *muqaddams*.[100] The *'āmil* or the revenue collector, had to deposit a copy of his detailed accounts of the collections, arrears and expenses with the *qānūngo* and the latter was required to check them with the accounts of the *zamīndārs* and others, in order to see whether the *'āmil* had correctly entered all the payments made to him.[101] In general, the imperial administration expected the *qānūngo* to ensure that the imperial regulations were faithfully followed by the assignees' agents and to act as "the friend of the peasants".[102] He was to report any illegal

[95] *Akhbārāt* 38/113.

[96] Cf. *Waqā'i' Ajmer*, 163, 171; *Ma'lūmātu-l Āfāq,* f. 174a; *Dastūru-l 'Amal-i Khāliṣa-i Sharīfa,* f. 32a; Add. 6603, f. 75b. The last work declares that if a *qānūngo* is asked to produce the revenue records for the previous hundred years he should be able to do so. In the documents relating to the case of the deposed *qānūngos* of Sahasram it is stated in their favour that they had in their possession the *muwāzana* papers dating from 1013 to 1074 *Faṣlī* (AD1604 to 1665) (*IHRC*, op. cit., 144-45).

[97] *A.N.*, II, 270; *Ā'īn*, I, 347; Jahāngīr's (forged) *farmān* in *IHRC*, XVIII (1942), 188-9; Shāhjahān's *farmān* in Blochet, Suppl. Pers. 482, f. 91a-b; *Nigārnāma-i Munshī,* ed., 91; *Hidāyatu-l Qawā'id,* f. 18b, Aligarh MS, f. 64a-b.

[98] *Ā'īn*, I, 288 (where it is the *bitikchī* whom the *qānūngo* supplies with the *muwāzana* papers); *Dastūru-l 'Amal-i 'Ālamgīrī*, f.36a-b; *Khulāṣatu-s Siyāq,* ff. 74a, 78a, Or. 2026, ff. 22b, 30a; *Hidāyatu-l Qawā'id,* f.10a-b. The last work recommends that the *amīn* should carefully check the area-figures supplied by the *qānūngo* by on-the-spot enquiries from the *muqaddams*. On the other hand, the *qānūngo* was required to deal with only the agents of those *jāgīrdārs* who possessed authentic certificates of assignment from the court (Sihunda Docs. 51, also 49).

[99] *Farmān* to Rasikdās, Preamble; *Dastūru-l 'Amal-i 'Ilm-i Navīsindagī*, f.153b; *Khulāṣatu-s Siyāq,* ff.74a, 78b, Or. 2026, ff.22b, 31a; *Farhang-i Kārdānī*, f.29a, Edinburgh no. 83, f. 54b; *Siyāqnāma,* 28.

[100] Cf. *Farhang-i Kārdānī,* 34a (specimen *qabūliyat*).

[101] *Hidāyatu-l Qawā'id,* ff. 18b-19a.

[102] *Ā'īn*, I, 300. The author of the *Maẓhar-i Shāhjahānī*, 189, however, doubts

exaction made by the *'āmil*, or risk his own removal.[103] And yet, paradoxically, the main purpose of his office is defined in an imperial order as being to facilitate the preparation of "the maximum revenue assessment" *(jama'-i kāmil o akmal).*[104]

The assignees' agents, being generally unfamiliar with the locality, usually depended heavily on the information supplied to them by the *qānūngo*. The *qānūngo* was therefore often placed in a position which he could greatly exploit for his own gain. An order issued by Aurangzeb recites that it was the general practice among the *qānūngos* to enter into collusion with the *'āmils* and, by making up fictitious accounts, share the embezzled amount among themselves. If an *'āmil* declined to fall in with them, they would persuade the *zamīndārs* not to pay him the revenue and then enrich themselves by acting as mediators. Finally, they used to recommend heavy reductions in the assessments levied upon the *zamīndārs,* for they often acted in collusion with them.[105] Elsewhere, the *qānūngos* of a *pargana* are said to have made a compact with a *faujdār* and reduced the *jama'* dishonestly.[106]

Abū-l Faẓl tells us that the *qānūngos* used formerly to be paid an allowance out of the revenue amounting to one per cent of it. But Akbar replaced this by fixed salaries, in lieu of which they were granted *jāgīrs*, that is, one may suppose, revenue-free lands.[107] But it seems that the *qānūngos* continued to receive allowances in

---

the ability of the *qānūngos* to fulfil this expectation, because "the *qānūngos* command little respect: they cannot restrain a *jāgīrdār* from practising oppression, but actually share in the oppression of the dominant *jāgīrdār*." He recognizes (p.51) that the imperial administration could make use of the papers maintained by the *qānūngos* to check the irregularities committed by the *jāgīrdārs* in collecting revenue but he also mentions (p.177) a case when a *jāgīrdār* of Sehwan simply prevented the *qānūngos* from obeying an order from the imperial court summoning them with their papers.

[103] *Nigārnāma-i Munshī,* ed., 80; *Khulāṣatu-l Inshā'*, ff. 111b-112a. Cf. *Tazkira Pīr Ḥassū Telī*, MS, CAS in History, ff.111b-112a, for the *amīn* summoning the *qānūngo* to enquire into extortions by a *shiqqdār* of the *pargana*.

[104] *Nigārnāma-i Munshī*, ed., 140. [105] Ibid. Cf. *Waqā'i' Ajmer*, 108, 218.

[106] *Akhbārāt* 38/113.

[107] *Ā'īn*, I, 300. It says that out of the *ṣad-doī* (2 per cent) allowance, the *paṭwārī* received half and half went to the *qānūngo*. In an early *farmān* (1563) of Akbar, the *qānūngo* of *sarkār* Nagaur was granted a *dastūr* or allowance of 2 per cent of the revenue variously collected in kind, in rupees and in *ṭankas* (copy in H.S. Mathur Coll., Bikaner, photostats, II, 113). In *madad-i ma'āsh* documents the *ṣad-doī-i qānūngoī* (or, sometimes, *ṣad-doī o qānūngoī*) constantly appears on the list of the cesses which the officials were prohibited from levying upon the grantees. The rates of pay which Akbar fixed for the three classes of the *qānūngos* amounted respectively to Rs 50, Rs 30 and Rs 20 per month (*Ā'īn*, op.cit.).

addition to the *nānkār* or *in'ām* land held by them.[108]

The *chaudhurī*, called *desāī* in Gujarat and *deshmukh* in the Dakhin,[109] was perhaps as important a functionary for the administration as the *qānūngo*. He was invariably a *zamīndār*.[110] In most cases he was the leading *zamīndār* of the locality,[111] but this does not always seem to have been the case.[112] The most powerful *zamīndār* might well be the least loyal;[113] and in such an event the office had probably to be entrusted to lesser men. The position was usually hereditary,[114] but an imperial *sanad* had to be

---

According to the *Maẓhar-i Shāhjahānī*, 186, the *qānūngos* in *sarkār* Sehwan (Sind) were entitled to realise *rusūm*, or a customary cess, amounting to one per cent of the revenue, from the peasants.

108 Cf. *Dastūru-l 'Amal-i Navīsindagī*, f. 40b; the Papal *pargana* records analysed in *IHRC*, 1929, 84-86; and Datta, nos. 27, 34, 322-3, 375, 381.

109 The identification of the *chaudhurī* with the *desāī* is based upon inference, and there is no direct statement to this effect in contemporary literature that I can cite. For the identification with *deshmukh*, see the *Ā'īn*, I, 476; *Ma'lūmātu-l Āfāq*, f.174a. As H. Fukazawa notes (*Medieval Deccan*, 43 n.35), the terms *deshmukh* and *desāī* were used interchangeably in Maharashtra.

The *Maẓhar-i Shāhjahānī* does not refer to the *chaudhurī*, but refers to an official called *arbāb*, who seems to have really been the counterpart of the *chaudhurī* in Sind (19-21, 101-2, 182, 185-6, 188, 191). Cf. *Factories, 1646-50*, 118-9, for a reference to "arbaubs and cheife men".

110 Add. 6603, f. 58a: "The title of *chaudhurī* is given to someone from amongst the *zamīndārs*, who is trustworthy." After the suppression of Khusrau's rebellion, Jahāngīr granted the *chaudhurāī* of the territory along the Chenab to *zamīndārs* who had rendered loyal service (*T.J.*, 32). A forged *farmān* of his, published in *IHRC*, XVIII (1942), 188-9, confers the simultaneous grant of "the service (i.e. office) of the *zamīndārī* and *chaudhurāī*" of certain *tappas* upon the same person. In the Malda Diary and Consultations the English describe Rajray, from whom they had purchased land for their new factory, alternatively as "Chowdry" and "Jimmedar" (*JASB*, N.S., XIV, 81, 122, 174, 182, 196, 202). Cf. also Elliott, *Chronicles of Oonao*, 112.

The *Maẓhar-i Shāhjahānī*, 191, says that the *zamīndārs* "also hold (lit. are connected with) the offices of *arbāb* and *muqaddam*". *Arbāb*, as explained in note no.109, was probably a synonym for *chaudhurī* in Sind.

111 Cf. Elliott, op. cit. That in the Dakhin the *deshmukh* used to be the dominant *zamīndār* of the area, appears from the case of Chanānerī *deshmukh*, already referred to in Chapter V, Section 4.

112 The *Dastūru-l 'Amal-i Khālisa-i Sharīfa* is a late 18th-century work written in Bengal, but, for what it may be worth, it defines *chaudhurī* as "a small *zamīndār*" (f.32b). Benett in his *Chief Clans of the Roy Bareilly District*, 58-9, is definite, in opposition to Elliott (who investigated the neighbouring district of Unao), that the office of the *chaudhurī* "was held by respectable, but thoroughly second-rate families".

113 The *Hidāyatu-l Qawā'id*, f. 7a, declares, as if it were a universal truth, that "the seditious *zamīndār* is the head of the *zamīndārs*."

114 Elliott, op. cit., 112. Jahāngīr's *farmān* (forged) (*IHRC*, XVIII, [1942] 188-

secured by each incumbent.[115]

The *chaudhurī* could also be deprived of his office by an imperial order. Aurangzeb ordered that if there were too many *chaudhurīs* in any *pargana,* all but two were to be dismissed.[116] The *chaudhurī* could also be removed for not reporting any illegal exactions levied by the *'āmils*[117] and also, perhaps, for other misdemeanours.

While the *qānūngo's* work was largely directed towards the preparation of revenue assessment, the *chaudhurī* was chiefly concerned with its collection. When the assignee's officials had drawn up the *jama'*, the *chaudhurī* affixed his signature on this and a separate document known as *qabūliyat.*[118] Similar *qabūliyats* for their respective villages were also taken from the *muqaddams.*[119] These documents contained an undertaking by the signatories to collect the amounts that had been assessed. The *chaudhurī* also stood surety for the lesser *zamīndārs.*[120] It is probable that the revenue was generally collected by the *chaudhurī* from the *muqaddams* and the *zamīndārs,* and was then passed on to the '*āmil.*[121] Deductions from the *jama'* for any loss to the crops from natural calamities were, as we have seen, frequently allowed,[122] but otherwise

89) grants the "*zamīndārī* and *chaudhurāī*" of some *tappas* in Bihar to one Hiran "together with his children". For the hereditary nature of the office of *deshmukh,* see Moreland in *JRAS*, 1938, 516: his study is based on certain original documents belonging to the period. Documentary evidence to similar effect will be found in *Ādāb-i 'Ālamgīrī*, ff. 161b-162b, ed., I, 636-9; Khare, *Persian Sources of Indian History*, II, 11-12; *IHRC*, 1948, 15-17.

[115] *Chār Chaman-i Barhaman*, op. cit.; *Akhbārāt* 44/13, 47/337. Kaiqubād Mahyār, *c.*1619, tells of how he obtained the post of *desāī* of two *parganas* of *sarkār* Surat through an imperial *farmān*, and how he was illegally deposed by two *jāgīrdārs* (*Dastūr Kaikobad Mahyar's Petition and Laudatory Poem*, 12-14).

[116] *Mir'āt*, I, 263; *Durru-l 'Ulūm*, f. 65b; Sihunda Docs. 22, 23, 41, 58. Cf. an order of the same emperor (Aurangzeb) cited in *Bulandshahr District Gazetteer* (1922), 148.

[117] *Nigārnāma-i Munshī*, ed., 80; *Khulāṣatu-l Inshā'*, ff. 111b-112a.

[118] He did so together with the *qānūngo*. See *Farhang-i Kārdānī*, f.34a.

[119] *Farhang-i Kārdānī*, f. 34a-b; *Khulāṣatu-s Siyāq*, ff.74a-75a, Or. 2026, ff.23a-24b.

[120] Add. 6603, f. 58a-b.

[121] In the specimen *bar-āmad* accounts reproduced in the *Dastūru-l 'Amal-i Navīsindagī*, ff. 41b-42b, the different itmes of deductions from the collections are first shown under the charges of the *chaudhurīs* and then distributed in detail among the *muqaddams*. Fryer, I, 300-301, says, while speaking of the villages around Surat, that the assignees holding them in "Jaggea" (*jāgīr*) "fail not once a-year to send to reap the Profit, which is received by the Hands of the Desie or Farmer who squeezes the Countryman."

[122] See Chapter VI, Sections 2 & 8.

any failure or refusal on the part of the *chaudhurīs* to collect the revenue could bring upon them the severest punishment. We thus read, incidentally, of an assignee's official's proposal in Akbar's time to keep the death of his master a secret in order that he might be able "to bring some of the refractory *chaudhurīs* to the fort (Chunar) and collect the arrears", obviously by subjecting them to some form of torture.[123] In the next (the seventeenth) century a European traveller saw in the same province of Ilahabad "a Fouzdare [*faujdār*] who carried with him certain Chowdrees or Chiefs of Townes [villages] prisoners, because either they will not or cannot satisfy the Kings Imposition".[124]

Apart from his principal function of collecting the revenue, the *chaudhurī* had also certain subsidiary duties. For instance, with the cooperation of the *muqaddams* he distributed, and stood surety for the repayment of, the *taqāvī* loans.[125] He was also used as a counter-check to the *qānūngo*, for he was required to see that the *muwāzana* papers and the record of local practices were sent regularly to the imperial court under the signature of that official.[126]

It is probable that the scale of remuneration allowed to the *chaudhurīs* varied considerably. The *Mir'āt* says the *desāīs* were first allowed 2.5 per cent of the revenue under Akbar, but this was later reduced to 1.25 per cent and, ultimately, to 5/8 per cent.[127] From specimen accounts contained in another work, it appears that the allowance, or *nānkār*, remitted to the *chaudhurī* out of the revenue was not very substantial.[128] But it is probable that he held

[123] Bāyazīd, 350. This happened in 1574-5, when Bāyazīd was Mun'im Khan's agent at Chunar.

[124] Mundy, 183. Princess Jahān Ārā, holding Surat in her *jāgīr*, ordered in 1639 that, in accordance with an imperial order *(ḥasbu-l ḥukm)*, the custody of *desāīs* held in prison was to be taken over by Mu'izzu-l Mulk, from the previous *mutaṣaddī*, Ḥakīm Masīḥu-l Mulk (Blochet, Suppl. Pers. 482, f.35a-b).

[125] See Chapter VI, Section 8.

[126] This is laid down in Jahāngīr's (forged) *farmān*, *IHRC*, VIII (1942), 188-89.

[127] *Mir'āt*, I, 173 and Supp., 228. The *Maẓhar-i Shāhjahānī*, 185, suggests a similar reduction made in the allowances of the *arbāb* in Sehwan (Sind). Under a *jāgīrdār* during Akbar's later years, the *arbābs* and *muqaddams* shared an allowance of 5 per cent out of the revenue. In the early years of Jahāngīr, another *jāgīrdār* reduced this to 2 per cent.

[128] In the *Dastūru-l 'Amal-i 'Ālamgīrī*, f.40b, the total revenue receipts are shown as amounting to Rs 4,338, out of which the *nānkār* allowed to two *chaudhurīs* amounted only to Rs 120. In Datta. No. 92 (AD1699), the *chaudhurī's nānkār* is fixed at Rs 175 per annum; and in No.104 (AD1646) at Rs 100, in No. 105 (AD1655) at Rs 70, and in No. 106 (AD1656) at Rs 250, presumably per annum.

extensive revenue-free (*in'ām*) lands.[129] Moreover, when he stood surety for the other *zamīndārs,* he is said to have generally taken a commission of 5 per cent (of the revenue) from them.[130]

By reserving to itself the power to retain or remove the *qānūngos* and *chaudhurīs*, the imperial government held one important instrument in its hands for exercising some measure of control over the administration of the assignments outside the *khāliṣa*. But apart from these local officials, who had a more or less permanent tenure, there were other regular imperial officials as well, the spheres of whose duties included an oversight of what went on within the *jāgīrs*. And these formed the third set of officials employed to make the assignment system work.

In the first place, there was the financial department represented by the *dīwān* in each province. One of the things expected of him was to prevent the oppression of the peasants by the *jāgīrdārs.*[131] He could report to the imperial court about maladministration in any of the *jāgīrs;*[132] and he himself might be required to enforce any orders issued by the emperor with regard to the conduct of the assignees or their agents.[133] Since the claims of the assignees against their own *'āmils* were settled in his *kachehrī* (court),[134] his authority over them must have been considerable.

It appears that under Akbar and Jahāngīr another officer was sometimes appointed, charged specifically with the duty of ensuring that the *jāgīrdārs* and their agents followed imperial regulations in collecting the revenue. He does not appear on the list of officers said to have been appointed to every province in 1580.[135] But four years later a high dignitary was appointed to Gujarat, alongside the governor and the *dīwān*, under the designation of *amīn.*[136] No statement is made anywhere in Abū-l Faẓl

[129] See the analysis of the records of the *pargana* of Papal in *IHRC*, (1929), 83-86; and Datta, Nos. 103,130,146 and 443. An oppressive *desāī* in *pargana* Sopa, *sarkār* Surat, cultivated land worth 7,000 *maḥmūdīs* (in revenue?), on which he paid nothing, transferring the burden to other peasants (*parwāncha* of Ṣādiq Khān, d. 1596-97, in Blochet, Suppl. Pers. 482. f. 171b). One may assume that such practices were not rare.

[130] Add. 6603, f. 58a.

[131] See the *parwāna* sent by the *dīwān* of Khandesh announcing the appointment of his agent in the *sarkār* of Baglana (4th regnal year of Aurangzeb) (*Daftar-i Dīwānī o Māl o Mulkī*, 186).

[132] Cf. *Akhbārāt* 36/15 for a report from the deputy *dīwān* of Berar.

[133] *Akhbārāt* 37/38.

[134] Cf. *Riyāẓu-l Wadād*, ff. 3b-4a; *Ruq'āt-i 'Ālamgīrī*, Kanpur edn., 41-42.

[135] *A.N.*, III, 282.

[136] *A.N.*, III, 403; *Ṭabaqāt-i Akbarī*, II, 368. For an *amīn* and *bakhshī* appointed

defining the jurisdiction and functions of this officer. But what his functions precisely were appears clearly from a long passage and sundry other references in the *Maẓhar-i Shāhjahānī*. It recommends that this officer, when appointed over a *sarkār*, should send his agents to every *pargana* to see whether any of the *jāgīrdārs* or local officials were exacting more than the sanctioned rates (*dastūru-l 'amal*) from the peasants. If he found any violation of imperial regulations anywhere, he was to draw the attention of the *jāgīrdār's* agent to it; if the agent did not heed his advice, he was to complain to the *jāgīrdār* himself; if the *jāgīrdār* too did not respond satisfactorily, he was to report the matter to the court, and the emperor would be well advised in taking stern action on his report. At the time the book was written (1634) the appointment of this officer appears to have ceased, it being thought (mistakenly, says our author) that the *qānūngos* were sufficient for the purpose.[137] With the creation of the revenue assessor under the designation of *amīn*, under Shāhjahān, the memory of the earlier holder of that designation seems to have become dimmer still, and no attempt was made at any time subsequently to revive his office.

The *faujdār* represented the military or police power of the imperial government. One of his main duties was to go to the aid of any *jāgīrdār* or *'āmil* of the *k͟hāliṣa* who was finding it difficult to deal, on his own, with local malcontents, that is with *zamīndārs* or peasants who refused to pay the revenue.[138] It seems that from the beginning, the bigger assignees were given *faujdārī* jurisdictions within their *jāgīrs*;[139] and under Aurangzeb this was certainly the general practice.[140] Such grants seriously reduced the powers of the imperial *faujdār*, for he was not entitled to interfere in the affairs of these *jāgīrs*.[141]

---

to Bengal in 1591-2, see *Inshā'-i Abū-l Faẓl*, 195; and for the post of *amīn* in *ṣūba* Berar in 1608-09, *Zak͟hīratu-l K͟hawānīn*, ed., I, 158.

[137] *Maẓhar-i Shāhjahānī*, 187-90; also 21-22, 51-2, 244. See also *Maẓhar-i Shāhjahānī*, Vol.I, MS, ff.26a-27b.

[138] *Ā'īn*, I, 283; *Durru-l 'Ulūm*, f.57b; *Ak͟hbārāt* 37/25; *Inshā'-i Roshan Kalām*, ff. 9a-b, 31a-b, 40b; *Siyāqnāma*, 67-68.

[139] For references to *faujdārs* appointed by *jāgīrdārs* in the reigns of Akbar and Jahāngīr, see Badāūnī, III, 94-5; *Ma'āṣir-i Raḥīmī*, III, 1643 and *Taẕkira-i Maik͟hāna*, 429.

[140] Aurangzeb observes in the *Kalimāt-i Ṭaiyabāt*, f.125a, that "the *faujdārī* of a *jāgīr* vests in the *jāgīrdār* of some *maḥals*". For specific cases of the grant of *faujdārī* to assignees, see *Inshā'-i Roshan Kalām*, f.24b; *Ak͟hbārāt* 36/15, 36/37, 38/24, 38/242, 47/367, 48/217; *Aḥkām-i 'Ālamgīrī*, f.43a-b.

[141] Cf. *Ak͟hbārāt* 43/113; *Inshā'-i Roshan Kalām*, f.13a-b.

The Mughal empire was honey-combed with a body of officials, known as *wāqi'a-navīs, sawāniḥ-nigār,* etc., who may best be designated news-writers.[142] They were specially charged with reporting cases of irregularities and oppression, and there are instances on record where they did, in fact, do so.[143] But they were widely reputed to be corrupt and to conceal or complain solely from interested motives.[144]

In theory both the peasants and the *zamīndārs* could complain directly to the imperial court or the provincial governor or *dīwān* against any act of oppression committed by a *jāgīrdār.*[145] But it was apparently considered a normal practice for the agents of the assignees to prevent the peasants physically from proceeding to the court with any complaint.[146]

In general, if the imperial government chose to take a serious view of any irregularity committed by an assignee, it could either transfer his *jāgīr*[147] or resume it without any compensatory assignment.[148] As we have seen, the assignee was free to appoint or remove his own officials, but he might still be directed to change his men under the threat of a resumption or transfer of his *jāgīrs.*[149] The punishments for the gravest acts of oppression committed by the *jāgīrdārs* could be light. The author of *Maẕhar-i Shāhjahānī,* indeed, protests that it was no punishment to transfer a *jāgīrdār* for oppressive conduct, from Sehwan to Multan: it did not indicate royal wrath, but favour![150] "Today," he laments, "the oppressed of

[142] *T.J.*, 120-21.

[143] E.g. *Maẕhar-i Shāhjahānī*, 164, 174, 176-7; *Akhbārāt* 37/38; *Inshā'-i Roshan Kalām*, ff. 38b-39b.

[144] Bernier, 231; Manucci, II, 452. In *Akhbārāt* 36/15 we have a reference to a report from the deputy *dīwān* of Berar, alleging that the "*wāqi'a-nigārs* take something from the agents of the *jāgīrdārs* and do not report the true facts." In the *Inshā'-i Roshan Kalām*, op.cit., Ra'd-andāz Khān claims that the *wāqi'a-nigār* of Lakhnau reported against a *sawāniḥ-nigār* for levying illegal cesses simply because he was in league with a "seditious" *zamīndār* and the agent of a *jāgīrdār* in that neighbourhood, who had grudges against the *sawāniḥ-nigār*.

[145] *Maẕhar-i Shāhjahānī*, 174; *Ādāb-i 'Ālamgīrī*, f.33a; *Ruq'āt-i 'Ālamgīr*, 119; Bālkrishan Brahman, ff.55b-57b, 63b-64a; *Waqā'i' Ajmer*, 217-19; Sihunda Docs.53; *Ruq'āt-i 'Ālamgīrī*, Kanpur edn., 40-41.

[146] Bālkrishan Brahman, f.60a.

[147] *Inshā'-i Abū-l Faẕl*, 66; *A.N.*, III, 743; *Maẕhar-i Shāhjahānī*, 164, 177; *Selected Documents*, 133; *Inshā'-i Roshan Kalām*, f.12a.

[148] *Maẕhar-i Shāhjahānī*, MS, I, f.26a; *Ruq'āt-i 'Ālamgīrī*, Kanpur edn., 40-41.

[149] Bāyazīd, 248-50; *Waqā'i' Ajmer*, 219; *Ruq'āt-i 'Ālamgīrī*, Kanpur edn., 40-41.

[150] *Maẕhar-i Shāhjahānī*, 177.

Sehwan are in the same state, while Aḥmad Beg Khān (the *jāgīrdār*) and his (tyrannical) brother are immersed in wealth and luxury."[151]

The result of this lenient attitude on the part of the imperial government was that there was little to deter a *jāgīrdār* from committing oppression. "If the *jāgīrdār* of Sehwan", declares our author, "unjustly slaughters and robs a hundred men, no one will restrain him. And if a poor man with great exertion, travels the long distance to the imperial court, lodges a complaint and brings an imperial *farmān,* it is not accepted here and is not acted upon. On the contrary, the man becomes an enemy for the informers of this country, who in little time will have him ruined at the hands of the *jāgīrdār*. And there is not one officer, whether the *ṣadr,* the *qāẓī*, the *qānūngo*, or the *arbāb*, who tells what is right at the proper time to the *jāgīrdār*. On the contrary, everyone acts looking to his own good. And so, amidst the cry of '(Save) me! (Save) me!', verily the tumult of the Last Day is being witnessed."[152]

[151] Ibid., 180. [152] Ibid., 173-4.

CHAPTER VIII

REVENUE GRANTS

Grants by which the king alienated his right to collect the land revenue and other taxes from a given area of land, for the lifetime of the grantee or in perpetuity, have an ancient history in India.[1] They were known in the Mughal period sometimes as *milk* and *imlāk* (terms inherited from the Dehli Sultanate),[2] and as *suyūrg͟hāl* (brought by the Mughals from Central Asia).[3] But the appellation usually employed both in official documents and other records was *madad-i ma'āsh* ("aid for subsistence").[4] A term which came into use later was *a'imma*, plural of *imām* ("[religious] leaders") for the grantees and applied by later extension to the land covered by grants.[5]

[1] For a study of such grants made in the Gupta period and later, see R.S. Sharma, *Aspects of Political Ideas and Institutions in Ancient India*, Delhi, 1959, 202 ff. Sharma (p.232) compares these grants with the *jāgīrs* of the Mughal period, but their real parallel lay in the *madad-i ma'āsh* grants. For such grants under the Dehli Sultans, see I. Habib, *Cambridge Economic History of India*, I, 75-6.

[2] The use of *milk* in the sense of land assigned in grants is referred to in the *Ā'īn*, I, 198. See also *Tārīk͟h-i Dāūdī*, 44. The plural, *imlāk*, seems to have been in more common use: see 'Ārif Qandahārī, 198; *Tārīk͟h-i Dāūdī*, 38; Bekas, f.31b. For use of *milk* in the same sense in the period of the Dehli Sultanate, see *Cambridge Economic History of India*, I, 75.

[3] See *Ā'īn*, I, 198, etc. Abū-l Fazl insists on using this term, though it is rarely used in the documents. One *farmān* of Bābur (I.O.4438:1) does, indeed, use it, but two of his other known land-grant *farmāns* (one in the Aligarh University Library, and the other printed in the *Oriental College Magazine*, V.IX(3) (1933), 121-2), have *madad-i ma'āsh* only. The text is damaged in the fourth surviving *farmān*: Bhojpur Coll.B, No.1. For *suyūrg͟hāl* in Iran, see Lambton, *Landlord and Peasant in Persia*, 102-4.

[4] See *Ā'īn*, I, 198. Almost all the *farmāns* and official documents concerning the grants, including those of Akbar, use this term and no other.

[5] The term *a'imma* seems to have been used first for the grantees, as a complimentary epithet as early as the 14th century ('Iṣāmī, *Futūḥu-s Salāṭīn*, 390; *Inshā'-i Māhrū*, 75), and, frequently, in 16th- and 17th-century texts and documents ('Ārif Qandahārī, 177; 'Abbās K͟hān, f.112b; Badāūnī, I, 384, II, 204, 254; *T.J.*, 5; *Maẓhar-i Shāhjahānī*, 146-7, 158, 180, 190; Aurangzeb's *farmāns*, Allahabad II, 53 and 55). Subsequently, while *a'imma* came to mean the land granted, the term *a'imma-dār* (holder of *a'imma*) was coined for the grantee (Ṣādiq K͟hān, Or. 174, f.186a, Or. 1671, f.91a; K͟hāfī K͟hān, I, 735n; *Fatḥiya-i 'Ibriya*, ff.117b-121a; *Dastūru-l 'Amal-i K͟hāliṣa Sharīfa*, ff.59b-60a; Add. 6603, f.48a; Yāsīn, f.48a). This linguistically indefensible usage led a late lexicographer, the author of the *G͟hiyāṣu-l Lug͟hāt* (1826-7), s.v. *a'imma*, to suggest that the correct word is not *a'imma-dār*,

There was a separate imperial department charged with looking after these grants. It was presided over by the *Ṣadr* or *Ṣadru-s Ṣudūr* at the imperial court, under whom were placed the provincial *ṣadrs* (*ṣadr-i juzv*) and, at a still lower level, officers known as *mutawallīs*.[6]

The *farmāns* issued to the holders of *madad-i ma'āsh* grants usually contained a passage which set out the rights and favours conferred upon them. A nearly set text of this passage came to be adopted from the earlier years of Akbar's reign onwards: The grantees were to enjoy the revenues (*ḥāṣilāt*) from the land, and they were exempted from all obligation to pay the land revenue (*māl-o-jihāt*) as well as *ikhrājāt*, the petty burdens imposed by officials, which are then specified in detail, and so, from "all fiscal obligations and royal demands" (*ḥuqūq-i dīwānī o muṭālibāt-i sulṭānī*).[7] In other words, what was granted was the right to collect the land revenue and to keep it.[8]

---

but *yimadār* from Turkish *yima*, "food and daily subsistence". But see G. Clauson, *Etymological Dictionary of pre-Thirteenth Century Turkish*, 934 (s.v. *ye:m*), for the original Turkish word and its subsequent forms and senses, in the various Turkic languages down to the 19th century, none of which includes land grants or pensions; cf. H.C. Hony, *Turkish-English Dictionary*, 382, s.v. *yem*. See also Rafat M. Bilgrami, *Religious and Quasi-Religious Departments of the Mughal Period*, New Delhi, 1984, 208-16.

[6] For the nature and history of this department see Ibn Hasan, *Central Structure of the Mughal Empire*, Chapter VIII, and Rafat M. Bilgrami, op.cit., Chapters II and III. That the *ṣadr-i juzv* meant the provincial *ṣadr*, appears from Allahabad 1187 (Shāhjahān's reign). Cf. also Lāhorī, II, 365-66. The *mutawallī* was an official at the *pargana* level, who kept a check on the grants (see, e.g., Allahabad 851).

[7] The standard list of obligations from which the grantees were exempted occurs first in Akbar's *farmān* of 1 December 1559, grant in *pargana* Fatehpur, *sarkār* Lakhnau (Lucknow), xerox copy in CAS in History library, Aligarh. From then on down to the last days of the Mughal chancery, the *farmāns* reproduce practically the same list with only slight variations.

It is not to be supposed, however, that no impost was levied on the grantees. There was one known as *muqarrarī-i a'imma* which they had to pay to the *jāgīrdār*. In one locality in Awadh, it amounted to half a rupee per *bīgha* of land actually cultivated (Allahabad 5, of AD 1650). This extortion was prohibited, along with certain other imposts, by Aurangzeb early in his reign (Rāja Raghunāth's *parwāna*, Allahabad II, 284, and *Mir'āt*, I, 287; see also Allahabad 1117). An undated document in *Jamm-i Badī'*, f.68a, mentions a levy upon grantees of half a rupee per *bīgha* by *faujdārs* in Sind, raised recently to a rupee and a *bahlolī (ṭanka?)*, against which a *farmān* had already been obtained. A cess known as *ṣadrāna*, levied on the grantees by the *ṣadr*, is also mentioned (Allahabad 1204 & 1230). The *mutawallī* too had his perquisites (Allahabad 1). There were a few other imposts besides (Allahabad 1117 and 1204). These documents show that the grantees might sometimes be exempted from these burdens, by the collecting officers themselves.

[8] A sale deed from Awadh, of AD 1764, actually identifies the *a'imma* grant,

The *madad-i ma'āsh* grant, therefore, did not invest the grantee with any rights not claimed previously by the administration. He could not legitimately demand a larger amount of land revenue than was authorized. An early *farmān* of Akbar specifically asks the cultivators "to pay their land revenue on the basis of measurement (*az qarār-i masāḥat*)."[9] Nor was the *madad-i ma'āsh* holder expected to interfere with the peasants already in occupation.[10] Thus in some *farmāns* and supplementary documents, the *ra'īyatī* (peasant-held) and *khwud-kāshta* lands (cultivated by the grantees themselves) are specified separately.[11] And the *Ā'īn* demands that the revenue collector should prevent *ra'īyatī* land from being converted into *khwud-kāshta* by the grantees.[12] Seventeenth-century records offer some instances where the peasants proved recalcitrant and refused to pay the land revenue to the grantees with the result that the grants had to be transferred to other villages.[13] The village headman, *muqaddam*, was also apparently independent of the grantees, even when the latter held the whole of the village.[14]

Similarly, the *madad-i ma'āsh* grant did not in any way affect

held by imperial order (*sanad*), with the right to collect the land revenue (*ḥaqq-i akhz-i kharāj*) (Allahabad 457).

9 *Farmān*, dated 3 October 1567, in Azad Library, Aligarh. The *Maẓhar-i Shāhjahānī*, 180, says that the grantees, in contrast to the *jāgīrdārs*, treated the peasants leniently in order to keep their lands under cultivation: they gave the peasants loans and remitted part of their share of the crop. But the author's good opinion of the grantees might have been coloured by the fact that he himself held *madad-ma'āsh* (p.122).

10 Cf. Qāẓī Muḥammad A'lā, *Risāla Aḥkām al-Ārāẓī*, MS 'A', f.46a.

11 See Akbar's *farmāns* of AH 966-983 (Allahabad II, 23. copy in Or. 1757, ff.39a-51b) and AH 983 (transcript in CAS, Aligarh), and Document No.4 in Modi's *Parsees at the Court of Akbar*, photo-print. The last is an official's report, dated 27 November 1596. It gives not only the area of the *ra'īyatī* land, but also the names of the peasants and the areas under different crops sown by them (see I. Habib in *PIHC*, 54th session, 1993, Mysore, 246-62).

12 *Ā'īn*, I, 287.

13 Bilhaur Docs., *Chaknāma* of AH 1056; and Allahabad 873 and 1213 (all of Shāhjahān's reign).

14 An incident recorded by Faiẓī Sirhindī, ff.148a-149a, is instructive. When Akbar passed by the village which Faiẓī Sirhindī held in *madad-i ma'āsh*, he entered into conversation with its *muqaddam*, to discover whether the grant had been obtained by fraud or use of favour. In Bekas, f.31b, the *muqaddam* is required to prevent the grantees from gathering anything from the fields unless they had obtained the necessary papers (*sanads*). Allahabad 881 describes the transfer of a grant from one village to another necessitated by the lack of amity between the *muqaddam* and the grantees. See *taḥqīqnāma* of 1080/1669 in *Tazkiratu-l Muttaqīn*, II, 180-81, regarding encroachment on grant-land by *muqaddams*.

the *zamīndārī* or *milkiyat* rights established over the land. This becomes clear from documents where the grantees are required to desist from interfering with these rights.[15] One of them, an official order, in fact declares that the grantees must pay the "proprietors" their *ḥaqq-i milkiyat*, "proprietary right", obviously meaning the claimants' established share in the produce.[16] Hostility of the "proprietors" sometimes also compelled the grantees to get their grants transferred elsewhere.[17]

The imperial *madad-i ma'āsh* grants were, as a rule, made in terms of definite areas stated in *bīghas*. But there are exceptions, becoming rarer with time, when not the area, but the revenue assigned is specified.[18] From the time of its introduction during Akbar's reign, the *gaz-i Ilāhī* seems to have been uniformly used to measure the *bīghas* of the grants.[19] When a new grant was issued,

[15] Allahabad 782 and 1203.

[16] Allahabad 1203. This distinction between the two rights is shown strikingly by an 18th-century document, Allahabad 457 (of 1764), which refers to the sale at different times of "the *milkiyat* and *zamīndārī*, that is *satārahī*" and "the right to collect the land-revenue" derived from an "*a'imma* grant" in the same two *bīghas* of land.

[17] Allahabad 1190.

[18] Three of Bābur's *farmāns* (I.O. 4438: (1); Azad Library, Aligarh; and Bhojpur Coll.B, No.1) simply name the village, and, in the first and third, its *jama'-i raqamī* (assessed revenue) is also stated. Later examples, where the *jama'* is stated, include Akbar's *farmāns* of 1567 (Azad Library) and 1575 (*Asnādu-s Ṣanādīd*, 157-62), Jahāngīr's *farmān*, R.Y. 22 (*Farāmīn-i Salāṭīn*, 8-9); Shāhjahān's *farmān*, R.Y. 10 (*Asnādu-s Ṣanādīd*, 167-70); and Aurangzeb's *farmān*, R.Y. 35 (I.O. 11,698). The last two *farmāns* specify both *jama'* and *ḥāṣil*. A *farmān* of Shāhjahān, R.Y.4 (*Farāmīn-i Salāṭīn*, 10-11) gives the *jama'* and *ḥāṣil-i kāmil* as well as the area of the grant.

In some provinces the area of the grant was specified in units other than the *bīgha*, for example: *juftwār* (plough-land?) in Bābur's *farmān* in Bhojpur Coll.B, No.1; *kharwār* (land yielding ass-load of grain) in Kashmir (*TJ*, 268), *qalba* (plough-land) in Kabul (*IHRC*, XVIII [1942], 242-3) and *chāvar* in the Dakhin (*Selected Documents*, 189-90).

[19] The areas held under previous grants were reduced by Akbar on the introduction of the bamboo *ṭānab*, and then of the *gaz-i Ilāhī*. The former reduction according to the standard allowance for shrinking of the measuring rope should have amounted to 13 per cent (*Ā'īn*, I, 297); we find it actually to have been 13.05 per cent. in the case of one grant (originally made in 1576, Sandila, National Archives: Acquired Docs. No.1441) and 13.03 per cent. in another (originally made, 1569, Batala, I.O. 4438:55); yet in a third (originally of 1581, Pathan[kot], *Jogis of Jakhbar*, 60) it amounts to 15 per cent. The reduction in the area of the grants upon the introduction of the *gaz-i Ilāhī* should have been 10.54 per cent. according to the standard calculation in the *Ā'īn*, I, 297, and numerous documents show it being made at about this rate (Moosvi, *Economy*, 97-98). The total reduction on both these counts should have been 22.17%, according to *Ā'īn*, I, 297, but it is

the *farmān* usually enjoined the local officials "to measure the said area and demarcate the *chak* (i.e. land of the grant)," in a particular village or anywhere in a *pargana*, as might be particularized in the *farmān*.[20] The *jāgīrdārs* and revenue officials, on their part, were naturally anxious that the grantees should confine their rights to the area of their grant and not occupy any area in excess (*taufīr*) of it.[21]

In 1574-75 Akbar issued an order for all lands of grants to be recorded with their current occupants, with a view to setting them apart from the tax-paying land (that is land "with the peasantry").[22] He found, apparently from this survey, that the system of assigning *madad-i ma'āsh* grants in widely scattered villages was open to much abuse. The grantees could sometimes fraudulently obtain lands in two or more places on the strength of the same grant; on the other hand, the holder of a petty grant in an ordinary village was liable to oppression from officials of the *jāgīrdārs* and the *khāliṣa*. He, therefore, decided in 1578 to concentrate the existing grants in certain villages within each locality and ordered that all new grants should also be made from the lands of these villages.[23]

set at the whole figure of 23% in Bhojpur Coll. (B), Nos. 3 and 5. Ṣādiq Khān, (Or.174, f.186a, Or. 1671, f.91a; Khāfī Khān, I, 734-5 n.) says that while the *bīgha-i daftarī*, based upon the *dir'a-i Shāhjahānī* (*dir'a* = *gaz*), was in use, by the middle of the 17th century, for measuring ordinary land, "the *bīgha* which is mentioned in the *farmāns* of royal grants to *a'imma-dārs* is the *bīgha-i Ilāhī*". The documents of Shāhjahān's and Aurangzeb's reigns in fact continue to mention *gaz-i Ilāhī* as the *gaz* by which the *bīgha* of the grant was measured (Allahabad 783, 881, 1190, etc.; CAS in History, Aligarh, MSS Nos.36 and 37; *Durru-l'Ulūm*, f.138a-b; also Bekas, ff.40a, 41a). See also Appendix A.

20 For the word *chak*, see Elliot, *Memoirs*, II, 79. It generally means a landholding. When the officials had measured out the area of the land assigned to the grantee they drew up a document, called *chaknāma*, laying down the area and boundaries of the land measured. For an early *chaknāma*, datable to 1569-70 from seals, see CAS in History, Aligarh, MS No.41. For 17th-century examples, see Allahabad 36, 869, 873, 874, 879, 881, 1190; I.O. 4438: 59. Cf. also Add 6603, f.58b.

21 Allahabad 179. See also Allahabad 36.

The *Maẕhar-i Shāhjahānī*, 146-7, refers to the "oppressive" proceedings of the agents of a *jāgīrdār* of Sehwan (during the last years of Jahāngīr) who remeasured the land and demanded revenue (from, presumably, the area in excess of that specified in the grants). The grantees went to the court, and the *jāgīrdār*, in order to satisfy them, issued orders (*parwānchas*) requiring his officials to honour the limits of the grants as previously established.

22 'Ārif Qandahārī, 177. Documents such as Allahabad II, 23 (=Or.1757, ff.39a-51b), *farmān* of AH 983 (transcript in CAS in History, Aligarh) and *farmān* in the *Ma'āṣiru-l Ajdād*, 481-3, all of 1575, were obviously generated by this survey.

23 *A.N.*, III, 240; *Ā'īn*, I, 198; Badāūnī, II, 254. We are fortunate in possessing in

Henceforward the practice of marking out certain villages in each *pargana* for *madad-i ma'āsh* grants became an established one in Mughal administration.[24]

The standing rule, says Abū-l Fazl, was to give half the area of the grant in land already cultivated and the other half in cultivable waste; and, if the latter was not available, the area of the grant was to be reduced by a fourth.[25] This rule is reflected in some early grants.[26] But some of these go further and stipulate that the whole grant was to consist of cultivable waste, not previously paying revenue.[27]

It was, probably, usually on the wasteland assigned to them that the grantees established their k̲h̲wud-kāshta holdings. This category (k̲h̲wud-kāshta) does not usually appear in original grants, and is found mainly in confirmatory orders.[28] It is also likely that

---

Allahabad 24 the original text of Akbar's order. It was issued on 13 June 1578, and stated that all villages where the grantees possessed "mosques, wells, houses, *chaupāls* (community sheds), orchards, etc." should be included among villages where the grants were to be concentrated, so that the grantees might not have to abandon any of their immovable possessions. But it may be doubted if attention was or could have always been paid to this. Badāūnī at least does not omit to tell us that the measure caused great distress to the grantees.

[24] Thus *Siyāqnāma*, 40, etc., and the *K̲h̲ulāsat-s Siyāq*, ff.78b, 82b, put a number of villages in the category of *dar-o-bast a'imma-i 'uzzām*, i.e. wholly assigned in imperial *a'imma* grants, and exclude them from those coming under revenue assessment. See also *Mir'āt*, I, 26, where 103 villages in Gujarat are assigned to *madad-i ma'āsh*; and the English revenue collector's report from Broach, 1776, showing seven villages in that *pargana* as "totally set apart" for the grants (*Selections from the Bombay Secretariat, Home* II, 183). A grantee who would wish to get the grant transferred to another *pargana* could lose a fourth of the grant (*chauthāī intiqāl-i parganātī*) (*Jamm-i Badī'*, f.82a).

[25] *Ā'īn*, I, 199.

[26] Akbar's grant of 200 *bīghas* to Gopāldās of Vrindaban, made in 1565, clearly specified that the grant was to be "half in cultivated land (*mazrū'*), half in waste (*uftāda*)" (Madan Mohan 55); the same formula was used in the original grant of 200 *bīghas* to Udant Nath in *pargana* Pathan(kot) in 1571 (confirmatory *farmān*, 1581: *Jogis of Jakhbar*, Doc.I). For Sher Shāh's *farmāns*, see *Oriental College Magazine*, IX(3), 121-2, 125-8, and Allahabad 318. See *chaknāma* of 1624 from Navsari in Gujarat (*JBBRAS*, NS, XXV, 464-5) for an explicit reference to this rule (*zābita*).

[27] The standard phrase being *zamīn-i uftāda lā'iq-i zirā'at k̲h̲ārij-i jama'*. See I.O. 4438: 3; Or. 11,697; Allahabad 874, 881; *Nigārnāma-i Munshī*, ed., 91; I.O. 4435; *Durru-l 'Ulūm*, f.138a-b; Bekas, f.31b (*banjar* used for *uftāda*). This emphasis on grant of wasteland was apparently no innovation of the Mughals. Cf. the 14th-century *Inshā'-i Māhrū*, 74.

The authorities seem also to have been anxious that the grantees should not draw away cultivators from the revenue-paying land. See Bekas, f.31b, for an undertaking by a *muqaddam* to prevent the sowing of the *imlāk* (or *madad-i ma'āsh* lands) so long as the rest of the land had not been brought under the plough.

[28] E.g. Akbar's *farmāns* of 1575: Allahabad II, 23 (Or. 1757, ff.39a-51b); tran-

the *khwud-kāshta* lands partly comprised orchards planted by the grantees.[29]

A *farmān* of Aurangzeb defines *madad-i ma'āsh* as something held on loan (*'āriyat*).[30] That is it was not transferred to the grantee in full proprietary possession, but was only held by him during the pleasure of the emperor.[31] No period of years was laid down in the *farmāns* of grant; and, normally, a grant was enjoyed by its recipient undisturbed in his lifetime.[32] But the right to resume it at any time always remained with the king; and already in Akbar's reign, the grants appear to have been substantially reduced after the death of the original grantees, very much as a matter of course.[33] In its later phase his reign presented the spectacle of wholesale resumptions and reductions of grants, either on suspicion that they had been obtained by corrupt or fraudulent means or simply as part

---

script, CAS in History, Aligarh; and *Ma'āṣiru-l Ajdād*, 481-3. In these *farmāns*, of a confirmatory nature, the land of each grant is divided into *uftāda* (waste) and *mazrū'* (cultivated); and, then, the latter into *ra'īyatī* and *khwud-kāshta*. In an early *farmān* (1562), while granting 100 *bīghas* of cultivated land to his master dyer, Rāmdās, Akbar took care to order that 37 *bīghas* of revenue-paying land already cultivated by him (*zirā'at-i khāṣa-i ū*) in that village should form part of the grant (*Akbar and his India*, 263-4, 272-3).

29 Abū-l Faẓl assures us that "owing to the appearance of peace and security", the grantees "planted orchards in their lands and obtained abundant profit" (*Ā'īn*, I, 199).

30 *Farmān* issued in the 34th year, Allahabad II, 53 and 55.

31 Such a view is attributed to certain contemporary scholars by Jalāluddīn Thānesarī (d.1582) in his *Risāla Taḥqīq Ārāẓī Hind*, fragment printed in *Baṣā'ir*, Karachi, II, (2) (1963), 3-4. They are said to have held that the *milk* grants of the rulers could not become the *milk* (property) of the grantees, it being unlawful to sell or transfer such grants. Thānesarī wrote his tract to refute such a view.

32 The *farmāns,* in fact, often direct that the grantee be allowed to hold the grant "year after year" (*sāl-ba-sāl*).

33 See Akbar's *farmān* of 1598 (original in National Archives and early copy in Govind-dev Coll.), granting land to temples in Vrindaban, etc. Its *ẓimn* tabulates grants given to five religious divines by a *farmān* of 1576. All the five grantees being dead by 1598, their grants had suffered the following reductions (areas in *bīghas*).

	Original grant	Area after reduction		Original grant	Area after reduction
1. Govardhan	40	35	4. Harbans	100	40
2. Kishandās	40	25	5. Rāmdās	100	35
3. Bhagwān	40	25	Total	[320]	160

In these cases the reduction does not follow a standard rate: perhaps, in each case, the merits of the heirs were separately judged.

of policy directed against certain classes of grantees.[34] By an order issued in 1579 all grants of 500 *bīghas* and above were to be held in abeyance until confirmation was obtained from the court;[35] and in 1603 an imperial decree required a reduction of all grants in Gujarat by a half.[36] The imperial right to resume is implicit in Jahāngīr's action of confirming all grants conferred by his father.[37] There was actually an attempt in Shāhjahān's reign to examine all the grants made till then and resume such of them as were held by persons found to be undeserving.[38] The *Maẕhar-i Shāhjahānī* shows that, even ordinarily, the *ṣadrs* were required to resume to the *khāliṣa* all grants of persons who had died or fled, or were found to have occupied land elsewhere using the same deed of grant, or had obtained the grant itself by fraud or forgery.[39] Its author demands that the genuine grantees be yet protected from harassment by the *jāgīrdārs*, who often resumed their grants and levied revenue upon them on one pretext or another.[40]

The non-proprietary nature of *madad-i ma'āsh* is also shown by the fact that its possession could not be transferred or sold by the grantee.[41] Similarly, it could not pass on to his heirs except in accordance with imperial orders. In the time of Akbar no regular provision seems to have been made for inheritance, and the heirs had to apply for a renewal of the grant, of which only a part was

[34] *A.N.*, III, 233-4; *Ā'īn*, I, 198-9; Badāūnī, I, 204-5, 274-7, 315, 343, 368; Faiẕī Sirhindī, ff.147a-149a, 185a-186a.

The use of corruption and fraud for obtaining grants, especially larger grants than authorized, was so widespread that Sher Shāh was compelled to take measures to protect the state against forged alterations in the *farmāns* ('Abbās Khān, ed., 225-6). It was reported to Aurangzeb that forged entries had been made even in the official record of grants (*yāddāsht-i a'imma-i madad-i ma'āsh*) (*Akhbārāt* 47/323).

[35] National Archives, Acquired Docs. No.1441 (where the general *farmān* is apparently misdated by one year, reading 988 instead of 987); 'Abbās Khān, ed., 167-8.

[36] Modi, *Parsees at the Court of Akbar*, Doc.II.

[37] *T.J.*, 21. Aurangzeb also issued a similar order: see reference to it in Rāja Raghunāth's *parwāna*, Allahabad II, 284.

[38] Lāhorī, II, 365-6; Ṣādiq Khān, Or. 174, ff.103b-104b; Or. 1671, ff.56b-57a. This measure was proposed in the 17th year of the reign, but proved abortive. Shāhjahān's favourite daughter, Jahān Ārā, was seriously injured by fire, and the superstitious father, attributing the mishap to the curses of the grantees, practically rescinded his order.

[39] *Maẕhar-i Shāhjahānī*, 192.

[40] Ibid., 191-2; also 158.

[41] A judicial decision (January 1666) states definitely "that by law (*shar'an*), the land of *madad-i ma'āsh* is not alienable (*qābil-i tamlīk nīst*)" (Allahabad 1189). "The imperial regulation is that the *a'imma* land cannot be sold" (Add. 6603, f.48a).

normally granted to them, as we have seen.[42] Under Jahāngīr, at least from his 8th regnal year, the rule was set that only half the area of the grant was to be allowed to the heirs upon the death of the grantee.[43] Shāhjahān's orders and those of Aurangzeb, early

---

Jalāl Thānesarī, *Risāla Taḥqīq Ārāẓī Hind*, op.cit., alleges that this prohibition was a recent innovation (presumably of Akbar's time); and that revenue officials were now seeking to deprive persons of their grant-lands if they had obtained these by purchase. Shamsabad Docs.1 (of 1530) may represent a transaction of the kind Thānesarī had in mind, for it records the "sale" of *kharāj-in'ām* (revenue-grant); but the actual terms suggest lease for an undefined period rather than outright sale (I. Habib in *IESHR*, IV(3), 210, 220-1). During the 17th century such sales are very rare: I have found only two documents, Amroha Docs. II(1) and (7), both from Aurangzeb's reign, that record sales of lands originally granted in *madad-i ma'āsh*.

In the 18th century, such sales begin to appear more frequently: see, for example, *JBBRAS*, NS, XXV (1917-21), 484-5, of 5th. R.Y. of Muḥammad Shāh; I.O. 4438: 69, of a date later than 1729-30; and Allahabad 457 of 1764. This is, perhaps, what one would expect from a period of administrative laxity.

While in the earlier conditions of greater administrative rigour, the grantees could not transfer their grants, they could still apparently transfer the land to someone for the duration that they themselves held it. Thus in Allahabad 296, of as early a date as 1596, a group of *madad-i ma'āsh* holders affirm that they had transferred 29 *bīghas* out of their grant to one Mīān Ḥamīduddīn in return for his undertaking the duty of *khaṣmāna*, i.e. protecting or guarding the rest of their land. The period of the grant was to be "as long as their *madad-i ma'āsh* in the village remained with the transferors" (cf. Allahabad 279 and 280). Ḥamīduddīn, therefore, established no independent right of his own in the land. The grantees could also lease or farm out their right for one year or a longer period (Allahabad 892 and 1230), but the lease or *ijāra* would presumably have lapsed as soon as the grant was resumed or went into other hands.

[42] The *Ā'īn*, I, 287, calls upon the revenue collector to resume (*bāzyāft*) the grant of any person who had died or absconded. It also says (I, 199) that it was decided that "if the grant had been made to a group and the share of each grantee was not specified on the *ẓimn*, and one of the grantees died, the *ṣadr* was to determine his share, and this share was to be resumed to the *khāliṣa*, till the survivors (heirs?) presented themselves (or their case?) at the Court". See Faiẓī Sirhindī's account of how when his father died, he had to obtain afresh the grant held by his father (ff.139b-141b). Akbar was apparently surprised at finding that the whole of the father's grant had been confirmed to the son (ff.148a-149a). Cf. also Badāūnī, II, 368, for grants resumed by Mīr Fatḥullāh Shīrāzī's *shiqqdār* from "widows and orphans" on the grounds of "disappearance" (i.e. death or flight) of the grantees. A *farmān* of Jahāngīr (5th R.Y.) deals with a grant in Bihar of 3,500 *bīghas*, whose holder had died. Only 1,000 *bīghas* were regranted: 700 to the widow and 300 to the son present at the court. No decision was made concerning the other son, who till then had made no representation (*IHRC*, XXVI, ii, 3-4).

[43] See Jahāngīr's *farmāns* of R.Ys. 8, 14 and 15, in favour of the attendants and dependants of the shrine of Mu'īnuddīn Chishtī at Ajmer (*Farāmīn-i Salāṭīn*, 4-8; *Asnādu-s Ṣanādīd*, 51-2, 59-65, 73-7, 79-82, 82-7, 92-6, 101-7, 118-24). See also a *parwāna* of 1617 from Bihar, which confirms to the heirs of a deceased woman grantee only half of her grant of 60 *bīghas* (Datta, p.111, no.505).

in his reign, are summarized in a *parwāna* issued by Rāja Raghunāth, the *dīwān*, in the 3rd regnal year of Aurangzeb:[44] By Shāhjahān's order of the 5th year, all grants of 30 *bīghas* or less were to be wholly distributed among heirs on the death of the grantee. If the grant was of a larger area, half of it was to be distributed among the heirs and the other half resumed, unless the heirs proved their deserts (*istiḥqāq*) before the imperial court and obtained *sanads* for this portion as well.[45] By an order of the 18th year, it was declared that only if the grant had contained the formula "with his offspring" after the name of the grantee, was half of it to be allowed to the heirs; otherwise the whole of it was to be resumed.[46] Aurangzeb, at the beginning of his reign, lifted this condition, and, in his 3rd year, went back practically to the position of Shāhjahān's order of the 5th year, but with this difference that the limit for passing the whole grant to the heirs was put at 20 *bīghas*. Of every grant above this, half was to be resumed as before, unless the heirs obtained it in a fresh grant from the court.[46a]

In his 34th year (1690), however, Aurangzeb issued a *farmān*, which made the *madad-i ma'āsh* completely hereditary. It declared that henceforth "the land of the imperial grantees (*a'imma-i 'uẓẓām*), conferred by valid *farmāns*, old and new, would be retained,

[44] Allahabad II, 284 (dated 10 January 1661).

[45] This is illustrated by a *parwāna* issued in Shāhjahān's 16th R.Y. concerning a grant originally conferred in 1571 in *pargana* Batala in the Panjab. All the persons in whose name it was made being dead, the previous *ṣadrs* had resumed 49 *bīghas* out of the total grant of 107 *bīghas*, 8 *biswas*, redistributing the remaining portion among the heirs. The latter having made fresh representations, the resumed portion (termed *bāzyāft-i mutawaffī*) was now ordered to be granted to them (I.O. 4438: 7).

[46] This is corroborated by *Ādāb-i 'Ālamgīrī*, f.155b. Lāhorī, II, 366, apparently referring to the same order, speaks as if the whole grant was to be left with the sons, if the words "with his offspring" had been used in the original *farmān* of any grant. But this is probably due to a slip of the pen. The formula "with his offspring" is comparatively rare in the *farmāns*. It occurs in Akbar's *farmān* of AH 983/AD 1575 (transcript in CAS in History, Aligarh), where out of the many earlier *farmāns* of grant listed, only three contain this formula; Jahāngīr's *farmāns* of R.Y.s 14,15 and 21 (*JBBRAS*, NS, XXV [1917-21], 423); *Asnādu-s Ṣanādīd*, 88-9, 153; and Hodivala, *Studies in Parsi History*, 175 (photocopy at end of the volume), etc. The severe terms of Shāhjahān's order seem to have been widely evaded, because Raghunāth's *parwāna* admits that the provincial *ṣadrs* (*ṣadr-i juzv*) had in some cases allowed the heirs above half, and sometimes the whole, of the original grant. Later *ṣadrs* tried to resume such grants, but this was forbidden by Aurangzeb's order of the 3rd year.

[46a] See *taṣḥīḥa* in *Jamm-i Badī'*, f.82a-b, showing reduction of a woman's grant in Siwistan (Sind) according to this rule.

completely and fully, without loss or reduction, by the heirs of the deceased grantees, generation after generation." The *farmān* nevertheless insisted that since *madad-i ma'āsh* was an article of loan (*'āriyat*), not property, its inheritance was to be governed by imperial orders, and not (by implication) by the *Sharī'at*. Thus it allowed a direct share to the grandson, if his father had predeceased his grandfather; it deprived a daughter of her share if she was married or otherwise provided for; and it laid down that a widow might keep her husband's grant for her lifetime, before its passing to her husband's heirs.[47]

The grant of *madad-i ma'āsh* was theoretically an act of charity for "the maintenance of the poor and indigent (creatures) of God".[48] All those who were engaged in service or in any trade and thus had other means of livelihood could not properly hold grants.[49] According to Abū-l Faẓl, there were four classes of persons for whom the grants were specially meant: men of learning; religious devotees; destitute persons without the capacity for obtaining livelihood; and persons of noble lineage, who would not, "out of ignorance", take to any employment.[50] Women, belonging to respectable Muslim families, were frequently recipients of the

[47] Allahabad II, 53 & 55 (two copies of the *farmān*). Allowing a share in the inheritance to the children of a son, who had predeceased his father, was not only in contravention of the *Sharī'at*, but also opposed to earlier practice. The terms of Shāhjahān's order of the 18th year summarised in Rāja Raghunāth's *parwāna* imply that a grandson could then have directly inherited only if the *farmān* had contained the words "with his offspring" after the name of the deceased grantee. There is a case on record in which a person, debarred from any share in his grandfather's grant, in the time of Shāhjahān, brought up his claims in 1697. These were not upheld, apparently because Aurangzeb's *farmān* of 1690 was not meant to have retrospective effect (Allahabad 1228 and 1229).

[48] See the preamble of Aurangzeb's *farmān* of 1690 (Allahabad II, 53 and 55).

[49] The grant was liable to forfeiture (*bāzyāft*) if the grantee was found to be "in service". (*naukar*) (*Ā'īn*, I, 287). Under the terms of Shāhjahān's order of the 18th year, a grantee could not be a "*kāsib* (i.e. engaged in any trade) or *naukar* (employed in service)". This is according to the summary of the order in Rāja Raghunāth's *parwāna*. Lāhorī, II, 366, referring to the same order, is more specific and only makes resumable the grants of those who were "soldiers and artisans".

[50] *Ā'īn*, I, 198. *Maẓhar-i Shāhjahānī*, 190-91, enumerates three classes properly qualified to receive *madad-i ma'āsh* grants: 1. Officials who received grants in lieu of salaries; 2. "Scholars and memorizers (of the *Qur'ān*)"; and 3. "Saiyids, Shaikhs and Mughals, by descent, who, eschewing the urge for greater gain, retire to a corner and are content with a little *madad-i ma'āsh* received from the court, and have no other means of livelihood." For the class of imperial officials (*qāẓīs*, etc.) receiving grants, see below.

grants,[51] but they are probably covered by Abū-l Faẓl's third category. Still, there were other grantees, though probably few in number, who did not fall into any of the four categories. A series of documents relating to a grant in Gujarat shows it to have been made for the particular reason that the beneficiaries were physicians, who treated "the poor and indigent" of the locality.[52] Officers, no longer able to perform their duties, owing to their age or some other reason, were also pensioned off with *madad-i ma'āsh* grants.[53] Then, too, grants were sometimes conferred upon imperial servants, petty officials and others as a sign of favour or as a reward for service rendered.[54]

However, the bulk of the *madad-i ma'āsh* grants seem to have been enjoyed by persons, who, in actual fact or by their pretensions, fell under Abū-l Faẓl's first two categories. Learning and religious devotion were then the monopoly of a single class among Muslims and it was the current belief, entertained by this class, that the *madad-i ma'āsh* grants were meant solely for its benefit.[55] That

[51] Jahāngīr appointed a foster-sister of his father as the special official in charge of grants to women (*T.J.*, 21). Abū-l Faẓl also speaks of grants held by "Īrānī and Tūrānī women" (*Ā'īn*, I, 198-9). For a few specific instances of original grants in favour of women, see *T.J.*, 83; Allahabad 5 and 874; I.O. 4435; and *Durru-l 'Ulūm*, f.138a-b. *Maẓhar-i Shāhjahānī*, 158, refers incidentally to two categories of *chaks* (lands) of the *a'imma*, the *chak-hā-i musammātī* (lands held by women) and *muzakkarātī* (held by men).

[52] See the documents (texts and trs.) in Hodivala, *Studies in Parsi History*, 167-188, especially the public testimony to this effect, given in a document of Aurangzeb's reign (text on pp.185-6, and photocopy at the end of the volume; and Hodivala's own comment on p.188).

[53] Lāhorī, II, 308-9; *Ādāb-i 'Ālamgīrī*, f.153b, also ed., II, 841-2, 847-8; Wāriṣ, a:f. 499a; b: ff.148b-149a.

[54] An early example of this is Akbar's grant of 100 *bīghas* as *in'ām* to his master dyer in 1562 (*Akbar and his India*, 274-5, 282-4). See also *Ṭabaqāt-i Akbarī*, II, 336 (*muqaddams*); *T.J.*, 32 (*zamīndārs* and *chaudhurīs*). Akbar deprived all *chaudhurīs* of their *suyūrghāl* (*Ā'īn*, I, 198).

According to the *Maẓhar-i Shāhjahānī*, 191, in addition to the three classes of grantees mentioned by it as proper recipients of grants (see note 50), there was a fourth class, consisting of "*zamīndārs*, who were also *arbābs* and *muqaddams*". It says that Akbar and Jahāngīr did not allow grants to be conferred on such persons, but under the regime of Nūr Jahān they obtained *farmāns* of grants by paying money. It deprecates this practice, because by making use of their authority these local officials got the best lands included in their grants and then compelled the peasants to cultivate them, without making any effort themselves.

[55] 'Abbās Khān, ed., 226, himself the son of a grantee, puts in the mouth of Sher Shāh the following: "It is incumbent upon the king to give *madad-i ma'āsh* to the *a'imma*, because the splendour of the cities of India is due to these religious men

the belief was not really far from the fact is shown by the use of the words *a'imma* and *makhādīm*, both meaning religious leaders, as general names for the grantees even in official documents.[56] Faiẓī Sirhindī has preserved for us an effective recipe for proving one's worth (*istiḥqāq*) for *madad-i ma'āsh*, and that was a display of knowledge in any of the petty obscurities of the *Sharī'at*.[57] Such knowledge was, however, not invariably essential for obtaining a grant. Descendants of saints or religious divines, and persons who had retired from the world, but, most frequently, those simply belonging to families reputed for learning or orthodoxy, or just held to be respectable, were regarded, without particular reference to their individual merits, as eligible for grants.[58] Part of the Mughal soldiery came from these families;[59] but the grantees themselves

---

(*a'imma o makhādīm*)." Āzād Bilgrāmī in a similar strain bemoans the disaster that fell to Muslim learning in Awadh and Ilahabad ("Pūrab") when after 1718 Sa'ādat Khān and Safdar Jang resumed cash and land grants (*waẓā'if o suyūrghālāt*) wholesale (*Ma'āṣiru-l Kirām*, I, 221-3). See also Badāūnī II, 204-5, for the belief that only Muslim theologians deserved to receive grants. According to him, the best claims to *madad-i ma'āsh* were those of "the teachers of *Hidāya* (the celebrated textbook of Muslim law) and other advanced books". He laments the fact that when in 1575 the grants were checked, even such men as these were granted at the most 100 *bīghas*, and that also after the greatest difficulty.

56 The use of the word *a'imma* has been discussed in note 5. For *makhādīm* used in the same sense, see Akbar's order concentrating the grants in demarcated villages (Allahabad 24). Cf. also 'Abbās Khān, ed., 225-6.

57 Faiẓī Sirhindī obtained on the death of his father, the whole of his grant, by writing and presenting to the *ṣadr*, Shaikh 'Abdu-n Nabī, a tract entitled *Ṣaidana Akbariya*. In this he collected together "reliable Traditions from trustworthy books" to establish the position of the *Sharī'at* on one important point, then (1575-76) a subject of controversy among Akbar's court theologians, namely how was a deer to be lawfully slaughtered when it was held by the neck by a cheetah! (Faiẓī Sirhindī, ff.139b-141b).

58 See *Maẓhar-i Shāhjahānī*, 190-91, for a description of its third class of grantees (see note 50 above). See Allahabad 8, for a grant on the basis of descent; and I.O. 4433 and Allahabad 1117 for a grant to persons who were supposed to have retired from the world. The vast majority of grants seem to have been conferred on Shaikhs and Saiyids. All of them are stated to possess sufficient "worth" (*istiḥqāq*), but the documents do not go into details regarding their specific attainments. Their only qualification, quite often, was just their "respectability". In an appeal for the confirmation of a cash-grant from the revenues of a *pargana*, the sole argument put forward is that "the establishing of respectable gentlemen (*shurafā'*), especially of the said person, in that desolate place [surely, in a figurative sense], indeed in all of that district, is requisite for (divine) favours and is a sign of blessings". (Muḥammad Ja'far, *Inshā'-i 'Ajīb*, compiled 1706-7, ed., 18).

59 When in 1573 Akbar suppressed a rebellion in Gujarat it was alleged that "the [rebel] soldiers were all kinsmen of the *a'imma*", who, in turn, pleaded that they were unable to maintain such relations out of their grants: hence the compulsion

largely formed a parasitic class, for, excluded from engaging in service or trade, and hardly capable of devoting all their time to religious studies, they seem to have looked upon land as the best object of ambition. Records of a seventeenth-century family from Awadh bring out vividly how persons who held large *madad-i ma'āsh* grants, freely acquired *zamīndārīs* and even acted as revenue-farmers.[60] Submerged in these worldly pursuits, their alarm was naturally very great whenever anyone suggested an investigation into their credentials.[61]

The state had its own interest in maintaining this class. Jahāngīr called it the "Army of Prayer",[62] and he is reported to have said that this army was as important for the empire as the real army.[63] The grantees were its creatures, and therefore its natural apologists and propagandists. But they were at the same time a bastion of conservatism, because they had nothing except their orthodoxy to justify their claims on the state's bounty. When Akbar began to formulate a new theoretical basis for imperial sovereignty in India and embarked on his policy of religious tolerance, it was inevitable that he should enter into a conflict with this class. The extreme liberality of his early years now gave place to successive measures to control and curtail the *madad-i ma'āsh* grants held by Muslim

---

for them to join (military) service (Abū Turāb, 89-90). Similarly, Āzād Bilgrāmī alleges that once their grants were taken away members of the scholarly families of Awadh and Ilahabad took to "the profession of soldiering" (*Ma'āṣiru-l Kirām*, II, 222).

60 This is the family of Saiyid Muḥammad 'Ārif, whose *zamīndārī* holdings in one or two *parganas* of the *sarkār* of Bahraich, Awadh, especially the Pasnajat group of villages, have been mentioned more than once in Chapter V, and giving full references here will be needless repetition. Allahabad 886, 889 and 890 are *ijāra* documents, in which Saiyid 'Ārif contracts for the revenues of a *pargana*, or parts of it, with different *jāgīrdārs* in different years. He held *madad-i ma'āsh* lands in the environs of Bahraich (Allahabad 879, 1202, 1217, 1228-30). When Shaikh Hidāyatullāh, described as a religious divine, died, he left behind *madad-i ma'āsh* rights over 14 villages and *zamīndārī* over 8¼ villages in *sarkār* Khairabad, also in Awadh (statement of division of inheritance prepared by the *qāẓī*, November 1717, *Nāma-i Muẓaffarī*, II, 170-3).

61 See Ṣādiq Khān's strong condemnation of the attempt to re-examine the grants in the time of Shāhjahān (Or. 174, ff.103b-104a; Or. 1671, ff. 56b-57a).

For a spirited modern defence of the class of grantees, see Noman Ahmad Siddiqi, *Land Revenue Administration under the Mughals (1700-1750)*, 131-4.

62 *T.J.*, 5. Cf. the use of the same term, *lashkar-i du'ā* in Shaikh Aḥmad Sirhindī, *Maktūbāt*, III, no.47. The *farmāns* of *madad-i ma'āsh* grants usually contain a clause requiring the grantees to pray for the eternal prosperity of the empire.

63 *Intikhāb-i Jahāngīr-Shāhī*, Or. 1648, f.182a-b.

theologians.[64] The benefits of the grants were at the same time extended to non-Muslim divines.[65] Jahāngīr probably moderated Akbar's stern policy a little, because he required the reputation for great generosity in bestowing these grants.[66] But it was Aurangzeb who principally modified Akbar's policy. He ordered,

[64] Badāūnī, II, 71, 204-5, 274, 315, 343. A characteristic instance of the antagonism between Akbar and the *makhādīm*, or theologians, is described by Faiẓī Sirhindī, ff.185a-186a. When Akbar passed by Sirhind in 1585, the *makhādīm* of the *parganas* around did not come to pay him respects. In his indignation Akbar ordered their *madad-i ma'āsh* grants to be resumed forthwith. It was only then that a few appeared, but, owing to Abū-l Faẓl's intervention, most received back their grants.

Sirhind has also the honour of producing Shaikh Aḥmad, who in Jahāngīr's reign embarked upon virulent attacks against Akbar, the Hindus and Shī'as. His arrogation of supreme status in religious matters to himself, alongside his belief that the world of the *Sharī'at* could be established only through winning over the emperor, marks him out as a representative of the *makhādīm*, whose self-importance was matched fully by their dependence upon the bounty of the ruling class. (Compare his own letters, *Maktūbāt imām-i Rabbānī,* I, no.11, & III, no.87, with ibid., III, no.47; but for an account of the outlook of the Shaikh and his grandsons by one of the best satirists of the time, see the *Waqā'i'* of Ni'mat Khān-i 'Ālī, litho., 25-30). Jahāngīr ordered the Shaikh to be imprisoned, ironically enough, in the custody of a Rajput officer and compelled him to express repentence (*T.J.*, 272-3, 308).

[65] Badāūnī, II, 205. The earliest known Hindu divine to benefit from Akbar's bounty was Gopāldās, priest of the Madan Mohan temple, Vrindaban, who received 200 *bīghas* by a *farmān* issued in January 1565 (Madan Mohan 55). In 1568-9 Mādho, another Vaishnavite figure at Vrindaban, received 100 *bīghas* (IVS 159). According to Akbar's *farmān* of September 1598 (National Archives; copy in Govind-dev coll.), further grants to Vrindaban divines were made in 1575 (700 *bīghas* to Chain Gopāl), 1576 (160 *bīghas* to Govardhan, and others) and 1580 (100 *bīghas* to Rāmdās). The *farmān* of 1598 consolidated these grants (including the one to Gopāldās) into a grant of 500 *bīgha ilāhī* and added 500 *bīghas* more, the beneficiaries being 31 Vaishnavite temples of Vrindaban, and the Braj district, divided into six groups (cf. T. Mukherjee and I. Habib in *PIHC*, 48th session, 1987, Goa, 234-50). The line of the *jogīs* of Jakhbar received its first grant, of 200 *bīghas*, in 1571 (*Jogis of Jakhbar*, Doc.I). Jhaveri, Doc. V, dated June 1593, purporting to be the grant of village Gokul to Gosāin Bithal Rāi does not seem to be genuine, so too Doc.IV. Kaiqubād, a Parsi priest of Navsari (Gujarat) had received a grant of 300 *bīghas*, which was confirmed in 1596 in favour of his son Mahyār (Modi, *Parsees at the Court of Akbar*, 93-6, 139-46).

[66] *Intikhāb-i Jahāngīr-Shāhī*, Or. 1648, ff.181b-182b. Jahāngīr was as liberal in his grants to non-Muslim religious men. He granted the village of Pushkar to the Brahmans of that village as *in'ām* (*Asnādu-ṣ Ṣanādīd*, 140-41); and gave *madad-i ma'āsh* grants to the Brahmans of Banaras (*Administrative Docs.* Nos.15, 33, 35). He conferred several new grants on the Vaishnavite priests at Vrindaban (T. Mukherji and I. Habib, *PIHC*, 49th session, 1988, Dharwad, 288-9, 293-5). A *farmān*(1619) of his, granting 100 *bīghas* in *madad-i ma'āsh* to two Parsi priests (*mullās*) in Gujarat, was published in *JBBRAS*, NS, XXV (1917-21), 422-8, by J.J. Modi.

in 1672-3, the resumption of all grants held by Hindus.[67] And, as we have seen, in 1690 he made the grants fully hereditary – an act which represented probably the last concession that could have been made to the grantees.

The bulk of the *madad-i ma'āsh* grants were conferred without imposing any obligation in return, being designed simply to maintain certain classes. But some grants were conditional (*mashrūṭ*). The office of the *qāẓī* (judge) always had a *madad-i ma'āsh* grant attached to it.[68] Some of Sher Shāh's grants prescribe a regular

---

For his grants to the Jesuit mission at Agra and Lahore, see Fr. Felix in *JPHS*, V(1), 12, 20-1.

[67] *Mir'āt*, I, 288 (cf. Bernier, 341). Documentary evidence of enforcement of this order comes from *Jogis of Jakhbar*, Doc. IX and, possibly, Doc.XII. The former, a *parwāna* of 1695, records the previous conversion of a *madad-i ma'āsh* grant, originally conferred on the *jogīs* by Jahāngīr, into land paying tax at a permanently fixed amount (*jama'-i istimrār*).

The order, however, was not enforced absolutely, without exceptions. In the first place, lands granted in return for services, were not affected. See *Mir'āt*, op.cit., and A'ẓam's *nishān*, transl. in *IHRC*, 1945, 53-55. The *madad-i ma'āsh* grant held by a family of Parsi physicians of Navsari in Gujarat was confirmed by *sanads* issued in 1664 and 1702, during the reign of Aurangzeb (Hodivala, *Studies in Parsi History*, 178). There were other exceptions too. We know from Vrindaban documents that at least two of the Vrindaban grants, one of 135 *bīghas* originally conferred by Akbar (1598) on the Govind-dev temple and, under Shāhjahān, transferred to the Amber house, for the use of that temple, and another of 89 *bīghas*, 9 *biswas*, initially conferred by Jahāngīr on a line of priests of the Madan Mohan temple, were retained by the grantees, with full official cognizance throughout Aurangzeb's reign. In a series of articles published in the *Journal of the Pakistan Historical Society*, V, iv, VI, i; & VII, i & ii, Jnan Chandra has drawn attention to a number of cash and land grants to non-Muslims, issued or confirmed by Aurangzeb. It may also be borne in mind that Aurangzeb's prohibition did not apply to *madad-i ma'āsh* grants made by *jāgīrdārs* from their assignments, such as are represented by documents calendared by Datta, Nos. 260, 262, 272-4, 278, 283, 308, 315, 316, 324-7, 330, 341, 364, 374 and 397, which relate to grants made to non-Muslims during Aurangzeb's reign.

[68] Or. 11,697; *Selected Documents*, 189-90; *Nigārnāma-i Munshī*, f.161a-b. ed., 83, and Bodl., ff.145b-146a; *Siyāqnāma*, 86; I.O. 4370; Or. 11,698. See Abū-l Faẓl's reference to grants held by *qāẓīs*, "these turban-wearers of evil heart and long-sleeved men of small minds" (*Ā'īn*, I, 198-9). Abū-l Faẓl's scorn had ample justification if the type of *qāẓī* depicted in Allahabad 782 and 1203 was at all common. This man had been assigned 750 *bīghas* in grant, but had possessed himself of 5,375 *bīghas*! Cf. Elliott, *Chronicles of Oonao*, 115.

Besides the *qāẓī* there were also other recipients of *madad-i ma'āsh* grants who held semi-judicial and semi-theological offices, viz. "*muftīs*, *ṣadrs* and *muḥtasibs*" (*Maẓhar-i Shāhjahānī*, 190). For land held on a hereditary basis (*zamīn-i maurūṣī*), but attached to the office of *khaṭīb* (Friday sermon-reader) at the *pargana* headquarters, see the two documents of 1558 and 1574 studied by S. Zaheer H. Jafri in *Akbar and his India*, 266-9.

exercise in archery for the grantees and oblige them to render assistance against local malefactors whenever required by officials.[69] When Badāūnī received a grant, he was obliged by its terms to maintain a small cavalry contingent.[70] Such conditions of military service are, however, not found in the *farmāns* of the seventeenth century, and so were probably no longer tacked on to *madad-i ma'āsh* grants.

There were certain grants which were not in name *madad-i ma'āsh*, but were in fact very similar. From the *al-tamghā jāgīrs* instituted by Jahāngīr, developed hereditary grants to officials' families, known as *in'ām-i āl-tamghā*.[71] There were also revenue-free lands held as *in'ām:* we hear of a village so held by members of the Chāran caste in Gujarat on the condition of performing police duties;[72] and in Malwa a village was similarly attached to the hereditary office of *nagar-seṭh* (head merchant of a town).[73] The line between *in'ām* and *madad-i ma'āsh* was always thin, both appellations being sometimes indifferently given to the same grant.[74] Then we have a purely unconditional remission of revenue, (at the last stage designated *in'ām āl-tamghā*), which is illustrated by a series of *sanads* of the reigns of Akbar (probably forged) and Shāhjahān, issued to a family of Vaishnavite divines in respect of two villages, one of which they are said to have purchased from

[69] Allahabad 318 and *farmān* printed in *Oriental College Magazine*, IX, 3 (May 1933), 127 (the other *farmān* of Sher Shāh printed in the same journal does not contain these conditions). The exercise in archery is prescribed in a peculiar fashion: the grantees were to offer all the five prayers in congregation in a mosque and discharge ten arrows each after every *ẓuhr* (afternoon) prayer. Cf. Elliott, *Chronicles of Oonao*, 95.

[70] He was granted 1,000 *bīghas* conditional upon his maintaining a contingent up to the standard of "a 20-rank" and attending the imperial court (1575-76). He failed lamentably to fulfil his obligation and was forced in 1579-80, on the threat of resumption of half of his grant, to begin attending the court again (Badāūnī, II, 206-7, 296-7, 342).

[71] For *āl-tamghā jāgīrs*, see Chapter VII, Section 1. Sujān Rāi, 74, tells us that a village near Sodhra was held as *in'ām-i āl-tamghā* by (the family of) 'Ālī Mardān Khān, for the maintenance of the garden and buildings of that grandee at Ibrahimabad. A *farmān* of Bahādur Shāh I (1710) conferring an *in'ām-i āl-tamghā* grant has survived (Or. 2285). This takes care to state the *ḥāṣil* (revenue) of the village granted, a detail usually missing in *madad-i ma'āsh* grants.

[72] *Mir'āt*, I, 288. See also W. Erskine, 'Journey in Gujarat, 1822-23', *JBBRAS*, XXV (1918), 406.

[73] *IHRC*, XXII (1945), 53-55.

[74] Thus Jahāngīr's *in'ām* grant to the Pushkar Brahmans is styled *madad-i ma'āsh* in Dārā Shukoh's *nishān* of May 1659 (*Asnādu-ṣ Ṣanādīd*, 140-1, 203).

zamīndārs. The *farmāns* exempted them from the land revenue and all other cesses, in language similar to that of the usual *madad-i ma'āsh* grants.[75]

There was still another category of grants, known as *auqāf* (plural of *waqf*).[76] The beneficiaries of these were not, directly, individuals but institutions. The revenues of certain lands were assigned permanently in trust (*waqf*) for the maintenance of religious shrines, tombs and *madrasas* – for their repair as also for the subsistence of their staff and for charities disbursed through them.[77]

The *Ā'īn* gives us the detailed figures, from *pargana* level upwards, of the revenues alienated through revenue grants (*suyūrghāl*).

[75] Jhaveri, Docs. IV, V, VII and XI. Docs. IV and V (both of Akbar) are obvious forgeries, though these might be the product of an attempt at making good the loss of genuine originals. When the grant was confirmed by Shāh 'Ālam II, it was described as *in'ām-i āl-tamghā* (Docs. XIV & XV).

[76] See Badāūnī, II, 71, 204, for reference to *auqāf* alongside *madad-i ma'āsh*. The term occurs in Baranī, as well, together with *milk* and *in'ām* (*Tārīkh-i Fīrūz-Shāhī*, 283).

[77] Once the emperor made a grant in *waqf*, he could naturally determine how and by whom it was managed. Akbar, who made the initial grant of 18 villages to the shrine of Mu'īnuddīn Chishtī at Ajmer (see *farmān* of 1575: *Asnādu-ṣ Ṣanādīd*, 167-70), not only decided the issue of succession of the spiritual head of the shrine (*sajjāda-nishīn*) (*Farāmīn-i Salāṭīn*, 9-10), but also appointed its *mutawallī*, or administrator (ibid., 2-4; Badāūnī, II, 400-1, and III, 89). Part of the *waqf* grant was reserved for distribution as *madad-i ma'āsh* among religious men, scholars and needy persons, as ordered or confirmed by the emperor, the terms being laid down in Jahāngīr's *farmān* of 1618 (*Mu'īnu-l Auliyā'*, 61-71; *Farāmīn-i Salāṭīn*, 4-8). The revenues of the remaining portion, according to this *farmān*, were to be used to meet the expenses of the upkeep of the shrine, and the *langar* (free kitchen and grain-store), illuminations and celebration (*'urs*), and the maintenance of the *sajjāda nishīn* himself. Out of this income too were met the pensions sanctioned by the imperial court to persons connected with the shrine (*Waqā'i' Ajmer*, 30-32).

Lāhorī, II, 330-31, tells us that the revenues from thirty villages and from shops of the market and inns built near it, were made *waqf* for the Taj Mahal. The income, estimated at more than 3 lakh rupees annually, was to be used for the repair of the Taj, disbursal of salaries of servants and the food prepared for the staff, the beggars and the poor. The emperor himself was to be the *mutawallī*.

Where the emperor granted land revenue-free for the upkeep of a shrine, repair of mosque, etc., as Akbar did in 1577 for the shrine of Maḥmūd Burrāqī in *pargana* Bhojpur, *sarkār* Kanauj, the imperial government retained a hand in recognizing every new head of the shrine (*sajjāda-nishīn*), who was also in each case the *mutawallī* (see Bhojpur Collection B, 3, 5 and 6).

A *waqf* for a slightly different purpose is described by Bāyazīd, 310-11: Bāyazīd established a *madrasa* at Banaras, and the emperor (Akbar) assigned two villages near the town to meet the allowances of its teachers.

It does so by first adding these figures to the *jama'* against which *jāgīrs* were assigned to yield the figures in the *naqdī/jama'* column, and, then, shows these separately in the *suyūrghāl* column.[78] It is possible that these estimates were made initially in 1578 when such estimation might have been deemed desirable for the purpose of allotting land in the select villages where grants were to be now concentrated.[79] One may also conjecture that a rate of one rupee, as minimum, might often have been applied either to the whole, or to the cultivated portions of the grant, to yield the figures the *Ā'īn* gives.[80] However, the considerable variations between the *ṣūba* figures of *suyūrghāl*, and the actual totals of the figures given for *sarkārs* and *parganas* within the respective *ṣūbas*[81] suggest that the estimates were revised periodically, to keep up with resumptions and new sanctions, the revisions affecting the detailed figures, while the *ṣūba* totals were overlooked.

Despite these inconsistencies, and possible incompleteness, the *Ā'īn's* figures of *suyurghāl* may still serve as rough indicators of its size. In relation to the total *jama'*, they are highest in the upper Gangetic provinces: 5.4 per cent in Dehli, 5.2 in Ilahabad, 4.2 in Awadh, and 3.9 in Agra. They fall off to 1.8 per cent in Lahor and Gujarat.[82] For the seventeenth century, no statistics of any kind concerning these grants are available for the whole empire, but we possess some information about Gujarat, through the *Mir'āt-i Aḥmadī*. This shows that there was no great change in the proportion of the revenues alienated through the grants, between the time of the *Ā'īn* and the reign of Muḥammad Shāh.[83] This should not be taken to mean that the proportion of the grants

[78] This is definitively established by Moosvi, 154-5, 169-72. That a record of these reductions was kept is shown by the revenue accounts of a *pargana*, reproduced by the *Dastūru-l 'Amal-i 'Ālamgīrī*, ff.126b-128b, the *jama'* of the *pargana* being put at Rs 6,058 from which Rs 20 are deducted as *a'imma-mu'āfī*.

[79] Cf. Moosvi, 155-8.

[80] "The income (*ḥāṣil*) from each *bīgha* [under *suyūrghāl*] is different in each locality (*qaṣba*); but does not fall below one rupee" (*Ā'īn*, I, 199). The same estimated rate of income from *madad-i ma'āsh* for Gujarat is used (1615) in *Ma'āṣir-i Raḥīmī*, II, 609.

[81] For these variations, see Moosvi, 159.

[82] Under Agra and Gujarat, the figures given in the *Ā'īn* for the province are inconsistent with those given under the individual *sarkārs*. I have, therefore, used the totals of the *sarkār* figures in both cases. Cf. Moosvi, 159.

[83] *Mir'āt*, I, 25-26: "1,20,00,000 *dāms*; 50,000 *bīghas* of land; and 103 villages; and Rs 40,000 in cash from the treasury – excluding the *in'āms* given by officials out of their *jāgīrs* – were assigned in *madad-i ma'āsh* and *in'ām*... in

to the total revenue remained uniformly static. For we know that a few years after the *Ā'īn's* statistics were compiled, Akbar ordered all grants in Gujarat to be reduced by half;[84] thus the next century really saw this reduction being fully restored.

There is no reason to believe that Gujarat was an exceptional case; and it will, therefore, be unsafe to assume that the period after Akbar saw any great enlargement of the area of the grants. The *Ā'īn* figures, read in relation to the total revenues, are, therefore, probably valid for the whole period. The modest percentages which represent the extent of revenue grants in the various provinces show that they could have covered only a very small portion of the total cultivated area of the empire. This should prevent anyone being misled, from the details discussed in this chapter, into supposing that the class of grantees had a very important position in the agrarian society of the time, or that they could have contributed appreciably to the increase in cultivation, or even that their presence interfered very greatly with the general pattern of land-revenue administration.

This impression is not much altered, even if we add to the number of imperial grantees, that of the beneficiaries of grants made by *jāgīrdārs*. There was nothing to prevent a *jāgīrdār* from declaring a particular area of land tax-free during the term of his own assignment.[85] These grants also commonly bore the designation of *madad-i ma'āsh* or *a'imma*, though other names might be used.[86]

---

accordance with imperial *farmāns*", etc. The figure of 1,20,00,000 *dāms* may be compared with the total of Gujarat *sarkār* figures of *suyūrghāl* in the *Ā'īn*, viz. 76,19,974 *dāms*. But the *jama'* had risen in the intervening period, so that the *Mir'āt's* figure came to 1.5 per cent of the *jama'dāmī* given by it for the whole province. As for the area, if we take the *Mir'āt's* area of grants to be stated in *bīgha-i Ilāhī*, and the area of cultivable land in *bīgha-i daftarī*, the former stood to the latter in the ratio of a little under 1 to 100. The number of villages held in grants may be compared with the total of 10,465 villages in the whole province, yielding about the same percentage as for the area.

[84] See a *ḥukm* of Khān-i Khānān, 48th year of Akbar: Doc.3 in Modi's *Parsees at the Court of Akbar.*

[85] Examples of such grants are offered by a *jāgīrdār's parwāna* to his *shiqqdār* in *pargana* Sandila, AD 1580 (I.O. 4433); Todar Mal's grant of 100 *bīghas* to a priest of Madan Mohan temple, Vrindaban, 1584 (Radhakund 154); *parwāna* of 1614 making a grant of 125 *bīghas* from the grantor's *jāgīr* in *pargana* Narauli (facsimile reprod. by Maḥmūd Ahmad, *Tārīkh-i Amroha*, facing p. 264); a *parwāna* of 1648, from a *jāgīrdār* granting a village to a Muslim divine out of the grantor's "share of the *jāgīr*" (Bhojpur Coll. B, 2); and a *chaknāma* of 1676-77, demarcating land of grant based on the *parwāna* issued by the *amīn* of the *maḥal* of a *jāgīrdār* (Bilhaur Docs.).

[86] Todar Mal described his grant of 1584 to Gopāldās as *khairāt* (charity gift)

The *jāgīrdārs* could also set some special terms and conditions.[87] Since a *jāgīrdār* could make a grant only for his own term of assignment, which seldom lasted beyond three or four years,[88] the grantees of this class lived in the greatest insecurity. A new *jāgīrdār* might or might not confirm the grant made by his predecessor, though it was probably customary to do so.[89] We read of the distress caused in Bengal when, on the instructions of its governor, Mīr Jumla (1660-63), all grants not derived from imperial orders were resumed both in the *jāgīrs* and the *khāliṣa*. The former grantees were asked to cultivate the land and pay the revenue like ordinary peasants. In the end, however, the next governor, Shā'ista Khān ruled that each *jāgīrdār* should allow such people to retain their grants, if the revenue so lost to him did not exceed 2½ per cent of the total revenue of his assignment.[90] Later in Aurangzeb's reign we come across revenue officials in Sorath (Gujarat) resuming all grants based upon the *sanads* of the previous governors and *jāgīrdārs* and insisting that the grants could be honoured only if they were backed by imperial *sanads*.[91] It is, therefore, hardly surprising that the revenues claimed by such grantees could fall well below 2½ per cent, as in the case Bengal that we have just considered; or that these grantees should be anxious to convert the *jāgīrdārs*' grants into imperial grants in order to be free of the constant threat of resumption at each new *jāgīr* assignment.[92]

The autonomous chiefs were free in their territories to make

(Radhakund 154). Citing the same *parwāna*, Jahāngīr's *farmān* of 1613 (Radhakund 166) says Todar Mal had made the grant "by way of *madad-i ma'āsh*".

[87] Diler Khān, while confirming a grant in favour of two sons of the deceased grantee in 1678, forbade the latter from interfering with the houses and cultivated lands held by anyone within the granted villages previous to the grant (*Nāma-i Muẓaffarī*, II, 151-2).

[88] Manuchy tells us, for example, that he obtained from the Mughal deputy governor of the Karnatak the grant of "the income of two villages and their hamlets to be held during the whole time he governed the province" (Manucci, III, 288).

[89] For two *parwānas* of *jāgīrdārs*, of 1683 and 1703, confirming grants that were held on the basis of "the *sanads* of the previous officials [assignees] (*ḥukkām-i sābiq*)," see *Nāma-i Muẓaffarī*, II, 146, 162. The *Riyāẓu-l Wadād* of Īzid Bakhsh Rasā (Or. 1725, f.12a) contains a letter from him to a *jāgīrdār*, recommending that the *madad-i ma'āsh* land held by a friend of his in the other's *jāgīr* be confirmed.

[90] *Fatḥiya-i 'Ibriya*, ff.117b-121a.

[91] *Mir'āt*, I, 319.

[92] Jahāngīr's *farmān* of 8 R.Y. (Rādhākund 143A; copy, Rādhākund 166) recites how the current *sevak* of Madan Mohan temple, successfully "petitioned and prayed for an imperial *farmān*" for the 100 *bīghas* granted to his predecessor by Todar

revenue grants. Rāja Jaswant Singh of Jodhpur used to remit the revenue to Brahmans, Chārans (bards) and falconers on the lands they tilled.[93] Rāja Anirudh Singh of Bundi in 1689-90 gave an entire village in "*madad-i ma'āsh*" to a member of the retinue of the Chishti shrine at Ajmer, the grant being of such permanence as to be recorded on a copper plate.[94] Ordinary *zamīndārs* also made grants, presumably out of the revenue-free lands held by them in *mālikana* and *nānkār*. Some were made in lieu of service,[95] but others out of charity only. The latter type is divided by a late eighteenth-century revenue glossary into two categories: *pīrpāl*, grants made by *zamīndārs* to their old retainers, and *brahmotar*, grants made to Brahmans.[96]

Mal (as *jāgīrdār*), which equalled 89 *bīghas* 2 *biswas* by *gaz-i Ilāhī*. A similar *farmān* by Aurangzeb, R.Y. 25, converts a grant by a *sanad* of Diler Khān (the *jāgīrdār*) into an imperial grant, since the recipient of Diler Khān's bounty had now "petitioned for an imperial *farmān*" (*Nāma-i Muẓaffarī*, I, 82-5). For reference to an imperial order of Aurangzeb's time, discouraging resumption by new assignees, whether the *khāliṣa* or *jāgīrdārs*, of long-held non-imperial grants, see *ṣadr's* note on Bhojpur Coll. B, 2, the main document being dated 1648.

[93] *Waqā'i' Ajmer*, 318. This is with regard to the *pargana* of Merta. When after Rāja Jaswant Singh's death Aurangzeb ordered the occupation of his territory, the imperial revenue officials disregarded the remissions granted by the Rāja.

[94] *Asnādu-ṣ Ṣanādīd*, 250.

[95] Thus Bekas, f.52b, speaks of the retainers of the *zamīndārs*, paid by grant of land or in cash. In two Awadh documents (Allahabad 279 and 280) we come across the grant of 50 *bīghas* in a village as *khidmatāna* (from *khidmat*, service) in return for the grantee's keeping watch over the *khaṣmāna* (i.e. the rights of the grantors) of the village. Neither the two original grantors nor the widow of one of them, who confirms their grant in the second document, states the nature of their own right over the village. They were probably its *zamīndārs*; but they could possibly have been *madad-i ma'āsh* holders as well (cf. Allahabad 296).

[96] Yāsīn, Add. 6603, f.51a-b. He tells us that the land given away by *zamīndārs* in charity was known as *ba'ẓī zamīn*. Yāsīn had experience of revenue administration of Dehli and Bengal; and, therefore, the terms *brahmotar* (or, as also spelt, *brahnmotar*) and *pīrpāl*, defined by him, were probably used in both regions. When he defines *bishn-parīt* (land dedicated to Vishnu and granted to Brahmans by *zamīndārs*), he is careful to note that this term existed only in Bengal (f.51b). A *sanad* in Nagari, of AD 1585, records the grant of *bishn-parīt* by Mukund Rām Sen, a local raja of Purnea, to a Vaishnavite divine, Sant Rām Gosāin (Datta, 81, no.352).

CHAPTER IX

THE AGRARIAN CRISIS OF THE MUGHAL EMPIRE

1. THE EMPIRE AND THE ASSIGNMENT SYSTEM

For a hundred and fifty years the Mughal Empire covered a whole subcontinent, united under a highly centralized administration. To what did it owe its great success? The development of firearms has been regarded by some authorities as the underlying cause of the formation of the great Asian empires of the sixteenth century.[1] The adequacy of this explanation in the case of the Indian Mughals may, however, be doubted. Artillery was not the decisive arm of their army and they were never able to employ it successfully against really strong forts. Their main strength initially lay in their cavalry, or rather mounted archers, and it was in the battle in the open field, and in rapid movements, that they remained invincible, until, that is, the Marathas found an answer in scattered and decentralized warfare, and muskets at long last (in the eighteenth century) replaced the bow and arrow as the soldier's main weapon, to give infantry a major advantage.[2] The principal obligation of the *manṣabdārs* was the maintenance of cavalry contingents with horses of standard breeds. There was, therefore, an intimate connexion between the military power of the Mughals and the system of *jāgīrs* or territorial assignments by which the *manṣabdārs* and their contingents were maintained. It was the great merit of the latter system that it made the *manṣabdārs* completely dependent upon the will of the emperor, so that the imperial government was able to assemble and despatch them with their contingents to any point at any time, whenever the need arose. Once the initial territorial advantage had been established, none of the provincial kingdoms could withstand the concentrated pressure of Mughal power. Akbar undoubtedly built partly upon the foundations of

[1] See V. Barthold, *Iran*, tr. G.K. Nariman, 142-3. The argument is further developed in Marshall G.S. Hodgson, *The Venture of Islam*, III, 17-27.

[2] On the issue of the bow-and-arrow *vs*. musket, see M. Athar Ali, introd. to *The Mughal Nobility under Aurangzeb*, revised edn., Delhi, 1997, xix-xx. Iqtidar Alam Khan has studied the nature and dissemination of handguns in Mughal India in his *Gunpowder and Firearms: Warfare in Medieval India*, New Delhi, 2004, pp.128-90.

the administration created by the Sūrs, but his own contribution to the creation of a centralized government was the most crucial. As he forged the main features of the assignment and *manṣab* system, and systematized provincial administration, he gave shape to a centralized apparatus through which an absolute monarchy could function.[3] There was one great struggle in protest from one section of the nobility – the revolt of 1580[4], – but once it had been quelled, the empire never really faced a serious revolt from within the ranks of its own ruling class. The major upheavals were caused by the wars of succession, which did not by themselves endanger the Mughal throne. Indeed, the very fact that neither in 1658-59 nor in 1707-09 could the partition of the empire be countenanced by the contenders reveals the great degree of cohesion in its basic structure. There were stresses and strains, it is true, within the various ethnic and caste elements forming the Mughal nobility;[5] and Aurangzeb's policy of religious discrimination possibly contributed to the Rājpūt revolt of 1679-80.[6] But even the effects of this revolt were relatively short-lived, and the Rajputs generally returned to their old allegiance.[7]

[3] As late as Aurangzeb's time it was recognized in the official history that Akbar was "the renovator of the rules of sovereignty and the architect of the regulations of this eternal state" (*'Ālamgīrnāma*, 387). The authority actually exercised by the Mughal emperor could lead Abū-l Faẓl to claim that "Royalty is a light emanating from God, a ray from the World-illuminating Sun" (*Ā'īn*, I, 2).

[4] The revolt in Bengal and Bihar was provoked by the imposition of the branding regulations and the reduction in the concession previously granted to the officers stationed there in allowing for a deterioration in the quality of the horses (*A.N.*, III, 284-6, 291-3; *Ṭabaqāt-i Akbarī*, II, 348-50; Monserrate, 68-69).

[5] Mirzā Ḥakīm is said to have vainly hoped, in 1581, to benefit from the disloyalty of the Īrānī and Tūrānī nobles and the cowardice of the Afghāns, Rājpūts and Shaikhzādas (Indian Muslims) serving under Akbar (*A.N.*, III, 366). Jahāngīr is reproached by Azīz Koka of discriminating against the Chaghatāī (Tūrānī) and Rājpūt nobles, while favouring the Khurāsānīs (Īrānīs) and Shaikhzādas. (*'Arẓdāsht-hā-i Muẓaffar*, f.19a-b. Cf. also Hawkins, *Early Travels*, 106-7). Shāhjahān seems to have been suspicious of the Afghāns (*Ādāb-i 'Ālamgīrī*, f.154a; ed., I, 604-5; *Dilkushā*, f.84a), while he had been critical of Aurangzeb's hostility, as a prince, to the Rājpūts (*Ādāb-i 'Ālamgīrī*, ff.37b-38a; ed., I, 146; *Ruq'āt-i 'Ālamgīr*, 114-5).

[6] Cf. M. Athar Ali, *Mughal Nobility under Aurangzeb*, 99-101.

[7] The fact that Akbar aimed at a religiously and ethnically composite nobility, without allowing any one faction to become too powerful, is noted in as early a work as the famous *Dabistān-i Maẕāhib* (*c.*1655), 431-2. The most comprehensive data yet on the various ethnic and religious groups composing the Mughal nobility are provided by M. Athar Ali in *Apparatus of Empire: Awards of Ranks, Offices and Titles to the Mughal Nobility, 1574-1658*, and *Mughal Nobility under Aurangzeb.*

The assignment system, as it was established and worked under the Great Mughals, necessarily presupposed the prevalence of a certain type of economic order. The *jāgīrs* were divorced, as far as possible, from any permanent rights to the land, and were essentially assignments of revenue, assessed in terms of money. This suited best an economy where the cash nexus was well established; but that in turn meant that agrarian trade should have been both brisk and extensive.[8] We have seen in Chapters II and VI that both these conditions were present in Mughal India. At the same time, commercial activity could prosper best under an imperial system with its uniform methods of tax collection and administration and its control of the routes. In so far, therefore, as the assignment system strengthened imperial power it also reinforced the economic foundations of its own existence. Unlike the feudal lord of Western Europe, the Mughal *jāgīrdār* might not have needed to harbour any fear of money and trade undermining his power.

2. OPPRESSION OF THE PEASANTRY

The unity and cohesion of the Mughal ruling class found its practical expression in the absolute power of the emperor. The *jāgīrdār* as an individual member of the governing class had theoretically no rights or privileges apart from those received from the emperor: he could not manage his *jāgīr* just as he pleased, and was required to conform to imperial regulations. The rate of the land revenue demand and the methods by which it was to be assessed and collected were all prescribed by the imperial administration.[1] The emperor also decreed what other taxes were to be collected.[2] The conduct of the *jāgīrdār* and his agents was supposed to be watched over and checked by officials such as *qānūngos* and *chaudhurīs*, and *faujdārs* and news-writers.[3]

Not all, nor even most, Rājpūt houses participated in the revolt of 1679-80 and Rājpūt contingents fought for the Mughal cause in the Dakhin. It is also apt to be forgotten that their position was largely restored after the death of Aurangzeb and the initial struggle with Bahādur Shāh I. In this the policy of the Saiyid brothers, who also had the *jizya* abolished, is particularly noteworthy. (See Satish Chandra, *Parties and Politics at the Mughal Court, 1707-1740*, 128-9, 166.)

[8] See W.C. Smith in *Islamic Culture* (1944), 358-9, for perhaps the first long comment on the economic implications of the prevalence of the cash nexus in Mughal India. Similar observations by K. Antanova in a Russian publication of 1957 are cited in V.I. Pavlov, *The Indian Capitalist Class: A Historial Study*, 10.

[1] Chapter VII, Section 2.

[2] Chapter VI, Section 7.

[3] Chapter VII, Section 2.

Imperial revenue policy was obviously shaped by two basic considerations. First, since military contingents were maintained by the *manṣabdārs* out of the revenues of their *jāgīrs,* the tendency was to set the revenue demand so high as to secure the greatest military strength for the empire. But, secondly, it was clear that if the revenue rate was raised so high as to leave the peasant not enough for his survival, the revenue collections could soon fall in absolute terms. The revenue demand as set by the imperial authorities was thus designed ideally to approximate to the surplus produce, leaving the peasant just the barest minimum needed for subsistence.[4]

It was this appropriation of the surplus produce that created the great wealth of the Mughal ruling class. The contrast was accordingly striking between "the rich in their great superfluity and the utter subjection and poverty of the common people".[5]

There seems, moreover, to have been a tendency, increasing in its effect with time, to press still harder upon the peasant. This tendency seemed to derive from the very nature of the *jāgīr* system. The imperial administration, which could contemplate the long-term interests of the empire and the ruling class, might even aspire to set a limit to the revenue demand. As we have seen in Chapter VI, the suggestion that a great increase in revenue demand was sanctioned by it in the course of the seventeenth century is based on an oversimplified view of the evidence; and there are indications that the increase in the cash rates did not outstrip the increase in the prices of agricultural produce.[6] But there was an element of contradiction between the interests of the imperial administration and the individual *jāgīrdār*. A *jāgīrdār*, whose assignment was liable to be transferred any moment and who never held the same *jāgīr* for more than three or four years at the most, could have no interest in following a far-sighted policy of agricultural development.[7] On the other hand, his personal interests

[4] Chapter VI, Section 1.

[5] Pelsaert, 60. Cf. Bernier, 230: "The country is ruined by the necessity of defraying the enormous charges required to maintain the splendour of a numerous court, and to pay a large army maintained for keeping the people in subjection. No adequate idea can be conveyed of the sufferings of that people. The cudgel and the whip compel them to incessant labour for the benefit of others."

[6] Chapter VI, Section 1.

[7] A recommendation made by Mīr Fatḥullāh Shīrāzī to Akbar was obviously inspired by the desire to offer some incentive to the *jāgīrdār* to improve the condition of his charge. It was proposed that if any assignee made his *iqṭā'* (*jāgīr*)

would sanction any act of oppression that conferred an immediate benefit upon him, even if it ruined the peasantry and so destroyed the revenue-paying capacity of that area for a long time.

This explains what a near-contemporary historian said of the doings of an influential noble, Murtaẓā Khān Bukhārī (d.1616), who had been one of Akbar's most powerful ministers: "He showed no compassion to the peasants *(ri'āyā)*. He expected his revenue collectors to raise the assessments *(jama')* by fifty per cent. If owing to this cause the peasants took to flight, he surrendered that *jāgīr* to take another bringing him gain in the exchange."[8] Yūsuf Mīrak, *c.*1634, similarly speaks of oppressive *jāgīrdārs*, who after devastating their *jāgīrs*, sustained no loss since they were then assigned other *jāgīrs*.[9]

European observers, beginning with J. Xavier (1609), Hawkins (1611) and Manrique (1640-41), ascribe similar conduct to Mughal nobles and revenue officers;[10] but it is Bernier whose argument is the most spirited. He describes the individual assignees' outlook in a well known passage (1660s):

> The Timariots [Bernier's term for the *jāgīrdārs*], Governors and Revenue-contractors on their part reason in this manner: "Why should the neglected state of this land create uneasiness in our minds? and why should we expend our money and time to render it fruitful? We may be deprived of it in a single moment, and our exertions would benefit neither ourselves nor our children. Let us draw from the soil all the money we can though the peasant should starve or abscond and we should leave it, when commanded to quit, a dreary wilderness."[11]

Owing to the constant and unpredictable transfers of *jāgīrs*,

---

populous (*ābād*) and increased its revenue, his rank was to be raised, so that by getting additional pay he might enjoy the fruits of his efforts (*A.N.*, III, 459). Much later we find Aurangzeb recommending a promotion for Rāo Karan on the ground that he had relinquished his previous *jāgīr* in a very improved condition (*Ādāb-i 'Alāmgīrī*, ff.36b-37a; ed., I, 142; *Ruq'āt-i 'Ālamgīr*, 112-3). It is clear that if a *jāgīrdār* was not promoted, any effort on his part to improve his *jāgīr* would not bring him any gain.

[8] *Zakhīratu'l Khawānīn*, I, 145-6; Aligarh MS, f.26a.

[9] *Maẓhar-i Shāhjahānī*, 52.

[10] Writing in 1609, Jerome Xavier noted that since the assignments were held at the king's pleasure, "during the time that someone holds certain lands he squeezes out of them whatever he can and the poor labourers desert them and run away" (tr. Hosten, *JASB*, N.S., XXIII (1927), 121. See Hawkins, *Early Travels*, 114, and Manrique, II, 272.

[11] Bernier, 227. The use of the term "timariot" for *jāgīrdār* is a piece of harmless Turkicism on Bernier's part; he identifies the Mughal "jah-ghir" with the Ottoman "timar" on p. 224.

Bhīmsen tells us late in Aurangzeb's reign, the agents of the *jāgīrdārs* had given up the practice of helping the peasantry (*ra'īyat parwarī*) or making firm arrangements (*istiqlāl*). Moreover, the *'āmils* of the *jāgīrdārs* were not sure of their own tenures of employment and so, "proceeding tyrannically", were unrelenting in the collection of revenue.[12] When the *jāgīrdār*, instead of appointing his own agents to collect the revenue, farmed out the *jāgīr*, the evil was worse still. The land was being laid waste, says Ṣādiq Khān, writing of Shāhjahān's reign, through bribery and revenue farming, as a result of which the peasantry was being robbed and plundered.[13]

These statements show that in the seventeenth century the belief had become deep-rooted that the system of *jāgīr* transfers led inexorably to a reckless exploitation of the peasantry. It was a result which the imperial administration might check for some time but could not ultimately prevent. As the imperial regulations stood, they left a considerable field of discretion to the *jāgīrdārs*. They might or might not give remissions or advance loans or otherwise help the peasants to tide over unfavourable seasons. Or, they might insist on realizing the revenue even before the harvest was cut.[14] But the regulations themselves could also be simply violated or evaded in practice. Some *jāgīrdārs* of Gujarat, according to a *farmān* of Aurangzeb (1665), were trying to extort more than the whole produce in revenue by the simple expedient of estimating the yield at two and a half times the actual one;[15] in such circumstances imperial regulations must often have been followed on paper only. Similarly, it was alleged that Aurangzeb's order prohibiting the imposition of numerous taxes by the *jāgīrdārs* was largely ineffective.[16]

It was inevitable that the actual burden on the peasantry should become so heavy in some areas as to encroach upon their means of survival. The collection of revenue of this magnitude from peasants, who had "no possessions or assets from which to pay",[17] could

[12] *Dilkushā*, f.139a.

[13] Ṣādiq Khān, Or.174, f.10b, Or.1671, f.6b. See also Khāfī Khān, I, 157-8, for the oppression of the *'āmils* in his own day (1731). Sometimes the agents of the *jāgīrdārs* were no better than common robbers, who carried out depredations upon the country around. Thus we find the *faujdār* of Baiswāra complaining of the lawlessness in "the *jāgīr* of 'Azīz Khān, whose agent Maḥmūd commands an army of robbers" (*Inshā-i Roshan Kalām*, f.24b; also ff.11b-12b, 40b-41b). Cf. also *Aḥkām-i 'Ālamgīrī*, f.90b.

[14] Chapter VI, Section 6. [15] *Mir'āt*, I, 263. [16] Khāfī Khān, II, 88-89.

[17] Manrique, II, 272.

not be a refined process. When the "arrayatos" (*ra'īyat*, peasants) could not pay the revenue, says Manrique, they were "beaten unmercifully and maltreated".[18] Manuchy, who on this occasion assumes the viewpoint of the ruling class, declares that "it is the peasants' habit to go on refusing payment, asserting that they have no money. The chastisements and instruments [of torture] are very severe. They are also made to endure hunger and thirst... They feign death (as sometimes really happens)... But this trick secures them no compassion..."[19]

Frequently, therefore, the peasants were compelled to sell their women, children and cattle in order to meet the revenue demand.[20] But the enslavement was not generally so voluntary as even this. "Villages," we are told, "which owing to some shortage of produce, are unable to pay the full amount of the revenue-farm, are made prize, so to speak, by their masters and governors, and wives and children sold on the pretext of a charge of rebellion."[21] "They (the peasants) are carried off, attached to heavy iron chains, to various markets and fairs (to be sold), with their poor, unhappy wives behind them carrying their small children in their arms, all crying and lamenting their evil plight."[22]

Failure to pay the revenue was not the only cause for which such punishment was inflicted upon the peasants. It was the general law in the Mughal Empire that if any robbery occurred within the assignment or jurisdiction, respectively, of a *jāgīrdār* or a *faujdār*, he was obliged to either trace the culprits and recover the loot, or make the restitution himself.[23] This was, perhaps, not an unwelcome duty in that it offered the potentates an excuse to sack any village they chose to suspect. The men were killed in such cases, says Mundy, and "the rest, with women and children, are carried away and sold for Slaves".[24] A petition to the imperial court shows that a village which had been once guilty of violence,

[18] Ibid. [19] Manucci, II, 450-51.

[20] Badāūnī, II, 189; *Maẓhar-i Shāhjahānī*, 21; Manucci, II, 451.

[21] Pelsaert, 47. [22] Manrique, II, 272. Cf. Bernier, 205.

[23] See Chapter II, Section 1.

[24] Mundy, 73-4. He says the villages were in most cases unable to prevent the thieves from establishing themselves in their midst and adds that those affected by the *faujdārs'* punitive expeditions were "sometymes... Innocent". These remarks are made in the course of a journey across the Doāb (1631). In Gujarat Shā'ista Khān is denounced in *Factories, 1646-50*, 127, for "his unheard of tiranie in depopulating whole townes [villages] of miserably pore people, under pretence of there harbouring theives and rogues (whilst those that are such may walke untoucht at noone day)".

remained ever onwards subject to depredations by *faujdārs*, who carried away both the cattle and the peasants.[25] Abū-l Faẓl says candidly that Akbar's orders prohibiting the seizure and sale of the women and children of combatants were issued because "many evil-hearted, avaricious men, either merely from ill-founded suspicion or only from a false imputation of disloyalty or because of sheer greed, make their way to the villages and *maḥals* of the countrymen and put them to sack. On being questioned they offer a thousand excuses and attempt delay or evasion."[26]

There is a continuous stream of statements in our authorities to the effect that the oppression increased with the passage of time, cultivation fell off and the number of absconding peasants grew. J. Xavier declared that both in Gujarat and Kashmir the Mughal conquest had greatly increased the misery of the rural population: "The lands are much spoiled which at an earlier period were taken by the Mogores: for they destroy everything with their oppressions."[27] In the central regions of the empire, Akbar's *'karorī* experiment' (1574) is said to have brought about such oppression as to have "dispersed" the peasants in various "directions" with a consequent fall in the revenues.[28]

In Jahāngīr's reign the peasants were "so cruelly and pitilessly oppressed" that "the fields lie unsown and grow into wildernesses".[29] Thus, says another observer, "the poor labourers desert them (the lands) and run away which is the reason why they are poorly peopled".[30] And yet the historian of the next reign declares

[25] *Durru-l 'Ulūm*, f.56a-b. This village was situated in the area around the Lakhi Jungle and the peasants belonged to the caste of Dogars.

[26] *A.N.*, II, 159-60. The *Siyāqnāma*, 88, contains a deed of sale of a woman who had been seized by a *faujdār* from a village reported to be in rebellion: she was accepted by a servant or trooper of his in lieu of his pay and then sold for Rs 40.

[27] This is said in respect of Gujarat in 1615 (letter transl. Hosten, *JASB*, N.S., XXIII, 125). When he visited Kashmir in 1597, he noted: "it is very much uncultivated and even depopulated from the time that this King (Akbar) took it and governs it through his captains, who tyrannise over it... and bleed the people by their extortions... And they say that before this King they were all sufficiently provided with food... Now everything is wanting for there are no cultivators on account of the violence done them" (ibid., 116).

Writing in 1634 the author of *Maẓhar-i Shāhjahānī*, 52, believed that Thatta (Sind) was happier under the Tarkhāns than under the succeeding *jāgīrdārs* appointed by the Mughals.

[28] Badāūnī, II, 189.

[29] Pelsaert, 47.

[30] Xavier's letter from Agra, 1609, transl. Hosten, op.cit., 121. See also the reference to the flight of peasants from their lands because of oppression, in Navsari (Gujarat), in the early years of Jahāngīr's reign, in *Dastur Kaikobad Mahyar's*

that "owing to natural calamities, the rebellions of seditious *zamīndārs* and the cruelty of ill-fated officials", vast lands became completely depopulated, and, despite the efforts of the emperor [Shāhjahān] and his able ministers, "the land appeared more desolate than during the time of Jannat Makānī (Jahāngīr)".[31] In Gujarat, a Dutch traveller noted in 1629 that "the peasants are more oppressed than formerly (and) frequently abscond", so that the revenues had fallen.[32] In 1634 we are told of Sehwan (Sind) that it had become the "land of the forsaken, of the cruel and the helpless", through the oppression of the *jāgīrdārs*.[33]

In the Dakhin the period preceding Aurangzeb's arrival as viceroy (1652) saw desolation stalking the land and the peasants "scattered", owing to "the oppression and neglect of the provincial governors".[34]

What the conditions were during the early years of Aurangzeb's reign may be judged from Bernier's long discourse on the ills of the Mughal Empire. He too declares that "a considerable portion of the good land remains untilled from the want of peasants", many of whom "perish in consequence of the bad treatment they receive from the Governors", or are left no choice but to "abandon the country".[35]

Finally, writing in 1731 in the early years of Muḥammad Shāh's reign – the twilight days of the Mughal empire – Khāfi Khān drew the following picture of the conditions of the peasantry and the decline in cultivation:

It is clear to the wise and experienced that now, according to the ways of the time, thoughtfulness in managing the affairs of state, (and the practice of) protecting the peasantry and encouraging the prosperity of the country and increase in produce, have all departed. Revenue collectors, who take the revenues on farm, having spent considerable amounts at the imperial court (to obtain it), proceed to the *maḥals* and become a scourge for the revenue-paying peasantry... Since they have no confidence that they will be confirmed in their office the next year, nay, even for the whole of the current year, they seize both parts of the produce [the state's share as well as the peasants'] and sell them away. It is a God-fearing

Petition and Laudatory Poem, ed. J.J. Modi, 13.

31 Ṣādiq Khān, Or. 174, f.10a-b; Or. 1671, f.6b.

32 Geleynssen, tr. Moreland, *JIH*, IV, 78.

33 *Maẓhar-i Shāhjahānī*, 173-4.

34 *Ādāb-i 'Ālamgīrī*, ff.26b, 30b-31a, 34a; *Ruq'āt-i 'Ālamgīr*, 69, 70, 84, 91.

35 Bernier, 205; also 226-27. The word "labourers" in this translation stands for "laboureurs" in the original, which really meant peasants in French usage (cf. Moreland, *Agrarian System*, 147n).

man, indeed, who limits himself to this and does not sell away the bullocks and carts (of the peasants), on which tillage depends, or, not contenting himself with extorting the amount of his expenses at the court, of his troopers and of the deficit on his pledge, does not sell away whatever remains with the peasantry, down to fruit-bearing trees and their proprietary and hereditary (rights in) land... Many *parganas* and townships, which used to yield full revenue, have, owing to the oppression of the men in authority (*ḥukkām*), been so far ruined and devastated that they have become forests infested by tigers and lions; and the villages are so utterly ruined and desolate that there is no sign of habitation on the routes. Although from greed and the ways of these evil times, the country becomes devastated every day and peasants are crushed by the oppression and cruelty of ill-fated revenue collectors, (while) the *jāgīrdārs* have to bear the scourge of the groans of the women and children of the oppressed peasants, the cruelty, oppression and injustice of the officials, who have no thought of God, has reached such a degree that if one wishes to describe a hundredth part of it, it will still defy description.[36]

One has here to take into account the universal human propensity to contrast the grim present with a rosier past. But no allowance made for such propensity can justify our neglecting the cumulative force of the statements we have just quoted, particularly since there is little other evidence by which it can be directly contradicted.

It is true that the area figures of Aurangzeb's reign generally exceed those of the *Ā'īn*, but, as has been explained in Chapter I, measurement having been extended in the intervening period to land previously unsurveyed, the larger figures do not necessarily imply a corresponding extension of cultivation. There are a few areas where land reclamation appears to have taken place on a large scale in Mughal times, such as the eastern portions of deltaic Bengal and parts of the Tarai.[37] But the development of one tract might well have been accompanied by varying degrees of desolation of previously cultivated land in other areas, so that a large net advance in cultivation cannot be established from the very limited number of reports of successful local reclamations.

[36] Khāfī Khān, I, 157-8. Khāfī Khān probably wrote this portion in or before 1720-21, although he completed his work in 1731. (See Storey, I, 468 & n.) In the passage translated here the text in the printed edition seems partly corrupt. For instance, the words "and peasants" are inserted after "greed" at the beginning of the last sentence. This is presumably due to a misreading of the original.

[37] See Chapter I, Section 1. In Bengal the reclamation followed Shā'ista Khān's successful expedition against Arakan. In the Tarai the most extensive clearing made in the Mughal period seems to have been that of the *maḥals* of Kant and Gola.

Revenue statistics may be thought of as another set of data relevant for our purpose. When Lāhorī singled out the first twenty years of Shāhjahān's reign (1628-47) as a period of "the abundant nourishing of the peasantry, the growth of populousness and increase in prosperity", he added that this was reflected in the increase of the *jama*'. In the old territories where the *jama*' was 700 crore *dāms* in 1628, there was an overall increase of 100 crores – despite the devastating famine of 1630-32, which had reduced the *jama*' in Gujarat and the Dakhin provinces.[38] But the question is whether the *jama*' enhancement was really reflective of an increase in cultivation, or whether an illusory prosperity was invoked to justify an increase in the *jama*', whereby, in fact, the real income of the *jāgīrdārs* had merely been reduced, with their *hāṣil* (actual tax realization) becoming an even smaller proportion of the *jama*' than formerly.[38a] There is, beyond this, the question as to how far the increase in *jama*' was due to price changes.[39] It is, therefore, not possible for one to infer just from an increase of one-seventh in the *jama*' over a twenty year period, that cultivation too extended at the same rate, unless some elucidation is forthcoming on how the *jama*' was determined and what happened to prices.

Price changes, at least, are a phenomenon to which *jama*' statistics must be adjusted before any further queries are set. This can be done by juxtaposing *jama*' changes over a long period (seventeenth century) to data about prices. Accordingly, in Tables 9.1 and 9.2 we present in an indexed form the *jama*'*dāmī* statistics for the period until the death of Aurangzeb (1707), based on the data collected in Appendix D, and attempt price indices based on material in Chapter II, Section 3, and Appendix C.

While the indexed *jama*' rose in the empire (excluding the Dakhin) by about 78 per cent between 1595-96 and 1707, gold prices rose by nearly 50 per cent with copper falling to less than half and then recovering, and commodity prices probably doubled in the

[38] Lāhorī, II, 711-12.

[38a] Cf. a verse of Mirzā Uvais Beg (1650) quoted in *Zakhīratu-l Khawānīn*, III, 75.

[39] Cf. Muzaffar Alam, *Crisis of Empire*, 252-54, where *jama*' figures of varying dates are compared with those of the *Ā'īn* to establish an "increase in agricultural production" in Uttar Pradesh without making any allowance for possible changes in prices. He claims that "over a number of years in Aurangzeb's reign, even in Awadh in most of the *maḥals*, the *hāṣil* approximated [to] the *jama*' figures, while in some *parganas* the former also exceeded the latter"; but the two sources he cites are of a much later time.

Table 9.1
RISE IN JAMA' DĀMĪ
(*Ā'īn*'s figures as base, = 100)

	Empire excl. Dakhin provinces	Bengal and Orissa	Bihar	Ilahabad	Awadh	Agra
1595-96	100.00	100.00	100.00	100.00	100.00	100.00
1605	115.54	97.99	118.41	143.27	113.93	141.05
1627	134.54	116.90	140.91	144.52	115.09	150.57
1628-36	130.00	141.00	136.70	142.80	128.75	141.05
1633-38	147.55	139.68	166.20	170.12	127.98	172.29
1646-47	170.36	163.67	180.25	188.30	148.69	164.76
1667	183.75	168.54	325.25(!)	214.92	158.64	192.53
1690	178.23	156.06	183.48	214.92	159.26	209.01
1709	178.23	156.05	183.48	214.92	159.26	209.02

	Dehli	Lahor	Kashmir	Multan and Sind	Ajmer	Malwa	Gujarat
1595-96	100.00	100.00	100.00	100.00	100.00	100.00	100.00
1605	104.09	115.60		116.74	107.46	106.93	107.40
1627	109.06	147.46		183.86	145.80	116.33	115.93
1628-36	104.09	115.71		152.14*	107.47	107.14	107.59
1633-38	122.89	150.91	192.20	154.32	187.36	150.61	106.06
1646-47	166.22	160.87	241.50	165.47	208.04	166.19	121.33
1667	194.21	162.12	343.04	147.23	220.84	176.77	102.76
1690	203.28	160.54	370.15	130.16	226.30	167.84	104.10
1709	203.28	160.54	370.15	134.76	226.54	167.84	104.10

* Multan province only

Table 9.2
RISE IN PRICES (IN RUPEES)
(*Ain's* prices as base)

Year	Value of minted gold	Value of minted copper	Value of agricultural produce (normal harvests)	Price of Bayana indigo
1595-6	100	100	100 Lahor/Agra	100*
1609	111	50 Gujarat		150
1614	119	39 to 42 Gujarat		
1615			64 to 70, or 78 to 86 Sugar: between Agra and Lahor	
1621	111			
1626	156	60 Agra		
1627				200
1628	142 & 145	80 Gujarat		
1633	138	80 Gujarat		
1636		75 Gujarat		
1637		80 Agra		
1638		69 Agra		
1639			164 Sugar: Lahor	281
1640	144	71 Bengal		
1641-2	156			
1644-5	156			
1646		86 Gujarat	141 Sugar: Agra	263
1651			141 Sugar: Agra	
1653	156			
1656		89 Sind		200
1658	183			
1659	167			
1661	161 to 163	129 Dakhin		
1662	167	125 Gujarat		
		136 Dakhin		
1666	178	119 Gujarat		
1667		123 Gujarat		325
1670	168 & 169	129 Gujarat	285 Wheat: Agra	
1671		133 Patna		
1676	167			
	133 & 122			
1677	153			
1680	138 & 144			
1684	138	86 Gujarat		
1690-93	156	114 Gujarat		
1695	147	127 Gujarat(?)		
1697	146	105 E. Raj.		
1702			285 Wheat: Lahor	

*The *Ā'īn's* maximum price of Rs 16 has been accepted as the base.
Note: This table is based on Chapter II, Section 3, and Appendix C.

central regions. There is, therefore, very little likelihood of the revenue assessments registering any substantial increase in real terms. In the rather unlikely case of the ratio between agricultural production and revenue assessment (adjusted to prices) having remained constant throughout the period, there would still hardly be any reason for postulating an extension of cultivation much beyond the rate of increase in population, estimated on other grounds at a modest 0.21 per cent per annum.[40]

The main fact, attested to, as we have just seen, by a number of contemporary observers, is that the flight of the peasants from their land was a common phenomenon, and that it was apparently growing in momentum with the passage of years. We have argued earlier that, with vast areas still unploughed, peasant migrations were probably a general feature of the agrarian life of our period.[41] Famines, as a rule, initiated wholesale movements of population.[42] But it was the man-made system, which, more than any other factor, lay at the root of the peasant's mobility. Flight alone might save him if the revenue arrears became impossible to pay.[43] He might even be able, when settling down at a new place, to obtain some concessions for bringing land under the plough.[44] It is obviously in respect of such cases that some official orders specially stipulate that peasants to be settled on land not yet under cultivation should be *ghair-jama'ī*, that is they should not previously have been paying revenue anywhere else.[45] Some peasants abandoned agriculture altogether. Bernier says, for example, that some left "the country" to "seek a more tolerable mode of existence either in the towns or in the camps; as bearers of burdens, carriers of water, or servants to horsemen".[46] The urban population was large, relatively speaking, and the countryside must have been the source of the innumerable "peons", and unskilled labourers who filled the

[40] Cf. Moosvi, 405-6. [41] See Chapter IV, Section 1.

[42] See Chapter III, Section 2.

[43] So Kabīr: Just as the physical attributes of man disappear at death, leaving the Soul alone to answer for the deeds done by them, so the peasants (*kirsān*) flee from the village leaving the headman (*mahtau*) by himself to answer for the arrears of revenue (*bāqī*) (*Gurū Granth Sāhib*, Nagari edn., 1104, lines 13-19). Official orders leave us in little doubt that the peasants' flight to evade payment of revenue was a common phenomenon (e.g. Blochet, Suppl. Pers. 482, ff.153a, 181a-182a; *Ādāb-i 'Ālamgīrī*, f.123b; *Nigārnāma-i Munshī*, ff.194b-195a, Bodl., f.145a-b; *Mir'āt*, I, 290-91).

[44] See Chapter VI, Section 8.

[45] *Nigārnāma-i Munshī*, ff.103b-104a, 187a-188a, ed., 81, 143-44.

[46] Bernier, 205.

towns.[47]

Nevertheless, as Manuchy says in the context of south India, the same oppression reigned everywhere, and the lot of the aimless migrant was not a happy one.[48] A point could accordingly arrive where there was no choice left to the peasant but that between starvation or slavery and armed resistance.[49]

3. ARMED RESISTANCE BY THE PEASANTRY

It may be superfluous to say that by inclination the mass of the people were anything but warlike. It is recorded as a peculiarity of Malwa that both the peasants and artisans of the province used to carry arms.[1] Pelsaert (*c.*1626) observed that despite so much misery and want "the people endure patiently, professing that they do not deserve anything better".[2]

Nevertheless, there was a limit to endurance. The classic act of defiance on the part of the peasants was the refusal to pay land revenue. But a particular act of oppression committed against them might also goad them into rebellion.[3] They are also frequently

[47] See Chapter II, Section 2, for the size of towns.

[48] Manucci, III, 47, 51.

[49] Among 18th-century writers Shāh Walīullāh of Dehli (d.1762-63) seems to have been greatly impressed by the connexion between growth of oppression and popular revolts. He thought that the "ruin of countries" in his age was due, first, to the strain on the Treasury from maintaining a large class of idlers. "The second cause," he says, "is the imposition of heavy taxes on the peasants, merchants and artisans, and, then, the oppression inflicted upon them, as a result of which the submissive ones flee and are destroyed and those who have got the strength to do so rise in rebellion. Surely, the peace of the country can only be obtained through reduced taxation" (*Hujjat Allāh al-Bāligha*, ed. Abū Muḥammad 'Abdu-l Ḥaq Ḥaqqānī, I, Karachi, n.d., 94). At another place in the same work he describes the luxurious mode of living at the ancient Persian and Byzantine courts and then adds that the same thing could be seen among "the rulers of countries" of his own time. Such luxury could subsist only on reckless oppression: "To obtain so much wealth it is necessary that the peasants, merchants and artisans be more heavily taxed and be severely treated; and if they do not pay, they are massacred and harmed in various ways; and if they remain obedient, they are kept as asses and oxen that are used for drawing water, ploughing and harvesting" (ibid., I, 225). It should not, however, be forgotten that Shāh Walīullāh's own sympathies were extremely limited. He was quite ready to imitate the Sassanids and the Byzantines in their treatment of peasants and labourers, if these happened to be non-Muslims. In an ideal Islamic order, he declares, the Imām "would put the ignoble Infidels to the task of harvesting the crops, threshing the grain and working at (different) crafts in a submissive and humble condition, like animals made to work in the fields and bear burden" (I, 257).

[1] *Ā'īn*, I, 455; *T.J.* 172. The *Ā'īn* has *baqqāl* (*banya*) instead of "artisan".

[2] Pelsaert, 60.

[3] Manucci, II, 451.

alleged to have taken to robbery; but, on some occasions, at least, they merely robbed Peter in order to pay Paul.[4]

Villages and areas, which thus went into rebellion or refused to pay taxes, were known as *mawās* and *zor-ṭalab*, as opposed to the revenue-paying villages, called *ra'īyatī*.[5] Usually, the villages,

[4] Ra'd-andāz Khān, the *faujdār* of Baiswāra, complains that in a particular *pargana* the villages of the peaceful peasants had been laid waste by "seditious highwaymen" who had started cultivating their lands. Whenever he expelled them they were able to return owing to the avarice of the agents of the *jāgīrdārs*, who apparently found their presence profitable to themselves (*Inshā'-i Roshan Kalām*, f.38a-b).

[5] The word *mawās*, also *mahwās*, is used in the sense of rebellious or non-revenue-paying territory. For instance, a specimen letter from a revenue collector to his *jāgīrdār* reads: "We reached the *pargana* of –. Some of the *chaudhurīs* and *qānūngos* and the peasants from the *ra'īyatī* villages have come, but those who are attached to (or, border upon) the *mawās* have not shown any inclination (to do so).... Sir! This *pargana* is rebellious (*zor-ṭalab*): one part *ra'īyatī*, three parts *mawās*. For keeping the peasants and rebels in order (and) collecting the full revenue, one needs a contingent" (Ḥadīqī, f.15a-b). See also *Akhbārāt A*, 233, where it is recorded that a certain *pargana* "is very *mawās* and *zor-ṭalab*". In *Tārīkh-i Ṭāhirī*, f.128b, ed., 272, the plural in the neuter gender occurs: *mawās-hā*, rebellious areas. Hence *mahwāsīān* (pl. of *mahwāsī*, inhabitant of *mahwās*, or rebel) in Abū Turāb, 90. But *mawās* itself also meant rebellious people. Thus 'Abbās Khān, 213, speaks of the peasantry of *sarkār* Sambhal as being "seditious and *mawās*". Similarly, Badāūnī, II, 219, has "*mawāsān* (plural, in human gender, of *mawās*) and rebels", "who never pay the revenue". So Mundy, 90, in respect of "a little towne whoe were Manasse [Mavasse] or Rebells".

Mawās is best traceable linguistically to Sanskrit *mahat+āshraya*, whence Hindi *maha+vās* shortened to *mawās*, meaning protection, retreat, wood, etc. (Platts, s.v. *mawās*). This sense appears well enough in the Sanskrit text from Gujarat, the *Dvaiāsharaya*, completed in 1174, where *mewās*, *mewāsī* can only mean forest, forester (*Indian Antiquary*, IV, 71-2, 74, 76). There is absolutely no connexion either with the Arabic word *mawāshī*, "cattle", suggested by J.C. Heesterman, *Inner Conflict of Tradition*, 243, or with another Arabic word *ma'ṣiya*, "rebellion", assumed by A. Wink, *Land and Sovereignty in India*, 65 & n., although both these writers have placed me in their debt by drawing attention respectively to the two authorities cited earlier in this paragraph.

The extension of the meaning of *mawās* from forest to a refuge for rebels, thence rebel territory, was already complete in popular usage by the 13th century, when the term occurs in the form *mawās*, with the territorial plural *mawāsāt*, in Minhāj Sirāj, *Ṭabaqāt-i Nāṣirī*, ed. 'Abdu-l Ḥaī Ḥabībī, I, 491, II, 18, 19, 27, 29, etc. For 14th-century use of the word in the same sense, see Ḥasan Sijzī, *Fawā'idu-l Fa'wād*, ed. M. Latif Malik, 227 (Katehr described as *mawās*), and 'Iṣāmī, *Futūḥu-s Salāṭīn*, ed. A.S. Usha, 606 ("the whole of Tirhut and Gaur" becoming *mawās* in defiance of Muḥammad Tughluq). See also H.G. Raverty's note in his translation of *Ṭabaqāt-i Nāṣirī*, London, 1881, 704-5; Maḥmūd Sherānī in *Oriental College Magazine*, XII (2), February 1936, 37-8; and S.H. Hodivala, *Studies in Indo-Muslim History*, 226-29.

For *ra'īyatī* in the sense of obedient or revenue-paying, see Ḥadīqī, f.15a-b, and

which were protected in some measure by ravines or forests or hills, were more likely to defy the authorities than those in the open plains.[6] Mundy, while saying that "of theis kinde of broyles [between the authorities and the peasants] there is perpetuallie in one part or other of India", adds that "most commonly the Gawares [*ganwārs*, villagers] goe to the worst though they may be able to stand out a while".[7] As may be imagined a terrible fate awaited the villagers when defeated:

> Everyone is killed that is met with and their wives, sons and daughters and cattle are carried off.[8]

Very often acts of defiance by the peasants were mere isolated incidents. The intensity of distress probably varied from village to village, according to the burden of the revenue demand imposed upon each. But distress to be translated into armed resistance required the presence of some other factors as well. Since weaponry was crucial to even the initial success of any act of defiance, the readiness of the upper strata of peasants, possessed of muskets or swords, might often determine whether such an act would take place at all.[9] It was also possible that while the peasants of one village rose and were slaughtered, their neighbours remained unconcerned. However, there were still two social forces working among the peasantry, which could help to ignite, and extend the scale of such peasant uprisings.

Hidāyat al-Qawā'id, Aligarh MS, f.63a-b, where too it is contrasted with *zor-ṭalab*.

6 "In some parts of the plains, there is thornbush jungle; the people of the *parganas*, relying on and taking refuge in this jungle and rebelling, do not pay the revenue (*māl*)" (*Bāburnāma*, ed. Mano, 440; I.O. 3714, f.378b; tr. Beveridge, II, 487).

7 Mundy, 172-3.

8 Manucci, II, 451. Abū-l Faẓl, while requiring the *faujdār* to take action against "the peasant, or revenue collector of the *khāliṣa* or (of) a *jāgīrdār*, who shows rebelliousness", makes no reference to the fate of the combatants or their families. He merely says that everything found in the village should be treated as booty, a fifth thereof being reserved for the *khāliṣa*. If there were any revenue arrears standing against the village, these were to be secured first from the booty (*Ā'īn*, I, 283). In an order issued in June 1671, Aurangzeb apparently seeks to modify the sternness of punishment customarily meted out to such "groups of rebels". All rebels captured or wounded were to be slain, if the enemy had not yet taken to flight. But when the rebel host had been dispersed, the prisoners were to be spared, and if they showed "repentance" the spoils were to be returned to them (*Mir'āt*, I, 280).

9 To this extent, one may, perhaps, agree with V.I. Pavlov, *Historical Premises for India's Transition to Capitalism*, Moscow, 1979, 40-41, that "the elite of the village community acted as the spearhead of armed resistance".

In the first place, there was the larger community of caste. That the ties of caste could have played an important role in rousing peasants to act collectively in the defence of their interests, has been well stressed by one of the most distinguished leaders of the Indian communist movement.[10] Caste must naturally have occupied a still more important place in the life of the peasant three hundred years ago. It brought him into contact with his peers in the most distant villages through a thousand ties of blood and rites. If they took to arms, he could not stand aloof. In the Jāṭ revolt we have, perhaps, the clearest instance of how a peasant rebellion proceeded along caste lines. The same influence is visible also in the violent activities attributed to such castes as the Mewātīs and the Wattūs and Dogars.

But many peasants in our period were finding a new basis for a community that was not complementary, but essentially opposed, to caste divisions. This was being created by the sects formed as part of the great monotheistic movement that had begun in the latter part of the fifteenth century. The leading ideas of most of these sects were identical: an uncompromising monotheism, the abandonment of ritualistic forms of worship, the denial of caste barriers and of communal differences. As important perhaps as the content of their ideas was the mode of their preaching. For this was entirely directed towards the masses: the new teaching was transmitted mostly through verses sung in vernacular dialects, and the preachers themselves belonged mostly to the lower classes. Kabīr (*c.*1500), the great monotheist, was a weaver; of his two younger contemporaries, Ravdās and Sain, the former was a remover of dead cattle, the latter a barber; Dādū (*c.*1575) was a village cotton-carder; Haridās (d.1645), a Jāṭ slave.[11] Only Nānak (d.1539), belonging to the mercantile Khatrī caste, came from a higher station. None of these teachers, least of all Kabīr and Nānak, preached any other code of conduct than that of humility and resignation; they certainly did not preach militancy or physical struggle. Most of the devotional sects did not, perhaps, ever assume the form of social movements. But when radical ideas, such as the contempt for caste and the sense of unity under a new and convincing

[10] E.M.S. Namboodiripad, *The National Question in Kerala*, 102-3.

[11] Gurū Arjan, composing in the name of Dhannā Jāṭ, proclaims the special claims of the lowly in access to God, on the basis of the occupations (specified) of Nāmdev, Kabīr, Ravdās, and Sain (*Gurū Granth Sāhib*, Nagari text, 487-8). For Kabīr, Dādū and Haridās, see also *Dabistān-i Mazāhib*, 246, 267-8.

PREACHING

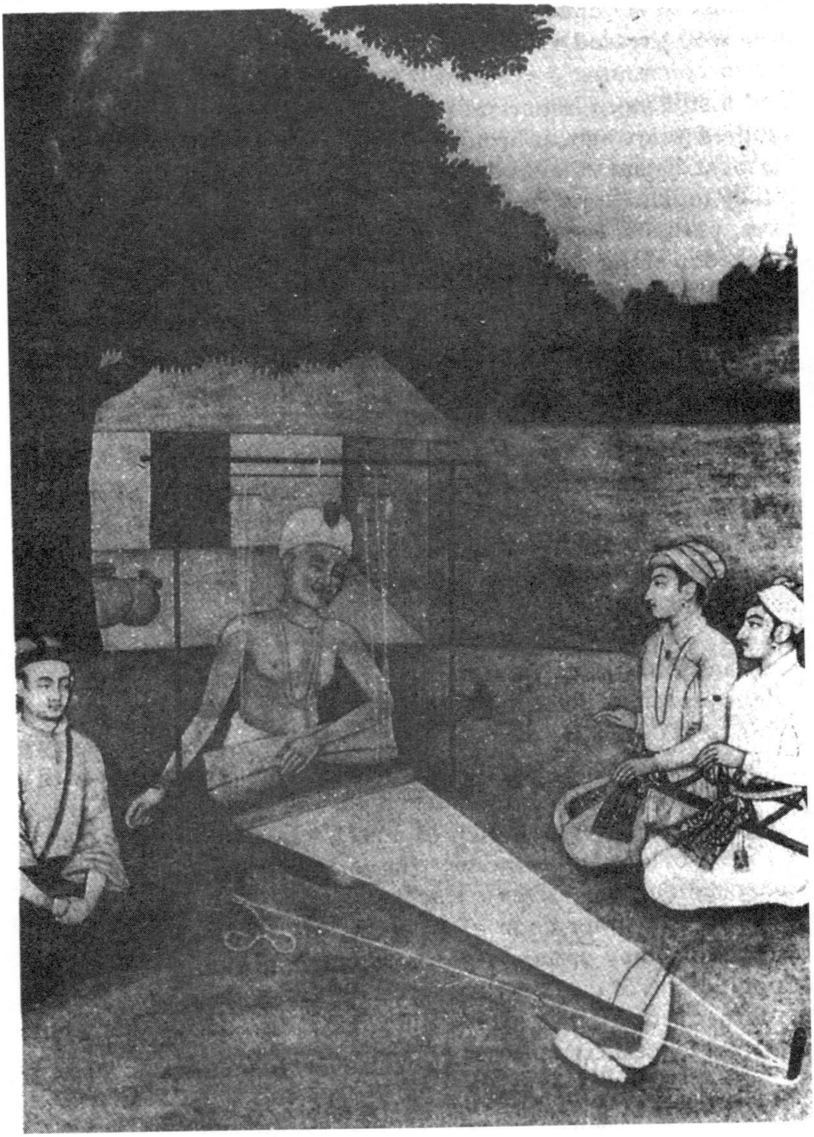

Kabīr, the weaver, at work while preaching, Mughal school, mid-17th century, miniature in the Leningrad Branch of the Institute of the Peoples of Asia.

COMMUNICATION

Peasant on roadside listening to two sufic singers. Painting by Bichitr, earlier part of 17th century. Victoria and Albert Museum, I.M. 27-1925.

faith, established themselves in the minds and hearts of their followers the sects could not always remain confined within their old mystic shell. In the event, they provided the inspiration for two of the most powerful revolts against Mughal authority, those of the Satnāmīs and the Sikhs.

But while the ties of castes and religious communities helped to enlarge the scale of peasant uprisings, they also perhaps tended to cloud or obscure their class nature. In any case, the real transformation of peasant unrest was probably brought about by the intervention of elements from the *zamīndār* class that had their own motives in opposing the Mughal ruling class. This came through two distinct processes: either the peasant rebellions, at some stage of their development, passed under the leadership of *zamīndārs* (or their own leaders assumed the status of *zamīndārs*), or, from the very beginning, the desperation of the peasants provided recruits for rebelling *zamīndārs*. The rising of the oppressed thus became inseparable from the conflict between two oppressing classes.

4. THE POLITICAL ROLE OF THE *ZAMĪNDĀRS*

In Chapter V, we found that the word *zamīndār* had a very wide connotation and could apply both to the ruler of a large kingdom and to a person who had only some rights over portions of a village. Nevertheless, in general, it would be correct to speak of the *zamīndārs* as a distinct class of potentates who had many features in common. For one thing, their rights did not originate from imperial grants, though there were some exceptions to this; secondly, command over armed retainers was usually a necessary complement of their right; and, thirdly, they were frequently leaders of caste groups. The main point of conflict between the imperial authorities and the *zamīndārs* was the size of the latter's share in the land revenue or in the surplus produce. In the imperial territories the *zamīndārs* were often treated as mere tax gatherers, on behalf of the state and the assignees, and a share was allowed to them as compensation for their work. Their exactions from the peasants were restricted not only by formal regulations, but much more by the high pitch of the revenue demand which left little with the peasants to be taken by anyone else. In such a situation it became difficult for the *zamīndār* to collect the revenue and pass it on to the authorities without harming his own interests. A similar dilemma confronted the autonomous chiefs. They too had to pay revenue or tribute or both. Nor were their states at any time free from the threat of annexation to the empire.[1] But, at the same time, since the *zamīndārs*, whether as tax gatherers or as chiefs, usually had armed force at their disposal, they could not be as easily dealt with by the administration as it would have wished, and they were always a thorn in its side.

Official texts frequently reflect an attitude of hostility towards the *zamīndārs* as a class. Abū-l Faẓl declares that "the custom of most of the *zamīndārs* of Hindustan is that leaving the path of single-mindedness they look to every side and whoever appears more powerful and tumult-raising, they join him".[2] Elsewhere, he remarks that Rāja Bhāramal "out of wisdom and good fortune, aspired to leave the ranks of *zamīndārs* and become one of the select of the Court", as if the two positions were mutually incompatible.[3] The court historian of Aurangzeb follows Abū-l Faẓl in using the word *zamīndārāna* in the sense of opportunism or disloyalty.[4] In documents written from the official point of view, it is assumed as a matter of course that the main danger to law and order came from the *zamīndārs*, who refused to pay the revenue and had to be subjugated by force either by the *faujdār* or the *jāgīrdār*.[5] The erection of a fort by any *zamīndār* could arouse the suspicions of the authorities and apparently be a sufficient justification for punitive action against him.[6]

How extensive became the conflicts with the *zamīndārs* in the later years of Aurangzeb is illustrated by the following information from diverse sources.

In Gujarat, Hamilton reported in connexion with an incident of 1705 and other disorders, that the "Gracias" (*girāsyas*, a species of *zamīndārs*) were dissatisfied with the "Nabobs" (*nawwāb*, "deputies", Mughal officials) over the "Ground Rents", and so "to put the Governors of Towns and Villages in mind of the Contract [with them, they] come in great numbers, and plunder or

[1] Within four years of Aurangzeb's accession, for instance, three large states were annexed; Kuch Bihar (1661), Palamau (1661) and Navanagar (1663).

[2] *A.N.*, II, 63.

[3] Ibid., 156.

[4] Rāja Karan Bhūrtiya of Bikaner, we are told, did not present himself at Aurangzeb's court because of "evil intentions and *zamīndārāna* considerations". (*'Ālamgīrnāma*, 571). For Abū-l Faẓl's use of the word, see *A.N.*, II, 63.

[5] *Hidāyatu-l Qawā'id*, f.7a-b (duties of a *faujdār*); *Bayāẓ-i Īzid Bakhsh "Rasā"* (?), I.O.4014, f.2a-b (the exploits of a *jāgīrdār* in a semi-humorous petition to God).

[6] *Aḥkām-i 'Ālamgīrī*, f.205a-b; *Inshā'-i Roshan Kalām*, f.6b. The forts were known in Hindi as *gaṛhīs*. See Chapter V, Section 2.

lay them in contribution".[7]

On the other side of the empire, in southwestern Bengal, Mughal authority was seriously shaken in 1695-98 by the rebellion of Sobhā Singh, "the *zamīndār* of Chitwa and Barda'(?)", who was joined by Raḥīm K͟hān, "the chief of the tribe of the perdition-marked Afghāns" of the area: the loyal *zamīndār* of Burdwan was killed, and the area on both sides of the Hugli river ravaged. It needed much effort before the rebellion could be stamped out, the lines of loyal *zamīndārs* reinstated, and the machinery of revenue collection re-established.[8]

The letters of Ra'd-andāz K͟hān, the *faujdār* of Baiswāra (?-1702) in Awadh, show this official, posted in an area in the plains quite close to the heart of the empire, constantly leading or sending expeditions against *zamīndārs* whose principal fault is usually stated to be their refusal to pay the revenue, though this is almost invariably coupled with the allegation that they were engaging in robbery and plunder.[9] Even in the vicinity of the capital city of Agra, at an earlier time the *zamīndārs* are said to have refused to pay the revenue to the authorities "without a fight".[10]

It is possible that the appointment of *zamīndārs* by grant from the court, a practice which comes into particular prominence during Aurangzeb's reign, was largely motivated by the desire to establish loyal supporters, in order to counterbalance the power of the old and potentially seditious *zamīndārs*.[11]

The struggle between the imperial administration and the *zamīndārs*, breaking out frequently into armed conflict, was thus an important feature of the political situation. Manuchy summed it up when he wrote in or about 1700: "Usually the viceroys and governors are in a constant state of quarrel with the Hindu princes and *zamīndārs* – with some because they wish to seize their lands; with others, to force them to pay more revenue than is customary."[12] He adds elsewhere that "usually there is some rebellion of the rajahs and *zamīndārs* going on in the Moghul kingdom".[13]

[7] Hamilton, I, 88. The Viceroy of Goa, in a letter of 1695, speaks of how the *desāis* in Mughal territories, who had their lands confiscated on refusal to pay revenue, "become thieves and make bold to rob and destroy" (*Portuguese Records on Rustom Manock*, 23-24).
[8] *Munshī* Salīmullāh, *Tārīkh-i Bangāla*, 5-29. Salīmullāh's late account is corrected and supplemented through use of French and English records by Aniruddha Ray, *Adventures, Land-owners and Rebels*, 117-57.
[9] *Inshā'-i Roshan Kalām*, ff.2a-4a, 6a-b.
[10] *Zak͟hīratu-l K͟hawānīn*, II, 358-9. [11] See Chapter V, Section 3.
[12] Manucci, II, 431-2. [13] Ibid., 462.

It was, probably, more than anything else, their position in this unequal contest with the imperial power that compelled many *zamīndārs* to adopt a conciliatory attitude towards their peasants whose support would have been indispensable to them for defence as well as in flight. Moreover, being local men, closely acquainted with the conditions and customs of the peasants, they were probably able generally to make more flexible arrangements with the peasants under their control than could the officials of the *khālisa* or the *jāgīrdārs*, who were generally outsiders and interested mainly in an immediate increase in assessment. Bernier noted that the peasants found "less oppression and [were] allowed a greater degree of comfort" in "the territories of a Rāja".[14] This is clearly recognized even by the official historian of Aurangzeb, who says that "the *zamīndārs* of the country of Hindustan, for considerations of policy – for winning the hearts of, and conciliating, the peasants, in order that they may not cease to obey or pay revenue to them –conduct themselves gently in exacting the revenue in the *maḥals* of their *zamīndārī*, and do not apply the regulations and laws followed in the imperial dominions."[15]

It came about, therefore, that the *zamīndārs* frequently attracted to their lands peasants absconding from areas directly under imperial administration. This was noted in general terms by Pelsaert and Bernier,[16] but a manual written in 1714 is even more explicit: The *manṣabdārs*, presumably holding *jāgīrs*, "strike their hand (of extortion) upon the peasants, and the peasants are without help. When the peasants become desperate for their lives, they abscond from the *ra'īyatī* country and, making their way to the country of rebellious *zamīndārs*, settle there. The country of the rebellious *zamīndārs* thus becomes well populated and the rebels gain in power every day."[17]

[14] Bernier, 205.

[15] '*Ālamgīrnāma*, 781 (cf. *Fatḥiya-i 'Ibriya*, ff.47b-48a; ed., 90). This statement is made with reference to Kuch Bihar. It is true that a contrary view is put forward by Hamilton, II, 14, with regard to Bengal generally: "the Gentiles are better contented to live under the Mogul's laws than under Pagan Princes, for the Mogul taxes them gently and every one knows what he must pay, but the Pagan Kings or Princes tax at Discretion making their own Avarice the Standard of Equity." By "Gentiles" here Hamilton might have had Hindu merchants rather than peasants in mind.

[16] Pelsaert, 47; Bernier, 205.

[17] *Hidāyatu-l Qawā'id*, Aligarh MS, f.56a-b. The word *ra'īyatī* in this passage can signify either peasant-held country directly under imperial administration or,

These general statements are illustrated by certain specific instances from the seventeenth century. When under A'ẓam Khān, governor of Gujarat (1632-42), the peasants suffered great oppression, "most of them fled and took refuge with the *zamīndārs* in distant places".[18] A'ẓam Khān thereupon led an expedition against Navanagar to compel its "*zamīndār*" to expel the peasants who had fled to his territory, so that they might return to their old homes.[19] In Malwa, in 1644, a similar campaign was organized against the "*zamīndār*" of Ginnur, not only because he did not "pay the revenue in the proper way", but also because "the peasants of some of the *maḥals* of the *jāgīr* of the governor, who had fled to the territory of Ginnur, evaded paying the revenue as well, being backed in this by those infidels".[20] In the reign of Aurangzeb we come across a complaint by the *thānadār* of Kalyan in the Konkan, to the effect that, first, a large number of the peasants had fled to the territories of the *zamīndārs*; and, then, when he had brought them back by force and settled 600 villages with them, the Portuguese of Salsette had enticed them away.[21]

The peasants and the *zamīndārs* thus frequently became associated in the struggle against Mughal authorities. When the kingdom of Kuch Bihar was annexed in 1661, the Mughal officials introduced there the methods of "revenue assessment and collection, according to the regulations followed in the *maḥals* of the imperial territories". This caused a general revulsion against the conquerors among the peasants, who were treated with much greater leniency by their deposed *rāja*, Bīm Narāyan. They, therefore, rose and expelled the Mughal troops and officials.[22] In the same way, when the

simply, revenue-paying country. The author attributes the increasing oppression of the peasantry by the *manṣabdārs* to the fact that the latter did not hold high *manṣabs* and, therefore, could not afford to maintain contingents large enough to deal with the seditious elements. They accordingly stood in need of money, and since they could not take anything from the powerful *zamīndārs*, their hand fell heavily upon the peasants.

A similar statement is made in the *Maẓhar-i Shāhjahānī*, 20-21. When the revenue demand imposed upon the *arbābs* (officials corresponding to *chaudhurīs* in Sind, who were mostly *zamīndārs*) became excessively heavy, they rebelled. In such cases the peasants always followed them and absconded from their lands, because if they stayed on upon their lands, they would have had to meet the high revenue demand imposed by the authorities, while the *arbābs* would come and kill them. The peasants followed the *arbābs* also because they belonged to the same places.

[18] *Mir'āt*, I, 216. [19] Lāhorī, II, 232; *Mir'āt*, I, 214. [20] Lāhorī, II, 370.

[21] *Kārnāma*, ff.243b-244a.

[22] '*Ālamgīrnāma*, 781-2; *Fatḥiya-i 'Ibriya*, ff.47b-48a.

Mughal authorities used force to obtain the return of fugitive peasants from the lands of the *zamīndārs*, the result in many cases might have been only to direct peasant migration towards "the rājas who are in rebellion", as Pelsaert says.[23]

These peasants would not only add to the resources of the *zamīndārs* by engaging in cultivation, but could also provide recruits for their armed bands. Such primitive troops were initially of little avail against the professional cavalrymen of the Mughal armies. But the diffusion of musket manufacture in the latter half of the seventeenth century, despite imperial bans on production of muskets in private smithies, posed a new challenge to the invincibility of Mughal cavalry.[24] Moreover, terrain and numbers still counted, as the Marathas were to show so strikingly. The new feature that comes to the fore in the reign of Aurangzeb is, indeed, that the *zamīndārs'* struggle against the Mughals is no longer merely defensive. As the number of starving, homeless peasants grew and the peasants took to arms themselves, it became possible for the *zamīndārs* to organize them into large bands, and even armies, and employ them in predatory warfare with the object of extending their own *zamīndārīs* or areas of dominance.

In the next section we shall study in some detail the extent of peasant participation in the major revolts against Mughal power. As we will see, the *zamīndārs'* leadership was not uniformly established over all the peasant risings; nor is there any reason to believe that all rebellious actions by *zamīndārs* were supported by the peasants. But the fact remains that two of the most successful revolts, those of the Marathas and the Jāṭs, were led by men, who were, or aspired to be, *zamīndārs*. The fact assumes particular importance when we consider the historical results of these revolts.

[23] Pelsaert, 47.

[24] For the imperial prohibitions, first recorded in the middle and later years of Aurangzeb, see *Nigārnāma-i Munshī*, ed., 135; *Documents of Aurangzeb's Reign*, 41 (the document belongs to the period 1686-1707, and not to Aurangzeb's 5th regnal year); *Document Forms*, ed. J.F. Richards, ff.217a, 218b, 226b, 227b. But already about 1650, the author of the *Z̲akh̲īratu-l Kh̲awānīn*, II, 358-9, noted that in certain localities near Agra, "the peasants (*ri'āyā*) who drive the plough, carry a musket (*bandūq*) slung on the neck with a (powder) pouch at the waist". In 1703 it was reported to the emperor that when the local *faujdār* sacked a village in *pargana* Palwal, near Dehli, killing 200 persons (Meos), he also seized 194 muskets, besides 76 horses, 750 swords, and 1064 bows (*Akh̲bārāt* 47/28). I am indebted to Professor Iqtidar A. Khan for drawing my attention to this new factor in the internal military situation of the empire.

5. AGRARIAN ASPECTS OF THE REVOLTS AGAINST THE MUGHAL EMPIRE

Various explanations are put forward for the revolts which brought about the collapse of the Mughal Empire. The study offered in this section lays no claim to being comprehensive or to having covered all aspects of the revolts. There has existed for a long time the thesis of "Hindu Reaction" as the main factor behind the revolts against Aurangzeb. Its proponents tend, however, to rely more on present sentiment than on contemporary evidence. For the rest, the reader may judge their case as presented in their own writings.[1] Here our main concern is with what our seventeenth- and early eighteenth-century texts have to say; and they, at any rate, put the greatest store by the economic and administrative causes of the upheaval and hardly ever refer to religious reaction or consciousness of nationality.

I. Revolts in the Agra Region, and the Jāṭs

Speaking of the province of Agra, Abū-l Faẓl observes that "owing to the peculiarity of its climate the peasant masses (*'umūm-i ri'āyā*) of that territory are notorious throughout the vast country of Hindustan for rebelliousness, bravery and courage".[2] Speaking of the tract across the Yamuna from Agra, an author writing about 1650 says the *zamīndārs* did not pay the revenue without a fight, and the peasants ("*ri'āyā* who drive the plough") carried firearms.[3] The area on both sides of the Yamuna figures constantly as the scene of military operations against rebellious peasantry. Akbar once personally led an attack on a village in this area;[4] and we read of a *rāja* in a *pargana* close to Agra, who used to engage in robbery and defended himself, when attacked, with the assistance of *ganwārs* or villagers.[5] In 1623 it was reported to the court that "the *ganwārs* and cultivators" on the eastern side of the Yamuna, near Mathura, "do not cease to commit highway robbery and, pro-

[1] The classic presentation of the case is in Jadunath Sarkar, *A History of Aurangzib*, III, 283-364.

[2] *A.N.*, III, 231.

[3] *Zakhīratu-l Khawānīn*, II, 358-9, in an account of Jahāngīr's noble Bikramājīt Bhadauriya, a *zamīndār* of the area.

[4] *A.N.*, II, 163. The village is in the *pargana* of Sāketa (*sarkār* of Kanauj) and the attack was made in the 7th year of the reign. Cf. also Manucci, I, 132-4.

[5] Badāūnī, II, 151-2. Jalesa, the name of the *pargana*, must be a misreading for Jalesar.

tected by dense jungle and fastnesses, live in rebellion, have no fear of anyone and do not pay the revenue to the *jāgīrdārs*". An expedition was despatched against them, as a result of which, "numbers of them were killed, their women and children taken captive and a great booty acquired by the victorious troops".[6] Yet over a decade later (1634) a campaign on a far more elaborate scale had to be organized against "the malefactors" on both sides of the Yamuna, who used to commit robberies on the Agra-Dehli route. "Ten thousand of those human-looking beasts" were slaughtered, and their women and children and cattle "beyond computation" were seized.[7] In 1645 the "rebels" near Mathura were apparently still out of control.[8] When Sa'dullāh Khān died in 1656 "the gamors [*ganwārs*] of severall his townes [i.e. villages in his *jāgīrs*] neare Agra rose in armes. But ... they were suddainely surprized by Abdall Nubby, his fouzdarr, their townes sacked and such as escaped not by flight, either slaine or imprisoned."[9]

Such had been the past history of the area which was to be the cradle of the Jāṭ revolt in the time of Aurangzeb. In the accounts of the earlier revolts, the revolting peasants are not identified as Jāṭs. The usual term for them is *ganwār*, or villager, and in one or two cases, at least, they were probably led by Rājpūt *zamīndārs*.[10] Nevertheless Manuchy, who treats of their revolts in some detail, knows the Jāṭ rebels of Aurangzeb's reign also as simply "peasants" and assumes them to be the partisans of the same cause as of those whom Akbar had oppressed.[11] The Jāṭs were *par excellence*, "a peasant caste";[12] they inhabited villages between Dehli and Agra[13] and are also entered as *zamīndārs*, under many *maḥals* in

[6] *T.J.*, 375-6.

[7] Qazwīnī, Add. 20734, 679-80; Or. 173, ff.237b, 239; Lāhorī, I, ii, 71-2, 76. The latter adds that 12,000 troops were deployed against the rebels, 7,000 to the east and 5,000 to the west of the Yamuna.

[8] Lāhorī, II, 425.

[9] *Factories, 1655-60*, 65.

[10] Thus the villagers against whom Akbar personally led an expedition are described as Rājpūts in Manucci, I, 132, who has here very probably drawn upon local tradition. This is likely too since the Chauhāns are entered as the *zamīndārs* of the *pargana* (Sāketa) in the *Ā'īn*, I, 446. Similarly in Jalesar, where the rebellion was organized by a *rāja*, the Guhilots, Sūraj (bansīs) and Bankras are shown as *zamīndārs* (ibid., 443).

[11] Manucci, I, 134; he says the "villagers" took their revenge upon Akbar when they desecrated his tomb in 1691 (*sic.* 1688).

[12] *Tashrīḥu-l Aqwām*, f.155a; Crooke, *The Tribes and Castes of the North-Western Provinces and Oudh*, Calcutta, 1896, III, 40.

[13] "The cultivators of villages between Dehli and Akbarabad (Agra) are of the Jāṭ caste" (Shāh Walīullāh, *Siyāsī Maktūbāt*, 48).

the Doāb and the trans-Yamuna plains, in the *Ā'īn*. It is, therefore, not unlikely that they had already participated in many of the previous conflicts with the authorities.

The Jāṭ rebellion, properly speaking, dates from the time when Gokulā Jāṭ, the *zamīndār* of Talpat near Mathura, "assembled a large army of Jāṭs and other villagers and raised a rebellion".[14] He was killed in 1670;[15] but the leadership passed to Rāja Rām Jāṭ (d.1688) and then to Chūrāman Jāṭ, who is said to have been the son of a *zamīndār* of eleven villages.[16] Over wide areas the peasants refused to pay revenue and took to arms. We thus learn from the grant of a *zamīndārī* near Mathura that the twenty-five villages covered by it were all inhabited by "evil-mannered rebels", and the grantee was required to expel them and settle new "revenue-paying" peasants.[17] In 1681 Multafat Khān, the *faujdār* of the district around Agra, was killed when leading an attack on a village whose peasants had refused to pay the revenue.[18] And later in the same decade we find a *jāgīrdār* complaining that for three years he could not obtain anything from his *jāgīrs* near Agra "owing to the rebellion".[19]

That the leadership of the Jāṭ rebellion lay in the hands of *zamīndārs* is established not only from the known antecedents of its chief men,[20] but also from their conduct. Chūrāman, for example, is said to have "seized a number of *Chamārs* [tanners], who are called the menials of the Hindus and entrusted [the upkeep of] the ditch [at Bharatpur] to them".[21] The assertion of a kind of

14 Īsardās, f.53a. A detailed description of the various phases of the Jāṭ rebellion is offered by Girish Chandra Dwivedi, *The Jats – Their Role in the Mughal Empire*, New Delhi, 1989.

15 *Ma'āṣir-i 'Ālamgīrī*, 93-94.

16 Saiyid Ghulam 'Alī Khān, *'Imādu-s Sa'ādat*, 54-55. The *zamīndār* and peasant dimensions of the Jāṭ revolt under Chūrāman are studied on the basis of Amber records now in the Rajasthan State Archives, Bikaner, by R.P. Rana in *IESHR*, XVIII (3-4), 287-326.

17 *Nigārnāma-i Munshī*, ed., 152. The grant was made on the recommendation of Ḥasan 'Alī Khān, the *faujdār* of Mathura, who had been responsible for the defeat and capture of Gokulā.

18 Manucci, II, 223-4; *Ma'āṣir-i 'Ālamgīrī*, 209.

19 *Riyāzu-l Wadād*, f.16b. The letter seems to have been written immediately after the campaign against "Bījāpūr and Ḥaidarābād".

20 As stated above, Gokulā was *zamīndār*, and Chūrāman, the son of a *zamīndār*. Of Sūrajmal (d.1763), Chūrāman's grandson, under whom Jāṭ power reached its zenith, it was said that "although he spoke the Braj dialect and wore the dress of a *zamīndār*, he possessed an intelligence that made him a Sage among his people" (*'Imādu-s Sa'ādat*, 55).

21 Ibid.

lordship over a semi-servile community is here unmistakable. It was also natural that the Jāṭ leaders should aspire to supplant other *zamīndārs* by themselves. It was said in mid-eighteenth century, when Jāṭ power was at its height, that "the lands that the Jāṭs have brought into their possession are not their own, but have been usurped from others. The (rightful) proprietors (*mālikān*) of those villages are still to be found". So that if a just king gave the old proprietors some assistance, they could be incited to fight against the Jāṭs.[22] One of the results of the Jāṭ rebellion was a great extension of Jāṭ *zamīndārī* in the Braj-speaking area. This can be seen from a comparison of the areas, for which Jāṭs were entered as the *zamīndār* caste in the *Ā'īn*, with the areas held by Jāṭ *zamīndārs* in pre-Mutiny days (1844).[23] (See maps next page.)

The Jāṭ revolt grew in time into a large plundering movement. This was, perhaps, inevitable under the narrow caste horizons of the peasants and the plundering instincts of their *zamīndār* leaders. The area devastated expanded from the one *pargana* of Sa'dabad, plundered by Gokulā,[24] and the *parganas* around Agra, sacked by Rāja Rām,[25] to its highest extent under Chūrāman, when "all the *parganas* under Agra and Dehli had been sacked and plundered and, from the tumult of that perdition-seeker, the routes and ways were blocked".[26]

So far as we know, the Jāṭ rebels (in spite of Harīdās) had no connexion with any particular religious movement. In the Satnāmī and Sikh rebellions, on the other hand, religion almost entirely

[22] Shāh Walīullāh, *Siyāsī Maktūbāt*, 50-1.

[23] See Elliot's Maps in *Memoirs*, II, 203. It will be noticed that the extension is very marked in the Middle Doāb, but not in the Upper, where, if anything, the area under Jāṭ *zamīndārī* would seem to have contracted. The obvious reason for this is that the Jāṭ rebellion was really a rebellion of the Jāṭs of the Braj country and did not affect the Upper Doab.

[24] *Ma'āṣir-i 'Ālamgīrī*, 93. [25] Īsardās, ff.98b, 131b.

[26] Ibid., f.135b. A concerted campaign under Bishan Singh in 1690-1 restored Mughal authority somewhat (ibid., ff.136a-137b). Kishan Charan Gosā'in, of the line of Rūp Goswāmi, at Vrindaban, was now able to return and reclaim his property, having been forced to flee earlier by the Jāṭ depredations (*futūr-i Jāṭān*) (NAI 267/14, dated 16 May 1694). But already in October 1691 there was some disquiet at the imperial court at the limited success attending Bishan Singh's efforts, and a *farmān* was issued assigning *faujdārī* jurisdiction over Hindaun, Bayana, etc., where Jāṭ resistance was still continuing, to Kamāluddīn Khān (*Nāma-i Muẓaffarī*, I, 255-7). Smouldering on, the Jāṭ revolt flared up once again under Chūrāman himself, after Aurangzeb's death (1707); and ultimately a Jāṭ kingdom was established, with its capital at Bharatpur, reaching its largest extent under Sūrajmal (1756-63).

AREAS OF JAT ZAMINDARI

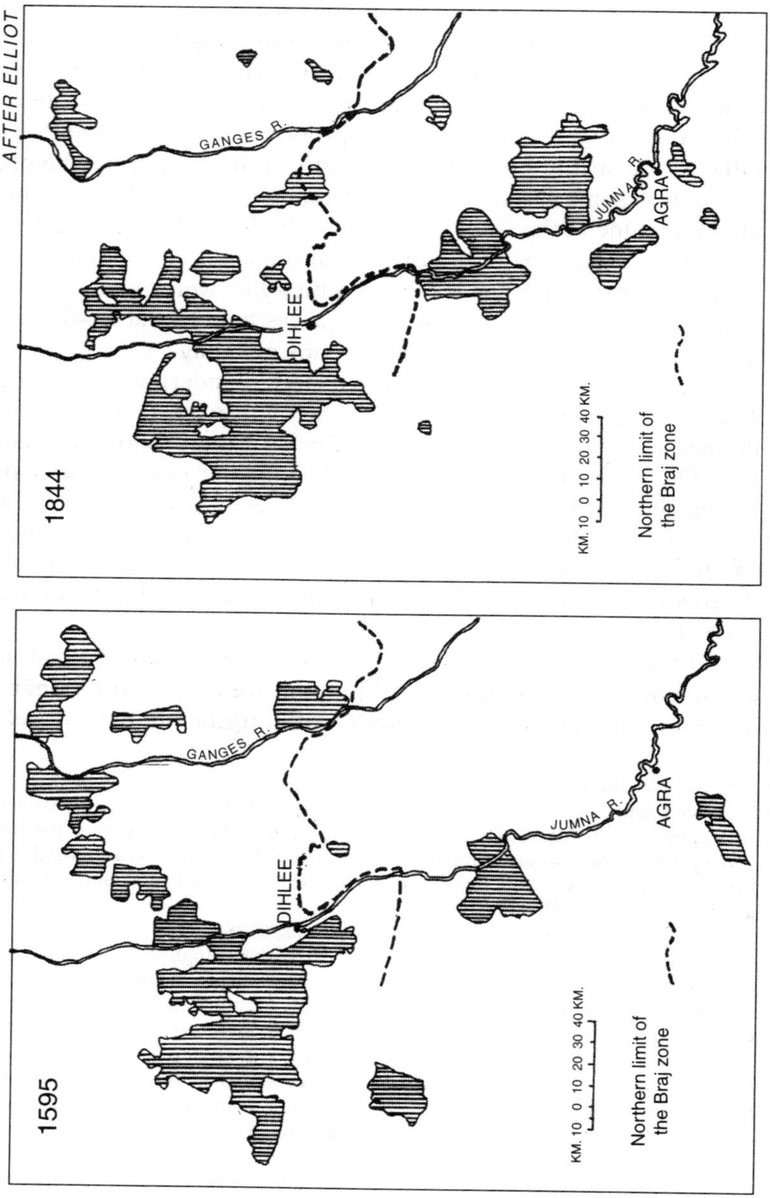

replaced caste as the cementing bond among rebel ranks.

II. The Satnāmīs

The Satnāmīs were a sect of the Bairāgīs. The traditional date of the foundation of this sect by a native of Narnaul is 1657. The Satnāmī beliefs, as stated in the sect's scripture, centred round an unalloyed monotheism. Ritual and superstition were alike condemned, and allegiance was explicitly rendered to Kabīr. There was also a definite social aspect of the message. Caste distinctions within the community of believers were forbidden; so also one's living on the charity of others. An attitude of sympathy with the poor and hostility towards authority and wealth is apparent from such commandments as the following: "Do not harass the poor... Shun the company of an unjust king and a wealthy and dishonest man; do not accept a gift from these or from kings."[27]

Such a religion could best appeal to the lower classes. The following description of its followers is from the pen of a contemporary historian:

> There is a group of Hindu mendicants, known as Satnāmīs, who are also called Mundiyas.[28] They consist of some four or five thousand householders in the *pargana* of Narnaul and Mewāt. Although those Mundiyas dress like mendicants, yet their livelihood and profession is usually agriculture and trade in the manner of Banyas [or tradesmen] with small capital.[29] Living according to the ways of their own community they aspire to reach the status of a good name (*nek-nām*), which is the meaning of the word *satnām*. But if anyone should want to impose tyranny and oppression upon them, in a display of courage or authority, they will not tolerate it; and most of them bear arms and weapons.[30]

[27] This entire passage is based on the MS of the scripture, *Satnām Sahāi (Pothī Giyān Bānī Sādh Satnāmī*), Royal Asiatic Society, London (Hind. 1). The language is Braj. The text is given in the Nagari as well as Arabic script. In the latter, an introductory portion in verse (running up to f.34b) is added.

The quotation is from f.44b (cf. also f.38a). The reference to Kabīr occurs on f.49 b.

In the beginning of the introductory portion, f.1a, the native place of the founder is said to be Bījhāsar in the country of Narnaul (Mahendragarh District, Haryana). In the colophon in Persian, at the end of the text of the scripture in Arabic characters, the date of the foundation of the sect is given as Baisākh, 1714 Samvat. This I have accepted the more readily since the prohibition of tobacco smoking (f.39b) practically precludes an earlier date for the scripture.

[28] Cf. *Dabistān-i Mazāhib*, 251: "The Bairāgīs are also called Mundiyas."

[29] *Baqqālān-i kam-māya* (Ma'mūrī). Khāfī Khān reads "tradesmen" instead of *baqqālān*, the usual Persian designation for Banyas.

[30] Ma'mūrī, f.148a-b, Khāfī Khān, II, 252.

Another contemporary writer castigates the community for being, "by its extreme dirtiness, rendered foul, filthy and impure". "Thus," says he, "under the rules of their sect they do not differentiate between Muslims and Hindus and eat pig's flesh and other disgusting things."[31]

In a possible reference to them made during the early years of Aurangzeb, a revenue official declared that though certain "cultivators" in a village in the *pargana* of Bhatnair were "living with their women, children, possessions and cattle in the garb of Bairāgīs", they were "not free from the thoughts of sedition and robbery".[32] The revolt in fact began (1672) as a rural affray. One of the Satnāmīs "was working in his fields when he exchanged hot words with a *piyāda* (foot-trooper), who was guarding the corn-heap. The *piyāda* broke the Satnāmī's head by a blow from his stick. Thereupon a crowd of that sect mobbed that *piyāda* and beat him so much as to reduce him almost to a corpse." The *shiqqdār* then sent a contingent of troops, and so the conflict began.[33]

The plebeian character of the revolt is perhaps best indicated in the following words of scorn which Sāqī Musta'idd Khān, the self-designated official chronicler of Aurangzeb, pours upon it:

> To the spectators of the wonderful works of Fate the occurrence of this event is a cause of amazement, i.e. what came into the head of this rebellious, murderous, destitute gang of goldsmiths (peasants?),[34] carpenters, sweepers and tanners and other mean and ignoble men of artisan castes that their conceited brains became so overclouded? Rebellious pride having found a place in their brains, their heads became too heavy for their shoulders. By their own legs they were caught in the snare of annihilation. To unveil this tale, this huge horde of mischief-makers of the region of Mewāt all of a sudden sprang up from the earth like moths and fell down from the sky like locusts....[35]

To a Hindi bard, praising a Mughal commander's prowess in battle against the Satnāmīs, the latter, indeed, appeared as an army (*dal*) of "a crore of *ganwārs* (villagers)".[36]

Despite its great initial success, the repeated defeats inflicted

[31] Īsardās, f.61b.

[32] Bālkrishan Brahman, f.56a-b.

[33] Ma'mūrī, f.148b, Khāfī Khān, II, 253.

[34] The printed text has *zargar* and is supported in this by Add.19,495, f.63a. But "goldsmith" is incongruous here and *zargar* is likely to be a mistake for *barzgar*, "peasant". The two words are almost indistinguishable in Persian if written in a rapid hand.

[35] *Ma'āṣir-i 'Alāmgīrī*, 114-15.

[36] Quoted in *Nāma-i Muẓaffarī*, I, 252, from the 18th-century work *Makhzan-i Akhbār* (of Sa'ādat Khān, cf. Marshall, *Mughals in India*, 421, no.1593).

on imperial troops and the occupation of Narnaul and Bairat, the rebels were finally destroyed by a large army sent from the imperial court. But they went down fighting bravely, and Sāqī Musta'idd Khān concedes that despite the lack of all materials of war, they repeated the scenes of the great war of Mahabharata.[37]

III. The Sikhs

Just as it has been said of Islam that it is a "religion for townspeople",[38] so it will, perhaps, not be wrong to say that Sikhism is a peasant religion. The verses of Gurū Nānak "are all in the language of the Jaṭṭs of the Punjab. And Jaṭṭ in the dialect of the Punjab means a villager, a rustic."[39] The author of the *Dabistān-i Mazāhib*, *c.*1655, who gives us an intimate account of the Sikhs, adds that "among them there is no such rule as that a Brahman should not be a disciple (*sikh*) of a Khatrī, for Nānak was a Khatrī... Similarly, they have made Khatrīs subordinate to the Jaṭṭs, who are the lowliest of the caste of Bais (*Vaishya*). Thus of the great *masands* (nobles, agents) of the Gurū most are Jaṭṭs."[40] Gurū Arjan (d.1606) took the first steps in creating a well-knit and disciplined organization. He appointed his agents in every town. "It has been ordained that an *udāsī*, or ascetic, is not a good believer. Owing to this some of the Sikhs of the Gurū engage in agriculture, others in trade and service; and every one according to his capacity pays a *nazar* (offering) each year to the *masand*", who received it on behalf of the Gurū.[41] The Sikhs became a military power under Gurū Hargobind (1606-45), who created an army of his own, and, as a result, came into armed collision with Mughal power.[42] He thus founded a tradition, which was doggedly continued by the last Gurū, Gobind Singh (1676-1708), till, finally, in 1709-10 Banda was able to put into the field in *sarkār* Sirhind "an army of innumerable men, like ants and locusts, belonging to the low castes of the Hindus and ready to die" at his orders.[43]

[37] *Ma'āṣir-i 'Ālamgīrī*, 115-16.

[38] F. Lokkegaard, *Islamic Taxation in the Classic Period*, 32. Cf. M. Habib, Introduction to Elliot and Dowson's *History of India*, II, Aligarh, 1952, 2-3.

[39] *Dabistān-i Mazāhib*, 285. Cf. Ibbetson, *Punjab Castes*, 105, for the use of the word *jaṭ* in the sense of "agriculturist".

[40] *Dabistān-i Mazāhib*, 286, also 214. Similarly, Khāfī Khān, II, 651: "Most of the followers of the *gurū* of that perdition-bound sect belonged to the castes of Jāṭs and Khatrīs of the Panjab and other lowly castes of the infidels."

[41] *Dabistān-i Mazāhib*, 286-7. Cf. also Khāfī Khān, II, 651-2.

[42] *Dabistān-i Mazāhib*, 288.

[43] Khāfī Khān, II, 672.

Other sources have similar statements regarding Banda's followers. Says Kāmwar Khān (1724): "Large numbers of scavengers and tanners and a class of *banjāras* (ox-transporters) and other lowly persons and cheats became his disciples and gathered (under him)."[44] Wārid (1733-34), while noting that letters were sent to *zamīndārs*, who owed allegiance to the deceased Gurū, to join Banda, insists that his followers were forced to accept a rough equality. Such Hindus and Muslims as joined him had to eat together "so that all distinction between the low and the high departed", and "scavengers and tanners, dirtier than whom there is no race in Hindustan, joining his service, received appointments to governments of their own places", whereat all persons of whatever class had to obey them.[45] Thus any *zamīndār* support was heavily diluted by a conscious appeal to the lower classes.[46] Even in the early nineteenth century, "most of the chiefs of the highest dignity" among the Sikhs were reputed to be "low-born persons, such as carpenters, shoe-makers and Jaṭṭs".[47]

IV. Other Revolts in Northern India

These three rebellions do not by any means exhaust the list of peasant revolts in northern India. Many of these are mentioned in our authorities as passing incidents. For example, we read that in 1575-6 the governor of Bhakkar levied the revenue at a uniform rate per *bīgha*, and "the peasants were subjected to oppression." The Mangcha tribe thereupon revolted and killed the tax gatherers. They were, however, defeated and expelled from their lands.[48] When Manuchy passed by Ilahabad in 1662, he found the governor absent "on a campaign against some villagers, who objected to pay their revenue without at least one fight".[49]

Of disorders of a different kind were those perpetrated by the Meos in Mewāt, who were constantly in rebellion and made plundering raids from their villages lying deep in the hills.[50] Ferocious campaigns were led against them in 1630 and 1649-50,[51]

[44] Muḥammad Hādī Kāmwar Khān, *Tazkiratu-s Salāṭīn-i Chaghatā*, 93.

[45] Muḥammad Shafī' Wārid, *Mir'āt-i Wāridāt*, Add. 6579, ff.117a-118b.

[46] These statements should seriously modify Muzaffar Alam's insistence (*Crisis of Empire*, 136) that "Banda Bahādur drew [his] principal strength from the support of the *zamīndārs*". Cf. Satish Chandra, *Parties and Politics at the Mughal Court, 1707-40*, 50-51.

[47] *'Imādu-s Sa'ādat*, 71.

[48] Ma'ṣūm, *Tārīkh-i Sind*, 245-6.

[49] Manucci, II, 83.

[50] Pelsaert, 15; Manucci, II, 458.

[51] *Zakhīratu-l Khawānīn*, III, 51-53; Wāriṣ: a: ff.433a-b, 435a-b, 435b; b: ff. 64a-67a; Ṣāliḥ, III, 110-12.

but they still survived to give trouble later on.[52] A vigorous campaign against "Ikrām, *zamīndār* of Mewāt", had to be organized in 1703, accompanied with the usual killings, and the seizures of horses, muskets, swords, and bows and arrows of the rebels.[53]

Similarly the peasants of the Lakhi Jungle were "notorious for rebellion and mischief". They belonged to the castes of Wattūs, Dogars and Gūjars, and were so well protected by the various channels thrown out by the Sutlej-Beas river and the forests created by the inundations, that most of the expeditions against them proved ineffectual.[54] In Aurangzeb's later days they are once said to have ravaged the whole *sarkār* of Dipalpur.[55]

In Gujarat, the Kolīs formed a species of lower peasantry, traditionally bearing arms and ready to commit depredations.[56] In 1636 when the Chunwāl Kolīs began to plunder the routes, the governor A'ẓam Khān conducted a campaign against the Kolīs "laying waste their cultivated fields and trees, and cutting down the jungle".[57] In early 1650s, however, Chunwāl Kolīs plundered villages of a large tract west of Ahmadabad.[58] In 1676 the English factors reported that "the Coolys [and] Rashpoots, appearing in bodies of 2-, or 3,000" were "carry[ing] whole Caphilaes away".[59]

The Bundela rebellion, which began after Shāhjahān's annexation of Orchha in 1635, and continued intermittently for the rest of our period, was essentially a dynastic affair, a war for the rights of a princely house. But two letters from the Mughal commander Khān Jahān Bārha show that here too the rebels were able, after a successful exploit, to call over to their side "*zamīndārs* and peasants" from "both the *ra'īyatī* and *mawās* areas". Moreover, the peasants took the opportunity to evade paying the revenue whenever the rebels became active.[60]

[52] Manucci, II, 458. [53] *Akhbārāt*, 47/28, 259, 299.

[54] Sujān Rāi, 63; Manucci, II, 457-8. Cf. also *Akhbārāt* 43/53. The Wattūs are a Bhaṭṭī clan (Ibbetson, *Punjab Castes*, 145-6).

[55] *Aḥkām-i 'Alāmgīrī*, f.215a.

[56] Bernier, 88-9. *Mir'āt*, Suppl. 132, puts Kolīs next to "Kuṁbīs or [ordinary] peasants" among the Hindu castes of Gujarat. But there were Kolī *zamīndārs* too, for the *Ā'īn*, I, 493-95, records Kolīs as *zamīndārs* in many *parganas* of *sarkārs* Ahmadabad and Patan.

[57] *Mir'āt*, I, 213. On the Chunvaliyas, identified as one of the main four divisions of the Gujarat Kolīs, with settlements around Viramgaon, between Ahmadabad and the Little Rann, see *Imperial Gazetteer*, New Edition (1908), XV, 388.

[58] *Mir'āt*, I, 230. [59] *Selections from Bombay Secretariat, Home*, I, 80.

[60] '*Arẓdāsht-hā-i Muẓaffar*, ff. 6a-7a, 115b. The first letter describes the sack of Dhamoni and Chanderi by Champat and Rāmsen.

V. The Marathas

The Marathas undoubtedly constituted the greatest single force responsible for the downfall of the Mughal Empire. On the history of their uprising, and the factors that contributed to its genesis and success, so much has been written that it would seem presumptuous to add to the mass. One can, however, legitimately draw attention to the agrarian contexts in which this momentous event took place.

In the year 1700, Bhīmsen, while writing his memoirs, set himself to explain the reasons for the success of these "malefactors and Marathas". Himself a native of Burhanpur, and with decades of service in the Dakhin behind him, his views on the subject are of great significance. He begins purely with a military argument. The Mughal commanders were not maintaining their contingents up to the standards required by the regulations. As a result the "malefactors" did not entertain any fear of the Mughal *faujdārs*, and so "those regions that have been assigned in pay to the *manṣabdārs* cannot be compelled to pay revenue". "The *zamīndārs* also, having obtained power, have allied themselves with the Marathas."

He turns to the second reason and here finds a connexion between the rise of the Maratha power and the oppression of the peasants in the imperial territories:

The agents of the *jāgīrdārs*, having apprehensions concerning the niggardly behaviour of the clerks of the imperial court, who on every excuse ... effect a transfer, do not have any hope of the confirmation (*ba-ḥālī*) of the *jāgīr* for the following year, and so abandon the habit of protecting the peasant (*ra'īyat-parwarī*) and of firmness (*istiqlāl*). The *jāgīrdār*, who sends a revenue collector (*'āmil*), owing to his own difficult circumstances, first takes something from him as deposit (*qabẓ*); and the latter, reaching the *jāgīr*, keeps thinking, perhaps another *'āmil* is coming behind him, who has paid a larger *qabẓ*, and, so proceeding tyrannically, is unrelenting in his exactions (*taḥṣīl*). Some peasants are not remiss in paying the authorized revenue (*māl-i wājib*), but are made desperate by the evil of this excruciating spoliation. It came to be represented [at the imperial court] that the Marathas obtain collaboration from the peasants of the imperial dominions. It was, thereupon, ordered that the horses and weapons found in every village should be confiscated. When this happened in most villages, the peasants, providing themselves with horses and arms, joined the Marathas.

Bhīmsen returns again to the subject of the oppression of the peasants and speaks of:

the tyranny of the *paṭṭīs* of the *faujdārs*, and the *zamīndārs*, who on every excuse collect money from the peasantry – and besides this the imperial tribute (*peshkash-i pādshāhī*) was fixed upon the *zamīndārs*, people being appointed to exact it and sent everywhere to obtain supplies. There is no limit to the oppression of these men. The *zamīndārs* do not give a *dām* or *diram* from their own purse, but pay it after exacting it from the peasants. And the *jizya* that has been imposed and collectors (*umnā'*) appointed: Of their oppression and cruelty what may one write? For no description can suffice ...

In addition to this, the conditions of the peasants were aggravated beyond endurance from Maratha depredations. For,

as the country has been divided into the *khāliṣa* and pay-assignments of the *jāgīrdārs*, so the Marathas too have distributed the very same country among their own "pseudo-chiefs":[61] On one land there came to be two *jāgīrdārs*. Quatrain: 'The village is ruined by a measuring rod with two measures", etc. The troops of the (Maratha) leaders who come in for the sake of plundering the country, extort money from every *pargana* and all places, in accordance with their desire, and let (their horses) graze and trample upon the cultivated fields... Order has disappeared... Now things have gone beyond every limit. The produce of the field does not reach the granary at all. They (the peasants?) are absolutely ruined.

This, apparently, drove the peasants still further into the arms of the Marathas: Thus "when many of Sīvā's[62] forts came into the possession of His Majesty (Aurangzeb), it became difficult for the Marathas to find a place to live and keep their dependants. (But) they have affinities with the peasants of the imperial dominions and left their families in their custody in inhabited places..." The passage closes with these words: "The peasants have abandoned cultivation and not a coin reaches the *jāgīrdārs*. Despairing and perplexed because of [their lack of] strength, many of the *manṣabdārs* of this country[63] have gone over to the Marathas."[64]

As a contemporary appraisal of the causes of Maratha success Bhīmsen's statements are invaluable. Such facts as we possess amply justify the leading lines of his argument. The peasants of the Dakhin had suffered for decades before Shivājī's rise to eminence from wars brought about by the steady pressure of the Mughals

[61] *Nā-sardārān*. This is the official term used for the Maratha commanders in Mughal documents.

[62] The author, of course, means Shivājī's successors, or simply Marathas.

[63] Bhīmsen has here probably in mind those Dakhinī nobles who had been serving formerly under the Bijapur and Golkunda governments.

[64] *Dilkushā*, ff. 138b-140a.

against the Dakhin kingdoms. Vast areas were ravaged by the invading armies, especially when no immediate annexation of the territory was foreseen: the grain was seized, the people slaughtered or enslaved.[65] Large armies were stationed in the Mughal Dakhin and maintained largely from assignments in its provinces so that even in peacetime the peasants were laid under a crippling burden.[66] And so, as we have already seen, the country was desolate and the peasants in flight, when Aurangzeb came to assume the viceroyalty of the Dakhin for the second time (1652).

Thus even at that early period the peasants had begun to render aid to Shivājī. Before he set out to win his throne in 1658, Aurangzeb urged his officials to mete out capital punishment to "peasants, *deshmukhs* and *paṭels* of the *parganas* of imperial territories, who have gone over to the side of the enemy [Shivājī and his associates] and have exerted themselves in guiding or abetting those ill-destined ones."[67]

At the same time, it will be a mistake to consider Shivājī and the Maratha chiefs as leaders of a peasant uprising. Shivājī was the son of a great Niẓāmshāhī (later 'Ādilshāhī) noble, and he himself began his career as a chieftain in the Konkan. The fiscal and political practices of the Marathas bore the deepest imprint of their *zamīndārī* origins. Thus the *chauth*, the customary demand of Maratha raiders, derived from the traditional claim of the *zamīndār* to a fourth part of the land revenue, on a pattern we know to have existed in Gujarat.[68] It was, probably, typical of their vision that when Tārābāī sought peace with Aurangzeb she asked for "the *deshmukhī* of the country of the Dakhin", the acme of the ambition of any *zamīndār*.[69] When by the mid-eighteenth

[65] Cf. Lāhorī, I, 316-17, 416-17, for such measures in territories belonging respectively to Ahmadnagar and Bijapur.

[66] This emerges most clearly from the letters Aurangzeb wrote as viceroy of the Dakhin. The *jama'* was considerably inflated, being over four times higher than the actual revenue (*Ādāb-i 'Ālamgīrī*, f.40b; ed., I, 157; *Ruq'āt-i 'Ālamgīr*, 121-2); and the *manṣabdārs* found it most difficult to maintain their contingents from the income of their assignments (*Ādāb-i 'Ālamgīrī*, ff.38a-b, 117b-118a; ed., I, 148-50; *Ruq'āt-i 'Ālamgīr*, 116-7 and passim).

[67] *Ādāb-i 'Ālamgīrī*, f.175a-b.

[68] See Chapter V, Section 1.

[69] *Akhbārāt* 47/73; Khāfī Khān, II, 627. The right demanded by Tārābāī is called *sardeshmukhī* (involving a claim to 9% of the revenue collected) in the latter work.

It is interesting to read in the English records of "a very great report of peace settled between the Mogull and Sevagee" in 1675, under which Shivājī was "to deliver up all the castles and country which he has taken from the Mogull" and in return "to be the Kings Desy of all his countrys of Deccan" (*English Records on*

century the Marathas had almost conquered an empire for themselves, their leaders still used their power to acquire *zamīndārī* rights everywhere. "The Marathas in general, but especially the Brahmans of the Dakhin," says a writer of that period, "have the peculiar desire to deprive all people of their means of livelihood and appropriate it for themselves. They do not spare the *zamīndārī* of *rājas*, nor even the *zamīndārī* of small people like headmen and village accountants. Uprooting most cruelly the heirs of ancient lineage, they establish their own possession and desire that the Brahmans of the Konkan should become the proprietors (*mālik*) of the whole world."[70]

There is no reason to believe, moreover, that the peasantry in the Maratha kingdom was free from oppression. How Shivājī treated the peasants in his dominions is described by Fryer, who visited parts of his kingdom in 1675-6. He demanded the revenue, we are told, at double the rates of former days,[71] leaving to "the Tiller hardly so much as will keep Life and Soul together".[72] And in Kanara "three-quarters of the Land lies unmanured (uncultivated) through the Tyranny of Seva Gi".[73] According to an English report of 1675, the hardships suffered by the peasants were so severe there that "all people pray that the Moors may regain the country".[74]

Shivājī had use for the peasants in a different sphere altogether. They were the "Naked Starved Rascals" who formed much of his army.[75] Armed with "only lances and long swords two inches wide",[76] they were "good at Surprising and Ransacking", but not "for a pitched Field".[77] They had to live by plunder only, for Shivājī's reputed maxim was: "No Plunder, no Pay."[78] This was the form of salvation which Shivājī and his successors held out to

---

Shivājī, II, 57). The offices of *deshmukh* and *desāī* are identical.

70 Āzād Bilgrāmī, <u>*Kh*</u>*izāna-i 'Āmira*, (1762-63), 47. The references to Dakhinī and Konkanī Brahmans were probably provoked by the fact that with the rise of the Peshwās, this caste of Brahmans tended to acquire a dominating position within the Maratha political system.

Though A. Wink in his *Land and Sovereignty in India: Agrarian Society and Politics under the Eighteenth Century Svarajya*, sets forth a theory of political processes in pre-colonial India, with which it is hard to agree, there is little to fault him with when he lays out evidence (pp.34-51), to establish that "Maratha svarājya was a form of '*zamīndārī* sovereignty'" (p.43).

71 Fryer, II, 4. 72 Ibid., I, 311-12; also II, 66. 73 Ibid., II, 86.

74 *Factories, N.S.*, I, 337. 75 Fryer II, 67.

76 Manucci, III, 505. 77 Fryer, II, 67, 68; Manucci, op.cit.

78 Fryer, I, 341.

the destitute peasantry of the Dakhin. As Bhīmsen's account shows, the military operations of the Marathas did not offer any relief to the cultivating peasants. On the contrary, they suffered grievously from the ravages of both the Maratha armies and their opponents. In 1671 the castellan of Udgir reported that owing to the operations of "the imperial forces and the villainous enemy" all the peasants had fled the *pargana* and for two years no revenues had been collected.[79] The Mughals too would burn villages, devastate the crops and enslave men and women.[80] As the range of the conflict grew, and the numbers of its victims increased, a still larger number of "naked starved rascals", themselves plundered, had no alternative left but to join the Marathas and become plunderers themselves.[81] And so the unending circle went on.

"There is no province or district," confesses Aurangzeb in his last years, "where the infidels have not raised a tumult and since they are not chastised, they have established themselves everywhere. Most of the country has been rendered desolate and if any place is inhabited, the peasants there have probably come to terms with the 'Robbers' [*Ashqiyā*, official Mughal name for the Marathas]..."[82]

If peasant distress was at the root of these rebellions that shook

[79] *Documents of Aurangzeb's Reign*, 86-87.

[80] Ibid., 27 (a report of 1662: 80 or 90 villages near Lohgarh ravaged, 1,000 or more heads of cattle seized, and about 300 men and women enslaved in one small expedition). See also Fryer, I, 310.

[81] The Maratha armies thus retained their low-class composition even when they had conquered the larger portion of India. Writing in 1762-3, Āzād Bilgrāmī tells us that "the army of the enemy (the Marathas) consists mostly of low-born people, like peasants, shepherds, carpenters and cobblers, while the army of the Muslims comprises mostly nobles and gentlemen. The success of the enemy is due to this that the enemy troops, being able to withstand great exertion, practise guerilla warfare (*jang-i qazzāqī*) and at the time of war cut off the supplies of grain and fodder of their opponent, reducing him to impotence... (although) there is no question of the low-born possessing the courage and dignity that is ingrained in the nature of the noble-born" (*Khizāna-i 'Āmira*, 49).

The way in which the Maratha depredations created a larger and larger recruiting ground for the Maratha armies may be illustrated by the example of the Pinḍārīs, who became prominent auxiliaries of the Maratha chiefs in the last phase of the Maratha regime. "The Pindarries were fed and nourished by the very miseries they created; for as their predatory invasions extended, property became insecure, and those who were ruined by their depredations, were afterwards compelled to have recourse to a life of violence, as the only means of subsistence left them. They joined the stream which they could not withstand and endeavoured to redeem their own losses by the plunder of others" (J. Malcolm, *Memoir of Central India*, 3rd edn., I, 429).

[82] *Aḥkām-i 'Alāmgīrī*, f.61b.

the Mughal empire to its foundations, the rebellions themselves represent a historical paradox in that the alleviation of such distress nowhere forms part of the rebels' proclaimed objectives or of their actual deeds and measures. This marks a singular difference between the agrarian revolts in India and those of China and Europe.[83] The weakness of the Indian peasants' class consciousness, an elementary failure on their part to recognize a peasant brotherhood out of the welter of castes and religious sects, calls for reflection. It can be partly attributed to the intervention of the *zamīndār* class, a leading component of many of the uprisings. But this by itself cannot be a sufficient explanation.

The success of the revolts, then, given the complexities of their genesis and the nature of ambitions of their diverse leaders, could not lead to the creation of any new order in the place of the empire that they helped to destroy.[84] In the period that followed the gates were opened to anarchy and colonial conquest. But the Mughal empire had, at least partly, been its own grave-digger; and what Sa'dī said of another great empire might well serve as its epitaph:

> Know ye of the emperors of Persia,
> Who oppressed the lower classes:
> Gone is their glory and empire;
> Gone their tyranny over the peasant![85]

[83] Cf. I. Habib, *Essays*, 257-8.

[84] It may here be instructive to refer to the history of China, for similar consequences of pre-modern agrarian uprisings. After enumerating a number of peasant revolts in China down to the Taiping Revolution (1851-64), Mao Zedong (1939) observed justly that "the scale of peasant uprisings and peasant wars in Chinese history has no parallel anywhere else". He added, however, that "since neither new productive forces, nor new relations of production, nor new class-forces, nor any advanced political party existed in those days [ancient and medieval times]... every peasant revolution failed, and the peasantry was invariably used by the landlords and the nobility, either during or after the revolution, as a lever for bringing about dynastic change" (*Selected Works of Mao Tse-tung*, Peking, 1967, II, 308-9).

[85] "*Khabar dārī az khusrawān-i 'Ajam*", etc., *Bostān*.

APPENDIX A

MEASURES OF LAND

1. GAZ-I SIKANDARĪ

The standard official unit of land measurement which Akbar's administration inherited from its predecessors was the *gaz-i Sikandarī* (or *Iskandarī*). According to the *Ā'īn*, it was first instituted by Sikandar Lodī, who made it equal to (the diameters of) 41½ of his *Sikandarī* pieces, the length being later increased to 42 by Humāyūn. The *gaz* continued in use under Sher Shāh and Islām Shāh, who, bringing the whole of Hindustan under *ẓabṭ*, are said to have "measured with this same *gaz*".[1] During Akbar's reign it remained the official standard till it was finally superseded by the *gaz-i Ilāhī* in 1586.[2]

Thomas found as a result of careful measurement that, the *Sikandarī* coins being placed in a row, "the completion of the 30th inch of our measure falls exactly opposite the centre of the 42nd coin", from which it follows that Humāyūn's *gaz-i Sikandarīs* was equal to 30.36 inches (77.01 cm). But the margin of error in such an experiment with coins only tolerably round, must obviously have been large; moreover, Thomas himself recognized that the length of the *gaz* might really have been greater than is indicated by his measurement, if allowance was to be made for the wear and tear the coins had suffered in the course of three and a half centuries.[3]

Abū-l Faẓl adds that Humāyūn's *gaz-i Sikandarī* consisted of

[1] *Ā'īn*, I, 296. It may perhaps be helpful here to indicate that in our Persian sources of the time *gaz*, *ẕirā'* and *dir'a* were fully interchangeable terms: the use of one word instead of another did not imply a different length for the yard. In three documents concerning *madad-i ma'āsh* grants of Sher Shāh's reign, it is stipulated that the area of the grant should be measured by the *gaz-i Sher Shāhī* (Allahabad 318; and texts of the other two documents, with photographic reproductions, printed in the *Oriental College Magazine*, IX, 3 [May 1933], 121-2, 125-8). Perhaps Sher Shāh made some slight change in the *gaz* length, which entitled him to call the *gaz-i Sikandarī* after his own name.

[2] *Ā'īn*, I, 296. *A.N.*, III, 529, assigns the introduction of the *gaz-i Ilāhī* to the beginning of the 33rd year (1588), and not 31st year as stated in the *Ā'īn*.

[3] Prinsep, *Useful Tables*, ed. Thomas, 123-4 n. Sikandar Lodī's coins are catalogued by H.N. Wright in his *Coinage and Metrology of the Sultans of Dehli*, 250-4. Abū-l Faẓl says that the *Sikandarīs* were "copper pieces with a silver alloy", and these must be the heavier issues comprising the larger number of Sikandar's coins.

32 *angushts* (digits);[4] and since the *gaz-i Ilāhī* had a length of 41 digits, this would imply that the former was just a little shorter than four-fifths of the latter. Though this has been accepted by some modern writers,[5] there can hardly be any doubt that the number 32 is due to a slip of the pen, for the ratio it suggests is directly contradicted by Abū-l Faẓl himself, when he defines the difference between a *bīgha* (i.e. a square of 60 *gaz*) of the *gaz-i Sikandarī* and that of the *gaz-i Ilāhī*.

He says, first of all, that previous to the introduction of the bamboo measuring rod in the 19th year (1574-75), the *bīgha* used to be 13 per cent smaller than its true size, because the hempen rope would shrink from the length of 60 *gaz* to 56.[6] The second change came with the promulgation of the *gaz-i Ilāhī*. According to the difference between the new and the superseded *bīgha* as given by Abū-l Faẓl, 87 *bīghas* of the latter unit should have been equal to 77.83 *bīghas* of the *gaz-i Ilāhī*, implying thereby that 9.32 *gaz-i Sikandarī* were equal to 8.8 *gaz-i Ilāhī*, so that 100 *gaz-i Sikandarī* were equal to 94.64 *gaz-i Ilāhī*.[7]

[4] *Ā'īn*, I, 296.

[5] Prinsep, *Useful Tables*, ed. Thomas, 123; cf. Thomas's n., ibid., 124.

[6] This statement in *Ā'īn*, I, 297 (see the following note for translation of the whole passage) appears at first sight to be illogical and arbitrary. Surely, not every rope would have been shrinking uniformly at the rate of 4 *gaz* in 60. Cf. Abū-l Faẓl's own remarks a little earlier, ibid., I, 296. The explanation is forthcoming, however, from a *parwāna* of 1757, which confirms a *madad-i ma'āsh* grant in the *pargana* of Batala, originally made in 1569, and reproduces the endorsements put upon the original document (I.O.4438:55). The endorsements show that the grant in the first instance was of 300 *bīghas*, but three reductions were successively made from it, the first being called "reduction [on account] of the measuring rod" (*quṣūr-i ṭanāb*). This amounts to 39 *bīghas*, two *biswas*, i.e. 13.03 per cent of the original grant. It seems, therefore, that when introducing the new *ṭanāb* it was anticipated that the actual *bīgha* as measured would now be larger, and to prevent the grantees from taking advantage of this, a definite scale was fixed for making reductions from the total area of their grants in order to offset, or, perhaps, more than offset, this increase. In the Batala grant the reduction is practically at the standard rate of 13% given by Abū-l Faẓl, but in the specified area of a grant originally made in 1571 in *pargana* Pathan(-kot) in the Punjab, the reduction made on account of the bamboo rod was as high as 15% (*Mughals and the Jogis of Jakhbar*, Docs. I and II).

[7] *Ā'īn*, I, 297. The whole passage reads: "One *bīgha* by the hempen rope (*ṭanāb-i san*) was smaller than the *bīgha* by the bamboo rod (*ṭanāb-i bāns*) by two *biswas* and twelve *biswānsas*. And in every hundred *bīghas* the difference amounted to thirteen *bīghas*. Although the hempen rope was also of sixty *gaz*, yet on being twisted it used to come to fifty-six *gaz* (only). And (the *bīgha* of) the *gaz-i Ilāhī* was larger than (that of) the *gaz-i Sikandarī* by one *biswa*, sixteen *biswānsas*, thirteen *taswānsas*, eight *tapwānsas* and four *answānsas*. The difference from both diminutions amounts in one *bīgha* to fourteen [sic! four] *biswas*, twenty [sic! eight;

Abū-l Faẓl's statements about the reduction by 10.54 per cent in the specified area in terms of the new *bīgha* consequent upon the introduction of the *gaz-i Ilāhī*[8] are confirmed by numerous endorsements found on *madad-i ma'āsh* documents. These show reductions in the area of the grants, specifically on account of the new measure, mostly amounting to 10.5 and 10.6 per cent of the original area.[9] Abū'l Faẓl's own standard reduction rate implies that the *bīgha-i Ilāhī* was 11.78 percent larger than the *bīgha* of *gaz-i Sikandarī*.

The ratio between the lengths of the two linear measures established from the difference in the relative sizes of their squares is nearly 41:38.78. The *gaz-i Ilāhī* being equal to 41 digits, Abū-l Faẓl's length of 32 digits for the *gaz-i Sikandarī* must, then, be a mistake (for 39?).

Calculating on the basis of the ratio 41:38.78 between the two measures, we can deduce the length of the *gaz-i Ilāhī* from that of the *gaz-i Sikandarī* as found by Thomas, to be 32.1 inches or 81.53 cm. In other words, a length of just over 32 inches or about 81.5 cm

---

for in Persian writing *hasht* (8) and *bist* (20) are often confounded] *biswānsas*, thirteen *taswānsas*, eight *tapwānsas* and four *answānsas*."

Abū-l Faẓl thus records a standard rate of reduction of 22.17% on an original grant stated in the earlier *bīgha* measured by the hempen rope, to convert it into a *bīgha* based on the *gaz-i Ilāhī* measured by the bamboo rod. But in the grants the total reductions show higher rates: 22.9% in a Vrindaban grant (IVS 159,191-2, Gopinath); 22.97% in a grant in *pargana* Unao, *sarkār* Lakhnau (Allahabad 154); 23% in a grant in Bhojpur, *sarkār* Kanauj (CAS in History, Aligarh MS No.36) and 25% in another in the same locality (same collection, No.37). These variations may be due mainly to variations in the rates of reduction on account of the bamboo-rod, for which, as we have seen in the preceding note, as high a rate as 15% is recorded.

8 See preceding note for passage from the *Ā'īn*, I, 297: a reduction of 0.0917 *bīgha* from 0.87 *bīgha*.

9 The reductions amounting to 10.5 per cent (described as *quṣūr-i tafāwat-i gaz-i Ilāhī*) appear in endorsements on documents belonging to the Batala series in the India Office, I.O. 4438: 7, 25 & 55. The reduction of 10.6 per cent for "*tafāwat-i gaz-i Ilāhī*" is shown on an endorsement on Allahabad 1177 and in the text of Allahabad 789, both documents relating to the *pargana* of Bahraich. A reduction of 10.55% was made in Todar Mal's grant of 1584 in *pargana* Mathura, when it was made an imperial grant in 1613, 100 *bīghas* "by the bamboo rod" being deemed equivalent to 89 *bīghas* 9 *biswas* by *gaz-i Ilāhī* (Radhakund 143A, 154, 166). In grants edited by A. Ansari, *Administrative Documents*, nos. 6,7 and 33, the reduction imposed on account of the *gaz-i Ilāhī* is set at 11%. See also *Mughals and the Jogis of Jakhbar*, Doc.III. In another endorsement on Allahabad 1177, the reduction is set at 11.6 per cent, but that this was an exceptional case is shown by the remark that this reduction was made "in accordance with the *parwāncha* (order) of Muẓaffar K͟hān". See also Moosvi; 97-99, where col.(d) in Table 4.1 is relevant for the diminutions of areas of grants and col.(e) for enhancement of tax per *bīgha*, since this represents the increase in the size of the *bīgha*.

would seem to be likely for the *gaz-i Ilāhī*, if Thomas's measurement of the *gaz-i Sikandarī* can be given any credit.[10] In the next section we shall try to see if this length is confirmed by the other evidence that we have.

2. GAZ-I ILĀHĪ

The controversy over the exact length of the *gaz-i Ilāhī* has a long history behind it. In the early 1820s it became a matter of some importance for the British government to discover its length in order to settle the areas of the various revenue-free lands in Mahalwari territories. The government finally declared in 1825-6 that it would consider one *gaz-i Ilāhī* equal to 33 inches. The decision arose partly, at least, from the convenience of converting *bīghas* based on a *gaz* of this length, into acres.[1] With the removal of its administrative significance the subject lost its topical interest and has received only sporadic attention since then. In the absence of a systematic study of contemporary evidence, proper distinction does not often seem to have been made between the *gaz-i Ilāhī* and certain other parallel units of measurement.

The only indication directly given by Abū-l Faẓl about the length of the *gaz-i Ilāhī* is that it was equal to 41 *angushts* or finger-breadths.[2] Unfortunately, there is no fixed length for a digit in India,[3] and the average derived from the actual measurement of fingers can at best be a very rough guide to the digit of the *Ā'īn* or the Mughal administration.[4]

[10] A late European traveller Marshall, 420 refers to the "Seecundrees Guz, called the Carpet Guz" and gives its length as 27 7/8 inches, while his value for the *gaz-i Ilāhī* is 31 1/3 inches. At Hugli in 1699 "the Secundree Guz" was given the length of 29 inches (Bodl. Rawlinson MS A 302, f.250a – reference owed to Dr Najaf Haider). But this may be a local unit only.

[1] Cf. Prinsep, *Useful Tables*, ed. Thomas, 125. [2] *Ā'īn*, I, 296.

[3] The English mode of reckoning whereby 41 digits equal 30.75 inches has no relevance, though this was accepted provisionally by Prinsep, op.cit., 124, and, following him, by Moreland, *JUPHS*, II (1919), i, 17.

[4] Col. A. Hodgson, then Surveyor-General of India, in an attempt to determine the length of the *gaz-i Ilāhī*, "measured at Futtehgur the breadth of the four fingers of the right hand of seventy-six men of different classes", and the average result was that, if measured at the middle joints, 41 finger-breadths would be equal to 31.549 inches, and, if across the knuckle-joints, 33.08 inches (Hodgson, 'Memoire on the Length of the Illahee Guz', *JRAS*, 1843, 45-49). "Six barleycorns being also generally understood to be the value of a finger", Halhed at Muradabad made an experiment with them and, striking an average, obtained the length of 31.843 inches for 41 digits (ibid., 49-50). The *Ā'īn* says that an *angusht* was considered by "some" to be equal to six barley-corns of moderate size joined in width (I, 295, 597) and by

Two direct statements belonging to the earlier part of the seventeenth century are, however, available that express the length of the *gaz-i Ilāhī* in terms of European units of measurement, whose values have remained constant since that period. In 1620-21 Robert Hughes, writing from Patna, speaks of the "elahye of Agra" as 4/5 of the "Jahanger coved", the length of which is stated to be 40.5 inches at one place and 40 inches at another.[5] The *gaz-i Ilāhī* should therefore have been either 32 or 32.4 inches long, but there is a distinct hint from Hughes himself that it was in fact 32.33 or 32.125 inches.[6] Less than six years later Pelsaert observed that "100 Akbarī *gaz* made 120 of our (i.e. Dutch) ells",[7] which means that its length was 32.126 inches. Both the sources, therefore, agree very closely, which is all the more significant inasmuch as they alone of our earlier European authorities have explicitly referred to this *gaz*.[8] Other references to unnamed "coveds" or "ells" then in vogue are by no means necessarily to be taken as applying to the *gaz-i Ilāhī*.

Thus in 1641 there were said to be two "covedas" or measures in use in the cloth trade in the Mughal dominions in general, one of 33 inches and the other of 27 inches. In 1616 Salbank and Fettiplace, writing from Agra and Ajmer, speak of a "covado" by which their cloth was sold at the court and in the general market, and whose

"the sages of Hind" to "8 barley-corns, stripped of husks, laid breadthwise" (I, 598).

Another means adopted by Halhed was to measure by "the mansuri pice", "42 of these being held to make a guz": the resultant value was 32.025 inches (*JRAS*, 1843, 50). But this apparently is based upon a misunderstanding of Abū-l Faẓl's statements, where the length of 42 *Sikandarī* pieces is given to the *gaz-i Sikandarī*, as modified by Humāyūn, and not to the *gaz-i Ilāhī*. The coins which were used for the experiment were, therefore, also the wrong ones.

[5] *Factories, 1618-21*, 192, 197, 236. This *gaz* was possibly the one brought into being by Jahāngīr, when, upon his accession in 1605, he ordered "an increase in the weights and the *gaz*" (*T.J.*, 96). A yard of the length of almost 40.5 inches remained in use in the retail trade at Patna as late as 1661 (*Early Annals*, I, 380).

[6] Ibid., 236. Hughes, writing to the Surat factors in reply to their letter, points out that "the 'Jehangery coved' of this place was 40 inches, not 32½ as stated" in their letter. Since Hughes had had previously to distinguish the *gaz-i Ilāhī* from the *Jahāngīrī* for the benefit of the same factors (ibid., 192), it is probable that the two units had now again been confounded.

[7] Pelsaert, 29. For the length of the Dutch ell, see Moreland, *Relations of Golconda*, 88.

[8] The only other traveller during the whole of the 17th century who gives the value of this *gaz* in explicit terms is Marshall. He speaks of "Eckbar Guz, called Taylors Guz, containing 31 1/8 inches" (Marshall, 420). His observations were made too late for him to be regarded as an authentic source for the length of the original unit. It is most likely that what he found was not the true *gaz-i Ilāhī*, but a modified or shorter form of it, adapted to a particular trade.

length was 7/8 of the English yard or 31.5 inches.[9] This ought to be read with a statement in Jahāngīr's Memoirs, where, under the 13th regnal year (1618-19), the *gaz-i Ilāhī* is stated to be equal to 40 *angushts*.[10]

Now, a reduction in the length of the *gaz-i Ilāhī* by one digit since the time of the *Ā'īn* is not impossible, but it seems more likely that Jahāngīr has loosely attributed to it the length that, in fact, belonged to a distinct, though almost equal, unit. Writing under the 10th regnal year of Shāhjahān (1636-37), while setting down the measurements of certain buildings at Agra, Lāhorī assigns the length of 40 digits not to the *gaz-i Ilāhī*, but to what he calls the *z̲irā'-i Pādshāhī*, the Royal Yard.[11] It is with this *z̲irā'*, probably, that the anonymous "covado" of Salbank and Fettiplace ought to be identified. It is true that the difference between the latter and the length of the *gaz-i Ilāhī* given by Hughes and Pelsaert is a little less than 1/41; but the equivalents in European measurements have obviously been given in approximate rather than exact terms, and a small difference in fractions need not cause us any surprise.

What is possibly a more precise means of discovering the length of the *z̲irā'i Pādshāhī* (from which that of the *gaz-i Ilāhī* can, of course, be deduced) is provided by the detailed measurements given by Lāhorī for the Tāj Maḥal. He sets these down under the 15th year of his patron's reign, when it was completed, though the foundations had been laid early in the 5th year (1632).[12] The measurements are stated simply in terms of an unspecified *z̲irā'*, but it seems certain that it is the same unit of 40 digits which Lāhorī had used to describe the measurements of other Agra buildings under the 10th year (1641-42). The measurements, though set down in the 15th year, obviously conform to the original plan that must have been prepared ten years earlier. This is apparent from the size given for the raised marble platform, 120x120 *z̲irā'*, or exactly 4 *bīghas*: a size which would naturally have occurred to the planners, but could hardly have been reached by a conversion of the figures of the original into those in terms of some other unit.

The comparative measurements at the Tāj Maḥal were made by A. Hodgson and his assistants in 1825. He found the raised marble platform to be both the most convenient for measurement and the simplest for comparison: the average length derived for the *z̲irā'*

[9] *Lett. Recd.*, IV, 231 & 238. [10] *T.J.*, 234. [11] Lāhorī, I, ii, 237.
[12] Lāhorī, II, 322-9.

from its measurements was 31.456 inches, while from those of the lower red sandstone platform, the corresponding length obtained was 31.464 inches.[13] If these figures are assumed to apply to the *zirā'-i Pādshāhī* of 40 digits, the length of the *gaz-i Ilāhī*, being 41 digits, should be taken to be about 32.24 inches (81.89 cm).

In the letters of English factors of 1647-8 there are two statements to the effect that in 1647 Shāhjahān reduced the length of "the Agra covett" by "at least" 2½ per cent, whereupon it became equal to "the Lahore covett";[14] and that its length now was "exactly 8/9ths of a yard or 32 inches".[15] Moreland has linked this change with the reference in Lāhorī, under the 10th year, to the *zirā'-i Pādshāhī*, and he suggests that Shāhjahān introduced a new unit which was smaller than the *gaz-i Ilāhī* by one digit, and that this was finally imposed on the markets of Agra in 1647. His conclusion, therefore, is that the *gaz-i Ilāhī*, being identical with the superseded "Agra covett", had a length of 32.8 inches.[16] However, as we have seen, the *zira'* of 40 digits was no innovation of Shāhjahān. Furthermore, by the time the change is said to have taken place at Agra, the *zirā'-i Pādshāhī* seems to have been increased to 42 digits.[17] It is true that this new length is mentioned only in connexion with the distances on the routes, but since it bore the same name as given to the older unit of 40 digits, it is very likely that it prevailed in the spheres of that unit as well. If so, it must have been in force in Agra by 1647 and the change in that year can be best interpreted only as a reduction in the size of the market (not administrative) unit by 2½ per cent, or

[13] The full details of all his measurements will be found in his 'Memoire on the Length of the Illahee Guz or Imperial Land Measure of Hindostan', *JRAS*, 1843, 45-53. He believed that the *zirā'* used in the Tāj was identical with the *gaz-i Ilāhī*, being apparently unaware of the *zirā'* of 40 digits. He knew, however, of the unit of 42 digits mentioned by Lāhorī, II, 534, 709, under the 19th and 20th years, but thought that the increase in the number of digits did not signify any increase in its absolute length, but only a proportional diminution of the length of each digit. It seems that the results of his measurements published earlier had pointed to a much larger length for the *zirā'* (cf. Prinsep, *Useful Tables*, ed. Thomas, 125). This drew a communication from W. Cracroft ('On the Measurement of the Illahy Guz of the Emperor Akber', *JASB*, 1834, 360-61), who observed that the measurements of the marble slabs in the *kursī* or raised platform of the Tāj had convinced him that they were cut to conform to the sizes of *gaz*-units or multiples thereof and that the mean length of the *gaz* so derived was just a fraction short of 32 inches (81.28 cm).

[14] *Factories*, 1646-50, 122. [15] Ibid., 190.

[16] W.H. Moreland, 'The Mogul Unit of Measurement', *JRAS*, N.S., 1927, 120-121.

[17] Lāhorī, II, 534, 709 (under the 19th and 20th regnal years, 1645-6 and 1646-7).

from 42 to 41 digits, which was the length precisely of the *gaz-i Ilāhī*. In that case, almost the reverse of what Moreland suggests would appear to have happened, and the length of the *gaz-i Ilāhī*, deduced from the factors' statements, works out at just 32, not 32.8 inches.[18]

A different method of ascertaining the length of the *gaz-i Ilāhī* was suggested by Elliot, who examined the distances between the old Mughal route-pillars or *mīnārs*, set up to mark each *kuroh* on the imperial highway near Dehli. Calculating on the basis of 5,000 *gaz* making a *kuroh*, he found that, on the average, the spacing of the *mīnārs* north of Dehli would conform to a *gaz* of 32.818 inches.[19] But he is, perhaps, hasty in assuming that the *kuroh* of these pillars is measured according to the *gaz-i Ilāhī*. Akbar began setting up the kos-mīnārs at distances of 5,000 *gaz* between Agra and Ajmer in 1573-74, long before he instituted the *gaz-i Ilāhī* in 1588;[20] and the *mīnārs* must, therefore, have been spaced at *kurohs* based on the *gaz-i Sikandarī*. The *Ā'īn* does say that Akbar's *kuroh* consisted of 5,000 *gaz-i Ilāhī*;[21] but it is unlikely that the earlier *kos*-marks were disturbed to accord with the new measure. Indeed, Jahāngīr says, under his 15th regnal year, that the *kuroh* in his reign was equal according to the regulation of his father, to 5,000 *dir'as*, one and a quarter of which *dir'as* equalled two *dir'a-i Shar'ī* of 24 digits each.[22] This means that the *dir'a* used in the *kuroh* consisted of about

[18] van Twist, writing c.1638, says that in Gujarat "they use two different ells: 19 of the larger make fully 23½ Dutch ells; the smaller differ from ours only by the breadth of a thumb" (tr. Moreland, *JIH*, XVI, 72). The Dutch ell being 26.77 inches, the larger ell must have been 33.11 inches in length. Moreland seeks to identify it with the *gaz-i Ilāhī* (73n.). It is conceivably the enlarged *zira'-i Pādshāhī*, but it appears more probable that there has been a mistake in putting down the figures and the larger *gaz* of Gujarat (which was about 35.5 inches but is once put down also as of 34 inches) is really meant. For the latter unit, see *Lett. Recd.*, I, 34, 241; II, 214 (refers to the "covad" at Ahmadabad of 34 inches); III, 11; Foster, *Supp. Cal.*, 47; and Fryer, II, 127.

[19] Elliot, *Memoirs*, II, 194. It is not the direct, but the "road distance" between the pillars which has naturally to be compared and it is accordingly the latter from which Elliot calculates. The distances in the Mathura district as given by him, seem to point to a lower value for the *gaz*: on an average, 32.432 inches; but 8 of the 12 distances mentioned suggest a uniform length of 32.371 inches only.

Kuroh is the Persian equivalent of the Sanskrit *krosa*, from which is derived the Hindi *kos*.

[20] 'Ārif Qandahārī, 46. [21] *Ā'īn*, I, 597.

[22] *T.J.*, 298. As Beveridge in his translation of *T.J.*, II, 141 n., notes, the printed text which makes one *dir'a* of the *kuroh* equal to two *dir'a-i Shar'ī* is contradicted by the MSS, which read one and a quarter instead of one.

38.4 digits – close enough to the *gaz-i Sikandarī* of 38.8 digits. Mu'tamad K͟hān also, while giving the distance between limits of Akbar's empire, explains that each *gaz* used in the *kuroh* comprised 38 digits.[23] Writing in 1631 Mundy describes the "auntient Course", "used by the Kinge and great men", as consisting of 5,000 "Coards", each of which was 4/5 yard or 28.8 inches.[24] Mundy has obviously given an approximate an equivalent to the *gaz*, but his statement leaves little doubt that in his day also it was the *gaz* of 38 digits, or, at any rate, a *gaz* substantially smaller than the *gaz-i Ilāhī*, that was used to measure the *kuroh*. The change-over to a longer unit is first signified by Lāhorī, under the 19th and 20th years of Shāhjahān, when he says that the distances given by him are in terms of *kurohs*, each of 5,000 *z̤irā'-i Pādshāhī*, the *zirā'* being equal to 42 *angushts*.[25] This enlarged unit continued in use, apparently, right through Aurangzeb's reign, for the *Mir'ātu-l 'Ālam*, written after the tenth year of his reign, and the *Ma'lūmātu-l Āfāq*, written shortly after his death, gave the same value to the *z̤irā'* making up the *kuroh-i Pādshāhī*.[26] It would thus appear that throughout the seventeenth century only two *dir'as* or *z̤irā's* had been in use for measuring the *kurohs*: in the earlier decades, one of 38 or 39 digits, and during the rest of the period, that of 42. It is, therefore, most improbable that the extant *kos-* pillars around Dehli are spaced according to the *kuroh* of the *gaz-i Ilāhī*, while it is very likely, on the other hand, that, while Shāhjahān was building his new capital of Shāhjahānābād at Dehli, the *kos-mīnārs* on both sides of Dehli were set up by him

23 *Iqbālnāma*, II, Or. 1834, f.231b. He makes a serious error, however, in stating that a *kuroh* consisted of 200 *jarīb* and each *jarīb* of 60 *gaz*, thereby making a *kuroh* equal to 12,000 *gaz*.

24 Mundy, 66-67.

25 Lāhorī, II, 534, 709. In I, ii, 15, however, he assigns the *z̤irā'* used for measuring the route, a length of 40 digits only. On the other hand, the value of 42 digits for the *gaz* used for the *kuroh-i Shāhjahānī* is confirmed by Ṣādiq Isfahānī, *Shāhid-i Ṣādiq*, Egerton 1016, f.332b, where he makes such a *gaz* equal to 1.75 *arash*, and each *arash* to a *dir'a* of 24 digits.

26 *Mir'ātu-l 'Ālam*, Aligarh MS, f.214a; *Ma'lūmātu-l Āfāq*, Or. 1741, f.83a. See also *Mir'āt*, Supp., 176. Marshall, 420-21, speaks of two distinct "courses", each consisting of 8,000 "Covets"; 8,000 is probably a mistake for 5,000. The value of the two "Covets" derived from his lengths of the respective "courses" are 31.7 and 29.7 inches. Like Mundy his lengths may not be accurate, yet he is probably here describing respectively the new and the superseded *gaz* lengths used for measuring the *kuroh*. Similarly Manucci, II, 442 (also tr.'s n.), who equates 10 European leagues with 12 of India and thus suggests 31.7 inches for the length of the *gaz*, would seem to have the new measure of distance in mind.

and so conform to the *zirā'-i Pādshāhī* of 42 digits.[27] It follows, then, that Elliot's length of 32.818 inches is really that of the latter unit, and such being the case, the value of the *gaz-i Ilāhī*, deduced proportionally, ought to be put around 32.04 inches (81.37 cm.).

We may recall now that working on the basis of Thomas's measurement of the *gaz-i Sikandarī*, we had found the length of the *gaz-i Ilāhī* to be about 32.10 inches. From the further evidence now brought together, it would seem that its length lay somewhere between 32.00 and 32.25 inches, that is approximately 81.5 cm. It is probably unsafe to attempt any greater precision, for that can be achieved only by preferring one source to another on rather arbitrary grounds. The *bīgha*, or the area of 60 *gaz* square, based on the *gaz-i Ilāhī* of a length within the limits set above, could not have been smaller than 0.5877 acre or larger than 0.5969. The difference between the two limits is insignificant, and there would not be much loss of accuracy, perhaps, if, for the sake of convenience calculation, we were to assume one *bīgha* of the *gaz-i Ilāhī* as equal to 0.59 acre, with the understanding that it was probably a little larger than this, and quite possibly 0.60 acre (or 0.24 hectare).

3. BĪGHA-I DAFTARĪ

The *gaz-i Ilāhī* was undoubtedly intended by Akbar to be the sole official standard unit of measurement in almost every sphere.[1] Its displacement of previous official units for measuring land, buildings and cloth is expressly recorded;[2] and the conversion of the areas of all *madad-i ma'āsh* grants, made before its introduction, into *bīghas* measured by this new unit is attested to by documents belonging to the period.[3] One can be equally certain that the *dastūrs* (i.e. the final land-revenue rates) and the *ārāẓī* (area) statistics of the *Ā'īn* are both given in terms of the *bīgha* of this *gaz*.[4]

[27] There is no reference in our sources to Akbar having laid out *kos-mīnārs* on the Agra-Dehli-Lahor route. Jahāngīr issued orders for their construction in 1619-20 (*TJ*, 277); but the earliest record of their actual existence on this highway belongs to the early years of Aurangzeb's reign (Bernier, 284; Thevenot, 57).

[1] *A.N.*, III, 529.

[2] See note no.9 to Section 1 of this appendix and Moosvi, 97-100, 119-20, who also shows that the *dastūrs* were revised upwards through a set schedule to conform to the larger area of the *bīgha* of taxable land after the introduction of the *gaz-i Ilāhī*.

[3] *Ā'īn*, i, 296. The one possible exception is, as we have seen, the measurement of the routes, though the *Ā'īn*, I, 597, declares that here also the *gaz-i Ilāhī* was in use.

[4] See references to these documents in notes to Section 1 of this appendix. For

The next change in the official unit of land measurement appears to have come in the reign of Shāhjahān. About this our knowledge is almost entirely derived from a single passage in Ṣādiq Khān's history of the reign. We are told that while the *madad-i ma'āsh* grants continued to be defined in terms of the *bīgha-i Ilāhī*, the standard official unit of measurement for purposes of revenue records generally was now the *dir'a-i Shāhjahānī*. The *bīgha* based on the new unit was known as the *bīgha-i daftarī*, or the *bīgha* of the registers, and was exactly, or nearly exactly, two-thirds of the *bīgha-i Ilāhī*; it was, at the same time, three times the size of the small *bīgha* used by the peasants in the neighbourhood of Dehli and Agra. Ṣādiq Khān declares that "the cultivation and computation (*ḥisāb*) of the land of the territories of the provinces and the dependencies of Shāhjahānābād are entirely based on the *bīgha-i daftarī*." In the provinces of the Dakhin too, though the unit recorded, in the first instance, was the local *aut*, it used to be converted "ultimately" into the *bīgha*, i.e., presumably, the *bīgha-i daftarī*.[5] From the relative sizes of the *bīgha-i daftarī* and *bīgha-i Ilāhī*,[6] it would appear that the length of the *dir'a-i Shāhjahānī* stood in relation to that of the *gaz-i Ilāhī* as 60 to 73.485, or that, in other words, it was equal to a little less than 33.5 digits.

Important corroboration of Ṣādiq Khān's statements comes from Aurangzeb's *farmān* to Muḥammad Hāshim, 1668-9, Art. 14. While dealing with the tax to be levied on orchards, according to Muslim law (*Sharī'at*), it equates the *bīgha-i Shar'ī*, being the square of 60 *gaz-i Shar'ī*, with a square of 45 *gaz-i Shāhjahānī*. From this one should infer that by this time the unit of area in use in measuring taxable land was a *bīgha* based on the *gaz-i Shāhjahānī*, and that, given the length of *gaz-i Shar'ī* as 24 digits,[7] the *gaz-i Shāhjahānī* had a length of 32 digits. This puts its length fairly close to the one

the use of the *gaz-i Ilāhī* in stating the areas of *madad-i ma'āsh* grants, see Chapter VIII.

[5] Ṣādiq Khān, Or. 174, f. 186b; Or. 1671, f.91a; Khāfī Khān copies the whole passage *verbatim* in the earlier versions of his work. It is printed in a foot-note in the Bibliotheca Indica ed., I, 734-5; cf. also Add. 6573, f.261b.

[6] The *bīgha-i daftarī* is said to have amounted to 3,600 square *Dir'a-i Shāhjahānī*, and the *bīgha-i Ilāhī* "a fraction above" 5,400. The natural assumption that this *bīgha-i Ilāhī* contained just 3,600 square *gaz-i Ilāhī* is confirmed by a *chaknāma*, or boundary-defining document, belonging to the Batala series (I.O. 4438: 59). It was itself prepared in the 49th regnal year of Aurangzeb, but it is concerned with a grant originally made in the 7th year of Shāhjahān. It expressly speaks of measuring with a sixty-*gaz jarīb*.

[7] *T.J.*, 298.

deduced for the *dir'a-i Shāhjahānī* from Ṣādiq K͟hān's statements (33.5 digits); and one may assume the two linear measures to be identical.

There is some other supporting evidence as well. There is a suggestion in Pelsaert that indigo cultivators in the neighbourhood of Agra used a *bīgha* based on a *gaz* five-sixths of the length of *gaz-i Ilāhī*, making it practically equal in size to, and, therefore, possibly the parent of, the *bīgha-i daftarī*.[8] In 1680, the land acquired by the English factory at Malda in Bengal was measured, under official auspices, by a *bīgha* which corresponds in size almost exactly to the *bīgha-i daftarī*.[9] Again, there is a statement in K͟hāfī K͟hān to the effect that the *bīgha* was measured in his day, i.e. in the earlier part of the eighteenth century, by the *dir'a-i Shāhjahānī*, which, he implies, was different from the unit in use in the time of Rāja Todar Māl.[10] In the statistics of the measured areas of the different provinces of Aurangzeb's empire the *bīgha* used is not specified,[11] but we can now see that the figures here must be stated in terms of the *bīgha-i daftarī*, since it was this measure which was in use for taxable land.

So far our evidence is clear enough. When, however, we turn to the accountancy and administrative manuals, from which some precise information might have been expected, we find instead the greatest confusion concerning the name and length of the *dir'a* used in measuring the land. One manual, belonging to Shāhjahān's reign, speaks of the *dir'a-i Ilāhī* as the unit whereby a *bīgha* ought to be measured;[12] another, of a later date, does not refer to the *gaz* or *dir'a* at all, but to cubits (*dasts*) of 24 digits each, one *bīgha* being

---

[8] Pelsaert, 10, speaks of indigo being sown "at the rate of 14 or 15 lb. of seed to the *bīgha* or 60 Holland ells"; so that the Dutch ell would have been exactly equal to the *gaz* by which this *bīgha* was measured. Now the ell, according to Pelsaert, 29, was 100/120 *gaz-i Ilāhī*, so that the ratio between the two was as 60 to 72 – almost the same as that between the *dir'a-i Shāhjahānī* and the *gaz-i Ilāhī*.

[9] 'Malda Diary & Consultations', *JASB*, N.S., XIV (1918), 81-2, 122-3. The size of the *bīgha* is thus stated (p.82): "each Begae qts eighty large Coveds of Nine Nailes of an English yard". It, therefore, consisted of 2,025 square yards or 0.418 acre. The *bīgha-i daftarī*, being two thirds of the *bīgha-i Ilāhī*, was probably equal to 0.400 acre.

[10] K͟hāfī K͟hān, I, 156; Add. 6573, f.69b. The Bib. Ind. ed. contains two serious misreadings, 'ṭanka' for 'bīgha' and 'ḥāṣil' for 'paimā'ish'.

[11] Under Orissa, equivalent area figures are also given in terms of two other much smaller units (Fraser 86, f. 60b; *Intik͟hāb-i Dastūru-l 'Amal-i Pādshāhī*, Edinburgh 224, f.11a).

[12] *Dastūru-l 'Amal-i Navīsindagī*, f.171a.

100 cubits square.[13] Of two other manuals, dating from the middle and later years of Aurangzeb's reign, one puts the length of the *dir'a* (unnamed) at 48 digits,[14] while the other says that the *dir'a-i Ilāhī* was used for "the measurement of the cultivated area", but gives its value as 36 digits.[15]

The confusion is compounded by Grant, who, writing in 1786, first confuses the "beghah duftery" with the one used by Todar Māl, and then says it was subsequently reduced to a third of its original size. He goes on to say that in Bengal in his day, "the common begah, now called 'Ryotti' contained no more than 16,000 square yards", but served as "almost the universal standard to estimate the annual farm or permanent transfer of territorial property".[16] This could be the *bīgha-i daftarī*, somewhat reduced (55.21% of the *bīgha-i Ilāhī* instead of 66.66%). At the same time, the *bīgha-i Ilāhī* also appeared firmly established as the only official measure, of area in use in much of northern India.[17] The survey officers of the British Government, who organized revenue settlements early in the following century also found the *gaz-i Ilāhī* to be the only common, or non-local, unit of land measurement used in the various districts of the present-day Uttar Pradesh.

Neither the discrepancies in the statements of the manuals, nor the solitary survival of the *gaz-i Ilāhī* need be regarded as obstacles to an acceptance of Ṣādiq Khān's statements. His *bīgha-i daftarī*, as its name (meaning "*bīgha* of the registers") signifies, was meant primarily to obtain uniformity in the records; and it can reasonably be conjectured that actual measurement generally continued to be made in terms of the local units, which, in the records, were converted at some stage into *bīgha-i daftarī*. With the disruption of the empire the *raison d'etre* of the *bīgha-i daftarī* would have disappeared and the local administrations would have gradually

[13] *Dastūru-l 'Amal-i 'Ālamgīrī*, f.2a-b.

[14] *Khulāṣatu-s Siyāq*, f.75a; Or. 2026, f.24b.

[15] *Farhang-i Kārdānī*, ff. 12a-13a, Edinburgh 83, f. 7a. It also mentions the *dir'a-i Shāhjahānī* which, it explains, was used for measuring cloth, stone, wood and buildings; it puts its length at 41 digits, exactly that of the *gaz-i Ilāhī*! That there was a larger unit promulgated by Shāhjahān for cloth appears, however, from Marshall, 420, who speaks of "Shaujahauns Guz, called the Mulmull Guz, containing 41¼ English inches".

[16] *Fifth Report*, 676-7.

[17] See a brief report in Persian on the local and official *bīghas* in use in the provinces of the Panjab, Shāhjahānābād, Awadh and Ilahabad, drawn up some time before 1788 for the benefit of the British administrators of Bengal (Add. 6586, f.164a-b). Cf. also Add. 6603, f.51b, which puts one *dir'a-i Ilāhī* at 40 digits.

dropped it from their records. The *bīgha-i Ilāhī*, on the other hand, had actually been in use for measuring the limits of the *madad-i ma'āsh* lands and as such enjoyed a universality denied to any of its rivals. The holders of grants as a class had a permanent interest in its survival in order to retain the original limits of their lands. It was therefore able to continue under the British regime in the garb of the standard *bīgha* of the United Provinces (Uttar Pradesh), being really the *bīgha-i Ilāhī* with just a trifling alteration in size.

APPENDIX B

WEIGHTS

1. STANDARD *MANS*

The customary Indian scale of weights for bulk, 40 *sers* = 1 *man*,[1] was used almost exclusively throughout the Mughal empire, except for certain regions in the east and north-west and in the Dakhin, where it either intermingled or coexisted with other systems of weights or capacity.

The *ser* in Hindustan, says Abū-l Faẓl, used formerly to be equal to the weight of either 18 *dāms*, or 22. From the beginning of Akbar's reign, however, the current standard *ser* was 28 *dāms* in weight, but it was raised to 30 *dāms* by the emperor some time before the *Ā'īn* was written.[2] The weight of the *dām* in terms of the *tola* scale is given elsewhere in the same work,[3] and the weight of the latter unit has been determined fairly precisely on the basis of numismatic and other evidence.[4] The *dām*, accordingly, should have weighed 322.7 grains, so that the *man* based on the *ser* of 28 *dāms* was equal to about 51.63 lb. avoirdupois (23.44 kg), and that of 30 *dāms* to

[1] The Anglicized monstrosity "maund", as old as the 17th century, was born apparently out of a fusion of the Indian name with the Portuguese corruption *mao* (*Hobson-Jobson*, ed. Crooke, 563-4). In the present book it has been applied only to the standard unit of weight under the British, which officially bore this name. The distinction might as well serve as a reminder that the British official "maund" (82.74 lb. avdp.) is no guide to the weights of the units in use in our period.

[2] *Ā'īn*, II, 60; also ibid, I, 284.

[3] Ibid, I, 26: 1 *dām* =1 *tolcha*, 8 *māsha*, 7 *surkh*; or 1.74/96 *tola*.

[4] S.H. Hodivala, *Historical Studies in Mughal Numismatics*, 224-34, fixes the weight of the *tola* at about 185.5 grains, after assembling almost the entire evidence directly bearing upon this point. He has, however, made no attempt to arrive at its value by working back from the weights of the *mans* found in European sources. This is noted here solely to clear the argument in the text in advance from any suspicion that the evidence adduced later on in its confirmation is really part of the material that led to the initial finding. Prinsep, who tried to determine the weight of the *man-i Akbarī*, confused the jewellers' weights with those of the bankers, and his value for it is accordingly impossibly low (*Useful Tables*, ed. Thomas, 111). Thomas steers clear of this confusion, but he uses Prinsep's value for the Mughal *tola* (186.0 grains), which, as he himself notes, is based on a misreading of the text by Gladwin (ibid., 19-20 & 20 n.; *Chronicles of the Pathan Kings*, 421, 425, 429-30). But the difference between Hodivala's and Prinsep's values for the *tola* is so small that Moreland could not go far wrong in his weights of the various *mans* which he determined on the basis of Prinsep's value (*India at the Death of Akbar*, 53; *Akbar to Aurangzeb*, 334).

the *ser* – called *Akbar-shāhī* or *Akbarī* – to about 55.32 lb. (25.11 kg). The values for the latter *man* in European sources seem to approximate to the same figure.[5]

On his accession Jahāngīr promulgated a new *man* (*man-i Jahāngīrī*) based upon the *ser* of 36 *dāms*. He withdrew it in or a little earlier than the 14th regnal year, but restored it finally during that year.[6] In terms of avoirdupois weights the new unit must have been equal to about 66.38 lb., or about 30.14 kg.[7]

Shāhjahān, in his turn, established a new *man*, raising its weight so that the *ser* equalled 40 *dāms* in weight.[8] The date when it was established does not appear in our sources, but the first references to it are found in Dutch and English commercial literature in 1634[9] and 1635.[10] Assuming that the *dām* weights correctly represented its real ratio with the *man-i Akbarī* – an assumption fortified by the definite testimony of a contemporary manual[11] – the *man-i*

[5] Ufflitt in 1614 noted that the "maund" based on "the Achabe [Akbarī] sera, equalling 30 pices" was equivalent to 56 lb. (avdp.) (Foster, *Supplementary Calendar*, 48). Pelsaert, 29, says "1 Akbarī *ser* weighs 30 pice, or 1¼ lb.", i.e., 1 *man-i Akbarī* = 50 lb. Holland or 54.5 lb. avdp. Hawkins (*Early Travels*, 105) is, probably, referring to the same *man* when he says, "every maune is five and fiftie pounds weight". Cf. Moreland, *India at the Death of Akbar*, 53-62; *Akbar to Aurangzeb*, 334, 342. A discordant note is struck by certain references in English records where the *man* is considered equal to 50 lb. avdp. (*Lett. Recd.*, III, 60, 87; *Factories, 1630-33*, 328). The first and third of these are expressly concerned with indigo trade and perhaps include an allowance of 9 per cent for dryness, a proportion estimated elsewhere in the same records (*Lett. Recd.*, VI, 326).

[6] *T.J.*, 96, 281. Jahāngīr's statements appear to have been misunderstood. Moreland, for instance, says that it was in 1619 that, on the advice of the mystic Jadrūp, he "promptly" ordered the *ser* to weigh 36 *dāms* (*Akbar to Aurangzeb*, 335). Jahāngīr does not speak, under the 14th year, of promulgating, but, in quite clear terms, of restoring his previous standard. To the original fixation at the accession there is an incidental reference under the 6th year (*T.J.*, 96). There are equally definite references in the English records of 1614 and 1615 to "the maund of Shawsalem, which is 36 pices to the seara" (Foster, *Supp. Calendar*, 43, 47, 48; *Lett. Recd.*, III, 11).

[7] Ufflitt puts its value at 65 lb. avdp. (Foster, *Supp. Calendar*, 48) and Pelsaert, 11, at 60 lb. Holland or 65.4 lb. avdp. Cf. also Moreland, *Akbar to Aurangzeb*, 335, 342, and the authorities cited there. Mundy, 237, equates "16 Maund Jehangueere" with "neere 1000 (lb.) weight English", thus suggesting that 1 *man*=62½ lb. avdp., but it ill accords with his own weight for the pice, or *dām*, viz. 22 pice =1 lb. given elsewhere (p.156), from which a weight of 65.45 lb. would be deduced for the *man-i Jahāngīrī*.

[8] *Dastūru-l 'Amal-i Navīsindagī*, f.179b; *Dastūru-l 'Amal-i 'Ālamgīrī*, f.2b; *Factories, 1634-36*, 156.

[9] *Dagh Register*, 22 October 1634, cited by Moreland, *Akbar to Aurangzeb*, 342.

[10] *Factories, 1634-36*, 129, 133.

[11] The *Dastūru-l 'Amal-i Navīsindagī*, f.179b, giving the arithmetical formula

Shāhjahānī should have been equal to about 73.75 lb. avoirdupois (33.48 kg).[12]

There seems good reason to believe that Aurangzeb did not introduce a new *man* of his own, in so far as this might imply a change in absolute weight.[13] A new difficulty must have arisen, however, with the discontinuance of the issue of the *dāms* at their old weights, the old ones being replaced in the very first decade of the reign by *dām* pieces lighter by a third.[14] If the weights were to go on being determined at the former ratios of the *dāms*, only old coins would now be available for use, and these would wear off with the passage of time. Apparently, the *ser* weight was not restated in terms of the new pieces,[15] but the rate in terms of the old was at length increased to 42 for the *ser-i Shāhjahānī*. Perhaps this also became outdated in course of time so that the rate of 43, and still later 44 *dāms*, was instituted, the units of weight being renamed *'Ālamgīrī*, although no alteration in real weight seems to have been intended.[16]

---

for converting the *man-i Shāhjahānī* into *man-i Akbarī* and *vice-versa* assumes that the former was equal to 11/3 of the latter. The late 17th-century manual, the *Ẓawābiṭ-i 'Ālamgīrī* (Ethe 415, f.170b; Or. 1641, f.50a; Add. 6598, f.153a) also sets down the weight of the *man-i Akbarī* in terms of the Shāhjahānī at 30 *ser*.

12 A Dutch record (apparently the same one in the *Dagh Register* as above cited) puts the value of this *man* at 67 lb. Dutch (i.e. 73.03 lb. avdp.) (Moreland, op.cit., 335). It is equated with 74 lb. in a Surat Consultation of 1639 (*Factories, 1637-41*, 192), but with 731/3 the next year (ibid., 274). In Tavernier, I, 32 (69 *livres*) and Thevenot, 25 (70 *livres*), if they are speaking of the same *man*, its weight seems to be overstated, even if we accept Moreland's value for the French *livre* of the period, rather than that of Ball (Moreland, op.cit., 333; Ball's Appendix, Tavernier, I, 331). Cf. also Hodivala, *Mughal Numismatics*, 231. Tavernier's value for the *man-i Akbarī*, viz. 53 *livres* (I, 132; II, 7), would similarly be a distinct overstatement of the real weight if converted into lb. avdp. according to Moreland's rate. But French equivalents are of little use in this period, in view of the great metrological chaos that prevailed in France before 1789, with local weights and measures constantly proliferating (Witold Kula, *Measures and Men*, transl. R. Szreter, 161-84).

13 The *Ẓawābiṭ-i 'Ālamgīrī* (op.cit.) shows the *man-i 'Ālamgīrī* as identical in weight with the *man-i Shāhjahānī*. In 1676 Fryer describes "The Maund Pucka at Agra" as "double" the Surat *man*, the latter based on the *ser* of 20 "Pice"; the only other "maund" at Agra, known to him, was the "Maund Ecbarry" (II, 126-7).

14 Cf. S.H. Hodivala, 'The Weights of Aurangzeb's Dams', *JASB*, NS, XIII (1917), 62-67. See also Appendix C.

15 For the clearest contemporary statement on this point, see Marshall, 416.

16 The argument of the passage is largely based on the tables of official weights given in the *Ẓawābiṭ-i 'Ālamgīrī*, op.cit. It gives their values in terms of the old *dāms* (*fulūs-i qadīm*) on one side and in those of the *man-i Shāhjahānī* on the other. In the former table, 30 *dāms* go to the *ser-i Akbarī*, 36 to *Jahāngīrī*, but 42 to *Shāhjahānī* and 43 to *'Ālamgīrī*; while, as we have already seen above, the *man-i*

2. THE *MANS* AND OTHER WEIGHTS USED IN THE VARIOUS REGIONS

The evidence we possess, being largely confined to incidental references, does not permit any comprehensive statement of the markets and lines of trade in which the standard and local weights were used at different times. Whatever information we have suggests that the successive official weights were widely enforced; that the enforcement did not come immediately upon the first introduction of the new unit, but was applied gradually in different markets or in specific trades; and that in many regions local weights and measures of capacity, sometimes officially recognized, or even altered, continued to exist, occasionally alone, but generally side by side with the imperial standards. To all this is to be added another factor, namely the varying customs of different trades and markets, whereby apparent variations in weight units and scales really represented commercial allowances or commissions to either party.[1]

It seems that the *man-i Akbarī* had come very near to being the single, universal unit of weight in the markets of the central regions

---

Akbarī is equated with 30 *ser-i Shāhjahānī* and the *man-i Jahāngīrī* with 36 (MS. var. 31), and the *man-i 'Ālamgīrī* is declared to be the same as the *man-i Shāhjahānī*. Writing on the basis of his observations in 1668-72 in Bengal and Bihar, Marshall, 421, says: "19¾ mass (*māsha*) make one pice Shawjahan, being copper, 42 which pice make one seer bazar weight." This weight for the *dām* is distinctly less than the standard weight given to it in our other authorities (20⅞ *māshas* in the *Ā'īn*, and, perhaps, less precisely, 21 *māshas* in the *Mir'āt-i Aḥmadī*, I, 267, 385; *Ẓawābiṭ-i 'Ālamgīrī*, Ethe 415, f. 170b, Or. 1641, f. 49b, Add. 6598, f. 48b). Assuming that Marshall's weight allows for the depreciation since the last issue of the old *dāms*, an increase in number of the *dāms* going to a *ser*, from 40 to 42 – the rate which he in fact himself gives here – must have become necessary, if the *ser* was to be prevented from gradually falling in weight. The *Farhang-i Kārdānī*, Edinburgh 83, f.5b, after giving the usual weights for the *ser-i Akbarī* and *Jahāngīrī* in terms of *dāms*, assigns 40 as well as 42 to the *ser-i Shāhjahānī*. Under the *ser-i Aurangshāhī*, we have 44 and 48 *dāms* to the *ser*. The first figure probably represents the result of a further depreciation in weight of the old *dāms*. The second figure is rather difficult to explain. The same manual, f. 6a, shows that the *dām* issued by Aurangzeb's mints in Bengal, where the work was written, was 18 *māshas* in weight, and it might be that these *dāms* were used in weighing *ser-i Aurangshāhī*. But in that case, 47 would have been more accurate than 48.

[1] To take two examples from the indigo trade of Ahmadabad: The English factors report in December 1614: "We here buy of good Sarques (Sarkhej) indigo for 11 rupees the maund, they allowing us 42 *seers* of the new (i.e. the less dry) and 41 *seers* of the old to the maund ..." (*Lett. Recd.*, II, 250). In 1647 over thirty years later the complaint is made from the same place of "the prejudicial custom of weighing (indigo) 40 s(e)r net introduced by the prince (Aurangzeb)" (*Factories, 1646-50*, 143).

of the empire. This view is certainly not backed by any explicit evidence, but is based rather upon the silence of our authorities in regard to any other unit. For instance, while giving prices of different commodities, Abū-l Faẓl might well have mentioned the presence of another weight, if such was used in the case of one or a few of them. Similarly, there is no reference at all in the English records of the early years of the seventeenth century to any unit in the markets of Agra or Ajmer, which may possibly be conjectured to have had an earlier origin than Akbar's *man*. Its monopoly went, however, with the promulgation of the *man-i Jahāngīrī*, though it was by no means entirely superseded. For a number of years afterwards the *man-i Akbarī* still continues to be referred to as the general unit in use in the Agra market.[2] In the indigo trade of the Agra region it lasted throughout our period, or at any rate till the 1670s.[3] It endured similarly in the trade in silk and "other fine Goods",[4] especially quicksilver and vermilion,[5] and musk.[6]

It is not clear in what lines of trade precisely the *man-i Jahāngīrī* was used. Most statements about its use in the Agra market are couched in general terms only. The one specific reference we have shows that it continued to be used in the cochineal trade down to about 1652, when it was finally displaced there by the *man-i Shāhjahānī*.[7]

Apart from its ultimate entry into this trade, the *man-i Shāhjahānī* was probably imposed chiefly upon the trade in foodstuffs and other rural produce (except indigo). We hear of its use at Agra in 1639 and 1646 in connexion with sugar and gum-lac;[8] and in the next half of the seventeenth century it comes to be spoken of as the "ordinary" *man* of the market.[9]

Turning eastward, we find that the Patna market responded to the changes in the official standard weights effectively enough, but with peculiar deviations of its own. In 1620, the English factors sent there reported that the unit used in the silk trade of the place was not the *man-i Akbarī*, but a *man* based upon the *ser* of 34½[10] or,

[2] Hawkins, *Early Travels*, 105; *Lett. Recd.*, III, 87 (refers to Ajmer while the court was there); and other references in the notes below.

[3] *Lett. Recd.*, III, 69; Pelsaert, 16-17; *Factories, 1622-23*, 284-5; *1630-33*, 328; *1642-45*, 84; *1646-50*, 202; Tavernier, I, 32; II, 7; Fryer, II, 127.

[4] Thus Fryer, II, 127. Also, *Factories, 1618-21*, 194, 213.

[5] *Factories, 1630-33*, 213.

[6] *Factories, 1618-21*, 47.

[7] *Factories, 1655-60*, 18.

[8] *Factories, 1637-41*, 192; *1646-50*, 62.

[9] Tavernier, I, 32; Thevenot, 25.

[10] *Factories, 1618-21*, 193-94.

as stated by themselves elsewhere, 33½ pice, or *dāms*,[11] by which, nevertheless, they apparently meant the *man-i Jahāngīrī*.[12] The lower value in terms of *dāms* may signify a sellers' allowance in the particular trade at that time. On the other hand, Mundy, who visited Patna in 1632, says that the *man* used there, apparently for all goods, was based upon the *ser* of 37 *dāms*,[13] and this would indicate an allowance in favour of the buyer.[14] The *man-i Jahāngīrī* was still in use there in 1661, though the *man-i Shāhjahānī* too had been introduced.[15] Within the next ten years only the latter remained, for Marshall (1668-72) speaks of the *man* current there as based on a *ser* weighing 42 *dāms*, and itself equivalent to 78 lb. avdp.; "but the custom of the place is to allow 2 seer in every maund".[16]

In Bengal we do not come across any reference to the actual use of the *man-i Akbarī*, but the *man-i Jahāngīrī* is frequently met with. In 1634 the English sold lead by its weight,[17] and in 1642 we find them charging freight on cloth and sugar, taken aboard at Balasore, at respectively the "maunds" of 64 and 128 lb. avdp.,[18] which are obviously single and double *man-i Jahāngīrī*. In a formal attestation in 1657, a Portuguese merchant equates the "*mao* of Bengala" with 64 "arates" or 64.64 lb. avdp.,[19] so that till this date at least it continued to hold its position in the province. But in 1659 the *man-i*

[11] Ibid., 205, 213.

[12] Thus when they refer to the despatch of goods, purchased by them, from Patna, they give the rate of payment for transport in terms of the "Jehanger maund". Moreland, *Akbar to Aurangzeb*, 335, seems to have misunderstood their statements for he cites one of them, Hughes, as saying that the *man-i Akbarī* was also current at Patna.

[13] Mundy, 156.

[14] Cf. Moreland, op.cit.

[15] *Early Annals*, I, 380. A third *man*, "of small weight", 28 "pice" to the "seer", apparently a variant of the *man-i Akbarī*, was in use as well.

[16] Marshall, 419. His statements are not consistent. If 2 *sers* were allowed in a *man*, the *man* would have weighed, in the result, nearly 82 lb. avdp., but elsewhere (127, 149, 143) he speaks of the *man* as weighing 80 lb. only. In any case he gives a very high value for the *man-i Shāhjahānī*. It is tempting to think that 42 *dām* weights per *ser* really signified an increase in the weight of the *man-i Shāhjahānī*, founded originally on the *ser* of 40 *dāms*. But this is belied by Marshall's own weight for the *dām* piece (p.421), which, as seen above, distinctly reveals loss from depreciation.

[17] *Factories, 1634-36*, 49.

[18] *Factories, 1642-45*, 72. Moreland says, "the Dutch records mention a maund of about 66 lb. (avdp.) at Hooghly in 1636 and at Balasore in 1642, but in 1645 the Shāhjahānī maund was used at the port of Pipli" (*Akbar to Aurangzeb*, 335). For the last statement he refers us to the page in the *Factories* given at the head of this note. It would appear that he has mixed up his Dutch and English authorities.

[19] Master, II, 62.

Shāhjahānī ("the maund of 75 lb.") is found in use for cotton yarn at Balasore,[20] although a manual belonging to the later years of Aurangzeb says the *man-i Jahāngīrī* was employed in Bengal and Orissa, presumably at the time it was written, chiefly in the trade of this very commodity.[21] Indeed, henceforth in the English commercial records, the *mans* of different markets in the province seem to be only either equivalents or minor variations of the *man-i Shāhjahānī*;[22] the greatest variation occurred in the grain trade, where the *man* continued to be based upon the *ser* of 40 *dāms* and so lost, with the depreciation of the old *dāms*, in terms of absolute weight and in relation to the *man* weights elsewhere.[23] We should not omit to note, however, the local scale of measures of capacity, based upon the *gaunī*, or basket, which is stated to have been in use in the provinces of Bengal and Orissa in the trade in foodgrains.[24]

We have little information about the weights used in the Lahor market. Prices current there of sugar and indigo are quoted in 1639 in terms of a "maen packa" and "the greate maen",[25] both of which, at that time, should have meant the *man-i Shāhjahānī*. The great "maen" is also used with reference to the prices of the same goods

20 *Factories, 1655-60*, 297.

21 *Farhang-i Kārdānī*, Edinburgh 83, f.6b-7a. The word used is *sūt* (cotton yarn).

22 The English factor Kenn reported in 1661 that the weight of the *man* at Hugli had recently been increased from 70 to 75 lb. (*Early Annals*, I, 380). But some years later, the *man* at Hugli is stated to have weighed 73 lb. avdp. by Marshall, 419, and 70 lb. by Bowrey, 217. The latter also gives the value of 75 lb. avdp. to the *man* at Balasore; and 68 lb. to that at Qasimbazar, which means that it was identical with the *man* used for foodstuffs. An interesting distinction is drawn by Marshall between two units: one, the *man* of which the *ser* weighed 42 pice "Shawjahaun", and each pice 19¾ *māshas*, it being known as the "buzar weight"; the other a *man* whereof the *ser* weighed 40 pice "Modussay", "or one old pice" of 18½ *māshas* the "factory weight" at Hugli (p.421). The latter would have come, according to the weight of the particular pice, to about 62.3 lb. avdp. But the weight of the *madhushāhī paisa* is stated to be 16 *māshas* in the *Farhang-i Kārdānī*, Edinburgh 83, f.6a. Perhaps Marshall meant the *Aurangshāhī paisa* (of local mintage?), which in the same manual is assigned the weight of 18 *māshas*.

23 *Farhang-i Kārdānī*, Edinburgh 83, ff.5b-6a: "In *baqqālī* (the *banyas*' profession, or grain trade) the established weight is in terms of the *muradī* (or *dām*) Shāhjahānī by the forty-weight." Cf. Bowrey, 217: "Graine, butter, Oyle, or any liquid things, all the River of Hugly over, allow but 68 pound to the maund."

24 Or.1840, f.187a; *Farhang-i Kārdānī*, Edinburgh 83, ff. 6b-7a. The *gaunī* appears in both these texts as *gaudi*. For this measure, see Wilson's *Glossary*, 170; *Cuttack Dist. Gazetteer*, (1906), 144, where it is stated that the weight of the *gaunī* varies from 1¾ to 7 seers the British standard. The measure now appears to be used in Orissa only.

25 *Factories, 1637-41*, 135.

at Multan.[26] The *Zawābiṭ-i 'Ālamgīrī* lists "the *mānī*, i.e. [sic!] the *topa*, a wooden measure", among the recognized weights; the weight of this is given at Lahor as 6, and at Multan, 12 *man* (*-i Shāhjahānī?*).[27] This measure of capacity, in slightly varying scales, has survived in the Panjab proper down to recent times, being used particularly in rural trade.[28]

The English factors, who visited Sind in 1635, found that while in Sehwan the *man-i Jahāngīrī* was still current in the indigo trade, the Thatta market had gone over to the *man-i Shāhjahānī*.[29] Subsequently, the latter unit alone is referred to, at any rate in the indigo trade of Sind,[30] and at the end of the century it was the prevalent measure of weight used in the province.[31] In this province we first come across the great rival of the *man* in the north-west, namely the k̲h̲arwār, or "ass-load".[32] We find it in use in 1634 in Sehwan for stating the quantity of all foodgrains. It was then equated with either 9 or 10 *man-i Jahāngīrī*, that is either 597.3 or 663.8 lb. avdp.[33] In 1635 the English factors considered the "corwaur" at Thatta as equal to 8 *man-i Shāhjahānī*, or some 590 lb. avdp.(268 kg).[34]

While in Sind the k̲h̲arwār coexisted with the *man*, in Kashmir it enjoyed exclusive dominance.[35] Abū-l Faẓl equates one k̲h̲arwār

---

[26] Ibid., 136.

[27] *Zawābiṭ-i 'Ālamgīrī*, Ethe 415; f. 171a; Or. 1641, f.50a; Add. 6598, f. 153a.

[28] The various local scales, as described in the *District Gazetteers*, show that whatever the size of the *topa*, its ratio to the next higher unit, the *pai*, is every-where the same, i.e. 4 *topas* make a *pai*. In Multan 80 *pais*, and in the old Montgomery district and the Rechna tract of the Lahore district 50 *pais* make a *mānī* or *mahni*. (See *Lahore Dist. Gaz.* (1893-4), 194-5; *Montgomery Dist. Gaz.* (1898-9), 182-3; *Multan Dist. Gaz.* (1901-2), 258.)

[29] *Factories, 1634-36*, 133. The *Maẓhar-i Shāhjahānī*, written in Sehwan in 1634, does not refer to *man-i Shāhjahānī* at all, but has two references to *man-i Jahāngīrī* (146, 182).

[30] *Factories, 1637-41*, 274, 276.

[31] Hamilton, II, Table of Weights, etc., p.4, at end of vol. He visited Sind in 1699-1700 and speaks of a "Maund-pucah" of 75 lb.

[32] *Maẓhar-i Shāhjahānī*, 182-5. A k̲h̲arwār consisted of 60 *kāsas* and a *kāsa* of 4 *toyas* (ibid., 182; also 146 & 172).

[33] The *Maẓhar-i Shāhjahānī* at one place (146) equates 5 *kāsas* with 30 *ser-i Jahāngīrī*, but says elsewhere (182) that one *kāsa*, "by the weight of stones", was equal to 65/8 *ser-i Jahāngīrī* and 1½ *dām*-weights.

[34] *Factories, 1634-36*, 133.

[35] The *Ā'īn*, I, 570, gives the following scale of the weights current in Kashmir: 2 *dāms*' weight=1 *pal*; 7½ *pal*=1 *ser*; 4 *sers*=1 *man*; 4 *mans*=1 *trak*; 16 *traks* =1 k̲h̲arwār. Blochmann's text makes a serious omission while giving this scale, whereby it makes 4 *sers* equal to one *trak*. (This remains uncorrected in Jarrett's tr., II, ed. Sarkar, 366.) MSS Add. 7652 & Add. 6552 are quite clear in their reading and they

of Kashmir with 3 *mans* and 8 *sers* in *Akbarshāhī* weight,[36] or 177.02 lb. avdp. (80.37 kg), which is nearly identical with the weight assigned to it by a modern authority, namely 177.74 lb.[37]

In the Mughal Dakhin the *man-i Jahāngīrī* was certainly in use at Burhanpur in 1622, when the English sold their lead by it.[38] However, the *man-i Akbarī* seems to have outlasted it even here, for in an official inventory of the royal stores, at the fort of Daulatabad, made in the 10th regnal year of Shāhjahān, the weights of a number of articles, cannon-balls, sulphur, etc., are expressly given in terms of *man-i Akbarī*.[39] The *man-i Shāhjahānī* is used for quantities at the end of the list, comprising some edible materials (betelnut, poppy-seed, *bhang* and bājrī-grains) and a cauldron.[40] In a document of *c.*1638, however, the *man-i Shāhjahānī* is used for reckoning the quantities of sulphur, charcoal and saltpetre as well.[41] And Bhīmsen uses the *man-i Shāhjahānī* in his reminiscences of the prices current in the Dakhin provinces during the early years of Aurangzeb's reign.[42]

In Gujarat, the prevalent *man* was probably of local origin, but it was kept, partly, at least, by administrative action, at exactly half the weight of the current imperial standard. There is one reference in 1611 to the "smaller" *man* at Surat of 27 or 27.5 lb., that is half the *man-i Akbarī*, and again in 1614, when it is said to have been in

are supported by *T.J.*, 315. The scale is the same today, for 30 *pals* are considered equal to one *manwata* (Lawrence, *The Valley of Kashmir*, 242).

[36] *A.N.*, III, 548; *Ā'īn*, I, 570.

[37] W.R. Lawrence, op.cit. Jahāngīr (*T.J.*, 297, 315), giving equivalents of the Kashmiri units in terms of the *man* scale has simply copied Abū-l Faẓl despite the fact that he himself had changed the official standard weight.

[38] *Factories, 1622-23*, 30: "maund of 36 pices to the ser and 42 sers to the maund", which means a trade allowance of 5% presumably.

[39] *Selected Documents of Shāh Jahān's Reign*, 92-98. Cf. also an undated document in ibid., 219-20.

[40] *Selected Documents of Shāh Jahān's Reign*, 98. The *man-i Shāhjahānī* is termed *man ba-wazn-i chihal-dāmī* ("the *man* by the forty *dām*-weight").

[41] Ibid., 223. Here the term *man ba-wazn-i Shāhjahānī* is actually used. The document is undated, but a reference to preparations for the expedition against Baglana enables us to determine its approximate date.

[42] *Dilkushā*, f.20b. From the *Ẓawābiṭ-i 'Ālamgīrī*, Ethe 415, f.71a, Or. 1641, f.50a, Add. 6598, f.153a, it appears that the southern unit, *khandī*, the "candy" of European commercial literature, was incorporated into the official scale of the Dakhin provinces at its usual value of 20 *mans*, which in this manual are specified as *man-i Shāhjahānī*. This large measure was probably convenient for use in laying cargo ships. Princess Jahān Ārā in her instructions issued in 1642 or 1643 regarding the cargo in her ship *Ṣāhibī*, bound from Surat for the Red Sea, asks 50 *gonī* of rice to

use "for elephant's teeth, gold and silver".[43] But it is not noticed afterwards and must have gone entirely out of use. Henceforth the "larger" *man* appears: it was based on the *ser* of 18 *dāms'* weight and was, therefore, half the *man-i Jahāngīrī*. Its weight must, accordingly, have been 33.19 lb. avdp. (15.07 kg), and the English and Dutch records generally confirm this value.[44] This *man* was used for everything – or, as one source puts it, "for butter, meat, sugar, indigo, saltpetre, wood, salt, etc. and everything that is weighable"[45] – and was current not only at Surat and Ahmadabad, but "practically throughout Gujarat".[46] The introduction of the *man-i Shāhjahānī*, in or before 1634, caused a corresponding change in the Gujarat *man* whose weight was now raised to 20 *dāms* per *ser*: the new weight was imposed at Ahmadabad in 1635 and at Surat early in the following year by an imperial *farmān*.[47] The value of the new *man* should have been 36.88 lb. (16.74 kg), and this again is confirmed by European evidence.[48] This *man* completely superseded the older one, which is not heard of after the change: not only were all the articles in which the European merchants were interested sold by the new *man*, but also "all sorts of Grain... and other Goods of Weight".[49] It does not appear to have been altered during the rest

be carried, each *gonī* put as equal to 20 *mans* by Shāhjahānī weight, and, therefore, identical with the *khandī* (Blochet, Suppl. Pers. 482, f.36a).

43 *Lett. Recd.*, I, 34; Foster, *Supplementary Calendar*, 47.

44 The English estimates range from 32 to 33 lb. avdp. (*Lett. Recd.*, I, 34, 241; II, 214, 238; III, 11; Foster, *Supp. Calendar*, 47; *Factories, 1618-21*, 60, 76; Fryer, II, 126), while one estimate (*Lett. Recd.*, III, 69) gives it as low a value as 30 lb. avdp. Pelsaert, 42, says its weight was 30 lb. Dutch, or 32.7 lb. avdp., but Broeke (*JIH*, xi, 10) and van Twist (*JIH*, xvi, 72) give 30½ lb. Dutch or 33.2 lb. avdp.

45 van Twist, *JIH*, xvi, 72.

46 Pelsaert, 42. This is also to be deduced from the fact that the factors dealing at Baroch or Baroda, for example, do not speak of a separate *man*. At Khambayat (Cambay), we are told, opium was sold by "the maund of 45 seer at 17 pice the seer", which seems to be the result of peculiar trade allowances (*Lett. Recd.*, III, 41).

47 *Factories, 1634-36*, 143, 156.

48 37 lb. avdp. in *Factories, 1646-50*, 206, and Fryer, II, 126; 36-2/3 lb. in *Factories, 1661-65*, 113. Moreland says, "the Dutch took it as 34½ (lb. Holland)" (*Akbar to Aurangzeb*, 336), which means it weighed 37.6 lb. avdp. Tavernier (II, 7, 14) puts its value at 34½ or 34 French *livres* (or, at Moreland's rate for the latter, slightly less than 37.6 or 37.06 lb. avdp. respectively). Thevenot, 25, says a *ser* of Surat equalled 14 oz. French, and the *man*, therefore, should have weighed 35 lb. French or 38.15 lb. avdp., which is much too high. On the other hand, Ovington, 133, certainly underrates it when he says, "a sear" = 13 1/3 oz. avdp., so that the *man* = 33.3 lb.

49 Fryer, II, p.126.

of our period.[50]

3. WEIGHTS USED IN EUROPEAN SOURCES

Since European weights are quite often used in the European authorities, their values must also be borne in mind. The English factors always used the avoirdupois ("English" or "haberdepoiz") weights, while the unit used by the Dutch was the Amsterdam pound, equal to 0.494 kilograms, or practically 1.09 lb. avdp.[1] Moreland says that the "French *livre* of the period was slightly less than the Dutch pound",[2] which suggests a value much less than that assigned to it by Ball.[3] But, as has been discussed in a footnote in connexion with the values for the *man-i Shāhjahānī* given by Tavernier and Thevenot, it would seem that even Moreland's rate is too high for the *livre* these two French travellers were using. The Portuguese used the "quintal" or "kintal" of about 130 lb. avdp.[4] and the "arratel" of 1.01 lb.[5]

European merchants and factors frequently use another set of terms with reference to indigo and sugar, namely "churl", "fardle", "bale", which signify a package of weight and size convenient, in the case of inland marts, for transport on pack-animals and roughly equivalent, therefore, to a full or half ox- or buffalo- or camel-load.[6] As such the terms by themselves do not denote definite weights, different weights being assigned to them for different goods at different places. The indigo at Agra, for example, was packed in churls or fardles of just slightly above 4 *man-i Akbarī*.[7] In Bengal the bale

[50] Cf. ibid. Does Ovington's value (AD 1690-93) for it, viz. 33.3 lb. avdp., signify a reduction in weight owing to the wearing off of the old *dāms*?

[1] *Akbar to Aurangzeb*, 333. [2] Ibid. [3] Tavernier, I, 331.

[4] *Akbar to Aurangzeb*, 334.

[5] *Relations*, 90. This is stated to be the value of the "new" arratel of 16 ounces. The old one of 14 ounces "was obsolete in India, except for the pepper trade, before the end of the sixteenth century".

[6] Cf. *Akbar to Aurangzeb*, 340-41. Mundy, 95, says that while journeying from Agra to Patna he saw oxen each carrying "4 great Maunds", which load, if the *man-i Jahāngīrī* is meant, would amount to 265.5 lb. avdp. On p.98, he puts the ox-load at 2½ cwt. or 280 lb. avdp. Tavernier, I, 32, says an ox could carry 300 or 350 *livres*, i.e. 327.0 or 381.5 lb. avdp. (but lb. value doubtful).

[7] In 1615 the Surat factors speak of indigo brought from Agra in terms of "fardles", each, "by estimation", of 6½ "maund", i.e. presumably the *man* of Surat, and so equivalent to a little below 4 *man-i Akbarī* (*Lett. Recd.*, II, 194). In 1617 Hughes at Agra gives figures of fardles and weights of indigo packed, which imply that a fardle contained 4.1 *man-i Akbarī* "net", i.e. apparently without counting the packing materials (*Lett. Recd.*, IV, 236). In 1621, in a complaint against the Mughal authorities one churl of Agra indigo is put at 4½ *man-i Akbarī*, but the occasion was

of sugar is stated at Hugli to be 2 "mds", 13 "seer", in *Shāhjahānī* weight ("40 Pice Seer") in 1661;[8] at Qasimbazar, "2 Maunds. 6½ seers, the Factory Weight" in 1683;[9] and in Bengal, generally, "2 maunds 5 seer" in 1684.[10] A bale of silk in Bengal weighed about two *man-i Shāhjahānī*.[11] In Gujarat the weight of a bale of indigo at Ahmadabad was fixed by the English in 1619 at 4 Surat *mans* (of 18 *dāms* per *ser*) as the maximum,[12] but there are later references to a slightly higher weight.[13] A bale of Gujarat sugar was taken in the Dutch records as the equivalent of 8 *mans* of 20 *dāms* per *ser*.[14]

such as naturally to breed exaggeration (*Factories, 1622-23*, 284-5). In 1633-4 and 1643 a "bale" of Bayana indigo is put at just 4 *mans* (*1634-36*, 1; *1642-45*, 48). Pelsaert, 16-17, also reckons a bale of Agra indigo as equal to 4 "maunds" net. Moreland (*Akbar to Aurangzeb*, 340-41) says the Dutch records give its weight as 230-240 lb. avdp., i.e. between 4.25 and 4.5 *man-i Akbarī*, the unit in use in this trade; but this might include packing materials as well.

[8] *Early Annals*, I, 380. [9] Hedges, I, 75. [10] *Early Annals*, I, 399.

[11] *Early Annals*, I, 395, 399. This is very close to the weight of the bale of Bengal silk (143 lb. avdp.) which Moreland (op.cit.) cites.

[12] *Factories, 1618-21*, 76.

[13] "4 maunds, 7 *seers*" in 1629 (*Factories, 1624-29*, 230). Moreland cites the Dutch records as giving a value of 145.155 lb. avdp. to the bale (*Akbar to Aurangzeb*, 340, 342). He also refers to an invoice in the "Old Correspondence" of 1656, where a bale of Gujarat indigo is reckoned as 148 lb. net, or, apparently, exactly 4 *mans* of 20 *dāms* to the *ser*.

[14] *Dagh Register*, 21 May 1641, cited by Moreland, *Akbar to Aurangzeb*, 340.

APPENDIX C

THE COINAGE, AND THE GOLD AND COPPER VALUES OF THE RUPEE

1. THE COINAGE

It must be regarded as a notable achievement for the time that the Mughals were able to establish a currency of a very high metallic standard and uniformity throughout their vast empire. They coined gold, silver and copper: the gold issues were almost wholly pure, while in the silver the proportion of the alloy never rose above 4 per cent.[1] The currency system, moreover, was one of 'free' coinage; that is, it was open to anyone to take bullion to the mint and, on payment of charges, get it converted into specie.[2] The coins, therefore, circulated at values practically corresponding to their weights in the respective metals, and the ratios at which one unit exchanged for another of a different metal was a matter to be determined by the market, and not by the administration.

In so far as both the administration and the commercial world were concerned, the basic unit for all cash transactions was the silver coin, *rūpya*, or, in its Anglicized form, the rupee. The silver fractional unit of *āna*, or anna, equivalent to one-sixteenth of the rupee, seems to have come into common use in the seventeenth century.[3] The gold *muhr*, known also as the *ashrafī*, was not in general commercial use, but mostly employed for hoarding purposes, especially by the aristocracy.[4] The main copper coin was the *dām*. In Akbar's reign it gradually replaced the copper *ṭanka*, of which it was supposed to be half in value.[5] The

[1] Cf. Hodivala, *Historical Studies in Mughal Numismatics*, 235-44.

[2] This follows from the *Ā'īn*, I, 16, 31-33 (cf. Hodivala, op.cit.) and the numerous instances scattered in English records (e.g. *Factories, 1634-36*, 68-9; *1646-50*, 185); also Tavernier, I, 7-8, 20. For a detailed study of Mughal minting system and minting costs, see Najaf Haider, 'Precious Metal Flows and Currency Circulation in the Mughal Empire', *JESHO*, XXXIX(3), 326-35.

[3] The two lowest fractional units of the rupee in the *Ā'īn*, I, 26, are the *sūkī*, 1/20, and the *kalā*, 1/16. It is uncertain when the latter, under the name *āna*, established itself as the basic fractional unit, but it was already in use in Bengal about 1600 (*Haft Iqlīm*, 94-95). It appears in commercial use as early as 1620 at Patna (*Factories, 1618-21*, 94, 204). It is definitely employed in the official accounts of Shāhjahān's reign (*Selected Documents*, 93, 97,180, 194-5, 216-18, 220).

[4] Pelsaert, 29; Tavernier, I, 15, 16.

[5] The copper *ṭanka* is sometimes also called *ṭanka-i Dehlī*, *ṭanka-i murādī* and

dām was also known as *paisa*, while the half-*dām* was called *adhela*.[6] The suspicion has been entertained that in the seventeenth century, with the disappearance of the old *ṭanka*, it became common to confuse the *ṭanka* with the official *dām*, and *paisa* with the old *adhela*.[7] (But see below.) Moreover, owing to the changes in the silver price of copper the standard ratio of 40 *dāms* to a rupee instituted under Akbar could no longer be maintained for purposes of actual payments. Since, however, the old rate continued to be used in the accounts, notably in connexion with the *jama*ʻ figures and the calculation of salaries, the *dām* of these accounts became an imaginary coin, a mere theoretical fixed fraction of the rupee.[8]

The weights of the rupee and the *muhr* remained practically unaltered throughout our period. Only Aurangzeb at his accession made a trifling increase in the weights of both coins, which, however, left their relative weights unaffected.[9] Jahāngīr gave currency to two heavier kinds of rupees and *muhrs*, but the innovation was short-lived and the new issues bore special names, so that there is usually

---

ṭanka-i siyāh. See Hodivala, *JASB*, NS, XXVIII, 80-96. To the authorities cited there we may add ʻĀrif Qandahārī, 179, and Muʻtamad K͟hān, *Iqbālnāma*, Or. 1834, f.232b.

6 *Āʼīn*, I, 27. It should be noted that Akbar's introduction of *dām* as half-*ṭanka* played havoc with the traditional Indian scale of copper money, which was as follows: 3 *dāms*=1 *damrī*, 4 *damrīs* =1 *adhela*, 2 *adhelas*= 1 *paisa*, 2 *paisas* = 1 *ṭanka*; but 1 *paisa* = 25 *dāms* and 1 *ṭanka* = 50 *dāms* (*Dastūru-l ʻAmal-i ʻĀlamgīrī*, ff. 3a, 17b, 19a; Marshall, 416; Or. 1840, f. 134a; *Farhang-i Kārdānī*, Edinburgh 83, f. 6a; Elliot, *Memoirs*, II, 296). The *dām* could suit this scale only if the *ṭanka* here is taken to be a silver *ṭanka* and so equivalent to a rupee. The *Āʼīn*, I, 196, does indeed refer to 48 *dāms* going to a rupee before Akbar set the value of the rupee finally at 40 *dāms*.

The *dām* is indisputably described as "pice" (or by numerous other corruptions of the word *paisa*) in the European records, when the reference is to *dām*-weight.

7 For such an interpretation of English references, see Hodivala, *Mughal Numismatics*, 140n., and Moreland, *Akbar to Aurangzeb*, 331, as also the two previous editions of the present book.

8 This *dām* came to be known as the *dām-i tank͟hwāhī*, "the *dām* of salaries" (*Dastūru-l ʻAmal-i ʻĀlamgīrī*, f.3a). Cf. Manucci, II, 374-5.

9 The heaviest of the rupees of Akbar, Jahāngīr and Shāhjahān weigh 178 grains troy, and *muhrs* 169 grains, in both the British Museum and Indian Museum collections. Those of Aurangzeb, on the other hand, reach 180 and 171 grains respectively. (See S. Lane-Poole, *The Coins of the Moghul Emperors of Hindustan in the British Museum*, and H.N. Wright, *Catalogue of the Coins in the Indian Museum*, Calcutta, III, Mughal Emperors.) The alteration in the weight of the rupee is noticed in the Surat factors' letters to Ahmadabad and to the Company, written in September 1659 (*Factories 1655-60*, 211-12 , 211n.).

no risk of confusion between them and the ordinary issues in contemporary references.[10] The weight of the *dām* was also kept at the same standard till the growing scarcity of copper compelled Aurangzeb to issue a new *dām* that was one-third lighter than the old. It began to be uttered from certain mints in the 1660s, and seems to have gradually superseded the old *dām*.[11]

Since the values of the coins closely corresponded to their weights in metal, a coin lost in value if it lost in weight through clipping or wear. A peculiarity of the Mughal currency system was that a coin also lost in value simply on account of its age. The year in which it was minted was inscribed on it, along with the name of the mint and the titles of the reigning emperor. The newly coined rupees were known as *sikka*. These bore a premium over those struck in the preceding years of the same reign which were known as *chalanī* or *peṭh*. These in turn had a higher value than the coins current from former reigns, known as *khazāna*. Normally, however, the discounts on account of age-depreciation were quite small.[12] They can be generally ignored when considering the prices of articles. Indeed, prices are often quoted in our sources without any specification of whether they were in terms of the newly coined or the older rupees. As for land revenue, regulations promulgated during Akbar's reign imply that the demand was assessed in terms of the *chalanī* rupees, since they prohibit any discount on the emperor's coins, if of "correct assay and full weight", whatever their age.[13]

[10] The question is best discussed in Hodivala, *Mughal Numismatics*, 132-146. To the authorities cited there one might add Pelsaert, 29, whose statements are exceptionally clear on the point.

[11] The lighter *dām* was first issued from the capital cities in 1663-4; it began to be uttered in Gujarat from 1665-6, and in Bihar its use was just spreading in 1671. The overwhelming majority of Aurangzeb's copper issues belongs to this type. See *Mir'āt*, I, 265, 267; Marshall, 416-17; *Ẓawābiṭ-i 'Ālamgīrī*, Ethe 415, f.170b. Or. 1641, f. 49b, and Add. 6598, f. 152b; *Farhang-i Kārdānī*, Edinburgh 83, f.6a. Cf. Hodivala, *JASB*, NS, XXVIII, 62-67.

[12] That the discounts were not large may be inferred, for example, from the rates in terms of copper money quoted for rupees of the different kinds at Aurangabad in 1661. The market rate for the *sikka* ('Ālamgīrī) rupee was 15 *ṭankas* to 14 7/8 *ṭankas*, for the *chalanī*, 14 57/100 to 14 7/16 *ṭankas*, and for the *khazāna*, 14 7/16 to 14 5/6 *ṭankas* (*Waqā'i' Dakhin*, 32-33: For an interpretation of copper money rates here, see note 26 in Section 3 of this appendix).

For a general discussion of the Mughal currency system, see I. Habib, *Medieval India Quarterly*, Aligarh, IV, 1-21.

[13] Todar Mal's Regulations of the 27th Year laid down that the mints were to exchange new coins for the old ones so that "the *karorīs*, *foṭadārs* and *ṣarrāfs* (bankers) changed new and old coins according to the prescribed regulations". The rates

The Mughals imposed their standard currency on all the regions that came under their sway, an achievement certainly of great importance for trade.[14] Yet in certain regions local currencies inherited from the previous regimes continued, although no longer uttered by the imperial mints. The most important of these were the silver coins of a rather heavy alloy which were current in Gujarat and western India and were very close to each other in worth. Malwa had *muẓaffarīs*, each worth less than half a rupee;[15] Berar had silver *ṭankas* worth 16 *dāms* or 2/5 of a rupee.[16] In Khandesh *ṭankas* were probably only units of account, for their value was arbitrarily raised by Akbar from 2/5 to 3/5 of a rupee.[17] In Gujarat the *maḥmūdī* continued to be used at the great port of Surat. Its value at the beginning of the seventeenth century was about 2/5 of a rupee, but it tended to rise, perhaps owing to the cessation of its mintage, to about four-ninths of a rupee.[18]

---

of discount which are then given allow only for loss in weight, "the *jāgīrdārs, karorīs* and *foṭadārs*" being again told to conform strictly to these rules (original text of the Regulations in *Akbarnāma*, Add.27,247, f.332b). In Abū-l Faẓl's paraphrase of Todar Mal's Regulations in his final draft, it is directly stated that "the revenue collectors and *ṣarrāfs* should not (the negative is omitted in the Bib. Ind. text, but is given in Add. 26,207. f.162a) levy discounts by distinguishing between the old and new coins" (*A.N.*, III, 383). But Abū-l Faẓl himself says elsewhere that up to the 39th year the revenue collectors of the *khāliṣa* and the *jāgīrdārs* used to demand the pure coin as defined by the money changers (*sikka-i ṣairafī*) and to charge *ṣarf*, or discount, on other coins of "correct assay and full weight". This was now prohibited (*A.N.*, III, 651: the printed text omits the key word *ṣarf*, although it occurs in Add. 26,207, f.275b, and most of the MSS consulted by the editor himself).

[14] Apart from the evidence of the existing collections which shows that the Mughals did not continue the mintage of the older currencies of the conquered provinces, one may refer to Lāhorī, II, 562-3, where an exception made with regard to Balkh and Badakhshan during their temporary occupation in 1646-7 is proclaimed as a great concession made in favour of the local inhabitants.

[15] The value of half rupee is deduced from a passage in Firishta, II, 287, by Hodivala, *Mughal Numismatics*, 350n., 351; but S. Bashir Hasan (*PIHC*, 56th session, 1995, Calcutta, 341-2), points out that Firishta does not mention the rupee coin at all and argues that a rate corresponding to that of the *maḥmūdī* (2/5 rupee) would suit better the ranges given in terms of *muẓaffarīs* and *dāms* in the *Ā'īn-i Akbarī*. He also shows (p.344) that the *muẓaffarī* was superseded by the rupee in the Malwa mints during the 1580s.

[16] *Ā'īn*, I, 478; *Żawābiṭ-i 'Ālamgīrī*, Ethe 415, f.171a, Or. 1641, f. 50a, Add. 6598, f.153a.

[17] *Ā'īn*, I, 474. The *Żawābiṭ-i 'Ālamgīrī*, op.cit., also equates it with 12 *ṭankas* or 24 *dāms*.

[18] The *maḥmūdīs* were minted by the chiefs of Baglana and Navanagar down to 1638 and 1640 respectively (cf. Hodivala, op.cit., 115-30).

2. GOLD VALUE OF THE RUPEE

In Chapter II, Section 3, where we tried to trace the main trends in agrarian prices during our period, we referred to the importance of a study of the changes in value of the silver rupee in terms of gold and copper from which the changes in its general purchasing power may be deduced. Our task is greatly simplified because, the Mughal monetary system being one of an unrestricted coinage of great metallic purity, the rates at which *muhrs* and *dāms* exchanged for rupees should have closely corresponded to the market values of the three metals.[1] In considering contemporary quotations of *muhr*-rupee rates, the possibility of variations at any given time among the different regions must, of course, be borne in mind; but so long as the routes remained open, these differences probably tended to be kept at the minimum, owing to the relatively low cost of transport of gold and silver.

At the time of the *Ā'īn* (1595) the *muhr* was considered to be worth exactly nine rupees,[2] and it had remained stationary at this value apparently for well over a decade.[3] Hawkins (1608-12) took an *ashrafī* of Akbar to be equal to ten rupees,[4] and it was quoted at the same rate in 1614.[5] Jahāngīr's statements indicate that the rate stood at Rs10.7 to the *muhr* in his tenth regnal year (1615-16),[6] but

---

Abū Turāb, 27, in 1584, equates the *maḥmūdī* with 5/12 of the rupee. The early English factors regarded it as equal to 2/5 of a rupee (e.g. *Lett. Recd.*, I, 306) and this was the rate accepted in English accounts (*Factories, 1633-34*, 209); the Dutch rate, however, seems to have conformed to the rate adopted by Abū Turāb (cf. Pelsaert, 42).

The new value of 4/9 of a rupee is first noticed in 1636, when it is said to have become established "of late yeares" (*Factories, 1634-36*, 224). In 1638 we have the definite statement that the book rate of 2½ *maḥmūdīs* to the rupee in English accounts was misleading since the actual rate was 2¼ (ibid., *1637-41*, 91). But both the market rate and the English book rate seem to have remained unchanged for the rest of the period (ibid., *1651-54*, 58; Fryer, II, 125-6).

[1] Both the rupee and the *muhr* were worth a little more than their weight in bullion. The amount of seigniorage may be gathered from the *Ā'īn*, I, 31-2, where the amount of bullion to be deposited in the mint for a certain number of minted pieces is specified.

[2] *Ā'īn*, I, 25, 196.

[3] Under the Regulations of Todar Māl, formulated in the 27th year, the *La'l-i Jalālī*, a gold coin, equal to 1 1/9 *muhrs* in weight, was rated at 400 *dāms*, while the square rupee was considered worth 40, and the round 39 *dāms* (*A.N.*, III, 383; original text in Add. 27,247, f.332b). Mān Singh's *parwāna* of 1608 (NAI-2671/2) equates one *ashrafī* with Rs 8 *muhrī* or Rs 9.6 of ordinary issue.

[4] *Early Travels*, 101.

[5] Foster, *Supp. Calendar*, 48.

[6] Hodivala examines two statements of the emperor of this year, the purport of which is that a special *Nūrjahānī muhr*, weighing 500 *tolchas*, was worth Rs 6,400.

was back at 10 in 1621.[7]

In the next five years, however, a great rise must have taken place in the silver-price of gold, for in 1626 the *muhr* is stated to have fetched Rs 14.[8] This is supported by the prices realized by foreign gold coins this year at Surat.[9] Indeed, it was thought an "unexpected cheapness of gold" when in 1628 the "sunneas" or *muhrs* at Ahmadabad could not be disposed of for more than Rs13, and, subsequently, for just 12¾ each.[10] From this year onwards gold seems to have stabilized at about these prices: in 1633 *muhrs* were sold at Jalor for Rs 12½ each,[11] and in 1640 the price prevailing in Bengal is stated to be about Rs 13.[12]

The value of the *muhr* was back at Rs.14 by 1641-2,[13] and this rate is quoted in 1644-5[14] and 1653.[15] Another rise seems to have begun during the early fifties,[16] and a writer remembered the rate to have reached Rs 16 2/5 at Aurangabad in 1658.[17] In May 1661 the market rate for the *ashrafī* was officially reported to be Rs.14, as. 10, to Rs.14, as. 9, at Aurangabad;[18] but in February 1662, the rate

---

In Jahāngīr's weights for the gold coins, an ordinary *muhr* weighed 10 *māshas*, so that the real equation suggested is 600 *muhrs* =Rs 6,400, or 1 *muhr* =Rs 10 2/3. Hodivala takes the given weight to be in terms of Akbar's weights, but admits that the result arrived at, viz. 1 *muhr*=Rs 11, as. 12, looks a little out of place (*Mughal Numismatics*, 249).

[7] *T.J.*, 286. The half-*muhr* was worth Rs 5 at Burhanpur this year (*Factories, 1618-21*, 320).

[8] Pelsaert, 29. His statements, it is true, are not above criticism. He describes the *muhr* as weighing "a tola, or 12 *māshas*", which would suggest that it was the *muhr-i Nūrjahānī*. But the minting of this coin had ceased almost 15 years earlier. Moreover, he also speaks of the "single" *muhr* (pp.7, 29), with a value of Rs 7, and this could only have been a half-piece of the ordinary *muhr*.

[9] Of these, the "Hungary ducketts", which fetched the highest price, were sold for 13¼ *maḥmūdīs* each (or, between Rs 12½ and 13 per *tola*) (*Factories, 1625-9*, 155-6), and we must remember that even this coin, which was bought like the rest for its bullion, was much less refined than the *muhr*. In 1628, when a *muhr* was worth Rs 13, the Hungarian ducat was sold for just Rs.13 per *tola* at Ahmadabad (ibid., 235).

[10] Ibid., 235, 270.

[11] Mundy, 290. But elsewhere (310-11) he gives equivalents in English money from which the equation 1 *muhr* = Rs 14 is to be deduced (cf. Hodivala, op.cit., 252).

[12] Manrique, II, 129.

[13] Lāhorī, II, 259, cited by Hodivala, op.cit, 250.

[14] Lāhorī, II, 396, cited by Hodivala, op.cit., 250n.

[15] Tavernier, I, 246; also 15-16.

[16] In December 1652, the Surat factors predicted that gold was "more likely to rise than to fall" (*Factories, 1651-54*, 141).

[17] *Dilkushā*, f.15b.

[18] *Waqā'i' Dakhin*, 32. The prices of the *ashrafī* are given in four pairs (each of

of Rs 15, as. 8, to Rs15, was reported from Ramgir in Bidar province.[19] It was probably generally rated at Rs 16 in 1666,[20] and we have the testimony of the English factors at Surat that the *muhr* had been usually worth Rs 15 some time before 1676,[21] while it had certainly passed this rate in Bengal in the 1670s.[22]

In 1676, however, there was a sudden crash in the gold market "all India over", and the *muhr* fell to Rs 12 and 11 – a fall attributed by market gossip to the dishoarding of his ancestral treasure by Aurangzeb.[23] But the real or main cause seems to have been an exceptional increase in gold imports from Japan as well as Europe.[24] There was a partial recovery in gold price soon afterwards, for in the following year the rate quoted at Surat was Rs 13¾ per *muhr*.[25] At Qasimbazar, in Bengal, the *muhr* sold at Rs 13 in 1678 and 12₁₄/₁₆ in 1679.[26] In the latter year, gold had again been at very low prices at Surat,[27] while a fall of Rs 2, as. 5, in the price of the *muhr* was reported from Bengal.[28] In 1680 the market rate was reported to be Rs13 in Ajmer province,[29] while it remained below Rs 13 and even touched Rs 12½ at Qasimbazar.[30] Gold was still at low rates at Surat in 1681.[31] In 1684 the *muhr* fetched Rs 12½ in Bengal and even less

---

maximum and minimum) for *ashrafīs* of Aurangzeb and Shāhjahān in both *'Ālamgīrī* and *Shāhjahānī* rupees. The differences among the four pairs of rates are very small: I have quoted rates in terms of the *'Ālamgīrī* rupees.

[19] *Daftar-i Dīwānī*, 173; *Waqā'i' Dakhin*, 75.

[20] Ma'mūrī, f.134b; K̲h̲āfī K̲h̲ān, II, 190, cited by Hodivala, op.cit., 250-51. K̲h̲āfī K̲h̲ān says a little earlier (II, 189) that a *muhr* was then equal to Rs 17, but this is not supported by Ma'mūrī. On the other hand, Thevenot in 1666-7 gives such values for the *muhr* and the rupee in terms of the French *livres* as suggest that 1 *muhr* = Rs 14.

[21] *JRAS*, 1925, 315.

[22] Bowrey, 217, speaking of Bengal and Orissa (1669-79), says, the *muhrs* "passe very current at 15¼ and 15½ rupees each".

[23] *JRAS*, 1925, 314-16 (W. Foster's communication); *Factories*, NS, I, 267-8.

[24] Discoveries of gold in Japan led to an "export boom" around 1670. The Dutch exported as much as 11.5 million florins worth of gold from Japan during the decade 1670-79 (Glamman, *Dutch Asiatic Trade*, 58, 63). For the spurt in the English East India Company's export of gold to the East, including India, from the early 1660s to about 1685, whereafter these fell shaply, see S. Moosvi, in *JESHO*, XXX, 67-68. See, however, Najaf Haider, *JESHO*, XXXIX, 352-55, who argues that the real reason for the crash in gold was a temporary scarcity of silver, rather than an addition to gold supplies.

[25] *Factories*, NS, I, 267n.

[26] Master, II, 304: by one reading accepted in the text, the latter figure would be Rs 12 only. See also *Early Annals*, I, 385.

[27] *Factories*, NS, III, 240.

[28] Ibid., IV, 219. This is, perhaps, an exaggeration.

[29] *Waqā'i' Ajmer*, 678-9.   [30] *Factories*, NS, IV, 243.   [31] Ibid., III, 270.

was being offered.[32]

Perhaps, the price of gold improved a little in the next decade. In the early nineties, the price quoted for Surat was Rs 14 per *muhr*;[33] in 1695, the *muhr* was said generally to have fetched Rs 13¼;[34] and in 1697 the English at Surat gave the value of Rs 13, as. 2, to the *muhr*.[35]

3. COPPER VALUE OF THE RUPEE

The *dām* was as much an index of the value of copper, as the rupee was of silver. It purchased 1.15 of its own weight in copper at the time of the *Ā'īn*,[1] and we may assume that this ratio remained about the same for the rest of the period. It must, however, be remembered that regional price variations attained a much greater importance in the case of this baser metal than in that of gold or silver. Although sea-borne imports of copper became important with time,[2] the main supplies appear to have come from inland mines, notably those situated on the northern and eastern slopes of the Aravalli range,[3] and proximity to these could play a large part in determining the extent of differences in price among various markets.[4]

The *dām* originally seems to have had its copper weight so fixed as to make it accord with the traditional Indian scale, whereby one silver *ṭanka* (rupee) equalled 48 *dāms*.[5] The value of copper then began to rise in relation to silver so that the rupees "passed forty [*dāms*]", falling to 35.[6] Some time before 1582, Akbar decreed the rate of 40 *dāms* to the rupee.[7] By the 27th Ilāhī year (1582), 39

[32] Ibid., IV, 342, 353-4. [34] Careri, 253. [33] Ovington, 131-2.
[35] Surat Persian Letters, I.O. 150, f. 63b. [1] *Ā'īn*, I, 33.

[2] Cf. Moreland, *Akbar to Aurangzeb*, 183-5.

[3] There were a number of mines in the *sarkār* of Narnaul of Agra province, all situated in the midst of, or under the ridges at the far northern end of, the Aravalli range (*Ā'īn*, I, 454). Wāriṣ, a: f.488a, b: f.129a, indicates that there were mines also at Bairat, which lay in the *sarkār* of Alwar (Agra province). In Ajmer province there were copper mines at Chainpur and other places in the *maḥal* of Mandal (*sarkār* of Chittor) (*Ā'īn*, I, 505; *Waqā'i' Ajmer*, 13).

[4] Tavernier, I, 23. On his journey from Rajmahal to Patna in 1671 Marshall obviously found the price of copper falling distinctly as he proceeded westwards. (Marshall, 118, 121, 122, 125-6).

[5] The earlier rate of 48 *dāms* to the rupee is mentioned in *Ā'īn*, I, 196. For the ratio of 1:48 between the main coin and its fractional units in the Dehli Sultanate, see H. Nelson Wright, *Coinage and Metrology of the Sultans of Delhi*, 395-97. See also note 6 to Section 1 of this Appendix.

[6] *Ā'īn*, I, 176.

[7] This would mean an advantage to such troopers as were previously receiving

dāms were regarded as equal to the round or ordinary rupee, and 40 to the square.[8] But two years later the former was also declared to be worth 40 *dāms*,[9] and when the *Ā'īn* was written (1595) the actual market rates still fluctuated around this figure.[10]

As the copper coins lost their position as the main units of currency (as evidenced by the dramatic decline in their minting in the reign of Jahāngīr), the demand for them contracted so greatly that the silver value of copper fell dramatically. In 1606 much to Kaiqubād Mahyār's distress, while the rate at the court at Kabul was still 19 *ṭankas* (double-*dāms*) to the rupee, he had been compelled to sell the *dāms* entrusted to him in India at as many as 64 *ṭankas* to the rupee.[11] By 1609 in Gujarāt 80 'pice' or *dāms* (or 40 *ṭankas*) was the current rate, but it fell further in 1614.[12] Indeed, copper prices

fewer rupees in pay in lieu of their cash salaries, at the rate of 48 *dāms* to the rupee (*Ā'īn*, I, 196). On the other hand, troops receiving charges for horses in *dāms*, and so needing to exchange them for rupees, would have to have their allowances raised by a seventh, if the market rate of 35 *dāms* to a rupee was altered administratively to 40 *dāms* to the rupee (*Ā'īn*, I, 176).

[8] *A.N.*, III, 383; *Ā'īn*, I, 28. [9] *Ā'īn*, I, 28. [10] *Ā'īn*, I, 26.

[11] *Dastur Kaikobad Mahyār's Petition and Laudatory Poem*, 11.

[12] In 1609 a *maḥmūdī* was stated at Surat to be worth "32 paisaes or 31", "varying also as copper riseth and falleth" (*Lett. Recd.*, I, 34); and in 1611, it was 32 (ibid., I, 141). Taking the rupee as equal to 2½ *maḥmūdīs*, the rupee should have been worth exactly 80 pice (or *dāms*), when the *maḥmūdī* was worth 32. But when, as was probably more frequently the case in the market, the rupee was but worth 22/5 *maḥmūdīs*, it could only have fetched 77 *dāms*. In 1614 at Ahmadabad, the rate assumed was 77 to the rupee; but within ten days of this despatch, it was reported to be 84 (*Lett. Recd.*, II, 214, 249-50). Ufflitt's value of "96 to 102 pices" is given for the ordinary rupee (which he distinguishes from *sawāī* and *Jahāngīrī*) at Agra in the same year (Foster, *Supp. Calendar*, 48). His value for the *maḥmūdī* was 32 to 34 "pice" (ibid., also p.46). Early next year the *maḥmūdī* was reckoned at Surat as equal to 34 "pice" or *dāms* (*Lett. Recd.*, III, 11), and at Khambayat the rupee was worth 76 pice (ibid., 41). At the same time the *sikka* rupee at Ahmadabad was said to be worth 86 "pisas" (ibid., 87). Mitford, writing from Ajmer, in 1615, says the *chalanī* rupee at Agra fetched 83 "pisas", and the *khazāna* just 80 "pisas". (*Lett. Recd.*, III, 87). The following equations were adopted permanently by the English factors for their accounts: 1 *maḥmūdī* = 32 "pice"; 1 rupee =80 pice (*Lett. Recd.*, III, 87; *Factories, 1633-34*, 209; Fryer, II, 126).

In the quotations given in this note and in the main text account has been taken of the important critique by Najaf Haider, 'The Quantity Theory and Mughal Monetary History', *Medieval History Journal*, Vol.2.2 (1999), 309-48, esp. 341-4, in which he contested the view previously in vogue and adopted in this book that the 'pice' meant a half-*dam* as a coin and a full *dam* as a unit of weight. Najaf Haider showed conclusively by a scrutiny of copper prices during the seventeenth century that a 'pice' represented the *dām* both in money and in weight.

in India fell so much upon its practical demonetization that in 1619 the English found it profitable to melt down copper coins at Surat and export the metal to Iran.[13]

But the nadir had been reached. With the flow of further supply of excess coinage into the market at last draining off, the rupee fetched no more than 58 pice at Agra in 1626.[14] This is reflected in the quotations from Gujarat, of the years 1628 and 1633, which show that the rupee was down to 50 pice, if not still lower.[15] In 1634 in Sehwan (Sind) a rupee fetched only 24 *ṭankas* or 48 *dāms*.[16]

A slight recovery in silver seems to have set in by 1636 in Gujarat, where the rupee is then quoted at 26 or 27 *ṭankas*.[17] At Agra, the *dām* rate for the rupee in the Dutch accounts rose steadily from 50 pice in January 1637, to 58 in October 1638.[18] In 1640 the rupee seems to have fetched 56 "paisas" at Rajmahal, although copper must have been dearer there than at Agra.[19] Quotations of prices of Japanese copper at Surat suggest that the decline in copper prices continued into the 1640s.[20]

[13] The Surat factors were looking this year for copper to send to Persia and they decided to melt down "ten maunds of pice". They were, however, deterred from this by an official prohibition and had to despatch the coins unmelted (*Factories, 1618-21*, 142, 144). For changes of copper values from now on see I. Habib, 'A System of Trimetallism in the Age of the Price Revolution', in J.F. Richards, ed., *The Imperial Monetary System of Mughal India*, 137-170, including a note on the decline in copper minting by John S. Deyell, ibid., 160-64.

[14] Pelsaert, 29, 60. He says, first, that a rupee was worth 58 pice or more; and, second, that 5 or 6 *ṭakas* (each worth 2 pice) were equal to 4 or 5 stivers, while 24 stivers equalled a rupee.

[15] In Ahmadabad, the rupee fetched only 51 pice in 1628 (*Factories, 1624-29*, 235); and at Surat, in 1633, the "pice" were "20 to a Mohmoodee, sometymes more, sometymes lesse" (Mundy, 311). This is supported by a statement in a letter from the Surat factors, of 1636, to the effect that before the Gujarat famine the *maḥmūdī* was not above "20, 21 and 22 pice" (*Factories, 1634-36*, 206).

[16] *Maẓhar-i Shāhjahānī*, 184.

[17] Thus van Twist, *JIH*, XVI, 72-3. He says, 1 *maḥmūdī* = 24 or 25 pice =12 or 13 *ṭankas*; and 1 rupee = 53 or 54 pice =26 or 27 *ṭankas*. According to the Surat factors the *maḥmūdī* had risen to 25 and 25½ "pice" by 1636 (*Factories, 1634-36*, 206).

[18] See Moreland in *JUPHS*, III, i, (1923), 151, and Brij Narain, *Indian Economic Life*, 17.

[19] This appears from the equations given in Manrique, II, 102, 136, 174.

[20] Rs 15 per *man* in 1645 and 1646, and Rs 11.50 in 1650 (K. Glamann, in *Scandinavian Economic History Review*, I (1), 1953, 64 (Table IV). It may be tempting to draw inferences from the prices given of silver ingots, in terms of "pice" per *tola*, for the years 1646 and 1647 (*Factories, 1646-50*, 187). But these pice are

The 1650s saw, however, a spectacular rise in the price of copper. A partial cause, at least, of this ascent lay in the failure of some of the copper mines in the Aravallis. The court historian tells us that there was such a serious fall in the output of the mines in Bairat and Singhana that a change in their management became necessary in 1655.[21] The next year the rupee was quoted at so low a rate as below 45 pice in Sind.[22] In 1660 the Surat factors declared that copper was "exceeding deare",[23] and a Dutch letter from Surat the following year attributed its scarcity to the disorganization of the inland mines and the inadequacy of foreign supplies.[24] Early in 1661 the administration complained that the *dām* was extremely scarce at Surat, the rupee fetching no more than 15½ *ṭankas* (or 31 *dāms*), because the imported copper after being coined into *dāms* was being secretly supplied to other parts of the country, and not sold to local "*ṣarrāfs* dealing in small change."[25] This year the market rate of the newly coined '*Ālamgīrī* rupee was reported to be 15 to 14 7/8 *ṭankas* from Aurangabad and 16 3/10 to 16 9/50 from Daulatabad.[26] Early next year the rate was 14½ to 14¼ *ṭankas* at Ramgir in Bidar province.[27] Later the same year, the rate at Surat was 31 *dāms* to the rupee (inferred from copper prices);[28] and early in 1663 the *maḥmūdī*, stated to have been worth 20 pice formerly, was rated at 14 pice or less.[29] In 1665-6 "copper had become so scarce that the *ṣarrāfs* of the city of Ahmadabad introduced an iron pice into circulation and sold it at high rates", a situation sought to be mitigated by the coining of the lighter *dāms* of Aurangzeb.[30] Thevenot says

---

clearly the pice of account, 80 of which were rated to the rupee in the books of the English factory. The prices expressed are therefore those of silver bullion in terms of silver specie.

[21] Wāriṣ, a: f. 488a; b: f. 129a. Singhana was a *maḥal* in the *sarkār* of Narnaul.

[22] *Factories, 1655-60*, 78.

[23] *Factories, 1655-60*, 306.

[24] Cited by Moreland, *Akbar to Aurangzeb*, 184.

[25] Rāja Raghunāth's *parwāna* of 28 February 1661: copy in Vatican-Persiano 33 (reader-print copy at CAS in History, Aligarh, 52).

[26] *Waqā'i' Dakhin*, 32-33, 59. The editor reads the copper values in "*ṭankas*" and "*dāms*". It may be remembered (see note 6 of Section 1 of this appendix) that in the traditional scale of copper money, the *ṭanka* was the highest and the *dām* the lowest unit, 50 *dāms* making a *ṭanka*.

[27] *Daftar-i Dīwānī*, 173; *Waqā'i' Dakhin*, 75. A second set of rates, viz. 19¼ and 19 *ṭankas*, is also given: these are possibly in terms of *ṭankas* based on the new lighter *dāms* minted by Aurangzeb.

[28] *Factories, 1661-64*, 112.

[29] Ibid., 121.

[30] *Mir'āt*, I, 265.

that when he landed at Surat in January 1666, the rupee was rated at 33½ "pechas" and when he left, in February 1667, at 32½ "pechas".[31] In 1671 Marshall rated the rupee at Patna at 30 "pice".[32] Quotations of copper prices similarly reflect the scarcity of the metal during this period. In 1635, the English had purchased copper at Surat at the rate of 20 *maḥmūdīs* for the *man* then in use, or for 22.2 *maḥmūdīs*, had the later *man* been in use.[33] The Surat price quoted in 1660, however, was no less than 45 *maḥmūdīs* per "maund".[34] It had risen to Rs 22¼ in 1662,[35] but was quoted at Rs 20 to 22 in 1664,[36] and Rs 20 or lower in 1665.[37] It was again at Rs 21½ per *man* in 1668, when further demand for copper was still anticipated.[38] The high level of copper prices is also reflected in Dutch records. Japanese copper sold by the Dutch at Surat fetched Rs 11.50 per *man* in 1650, but Rs 20 in 1661, whereafter the price stayed around that figure until 1668, when it rose to Rs 21.25, the peak price of Rs 22.50 being attained in 1670 and 1671.[39] The rise was as remarkable in Bengal, from where the Balasore factors reported in 1669 that "copper usually fetched from 36 to 42 rupees per maund [which was about double the Surat *man*], but was for the moment at 50 rupees",[40] implying that a rupee was worth just 28 *dāms*.

The introduction of lighter *dāms* by Aurangzeb in the 1660s undoubtedly introduced some confusion in our evidence, which makes some of it difficult to interpret. Fryer, for example, quoted rates ranging as widely as from 12 to 24 "Pice" to the "Mamoodie".[41] But the Dutch quotations for Japanese copper at Surat indicate a gradual decline in its price from Rs 22.50 per *man* in 1671 to Rs 15

[31] Thevenot, 25-26. Tavernier, I, 22-23, says, however, that on his last journey (1665-7) the rupee at Surat was quoted at 49 *paisa*, but "there are times when it falls to 46". Probably he has made a slip and means an earlier journey, for he had been travelling in these parts since 1640.

[32] Marshall, 416. Marshall, 118, 121, 122, 125, 126, also gives the rates at various places between Rajmahal and Patna, ranging from 28 to 33½ "pice". His text, 416-7, makes it clear that he meant by "pice" the full *dām*.

[33] *Factories, 1634-46*, 148.

[34] *Factories, 1655-60*, 306.

[35] *Factories, 1661-64*, 113.

[36] Ibid., 210.

[37] *Factories, 1665-67*, 31, 77.

[38] *Factories, 1668-69*, 24.

[39] Glamann, *Scandinavian Economic History Review*, I(1) (1953), 64. There is no quotation for 1669.

[40] Ibid., 311. Cf. Bowrey, 232-3.

[41] "Pice, a sort of Copper Mony current among the Poorer sort of People; of these sometimes 12, 13, 14, 15, 16, 19, to 24 make, or are reckoned to a Mamoodie" (Fryer, II, 126).

in 1684. Despite a recovery during the 1690s the price continued to stay around Rs 15 during the early years of the next century.[42] In 1678 the rupee was rated at 36 *paisa*, which again suggests an improvement in the price of silver.[43] Other subsequent quotations, in terms of older *dāms*, are 42.7 to the rupee in 1691-2 on the western coast,[44] 35 (±0.5) in 1690-93 at Surat,[45] and 31.5 in 1695,[46] the latter two figures representing conversions from quotations given presumably in the new, lighter *dāms*. Because of the different localities and doubt surrounding what exactly was the copper coin in whose terms the value of the rupee is stated, the decline in the copper value these show may appear somewhat dubious. But a firmer index of copper price movements comes from eastern Rajasthan. Here the *ṭaka*, standing for the old double *dām,* slowly declined in value, as the number of *ṭakas* going to the rupee rose from 16.18 in 1665 to 20.25 in 1687, whereafter until 1706, the rate remained stable at 19±0.50.[47] It is possible, perhaps, to attribute this decline, and then stability, in copper prices partly to heavy Dutch imports into India of Japanese copper, which reached the level of 816.5 metric tons annually during the years 1679-84.[48]

Our information, large and complex as it is, is full of ascents, plateaux and descents in the silver price of copper; but there should be little doubt that at the close of the seventeenth century, copper had more than recovered the value it had lost in relation to silver in the first two decades of the century.

[42] Glamann in *Scandinavian Economic History Review*, I(1), 64-5, 68 (Tables IV and V). Table IV gives the sale prices of Japanese copper during the period 1645-84 in rupees per *man*; and Table V those from 1678-79 to 1738-39, in florins per 1000 lb. Dutch. In reconverting the latter rates into Rs per *man*, I have assumed 30 stuivers to be worth a rupee (ibid., 63) and 34½ lb. Dutch to equal one *man* (ibid., Table IV).

[43] *Waqā'i' Ajmer*, 14.

[44] Ṣādiq Khān's continuator (Ma'mūrī, f. 183b-184a; Khāfī Khān, II, 401-2) writes, under AH 1103 (AD 1691-92), that the coins current in the Portuguese possessions on the western coast were an "*ashrafī* ", worth 9 *ānas*, and a *bazurk*, worth ¼ *fulūs* (*ṭanka*). The "zeraphin" consisted of 48 "Bugerookes" (or 24 "Pice") (Fryer, II, 131), so that the rate to be deduced from the above equations would be 9/16 Rupee=12 *fulūs* = 24 pice.

[45] Ovington, 132: "Pice... Sixty of which sometimes two or three more or less".

[46] Careri, 253: "Pieces, call'd Pesies, 54 whereof make a Roupie".

[47] Cf. S.P. Gupta and S. Moosvi, 'Weighted Price and Revenue Rate Indices of Eastern Rajasthan (*c.*1665-1750)', *IESHR*, XII (2) (1975), 191 (Table 3).

[48] Glamann, *Scandinavian Economic History Review*, I(1), 51, 64-65. I have converted the Dutch lb. into lb. avdp. by adopting the rate of 1 lb. Dutch = 1.09 lb. avdp.

4. THE 'PRICE REVOLUTION' IN INDIA

From the changes in the value of the rupee in terms of gold and copper coins, as traced above, it becomes obvious that silver depreciated very greatly in relation to both the other money metals between *c.*1550 and *c.*1700. We can see that there were three great falls in the value of silver. The first took place during Akbar's reign before 1582, when the rupee:*dām* ratio changed from the previous 1:48 to 1:35, a fall of well over a quarter in the value of silver in terms of copper, then the main currency medium. After a period (*c.* 1605-20) in which copper fell heavily in value, a second decline in the value of silver began in the 1620s, when (with the *Ā'īn's* rates for the rupee as the base = 100) gold rose to 156 (in 1626) and copper began its recovery, reaching 60 (in 1628). After a slight recovery, a fresh fall in the value of silver began in the 1640s and continued till the 1660s, when gold stood at 178 (in 1666) and copper reached 129 (in 1662). From the later seventies silver showed sharp recovery, at least in terms of gold, but by the end of the century, gold again approached 150 and copper stood at above 110.

There is no discussion in contemporary sources about why this secular depreciation in the value of silver took place. The rise in the price of copper in the late 1650s and early 1660s was attributed, as we have seen, to the failure of inland mines. Similarly, the recovery of silver in relation to gold in 1676 was ascribed to Aurangzeb's dishoarding of the gold accumulated by his ancestors. Such explanations were, however, given, and can be accepted only, if at all, for temporary fluctuations in the price of either metal. But the real factor behind the general upward trend was a fall in the value of silver, from which both gold and copper benefited. This is shown best by the fact that the ascents in the prices of both the metals, during the 1620s and around 1650, closely synchronize, though it is true that copper fluctuated considerably more in value than did gold.

Writing in 1784 James Grant was probably the first writer to argue that the influx of silver and gold from the New World, which had led to a great rise in prices in Europe during the sixteenth and seventeenth centuries, was bound to make its impact on prices and metal-values in India in the same manner as it had done in Europe.[1]

[1] *Fifth Report*, 649-50. He thought that the gold:silver ratio altered, as a result of the silver imports, from 1:10 to 1:15 between the reigns of Akbar and Aurangzeb. Writers after him tended to ignore this factor altogether. Moreland, for example, notices the rise in the price of copper, but insists that its cause was "connected with copper and not with silver" and so denies any fall in the value of silver generally

Imports of American silver and gold into Europe had begun with the Spaniards' plunder of the wealth of the Aztecs and Incas in the first part of the sixteenth century. But it was the discovery and working of the rich silver mines in Mexico and Peru round about 1550 and their exploitation by the genocidal use of Amerindian labour, along with the application of the mercury amalgam process, that created an enormous regular flow of silver to Europe. American silver output continued to increase till 1630, after which a decline set in. American supplies of gold to Europe during this period were on a much smaller scale compared to those of silver, so that gold appreciated in terms of silver during this period.[2]

Part of this influx of American silver and gold was increasingly passed on by Europe to the East in the latter half of the sixteenth and the seventeenth century. A great controversy developed in western Europe about this drain of bullion eastwards, the total worth of which was estimated at £100 million at the close of the seventeenth century.[3] India stood out as the greatest among the recipients of this treasure. "India is rich in silver for all nations bring coyne and carry away commodities for the same," wrote Hawkins in 1613.[4] In the 1660s Bernier analysed at length the pattern of trade which drew bullion inexorably into India.[5] About the time that the imposition of the Tribute after the British conquest of Bengal (1757) was, at long last, changing the entire situation, an Indian author still claimed that while ships from foreign lands brought precious metals to India, they took away only merchandise, not treasure.[6]

The large silver imports should have led to an expansion of rupee output, an increase first sought to be quantified, on the basis of

(*Akbar to Aurangzeb*, 185). This was, perhaps, partly due to the fact that his investigation of the changes in the gold:silver ratio was so cursory (ibid., 182).

[2] On this entire subject, see Pierre Vilar, *A History of Gold and Money, 1450-1920*, Eng. transl, esp. 117-18, 121, for silver production in the Americas, 103-4, 193, for bullion (gold and silver) flow from the Americas to Europe, and 105 for alteration of gold silver ratio from 1:10.11 in 1536 to 1:12.12 in 1566-1608 in Spain. See also Ward Barrett, 'World Bullion Flows' in James D. Tracy (ed.), *The Rise of Merchant Empires*, 224-54, for revised data and references to work subsequent to Vilar as well as earlier.

[3] See for the contemporary controversy, J.R. McCulloch (ed.), *Early English Tracts on Commerce*, esp. 18-19, 340, for certain statistical data. Cf. E. Lipson, *Economic History of England*, II, 277-82; K. Glamann, *Dutch Asiatic Trade*, 56-57, 61; and K.N. Chaudhuri, *East India Company: The Study of an Early Joint-Stock Company, 1600-1640*, 118-21.

[4] *Early Travels*, 112.

[5] Bernier, 202-4. Cf. Fryer, I, 282-83.

[6] Āzād Bilgrāmī, *Khizāna-i 'Āmira*, 111.

museum collections by Aziza Hasan.[7] The estimate has been revised by Shireen Moosvi, who has also used coin-hoard evidence; she goes on to attempt absolute figures of currency output and quantify the flow of treasure imports.[8] Najaf Haider has gone over the ground once again, though his arguments for lower levels of output from Mughal mints as compared with those estimated by Moosvi, themselves quite conservative, do not seem to be sufficiently persuasive.[9] All the three studies, however, bring up enough evidence to show a substantial expansion in Mughal silver coinage.

The effect of such expansion on general prices involves, first, the question whether the prices were primarily quoted in terms of silver. Over large parts of northern India in the latter half of the sixteenth century, it was copper (or, billon) money in which prices of commodities and wages were set. It was only in the late years of Akbar that rupees began to be used in transactions of this sort; the full shift to the silver money was seemingly completed only in the early years of the seventeenth century.[10] So long as copper provided the medium in which commodity prices were mainly expressed, a fall in the value of silver could not affect them very much. Rather, the continuously increasing demand for copper, for use in artillery, musketry, tools and instruments, utensils, etc., should have constantly expanded the market for copper.[11] But, as silver displaced copper as the major currency medium during *c.*1580-*c.*1620,

[7] 'Silver Currency Output of the Mughal Empire', *IESHR*, IV(1) (1969), 85-116.

[8] 'Silver Influx, Money Supply, Prices and Revenue Extraction in Mughal India', *JESHO*, XXX(1) (1987), 47-94 (reprinted in Moosvi, *People, Taxation and Trade*, 35-80).

[9] Haider, 'Precious Metal Flows and Currency Circulation in the Mughal Empire', *JESHO*, XXIX(3) (1996), 298-304. Haider's own estimate of bullion imports is of broadly the same range as Moosvi's. He thus estimates the annual bullion imports (silver equivalents) during 1679-85 at 130.8 metric tons (p.323); but his annual estimate for rupee output during the whole decade 1676-85 is only 53.21 metric tons (p.340) as against Moosvi's (op.cit., 58) estimate of 82.8 tons. He estimates annual rupee output during 1696-1705 at just (the equivalent of) Rs 1.1 crore (p.340), as against Moosvi's (p.58), Rs 1.7 crore. But Grant, *Fifth Report*, 323, estimated the annual mint output of Bengal and Bihar mints under Mir Qasim alone at Rs 1.5 crore.

[10] Cf. I. Habib, 'A System of Trimetallism', in J.F. Richards, ed., *Imperial Monetary System of Mughal India*, 142-47.

[11] As Vilar, *History of Gold and Money*, 97-98, notes, "the industrial price of copper [in Europe] tended to rise above the monetary price offered in the East". There was "massive" minting of copper by Spain in early 17th century, exactly when copper coinage in India was on the retreat; and henceforward Europe became a net importer of copper, some of it drawn from as far as Japan (ibid., 98).

while silver could maintain its value because of the increasing monetary demand, copper underwent a sharp decline in its value since the industrial demand for it could not offset the heavy contraction of copper mintage. When the displacement of copper money by silver was complete, any further influx of silver now was bound to affect the general level of prices.[12] Gold had thus already begun to rise by *c.*1610, as we have seen, and copper began to recover from its fall after 1620.

It seems rather wilful to insist that the enormous silver imports into Mughal India did not necessarily have any impact on prices, just because the other factors of the Fisher equation (PT=MV) remain largely unknown.[13] But it is certainly valid to restrict the period of the impact to one beginning from the early years of the seventeenth century, and to ask whether the rise in prices owing to further silver influx was on a scale large enough to merit comparison with the European Price Revolution of the sixteenth and seventeenth centuries.[14]

Moosvi suggests a useful device for measuring the increase in silver-money supply by constructing an index of coined silver stock per capita. This she has done on the basis of the number of surviving rupee coins in treasure-troves and by assuming the population to have increased at the rate of 0.211 per cent per annum. The problem is, from what date should one count. If one assumes that the prices were largely being expressed in rupees by 1600, the per-capita stock by 1705 should, by her estimates, have grown by 61.9 per cent; if one takes 1610 (by which date the earlier standard gold:silver ratio had been breached), the increase would be 35.9 per cent; if, following Moosvi, one takes the initial date as 1615 (by which copper prices had dipped heavily), the increase would be just 23.6 per cent.[15] These alternatives set a range of about a quarter to two-fifths for the increase in silver-money supply per head: prices should have fundamentally increased in this range, during the seventeenth

[12] Cf. I. Habib, in Richards, ed., *Imperial Monetary System of Mughal India*, 146-47, 156-59.

[13] See Sanjay Subrahmanyam in *Studies in History*, VII(1) (1991), 79-105.

[14] For which see the classic discussion by P. Braudel and F.C. Spooner in E.E. Rich and C.H. Wilson, eds., *Cambridge Economic History of Europe*, IV, 378-486. See also Immanuel Wallerstein, *The Modern World System: Capitalist Agriculture and the European World Economy*, 67 ff., for a good summary of the debate over the factors behind the European Price Revolution.

[15] Moosvi, in *JESHO*, XXX, 74-81, 83-86.

century, if money velocity and per-capita productivity remained unchanged. By and large, this suggests that the rise in the silver price of gold (of about 50 per cent over the seventeenth century) might represent the general price increase better than the heavily fluctuating values of copper.

APPENDIX D

REVENUE STATISTICS

1. *JAMA'*

No other statistics, comparable in detail and spread to those of the *Ā'īn*, have survived from Mughal times, but a large number of tables setting out the *jama'dāmī* figures for the various provinces of the empire are preserved in the literature of the seventeenth century. They appear in the most unexpected places – in administrative manuals, in historical works, in travellers' accounts, and once even in a work on household management.

Thomas attempted a study of these statistics;[1] and Sarkar[2] and Moreland[3] followed in his footsteps. The information that they have collected is not inconsiderable but can still be supplemented from a number of sources not used by them. Moreover, the chronology of the statistical tables seems to require reconsideration. In some cases these are more or less definitely dated by statements in the sources themselves;[4] but most tables carry no explicit indication of their exact date. This is not surprising since the *jama'* figures represent the standard assessments and not the revenue receipts of particular years. Thomas and Moreland have as a rule assigned such undated statistics to the time when the works containing them were compiled. This is, however, open to the objection that the tables might really have been long out of date when they were copied into our sources, whether the authors of the latter abstracted them from semi-official papers or from earlier works. The dates of the works themselves are, therefore, of value only as setting the lowest time-limits for the respective tables.

It is, then, the internal evidence of the statistics on which we

[1] Edward Thomas, *The Chronicles of the Pathan Kings of Dehli*, 431-50; and *The Revenue Resources of the Mughal Empire in India*.

[2] *The India of Aurangzib*, xxix ff.

[3] *Akbar to Aurangzeb*, 322-28.

[4] *Ā'īn*, I, 386, indicates that the statistics given under the "Account of the Twelve Provinces" relate to the 40th *Ilāhī* year. *Iqbālnāma*, II, Or.1834, f.231b, says of the statistics given in it that they were placed before Jahāngīr after his accession in 1605; and Jagjīvandās (Add.26,253, f.51a) tells us that the revenue statistics reproduced by him had been submitted to Bahādur Shāh I, after the war of sucession, i.e. in or about 1709.

must largely rely. Significant clues are provided, for example, by the inclusion or omission of certain provinces. Thus any list containing figures for the province of Telangana could only have been compiled before 1657 (and probably not earlier than 1633), since it became a part of the newly formed province of Ẓafarābād Bidar in 1657.[5] Similarly, Baglana could only appear on tables prepared between 1638 and 1658, the two decades that it remained a separate province *(mulk)* by itself.[6] The inclusion of Balkh and Badakhshan, occupied temporarily in 1646-7, would be a still more precise indication, but that of Qandahar may be less significant since it probably continued to be claimed for the empire even after the the last siege of 1653. Finally, Bijapur and Haidarabad became provinces of the Empire in 1686 and 1687, and their omission or inclusion again provides a useful key for dating statistics. A study of the number of *sarkārs* and *maḥals* assigned to each province in the tables may also be of some help. Khandesh consisted of only one *sarkār* till 1632, when Galna was added as a separate *sarkār*;[7] then, towards the close of 1633 it received further accession of territory through the transfer of two whole *sarkārs* and a large portion of a third from Malwa.[8] No table showing three or more *sarkārs* under Khandesh can, therefore, be dated earlier than 1633. Similarly, since we know that certain *sarkārs* like Mu'izzābād in *ṣūba* Multan, and Islāmābād-Mathurā in *ṣūba* Agra, were created in the last years of Aurangzeb's reign, any statistics entering either of these as *sarkārs* could not be earlier than 1696.[9] Changes in nomenclature may serve as a guide as well. Agra was renamed Akbarābād in 1629,[10] and Dehli became Shāhjahānābād in 1648.[11] The old province of Ahmadnagar was renamed after

[5] *Dastūru-l'Amal-i Shāhanshāhī*, ff.79a-89a. Telangana appears as a *sarkār* of the Berar province in the *Ā'īn* and first appears as a separate province only in the reign of Shāhjahān (Lāhorī, I, ii, 62-3, 205; II, 711-12.) For the annexation of Bidar, and its new name, see Sāliḥ, III, 249-52, 261.

[6] Cf. Ṣādiq Khān, Or. 174, ff.60b-61a, 87b-88a, Or.1671, ff.34a, 48a.

[7] Ṣādiq Khān, Or.174, f.60a-b, Or.1671, ff.33b-34a; also *Dastūru-l'Amal-i Shāhanshāhī*, f.28a.

[8] Lāhorī, I, ii, 62-3; also Ṣādiq Khān, op. cit.

[9] *Sarkār* Mu'izzābād was created and named after Prince Mu'izzuddīn, who undertook a campaign to subjugate the area, when he was governor of Multan: he held the governorship from 1696-97 to 1707 (see M. Athar Ali in *Medieval India – A Miscellany*, I, 117-18). The Vrindaban Docs. enable us to narrow the period of the existence of Islāmābād-Mathurā as a separate *sarkār* to within the years 1696-1711.

[10] Ṣādiq Khān, Or.174, f.9a, Or.1671, f.5b.

[11] Ibid., Or.174, ff.155a, 156b-157a, Or.1671, ff.79a-80.

Daulatabad in 1636;[12] subsequently, it assumed the name of Aurangabad. The later names, it is true, could be put by a scribe or copyist on an earlier list, but a table belonging to the later period is not likely to carry the earlier names.

Owing to limitations of space it is not possible to discuss the date of each of the *jama*‘ tables that has come down to us. However, by proceeding on the lines outlined above we have been able to assign most of them to periods within reasonably narrow limits. These are shown in the following list which presents the statistics serially in a chronological order:

No.	Date	Source
1.	1595-96	*Ā’īn*, I, 386ff.
2.	1605	*Iqbālnāma-i Jahāngīrī*, II, Or.1834, ff.231b-232b.
3.	pre-1627	*Majālisu-s Salāṭīn*, Or.1903, ff.114a-115b.
4.	1628-36	*Bayāẓ-i Khwushbū’ī*, I.O.828, ff.180-181a.
5.	1633-38	*Farhang-i Kārdānī*, Aligarh MS, Abdus Salam, Fārsiya 85/315, ff.19a-20b.
6.	1646-47	Add.16,863, ff.120a-121a.
7.	,,	Lāhorī, II, 709-12.
8.	,,	Ṣādiq Khān, Or.174, f.151a-b, Or.1671, f.77a-b.
9.	1638-56	Bernier, 455-8.
10.	,,	Thevenot, passim.
11.	,,	Or.1840, ff.138a-140a.
12.	,,	*Dastūru-l‘Amal-i ‘Ilm-i Navīsindagī*, ff.143a-144b.
13.	,,	Bodl. Ousely 390, ff.9a-30a.
14.	,,	Sujān Rāi, passim.
15.	,,	Manucci, II, 413-15.
16.	,,	*Farhang-i Kārdānī o Kār-āmozī*, Edinburgh 83, ff.15b-17a.
17.	,,	*Siyāqnāma*, 102-104.
18.	,,	*Dastūru-l ‘Amal-i ‘Ālamgīrī*, ff.118b-120b (Dakhin provinces)
19.	1646-56	*Dastūru-l‘Amal-i Navīsindagī*, ff.166-b-167b.
20.	*c*.1667	*Mir’ātu-l ‘Ālam*, Add.7657, ff.445b-446a; Aligarh MS, ff.214b-215b.

[12] Lāhorī, II, 712. It seems to have been known officially as simply the province of the "Dakhin", as in 1645 (*Selected Documents*, 158).

21.	1687-*c*.1691	*Ẓawābiṭ-i 'Ālamgīrī*, Add.6598, ff.130b-132a, Or.1641, ff.4a-6b.
22.	1687-*c*.1695	Fraser 86, ff.57b-61b.
23.	1687-?	*Intikhāb-i Dastūru-l'Amal-i Pādshāhī*, Edinburgh 224, ff.1b-3b, 3a-11b.
24.	1701-02	*Dastūru-l'Amal-i Shāhjahānī*, Add.6588, ff.17a-39a; Aligarh, Sir S. Sulaiman Coll., ff.202b-218a.[13]
25.	*c*.1709	Jagjīvandās, *Muntakhabu-t Tawārīkh*, Add. 26,253, ff.51a-54a.
26.	1700-11	*Dastūru-l 'Amal-i 'Ālamgīrī*, ff.109a-118b, 120b (north Indian provinces).[14]

Some of the entries on this list call for special comment. The *jama'* in No.1 includes *suyūrghāl*, but deducting *suyūrghāl* figures from the *jama'* in each *sūba* will make only a marginal difference; and this, therefore, has not been attempted. Nos. 2 and 3 describe the figures given by them as *ḥāṣil* or *ḥāl-i ḥāṣil*. But the figures are expressed in *dāms* and not rupees; and it is, therefore, certain that they really represent the *jama'*, the word *ḥāṣil* having been only loosely used. This is certainly the case in No. 6 where the *jama'* figures in *dāms* are followed by "*ḥāṣil*" figures in rupees, though the latter are the exact equivalents of the former, at the standard rate of 1 Re = 40 *dāms*.

Nos.9, 10 and 15 are preserved in accounts of foreign travellers. It is to be assumed that they are ultimately derived from some *jama'-dāmī* tables. The figures are expressed in terms of rupees in Nos. 9 and 15 and in those of livres in No.10. Converted back into *dāms*, these were reproduced in the following tables in the first edition of this book. But these are essentially curiosities, of little real authority in themselves, and have been omitted in the tables in this edition. Also omitted are the figures from No. 8, for they are merely careless borrowings from the rounded figures provided by Lāhorī (No.7).

[13] Some figures in this source are used by James Grant in his 'Analysis', *Fifth Report*, 421, 440-41; but he is in slight error in supposing that the statistics belong to 1685. Not only do the separate entries for *sarkārs* Mu'izzābād and Islāmābād-Mathurā rule out a date before 1696, but the *ḥāṣil* statistics being expressly assigned to the year AH 1113 (AD1701-02), and references to two Rājpūt rulers, Amar Singh of Mewar (1700-16) and Rāo Amar Singh of Jaisalmer (d.1702) enable us to date them still more precisely to 1701-2.

[14] There is some difficulty in dating the statistics contained in the *Dastūru-l 'Amal-i 'Ālamgīrī*. While those of the Dakhin provinces clearly belong to the period 1638-

With these omissions, the *jama'* figures given for the Empire and the different provinces are reproduced from the sources listed above. Information incidentally supplied by other sources has also been included.[15] Statistics for the provinces of Kabul, Qandahar, Balkh and Badakhshan are not tabulated.

Authorities included in the list above are cited by the serial numbers assigned to them in that list.

The *Jama'* of the Empire

Source	Date	Amount in *dāms*
Ā'īn-i Akbarī, I, 386	1580	3,62,97,55,246[16]
Ṭabaqāt-i Akbarī, III, 546	1593-4	4,40,06,00,000[17]
1.	1595-6	4,94,22,08,084[18]
2.	1605	5,83,46,90,344
3.	pre-1627	6,66,91,00,000[19]
Lāhorī, II, 711	1628	7,00,00,00,000
4.	1628-36	6,57,73,57,625[20]

56 (with Telangana as a separate *ṣūba*, and Baglana, a separate territory), its statistics for north India are clearly post-1696, owing to its containing entries for *sarkārs* Mu'izzābād and Islāmābād-Mathurā, besides bearing other indications of a late date. In the first edition of this book, I was clearly in error in assigning these statistics to *c.*1656.

15 At different places in his Memoirs Jahāngīr mentions the *jama'* of some of the provinces. We may expect that his should have been the most authoritative information, giving us the *jama'* as it stood in the year when he was writing. But in every case he seems to have merely borrowed from the *Ā'īn*, the only difference being that he converts the *Ā'īn's* figures into round numbers. See *T.J.*, 101 (Bengal & Orissa), 172 (Malwa), 299 (Kashmir).

16 The *Ā'īn* gives this figure as representing the total of the *jama'-i dah-sāla*, and not of the *jama'* of the empire at the time the *Ā'īn* itself was completed. The *jama'-i dah-sāla* had been established in 1580.

17 This figure must be used with the greatest caution. Apart from the number-symbols being confusedly written, it is stated to be of *ḥāṣil*, not *jama'*. Moreover, the amount is shown in *ṭanka-i murādī*, or double-*dām*. It has been assumed here that the *dām* is meant.

18 This figure represents the total of the *Ā'īn's* figures for the various provinces set out in this Appendix, plus the figure for the *sarkār* of Kabul. In the case of Kabul the figure of 8,05,07,465 given in the statistical tables for the *sarkār* has been accepted and not the amount (6,73,06,983 *dāms*) given in the text preceding the table (*Ā'īn*, I, 594). Owing to the miscellaneous nature of the units of money and kinds of goods in which the revenues of Qandahar are stated (*Ā'īn*, I, 588), our figure for the *jama'* of the empire excludes the *jama'* of Qandahar.

19 This is the aggregate of the *ṣūba* figures; it much exceeds the total for the empire given in the source itself, viz. 6,30,00,00,000 *dāms*.

20 The total as stated in the source; the actual aggregate of *ṣūba* figures comes to 6,75,51,44,324 *dāms*.

5.	1633-8	7,77,60,03,662[21]
6.	1646-7	9,15,09,90,776[22]
7.	,,	8,80,00,00,000
11.	1638-56	7,82,30,49,662
12.	,,	9,70,71,81,000
13.	,,	7,84,99,47,640
14.	,,	8,68,26,80,573
16.	,,	7,82,00,49,662
19.	1646-56	8,90,00,00,000
20.	*c.*1667	10,49,57,80,331[23]
21.	1687-*c.*1691	13,80,23,56,000
22.	1687-*c.*1695	12,07,18,76,841
23.	1687-?	13,21,98,53,981[24]
24.	1700-2	1,13,26,56,263(!)
25.	*c.*1709	13,33,99,91,841

Bengal and Orissa
(Undivided)

Source	Date	Amount in *dāms*
1.	1595-6	42,77,26,681[25]
2.	1605	41,91,07,870
3.	pre-1627	50,00,00,000

[21] Aggregate of *ṣūba* figures: the total for the empire is not stated in the source.

[22] This is the total for the empire given in the source. From this it deducts 18,45,00,000 *dāms* as the *jama'* of Qandahar, Balkh and Badakhshan, "remitted to the *zamīndārs*", to bring down the total to 8,96,64,90,776 *dāms*. From this figure it makes a further deduction of 59,08,36,042 *dāms* as temporary remissions of *jama'* granted for "relief of the peasantry", the net total now coming to 8,37,56,54,734 *dāms*. Apparently, its *ṣūba* figures (e.g., the high figure for the Dakhin *ṣūbas*, 2,19,00,87,798 *dāms*) include these remissions, while Lāhorī (no.7) excludes them. Hence part of the difference between his figures for the total for the Empire, and the *jama'* of the Dakhin provinces, and those in our source no.6.

[23] This is the total of the *ṣūba* figures. The stated total is 9,24,17,16,082 *dāms* only. In counting the aggregate of the *ṣūba* figures, Beveridge, *JRAS*, 1906, 351-2, makes a slip of a full one "arb" (100 crore).

[24] The *jama'* of the empire given in this work excludes Bijapur and Haidarabad. The figures for these have been added to arrive at the figure in our table.

[25] I concur with Moosvi, 15, 26-27, that the *jama'* for Orissa has been included twice over in the total stated in the *Ā'īn* for Bengal and Orissa. The total entered here is, therefore, the stated total minus the *jama'* of Orissa. *T.J.*, 101, in giving 60 crore *dāms* as the *jama'* of Bengal and Orissa, merely copies the *Ā'īn*'s error.

Source	Date	Bengal *dāms*	Orissa *dāms*
1.	1595-6	25,69,94,043[26]	17,07,32,638[27]
Manrique, II, 395	1632	36,00,00,000	
4.	1628-36	40,25,20,000	20,05,45,000
5.	1633-8	42,71,91,000	17,02,04,000[28]
6.	1646-7	44,73,90,000	28,02,40,000
7.	,,	50,00,00,000	20,00,00,000
11.	1638-56	42,71,91,000	18,02,40,000
12.	,,	72,71,91,000(!)	19,10,00,000
13.	,,	42,71,91,000	18,02,40,000
14.	,,	46,29,00,000	40,41,05,000(!)
16.	,,	42,71,00,000	18,02,00,000
17.	,,	44,00,00,000	39,10,00,000
19.	1646-56		19,10,00,000
20.	c.1667	52,37,39,110	19,71,00,000
21.	1687-*c*.1691	52,46,36,240	14,28,21,000
22.	1687-*c*.1695	52,46,36,240	14,28,21,000
23.	1687-?	52,46,36,240	14,28,21,000
24.	1701-2	52,46,36,104	18,28,41,000
25.	*c*.1709	52,46,36,240	14,28,11,000
26.	1700-11	45,78,58,000	12,55,80,000

Source	Date	Bihar *dāms*	Ilahabad *dāms*
1.	1595-6	22,19,19,404½[29]	21,24,27,819[30]
2.	1605	26,27,74,167	30,43,55,746
3.	pre-1627	31,27,00,000	30,70,00,000
4.	1628-36	30,33,55,744	30,33,55,744
5.	1633-8	36,88,30,000[31]	36,13,90,000

[26] This represents the corrected *jama'* figure of Bengal and Orissa (undivided) less that of Orissa shown in the accompanying column.

[27] This is made up of figures given separately for the *sarkārs* of Orissa.

[28] The amount stated in rupees is equal to 18,02,04,000 *dāms*.

[29] This is the *jama'* given in the *Ā'īn*, for the province as a whole. The total for the figure of the various *sarkārs* of the province amounts, however, to 30,18,48,096 *dāms*.

[30] Almost all statistical tables from the *Ā'īn* onwards assign to the *jama'* of Ilahabad, in addition to the cash amounts, a quantity of 12,00,000 betel leaves.

[31] This is the equivalent in *dāms* of the figure given in rupees. The amount

6.	1646-7	37,56,92,299	37,36,04,358
7.	,,	40,00,00,000	40,00,00,000
11.	1638-56	36,88,30,000	36,13,90,000
12.	,,	38,32,00,000	37,88,00,000
13.	,,	36,88,30,000	46,90,00,000
14.	,,	38,07,30,000	37,60,61,000
16.	,,	36,88,30,000	
17.	,,	38,22,00,000	37,88,00,000
19.	1646-56	38,32,00,000	37,88,00,000
20.	*c*.1667	72,17,97,019(!)[32]	43,66,88,072
21.	1687-*c*.1691	40,71,81,000	45,65,43,278
22.	1687-*c*.1695	40,71,81,000	45,65,43,248
23.	1687-?	40,71,81,000	45,65,43,248
24.	1701-2	39,43,44,532	42,23,46,932
25.	*c*.1709	40,71,81,000	45,65,43,248
26.	1700-11	54,53,00,335	52,78,81,196

Source	Date	Awadh *dāms*	Agra *dāms*
1.	1595-6	20,17,58,172	54,62,50,304
2.	1605	22,98,65,014	77,04,89,055
3.	pre-1627	23,22,00,000	82,25,00,000
4.	1628-36	25,97,58,140	77,04,89,055
5.	1633-38	25,82,10,000	94,11,60,000
6.	1646-47	26,35,00,565	96,99,27,705
7.	,,	30,00,00,000	90,00,00,000
11.	1638-56	25,82,10,000	94,11,00,000
12.	,,	25,82,10,000	1,00,90,00,000
13.	,,	25,82,10,000	94,11,60,000
14.	,,	26,45,40,000	98,18,65,600
16.	,,	25,82,10,000	94,11,60,000
17.	,,	27,32,00,000	1,90,80,00,000[33]
19.	1646-56	27,32,00,000	1,00,90,00,000
20.	*c*.1667	32,00,72,193	1,05,17,09,283
21.	1687-*c*.1691	32,13,17,119	1,14,17,00,157
22.	1687-*c*.1695	32,13,17,819	1,14,17,60,157
23.	1687-?	32,13,17,719	1,14,17,00,157

stated in *dāms* in the source is only 16,88,30,000, an obvious error.

[32] Aligarh MS var.: 70,17,97,110.

[33] Probably an error for 1,01,90,80,000.

24.	1701-2	27,95,79,919	96,12,67,015
25.	*c*.1709	32,13,17,119	1,14,17,60,057
26.	1700-11	36,39,82,859	1,36,46,02,117

Source	Date	Delhi *dāms*	Lahor *dāms*
1.	1595-6	60,16,15,555	55,94,58,423
2.	1605	62,62,33,956	64,67,30,311
3.	pre-1627	65,61,00,000	82,50,00,000
4.	1628-36	62,62,33,753	64,73,30,611
5.	1633-8	73,93,10,000	84,42,90,000
6.	1646-7	96,94,24,481[34]	89,22,18,399
7.	"	1,00,00,00,000	90,00,00,000
11.	1638-56	78,93,00,000	84,42,90,000
12.	"	78,20,00,000	93,48,00,000
13.	"	73,93,00,000[35]	87,71,90,000
14.	"	74,63,35,000	89,33,70,000
16.	"	93,00,000(!)	84,41,90,000
17.	"	77,20,00,000	93,48,00,000
19.	1646-56	78,28,00,000	93,78,00,000
20.	*c*.1667	1,16,83,98,269	90,70,16,125
21.	1687-*c*.1691	1,22,29,50,177	89,89,32,170
22.	1687-*c*.1695	1,22,29,50,137	89,81,32,170
23.	1687-?	1,22,29,50,137	89,81,32,170
24.	1701-2	1,22,29,50,137	89,30,39,419
25.	*c*.1709	1,22,29,50,658	89,81,32,107
26.	1700-11	1,55,88,39,127	1,08,97,59,776

[34] The figure in the source is 36,94,24,481, confirmed by an equivalent stated in rupees. While it is true that if we adopt the reading as given in the MS and add it to the other *ṣūba* figures, the aggregate we get for the empire (8,37,76,53,556 *dāms*) would be close enough to the net total stated in the source (8,37,56,54,734 *dāms*), it is also noteworthy that if we read the first digit as 9 instead of 3, not impossible in *raqam* notation, we get an aggregate of *ṣūba* figures (8,97,76,53,556 *dāms*) which is quite close to the total given for the empire (8,96,64,90,776 *dāms*) before deducting certain temporary remissions from the *jama'* granted for "the relief of the peasantry".

[35] The figure expressed in *dāms* has been corrected by reference to the rupee equivalent given under it.

Multan and Thatta
(Undivided)

Source	Date	*Dāms*
1.	1595-6	21,75,56,012[36]
2.	1605	25,39,64,173
3.	pre-1627	40,00,00,000

Source	Date	Multan *dāms*	Thatta *dāms*
1.	1595-6	16,69,50,427[37]	5,06,05,585[38]
4.	1628-36	25,39,97,855	41,51,70,790(!)
5.	1633-8	24,27,00,000[39]	9,30,28,000[40]
6.	1646-7	25,46,04,499	9,23,40,000
7.	,,	28,00,00,000	8,00,00,000
11.	1638-56	24,47,00,000	9,20,00,000
12.	,,	22,55,00,000	9,28,00,000
13.	,,	24,47,00,000	9,20,00,000
14.	,,	24,46,55,000	9,49,70,000
16.	,,	24,48,47,000	9,20,00,000
17.	,,	26,56,00,000	9,18,00,000
19.	1646-56	26,56,00,000	9,28,00,000
20.	*c.*1667	24,53,18,505	7,49,86,900
21.	1687-*c.*1691	21,43,49,896	6,88,16,810
22.	1687-*c.*1695	11,43,42,896(!)	6,88,16,810
24.	1701-2	21,98,02,418	6,01,01,988
25.	*c.*1709	22,43,49,893	6,88,16,800
26.	1700-11	33,84,21,178	8,92,30,000

[36] This is the stated figure for the Multan province, plus the stated total for the sub-province of Thatta.

[37] This is the stated total for the *ṣūba* of Multan plus the stated total for *sarkār* Siwistan, but excluding the other *sarkārs* under Thatta. The stated totals of the *sarkārs* of *ṣūba* Multan yield a much higher total for that *ṣūba*, but the difference is explained by the very high figure for *sarkār* Dipalpur, exceeding by roughly the same amount the total of the figures for the *parganas* within that *sarkār* (cf. Moosvi, 31).

[38] The figure given in the *Ā'īn* for the *sarkārs* of *ṣūba* Thatta less that given for *sarkār* Siwistan.

[39] The amount stated in rupees is, however, equal to 24,47,00,000 *dāms*.

[40] The amount stated in rupees is equal to 9,01,20,000 *dāms*.

Source	Date	Ajmer *dāms*	Kashmir *dāms*
Ā'īn, i, 570-71	1592-3		7,46,70,411
Ibid.	1594-5		7,63,72,165¾
6,22,02,203¼[41]			
1.	1595-6	28,84,01,557	6,21,13,045
2.	1605	30,99,17,724	
3.	pre-1627	42,05,00,000	
4.	1628-36	30,99,37,734	
5.	1633-8	54,03,50,000	11,93,80,000[42]
6.	1646-7	56,66,21,310	13,64,12,039
7.	,,	60,00,00,000	15,00,00,000
11.	1638-56	54,00,50,000	11,43,80,000
12.	,,	87,68,00,000	14,02,00,000
13.	,,	54,00,50,000	11,71,80,000
14.	,,	55,53,60,000	12,62,85,000
16.	,,	54,00,00,000	11,43,80,000
17.	,,	87,68,00,000	14,02,01,900
19.	1646-56	98,68,00,000	14,02,00,000
20.	*c*.1667	63,68,94,883	21,30,74,826
21.	1687-*c*.1691	65,26,45,602[43]	22,99,11,397[44]
22.	1687-*c*.1695	65,23,45,382	22,99,11,397
23.	1687-?	65,53,45,702	22,99,11,397
24.	1701-2	60,29,10,270	27,79,11,397
25.	*c*.1709	65,33,45,702	22,99,11,300
26.	1700-11	64,87,61,685	11,43,90,000(!)

[41] These two figures represent the *jama'* worked out by Āṣaf Khān while the figure against 1592-3 represents that determined by Qāẓī 'Alī Baghdādī. The *jama'* of Kashmir was fixed in terms of *kharwārs* (ass-loads) of rice which were then converted into *dāms*. At the rates of conversion used by Qāẓī 'Alī, Āṣaf Khān's *jama'* should have amounted to 7,63,72,165¾ *dāms*. A remission of *bāj* and *tamghā* (tolls and cesses) caused a reduction of 8,98,400 *dāms*. Then for the revenues paid in grain the number of *dāms* rated to a *kharwār* (hitherto 29 to 1) was reduced by 5. This together with the tax remissions would have brought the *jama'* down to 6,22,02,203¼ *dāms*. It is not clear how Abū-l Faẓl can say that after these reductions the *jama'* of Āṣaf Khān was only 8,60,304½ *dāms* (not 1,24,68,107¾ *dāms*) smaller than the *jama'* of Qāẓī 'Alī.

[42] The amount stated in rupees is, however, equal to 11,43,80,000 *dāms*.

[43] MS var.: 85,26,45,702.

[44] MS vars.: 27,99,21,397 and 22,40,11,687.

Source	Date	Malwa *dāms*	Gujarat *dāms*
1.	1595-6	24,06,95,052	43,68,22,301
2.	1605	25,73,78,201	46,91,59,424
3.	pre-1627	28,00,00,000	50,64,00,000
4.	1628-36	25,78,78,361	46,99,59,421
5.	1633-8	36,25,10,000	46,32,80,000
6.	1646-7	39,81,53,749	53,37,91,485
7.	,,	40,00,00,000	53,00,00,000
11.	1638-56	36,25,10,000	46,32,80,000
12.	,,	39,85,00,000	53,00,00,000
13.	,,	36,35,10,000	46,32,60,000
14.	,,	36,90,70,000	58,37,90,000
16.	,,		46,32,60,000
17.	,,	39,85,00,000	53,58,00,000
19.	1646-56	39,85,00,000	53,58,00,000
20.	*c.*1667	42,54,76,670	44,88,83,096
21.	1687-*c.*1691	40,39,80,658	45,47,49,135
22.	1687-*c.*1695	40,39,01,658	45,47,49,135
23.	1687-?	40,39,80,653	45,47,49,135
24.	1701-2	40,83,46,718	53,65,25,000
25.	c.1709	40,39,80,658	45,47,44,135
26.	1700-11	55,73,17,320	86,92,88,069
Mir'āt, I, 25	*c.*1719		79,96,45,213

The Dakhin

Note: An asterisk in the table below indicates that the figure is not directly stated in the source, but is the total of the figures given in it for the different provinces of the Dakhin, for which see the tables that follow.

Source	Date	*Dāms*
1.	1595-6	84,49,56,264*
1. (after enhancement)	1601	94,61,32,758*
2.	1605	1,10,08,16,547*
3.	pre-1627	1,15,67,00,000*
4.	1628-36	1,25,08,05,955*
5.	1633-8	1,73,04,72,000*
Lāhorī, I, ii, 62-63	1635	2,12,00,00,000*
Ibid., 205	1636	2,00,00,00,000
6.	1646-7	2,19,00,87,798

7. *Ādāb-i 'Ālamgīrī*, f.40b; ed., I, 157; *Ruq'āt-i 'Ālamgīr*, 121-2	"	1,82,00,00,000*
	1653-4	1,44,90,00,000
11.	1638-56	1,57,77,90,000*
12.	"	2,56,55,00,000*
13.	"	2,13,62,70,000*
14.	"	1,56,71,69,000*
16.	"	1,52,56,40,000*
17.	"	2,42,51,00,000*
18.	"	1,85,64,48,000*
19.	1646-56	2,06,55,00,000*
20.	*c.*1667	2,96,70,00,000
21.	1687-*c.*1691	6,00,22,22,140
22.	1687-*c.*1695	5,86,99,94,307*
23.	1687-?	5,91,72,36,140*
24.	1701-2	6,50,22,22,140
25.	*c.*1709	6,03,73,74,000

Nos.21-24 above include the figures for *ṣūbas* Bijapur and Haidarabad. If these are deducted for convenience of comparison, the net figures for Mughal Dakhin in these sources would stand as follows:

21.	1687-*c.*1691	2,65,45,30,000*
22.	1687-*c.*1695	2,56,69,74,307*
23.	1687-?	2,57,05,74,000
24.	1701-2	3,15,46,60,036
25.	*c.*1709	2,57,05,74,000*

The *jama'* statistics for the individual Dakhin provinces are tabulated below.

Source	Date	Berar *dāms*	Khandesh *dāms*
1.	1595-96[45]	64,26,03,270	20,23,52,992

[45] The *jama'* figures for both Berar and Khandesh, presumably in force in 1595-6, are stated in *ṭanka-i Barārī*, valued at 16 *dāms* (*Ā'īn*, I, 478). (In the *jama'* table for Khandesh, the *ṭanka* is termed '*ṭanka-i Dāndesh*' in the MSS, though not in Blochmann's edn.).

Ā'īn	1601[46]		30,35,29,488
2.	1605	63,99,56,928	29,70,18,561
4.	1628-36	38,99,56,308	29,70,16,566
5.	1633-8	60,00,58,000	41,98,04,000
7.	1646-7	55,00,00,000	40,00,00,000
11.	1638-56	60,58,00,000[47]	36,15,10,000
12.	,,	63,50,00,000	44,60,00,000
13.	,,	60,58,00,000[47]	41,98,40,000
14.	,,	60,72,70,000	44,36,19,000
16.	,,	60,58,00,000	41,98,40,000
17.	,,	63,50,00,000	44,60,00,000
18.	,,	63,77,52,000	49,69,30,000
19.	1646-56	63,50,00,000	44,60,00,000
21.	1687-*c*.1691	92,65,45,000	42,36,00,000
22.	1687-*c*.1695	81,04,25,000	34,86,30,000
23.	1687-?	81,40,25,000	34,66,30,000
24.	1701-02	92,65,45,000	1,41,00,00,000(!)
25.	1709		34,86,30,200

Source	Date	Ahmadnagar/Daulatabad/ Aurangabad *dāms*	Telangana/ Bidar *dāms*
2	1605	16,38,41,058	
3.	Pre-1627	28,35,00,000	
4.	1628-36	56,38,41,066	
5.	1633-8	50,71,60,000	20,34,50,000
6.	1646-7		
7.	"	55,00,00,000	30,00,00,000
11.	1638-56	50,70,80,000	10,34,50,000(!)

[46] Upon the capture of Asirgarh this year, Akbar decreed an enhancement of the *jama'* of Khandesh by 50 per cent through raising the value of the *ṭanka-i Barārī* (now apparently a money of account) to 24 *dāms* (*Ā'īn*, I, 474). The MSS consulted by me (Add.7652, 6552 and 5645) do not contain the statement added in parenthesis by Blochmann that this enhancement raised the *jama'* of Khandesh to the equivalent of 45,52,94,230 '*dām-i Akbarī*', which would yield a rate of 36, not 24, *dāms* for the *ṭanka-i Barārī*. Moosvi, 29-30 *n*., notes this error, but is a little hasty in ascribing it to Abū-l Faẓl – the error is that of his editor.

[47] In both nos.11 and 13, Berar is given the name of 'Berar *alias* Daulatabad'; *ṣūba* Daulatabad appears as Dakhin-Baglana; and separate figures are not provided for Baglana. This shows that nos.11 and 13 are derived from a common source, where the same transcriptional error in *ṣūba* headings had been committed.

12. 1638-56	68,41,00,000	27,54,00,000
13. ,,	50,71,80,000	10,34,50,000(!)
14. ,,	51,62,80,000	
16. ,,		
17. ,,	68,91,00,000	63,50,00,000(!)
18. ,,	50,71,60,000	19,46,06,000
19. 1646-56	68,91,00,000	27,54,00,000
21. 1687-*c*.1691	1,18,30,65,000	62,05,50,000(!)
22. 1687-*c*.1695	1,03,49,45,000	37,29,74,370
23. *c*.1687	1,57,05,74,000	37,29,74,770
24. 1701-02	1,18,73,35,000	62,05,50,000(!)
25. 1709		37,29,74,307

Source	Date	Bijapur *dāms*	Haidarabad *dāms*
21.	1687-*c*.1691	2,25,48,27,140	1,09,28,65,000
22.	1687-*c*.1695	2,19,26,85,000	1,11,13,35,000
23.	1687-?	2,25,47,27,104	1,09,18,35,000
24.	1701-02	2,25,47,27,104	1,09,28,35,000
25.	1709	2,35,55,00,000	1,11,13,00,000

	Baglana	*dāms*
2.		50,00,000[48]
Lāhorī, II, 108-9	1638	1,60,00,000
7.	1646-47	2,00,00,000
Wāriṣ, MS. 'A' f.461a	1652	2,00,00,000
12.	1638-56	2,00,00,000
17.	,,	2,00,00,000
18.	,,	2,00,00,000

2. ḤĀṢIL

We have seen in the previous section that certain earlier works style as *ḥāṣil* what are really *jama'* statistics. It is only in four sources belonging to the last two decades of our period that the *ḥāṣil* figures given alongside the *jama' dāmī* statistics can inspire any degree of confidence. One set of these figures is designated *ḥāṣil-i san-i kāmil*, or simply *ḥāṣil-i kāmil*, the collection of the "best" year. Other *ḥāṣil* figures are assigned to particular years,

[48] Stated to be equal to 25 lakh *ṭankas*.

but in some cases there is no reference to date or time at all. These figures are uniformly given in rupees.

The four sources are: the *Ẓawābiṭ-i 'Ālamgīrī;* Fraser 86; *Dastūru-l'Amal-i Shāhjahānī*; and Jagjīvandās. These are cited, as in the previous section, as Nos.21, 22, 24, and 25 respectively. The *ḥāṣil* statistics in the *Intikhāb-i Dastūru-l 'Amal-i Pādshāhī* (No.23) are so close to those of No.22, that they are here omitted.

ḤĀṢIL-I (SĀN-I) KĀMIL
(in Rupees)

	No.21 (1687-91)	No.22 (1687-95)	No.24 (1701-2)	No.25 (1709)
The Empire, excluding Bijapur and Haidarabad		17,51,02,039		17,51,02,039
Dehli	3,10,12,154	3,10,12,154	3,10,12,154	68,49,110(!)
Agra	2,06,97,371	2,00,71,103	2,16,84,470	1,30,97,371
Ajmer	1,06,96,393	6,00,97,341(!)	80,94,861	1,06,97,371
Lahor	1,67,06,386	1,87,04,383	1,65,67,596	87,04,383
Multan	51,59,699[1]	51,69,399	52,46,937	51,69,389
Thatta	91,25,551	13,65,397	11,76,041	93,65,397
Kashmir	24,58,384	24,31,339	24,58,754	24,62,593
Illahabad	1,05,97,671	1,05,97,341	99,68,016	1,05,98,371
Awadh	91,25,511	92,25,591	83,57,876	91,25,651
Bihar	93,05,431	93,25,551	85,15,983	93,05,431
Bengal	86,19,247[2]	86,19,247[3]	3,86,19,247(!)	86,19,267[4]
Orissa	16,58,116[2]	16,58,856[3]	16,58,816	16,57,826
Malwa	84,72,299	84,72,299	1,34,19,048	84,72,291
Gujarat[5]	83,49,103	89,62,830	1,21,83,953	89,65,806
The Dakhin Provinces:				
Aurangabad		1,00,50,000		1,00,50,000
Berar		96,16,309		90,16,309
Bidar		31,00,000		
Khandesh		40,86,719		40,80,019

OTHER *ḤĀṢIL* STATISTICS

The regnal years, presumably of Aurangzeb, to which some of the *ḥāṣil* figures are assigned, are indicated by Roman numerals. The figures given in No.25 are uniformly termed "*ḥāṣil-i ākhir*", or the latest receipts, and may accordingly be dated about 1708-9.

[1] Styled simply "*ḥāṣil*" in the original.
[2] Styled "*ḥāṣil*" in the original.
[3] Described as "*ḥāṣil-i kāmil* of the 9th (regnal) year (of Aurangzeb?)".
[4] Described as "*ḥāṣil-i ākhir*" in the original.
[5] The *Mir'āt*, I, p.26, puts the *ḥāṣil-i sāl-i akmal* of Gujarat at Rs1,23,56,000

(In Rupees)

	No.21 (1687-91)	No.22 (1687-95)	No.24 (1701-2)	No.25 (1709)
The Empire	23,24,18,890	24,14,01,391	27,24,28,855	26,17,72,029
Delhi		2,22,56,400 (XVIII)		94,04,030
Agra		1,82,67,000 ,,		68,92,897
Ajmer		68,92,877 ,,		68,92,895
Lahor		1,30,42,327 ,,		30,42,327
Multan		24,75,349 ,,		24,75,649
Thatta		4,49,675 ,,		34,49,657
Kashmir		17,11,324 ,,		24,08,389
Illahabad		68,82,897 ,,		68,92,890
Awadh		98,85,771 ,,		47,85,871
Bihar		48,85,571 ,,		57,14,873
Bengal & Orissa				
Malwa		48,13,283 ,,		48,13,283
Gujarat[6]		71,84,685 ,,		71,84,685
The Dakhin Provinces[7]	8,39,68,648		11,26,20,223	
Aurangabad	1,28,36,043	96,99,000 (XVIII)	1,28,33,173	96,99,005
Berar	1,09,46,641	75,89,220 ,,	1,09,46,942	75,89,220
Bidar	66,59,811	31,00,000 (XVI)	66,59,811	46,42,732
		42,42,332 (XIX)		
Khandesh	47,39,562	41,19,067 (XVIII)	46,39,562	31,19,017
Bijapur	3,33,94,771	4,57,46,000	3,36,64,371	5,88,87,500
Haidarabad	2,00,94,478	2,05,53,352	2,00,94,978	2,47,82,500

and *sāl-i kāmil* at Rs 1,00,00,000. *San* and *sāl* are synonyms, and *akmal* probably signifies a year better than the previous best.

6 Cf. *Mir'āt*, I, 26, where it is stated that "in years past" the revenue collection sometimes amounted to Rs 60,00,000.

7 According to Aurangzeb the collection in the Dakhin provinces, which did not then include Bijapur, Haidarabad and the larger portion of Bidar, amounted in the 27th year of Shahjahan (1653-4) to no more than Rs 1,00,00,000 (*Ādāb-i 'Ālamgīrī*, f.40b; ed., I, 157; *Ruq'āt-i 'Ālamgīr*, 121-2).

BIBLIOGRAPHY

In the following list the items are numbered serially for convenience of cross-reference. When the serial number is followed by another number, prefaced with a capital S and placed within brackets, this indicates that the particular work has been described in C.A. Storey's *Persian Literature – A Bio-bibliographical Survey*, Vol.I, under that number. (Nos. of Storey's Vol.II begin with 'II' inserted before the Arabic numerals.) This dispenses with the need for offering particulars already supplied there.

Manuscripts are generally identified by their press-marks. When a MS belongs to any collection of the British Museum (now of the British Library) other than the Additional or Oriental, the abbreviation 'Br.M.', for British Museum, is put before the name of the collection and the press-mark. But all MSS simply designated 'Add.' or 'Or.' should be assumed to belong respectively to the Additional or Oriental Collection of the British Museum (British Library). 'Aligarh' stands for the Maulana Azad Library (Arabic & Persian MSS Section), Aligarh Muslim University; 'Allahabad', for the Central Record Office (Uttar Pradesh), Allahabad; 'Bodl.', for the Bodleian Library, Oxford; 'Cambridge', for the Cambridge University Library, Persian MSS; 'CAS in History' for the library of the Centre of Advanced Study in History, Aligarh Muslim University; 'Edinburgh', for the Edinburgh University Library, Persian Collection; 'I.O.', for the India Office Library, London; 'Kuwait', for the Dār al-Āthār al-Islāmiyyah (Islamic Art Museum), Kuwait; 'Lindesiana', for the collection of this name in John Rylands Library, Manchester; 'NAI', for the National Archives of India, New Delhi; and 'R.A.S.', for the Library of the Royal Asiatic Society, London. Some MSS have been identified by the numbers in the printed catalogues and not by their press-marks: in the case of the India Office, the catalogue numbers whenever given are prefaced by the name 'Ethé'; in that of the Bodleian MSS, the numbers are preceded by the abbreviation 'Bodl.' standing alone; and in that of Bibliothique Nationale, Paris, by 'Blochet'.

When more than one MS or edition is listed under any work, but only one or some of them have been cited in the footnotes of this book, such are asterisked. Abbreviations or letters as are used to indicate particular MSS and editions in the footnotes are in this

Bibliography put within brackets after the specifications of the respective MSS or editions. Where no such indication is given after an asterisked MS or edition, it is to be assumed that it is the asterisked MS or edition that is cited in the footnotes, and the folio or page references following immediately upon the title of the work (or its abbreviation) apply to that MS or ediction.

Translations seen, but not used, are not indicated if these have been listed by Storey. Texts and documents seen by me, but not cited in this book, are ordinarily omitted.

1. CONTEMPORARY AND EARLIER SOURCES

A. AGRICULTURE

1. *Nuskha dar Fan-i Falāḥat*, I.O.4702*; Or.1741, ff.25a-48a; Aligarh, Lytton: Farsiya 'Ulūm, 51. The initial words of the text in the I.O. and Br. M. MSS suggest that here we have the 11th chapter ('*amal*) of a larger work. The colophon of the Aligarh MS, which was transcribed in 1793 (but is incomplete at both ends), says it is a fragment of the *Ganj-i Bādāwurd* of Dārā Shukoh. A statement made in the *Risāla-i Nakhlbandiya* (Add.16,662, f.95b), written in 1790-91, and practically a copy of this tract, gives the same title to its parent work, but ascribes it to Amānullāh Khān Ḥusainī. This ascription is probably correct because Amānullāh Ḥusainī Khānazād Khān, son of Jahāngīr's great noble, Mahābat Khān, is in fact said to have left "a *majmū'a* called Ganj-i Bādāvard" (Rieu, II, 509b).

   Our author acknowledges his debt to a work which he calls the *Kitāb-i Shajaratu-n Nihāl*, which is almost certainly identical with the work preserved in Lindesiana 484, Add. 23,542 (fragment) and Add.1771. The latter work had obviously been written in Persia, and Amānullāh seems to have revised and enlarged it to include information about the produce (fruits and crops) of India.

B. ADMINISTRATIVE LITERATURE

1. General Works

2. (S.702:2) Abū-l Faẓl, *Ā'īn-i, Akbarī*, ed. H. Blochmann, Bib. Ind., Calcutta, 1867-77*. Blochmann's edition, though a very painstaking work and far superior to the two previous editions (Saiyid Ahmad's edn., Delhi, 1855, and Nawal Kishor's edn., Lucknow, 1869), was unfortunately not based on the best available MSS. Nawal Kishor's edns. of 1882 and 1892, 3 vols., are practically verbatim reproductions of Blochmann's edition. I have collated Blochmann's edition throughout with two 17th-century MSS, Add. 7652 and Add. 6552, which are by far the most accurate of all the MSS that I have seen. I.O. 6 (Ethé 264), also of an early date, is only a copy of Add. 7652. I have also occasionally consulted Add.6546 (transcribed, 1718). R.A.S. Persian 121 (Morley 161), though dated 1656, is carelessly written. The dates assigned to the *Ā'īn* MSS in Lindesiana by its catalogue are misleading: Lindesiana 170 was transcribed in 1680, not 1626-7 (and it is an inferior

copy anyway); and there are no grounds at all for assigning Lindesiana 800 to 1627-8. Lindesiana 223 is not a copy of the *Ā'īn* at all. Browne's *Supplementary Handlist,* 16, seems to imply that King's College Or. MSS no.31 contains a very early (1598-99) copy of the *Ā'īn*, but Palmer's catalogue of this collection (*JRAS*, 1867, p.108) indicates that it is only a part of a copy of the *Akbarnāma* which has been bound in three volumes.

See Moosvi, 3-9, for a discussion of the chronology of the preparation of the *Ā'īn-i Akbarī*. While in the *khātima* (epilogue) (*Ā'īn*, ed. Blochmann, II, 278), the current date is given as 20 March 1598, the revenue statistics mainly belong to Akbar's 40th R.Y. (1595-6), and there were additions and revisions made until at least 1601.

It has not always been possible, especially when using a large number of figures from the statistical portion of the *Ā'īn*, to indicate where and why I have departed from Blochmann's text. As a rule, I have always preferred the reading on which both Add.7652 and Add.6552 are agreed to that of Blochmann. The translations, when cited, are those of Blochmann, revised and edited by D.C. Phillott, Vol.I, Calcutta, 1927 and 1939, and H.S. Jarrett, revised by J. Sarkar, Vol.II, Calcutta, 1949 and Vol.III, Calcutta, 1948.

3. Yūsuf Mīrak, son of Abū-l Qāsim "Namakīn", *Tārīkh-i Maẓhar-i Shāhjahānī*, AD1634, Vol.II, ed. Saiyid Ḥusāmuddīn Rāshidī, Karachi, 1962;* transl. Muhammad Saleem Akhtar, *Sind under the Mughals*, Islamabad and Karachi, 1990, with a detailed introduction and valuable commentary. This is essentially an administrative history of Sind under the Mughals, down to 1634, with separate accounts of Bhakkar, Thatta and Sehwan.

I have not been able to use Vol.I (still unpublished), contained in the Punjab University Library (Lahore) MS: Arabic Sec., No.7743, Azur Coll. The late Dr (Mrs) Rafat Bilgrami kindly let me use the notes she had made from the earlier part of this MS.

4. (S.730) Rai Chandrabhān Brahman, *Chār Chaman-i Barhaman*, *c.*1656, ed. S.M.Y. Ja'fery, New Delhi, 2007. MSS: Add.18,863 ('A')*; Or 1892 ('B')*.

5. Munhtā Nainsī, *Mārwār rā parganāṅ rī Vigat*, ed. Narāin Singh Bhāṭī, 2 vols., Jodhpur, 1968, 1969. This remarkable survey of Mārwār, containing descriptions of its fiscal administration, revenue statistics, lists of crops, numbers of wells, names of castes, numbers of houses, etc., carried down to individual villages, was apparently completed in, or soon after 1664, since Samvat 1721 is the last year to which annual statistics are usually brought down.

2. Tracts on Agrarian Rights

6. Jalāluddīn Thānesarī (d.1582), *Risāla Taḥqīq Ārāẓī Hind*, ed. S. Moinul Haq in *Baṣā'ir*, II(2) (April 1963), Karachi, Arabic text with Urdu translation. For date of the author's death see Badāūnī, III, 312, and 'Abdul-l Ḥaqq, *Akhbāru-l Akhyār*, Deoband, n.d., 273.

7. Opinion of a *muftī* on the position of inherited right in land in *pargana* Sandīla, 1701, NAI, 2694/28.

8. Qāẓī Muḥammad A'lā (fl.1745), *Risāla Aḥkām al-Ārāẓī*, MSS, Aligarh: Abdus Salam 'Arabiya (4) 331, & Lytton 'Arabiya Mazhab (2) 62. Partly in Arabic, partly in Persian. For the author's biography, see 'Abdu-l Ḥaiy, *Nuzhatu-l Khawāṭir*, Hyderabad-Deccan, 2nd edn., VI, 278. I am indebted for this reference to the late Mr Sibtul Hasan, Deputy Librarian, Maulana Azad Library.

3. Administrative and Accountancy Manuals, Statistical Tables, etc.

A large number of works were written in our period for the guidance of persons seeking to acquire proficiency in accountancy (*siyāq*), clerical work (*navīsindagī*), and knowledge of details of administrative procedure (*dastūru-l 'amal*). They were in the nature of textbooks for candidates for clerical offices in the administration, and some of them aim at being comprehensive enough to be of use to persons working under any official of the empire in any department. Thus the functions of various officials, the papers prepared under them, the mode of drawing up such papers, explanations of various terms used, tables of pay scales of *manṣabdārs* and details of obligations, fines, etc., imposed upon them, account for the larger part of the contents of these works. Sometimes information of a miscellaneous nature is also provided, such as revenue statistics, tables of routes, or lists of titles of nobles. These works, though often written by persons who were serving, or had served, as officials, were not official manuals but written by their authors in their private capacity. But they often reproduce official papers to serve as illustrations, and sometimes seem to have copied verbatim detailed official regulations. It has been found convenient to group with these works independent revenue tables (often anonymous) that have come down to us.

Nos.111 and 142 below can also be assigned to this class of texts.

9. *Yād-dāsht-i Mujmil-i Jama'*, revenue tables, etc., *c.*1646-47. Add.16,863.
10. *Dastūru-l 'Amal-i Navīsindagī*, *c.*1646-48, Add.6641, ff.150-195.
11. Tables of revenue statistics, etc., Bodl. Ouseley 390. The heading attributes the statistics to the reign of Aurangzeb, but internal evidence suggests that they belong to the period 1638-56.
12. *Dastūru-l 'Amal-i 'Ālamgīrī*, c.1659. Add.6598, ff.1a-128b*; Add.6599, ff.1b-132a (wrongly supposed by Rieu, I, 404, to be a MS of the *Ẕawābiṭ-i 'Ālamgīrī*). Its date presents some difficulty. According to its text it was written in "the third regnal (year)" of Aurangzeb, which is said to have corresponded to 1069 *Faṣlī* and AH 1065, none of which years actually correspond. One must assume that the awkward phrase *sih julūsī* is a scribe's error for *san-i julūs* ("the year of accession"), and that the eras of 1069 and 1065 have been interchanged: the work would then have been actually written in Aurangzeb's first regnal year, 1069 AH and 1065 *Faṣlī*, all of which correspond to 1659 AD. Yet its revenue statistics in large part belong to the very late years of Aurangzeb, so that either its claimed date is wrong, or the statistical material was put into it at a later stage.
13. *Dastūru-l 'Amal-i Mumālik-i Maḥrūsa-i Hindūstān*, Aurangzeb: post-1671. Or.1840, ff.133a-144b.
14. *Dastūru-l 'Amal-i 'Ilm-i Navīsindagī*, Aurangzeb: post-1676. Add.6599, ff.133b-185a.

15. Jagat Rā'i Shujā'ī Kāyath Saksena, *Farhang-i Kārdānī*, 1679. Aligarh, Abdus Salam, Fārsiya 85/315.
16. *Intikhāb-i Dastūru-l 'Amal-i Pādshāhī*, Aurangzeb: post-1686. Edinburgh 224.
17. *Ẓawābiṭ-i 'Ālamgīrī*, Aurangzeb: post-1691. Add.6598; Or.1641; Ethé 432; Ethé 415, ff.161a, ff.(fragment).
18. *Dastūru-l 'Amal*, Aurangzeb: post-1696. Bodl. Fraser 86.
19. Munshī Nand Rām Kāyasth Shrivāstavya, *Siyāqnāma*, AD1694-6. Lithograph, Nawal Kishor, Lucknow, 1879.
20. Udai Chand, *Farhang-i Kārdānī o Kār-āmozī*, AD1699. Edinburgh 83. This work is partly based on No.15.
21. *Khulāṣatu-s Siyāq*, AD1703, Add.6588, ff.64a-94a (slightly defective)*; Aligarh, Sir S. Sulaiman 410/143 ('Aligarh MS.')*.
22. *Dastūru-l 'Amal*, Aurangzeb: post-1703. Or.2026. Practically an unacknowledged copy of no.21.
23. *Dastūru-l 'Amal-i Shāhjahānī*. Late Aurangzeb. Ethé 415, ff.23b-109b; Add.6588, ff.15a-47b; Aligarh, Sir S. Sulaiman 675/53.
24. Revenue statistics of the Mughal Empire, with detailed *maḥal*-wise statistics of the Ajmer province, Aurangzeb (?). R.A.S. Persian 173.
25. Muḥammad Laṭīf, *Mir'ātu-l Hind*, Or.4776, ff.a-56 b. Revenue statistics of Gujarat and five other provinces (*pargana*-wise), possibly of the reign of Aurangzeb.
26. Statistical account of the area, divisions and revenues of the provinces of the Mughal Empire, drawing upon the *Ā'īn* and the village and area statistics of Aurangzeb's reign. Compiled after the death of Aurangzeb. Or.1286, ff.310b-343a.
27. Hidāyatullāh Bihārī, *Hidāyatu-l Qawā'id*, 1714. I.O.3996A*; Aligarh, Abdus Salam, 149/339 ('Aligarh MS.')*. The texts of these two MSS vary considerably, the contents of the Aligarh MS being more extensive.
28. Jawāhar Nāth 'Bekas' Sahaswānī, *Dastūru-l 'Amal*, 1732. Aligarh, Subhanullah 954/4.
29. *Risāla-i Zirā'at*, *c.*1750. Edinburgh 144. Contrary to its title it belongs not to the genre of agricultural literature, but to administrative manuals. The preface shows it was written in Bengal probably a little before the British conquest.
30. Braj Rā'i, *Dastūru-l 'Amal-i Shahanshāhī*, *c.*1727, enlarged by Ṭhākur Lāl, 1779, Add.22,831.
31. Lachhmī Narāin "Shafiq", *Khulāṣatu-l Hind*, transcript from Asafiya MS 786/492, in CAS in History, Aligarh. Contains *pargana*-wise revenue statistics of the Dakhin provinces, ascribed to 1731 and earlier years, but arranged and edited by the author in 1789-90, with addition of much other matter.

C. PRIMARY DOCUMENTS, INCLUDING ADMINISTRATIVE RECORDS

No attempt at completeness has been made in this subsection. Documents of which I have only seen a translation, analysis or description, but not the text, have (with one or two exceptions) been excluded. Stray documents, cited with adequate reference in the book, are also omitted, especially if belonging to later years.

32. Persian documents, etc., relating to land and cash allowances granted to a family of Parsi physicians of Navsari, Gujarat, 1517-1671; and papers, in

Gujarati, of property and financial transactions of another Parsi family of Navsari, 16th and 17th centuries. Published and translated with a discussion of their significance in S.H. Hodivala, *Studies in Parsi History* (Bombay, 1929), 149-253, with photographic reproductions of a number of documents at the end of the volume.

33. *Farmāns, parwānas* and other papers relating chiefly to *madad-i ma'āsh* grants in the *pargana* of Batala (Punjab), 1527-1758. I.O.4438: 1-70. Collection described, with texts of four of the docs. (including a *farmān* of Bābur) pub. by P. Holt in *Epigraphia Indica*, II, 472-80. Bābur's *farmān* was also published by Muhiuddin Momin in *IHRC* (1961), 49-54.
34. Bābur, *farmān* confirming *madal-i ma'āsh*, 1527. Original: Aligarh, Farsiya 6-30.
35. Documents from Bilgram (Awadh), 16th century onwards, including a MS of *Sharā'if-i 'Uṣmānī* (no.212 below), containing texts of many documents from Bilgram and its vicinity, CAS in History, Aligarh. See my calendar, with commentary, of the earlier set of these docs. in *IESHR*, IV(3) (1967), 205-32.
36. Documents (earliest dated 1530) relating to *pargana* Shamsabad, *sarkār* Kanauj, 16th and 17th centuries, originals in possessions of Mr Ibrahim Ahmad Khan, Vil. Kalan Khail, Qaimganj, Dist. Farrukhabad (U.P.); photocopies in CAS in History, Aligarh. Early docs. of this collection were calendared by me in *IESHR*, IV(3) (1967), 205-32.
37. Collection of documents relating to a *ṣūfī* shrine in *pargana* Bhojpur, *sarkār* Kanauj, beginning with *farmān* of Bābur (date damaged) and ending with a *ḥasbu-l ḥukm* of 1709: xerox copies ('Bhojpur Collection B': 1-6) in CAS in History, Aligarh.
38. *Farmāns* of Bābur, Sher Shāh and Humāyūn, printed in the *Oriental College Magazine*, Lahore, Vol.IX, No.3 (May 1933), 115-28, by Maulvi Muḥammad Shafī'.
39. Documents in the Central Record Office (U.P.), Allahabad, arranged in two series: (I) Accessioned in the Accession Register of the U.P. Regional Records Survey Committee, till March 31, 1958*; (II) Accessioned in the Register of the Committee, from April 1, 1958 ('II')*.

    The Persian records in these two collections consist largely of *farmāns* and other documents concerning land grants, sale deeds, legal depositions, judgements, revenue papers, etc. They date from the 16th century onwards, beginning with a *farmān* of Sher Shāh (Series I: No.318). I have used the following documents: Series I: 1, 5, 8, 24, 36, 154, 179-80, 317-8, 323, 329, 359, 362, 370, 375, 414, 421, 424, 435, 457, 464, 782, 786, 789, 810, 851, 869, 873-74, 879, 881, 884-94, 896-97, 1177, 1180, 1183, 1185-87, 1189-92, 1194-98, 1200-06, 1208, 1210-17, 1219-25, 1227-28, 1231-32, & 1234. Series II: 23, 53, 55, 56, & 284. Docs. of Series I are cited as 'Allahabad', followed by their nos., and Docs. of Series II as 'Allahabad, II,' followed by nos.
40. Documents connected mostly with revenue grants of keepers of shrine of Saiyid Badī'uddīn at Makanpur, *pargana* Bilhaur, *sarkār* Kanauj, beginning with a *farmān* of Islām Shāh. Texts printed in (S.1410) Muḥammad Amīr Ḥasan Madārī Fanṣūrī, *Tazkiratu-l Muttaqīn*, II, (Kanpur, 1323/1905), 171-90.
41. Akbar, *farmān* conferring *madad-i ma'āsh*, 1558-59, with a listing of grants in the locality, 1575. Allahabad II, 23 (original); Or.1757, ff.39-51 (copy).

42. Bairam Khān, *ḥukm*, 1558-59, granting (on behalf of the emperor) 150 *bighas* of land. I have used photocopy of the original in U.P. State Archives; it is calendared in S.A.I. Tirmizi, *Mughal Documents (1526-1627)* (New Delhi, 1989), 47, no.8.
43. Akbar, *farmān*, Nov.-Dec.1558, ordering protection of a petitioner's hereditary land. I have seen a xerox copy of the original, now in the National Archives. For a translation with commentary, see S.Z.H. Jafri in I. Habib, ed., *Akbar and his India*, 266-69.
44. Akbar, *farmān* granting land to an ancestor of the Firangī Maḥal family, Dec.1559, photocopy in CAS in History, Aligarh.
45. *Farmāns* in favour of Rāmdās, for (1) assignment of *jāgīr*, April 1561; (2) for grant of land in *in'ām*, May 1562; and (3) for recovery of loan advanced by him, March-April 1569. Reproduced with translation and commentary by I. Habib in *Akbar and his India*, 271-87, where (in the first printing) *farmān* (1) was by mistake reproduced as *farmān* (2) and vice versa. The slip has been corrected in reprint.
46. Documents relating to, and originally in possession of, priests of the Chaitanya sect at Vrindaban, most of them in Persian, some in Braj and some bilingual, now preserved in (1) the Vrindaban Research Institute (where archives of the Madan Mohan and Rādhā Dāmodar temples are desposited); (2) Govind-dev temples (at Vrindaban and Jaipur) and Rādhākund temple; (3) the strong-room of the Mathura district court; (4) the Gopīnāth temple, Jaipur; and (5) the National Archives, New Delhi (NAI). The late Dr Tarapada Mukherjee generously furnished me with photocopies of all the Persian and bilingual documents in repositories (1), (2) and (3). He also gave me xerox copies of documents in (4) received through courtesy of the Institute of Vaishnav Studies, a US organization (cited by me as 'IVS'). Professor J.C. Wright kindly supplied me with his roman transcriptions and English translations of the Braj documents (cited as 'Wright'), drawn from repositories (1) and (2). Mr Zakir Ḥusain gave me transcripts of some of the documents in (5), besides those that I had read and transcribed myself. Unfortunately, the photographs of many docs. drawn from repositories (1), (2) and (3) did not carry any nos. or even, in some cases, the name of the collection; in such cases, the date supplies the only means by which a doc. can be traced; and I hope to place in due course a chronologically arranged set of photographs of the documents along with their transcripts in a suitable public repository.

    Studies of these docs. were published by the late Tarapada Mukherjee and myself in *PIHC*, 48th session (1987), 234-50; 49th session (1988), 287-300; and 50th session (1989-90), 236-55; and what essentially is a calendar of these docs., arranged according to individuals concerned, was pubished by me in *Govindadeva, a Dialolgue in Stone*, ed. Margaret H. Case (New Delhi, 1996), 131-59.
47. *Farāmīn-i Salāṭīn*, a large but rather ill-arranged collection of *farmāns* and other documents of the Mughal period, ed. Bashīruddīn Aḥmad, Delhi, 1344/1926. The collection includes a *farmān* of Akbar, 1562. This and other documents relating to Ajmer were derived by Bashiruddin Ahmad from (S. 1406) Qāẓī Sayyid 'Imāmu-ddīn Khān, *Mu'īnu-l Auliyā*, Ajmer, 1312/1894, a Persian work, in which the documents are printed on pp.64-125.
48. Hardayal Singh Mathur Collection, Bundle 1, in Rajasthan State Archives, Bikaner; photocopies in two bound vols. in CAS in History, Aligarh. Beginning with a *farmān* of Akbar, 1563, the documents come down to the reign of Muḥammad Shāh.

49. *Administraive Documents of Mughal India*, ed. and translated with introd. by M. Azhar Ansari, Delhi, 1984. A collection of 41 documents beginning with one of 1563-64, some reproduced in readable photo-prints, the rest printed according to the editor's transcriptions made at various times, and subject to "every possibility of mistakes which do occur while copying".
50. Mun'im Khān Khān-i Khānān, *ḥukm* to officers to protect land conferred by imperial grant, 1566. Original in CAS in History, Aligarh; reprod. in Iqtidar A. Khan, *Political Biography of a Mughal Noble. Mun'im Khan Khan-i Khanan*, New Delhi, 1973, facing p.95; text, p.159, and transl., pp.96-97.
51. Akbar, *Farmān* confirming *madad-i ma'āsh* grant in *pargana* Kota (Rajasthan), 1567. Photocopy of an apparently much damaged original, in possession of Professor Iqbal Husain, Aligarh.
52. Akbar, *farmān* transferring *madad-i ma'āsh* grant, 1567-68. Original: Aligarh, display case.
53. Collection of twelve documents from Khairabad (U.P.), four of which range from 1569-70 to 1673-74. Photographs in CAS in History, Aligarh, obtained through the kindness of Mr Mohammad Usman of Khairabad.
54. Akbar, *farmān*, 1569-70, on excavation of canal to serve Hansi and Hisar; Original text no longer traceable, but surviving in transl. by Lieut. [H.] Yule, 'A Canal Act of the Emperor Akbar, with some Notes and Remarks on the Western Jumna Canals', *JASB*, XV (1846), 213-23; reprinted in W.E. Baker, *Memoranda on the Western Jumna Canals*, (London, 1849), 95-102.
55. Collection of seven documents relating to *pargana* Bhojpur, beginning with a *chaknāma* of *c*.1569-70, in CAS in History, Aligarh, MSS 35-41: ('Bhojpur Coll.').
56. Akbar, *farmān* ordering restitution of money seized by assignees' officials from petitioner, 1572, Aligarh: Subhanullah, Farāmīn (1).
57. Mughal-period documents from Maham (District Rohtak, Haryana), beginning with Akbar's *farmān* conferring and recording *madad-i ma'āsh* grants, 1575, printed in Manẓūru-l Ḥaqq Ṣiddīqī, *Ma'āṣiru-l Ajdād* (Lahore, 1383/ 1964), 473 ff.
58. A large collection of documents relating to the shrine of Mu'īnuddīn Chishtī at Ajmer, beginning with a *farmān* of Akbar, 1575-76, compiled and edited by 'Abū-l Bārī "Ma'nī", under the title *Asnādu-s Ṣanādīd*, Ajmer(?), 1952. Some of the docs. have been reproduced in photo-plates; the original texts of all are given with translations and commentary in Urdu.
59. Akbar, *farmān* recording *madad-i ma'āsh* grants, 1575. Original in possession of Mr Mohd. Akbar Ali, Vakil, Gorakhpur. Transcript in CAS in History, Aligarh.
59a. Official documents relating to the *chaudhurīs* of Dhar, Malwa, 1576-77 to 1685, Kuwait, LNS 235, MSa-qq. Xerox copies obtained through courtesy of Mrs Henrietta Sharp Cockrell.
60. *Imperial Farmāns (A.D.1577 to A.D.1805) granted to the Ancestors of... the Tikayat Maharaj*, photographic reproductions of the originals and their translations in English, Hindi and Gujarati, with notes, by K.M. Jhaveri, Bombay, 1928. Docs.IV and V in this collection are forgeries, but the other docs. are genuine.
61. Copy of Akbar's *farmān* confirming *madad-i ma'āsh* grant, *pargana* Sandīla, *sarkār* Lakhnau, 1580. NAI, Acquired Docs. No.1441.
62. *Parwāncha* concerning a land-revenue grant, 1580. I.O. 4433.
63. Documents relating to grants to the Jogis of Jakhbar, Dist. Gurdaspur, Punjab,

edited (with facsimile reprods.), and translated by B.N. Goswamy and J.S. Grewal, *The Mughals and the Jogis of Jakhbar: Some Madad-i Ma'ash and other Documents*, Simla, 1967. The earliest doc., preserved in copy, is a *farmān* of Akbar, 1581.

64. Rāja Todar Mal's memorandum on revenue administration, with the emperor's observations thereon, 26 Isfandārmuz̲ 26 Ilāhī (2 March 1582). Original text in *Akbarnāma*, earlier version, Add.27,247, ff.331b-332b, summarized by Abū'l Fazl in *AN*, III, 381-3 (under 27 Ilāhī); transl., with analysis, Shireen Moosvi, *People, Taxation and Trade in Mughal India*, New Delhi, 2008, pp.159-74.

65. *Farmāns* and other documents of Akbar's reign relating to a *madad-i ma'āsh* grant in Gujarat. Texts printed with facsimile reproductions of the originals, translated and copiously annotated by Jivanji Jamshedji Modi, *The Parsees at the Court of Akbar,* (Bombay, 1903), 91ff. Doc. No.4 in this collection, only partly deciphered by the editor, is translated and analysed in my paper 'Agricultural and Agrarian Conditions of South Gujarat, 1596', *PIHC*, 54th session, 1993, Mysore, 246-62.

66. The Rev. Father Felix, O.C. (ed.), 'Mughal Farmāns, Parwānahs, and Sanads issued in favour of the Jesuit Missionaries', *Jour. of the Punjab Hist. Soc.*, V(i) (1916), 1-53. Doc.I belongs to Akbar's reign (1597).

67. Jahāngīr, *farmān* granting *al-tamg̲hā* in *pargana* Ilahabad, 1609, litho. Namwar Press, Allahabad, n.d.

68. Collection of documents relating to Sihunda, *sarkār* Kalinjar, originals in private possession, photographs in CAS in History, Aligarh. Includes a *farmān* of Jahāngīr, 1612-13.

69. Maryam Zamānī (d.1623), *ḥukm*, exhorting officials to protect the interests of a *jāgīrdār* from encroachments by a refractory *zamīndār*, Jahāngīr's reign. Photographic copy and text printed in *IHRC*, VIII, 1925, 167-69, by Zafar Hasan.

70. Jahāngīr, *farmān* granting rights of *zamīndārī* and *chaudhurāī* in *pargana* Khalgaon, *sarkār* Mungir (Bihar), 1618. Text printed in *IHRC*, XVIII, 1942, 188-96, by M.L. Roy Chaudhuri, who misdated it 1613. When through the kindness of Professor Surendra Gopal, Patna, I received a xerox copy of this document, I discovered that though it copies the style of the imperial *farmans*, it is in fact a forgery: its quality of writing is bad, it has misspellings, and has a wrong Hijri date in the *ẓimn*.

71. Jahāngīr, *farmān*, 1619, conferring *madad-i ma'āsh* on two Parsis of Navsari, Gujarat; a *chaknāma* of 1624 delimiting the same grant; and later documents. Reprod. in fascimile, ed. and transl. by J.J. Modi in *JBBRAS*, NS, XXV (1917-21), 419-90.

71a. Miscellaneous documents relating to *pargana* Bilhaur (cf. no.40 above), the earliest, a *taḥqīqnāma* dated 1030/1621. Photographs in CAS in History, Aligarh.

72. Nūr Jahān, *ḥukm* concerning *madad-i ma'āsh* grant, 1627. Transl. with photograph of original, by A.I. Tirmizi, *IHRC*, XXXV (ii), 196-202.

73. Miscellaneous 17th-century (and earlier) documents, relating to Amroha, *ṣūba* Dehli, in CAS in History, Amroha Coll. II, Nos.1-13.

74. Shāhjahān, *farmān*, 1628, deciding a complaint regarding customary rights of an astrologer (*joshī*) in certain villages of *pargana* Manglaur (Mangrol), *sarkār* Basim, Berar. Facsimile reprod. with transl. and commentary by G.T. Kulkarni in *PIHC*, 53rd session, 1992-93, Warangal, 199-204. Inspection of

the original document, through the courtesy of Mr G.B. Mehendale of Pune, has shown that the seal (containing the only date in the document: AH 1037) and *ṭughrā* are genuine, but the present text on the front has been written after the short text of the original had been washed and scratched off; moreover the *ẓimn*-text was written in only after the top portion of the original *farmān* had been lost. The absence of dates and the normal formula in the *ẓimn* also adds to suspicions of forgery. Yet the detailed nature of its contents suggests that the forger could have been drawing upon some genuine material, which was transferred with some linguistic or other changes to the paper of an early *farmān* that had much blank space on it.

75. Shāhjahān, *farmān* appointing a *qāẓī*, with grant of *madad-i ma'āsh*, 1629. Original: Or.11697.
76. Shāhjahān, *farmān*, 1633, forbidding oppresive practices in Kashmīr: inscription on gateway of the Jami' Masjid, Srinagar (copied by me), text pub. by Rev. Lowenthal, *JASB*, XXXIII (1865), 287-90 (reference owed to Dr Z.A. Desai), and (with errors and omissions) in Pīr Ghulām Ḥasan Koyhāmī, *Tārīkh-i Ḥasan*, Srinagar, n.d., II, 500-01. Variant versions in Qazwīnī, CAS in History, Aligarh transcript, 509-10, and Ṣāliḥ, I, 543-5. Transl. and analysis by Shireen Moosvi, *People, Taxation and Trade in Mughal India*, New Delhi, 2008, pp.186-98.
77. *Persian Sources of Indian History*, collected and edited, and translated into Marathi, by G.H. Khare, Vols.II-VI Poona, 1937-73. Mughal documents will be found on pp.1-19 of Vol.II. The bulk of the documents in this volume and in Vol.III (Poona, 1939) belong to the 'Ādilshāhī administration. Vol.VI contains a selection from the *Akhbārāt-i Darbār-i Mu'allā* of Aurangzeb's time (see no.83). I have not seen Vol.I.
78. Volume of documents, mostly relating to Surat and neighbouring localities in Gujarat, ranging over the period 1583-1648, and probably transcribed, *c.*1650. Blochet, Suppl. Pers.482 (microfilm in CAS in History, Aligarh).
79. *Selected Documents of Shāh Jahān's Reign*, ed. Yūsuf Ḥusain Khān, Daftar-i Dīwānī, Hyderabad-Deccan 1950. The documents (from 1634 onwards) now preserved in the State Archives (Andhra Pradesh), Hyderabad, have been excellently deciphered and printed; there are also some photographic reproductions. The editor's commentary should be treated with caution.

    Texts and reproductions of certain documents of Shāhjahān's reign from the same repository are also given in Shakeb's *Catalogue* (no.537 below).
80. *Daftar-i Dīwānī o Māl o Mulkī-i Sarkār-i A'lā*, Hyderabad, 1939. Texts and facsimile reproductions of Persian and Urdu documents, arranged in inverse chronological order, including documents of the reigns of Shāhjahān (pp.253-81) and Aurangzeb (pp.155-251). The originals are in the State Archives (Andhra Pradesh), Hyderabad.
81. Miscellaneous Persian docs., transcribed from various registers of the Jaipur archives in the Rajasthan State Archives, Bikaner, from 1638 to the reign of Muḥammad Shāh, CAS in History, Aligarh, Transcript no.85.

81a. Shāhjahān, *farmān* in favour of certain moneylenders. Text with translation printed in *IHRC* (Dec.1942), 59-60, by A. Halim.

82. Lashkar Khān, *parwāna* appointing a *shiqqdār*, 1658-59. I.O. 4434.
83. *Akhbārāt-i Darbār-i Mu'allā*. (1) News-letters from the imperial court, Aurangzeb's reign. 9 volumes in Case 47 at the R.A.S. (Morley 133). These include some of Bahādur Shāh's reign as well, although Morley seemed unaware of this, and they have actually been bound with those of Aurangzeb's

early years in the first volume. These *akhbārāt* have been cited by their year and the serial number put on them in the R.A.S. Library. (2) The residue of the *akhbārāt*, not taken to London by James Tod, now at the Rajasthan State Archives, Bikaner; transcripts at the Sitamau Library, Sitamau (Dist. Mandsaur, M.P.) and the National Library, Calcutta. I have used microfilms of the National Library transcripts at the CAS in History, Aligarh: these are best cited by dates. (3) G.H. Khare, *Persian Sources of Indian History*, VI, Poona, 1973, containing a selection of *akhbārāt* (down to R.Y.28/1684) drawn from both the above collections, through the Sitamau transcripts. Khare's Christian-era dates could in many cases be a year in advance of the real dates, since he takes 1 Muḥarram, not 1 Ramaẓān, as the beginning of Aurangzeb's regnal year.

83a. *Akhbārāt* of Prince A'zam's headquarters in Gujarat, R.Y. 46 and 47 of Aurangzeb, bound in one vol. of no.83(1) (Morley 133),the sheets marked A1 to A147 and A174 to A271. Some *akhbārāt* of A'ẓam's headquarters occur also in the R.Y.s 49-50 volume.

84. *Selected Documents of Aurangzeb's Reign, 1659-1706*, ed. Yusuf Husain Khan, Hyderabad, 1958. The texts of the documents, all from the State Archives (A.P.), Hyderabad, are given in full with a few photographic reproductions of the originals.

85. Numerous documents, the earliest dated 1659, concerned with the affairs of, or issued by, Diler Khān and his descendants, who had their seat at Shāhābād in *sarkār* Khairabad, Awadh. Texts printed in Munshī Muḥammad Muẓaffar Ḥusain, *Nāma-i Muẓaffarī* (Urdu), 2 vols., Lucknow, 1326/1917.

86. *Selected Waqai' of the Deccan (1660-1671)*, ed. Y.H. Khan Central Records Office, Hyderabad, 1953. Texts of the *wāqā'i'* printed with introduction, and a calendar of the documents and notes in English.

87. Miscellaneous documents, including a *parwāna* of Rāja Raghunāth on scarcity of copper coins at Surat, 1661, bound with a Persian transl. of a Latin tract on astronomy by Pietro della Valle, 1624, in Biblioteca Apostolica Vaticana, Rome: Vat. Persiano 33. The sheets in the original vol. being badly arranged, these have been rearranged and renumbered in the reader-print copy at CAS in History, Aligarh.

88. Transcripts of *arsaṭhas* and other papers of accounts (*arsaṭha bhaumī, jama, jamabandī, awārija mutāliba*) of *parganas* held in *jāgīr* by the Amber rulers (Chatsu, Malarna, Narayana, Jaitpur), of 1663-4, 1691-2, 1693-4, 1729-30, from Jaipur District records (now in Rajasthan State Archives, Bikaner), CAS in History Aligarh: Transcripts nos.49-50 (Urdu transcription), 63-75 (Nagari).

89. *Parwānas* sanctioning cash grants to family of Brahman priests [of Ujjain] in Malwa, 1664-1704, texts pub. with transl. by Jnan Chandra, *Journal of the Pakistan Historical Society*, VI (1), 1958, 55-65.

89a. *Taksīm dahai-sālā* of *pargana* Udehi (in Rajasthani), containing area and revenue data of years VS 1708-22/AD1651-66, partially reproduced in S.P. Gupta and S.H. Khan, *Mughal Documents: Taqsim (c.1649-c.1800)*, (Jaipur, 1996), 308-20.

90. Aurangzeb, *farmān* to Rasikdās, 8th regnal year (1665-66). Text published by Jadunath Sarkar, from MS in Berlin and one in his own possession, in *JASB*, N.S., II (1906), 223-55. I have collated this with the texts of the *farmān* contained in the following MSS: I.O.1146; I.O.1566; I.O.4014, ff.8a-11b; Add.19,503, ff.62a-63b; *Nigārnama-i Munshī*, Or.1735, ff.162b-164b, 129a-132b (ed., 123-4, 99-102). Detailed references to the various copies have

been avoided by citing only the relevant articles (or preamble). Sarkar's transl. in *JASB*, op. cit., has now been superseded by Shireen Moosvi's transl., in her *People, Taxation and Trade in Mughal India*, New Delhi, 2008, pp.175-85.

91. *Parwānas* concerning *madad-i ma'āsh* grants in *ṣūba* Lahor, 1667-1701, texts ed. M. Abdullah Chaghatai in *Jour. Pak. Hist. Soc.*, X(1)(1962), 25-37.

92. Aurangzeb, *farmān* to Muḥammad Hāshim, 1668-69. I have used the text published by Jadunath Sarkar in *JASB*, N.S., II (1906), 238-49, collating it with the texts in *Oriental Miscellany*, Calcutta, I (1798), 50-68; *Durru-l 'Ulūm*, ff.139b-149b; and *Mir'āt-i Aḥmadī*, ed. Nawab Ali, I, 268-72 (MSS: I.O., 222, ff.172b-175b; I.O., P.3597, ff.156a-159a). This *farmān*, like the one to Rasikdās, at no.90, has serially numbered articles, which have been usually cited in all references to it.

93. Aurangzeb, *farmāns* conferring *madad-i ma'āsh* on a religious family of Salon, *sarkār* Manikpur, *ṣūba* Ilahabad, 1675 and 1679. I transcribed these two *farmāns*, preserved in *qāẓī*-authenticated copies, through the courtesy of Dr Zaheer Husain Jafri, then a student. The documents themselves were unfortunately destroyed in an incident of arson at AMU in August 1981.

94. Aurangzeb, *farmāns* concerning *madad-i ma'āsh* grants in *pargana* Sandila, AD1677 (I.O.4436) and 1683 (I.O.4435).

95. Aurangzeb, *farmān* appointing a *qāẓī* with grant of *madad-i ma'āsh*, 1677, I.O.4370.

96. *Waqā'i' Ajmer*, & c., A.D.1678-80. Asafiya Library, Hyderabad, *Fan-i Tārīkh*, 2242; transcript in CAS in History, Aligarh, nos.15 & 16 (2 vols.)*. In the beginning there are a few reports sent from Ranthambhor. The writer was then appointed *waqā'i' navīs* of Ajmer and finally accompanied the army of Pādshāh Qulī Khān, as news-writer, in the Rajput War.

97. Shāhwardī Khān, *faujdār* of Sorath (Gujarat), proclamation (1686) of pledge to refrain from forced sale of grain from his *jāgīr* to merchants at high prices, and from imposing prohibited exactions, inscribed at Prabhas Patan, Mangrol and Junagadh. Ed. Z.A. Desai in *Epigraphia Indica, Arabic & Persian Supplement*, (1955-56), 99-101.

97a. 'Ādilshāhī *farmāns* 1577-1689, published under title *Ādilshāhī Pharmāne* eds. G.B. Mehendale, R. Lonkar and N. Bedekar, with Marathi commentary, Pune, 2007.

98. Aurangzeb, *farmān* appointing a *qāẓī* with *madad-i ma'āsh* grant, 1692. Or.11,698.

99. Copies of *farmāns* and official letters concerning affairs in the Carnatic, 17th century. 2 vols., Br. M. Sloane, 4092 & 3582, dates of docs. ranging from 1652 to 1689.

100. Documents printed in B.N. Goswamy and J.S. Grewal (eds.), *The Mughal and Sikh Rulers and the Vaishnavas of Pindori – A Historical Interpretaton of 52 Persian Documents*, Simla, 1969. The earliest document is datable to 1695-96.

101. Mu'aẓẓam, *nishān* concerning *madad-i ma'āsh* grant, 1696-97. Printed in *IHRC*, XVIII (1942), 236-45.

102. Copies of *farmāns, nishāns* and *parwānas* issued in favour of the English East India Company, 1633-1712, Add. 24,039. Of special interest are the documents of 1698-99 (ff.36a-b, 37a and 39a) relating to the English purchase of the *zamīndārī* of the three villages forming the nucleus of the future city of Calcutta.

103. Letters of the deputy of the *faujdār* of Talkokan to Portuguese officials about local *zamīndārs*, and other Persian documents, 1700-01 (some, not dated may be earlier). Biblioteca da Ajuda, Lisbon: Codice: 51-V-49, Colecção Governeo de Portugal. Ms Melba Ferreira da Costa of the Portuguese Archives very kindly presented photocopies of these twenty documents to CAS in History, Aligarh.

103a. Documents relating to *jāgīr* and *zamīndārī* of Shahdād Balūch, *Jour. Pak. Hist. Soc.*, *LIX*(4) (2011), 55-72.

104. 'Ināyat Jang Collection, NAI. This massive collection ("more than 130,000 records") of Mughal official archives in the Dakhin, covering the period 1685-1774, is described by A.I. Tirmizi in *Studies in Islām*, I(3), (1964), Delhi, 174-84. I regret I have not been able to explore this rich material.

105. (1) *Selections from the Peshwa Daftar,* Vol.31, ed. G.S. Sardesai, Bombay, 1933. (2) M. Nazim, ed., *Selections from the Peshwa's Daftar (Persian): Miscellaneous Papers*, Bombay, 1933: the earliest document is dated 1699.

105a. Bahādur Shāh, *farmān* conferring *āl-tamghā* grant, 1710. Or. 2285.

D. EPISTOLARY COLLECTIONS

Listed below are various collections of copies of personal and official letters and documents (including specimen papers), which have come down to us ordinarily in the form of compilations prepared for circulation.

106. 'Ainu-l Mulk 'Māhrū', *Inshā'i Māhrū*, ed. Sh. Abdur Rashīd and M. Bashir Husain, Lahore, 1965. This is a collection of administrative documents and official and personal letters of the author, who was a high officer under the Tughluq dynasty until *c.*1360 when he held the governorship of Multan.

107. Ḥakīm Abū-l Fatḥ Gīlānī (d.1589), *Ruq'āt-i Hakīm Abū-l Fatḥ Gīlānī*, also known as *Chārbāgh*, ed. M. Bashir Husain, Lahore, 1968.

108. Abū-l Qāsim Khān al-Ḥusainī 'Namakīn', *Munshāt-i Namakīn*, a collection of imperial orders, important administrative and diplomatic letters and private correspondence, the collection completed in 1594. Aligarh: Lytton F-3-26 & 27 (2 vols.).* Ed. (selection only) L.A. Zilli, New Delhi, 2007.

109. (S.709) Abū-l Faẓl, *Inshā'-i Abū-l Faẓl*. Collection made by 'Abdu-ṣ Ṣamad. Litho., Nawal Kishor, Kanpur, 1872.

110. Khānazād Khān, *Inshā'-i Khānazād Khān*, Jahāngīr's reign. Or.1410.

111. Har Karan, *Inshā'-i Har Karan*, comprising models of various official documents, Jahāngīr's reign, ed. and transl. Francis Balfour, Calcutta, 1781*; reprinted, 1881. The texts of the MSS vary greatly in later portions.

112. Shaikh Aḥmad Sirhindī, *Maktūbāt-i Imām-i Rabbānī*, collected by Yār Muḥammad Badakhshī, 'Abdu-l Ḥaiy and Muḥammad Hāshim, 3 vols. (last vol. compiled, 1622), litho., Nawal Kishor, Kanpur, n.d. (letters cited by nos.).

113. Letters written on behalf of Saif Khān, *Inshā'-i Munīr*, collected in 1641. Aligarh, Subhanullah, Fārsiya 891.5528/15*; litho., Muhammadi Press, Kanpur, n.d., and Nawal Kishor, Kanpur, 1885.

114. Khān Jahān Saiyid Muẓaffar Khān Bārha, *'Arzdāsht-hā-i Muẓaffar*, Shāhjahān: pre-1656. Add. 16,859, ff.1a-25a & 109b-122b. This collection includes an interesting letter written by Khān-i A'ẓam 'Azīz Koka to Jahāngīr, ff.17a-19b.

115. Bālkrishan Brahman, letters and other papers written by Shaikh Jalāl Ḥisārī

and by himself, late years of Shāhjahān and early years of Aurangzeb. Add.16,859, ff.27a-109b & 122b-127a. Rieu (ii, 837) failed to identify these letters or to distinguish them from No.114. Jalāl Ḥiṣārī was a servant of K͟hān Jahān Bārha; and Bālkrishan Brahman was a pupil of Jalāl Ḥiṣārī.

116. Aurangzeb, *Ādāb-i 'Ālamgīrī*, a collection of letters written on behalf of Aurangzeb before his accession by Abū-l Fatḥ Qābil K͟hān, to which are appended a collection of letters written on behalf of Prince Akbar, *c*.1680, by Muḥammad Ṣādiq, who finally edited this whole collection in 1703-4. Or. 177*; Add. 16,847. Edited by 'Abdu-l G͟hafūr Chaudhurī, 2 vols., Lahore, 1971 ('ed.')*. This edition, based on a single MS (Public Library, Lahore) needs to be collated with the other MSS: it has errors and omissions and an occasionally misleading Urdu commentary.

117. Aurangzeb, *Ruq'āt-i 'Ālamgīr*: correspondence of Aurangzeb with Shāhjahān, princess Jahān Ārā and other princes before his accession, largely extracted from No.116. Edited by Saiyid Najīb Ashraf Nadvī, Vol. I, Azamgarh, 1930. No further volumes published.

118. Jai Singh, '*arẓdāshts* (petitions) to the court and princes, 1655-58, R.A.S., Pers. Cat. 173, ff.8-76. The collection also includes a few '*arẓdāshts* from other nobles.

119. Munshī Bhāgchand, *Jāmi'u-l Inshā'*, a collection of letters, the bulk consisting of letters written by Jai Singh and correspondence between the Mughal and Persian courts. Compiled during Aurangzeb's reign. Or.1702.

120. (S. 738) Muḥammad Ṣāliḥ Kanbū Lāhorī, *Bahār-i Suk͟hun*, 1663-64. Add.5557; Or.178.

121. "Ḥadīqī", Collection of specimen letters, 1667. Br. M. Royal 16, B XXIII.

122. Abū-l Ḥasan "Ḥasan", *Muraqqa'āt-i Ḥasan*, letters written on behalf of Tarbiyat K͟hān, governor of Orissa, collected, 1678. Riza Library, Rampur, *Fan-i Inshā'* 2820 (microfilm and transcript in CAS in History, Aligarh).

123. Jahān Ārā, letters to Rāja Budh Prakāsh of Sirmur, 13th-23rd regnal years of Aurangzeb. Communicated by H.A. Rose, *JASB*, N.S., VII (1911), 449-58.

124. "Malikzāda", *Nigārnāma-i Munshī*, a collection of administrative documents, letters, etc., A.D. 1684. Litho., Nawal Kishor, Lucknow, 1882 ('ed.')*; MSS: Or. 1735*; Or. 2018; Bodl. MS. Pers. e-1 ('Bodl.')*.

125. *Durru-l 'Ulūm*, a collection of papers belonging to Munshī Gopāl Rā'i Sūrdaj, arranged by Ṣāḥib Rā'i Sūrdaj, 1688-89. Bodl. Walker 104.

126. *K͟hulāṣatu-l Inshā'*, 1691-92. Or. 1750, ff.107b-162a (extracts).

127. Īzid Bak͟hsh 'Rasā', *Riyāẓu-l Wadād*, 1673-95. Or. 1725.

128. *Bayāẓ*, attributed to Īzid Bak͟hsh "Rasā". I.O. 4014.

129. English Factory at Surat, Persian correspondence, 1695-97. I.O. 150.

130. Chathmal "Hindū", *Kārnāma*, a collection of letters written on behalf of Luṭfullāh Mu'tabar K͟hān, *c*.1688-98. I.O. 2007. Mu'tabar K͟hān is mentioned in *Ak͟hbārāt* 43/191 & 46/154 as the *thānadar* of Kalyan (Konkan).

131. Bhūpat Rā'i, *Inshā'-i Roshan Kalām*, letters written on behalf of Ra'd-andāz K͟hān, *faujdār* of Baiswāra, 1698-1702, and of his son and deputy, Sher-andāz K͟hān. I.O. 4011*; Aligarh, Abdus Salam, 109/339; Aligarh, Sir Shah Sulaiman, 394/82. The letters are undated, but the period with which they are concerned is established from their references to contemporary events, and from references to Ra'd-andāz K͟hān in *Ak͟hbārāt* 45/232 & 267.

132. Aurangzeb, *Raqā'im-i Karā'im*, letters to Amīr K͟hān (d.1698). MSS: C.A.S. in History (very early MS, 1708); Bodl. Ouseley 168 & 330; Add. 26,239. Ed. S.M. Azizuddin Husain, Delhi, 1990.

133. Aurangzeb, *Kalimāt-i Ṭaiyabāt*, letters and orders collected by 'Ināyatullāh Khān, 1719. Bodl. Fraser 157; Cambridge: King's Coll. 205.
134. Aurangzeb, *Aḥkām-i 'Ālamgīrī*, letters and orders collected by 'Ināyatullāh Khān (d.1725). I.O. 3887. This must be distinguished from (S.754) the unreliable anecdotes of Aurangzeb also entitled *Aḥkām-i 'Ālamgīrī*, preserved in I.O. 4071, and attributed by Jadunath Sarkar to Ḥamīdu-ddīn Khān "Nīmcha-i 'Ālamgīrī": the latter collection has been edited and translated by Sarkar as *Anecdotes of Aurangzib*, Calcutta, 1912.
135. Aurangzeb, *Ramz o Ishāra-hā-i 'Ālamgīrī*, letters and orders collected by Sabadmal (?), 1739-40. Add. 26,240.
136. Aurangzeb, *Dastūru-l 'Amal-i Āgahī*, letters and orders collected in 1743-44. Add. 26,237*; Add. 18,422.
137. Aurangzeb, *Ruq'āt-i 'Ālamgīrī*, letters and orders. This is the popular collection, deriving its materials from earlier compilations but containing some letters not found elsewhere. Add. 18,881 contains this collection, although at the beginning for a few pages it follows No.136. Litho., Kanpur, 1267/1851 ('Kanpur edn.')*; and Nawal Kishor (5th ed.), Kanpur, 1879.

Almost identical with this collection is the one compiled by Muḥammad Ṣāliḥ/Ṣalāh Ja'frī, who contributes a useful preface. Cambridge: Browne, p.195 (no.CXVII) (Add. 420).
138. Muḥammad Ja'far Qādirī, *Inshā'-i 'Ajīb*, letters written by the compiler himself and by his brothers and others, largely on private matters, 1706-7. Litho., Nawal Kishor, Kanpur, 1912.
139. Lekhrāj Munshī, *Matīn-i Inshā'* or *Mufīdu-l Inshā'*, letters written on behalf of Kāmgār Khān and (in fact almost entirely) on behalf of 'Alī Qulī Khān. Collected by Champat Rā'i in 1700-01, according to a chronogram, but includes letters of later date. Bodl., Bodl. 679. 'Alī Qulī Khān was the *faujdār* of Kuch Bihar, and he is mentioned in *Akhbārāt* 46/93.
140. Miscellaneous collection of letters, from the reigns of Akbar to Aurangzeb. I.O. 2678. The letters of Haridairām "Rām" Munshī, ff.77a onwards, belonging to the earlier part of the 17th century, appear to be of particular interest. I regret I have not been able to make full use of this collection.
141. Miscellaneous collection of letters of the reigns of Aurangzeb and Bahādur Shāh, including five letters from Shivājī. R.A.S. Morley 81 (Pers. Cat. 71).
142. Or. 1779, ff.214b-240a. Forms of orders of officials' appointment, *c*.1710, ed. & transl. J.F. Richards, *Document Forms for Official Orders of Appointment in the Mughal Empire*, Cambridge, 1986.
143. 'Ibādullāh Faiyāẓ, ed., *Faiyāẓu-l Qawānīn*, letters of Mughal emperors, princes, nobles and other rulers, collected, 1723-24. Or. 9617 (2 vols.).
144. Jān Muḥammad *b*. Muḥammad 'Ārif, *Jamm-i Badī'*, letters and administrative documents, relating mainly to Sind and Multan, collected, *c*.1733-34. The only MS known to me is in my possession, transcribed originally in 1911 (a xerox copy of this is now with CAS in History, Aligarh).
145. Shāh Walī-ullāh, Political letters, to *c*.1761, ed. with Urdu transl., *Shāh Walī-ullāh ke Siyāsī Maktūbāt*, by K.A. Nizami, Aligarh, 1950.

E. HISTORICAL WORKS

146. (S.698) Ẓahīruddīn Muḥammad Bābur, *Bāburnāma*: (1) Chaghatai Turki text: Hyderabad Codex, facsimile ed. by Annette Susannah Beveridge, Leyden and London, 1905; romanized text, ed. W.M. Thackston, Cambridge, Mass, 1993; critical ed. by Eiji Mano, Kyoto, 1995 ('ed.')*; (2) literal Persian translation

by 'Abdu-r Raḥīm K͟hān-i K͟hānān (1589): Or. 3174[*]; litho., Bombay, 1308/ 1890 (many errors); ed. W.M. Thackston, in same volume as the romanized Turki text, Cambridge, Mass, 1993; (3) English translations: (i) John Leyden and W. Erskine (1826, 1844), revised by L. King, Oxford, 1921 (richly annotated); (ii) Annette Susannah Beveridge, 2 vols. London, 1921 (directly from Turki and well annotated) ('Bev.');[*] (iii) Wheeler M. Thackston, New York, 1996 (poorly annotated).

While the use of the Beveridge translation is still recommended, one must guard against an unexpectedly large number of inadvertent slips (omissions of words and place-names, wrong transcriptions and inaccurate renderings of Persian words and terms used by Bābur). I have checked it throughout with Mano's text as well as 'Abdu-r Raḥim's translation as contained in Or. 3174, a splendid MS prepared for Akbar's library and illustrated by some of his best painters.

147. (S.698: 1) Shaik͟h Zain "Wafā'ī" K͟hwāfī, *Ṭabaqāt-i Bāburī*. Or. 1990.

148. Ḥasan 'Ali K͟hān, *Tawārīk͟h-i Daulat-i Sher Shāhī*. A fragment of the text and R.P. Tripathi's translation of a portion of the original which is not now traceable, have been published by S.A. Rashīd in *Medieval India Quarterly*, I(1) (1950). The endorsements on the fly-leaf of the surviving fragment are later forgeries, and there is good reason to doubt the genuineness of the main body of the work whose author claims improbably to have been a companion of Sher Shāh from his youth. But it is still a seemingly 17th-century composition.

149. (S.671) Rizqullāh "Mushtāqī", *Wāqi'āt-i Mushtāqī*. Add.11,633[*]; Or.1929. Ed. Iqtidar Husain Siddiqui and Waqarul Hasan Siddiqi, Rampur, 2002; transl. Iqtidar Husain Siddiqui, New Delhi, 1993.

150. (S. 672). 'Abbās K͟hān Sarwānī, *Tuhfa-i Akbar Shāhī*. I.O. 218 (Ethé 219)[*]; ed. S.M. Imamuddin, *Tarīk͟h-i Sher Shāhī*, I (text), Dacca, 1964 ('ed.')[*]. Since the author refers to the *Ilāhī* year, while the *Ilāhī* calendar was instituted only in 1584-85, and also mentions the death of Saiyid Ḥamīd Buk͟hārī (1586), the work could not have been completed before 1586.

151. (S.701) Mihtar Jauhar, *Taz̤kirātu-l Wāqi'āt*. Add. 16,711.

152. (S. 702) Bāyazid Bayāt, *Taz̤kira-i Humāyūn o Akbar*, ed. M. Hidayat Hosain, Bib. Ind., Calcutta, 1941.

153. (S. 707) 'Ārif Qandahārī, *Tārīk͟h-i Akbarī*, ed. Muinuddin Nadwi, Azhar Ali Dihlawi, and Imtiyaz Ali Arshi, Rampur, 1962[*]; transl. Tasneem Aḥmad, Delhi, 1993.

154. (S. 982) Mir Abū Turāb Walī, *Tārīk͟h-i Gujarāt*, ed. E. Denison Ross, Bib. Ind., Calcutta, 1905.

154a.(S. 1298:1) 'Abdu'l Ḥaqq, *Ak͟hbāru-l Ak͟hyār*, Deoband, n.d.

155. (S. 613) Niz̤āmu-ddīn Aḥmad, *Ṭabaqāt-i Akbarī*, ed. B. De, Bib. Ind., 3 vols. (Vol.III revised and partly edited by M. Hidayat Hosain), Calcutta, 1913, 1927, 1931 & 1935.

156. (S. 614) 'Abdu-l Qādir Badāūnī, *Muntak͟habu-t Tawārīk͟h*, ed. Ali, Ahmad and Lees, Bib. Ind., 3 vols., Calcutta, 1864-69.

157. (S. 709:1) Abū-l Faẓl, *Akbarnāma*, ed. Agha Ahmad Ali and Abdu-r Rahim, Bib. Ind., 3 vols., Calcutta, 1873-87[*]. I have collated the Bib. Ind. text extensively with Add. 26,207, an early MS corrected here and there in a fortunately distinct hand by the poet Shaidā in 1628-29. Beveridge collated some MSS for his translation, Bib. Ind., Calcutta, 1897-1921, and his notes on MS variants are often very helpful.

In Add. 27,247 we have the text of an earlier draft of the *Akbarnāma*. Its language, though sometimes identical with that of the final version, is generally less polished, and it has also many lacunae. On the other hand, in some places it is much fuller: it gives us the original text of Todar Mal's recommendations of 1582 concerning land-revenue administration and Akbar's comments thereon (ff.331b-332b) (see no.64 above). Another document of interest, and one not found anywhere else, is the text of Akbar's order issued to Prince Murād in answer to his queries about recruitment of *manṣabdārs*, and other matters (f.401b). I have generally cited Add.27,247 for these documents, but in other cases only when it has disclosed any important variation from the final version.

158. (S.824) Mīr Ma'ṣūm, *Tārīkh-i Sind*, ed. U.M. Daudpota, Poona, 1938.
159. (S.710) Ilāh-dād Faiẓī Sirhindī, *Akbarnāma*. Or. 169.
160. (S.712) Asad Beg Qazwīnī, Memoirs Or.1996.
161. (S.137) Ṭāhir Muḥammad Sabzwārī, *Rauẓatu-t Ṭāhirīn* (completed, 1605). Or.168.
162. (S.673) 'Abdullāh, *Tārīkh-i Dāūdī*, ed. S.A. Rashīd, Aligarh, 1954.
163. (S.674) Aḥmad Yādgār, *Tārīkh-i Salāṭīn-i Afāghina*, ed. M. Hidayat Hosain, Bib. Ind., Calcutta, 1939.
164. (S.825) "Idrākī" Tattawī, *Beglārnāma*, ed. N.A. Baloch, Hyderabad-Sind, 1980.
165. (S.826) Mīr Ṭāhir Muḥammad Nisyānī, *Tārīkh-i Ṭāhirī*. Or 1685*; ed. N.A. Baloch, Hyderabad-Sind, 1964 ('ed.')*.
166. (S.1013) Rafī'uddīn Ibrāhīm Shīrāzī, *Tazkiratu-l Mulūk*. Add.23,883: I have used the microfilm in CAS in History, Aligarh, containing a portion of this MS, ff.156b-238a.
167. (S.983) Sikandar "Manjhū", *Mir'āt-i Sikandarī*, ed. S.C. Misra and M.L. Rahman, Baroda, 1961.
168. (S.617) Muḥammad Qāsim Hindū Shāh "Firishta", *Gulshan-i Ibrāhīmī* or *Tārīkh-i Firishta*, litho., 2 vols., Kanpur, 1290/1874.
169. (S.544(1)) Khwāja Ni'matullāh al-Harawī, *Tārīkh-i Khānjahānī* or *Makhzan-i Afghānī*, ed. S.M. Imām al-Din, 2 vols., Dacca, 1960 and 1962.
170. Dastūr Kaiqubād, son of Mahyār, *Petition and Laudatory Poem addressed to Jahāngīr and Shāh Jahān*, [1617], ed. & transl. Jivanji Jamshedji Modi, Bombay, 1930.
171. (S.711) 'Abdu-l Bāqī Nihāwandī, *Ma'āṣir-i Raḥīmī*, ed. M. Hidayat Hosain, Bib. Ind., 3 vols., Calcutta, 1910-31.
172. (S.616) Nūru-l Ḥaqq Dihlawī, *Zubdatu-t Tawārīkh*. Add.10,583.
173. (S.715) Jahāngīr, *Jahāngīr-nāma* or *Tuzuk-i Jahāngīrī*, ed. Saiyid Ahmad, Ghazipur and Aligarh, 1863-64*. Some slips and errors of this edn. are corrected in the transl. by A. Rogers and H. Beveridge, 2 vols., London, 1909-14; but neither their transl. nor that of W.M. Thackston, New York, 1999, is free from inaccuracies. I have, on points of doubt, checked the printed text with the MS presented from Jahāngīr's own library to Saif Khān, now in Central Record Office, Hyderabad (photocopy in CAS in History, Aligarh); this breaks off at a point in R.Y.13.

    The fabricated version of the Memoirs (S.715:I) is now available in facsimile ed. of Khuda Bakhsh Library MS (*Jahangir Namah*, Patna, 2000). I have used Riza Library, Rampur, MS: History Persian No.175, transcript in CAS in History, Aligarh. The spurious version in R.A.S., P.122 (=Morley 117) incorporates and enlarges this earlier fabrication.

173a. 'Abdu-s Sattār, [*Majālis-i Jahāngīrī*,] Consersations of Jahāngīr, 1608-11, ed. 'A. Naushahi and M. Nizāmī, Tehran, 2006.

174. (S.1115) 'Abdu-n Nabī Fakhruzzamānī Qazwīnī, *Tazkira-i Maikhāna*, ed. Ahmad Gulchīn Ma'ānī, Tehīran(?), 1340 Shamsī/1962.

175. (S.955) 'Alā'u-ddīn "Ghaibī" Isfahānī "Mirzā Nathan", *Bahāristān-i Ghaibī*, transl. M.I. Borah, 2 vols., Gauhati, 1936. I regret I have not been able to check it with the unique MS of the work, Blochet, I, 617.

176. (S.717) Mu'tamad Khān, *Iqbālnāma-i Jahāngīrī*, 3 vols. I have consulted Vol.II (account of Akbar's reign), completed in 1620, for which I have used Nawal Kishor's litho. edn. of the entire work, Lucknow, 1870, Vol.II, checking it with MSS Or.1786 and Or.1834. The latter MS is unique in containing a supplement to Vol.II, setting out revenue statistics, *manṣab* pay schedules, etc. at Akbar's death. For Vol.III (account of Jahāngīr's reign) written in the early years of Shāhjahān's reign, I have used the edition of Abd al-Haiy and Ahmad Ali, Bib. Ind., Calcutta, 1865.

177. (S.619) Muḥammad Sharīf Najafī, *Majālisu-s Salāṭīn*. Or.1903.

178. (S.718) Kāmgār Ḥusainī, *Ma'āṣir-i Jahāngīrī*. Or.171; ed. Azra Alavi, Bombay, 1978.

179. (S.720) Anonymous, *Intikhāb-i Jahāngīr Shāhī*. Or.1648, ff.181b-201b (extracts). Though puporting to be written by a contemporary, it is probably an 18th-century fabrication.

180. (S.274) Amīn Qazwīnī, *Pādshāhnāma*. Or.173*; Add.20,734; transcript of MS of Riza Library, Rampur, in CAS in History, Aligarh (Nos.19-21) ('Aligarh transcript')*.

181. Banārasīdās, *Ardhakathānak* (composed, 1641): ed., with English transl., introd. & annotation by Mukund Lath, *Half a Tale*, Jaipur, 1981.

182. (S.674) Aḥmad Yādgār, *Tārīkh-i Salāṭīn-i Afāghina* or *Tārīkh-i Shāhī*, ed. M. Hidayat Hosain, Bib. Ind., Calcutta, 1939. The author's colophon gives 1644 as the year of completion (p.369).

183. (S.675) Muḥammad Kabīr, *Afsāna-i Shāhān*, Add.24,409.

184. (S.355) Abū Ṭālib Ḥusainī's Persian translation of the alleged Turkish Memoirs of Timūr, the *Tuzuk-i Timūrī* or *Malfūẓāt-i Timūrī*, presented to Shāhjahān in 1637; part of the "letters" (*tuzukāt*) section, pub. as *Institutes, political and military, written... by the great Timour*, ed., transl. and annotated by Major Davy and Joseph White, London, 1783. It is necessary to distinguish this text from the confessedly spurious memoirs of Timūr, written by Muḥammad Afẓal Bukhārī (MS Aligarh: Lytton, F. Akhbār, 44) on Shāhjahān's orders. See I. Habib, 'Timūr in the Political Tradition and Historiography of Mughal India', *L'Heritage Timouride*, ed. Maria Szuppe (Tashkent, 1997), 305-9.

185. (S.734) 'Abdu-l Ḥamīd Lāhorī, *Pādshāhnāma*, 2 vols., ed. Kabīr Al-Din Aḥmad, Abd Al-Raḥīm and W.N. Lees, Bib. Ind., Calcutta, 1866-72. Each vol. covers ten years (lunar) of Shāhjahān's reign. In the Bib. Ind. edn., Vol.I is divided into two parts separately paginated ('I' and 'I,ii' in our references).

186. (S.1465) Shaikh Farīd Bhakkarī, *Zakhīratu-l Khawānīn*, completed, 1650. Aligarh: Habibganj Fārsī 32/74 ('Aligarh MS')*; ed. Syed Moinul Haq, 3 vols., Karachi, 1961, 1970, 1974*; Vol.I, transl. Ziyauddin Desai, Delhi, 1993.

187. (S.734) Muḥammad Wāriṣ, *Pādshāhnāma*, being Vol.III of No.185. MSS: Add.6556 ('A'),* Or.1675 ('B')*.

188. (S.735) Muḥammad Ṣādiq Khān, *Shāhjahān-nāma*. Or.174; Or.1671. The author hides behind a pseudonym, and the autobiographical facts he gives appear to be fictitious. Yet it is a contemporary work of considerable importance.

189. (S.738:1) Ṣāliḥ Kanbū Lāhorī, *'Amal-i Ṣāliḥ*, ed. G. Yazdani, 4 vols. (Vol.IV: Index), Bib. Ind., Calcutta, 1912-46.

190. Munhta Nainsī, *Muhntā Nainsī rī Khyāt*, ed. Badarīprasād Sākariyā, Jodhpur, 1984, 3 vols., comprising historical fragments, genealogies, geographical accounts of areas of Rajput clans, etc., compiled, *c*.1660, by the author of the *Vigat* (No.5 above).

191. (S.743) Shihābuddīn Tālish, *Fatḥiya-i 'Ibriya*. Bodl. Or.589*. This MS is unique for its text of the continuation (to 1666). The first portion of this work is preserved in numerous MSS, and has been printed as *Tārīkh-i Mulk-i Āshām*, Calcutta, 1847.

192. (S.745) Muḥammad Kāẓim, *'Ālamgīrnāma*, ed. Khadim Husain and Abdu-l Hai, Bib. Ind., Calcutta, 1865-73.

193. (S.151:2) Shaikh Muḥammad "Baqā", ghost-writing for his patron, Bakhtāwar Khān, *Mir'ātu-l 'Ālam*, MSS: Add.7657*; Aligarh, Abdus Salam, 84/314; ed. Sajida S. Alvi, 2 vols., Lahore, 1979. There are considerable divergences between the Aligarh MS and Sajida S. Alvi's edn., where (II, 554) even Baqā's own death in 1094/1683 is mentioned.

194. Anonymous, *Pādshāh Burunjī*, Assamese chronicle, transl. S.K. Bhuyan, *Annals of the Delhi Badshahate*, Gauhati, 1947.

195. (S.751:1) Ni'mat Khān-i 'Ālī, *Waqā'i'*, litho. Naval Kishor, Lucknow, 1928, with important marginal annotation by the anonymous editor.

196. (S.748) Mehta Īsardās Nāgar, *Futūḥāt-i 'Ālamgīrī*. Add.23,884*; transl. Tasneem Ahmad, Delhi, 1978.

197. (S.622) Sujān Rā'i Bhanḍārī, *Khulāṣatu-t Tawārīkh*, ed. Zafar Ḥasan, Delhi, 1918*. I have also used MSS Add.16,680('A')*, Add.18,407('B')* and Or.1625 ('C')*, which I have cited only in case of any obscurity in the printed text.

198. (S.753) Abū-l Faẓl Ma'mūrī, Continuation of Ṣādiq Khān's *Shāhjahān-nāma* (no.188), Or.1671. The author wrote the continuation to give a history of the reign of Aruangzeb; like Ṣādiq Khān, his own identity is not established, for the numerous autobiographical details that he provides remain uncorroborated.

199. (S.750) Bhīmsen, *Nuskha-i Dilkushā*, Or.23*. Transl. J. Sarkar [and V.G. Khobrekar], ed. with notes & introd. by V.G. Khobrekar, Bombay, 1971. The transl. omits the last portion of the work, dealing with events after Aurangzeb's death.

200. (S.752) Ṣāqī Musta'idd Khān, *Ma'āṣir-i 'Ālamgīrī*, Bib. Ind. ed., Calcutta, 1870-73*. I have also consulted MS Add.19,495.

201. (S.623) Jagjīvandās Gujarātī, *Muntakhabu-t Tawārīkh*, Add.26,253.

202. (S.681) Muḥammad Hādī Kāmwar Khān, *Tazkiratu-s Salāṭīn-i Chaghata*, ed. Muzaffar Alam [portion dealing with the period 1707-24 only], Bombay, 1980.

203. Ḥaqq Muḥammad I'timād 'Alī Khān, *Mir'ātu-l Ḥaqā'iq*, Bodl. Fraser 124. The vol. contains a number of interesting memoirs, official papers and statistics, but the most important part is the author's diary, 1718-27 (ff.129a-489b), covering his travels as well as life in later years at Surat.

204. (S.627) Muḥammad Hāshim Khāfī Khān, *Muntakhabu-l Lubāb*, Vol.II and Vol.III (portions relating to the Dakhin), ed. Kabīr al-Din Aḥmad and Wolseley Haig, Bib. Ind., Calcutta, 1860-74, 1905-25*; transl. (portion only) by Anees Jahān Syed, *Aurangzeb in Muntakhabu-l Lubab*, Bombay, 1977.

Khāfī Khān has plagiarized extensively from Ṣādiq Khān's *Shāhjahān-nāma* (no.188) and its continuation by Abū-l Faẓl Ma'mūrī (no.198), the plagia-

rism being still more evident in the first version of K͟hāfī K͟hān's work, MSS Add.6573 and 6574.
205. (S.779: 1) Muḥammad Shāfī' "Wārid", *Mir'āt-i Wāridāt*, Add.6579.
206. (S.629) Yaḥyā K͟hān, *Tazkiratu-l Mulūk*, I.O.1147.
207. (S.880) Muḥammad A'ẓam, *Wāqi'āt-i Kashmīr*, completed, 1747. Printed ed., Lahore, 1886 (not seen). I was able, to examine a MS in private possession. The work in its k͟hātima gives a list of the *parganas*, with *jama'*, of the *ṣūba* of Kashmir.
207a.(S.1162:14 & 1362:a) Mir G͟hulām 'Alī Āzād Ḥusainī Bilgrāmī, *Ma'āṣiru-l Kirām*, completed, 1752-53, I, ed. 'Abdullāh K͟hān, Hyderabad (Dn.), 1910.
208. (S.984) 'Alī Muḥammad K͟hān, *Mir'āt-i Ahmadī*, ed. Nawab Ali, 2 vols. & Supplement, Baroda, 1927-28, 1930*. Nawab Ali's edition was based on the author's own MS, transcribed by his secretary, but the edition is not free from printing errors. I have checked some passages with MSS I.O.222 and I.O.2597-9.
209. (S.1471) Shāh Nawāz K͟hān, *Ma'āṣiru-l Umarā*', 'Abdu-l Ḥaiy's recension, ed. Abdu-r Rahim and Ashraf Ali, Bib. Ind., 3 vols., Calcutta, 1888-91.
210. (S.1162:17) Mir G͟hulām 'Alī Āzād Ḥusainī Bilgrāmī, *K͟hizāna-i 'Āmira* (1762-63), Nawal Kishor, Kanpur, 1871.
211. (S.958) Munshī Salīmullāh, *Tā'rīk͟h-i Bangāla*, 1763, ed. S.M. Imamuddin, Dacca, 1979.
212. (S.1509) G͟hulām Ḥusain "Ṣamīn", *Sharā'if-i 'Us̱mānī*, MS in CAS in History, Aligarh. A history of Bilgram, completed in 1765-6, giving texts of a very large number of Mughal-period documents, relating to Bilgrām and its vicinity.
213. (S.828:1) 'Alī Sher "Qāni'" Tattawī, *Tuḥfatu-l Kirām*, Vol.III (a history of Sind, completed, 1767-68, though later dates occur), Dalha'i (Lucknow?), 1886-87(?).

For the period before the sixteenth century, the historical works cited include:

214. (S.823) *Chachnāma* [Arabic, 9th century?], transl. into Persian by 'Alī Kūfī, c.1216-17, ed. Umar bin Muhammad Daudpota, Delhi, 1939.
215. Kalhaṇa, *Rājataraṅgiṇi*, history of Kashmir, to 1149-50, transl. M.A. Stein, 2 vols., London, 1900.
216. (S.104) Minhāj Sirāj, *Ṭabaqāt-i Nāṣirī*, ed. Abdul Hai Habibi, 2 vols., 2nd edn., Kabul, 1963, 1964.
217. Ḥasan 'Alā' Sijzī, *Fawāidu-l Fawād*, conversations of Shaik͟h Niẓāmuddīn at Dehli, 1308-22, ed. M. Latif Malik, Lahore, 1966.
218. (S.612) 'Iṣāmī, *Futūḥu-s Salāṭīn*, ed. A.S. Usha, Madras, 1948.
219. (S.666). Ẕiyā'[u-ddin] Baranī, *Tārīk͟h-i Fīrūz Shāhī*, ed. Saiyid Aḥmad K͟hān, W. Nassau Lees and Kabīr al-Din, Bib. Ind., Calcutta, 1862.
220. (S.669) Shams Sirāj 'Afīf, *Tārīk͟h-i Fīrūz-Shāhī*, ed. Wilayat Husain, Bib. Ind., Calcutta, 1891.
221. (S.356) Sharafuddīn 'Alī Yazdī, *Ẕafarnāma*, ed. Muḥammad Ilahdad, Bib. Ind., Calcutta, 1885-88, 2 vols.
222. (S.670) Yaḥyā Sirhindī, *Tārīk͟h-i Mubārakshāhī*, ed. M. Hidayat Hosain, Bib. Ind., Calcutta, 1931.

F. GEOGRAPHICAL WORKS

223. Ma Huan, *Yang-yai Sheng-lan, The Over-all Survey of the Ocean Shores*, transl. from Chinese by J.V.G. Mills, Cambridge, 1970.

224. (S.1649) Amīn Aḥmad Rāzī, *Haft Iqlīm*, Or.204; Add.16,734; Vol.I, ed. Ross, Harley and Haqq, Calcutta, 1918, 1927, 1939; II, ed. M. Ishaque, Calcutta, 1963; V, ed. S.B. Samadi, Calcutta, 1972, all in Bib. Ind. series*.

225. 'Abdu-l Laṭīf, Journey to Bengal, 1608-9, Persian original now untraceable; abridged transl. of fragment by J. Sarkar in *Bengal Past and Present*, XXXV (2)(1928), 143-46.

226. (S.II, 207) Ṣādiq Ṣāliḥ Isfahānī, *Shāhid-i Ṣādiq*, encyclopaedic work, with much geographical material, begun 1644-45, completed three years later, Br. M. Egerton 1016 (complete); Or.1626.

227. (S.II, 213) Amīnuddin Khān, *Ma'lūmātu-l Āfāq*, MS Aligarh: Subhanullah, 362/124, a magnificent copy transcribed for the author himself.

228. (S.780:9:3) Ānand Rām "Mukhliṣ", *Safarnāma-i Mukhliṣ*, ed. S. Azhar Ali, Rampur, 1946.

229. (S.631) Rā'i Chaturman Saksena, *Chahār Gulshan* or *Akhbār-i Nawādir*, ed. Chander Shekhar, New Delhi, 2011; MS Bodl. Eliot 366*. Portion transl. J. Sarkar in *India of Aurangzib*, Calcutta, 1901 ('Sarkar')*.

G. DICTIONARIES

230. Fakhruddīn Mubārak Qawwās, *Farhang-i Qawwās*, c.1342-43, ed. Nazir Ahmad, Tehran, 1974.

231. Muḥammad Shādīābādī, *Miftāḥu-l Fuẓalā,* written presumably at Mandu (Shādīābād), 1468-69. Its unique MS, Or. 3299, contains over 170 illustrations in the (pre-Mughal) Malwa style.

232. Jamāluddīn Ḥusain Injū, *Farhang-i Jahāngīrī*, 1608-9, Samar-i Hind Press, Lucknow, 1876.

232a. Muḥammad Ḥusain "Burhān", *Burhān-i Qāṭi'*, 1652, ed. Saiyid Muhammad "Ma'shūq", Lucknow, 1273/1856.

233. 'Abdu-r Rashīd al-Tattawī, *Farhang-i Rashīdī*, 1653-54, ed. Abu Tahir Zulfiqar Ali Murshidabadi, Asiatic Society of Bengal, Calcutta, 1872.

234. Tek Chand "Bahār", *Bahār-i 'Ajam*, 1739-40, litho. Nawal Kishor, [Lucknow], 1336/1916. Perhaps, the most authoritative and comprehensive of old Persian dictionaries, with an exceptionally rich stock of citations.

235. (S.834:22) Sirājuddīn 'Alī "Ārzū", *Chirāgh-i Hidāyat* (Vol.II of *Sirāju-l Lughāt*), 1740, printed on margins of edns. of *Ghiyāṣu-l Lughāt*, Naval Kishor, Kanpur, 1882; Intizami Press, Kanpur, 1317/1899.

236. (S. 780:2) Ānand Rām "Mukhliṣ", *Mir'ātu-l Iṣṭilāḥ*, 1745, Or. 1813.

H. RELIGION, ETHICS

Nos.154a and 217 above can also be listed under this class.

237. *Manusmriti*, transl. G. Buhler, *The Laws of Manu*, Sacred Books of the East Series, XXV, Oxford, 1886.

238. *Milindapañho*, Pali text ed. V. Trenckner, London, 1880, reprinted with index, etc., London, 1962; transl. T.W. Rhys Davids, *The Questions of Milinda*, 2 vols., Oxford, 1890, 1894.

239. Kabīr, *Kabīr Granthāvalī*, ed. Shyamsundardas, Kashi, 2008 v.s./1950-51.

240. *Shrī Gurū Granth Sāhib*, text in Nagari characters, pub. Shiromani Gurudwara

Prabandhak Committee, 2 vols., Amritsar, 1951*; transl. M.A. Macauliffe, *The Sikh Religion – its Gurus, Sacred Writings and Authors*, 6 vols., Oxford, 1909 ('Macauliffe')*.

241. (S 614: 6) 'Abdu-l Qādir Badāūnī, *Nijātu-r Rashīd*, AD 1591, ed. S. Moinul Haq, Lahore, 1972.

242. Ṣūrat Singh, *Tazkira Pīr Ḥassū Telī*, AD 1647, MS (prob. autograph), CAS in History, Aligarh: a metrical work about Ḥassū *Telī* (d.1603) and his successor Shaikh Kamāl of Lahor.

243. [Kaikhusrau Isfandyār, pseudomym: Zu'lfiqār] "Mobad", *Dabistān*[-*i Mazāhib*], work on various religions and religious sects, completed in 1653 or soon after, ed. Nazar Ashraf, Calcutta, 1809*; litho. pub. Ibrāhīm *bin* Nūr Muḥammad, Bombay, 1857, facsimile reprint, Tehran, 1361 Shamsī, with introd. by 'Ali Asghar Mustaufī) ('Bombay ed'.)*; Bombay text, ed. with extensive annotation by Raḥīm Riẓāzādeh Malik, Tehran, 1983, 2 vols; facsimile ed. of MS carrying early version, ed. Karim Najafi Barzgar, New Delhi, 2010. English transl. by D. Shea and A. Troyer, London, 1843, a brave attempt, is now obsolete.

244. *Satnām Sahāi* or *Pothī Gyān Bānī Sādh Satnāmī*, *c*.1657, MS: RAS, Hindustani 1, giving the Braj text in both Nagari and Arabic characters.

245. Shāh Walī-ullāh (d.1762-63), *Ḥujjat Allāh al-Bāligha*, Arabic text with Abū Muḥammad 'Abdu-l Ḥaqq Ḥaqqānī's Urdu transl. in parallel columns, 2 vols., Karachi, n.d.

I. DIET, DRUGS

246. (S. II(2) 438:2) Qāẓī *bin* Kāshifuddīn Muḥammad Yazdī, *Risāla-i Chūb-i Chīnī* (*o Qahwa o Chā*), Add. 19,619. This tract on china-root, coffee and tea was written in Iran for Shāh 'Abbās I, d.1629.

247. Anonymous, *Bayāẓ-i Khwushbū'ī*, I.O. 828. The MS was transcribed, 1697-98, but from internal evidence, the work can be assigned to the first two decades of Shāhjahān's reign. Its contents range from recipes for dishes to medicinal aids, perfumes, pen and paper, lay-out of stables and gardens, revenue statistics, etc.

248. Anonymous, *Khulāṣatu-l Mākūlāt o Mashrūbāt*, Add. 17,959, the MS dated 1765-66 being probably an autograph. Very detailed cookery recipes are provided.

J. EUROPEAN SOURCES

248a. Duarte Barbosa, *The Book of Duarte Barbosa*, transl. from Portuguese by M. Longworth Dames, 2 vols., London, 1918 & 1921.

249. Caesar Frederick (Caesar de Frederici), "Extracts of ... his eighteen years Indian Observations", 1563-81, *Purchas his Pilgrimes*, pub. MacLehose, Glasgow, 1905, X, 88-143.

250. Fr. A. Monserrate, 'Informacion de los X'pianos de S. Thome', 1579. Portions transl. H. Hosten, *JASB*, NS, XVIII (1922), 349-69.

251. *Letters from the Mughal Court: the first Jesuit Mission to Akbar (1580-83)*, transl. John Correia-Afonso, Bombay/Anand, 1980, the letters extracted from Joseph Wicki, ed., *Documenta Indica*, XII, Rome, 1972.

252. Fr. A. Monserrate, *Commentary on his Journey to the Court of Akbar*, transl. J.S. Hoyland, annotated by S.N. Banerjee, Cuttack, 1922.

253. Du Jarric's account of the Jesuit missions to the court of Akbar, transl. C.H. Payne, *Akbar and the Jesuits*, London, 1926.
254. J.H. van Linschoten, The *Voyage of John Huyghen van Linschoten to the East Indies*, from the old English translation of 1598, ed. A.C. Burnell (Vol.I) and P.A. Tiele (Vol.II), Hakluyt Society, Vols.70-71, London, 1885.
255. *Early Travels in India (1583-1619)*, collection of the narratives of Fitch (1-47), Mildenhall (48-59), Hawkins (60-121), Finch (122-87), Withington (188-233), Coryat (234-87), and Terry (288-332), ed. W. Foster, London, 1927.
    Fitch's narrative is also published by J.H. Ryley, ed., *Ralph Fitch, England's Pioneer to India and Burma*, London, 1899 ('ed. Ryley')*.
256. Fr. J. Xavier, Letters, 1593-1617, transl. H. Hosten, *JASB*, NS, XXIII (1927), 109-30.
257. Francesco Carletti, 'Ragionamenti', transl. Herbert Weinstock, *My Voyage Round the World by Francesco Carletti, a 16th-century Florentine Merchant*, New York, 1964/ London, 1965. Carletti was in India, 1599-1601.
258. *A Supplementary Calendar of Documents in the India Office Relating to India or to the Home Affairs of the East India Company, 1600-1640*, by W. Foster, London, 1928.
259. *Letters Received by the East India Company from its Servants in the East*, 1602-17. 6 vols.: vol.I, ed., F.C. Danvers; vols. II-VI, ed. W. Foster, London, 1896-1902.
260. Francois Pyrard of Laval, *The Voyage of Francois Pyrard of Laval to the East Indies, the Maldives, Moluccas and Brazil*, transl. (from the French 1619 edn.) by Albert Gray and H.C.P. Bell, Hakluyt Society, 2 vols., London, 1887. The author was in India and Maldives, 1602-10. I have read Vol.I and II, i; all my references to Vol.II are to be construed as references to II, i.
261. Robert Coverte, *A True and Almost Incredible Report of an Englishman*, London, 1612; reprint ed. Bois Penrose, *The Travels of Captain Robert Coverte*, Philadelphia, 1931*.
262. Fernao Guerreiro, *Relations*. Portions transl. C.H. Payne, *Jahāngīr and the Jesuits*, London, 1930.
263. *Relations of Golconda in the Early Seventeenth Century*, a collection of the 'relations' of Methwold (1-50), Schorer (51-65) and an anonymous Dutch factor (67-95). Ed. & transl. W.H. Moreland, Hakluyt Society, London, 1931.
264. John Jourdain, *Journal, 1608-17*, ed. W. Foster, Hakluyt Society, 2nd Series, No.XVI, Cambridge, 1905.
265. Joseph Salbancke, 'Voyage', 1609, *Purchas his Pilgrimes*, pub. MacLehose, III, 82-89.
266. Manuel Godinho de Eredia, 'Discourse on the Province of Indostan', 1611. Transl. Hosten, *JASB*, Letters, IV, 1938, 533-66.
267. Peter Floris, *His Voyage to the East Indies in the 'Globe'*, 1611-15. Contemporary translation of his Journal, ed. W.H. Moreland, Hakluyt Society, 2nd Series, LXXIV, London, 1934.
268. Thomas Roe, *The Embassy of Sir Thomas Roe, 1615-19, as Narrated in his Journal & Correspondence*, ed. W. Foster, London, 1926.
269. Richard Steel and John Crowther, 'Journall', 1615-16, *Purchas his Pilgrimes*, pub. MacLehose, Glasgow, 1905, IV, 266-80.
270. Edward Terry, *A Voyage to East India, & c., 1616-19*, enlarged version, London, 1655; reprinted, 1777*. Earlier version from *Purchas his Pilgrimes* printed in Foster (ed.), *Early Travels* (no.255 above).
271. *The English Factories in India, 1618-69*, ed. W. Foster, 13 vols., Oxford,

1906-27. The volumes are not numbered and have, therefore, been cited by the years allotted to each, given beneath the title in each individual volume.

272. Pietro Della Valle, *The Travels of Pietro della Valle in India*, transl. Edward Grey, Hakluyt Society, 2 vols., London, 1892. (Travelled in India, 1623-24.)

272a. Samuel Purchas, *Hakluytus Posthumus or Purchas his Pilgrimes*, London, 1625; pub. James MacLehose, Glasgow, 20 vols., 1905*. Vols.III, IV and X of the MacLehose edition contain 'relations' concerned with India. Cited only for 'relations' not elsewhere published.

273. Pieter van den Broeke, Surat 'Diary', 1620-29, transl. W.H. Moreland, *JIH*, X, 235-50; XI, 1-16, 203-18.

274. Francisco Pelsaert, 'Remonstrantie', *c*.1626, pub. in D.H.A. Kolff and H.W. van Santen, eds., *De geschriften van Francisco Pelsaert over Mughal Indië, 1627, Kroniek en Remonstrantie*, ('S-Gravenhage, 1979), 243-335; transl. W.H. Moreland and P. Geyl, *Jahāngīr's India*, Cambridge, 1925*.

275. Wollebrand Geleynssen de Jongh, 'Verclaringe ende Bevinding', etc., extracts transl. W.H. Moreland, *JIH*, IV (1925-26), 69-83.

276. Surat factory records: Outward letters, 1630; Inward letters, 1656-57; Diary, 1660-68. Maharashtra State Archives, Bombay. Ed. Ruby Maloni, *European Merchant Capital and the Indian Economy: Surat Factory Records*, New Delhi, 1992.

277. *Selections from the Letters, Despatches and other State Papers preserved in the Bombay Secretariat, Home Series*, George W. Forrest, Bombay, 1887. Vol.I contains selections from Surat letters, 1630-1700; Bombay letters, 1677-1742; Surat Diaries, 1660-1781. Vol.II, contains Bombay Diaries, 1722-88, and other documents.

278. Joannes De Laet, 'De Imperio Magni Mogolis', etc., 1631, transl. J.S. Hoyland, annotated by S.N. Banerjee, *The Empire of the Great Mogul*, Bombay, 1928. The discovery and publication of the many sources of this work have deprived it of its old authority.

279. Peter Mundy, *Travels*, Vol.II, 'Travels in Asia, 1630-34', ed. Sir R.C. Temple, Hakluyt Society, 2nd Series, XXXV, London, 1914; and Vol.V (including account of travel to India, 1655-56), ed. L.M. Anstey, same series, LXXVIII, London, 1936. All references to Mundy without specification of volume are to Vol.II.

280. Fray Sebastian Manrique, *Travels, 1629-43*, transl. C.E. Luard assisted by H. Hosten, 2 vols., Hakluyt Society, London, 1927.

281. Antonio Bocarro, 'Livro des plantas', etc., 1635, extracts transl. Fr. Achilles Meersman, 'Antonio Bocarro's Description of Sind', *Jour. Sind Historical Soc.*, IV(4) (1940), 199-204.

282. John van Twist, 'A General Description of India', *c*.1638, extracts transl. W.H. Moreland, *JIH*, XVI (1937), 63-77.

283. Jean-Baptiste Tavernier, *Travels in India*, 1640-67, transl. V. Ball, 2nd edition revised by W. Crooke, 2 vols., London, 1925.

284. Francois Bernier, *Travels in the Mogul Empire 1656-68*, transl. on the basis of Irving Brock's version by A. Constable, with notes, 2nd edition revised by V.A. Smith, London, 1916.

285. *English Records on Shivājī (1659-1682)*, ed. with introd. by B.J. Pranjpe, 2 vols., Poona, 1931.

286. Dircq van Andrichem, *Journaal van Dircq van Andrichem's Hofreis naar den Groot-Mogol Aurangzeb, 1662*, ed. A.J. Bernet Kempers, The Hague, 1941.

287. Fr. Manuel Godinho, 'Relacao de Novo Cominho', etc., transl. Vitalio Lobo

and John Correa-Afonso, *Intrepid Itinerant: Manuel Godinho and his Journey from India to Portugal in 1663*, Bombay, 1990.

288. Jean de Thevenot, 'Relation de Hindostan, 1666-67'. A. Lovell's transl. of 1687, reprinted with corrections, notes and an introduction by S.N. Sen in *The Indian Travels of Thevenot and Careri*, New Delhi, 1949.
289. John Marshall, 'Notes & Observations on East India', ed. S.A. Khan, *John Marshall in India – Notes & Observations in Bengal, 1668-72*, London, 1927.
290. Thomas Bowrey, *A Geographical Account of Countries Round the Bay of Bengal, 1669 to 1679*, ed. R.C. Temple, Cambridge, 1905.
291. Abbé Carre, MS journal, transl. Lady Fawcett, ed. Sir Charles Fawcett, *The Travels of the Abbe Carre in India and the Near East, 1672 to 1674*, 3 vols., Hakluyt Soc., London, 1947, 1947-48.
292. John Fryer, *A New Account of East India and Persia being Nine Years' Travels, 1672-81*, ed. W. Crooke, 3 vols., Hakluyt Society, 2nd Series, XIX, XX, XXXIX, London, 1909, 1912, 1915.
293. Streynsham Master, *The Diaries of Streynsham Master, 1675-80, & other Contemporary Papers Relating Thereto*, ed. R.C. Temple, Indian Records Series, 2 vols., London, 1911.
294. Georges Roques, 'La manière de nègocier dans les Indes Orientales' [written, 1678-80]. (1) Transl. of portion on cotton-printing at Ahmadabad and original index of subjects by Margaret Hall, with introd. & notes by Paul R. Schwartz, pub. as work by Paul R. Schwartz, *Printing on Cotton in Ahmedabad, India, in 1678*, Ahmedabad, 1969. (2) Portion on trade and traders of Ahmadabad, together with Roques's Preface, transl. Indrani Ray, 'Of Trade and Traders in Seventeenth-Century India', *IHR*, IX(1-2) (1982-83), 74-120. (3) Further portions on trade, transl. Ruqaiya K. Husain, *PIHC*, 55th session, 1994, Aligarh, 938-48.
295. 'Maulda Diary and Consultation Booke' & 'Maulda and Englezavad Diary', 1680-82, ed. Walter K. Firminger, *JASB*, NS, XIV (1918), 1-241.
296. William Hedges, *The Diary of William Hedges, Esq., during his Agency in Bengal*, transcribed and annotated by R. Barlow and illustrated by copious extracts from unpublished records by Col. Henry Yule, 3 vols., Hakluyt Society, nos.74, 75 & 78, London, 1887-89. I have only cited Vol.I, which contains Hedges's diary. Vols.II & III largely consist of biographical material.
297. J. Ovington, *A Voyage to Surat in the Year 1689*, ed. H.G. Rawlinson, London, 1929*. This edn. unfortunately omits the valuable Appendix on sericulture, for which I have cited the original edition, London, 1696.
298. *Portuguese Records on Rustamji Manockji, the Parsi Broker of Surat*, ed. S.S. Pissurlencar, transl. S.B. D'Silva, Bombay, 1936. The Portuguese letters date from 1691 to 1708; the last two are dated 1727 and 1728.
299. Giovanni Francesco Gamelli Careri, 'Giro del Mondo'. Careri visited India in 1695. 'Early English version' of portions of Careri's work relating to India reprinted in *The Indian Travels of Thevenot and Careri*, ed. S.N. Sen, New Delhi, 1949.
300. Nicolao Manuchy (Manucci), *Storia do Mogor, 1656-1712*, transl. W. Irvine, 4 vols., Indian Texts Series, Government of India, London, 1907-8. I have followed the spelling of the author's name found in his signatures preserved at Pondicherry (*IHRC*, 1925, 175). But in citing Irvine's translation, I have used the form 'Manucci', this being the spelling adopted by Irvine.
301. Alexander Hamilton, *A New Account of the East Indies... from the Year 1688*

to 1723, 2nd ed., 2 vols., London, 1739 (photo reprint, New Delhi, 1995)*; ed. W. Foster, 2 vols., London, 1930.

302. *The Early Annals of the English in Bengal, being the Bengal Public Consultations for the first half of the Eighteenth Century*, ed. C.R. Wilson, 2 vols., London, 1895. Vol.II, Part 2, Calcutta, 1911 (reprinted, 1963), contains documents concerned with the Surman embassy sent to Dehli, 1714-17.
303. John Burnell, Letters (1710-12) and an account of Bengal (1712-13), collected in *Bombay in the Days of Queen Anne*, ed. Samuel T. Sheppard, William Foster, Evan Cotton and L.M. Anstey, Hakluyt Society, London, 1933.
304. Ippolito Desideri, 'Il Tibet', transl. Philippo de Filippi, *An Account of Tibet: the Travels of Ippolito Desideri, S.J., 1712-1727*, London, 1932.

2. MODERN WORKS

A. AGRICULTURE, AGRICULTURAL PRODUCE, & STATISTICS

305. George Watt (assisted by numerous contributors), *Dictionary of the Economic Products of India*, 6 vols. (Vol.VI being issued in 4 parts), Calcutta, 1889-93.
306. *The Agricultural Statistics of India*, issued by the Department of Revenue & Agriculture [and successors], Government of India, as a series at uneven intervals from 1884-85 onwards.
307. John Augustus Voelcker, *Report on the Improvement of Indian Agriculture*, London, 1893.
308. Government of India, *Prices and Wages in India*, 12th issue, Calcutta, 1895.
309. George Watt, *The Commercial Products of India*, London, 1908.
310. N.G. Mukerji, *Handbook of Indian Agriculture*, Calcutta, 1915.
311. W.H. Moreland, *Notes on the Agricultural Conditions of the United Provinces and of its Districts*, Allahabad, 1913. Notes on each district separately paginated.
312. The Royal Commission on Agriculture in India, *Report*, London, 1928.
313. Government of India, *Agricultural Prices in India, 1951 and 1952*, and Supplement: *Farm (Harvest) Prices of Principal Crops, 1947-48 to 1951-52*, New Delhi.
314. Commonwealth Economic Committee, *Industrial Fibres – A Review*, London, 1965.

B. LAND SYSTEM & LAND-REVENUE ADMINISTRATION

315. Khwāja Yāsīn of Dehli, Glossary of revenue and administrative terms, in Persian. Add. 6603, ff.40-84*. The author claims to have had experience of revenue administration in Dehli and sets out to explain terms in use in both Dehli and Bengal for the benefit of the English officials in charge of revenue matters; and he is, therefore, definitely writing after 1772, when the "dual government" ended, and the English collectors took over. A second version of this work, in a MS from Purnea (photocopy in C.A.S. in History: R.244), was described in an unpublished paper by Qeyamuddin Ahmad submitted to the Indian History Congress, Mysore session (1966). The author says in the preface in this MS that he compiled the work at the request of James Grant (*c.* 1784?). It is yet to be established whether Add. 6603 or the Purnea MS contains the later (and, therefore, revised) version.
316. Report (in Persian) on the pre-British system of administration in Bengal, prepared by the Rā'i Rāyān and the *qānūngos* under instructions of the Gov-

ernor-General & Council, 4 January 1777. Add.6592, ff.75b-114b; Add.6586, ff.53a-72b.

317. *Dastūru-l 'Amal-i Khāliṣa-i Sharīfa*, a work of late 18th century, containing a glossary of administrative and revenue terms. Edinburgh 230.
318. Miscellaneous papers relating chiefly to revenue administration in Bengal, mostly in Persian, late 18th century. Add.6586, and Add.19,502-04.
319. *The Fifth Report* from the Select Committee on the Affairs of the East India Company, with Glossary, London, 1812-13 (photoreprint, Irish University Press, Shannon, 1969)*. W.K. Firminger's edn., 3 vols., reprint, Calcutta, 1918, has been used only for documents not found in the original *Fifth Report*.
320. *Selections from the Revenue Records of the North-west Provinces, 1818-20, pending the enactment of Regulations VII, 1822*, Calcutta, 1866.
321. Chhatar Mal, *Dīwān Pasand*, Or. 2011. Written at Agra after 1809-10 and before 1824. For the latter date, see Asiya Siddiqi, *Agrarian Change in a North Indian State*, 180.
322. H.M. Elliot, *Memoirs on the ... Races of the North-Western Provinces of India*, being an amplified edition of his original *Supplemental Glossary*, revised by John Beames, 2 vols., London, 1869.
323. H.H. Wilson, *A Glossary of Judicial and Revenue Terms ... of British India*, London, 1875.
324. B.H. Baden-Powell, *Land Systems of British India*, 3 vols., Oxford, 1892.
325. Alexander Rogers, *The Land Revenue of Bombay, a History of its Administration, Rise and Progress*, 2 vols., London, 1892.
326. Ranajit Guha, *A Rule of Property for Bengal: An Essay on the Idea of Permanent Settlement*, Paris, 1963 (photo reprint, New Delhi, 1982).
327. Asiya Siddiqi, *Agrarian Change in a North Indian State: Uttar Pradesh, 1819-1833*, Oxford, 1973.

C. AGRARIAN SOCIETY

328. (S.688) Col. James Skinner, *Tashrīḥu-l Aqwām*, 1825. MS Add.27,255 (magnificently illustrated, 1825).
329. Henry Sumner Maine, *Village-Communities in the East and West*, 3rd edn., London, 1876 (photo-reprint, Delhi, 1985).
330. George A. Grierson, *Bihar Peasant Life, Being a Discursive Catalogue of the Surroundings of the People of that Province*, Calcutta, 1885.
331. W. Crooke, *The Tribes and Castes of the North-Western Provinces and Oudh*, 4 vols., Calcutta, 1896.
332. B.H. Baden-Powell, *The Indian Village Community*, London, 1896.
333. William Wilson Hunter, *Annals of Rural Bengal*, 7th edn., London, 1897.
334. D. Ibbetson, *Punjab Castes*, Lahore, 1916.
335. W.H. Wiser, *The Hindu Jajmani System*, Lucknow, 1936.
336. Surendra J. Patel, *Agricultural Labourers in Modern India and Pakistan*, Bombay, 1952.
337. Louis Dumont, *Homo Hierarchicus*, English transl., London, 1972.
338. J.C. Heesterman, *The Inner Conflict of Tradition: Essays in Indian Ritual, Kingship and Society*, Delhi, 1985.
339. Bernard S. Cohn, *An Anthropologist among the Historians, and Other Essays*, Delhi, 1987.

D. LOCAL HISTORY, DISTRICT GAZETTEERS

340. J. Taylor, 'An Account of the District of Dacca, dated 1800', ed. Abdul Karim, *Jour. As. Soc. Pak.*, VIII(2) (1962), 290-341.

341. (S.626) Muftī G̲h̲ulām Ḥaẓarat, *Kawāi'if-i Ẓila'-i Gorakhpūr*, 1810, I.O.4540[*]; Aligarh, Subhanullah 954/12 ('Aligarh MS')[*]. The Aligarh MS contains some passages not found in I.O.4540.

342. (S.927) Girdhārī, *Intiẓām-i Rāj-i A'ẓamgaṛh*, early 19th century, Edinburgh 237.

343. Francis Buchanan, ed. Montgomery Martin, *The History, Antiquities, Topography, and Statistics of Eastern India, comprising the Districts of Behar, Shahabad, Bhagalpur, Goruckpoor, Dinajepoor, Puraniya, Rungpoor and Assam* (1801-12), 3 vols., London, 1838. This is an excellent abridgement, of Buchanan's original reports, though, by some slip, Buchanan's authorship is but poorly acknowledged. Some of Buchanan's original reports have been published separately: (1) *An Account of the District of Purnea in 1809-10*, Patna, 1928; (2) *An Account of the District of Bhagalpur in 1810-11*, Patna, 1939; and (3) *An Account of the Districts of Bihar and Patna in 1811-12*, Patna, n.d.

344. Donald Butter, *Outlines of the Topography and Statistics of the Southern Districts of Ou'dh*, Calcutta, 1839.

345. C.W.M. Hearn, *Statistical Report of the Colaba Agency*, Bombay, 1854.

346. R. Hughes Thomas, ed., *Memoirs on Shikarpoor, the Syuds of Roree & Buckur*, Selections from the Records of the Bombay Government, No.XVII, New Series, Bombay, 1855; reprinted as *Memoirs on Sind*, 2 vols., Delhi, n.d.[*]

347. Charles Elliott, *Chronicles of Oonao*, Allahabad, 1862.

348. W.C. Benett, *A Report on the Family History of the Chief Clans of Roy Bareilly District*, Lucknow, 1870.

349. (S.928) Saiyid Amīr 'Alī Riẓawī, *Sarguzasht-i Rāja-hā-i A'ẓamgaṛh*, 1872. Edinburgh 238.

350. Muḥammad Mak̲h̲dūm T̲h̲ānawī, *Arzang-i Tijāra* [written 1873-74], litho., n.d.

351. Kuar Lachman Singh, *Memoir of Zila Bulandshahar*, Allahabad, 1874.

352. Edwin T. Atkinson, et al, eds., *Descriptive and Historical Account of the North-western Provinces of India*, series of vols. [one for each Division], Allahabad, 1875-84.

353. H. Beveridge, *The District of Bakarganj [Bengal]: Its History and Statistics*, London, 1876.

354. W.W. Hunter, *A Statistical Account of Bengal*, 20 vols. [one for each district], London, 1875-77.

355. H.D. Watson, *Gazetteer of the Hazara District, 1907*, London, 1908.

356. *District Gazetteers*, issued at various times (in different series) by Provincial Governments. I have chiefly consulted the volumes of: (1) *Gazetteers of the Bombay Presidency*, ed. James A. Campbell and others, Bombay, 1874-84; (2) *District Gazetteers of the United Provinces of Agra and Oudh*, most vols. written by H.R. Nevill, a few by D.L. Drake-Brockman, Allahabad, 1909-30; and (3) *Punjab District Gazetteers*, by various writers, 1st/2nd /3rd edns., the substantive portions of these Gazetteers (Pakistan districts only), reprinted (offset), 2 vols., Lahore, 1976, 1977.

357. Durgā Prasād, *Tārīk̲h̲-i Sandīla* (Urdu), Lucknow, 1916.

358. Qāẓī Raḥmān Bak̲h̲sh, *Ifāẓāt-i Ḥamīd* (Urdu), Delhi, 1346/1927-28, local history of Nagaur. Contains copies of interesting Mughal-period docs.

359. Maḥmūd Aḥmad 'Abbāsī, *Tārīkh-i Amroha* (Urdu), 2 vols., Delhi, 1930, 1932.
360. Maḥmūd "Ḥamd" Bilgrāmī and Sharīfu-l Ḥasan Bilgrāmī, *Tārīkh-i Khiṭṭa-i Pāk-i Bilgrām* (Urdu), Aligarh, 1960. Contains texts of a number of Mughal-period documents.

E. MAPS

361. James Rennell, *A Bengal Atlas, Containing Maps of the Theatre of War & Commerce on that Side of Hindostan*, [London], 1781.
362. James Rennell, *Memoir of a Map of Hindoostan or the Mogul Empire*, London, 1792.
363. Irfan Habib, *An Atlas of the Mughal Empire: Political and Economic Maps*, Delhi, 1982.

F. TRAVEL

364. Francis Buchanan, *A Journey from Madras through the Countries of Mysore, Canara, and Malabar, etc.* [1800-01], 3 vols., London, 1807.
365. Mountstuart Elphinstone, *An Account of the Kingdom of Caubul and its Dependencies in Persia, Tartary and India* [based on information collected during his mission to Peshawar, 1808-9], 'new and revised' edn., 2 vols., London, 1839.
366. William Moorcroft and George Trebeck, *Travels in the Himalayan Provinces of Hindustan and the Panjab; in Ladakh and Kashmir; in Peshawar, Kabul, Kunduz and Bokhara, ... from 1819 to 1825*, ed. H.H. Wilson, 2 vols., London, 1837; offset reprint, New Delhi, 1971.
367. Alexander Burnes, *Travels into Bokhara, Together with a Narrative of a Voyage on the Indus* [1831-33], 3 vols., London, 1834; offset reprint, with introd. by James Lunt, Karachi, 1973.
368. Baron Charles Hugel, *Travels in Kashmir and the Panjab* [1835-36], transl. (from German) T.B. Jervis, London, 1845; offset reprint, Jammu, 1972 (lacks map).
369. G.R. Elsmie, *Thirty-five Years in the Punjab*, 1858-93, Edinburgh, 1908.

G. MUGHAL INDIA

1. Commentaries on Sources, Calendars

370. Najaf 'Alī Khān, *Sharḥ-i Ā'īn-i Akbarī*, 1851. Or. 1667.
371. H.M. Elliot & John Dowson, *History of India as Told by Its own Historians*, 8 vols., London, 1867-77.
372. C. Wessels, *The Early Jesuit Travellers in Central Asia, 1603-1721*, The Hague, 1924.
373. S. Commissariat, *Mandelslo's Travels in Western India (A.D. 1638-9)*, London, 1931.
374. S.H. Hodivala, *Studies in Indo-Muslim History: A Critical Commentary on Elliot and Dowson's History of India as Told by Its own Historians* (Vol.I), Bombay, 1939; Supplement (=Vol.II), Bombay, 1957.
375. K.K. Datta, ed., *Some Firmāns, Sanads and Parwānas (1578-1802 A.D.)*, Patna, 1962. This is a calendar, pub. by Bihar State Central Record Office, Patna, of docs. preserved in various government offices in Bihar. These are classified in two series: I: 'Firmans', pp.1-20, and II: 'Sanads, Parwānas, etc.', pp.21-129. All my references are confined to docs. in Series II.

376. Momin Muhiuddin, *The Chancellory and Persian Epistolography under the Mughals*, Calcutta, 1971.
376a. S.A.I. Tirmizi, *Mughal Documents (1526-1627)* [a calendar], New Delhi, 1989.

2. Agrarian History

377. W.H. Moreland, *The Agrarian System of Moslem India*, Cambridge, 1929.
378. S. Nurul Hasan, *Thoughts on Agrarian Relations in Mughal India*, New Delhi, 1973.
379. Satya Prakash Gupta, *The Agrarian System of Eastern Rajasthan (c.1650-1750)*, Delhi, 1986.
380. David Ludden, *Peasant History in South India*, Princeton, N.J., 1985/reprint, Delhi, 1989.
381. Dirk H. Kolff, *Naukar, Rajput and Sepoy: The Ethnohistory of the Military Labour Market in Hindustan, 1450-1850*, Cambridge, 1990.
382. Hiroshi Fukazawa, *The Medieval Deccan: Peasants, Social Systems and States, Sixteenth to Eighteenth Centuries*, Delhi, 1991.
383. A.R. Kulkarni, *Medieval Maharashtra*, New Delhi, 1996.
384. Vijay Kumar Thakur and Ashok Ounshuman, eds., *Peasants in Indian History: Theoretical Issues and Structural Enquiries*, Patna, 1996.

3. Economic History

385. Edward Thomas, *Revenue Resources of the Mughal Empire in India, from A.D.1593 to 1707*, London, 1871.
386. Edward Thomas, *The Chronicles of the Pathan Kings of Dehli*, London, 1871. [The pioneering work on pre-Mughal numismatic history.]
387. H. Terpstra, *De Opkomst der Westerwatieren van de Oost-Indische Compagnie (Suratte, Arabie, Perzie)*, S'Gravenhage (The Hague), 1918.
388. W.H. Moreland, *India at the Death of Akbar*, London, 1920.
389. W.H. Moreland, *From Akbar to Aurangzeb*, London, 1923.
390. S.H. Hodivala, *Historical Studies in Mughal Numismatics*, Calcutta, 1923*; reprint, Bombay, 1976.
391. Bal Krishna, *Commerical Relations between India and England (1601 to 1757)*, London, 1924.
392. Brij Narain, *Indian Economic Life, Past and Present*, Lahore, 1929.
393. Radhakamal Mukerjee, *The Economic History of India, 1600-1800*, published in *JUPHS*, XIV (1934); separately printed, Allahabad, 1967.
394. K.M. Ashraf, *Life and Conditions of the People of Hindustan* [under the Sultans before Akbar], 2nd edition, Delhi, 1959.
394a. H. Nelson Wright, *The Coinage and Metrology of the Sulṭāns of Dehli*, London, 1936; offset reprint, Delhi, 1974.
395. Sir Charles Fawcett, *The English Factories in India: New Series*, 3 vols., Oxford, 1936, 1952, 1954.
396. Kristof Glamann, *Dutch Asiatic Trade, 1620-1740*, Copenhagen/the Hague, 1958.
397. Tapan Raychaudhuri, *Jan Company in Coromandel, 1605-1690*, S'Gravenhage, 1962.
398. V.I. Pavlov, *The Indian Capitalist Class: A Historical Study*, English transl., Delhi, 1964.
399. K.N. Chaudhuri, *The East India Company: The Study of an Early Joint-stock*

Company, 1600-1640, London, 1965.

400. Susil Chaudhuri [Sushil Chaudhury], *Trade and Commerical Organisation in Bengal, 1650-1720*, Calcutta, 1975.
401. K.N. Chaudhuri, *The Trading World of Asia, and the English East India Company, 1660-1760*, Cambridge, 1978.
402. V.I. Pavlov, *Historical Premises for India's Transition to Capitalism, late 18th to mid-19th Century*, Moscow, 1979.
403. Tapan Raychaudhuri and Irfan Habib, eds., *The Cambridge Economic History of India, I: c.1200-c.1750*, Cambridge, 1982.
404. H.W. van Santen, *De Verenigde Oost-Indische Compagnie in Gujarat en Hindostan, 1620-1660*, Ph.D. thesis, Leiden University, 1982. I owe access to this work through the courtesy of Dr. Ishrat Alam.
405. Sinnappah Arasaratnam, *Merchants, Companies and Commerce on the Coromandel Coast, 1650-1740*, Delhi, 1986.
406. J.F. Richards, ed., *The Imperial Monetary System of Mughal India*, Delhi, 1987.
407. Shireen Moosvi, *The Economy of the Mughal Empire, c.1595: A Statistical Study*, Delhi, 1987.
408. Om Prakash, *The Dutch East India Company and the Economy of Bengal, 1630-1720*, Delhi, 1988.
409. Sanjay Subrahmanyam, ed., *Money and the Market in India, 1100-1700*, Delhi, 1994.
410. Irfan Habib, *Essays in Indian History: Towards a Marxist Perception*, New Delhi, 1995.

410a. Shireen Moosvi, *People, Taxation and Trade in Mughal India*, New Delhi, 2008.

4. Administrative History

411. W. Irvine, *The Army of the Indian Moghuls: Its Organisation and Administration*, London, 1903.
412. J. Sarkar, *Mughal Administration*, Calcutta, 1920.
413. R.P. Tripathi, *Some Aspects of Muslim Administration*, Allahabad, 1936*; reprinted, Allahabad, 1956.
414. Ibn Hasan, *The Central Structure of the Mughal Empire and its Practical Working up to the Year 1657*, London, 1936; offset reprint, New Delhi, 1970.
415. P. Saran, *The Provincial Government of the Mughals (1526-1658)*, Allahabad, 1941.
416. I.H. Qureshi, *The Administration of the Sultanate of Dehli*, 2nd edition (revised), Lahore, 1944.
417. Abdul Aziz, *The Mansabdari System and the Mughal Army*, Lahore, 1945.
418. S.N. Sen, *The Military System of the Marathas*, Bombay, 1958.

418a. M. Athar Ali, *The Mughal Nobility under Aurangzeb*, Bombay, 1966; 2nd edn., offset reprint with new introd., Delhi, 1997.

419. Ishtiaq Husain Qureshi, *The Administration of the Mughal Empire*, Karachi, 1966.
420. J.F. Richards, *Mughal Administration in Golconda*, Oxford, 1975.
421. G.D. Sharma, *Rajput Polity: A Study of Politics and Administration of the Sate of Mārwār, 1638-1749*, New Delhi, 1977.
422. Ahsan Raza Khan, *Chieftains in the Mughal Empire During the Reign of Akbar*, Simla, 1977.
423. Rafat M. Bilgrami, *Religious and Quasi-Religious Departments of the Mughal*

Period, 1556-1707, New Delhi, 1984.

424. M. Athar Ali, *The Apparatus of Empire: Awards of Ranks, Offices and Titles to the Mughal Nobility (1574-1658)*, Delhi, 1985.

424a. Muzaffar Alam and Sanjay Subrahmanyam (eds.), *The Mughal State, 1526-1750*, Delhi, 1998.

5. Eighteenth Century

425. W. Francklin, *The History of the Reign of Shah-Aulum, the Present Emperor of Hindostan*, London, 1798.

426. (S.938) Saiyid Ghulām 'Alī Naqavī, *'Imādu-s Sa'ādat*, completed in 1808. Litho. Nawal Kishor, Lucknow, 1897.

427. Satish Chandra, *Parties and Politics at the Mughal Court, 1707-40*, Aligarh, 1959.

428. Noman Aḥmad Siddiqi, *Land Revenue Administration under the Mughals (1700-1750)*, Bombay, 1970.

429. Indu Banga, *Agrarian System of the Sikhs, Late Eighteenth Century and Early Nineteenth Century*, New Delhi, 1978.

430. Ashin Das Gupta, *Indian Merchants and the Decline of Surat, c.1700-1750*, Wiesbaden, 1979.

431. C.A. Bayly, *Rulers, Townsmen and Bazars: North Indian Society in the Age of Expansion, 1770-1870*, Cambridge, 1983.

432. Muzaffar Alam, *The Crisis of Empire in Mughal North India: Awadh and the Punjab, 1707-48*, Delhi, 1986.

433. André Wink, *Land and Sovereignty in India: Agrarian Society and Politics under the Eighteenth-century Maratha Svarājya*, Cambridge, 1986.

434. B.L. Gupta, *Trade and Commerce in Rajasthan During the 18th Century*, Jaipur, 1987.

435. Girish Chandra Dwivedi, *The Jats: Their Role in the Mughal Empire*, New Delhi, 1989.

436. Dilbagh Singh, *The State, Landlords and Peasants: Rajasthan in the 18th Century*, New Delhi, 1990.

437. Iqbal Husain, *The Ruhela Chieftaincies, the Rise and Fall of Ruhela Power in India in the Eigteenth Century*, Delhi, 1994.

438. Sushil Chaudhury, *From Prosperity to Decline – Eighteenth-Century Bengal*, New Delhi, 1995.

438a. R.P. Rana, *Rebels to Rulers, The Rise of Jat Power in Medieval India, c.* 1665-1735, New Delhi, 2006.

6. Regional History

439. (S.963) Ghulām Ḥusain Salīm Zaidpūrī, *Riyāẓu-s Salāṭīn*, a history of Bengal, written 1786-88, ed. Abdul Hak Abid, Bib., Ind., Calcutta, 1890.

440. James Tod, *Annals and Antiquities of Rajasthan*, London, 1829; Popular edn., 2 vols., London, 1914*.

441. (Sir) John Malcolm, *A Memoir of Central India, including Malwa*, 2 vols., 2nd. edn., London, 1824*; 3rd ed., London, 1832.

442. James Grant Duff, *History of the Maharattas*, 3 vols., London, 1826; London, 1863 (reprint, Delhi, 1990)*.

443. Anonymous, *Jodhpur Rājya kī khyāt*, [*c.*1840], ed. Raghubir Singh and Manohar Singh Ranawat, New Delhi, 1988.

444. Henry T. Prinsep, *History of the Punjab*, London, 1846.

445. M.R. Haig, *Indus Delta Country: A Memoir, Chiefly on its Ancient Geography, History and Topography*, London, 1887.
446. Pīr Ghulām Ḥasan Khoyhāmī, *Tārīkh-i Ḥasan* [in Persian, completed, 1885], ed. Sahibzada Hasan Shah, 2 vols., Srinagar, 1954. Vols. III and IV do not appear to have been published.
447. Walter R. Lawrence, *Valley of Kashmīr*, Oxford, 1895.
448. W.Crooke, *The North-Western Provinces of India: their History, Ethnology and Administration*, London, 1897.
449. Kavirāj Shyāmaldās, *Vīr Vinod*, 4 vols., Udaipur, n.d. [*c.*1900?]. This great Hindi history of Mewar is based largely on Udaipur records, but also uses other Persian and Rajasthani sources. A particular merit of the work is that it gives full-length translations, and sometimes the texts as well, of documents from Udaipur archives that have not been generally accessible.
450. J.N. Das Gupta, *Bengal in the Sixteenth Century A.D.*, Calcutta, 1914.
451. M.S. Commissariat, *Studies in the History of Gujarat*, Bombay, 1935; photo reprint, Ahmedabad, 1987.
452. E.M.S. Namboodiripad, *The National Question in Kerala*, Bombay, 1952.
453. T. Raychaudhuri, *Bengal under Akbar and Jahāngīr*, Calcutta, 1953*; 2nd impression with introductory note, Delhi, 1969.
454. Mohibbul Hasan, *Kashmīr under the Sultans*, Calcutta, 1959.
455. Sukumar Sen, *History of Bengali Literature*, New Delhi, 1960.
456. Richard Eaton, *Rise of Islām and the Bengal Frontier*, Delhi, 1994.
457. Aniruddha Ray, *Adventurers, Land-owners and Rebels: Bengal, c.1575-c.1715*, New Delhi, 1998.

7. Archaeological Remains, Including Gardens

458. Major W.E. Baker, *Memoranda on the Western Jumna Canals in the North-western Provinces of the Bengal Presidency*, London, 1849.
459. Alexander Cunningham, *Archaeological Survey of India: Reports*, 1862-84, 24 vols. (last vol. containing index). Offset reprint, Varanasi, 1966-69.
460. James Burgess, *Report on the Antiquities of Kathiawar and Kachh*, 1874-75; reprint, Varanasi, 1971*.
461. A. Fuhrer, *The Monumental Antiquities and Inscriptions in the North-western Provinces and Oudh*, Allahabad, 1891.
462. C.M. Villiers Stuart, *Gardens of the Great Mughals*, London, 1913.
463. G. Sanderson, *A Guide to the Buildings and Gardens: Delhi*, 4th edn., Delhi, 1936-37.
464. Thorkild Schioler, *Roman and Islamic Water-lifting Wheels*, Odense, 1973.
465. Jean Deloche, *Ancient Bridges of India*, New Delhi, 1982.
466. James L. Wescoat and Joachim Wolschke-Bulmahn, eds., *Mughal Gardens: Sources, Places, Representations and Prospects*, Washington, 1996.

8. General

467. Durgā Prasād Sandīlī, *Gulistān-i Hind* (in Persian), 4 vols., Sandila, 1897. Vol.II & Vol.II Suppl. deal with Mughal India. A merit of this work is the extracts it gives from little-known historical works of the Mughal period.
468. Jadunath Sarkar, *A History of Aurangzib*, 5 vols., first edn., Calcutta, 1912-24.
469. Jadunath Sarkar, *Shivājī and his Times*, Calcutta, 1919; 5th edn. (revised and enlarged), Calcutta, 1952*.
470. P. Saran, *Studies in Medieval History*, Delhi, n.d. [1952?].

471. Sri Ram Sharma, *Studies in Medieval Indian History*, Sholapur, 1956.
472. Sri Ram Sharma, *The Religious Policy of the Mughal Emperors*, 3rd edn. (revised and enlarged), Bombay, 1972.
473. A.L. Srivastava, *Akbar the Great*, 3 vols., Agra, 1973.
474. Som Prakash Verma, *Art and Material Culture in the Paintings of Akbar's Court*, New Delhi, 1978.
474a. John F. Richards, *The Mughal Empire* (Vol.1.5 of *The New Cambridge History of India*), Cambridge/New Delhi, 1993.
475. Irfan Habib, ed., *Akbar and his India*, Delhi, 1997.
475a. Iqtidar Alam Khan, *Gunpowder and Firearms: Warfare in Medieval India*, New Delhi, 2004.
475b. M. Athar Ali, *Mughal India: Studies in Polity, Ideas, Society and Culture*, New Delhi, 2006.
475c. Osama Kondo, *The Early Modern Monarchism in Mughal India*, Kyoto, 2012.

H. OTHER BOOKS ON INDIAN HISTORY

476. Lt. Col. Mark Wilks, *Historical Sketches of South India*, 2 vols., London, 1810, 1817; ed. Murray Hammick, 2 vols., Mysore, 1930*.
477. James Mill, *The History of British India*, London, 1817; ed. Horace Hayman Wilson, 8 vols., London, 1840*.
478. Karl Marx and Frederick Engels, *On Colonialism*, 4th edn., Moscow, 1968 (several reprints). This collection includes Marx's articles printed in the *New York Daily Tribune*, 1853-58.
479. Romesh Dutt, *The Economic History of India under Early British Rule*, London, 1901; 6th ed., London, n.d.*
480. Romesh Dutt, *The Economic History of India in the Victorian Age*, London, 1903; 7th ed., London, 1950*.
481. Vincent A. Smith, *Oxford History of India*, Oxford, 1923.
482. D.R. Gadgil, *The Industrial Evolution of India in Recent Times*, 4th ed., London, 1942.
483. Jawaharlal Nehru, *The Discovery of India*, London, 1946; 4th ed., London, 1956*.
484. Mohammad Habib, Introduction to reprint of Elliot and Dowson, *History of India as Told by Its own Historians*, II (Aligarh, 1952), 1-102.
485. L. Natarajan, *Peasant Uprisings in India (1850-1900)*, Bombay, 1953.
486. Damodar Dharmanand Kosambi, *An Introduction to the Study of Indian History*, Bombay, 1956.
487. Ram Sharan Sharma, *Aspects of Political Ideas and Institutions in Ancient India*, Delhi, 1959.
488. P.K. Gode, *Studies in Indian Cultural History*, 3 vols.: Vol.I, Hoshiarpur, 1961; Vols.II and III, Poona, 1960, 1969.
489. Dharma Kumar and Meghnad Desai, eds., *The Cambridge Economic History of India*, II: *c.1757-c.1970*, Cambridge, 1983.
490. Michelle B. McAlpin, *Subject to Famine*, Princeton, 1983.
491. Prabhat Kumar Shukla, *Indigo and the Raj: Peasant Protests in Bihar, 1780-1917*, Delhi, 1993.

I. HISTORY OF OTHER COUNTRIES

492. V. Barthold, *Iran*, transl. G.K. Nariman, in S.H. Jhabvala, ed., *Posthumous Works of G.K. Nariman*, Bombay, 1935.
493. Mao Zedong, 'The Chinese Revolution and the Chinese Communist Party',

written, 1939, transl. in *Selected Works of Mao Tse-tung*, II, Peking, 1967, 305-334.
494. E. Lipson, *Economic History of England*, II, London, 1947.
495. F. Lokkegaard, *Islamic Taxation in the Classic Period*, Copenhagen, 1950.
496. A.K.S. Lambton, *Landlord and Peasant in Persia*, London, 1953.
497. Jaquetta Hawkes, *Prehistory* (Vol.I of UNESCO *History of Mankind*), London, 1965.
498. E.E. Rich and C.H. Wilson, eds., *Cambridge Economic History of Europe*, IV, Cambridge, 1967.
499. Marshall G.S. Hodgson, *The Venture of Islām*, III ('The Gunpowder Empires and Modern Times'), Chicago, 1974.
500. Immanuel Wallerstein, *The Modern World System: Capitalist Agriculture and the European World Economy*, New York, 1974.
501. Fernand Braudel, *The Mediterranean and the Mediterranean World in the Age of Philip II*, English transl., 2 vols., London, 1975.
502. Carlo M. Cipolla, *Before the Industrial Revolution: European Society and Economy, 1000-1700*, 2nd edn., London, 1981.
503. Pierre Vilar, *History of Gold and Money, 1450-1920*, English transl., London, 1984.
504. Witold Kula, *Measures and Men*, transl. R. Szreter, Princeton, 1986.
505. Dieter Kuhn, *Textile Chronology: Spinning and Reeling*, Vol.5(9) of Joseph Needham, *Science and Civilization in China*, Cambridge, 1988.
506. James D. Tracy, ed., *The Rise of Merchant Empires: Long-distance Trade in the Early Modern World, 1350-1750*, Cambridge, 1990.
507. S.J. De Laet, ed., *Prehistory and the Beginnings of Civilization* (Vol.I of UNESCO *History of Humanity*), Paris/London, 1994.

J. ECONOMIC AND SOCIAL THEORY

508. J.R. McCulloch, ed., *Early English Tracts on Commerce* [1621-1701], London, 1856 (reprint, Cambridge, 1952*).
509. G.W. Friedrich Hegel, *The Philosophy of History* (1830), transl. J. Sibree, New York, 1956.
510. Karl Marx, *Capital*, I, transl. Samuel Moore and Edward Aveling, ed. Frederick Engels, London, 1887 (page-to-page reprint with Supplement, ed. Dona Torr, London, 1938).
511. Karl Marx and Frederick Engels, *Collected Works*, XXIV (1874-83), Moscow, 1989.
512. Rosa Luxemburg, *The Accumulation of Capital* [1912], English transl., London, 1951.
513. Utsa Patnaik, *The Long Transition: Essays on Political Economy*, New Delhi, 1999.

K. WORKS OF REFERENCE, INCLUDING DICTIONARIES AND CATALOGUES

Works of this nature already listed in this Bibliography under other headings (eg. nos.323 and 330) are omitted here.

514. Muḥammad G͟hiyāṣuddīn of Rampur, *G͟hiyāṣu-l Lug͟hāt*, 1826-27, printed on margins of Sirājī Press edn. of Tek Chand "Bahār", *Bahār-i 'Ajam*, Delhi, 1282/1865-66.

515. W.H. Morley, *Descriptive Catalogue of the Historical Manuscripts Preserved in the Library of the Royal Asiatic Society of Great Britain and Ireland*, London, 1854.
516. A. James Prinsep, *Useful Tables Illustrative of the Coins, Weights and Measures of British India, Together with Chronological Tables and Genealogical Lists,* ed. with notes and additional matter by Edward Thomas, London, 1858.
517. S.W. Fallon, *New Hindustani Dictionary, with Illustrations from Hindustani Literature and Folklore*, Banaras, 1879 /reprint, Lucknow, 1986.
518. Charles Rieu, *Catalogue of the Persian Manuscripts in the British Museum*, 3 vols., London, 1879, 1881, 1883.
519. John T. Platts, *A Dictionary of Urdu, Classical Hindi, and English*, London, 1884.
520. Hermann Ethé, *Catalogue of the Persian, Turkish, Hindustani and Pushtu Manuscripts in the Bodleian Library* [*Oxford*], 3 vols., Oxford, 1889, 1930, 1954. [Vol. I partly by Ed. Sachau, and Vol.III by A.F.L. Beeston].
521. James A.H. Murray, *et. al.*, eds., *The Oxford English Dictionary*, 125 fasciculi, Oxford, 1884-1928; 2nd edn., 20 vols. Oxford, 1933; compact ed. (micrographic reprod. of whole 2nd edn. and Supplement), 2 vols., Oxford, 1971*.
522. O. Codrington, *Catalogue of Arabic, Persian, Hindustani and Turkish MSS in the Library of the Royal Asiatic Society*, London, 1892.
523. F. Steingass, *A Comprehensive Persian-English Dictionary*, London, 1892.
523a. Stanley Lane-Poole, *Coins of the Mughal Emperors of Hindustan in the British Museum, London,* London, 1892.
524. Bhai Maya Singh, *Punjabi Dictionary*, Lahore, 1895 (photo-reprint, Delhi, 1988, with author's name as Mayya Singh).
525. E.G. Browne, (1) *A Catalogue of the Persian Manuscripts in the Library of the University of Cambridge*, Cambridge, 1896. (2) *Supplementary Handlist of the Muhammadan Manuscripts in the Libraries of the University and Colleges of Cambridge*, Cambridge, 1922.
526. Henry Yule and A.C. Burnell, *Hobson-Jobson, a Glossary of Colloquial Anglo-Indian Words and Phrases*, new edn., ed. William Crooke, London, 1903.
527. Hermann Ethé, *Catalogue of the Persian Manuscripts in the Library of the India Office*, 2 vols., Oxford, 1903, 1937 [Vol.II revised and completed by Edward Edwardes.]
528. G.A. Grierson, ed., *Linguistic Survey of India*, 11 vols., orig. pub. 1903-28; reprint, Delhi, 1990*.
529. E. Blochet, *Catelogue de Manuscrits persans de la Bibliotheque Nationale*, Paris, 1905-.
530. 'Abdu-l Ḥaiy, *Nuzhatu-l Khawāṭir* [Arabic], 8 vols., 1st ed., 1907, etc.; 2nd edn., Hyderabad-Deccan, 1962-79*. A biographical dictionary of Indian Islamic scholars.
530a. H. Nelson Wright, *Catalogue of the Coins in the Indian Museum, Calcutta, including the Cabinet of the Asiatic Society of Bengal,* Vol.II (The Sultans of Dehli, etc.), Oxford, 1907; Vol.III (Mughal Emperors of India), Oxford, 1908.
531. *The Imperial Gazetteer of India*, new (2nd.) edn., 26 vols., Oxford, 1908-9.
532. C.A. Storey, *Persian Literature: A Bio-bibliographical Survey*, London, 1927-77. Vol. I (Quranic Literature; History and Biography) Part I (mainly History) issued in four fasciculi, London, 1927-39; and Part II (Biography), London, 1953. Vol. II, Part I (Mathematics, Astronomy, Geography), London, 1958. Part II (Medicine) London, 1971; Part III (Encyclopaedias, etc.), Leiden, 1977. Storey died in 1967, but the project is being continued by the Royal

Asiatic Society, London. I regret I have not been able to use any parts so far published of Vols.III and V.

533. H.C. Hony, *Turkish-English Dictionary*, Oxford, 1947.

534. H.G. Cattenoz, *Tables de Concordance des Eres Chrétienne et Hégirienne*, 2nd edn., Rabat, 1954. All conversions of Hijri dates into Christian-era dates in my book are based on this very detailed concordance.

535. D.N. Marshall, *Mughals in India: A Bibliographical Survey*, Vol.I (Manuscripts), Bombay, 1967; Supplement to Vol.I, New Delhi, 1996.

536. Sir Gerard Clauson, *An Etymological Dictionary of Pre-Thirteenth-Century Turkish*, Oxford, 1972. Despite the restrictive title, this richly documented dictionary gives citations and senses for each word included, down to modern times.

537. Mohd. Ziauddin Ahmed "Shakeb", ed., *Mughal Archives: A Descriptive Catalogue of the Documents pertaining to the reign of Shāh Jahān (1628-1658)*, I (Durbar papers and a miscellany of 'singular' documents), State Archives (A.P.), Hyderabad, 1977.

538. Som Prakash Verma, *Mughal Painters and their Work: A Biographical Survey and Comprehensive Catalogue*, Delhi, 1994.

L. PERIODICAL LITERATURE

The following is a list of journals, alphabetically arranged, containing articles cited in this book. Articles giving texts or translations of sources, or commentaries thereon, and already listed in Section 1 of this Bibliography, are not listed here. Also omitted are many papers originally published in journals, but later incorporated into books or included in volumes of collectanea (already listed in this Bibliography), in case they are cited in the footnotes from the latter volumes alone.

539. *Aligarh Journal of Oriental Studies*, Aligarh.
II(1-2) (1985), 197-222: Irfan Habib, 'Medieval Technology: Exchanges between India and the Islamic World.'

540. *Bulletin of the School of Oriental and African Studies*, London.
IX (1937-39), 927-60: V. Minorsky, 'A Soyūrghāl of Qāsim b. Jahāngīr Āq-Qoyunlū.'

541. *Comparative Studies in Society and History*, the Hague.
VI(4) (1964), 393-419: Irfan Habib, 'Usury in Medieval India.'

542. *Citi-Vithika*, Allahabad.
I(i), (1995-96), 64-77: Iqtidar Alam Khān, 'Socio-Political Implications of the dissemination of Handgun in Mughal India.'

543. *Contributions to Indian Economic History*, ed. T. Raychaudhuri, Calcutta.
I, 1960, 1-20: Irfan Habib, 'Banking in Mughal India'.

544. *Indian Antiquary*.
II, 1873, 33-37: F.N. Wright, 'The Chandel Thakurs.'
IV, 1875, 71-77, 110-14, 232-36, 265-69: Anonymous, 'The *Dvaiāsharaya*' [a summary of historical work in Sanskrit, completed, 1255].

545. *Indian Culture* Calcutta.
III(3), (1937), 543-5: Sri Ram Sharma, 'Nasaq as a System of Land Revenue Assessment in Muhgal Times.'
XIII(1), (1946), 25-34: P.K. Gode, 'History of the Art of Grafting Plants.'

546. *Indian Economic and Social History Review*, Delhi.
I (1) (1963), 1-23: B.R. Grover, 'Nature of Land Rights in Mughal India.'
I(3) (1964), 64-72: Irfan Habib, 'Evidence for Sixteenth-Century Agrarian Conditions in the Gurū Granth Sāhib.'
Ibid., I(3), (1964), 73-83: Noman Ahmad Siddiqi, 'The Classification of Villages under the Mughals.'
IV(3) (1967), 205-32: Irfan Habib, 'Aspects of Agrarian Relations and Economy in a Region of Uttar Pradesh during the 16th Century.'
XVII(i), (1980) 1-34: Irfan Habib, 'The Technology and Economy of Mughal India.'
XVIII(3-4) (1981), 287-326: R.P. Rana, 'Agrarian Revolts in Northern India during the Late 17th and Early 18th Century.'

547. *Indian Historical Review*, Delhi.
I(1) (1974), 51-64: Satish Chandra, 'Some Aspects of Indian Village Society in Northern India during the 18th Century – the Position and Role of *Khud-kasht* and *Pahi-kasht*.'
II(2) (1976), 299-311: Dilbagh Singh, 'Caste and the Structure of Village Society in Eastern Rajasthan during the Eigtheenth Century.'
IV(2) (1978), 336-53: Zahoor Ali Khān, 'Railways and the Creation of National Market in Foodgrains: A Study of Regional Price-levels.'
V(1-2) (1978-79), 152-74: Irfan Habib, 'Technology and Barriers to Social [*rect.* Technological] Change in Mughal India.'
VI(1-2) (1979-80), 141-53: B.L. Bhadani, 'The "Allodial Proprietors" (?) – the Bhumias of Mārwār.'
XIII (1-2) (1986-87), 1-36: Vivekanand Jha, 'Caṇḍāla and the Origin of Untouchability.'
XIV(1-2) (1987-88), 111-37: Iqtidar Alam Khan, 'The Karwansarays of Mughal India: A Study of Surviving Structures.'

548. *Indian Journal of Economics*, Allahabad.
I, (1916), 44-53: W.H. Moreland, 'The *Ā'īn-i Akbarī* – A Possible Base-line for the Economic History of Modern India.'

549. *Islamic Culure*, Hyderabad.
1938, 61-75: M. Sadiq Khan, 'A Study in Mughal Land Revenue System.'
1944, 349-63: W.C. Smith, 'The Mughal Empire and the Middle Classes.'
1946, 21-40: W.C. Smith, 'Lower Class Uprisings in the Mughal Empire.'
1985, 202-28: Irfan Habib, '*Manṣab* Salary Scales under Jahāngīr and Shāhjahān'.

550. *Journal of the Bombay Branch of the Royal Asiatic Society*, Bombay.
XXV (1918): W. Erskine, 'Journey in Gujarat, 1822-23.'

551. *Journal of the Economic and Social History of the Orient*, Leiden.
XII (1969), 322-40: Satish Chandra, 'Jizyah and the State in India during the 17th Century.'
XXX(1987), 47-94: Shireen Moosvi, 'The Silver Influx, Money Supply, Prices and Revenue Extraction in Mughal India.'
XXXIX (1996), 298-364: Najaf Haider, 'Precious Metal Flows and Currency Circulation in the Mughal Empire.'

552. *Journal of Indian History*, Allahabad, Madras, Trivandrum.
VIII, i, 1-8: W.H. Moreland, 'Feudalism (?) in the Moslem Kingdom of Delhi.'

553. *Journal of the Islamic Environmental Design*, Rome.
1988, 92-98: Iqtidar Alam Khan, 'Pre-Modern Indigo Vats of Bayana.'

554. *Journal of the Oriental Institute*, Baroda.

XIII (1-2), 20-38: R.N. Mehta, [Survey of Sudarsan Lake, Saurashtra].

555. *Journal of the Pakistan Historical Society*, Karachi.
I(1953), 205-17: I.H. Qureshi, 'Akbar's Revenue Reforms.'

556. *Journal of the (Royal) Asiatic Society of Bengal*, Calcutta.
XLII (1873), 209-310; XLIII (1874), 280-309; and XLIV (1875), 275-306: H. Blochmann, 'Contributions to the Geography and History of Bengal (Muhammadan Period).'
LIII (1884), 162-82: John Beames, 'On the Geography of India in the Reign of Akbar', 2 parts: Awadh and Bihar.
LXI (1892), i, 155-297: H.G. Raverty, 'The Mihran of Sind and its Tributaries: A Geographical and Historical Study.'
NS IX (1913), 436-49: H. Hosten, 'The Twelve Bhuiyas or Landlords of Bengal.'
NS, XII (1916), 29-56: Rai Manmohan Chakravarti Bahadur, 'Notes on the Geography of Orissa in the Sixteenth Century.'
NS, XV (1919), 197-262: C.U. Wills, 'The Territorial System of the Rajput Kingdoms of Chhattisgarh.'

557. *Journal of the Royal Asiatic Society*, London.
1843, 42-53: J.A. Hodgson, 'Memoir on the Length of the Illahee Guz, or Imperial Land Measure of Hindostan.'
1867, 105-31: K. Palmer, 'Catalogue of the Oriental Manuscripts in the Library of King's College, Cambridge.'
1896, 83-136, 743-65: John Beames, 'Notes on Akbar's Ṣūbahs with reference to the *Ā'īn-i Akbarī'*: Bengal and Orissa.
1900, 261-91: B.H. Baden-Powell, 'The Villages of Goa in the Early Sixteenth Century'.
1906, 349-53: H. Beveridge, 'Aurangzeb's Revenues.'
1917, 815-25: W.H. Moreland, 'Prices and Wages under Akbar.'
1918, 1-42: Moreland and A. Yusuf Ali, 'Akbar's Land Revenue System as Described by the *Ā'īn-i Akbarī*.'
1918, 375-85: Moreland, 'The Value of Money at the Court of Akbar.'
1922, 19-35: Moreland, 'The Development of the Land Revenue System of the Mogul Empire.'
1926, 43-56: Moreland, 'Akbar's Land Revenue Arrangements in Bengal.'
1936, 641-65: Moreland, 'Rank (*Manṣab*) in the Mogul State Service.'
1938, 511-21: Moreland, 'The Pargana Headman (Chaudhri) of the Mogul Empire.'
1968, 29-36: Iqtidar Alam Khan, 'The Nobility under Akbar and the Development of his Religious Policy.'
1981, 173-85: Shireen Moosvi, 'The Evolution of the *Manṣab* System under Akbar until 1596-7.'

558. *Journal of the Sind Historical Society*, Karachi.
III (1937), i, 14-31: H.T. Lambrick, 'Early Canal Administration in Sind.'

559. *Journal of the U.P. Historical Society*, Lucknow.
II, i (1922), 1-39: W.H. Moreland, 'The Agricultural Statistics of Akbar's Empire'.
III, i, (1923), 146-61: Moreland, 'Some Side-lights on Life in Agra, 1637-39.'

559a. *Medieval History Journal*, New Delhi.
2.2 (1999), 309-48: Najaf Haider, 'The Quantity Theory of Money and Mughal

Monetary History.'

560. *Medieval India*, Aligarh/Delhi.
I. (*Medieval India-1*) (1992), 49-61: Abha Singh, 'Irrigating Haryana: The Pre-Modern History of the Western Yamuna Canal.'
Ibid., 62-128: Iqtidar Alam Khān, 'The Mughal Assignment System during Akbar's Early Years, 1556-1575.'

561. *Medieval India, a Miscellany*, Aligarh/Bombay.
I (1969), 96-133: M. Athar Ali, 'Provincial Governors under Aurangzeb – an Analysis.'
IV (1977), 168-76: S.P. Gupta, 'Khasra Documents in Rajasthan.'

562. *Medieval India Quarterly,* Aligarh.
I(1) (1950), 49-57: S. Nurul Ḥasan, *'Latai'if-i Quddusi*, A Contemporary Afghan Source for the Study of Afghan-Mughal Conflict.'

563. *Muslim University Journal*, Aligarh.
I, No.(1), 93-118, No.(2), 156-88, No.(3), 401-435, No.(4), 563-95; and II, No.(1), 29-51: Ibadur Rahman Khan, 'Historical Geography of the Panjab and Sind.'

563a. *The Panjab Past and Present,* Patiala.
XVI(1) (1982), 108-25: M.S. Ahluwalia and Subhash Parihar, 'Mughal Sarais in the Punjab and Haryana'.

564. *Proceedings of the Indian Historical Records Commission*,
XII, 1929, 81-87: Y.K. Deshpande, 'Revenue Administration of Berar in the Reign of Aurangzeb (1679 A.D.). '
XXII (1945), 10-11: G.H. Khare, 'A Letter of Assurance of Ali Adil Shāh I - 974 A.H.(1566 A.D.).'
XXVI (1949), ii, 1-7: S. Ḥasan Askari, 'Documents relating to an Old Family of Sufi Saints of Bihar.'
XXVII (1951), ii, 1-7: S.H. Askari, 'Gleanings from Miscelaneous Collection of Village Amathua in Gaya.'
XXXI (1955), ii, 142-47: Qeyamuddin Ahmad, 'Public Opinion as a Factor in the Government Appointments in the Mughal State.'
XXXVI (1961), 55-60: B.R. Grover, 'Raqba-bandi Documents of Akbar's Reign'.

565. *Proceedings of the Indian History Congress*.
21st session, 1958, Trivandrum, 320-24; Irfan Habib, 'The Zamindars in the *Ā'īn*[*-i-Akbarī*].'
24th session, 1961, Delhi, 150-55; B.R. Grover. 'The Position of Desai in the Pargana Administration of Subah Gujarat under the Mughals.'
Ibid., 157-62: Noman Aḥmad Siddiqi, 'Implications of the Month Scales in the Mansabdari System.'
Ibid., 145-49: Iqtidar Husain Siddiqui, 'Iqta System under the Lodis'.
28th session, 1966, Mysore, 245-64: S. Nurul Hasan, K.N. Hasan and S.P. Gupta,'The Pattern of Agricultural Production in the Territories of Amber (c.1650-1750).'
29th session, 1967, Patiala, I(1), 221-42: Irfan Habib, 'The Manṣab System, 1595-1637.'
Ibid., I (2) 350-71: S. Nurul Hasan and Satya Prakash Gupta, 'Prices of Foodgrains in the Territories of Amber (c.1650-1750).'
33rd session, 1972, Muzaffarpur, 290-303: Irfan Habib, 'The System of Bills of Exchange in the Mughal Empire.'
Ibid., 196-203: Satish Chandra and Dilbagh Singh, 'Structure and Stratifica-

tion in Village Society in Eastern Rajasthan.'

48th session, 1987, Goa, 234-50: Tarapada Mukherjee and Irfan Habib, 'Akbar and the Temples of Mathura and its Environs.'

49th session, 1988, Dharwad, 277-86: S.Z.H. Jafri, 'Rural Bureaucracy in Cooch Bihar and Assam under the Mughals: Archival Evidence.'

Ibid., 287-300: Tarapada Mukherjee and Irfan Habib , 'The Mughal Administration and the Temples of Vrindaban during the reigns of Jahāngīr and Shāhjahān'.

50th session, 1989-90, Gorakhpur, 236-55: Tarapada Mukherjee and Irfan Habib, 'Land Rights in the Reign of Akbar: the Evidence of Sale-deeds of Vrindaban and Aritha.'

Ibid., 294-311: B.L.Bhadani, 'The Semi-serfs (Basīs) and their Masters in 17th-Century Mārwār.'

52nd session, 1991-92, New Delhi, 1-42: A.R. Kulkarni, 'The Indian Village with Special Reference to Medieval Deccan (Maratha Country)'.

Ibid., 378-89: Iqtidar A. Khan, 'Nature of Handguns in Mughal India.'

54th session, 1993, Mysore, 246-62: Irfan Habib, 'Agriculture and Agrarian Conditions in South Gujarāt, 1596.'

56th session 1995, Calcutta, 358-78: Irfan Habib: 'The Eighteenth Century in Indian Economic History.'

Ibid., 338-52: S. Bashir Hasan, 'The *Muzaffaris* in Malwa and the shift to Imperial Currency.'

71st session, 2010-11, Malda, 284-99: Irfan Habib, 'From Arith to Radhakund: the History of a Braj Village in Mughal times'.

566. *The Scandinavian Economic History Review*, Stockholm.

I(i), (1953), 41-79: Kristof Glamann, 'The Dutch East India Company's Trade in Japanese Copper, 1645-1735.'

567. *Studies in History*, Delhi.

I(1) (1985), 45-55: Shireen Moosvi, 'Scarcities, Prices and Exploitation: The Agrarian Crisis, 1658-70.'

VIII(1) (1991), 79-105: Sanjay Subrahmanyam, 'Precious Metal Flows and Prices in Western and Southern Asia, 1500-1750.'

568. *Transactions of the Literary Society of Bombay*.

III (London, 1823), 172-264: Thomas Coats, 'Account of the Present State of the Township of Lony [1820].'

Ibid., 331-90: Thomas Marshall, 'A Statistical Account of the Pergunna of Jumboosur.'

Other journals from which articles have been cited in this book include:

569. *Bengal Past and Present*, Calcutta.
570. *Epigraphia Indica*, Calcutta/Delhi.
571. *Epigraphia Indo-Moslemica*, Calcutta/Delhi, now *Epigraphia Indica, Arabic and Persian Supplement*, Delhi.
572. *Journal of the Asiatic Society of Pakistan/Bangladesh*, Dacca/Dhaka.
573. *Journal of the Punjab Historical Society*, Lahore.
574. *Ma'ārif*, Azamgarh.
575. *Oriental College Magazine*, Lahore.
576. *Studies in Islam*, New Delhi.

ABBREVIATIONS

Most of the sources and secondary works used in this book have been cited in the footnotes (and in references in the Bibliography) by various kinds of abbreviations, such as shortened titles, authors' names only, or MS nos. This list is designed to guide the reader to the appropriate entry for each such text or work appearing in the Bibliography, which provides the minimum necessary information for location (in the case of MSS) and publication details (in the case of printed works). For this purpose the entries in the Bibliography have been serially numbered, and these numbers are placed against the respective abbreviations in the following list.

The reader, who wishes to track down a text or work from the reference in a footnote to the right entry in the Bibliography, would find it convenient to use this list, but he may locate his quarry more quickly if he were to proceed according to the following rules: (1) Where the footnote reference consists of italicized words only, bearing the full or shortened title of a work or volume, please look for its alphabetical position in the list, ignoring, however, any initial article (*A*, *An* or *The*) with which the title in the reference might begin, since these are omitted in the following list. (2) Where the reference consists of both the name of the author (or editor) and italicized title (full or shortened) (e.g. 'Buchanan, *Journey from Madras*'), please ignore the name of the author (or editor) and locate the work referred to simply on the basis of the italicized title, as under Rule (1). The names of the authors or editors in certain cases have still been given within square brackets prefacing the titles for convenience; but these square-bracketed names do not affect the alphabetical position of the works in the list. (3) Where our references contain the authors' names only (e.g. 'Badāūnī', 'Saran') or the names of MS collections' (and nos.) only (e.g. 'Add. 27,247', 'Rādhākund', 'Sihunda Docs.'), without any italicized titles, please look directly for the names of the authors or collections at their expected alphabetical places in the list. (4) Where there is no italicized title, but essentially a description of contents in roman (eg. 'Tract on Agriculture', 'Aurangzeb's *farmān* to Rasikdās', 'Yāsīn's Glossary'), the entries occur in the list according to the initial words or names as under Rule (3). Note: '*Report*' is treated as a shortened title, and is thus covered by Rule (2).

The abbreviations used for the various archives and major MS collections in the Bibliography (as well as in the footnotes) are explained in the initial paragraphs of the Bibliography. Also explained there is the use of the asterisk and of the indications employed where more than one MS, edition or translation of the same work or document are cited. In this list only the abbreviation for the main work would normally be given. Thus, in case of a reference to '*Bāburnāma*, Bev.,' the reader may look up only *Bāburnāma* in the following list, which will direct him to entry no.146 in the Bibliography'; there he will find the abbreviation 'Bev.' marked with an asterisk and shown to stand for A.S. Beveridge's translation of the *Bāburnāma*

'Abbās Khān	150
Abbé Carre	291
Abū Turāb	154
[Elphinstone,] *Account of the Kingdom of Caubul*	365
[Luxemburg,] *Accumulation of Capital*	512
Ādāb-i 'Ālamgīrī	116
Add. 6,586	318
Add. 6,603	315
Add. 16,859	114
Add. 16,863	9
Add. 19,502/Add.19,503/ Add.19,504	318
Add. 27,247	157
Add. 22,831	30
Add. 24,039	102
Ādilshāhī Pharmāne	97a
[Qureshi,] *Administration of the Mughal Empire*	419
[Qureshi,] *Administration of the Sultanate of Dehli*	416
Administrative Docs.	49
Afsāna-i Shāhān	183
[Siddiqi,] *Agrarian Change in a North Indian State*	327
[Moreland,] *Agrarian System*	377
[Gupta,] *Agrarian System of Eastern Rajasthan*	379
[Moreland,] *Agricultural Conditions [in the United Provinces & Districts]*	311
[Patel,] *Agricultural Labourers of India and Pakistan*	336
Agricultural Prices in India, 1951 and 1952	313
Agricultural Statistics [of India]	306
Aḥkām-i 'Ālamgīrī	134
Aḥmad Yādgār	182
Ā'īn	2
Akbar and his India	475
Akbar and the Jesuits	253
Akbarnāma	157
[Srivastava,] *Akbar the Great*	473
[Moreland,] *Akbar to Aurangzeb*	389
Akhbārāt	83
Akhbārāt A	83a
'Ālamgīrnāma	192
Aligarh Jour. of Oriental Studies	539
Allahabad	39
'Amal-i Ṣāliḥ	189
A.N.	157
[Deloche,] *Ancient Bridges of India*	465
[Tod,] *Annals and Antiquities*	440
[Hunter,] *Annals of Rural Bengal*	333
[Athar Ali,] *Apparatus of Empire*	424
[Cunningham,] *Archaeological Survey Reports*	459
Ardhakathānak	181
'Ārif Qandahārī	153
Verma, *Art and Material Culture*	474
'Arzdāsht-hā-i Muẓaffar	114
Asad Beg	160
Asnādu-s Ṣanādīd	58
[I. Habib,] *Atlas*	363
Aurangzeb's *farmān* to Muḥammad Hāshim	92
Aurangzeb's *farmān* to Rasikdās	90
Bāburnāma	146

INDEX

This Index is designed to serve also as a glossary of technical terms, which are duly italicized. The definitions are usually short, but are extended wherever this has been found necessary. The sign = indicates that the term is synonymous with the one to which it is equated, and that for information on the subject, the entry under the latter should also be seen.

Reign periods are furnished in the entries for all the Mughal emperors and other important rulers. This has seemed desirable because specific dates could not always be given in the main text, where persons, documents and events have often been referred to the reigns of particular rulers.

'ummāl), 75n., 210, 212-3, 218n., 239n., 257, 271, 272n., 281, 282 & n., 283n., 288, 290-91, 318, 319 & n., 320 n., 321-4 & nn., 325, 327-30 & nn., 331n., 333, 336, 338, 369 & n., 400

amīn (1), revenue assessor, = *munṣif*, 212, 218n., 262n., 295, 318-20 & nn., 321, 322-3 & nn., 324, 325 & n., 327 & n., 333, 334n.

amīn (2), head of measuring party, 319 & n.

amīn (3), imperial officer ensuring conformity with imperial regulations in the *khāliṣa* and *jāgīrs*, 338 & n., 339

amīn o faujdār, officer holding the twin offices of *amīn* (1) and *faujdār*, 219n., 320

Amkhora [Indargarh], *sarkār* Ranthambhor, 216n.

Amroha, Rohilkhand, 15n.

āna, anna, one-sixteenth of rupee, 432 &n.

Ānand Rām "Mukhliṣ", lexicographer, 18th century, 173

angusht, finger-breadth, digit, as measure of length, 409 & n., 410n.

aniseed (*ajwā'in*), 106n., 251n.

Ankleshwar. See Uklesar

ankora, custom of seizing dead peasant's family and property (Bengal), 287

Antrī, near Gwalior, 52n.

Aonla, town, *sarkār* Badāūn, 15 & n.

apricot, 56

Arakan, Araccan, Rakhang, 10, 212, 228 & n., 373n.

arbāb, local headman (Sind), counterpart of *chaudhurī*, 335n., 337n., 341, 353n.

arbāb-i zamīn, land-holders, 126

area and village statistics of Aurangzeb's reign, 2-3 & nn., 4, 270, 417

arhar, pulse, 42n.

'Ārif. See Saiyid Muḥammad 'Ārif

arindi or eri silk, *ṭāṭband*, 46n. 52 & n.

Aritha (Rādhākunḍ), *pargana* Sahār, 148-9, 151, 160n., 161, 195n.

Arjan, Gurū (d.1606), 137, 141, 165, 172n., 397

arṣaṭṭha, abstract of accounts of revenue receipts and expenditure for each harvest, 88

artisans, of villages, 63-67; at Āgra, 104n., 110; among rebels, 396, 398, 404n.

Asad Beg, author of memoirs, 50 & n.

Āṣaf Khān, Ja'far Beg, minister under Akbar, 460n.

Āṣaf Khān, high noble under Jahāngīr & Shāhjahān, 39n.

Aṣālat Khān, 35n.

āsāmī, individual peasant, 135, 137, 139, 253, 271-2.

ashrafī (1), Mughal gold coin, = *muhr*, 432

ashrafī (2), Portuguese Indian silver coin, = Zeraphin, 444n.

Asīrgaṛh, Khāndesh province, 463n.

aṣlī, original (village), 293n.

Aśoka, Mauryan emperor, *c.*270-34 B.C., 30n.

Assam, 105 & n., 106, 108n., 109n.; produce of, 40, 45n., 51, 55n., 58 & n., 105, 106 & n.

auqāf. See *Waqf*

Aurangābād, city, 60, 100 n., 434n.

Aurangābād, province, 59n., village & measured area statistics, 4, 21, 269; crops of, 43-44n., 45n.; revenue statistics, 463-66

Aurangshāhī paisa, copper coin, 426n.

Aurangzeb ('Ālamgīr), emperor (1659-1707), 3-4, 38, 50n., 185n., 238, 268-9, 300n., 306-07nn., 325n., 332, 336, 349n., 368n., 389, 438, 444; taxes and exactions under, 69n., 72n., 73 & n., 285-7; and *zamīndārs*, 220-21, 385 & n., 386; land revenue administration under, 233-4, 235 & n., 236, 267-8 (see also Aurangzeb's *farmān* to Rasikdās); *jāgīrs* and *khāliṣa* under, 312, 313n., 315-6 & nn., 329; *madad-i ma'āsh* under, 349n., 350, 351-2 & nn., 356, 357 & n.; religious policy of, 222, 332, 356-7, 365; oppression under, 372, 380n., 401; and Marathas, 401-4; weights under, 422, 423n., 426;

pān. See Betel leaf
panch, panch mukadamman, village oligarchs, 148-59, 175n.
panchai, = *panchāyat*, 158n.
panchāyat, body of village oligarchs, public assembly, 149, 155, 158
Panjāb. See Lāhor, province, and Multān, province (also: Multān, *sarkār*, and Dīpālpūr, *sarkār*)
Panjnad, river, 32&n.
Papal, *pargana*, Berār, 6n., 269, 276n.
papaya, 55
parauṭī, land only rarely allowed to lie fallow, 240, 293n.
pargana, territory delimited by Mughal administration for revenue and administrative purposes (cf. *maḥal*), 2, 300, 332, 336; and *zamīndār* castes, 198-9; and *jāgīrdārs*, 303n., 328n.
Paris, city, 83
Parsis, 356-7nn.
Partāb, *zamīndār* of Pālama'ū, 224n.
Pasnājat village, *sarkar* Bahrā'ich, 188, 189n., 192-3&nn., 194, 204n., 355n.
paṭel, village headman (Gujarāt), (cf. *muqaddam*), 85n., 160&n., 161n., 295, 402
Paṭel, S.J., 141n.
Paṭels, peasant caste, 147
Pathal, *bairāgī*, 152
Paṭhan, Paṭhānkot, Panjāb, 36, 345n., 347n.
Patlād, *pargana*, Gujarat, 86n., 132, 278
Patna, city, 44n., 156, 410, 424-5, 439n., 443; trade of, 70&n., 79-80; population of, 83&n., 84n.; famine at, 83-4n., 119
paṭṭa (1), document stating revenue demand assessed upon village or individual, 167&n., 237&n., 271
paṭṭa (2), territorial revenue assignment (Rājasthān), 226&n.
paṭṭa (3), or *patta*, unit of area (Kashmīr), 241n., 263
paṭṭadārī, official's fee or perquisite when issuing *paṭṭa* (1), 288
Paṭṭan, town, Gujarāt, 86n., 120
paṭṭāwat, holder of *paṭṭa* (2) (Rajasthan), 177, 266n.
paṭṭī (1), demarcated division of land within village, 193-4&nn.
paṭṭī (2), agent, 401
Paṭṭi Haibatpūr (mod. Patti), Panjāb, 36&n.
paṭwārī, village accountant, 323&n.; designation, position and functions of, 152-3, 166-8&nn., 283&n.; perquisites and income of, 154, 167&n., 334n.
paunda sugarcane, 45n., 248n., 251n.
pear, 55n.
peas, green, *maṭar*, 42n., 251n.
peasant, peasantry, and cultivation, 1, 22, 24-27; and irrigation, 28-30, 35n.; and market, 66, 85-89&nn.; and credit/debt, 85-6, 86n., 112, 154n., 295-6&nn.; conditions of life of, 103-10, 230; migrations of, 120, 122, 130-34, 377, 387-8; his right over land, 126-30, 134-5, 174-9, 344; semi-serf, 130, 132-4; and caste, 126&n., 141, 143-4, 145-6 &nn., 147, 149, 381, 391-2; stratification, 136-41; and land revenue, 208-9, 214, 230-36, 271-3, 281-2, 291, 293-4; oppression of, 168, 340-41, 367-73, 400-01; and grantees, 344&n.; flight from land, 377&n., 378; and *zamīndārs*, 177-8, 387-9; participation in revolts, 378-81&nn., 384, 389-405
Pelsaert, Francisco, Dutch factor, 13-14, 29, 104n.; 227-8, 190; on indigo, 48n., 86n.; on peasants, 378, 387; on weights and measures, 410-11, 417&n.
pepper, round, 51, 51-52n.; trade and consumption of, 80-82, 106&n.
pepper, long, 51, 51-2n., 78n.
Persia, Iran, 57n., 297n., 299n.; trade with, 78, 81. 441n. See also Middle East.
Persian empire, ancient, 378n., 405
Persian wheel, *arhaṭ*, 25 (miniature), 28&n., 38, 157
peshkash, offering, present, tribute, 221, 225&n., 332, 401
peṭh, market, whence rupee current in market, =*chalanī*, 434
phad, system of cooperative manage-

zābiṭāna, cess per *bīgha* for meeting expenses of measuring party, 253-4, 254n., 287
zabṭ, measurement of land; revenue assessment by use of measurement and application of tax-rate (crop-wise) per unit of area, 211, 278n.; size of revenue demand under, 231-2, 235-6, 240; mode of assessment of revenue under, 240-54&nn.; enforcement of, 240, 246, 259-62, 264-6; *nasaq* under, 255-7, 259, 265-6
zabṭ-i har-sāla, annual measurement, 254, 256&n.
zabṭī provinces, 41n., 50n., 227, 276, 304
"zabti" rents (mod.), cash rents varying with crops, 253n.
zakāt, transit duty, 72, 73n.
zamīndār (1), hereditary, superior, non-peasant holder of varied claims to shares in produce of land, and/or part of land revenue, 353n.; meaning & history of term, 169-70 & nn.; nature of right of, 126-7, 134-5, 171-4, 190-91, 222; and peasants, 174-9; income of, 179-90; salability of right of, 125-6, 194-6; genesis and composition of class of, 198-202; armed power of, 202-08; position of class of, 208, 229, 384-5; and land revenue, 208-19, 270, 270-1n., 273, 282, 336, 384; 400-01; control of administration over, 219-22, 340; and revenue officials, 330, 333-4, 335&n., 336; & *madad-i ma'āsh*, 344-5, 353n., 355&n.; subversive tendencies of, 335&n., 385-6; grants by, 363&n.; his role in agrarian revolts, 384-9, 391-3, 399, 400, 402-3, 387-9
zamīndār (2), chief, 169&n., 170, 208, 222-4&nn., 362-3
zamīndārī villages, 174-8, 214-5
Zasulich, Vera, 136
z̲āt, numerical rank (*manṣab*) indicating status and personal pay (*k̲h̲āṣa*), 299
Ẓawābiṭ-i 'Ālamgīrī, 453
"Zeraphin", *ashrafī* (2), coin of Portuguese possessions, 444n.
z̲irā', unit of length, = *dir'a/gaz*, 414
zirā'-i pādshāhī, unit of length, 411-15
zor-ṭalab, (usually, of territory) "force-demanding", seditious, not paying revenue unless forcibly compelled to do so, = *mawās*, 327n., 379&n.